Software Engineering   Sixth Edition

International Computer Science Series

Consulting Editor **A D McGettrick** *University of Strathclyde*

Selected titles in the series

Software Development with Z
J B Wordsworth

Program Verification
N Francez

Concurrent Systems: An Integrated Approach to
Operating Systems, Database, and Distributed Systems
(2nd edn)
J Bacon

Concurrent Programming
A Burns and G Davies

Comparative Programming Languages (2nd edn)
L B Wilson and R G Clark

Programming in Ada 95 (2nd Edn)
J G P Barnes

Software Design *D Budgen*

Ada 95 From the Beginning (3rd edn)
J Skansholm

Programming Language Essentials
H E Bal and D Grune

Human-Computer Interaction
J Preece et al.

Distributed Systems: Concepts and Design (3rd edn)
G Coulouris, J Dollimore and T Kindberg

Fortran 90 Programming
T M R Ellis, I R Philips and T M Lahey

Foundations of Computing: System Development
with Set Theory and Logic
T Scheurer

Principles of Object-Oriented Software Development
(2nd edn)
A Eliëns

Object-Oriented Programming in Eiffel (2nd edn)
P Thomas and R Weedon

Compiler Design
R Wilhelm and D Maurer

Miranda: The Craft of Functional Programming
S Thompson

Haskell: The Craft of Functional Programming (2nd edn)
S Thompson

Software Engineering (6th edn)
I Sommerville

Compiler Construction
N Wirth

Software Engineering with B
J B Wordsworth

Functional C
P Hartel and H Muller

Java Gently: Programming Principles Explained (2nd Edn)
J Bishop

C++ From the Beginning
J Skansholm

Ada 95 for C and C++ Programmers
S Johnston

Algorithms and Data Structures: Design, Correctness,
Analysis (2nd edn)
J Kingston

Discover Delphi: Programming Principles Explained
S Williams and S Walmsley

Introductory Logic and Sets for Computer Scientists
N Nissanke

Discrete Mathematics for Computer Scientists (2nd edn)
J K Truss

Introduction to Programming using SML
M Hansen and H Rischel

Algorithms: a Functional Programming Approach
F Rabhi and G Lapalme

Software Engineering

Sixth Edition

Ian Sommerville

Addison-Wesley

An imprint of **PEARSON EDUCATION**

Harlow, England · London · New York · Reading, Massachusetts · San Francisco · Toronto · Don Mills, Ontario · Sydney
Tokyo · Singapore · Hong Kong · Seoul · Taipei · Cape Town · Madrid · Mexico City · Amsterdam · Munich · Paris · Milan

Pearson Education Limited
Edinburgh Gate
Harlow
Essex CM20 2JE
England

and Associated Companies throughout the world

Visit us on the World Wide Web at:
www.pearsoneduc.com

———————————

First published 1982
Second Edition 1984
Third Edition 1989
Fourth Edition 1992
Fifth Edition 1995
Sixth Edition 2001

© Addison-Wesley Publishers Limited 1982, 1984
© Pearson Education Limited 1989, 2001

ISBN 0 201 39815 X

British Library Cataloguing-in-Publication Data
A catalogue record for this book can be obtained from the British Library

Library of Congress Cataloging-in-Publication Data
Sommerville, Ian, 1951–
    Software engineering / Ian Sommerville. – 6th ed.
        p. cm. – (International computer science series)
    Includes bibliographical references and index.
    ISBN 0-201-39815-X
        1. Software engineering.   I. Title.   II. Series.
    QA76.758. S.657 2000
    005.1–dc21   00-033197

10 9 8 7 6 5
06 05 04 03 02

Typeset by 35 in 10/12.5pt Times
Printed and bound in the United States of America

Preface

Software systems are now ubiquitous. Virtually all electrical equipment now includes some kind of software; software is used to help run manufacturing industry, schools and universities, health care, finance and government; many people use software of different kinds for entertainment and education. The specification, development, management and evolution of these software systems make up the discipline of *software engineering*.

Even simple software systems have a high inherent complexity, so engineering principles have to be used in their development. Software engineering is therefore an engineering discipline where software engineers use methods and theory from computer science and apply this cost-effectively to solve difficult problems. These difficult problems have meant that many software development projects have not been successful. However, most modern software provides good service to its users; we should not let high-profile failures obscure the real successes of software engineers over the past 30 years.

Software engineering was developed in response to the problems of building large, custom software systems for defence, government and industrial applications. We now develop a much wider range of software, from games on specialised consoles through personal PC products and web-based systems to very large-scale distributed systems. Although some techniques that are appropriate for custom systems, such as object-oriented development, are universal, new software engineering techniques are evolving for different types of software. It is not possible to cover everything in one book, so I have concentrated on universal techniques and techniques for developing large-scale systems rather than individual software products.

Although the book is intended as a general introduction to software engineering, it is oriented towards my own interests in system requirements engineering and critical systems. I think these are particularly important for software engineering in the 21st century where the challenge we face is to ensure that our software meets the real needs of its users without causing damage to them or to the environment.

The approach that I take in this book is to present a broad perspective on software engineering and I don't concentrate on any specific methods or tools. I dislike zealots of any kind whether they are academics preaching the benefits of formal methods or salesmen trying to convince me that some tool or method is the answer to software development problems. There are no simple solutions to the problems of software engineering and we need a wide spectrum of tools and techniques to solve software engineering problems.

Books inevitably reflect the opinions and prejudices of their authors. Some readers will inevitably disagree with my opinions and with my choice of material. Such disagreement is a healthy reflection of the diversity of the discipline and is essential for its evolution. Nevertheless, I hope that all software engineers and software engineering students can find something of interest here.

Changes from the fifth edition

Like many software systems, this book has grown and changed since its first edition was published in 1982. One of my goals in preparing this edition was to reduce rather than increase the size of the book and this has entailed some reorganisation and difficult decisions on what to cut out while still including important new material. The end result is a book that is about 10% shorter than the fifth edition.

- The book has been restructured into seven rather than eight parts covering an introduction to software engineering, specification, design, critical systems development, verification and validation, management, and software evolution.

- There are new chapters covering software processes, distributed systems architectures, dependability and legacy systems. The section on formal specification has been cut to a single chapter and material on CASE has been reduced and distributed to different chapters. Coverage of functional design is now included in the new chapter on legacy systems. Chapters on verification and validation have been amalgamated.

- All chapters have been updated and several chapters have been extensively rewritten. Reuse now focuses on development with reuse, with material on patterns and component-based development; object-oriented design has more of a process focus; the chapters on requirements have been separated into chapters on the requirements themselves and chapters on the requirements engineering process; cost estimation has been updated to COCOMO 2.

- The introductory part now includes four chapters. I have taken introductory material that was distributed throughout the book in the fifth edition and covered it all in this part. Chapter 1 has been completely rewritten as a set of frequently asked questions about software engineering.

• The material on critical systems has been restructured and integrated so that reliability, safety and availability are not covered as separate topics. I have introduced some material on security as an attribute of a critical system.

• Program examples are now in Java and object models are described in the UML. Ada and C++ examples have been removed from the text but are available from my web site.

The further reading associated with each chapter has been updated from previous editions. However, in many cases, articles written in the 1980s are still the best introduction to some topics.

Readership

The book is aimed at students taking undergraduate and graduate courses and at software engineers in commerce and industry. It may be used in general software engineering courses or in courses such as advanced programming, software specification, software design or management. Practitioners may find the book useful as general reading and as a means of updating their knowledge on particular topics such as requirements engineering, architectural design, dependable systems development and process improvement. Wherever practicable, the examples in the text have been given a practical bias to reflect the type of applications which software engineers must develop.

I assume that readers have a basic familiarity with programming and modern computer systems and knowledge of basic data structures such as stacks, lists and queues.

Using the book as a course text

There are three main types of software engineering courses where this book can be used:

1. *General introductory courses in software engineering*   For students who have no previous software engineering experience, you can start with the introductory section, then pick and choose the chapters from the different sections of the book. This will give students a general overview of the subject with the opportunity of more detailed study for those students who are interested.

2. *Introductory or intermediate courses on specific software engineering topics*
   The book supports courses in software requirements specification, software design, software engineering management, dependable systems development and software evolution. Each of the parts in the book can serve as a text in its own right for an introductory or intermediate course on that topic. Some additional reading is suggested for these courses.

3. *More advanced courses in specific software engineering topics* In this case, the chapters in the book form a foundation for the course which must be supplemented with further reading which explores the topic in more detail. All chapters include my suggestions for further reading and additional reading is suggested on my web site.

The benefit of a general text like this is that it can be used in several different related courses. At Lancaster, we use the text in an introductory software engineering course, in courses on specification, design and critical systems and in a software management course where it is supplemented with further reading. With a single text, students are presented with a consistent view of the subject. They also like the extensive coverage because they don't have to buy several different books.

This book covers all suggested material in the SE Software Engineering component of the draft computer science body of knowledge proposed by the ACM/IEEE in the Computing Curricula 2001 document. The book is also consistent with the forthcoming IEEE/ACM 'Software Engineering Body of Knowledge' document which is due for publication sometime in 2000 or 2001.

Web site

My web site is http://www.software-engin.com and this includes links to material to support the use of this book in teaching and personal study. The following downloadable supplements are available:

- An instructor's guide including hints on teaching using the book, class and term project suggestions, case studies and examples and some solutions to the exercises. This is available in Adobe PDF format.

- A set of overhead projector transparencies for each chapter. These are available in Adobe PDF and in Microsoft PowerPoint format. Instructors may adapt and modify the presentations as they wish.

- Source code in Java for most of the individual program examples, including supplementary code required for compilation.

- Additional material based on chapters from previous editions on algebraic specification, Z and function-oriented design. Ada and C++ examples as used in the
fifth edition are also available.

This page also includes links to copies of slides and papers on systems engineering, links to other software engineering sites, information on other books and
suggestions for additional further reading.

I am always pleased to receive feedback on my books and you can contact me
by e-mail at ian@software-engin.com. However, I regret that I don't have time to
give advice to individual students on their homework.

Acknowledgements

A large number of people have contributed over the years to the evolution of this
book and I'd first like to thank everyone who has commented on previous editions
and made suggestions for change. I am grateful to the reviewers of initial drafts of
this text for their helpful comments and suggestions which helped me a great deal
when completing the final version.

The reviewers of the first draft were Andy Gillies and Lindsey Gillies of the
University of the West of England, Joe Lambert of Penn. State University, Frank
Maddix of the University of the West of England, Nancy Mead of the Software
Engineering Institute, Pittsburgh, Chris Price of the University of Wales,
Aberystwyth, Gregg Rothermel of Oregon State University and Guus Schreiber of
the University of Amsterdam. I'd particularly like to thank my friends Ron
Morrison of St Andrews University and Ray Welland of Glasgow University who
have reviewed previous editions and again volunteered to review this text.

Finally, my family has put up with my absence for more evenings than I like to
think while I finished this book. Thanks to my wife Anne and my daughters Ali
and Jane for their coffee and tolerance.

Ian Sommerville
Lancaster, February 2000

Contents at a glance

	Preface	v
Part 1	Overview	1
	Chapter 1 Introduction	3
	Chapter 2 Computer-based system engineering	20
	Chapter 3 Software processes	42
	Chapter 4 Project management	71
Part 2	Requirements	95
	Chapter 5 Software requirements	97
	Chapter 6 Requirements engineering processes	121
	Chapter 7 System models	148
	Chapter 8 Software prototyping	171
	Chapter 9 Formal specification	192
Part 3	Design	213
	Chapter 10 Architectural design	215
	Chapter 11 Distributed systems architectures	239
	Chapter 12 Object-oriented design	260
	Chapter 13 Real-time software design	285
	Chapter 14 Design with reuse	306
	Chapter 15 User interface design	327
Part 4	Critical Systems	351
	Chapter 16 Dependability	353
	Chapter 17 Critical systems specification	371
	Chapter 18 Critical systems development	392
Part 5	Verification and Validation	417
	Chapter 19 Verification and validation	419
	Chapter 20 Software testing	440
	Chapter 21 Critical systems validation	467
Part 6	Management	487
	Chapter 22 Managing people	489
	Chapter 23 Software cost estimation	511
	Chapter 24 Quality management	535
	Chapter 25 Process improvement	557
Part 7	Evolution	579
	Chapter 26 Legacy systems	581
	Chapter 27 Software change	601
	Chapter 28 Software re-engineering	622
	Chapter 29 Configuration management	641
	References	663
	Index	679

Contents

Preface   v

Part 1 Overview   1

Chapter 1 Introduction   3

    1.1   FAQs about software engineering   5

    1.2   Professional and ethical responsibility   14

    Key points   17
    Further reading   18
    Exercises   18

Chapter 2 Computer-based system engineering   20

    2.1   Emergent system properties   22

    2.2   Systems and their environment   24

    2.3   System modelling   26

    2.4   The system engineering process   29

    2.5   System procurement   37

Key points	39
Further reading	40
Exercises	40

Chapter 3 Software processes 42

3.1	Software process models	44
3.2	Process iteration	51
3.3	Software specification	55
3.4	Software design and implementation	56
3.5	Software validation	60
3.6	Software evolution	63
3.7	Automated process support	63
	Key points	68
	Further reading	68
	Exercises	69

Chapter 4 Project management 71

4.1	Management activities	73
4.2	Project planning	75
4.3	Project scheduling	78
4.4	Risk management	84
	Key points	90
	Further reading	91
	Exercises	92

Part 2 Requirements 95

Chapter 5 Software requirements 97

5.1	Functional and non-functional requirements	100
5.2	User requirements	106
5.3	System requirements	109

5.4   The software requirements document   115

Key points   119
Further reading   119
Exercises   120

Chapter 6   Requirements engineering processes   121

6.1   Feasibility studies   123

6.2   Requirements elicitation and analysis   124

6.3   Requirements validation   137

6.4   Requirements management   139

Key points   145
Further reading   145
Exercises   146

Chapter 7   System models   148

7.1   Context models   150

7.2   Behavioural models   153

7.3   Data models   158

7.4   Object models   160

7.5   CASE workbenches   166

Key points   168
Further reading   169
Exercises   169

Chapter 8   Software prototyping   171

8.1   Prototyping in the software process   174

8.2   Rapid prototyping techniques   180

8.3   User interface prototyping   188

Key points   189
Further reading   190
Exercises   190

Chapter 9   Formal specification   192

            9.1   Formal specification in the software process   194

            9.2   Interface specification   197

            9.3   Behavioural specification   204

            Key points   209
            Further reading   210
            Exercises   210

Part 3   Design   213

Chapter 10   Architectural design   215

            10.1   System structuring   219

            10.2   Control models   224

            10.3   Modular decomposition   229

            10.4   Domain-specific architectures   233

            Key points   236
            Further reading   237
            Exercises   237

Chapter 11   Distributed systems architectures   239

            11.1   Multiprocessor architectures   243

            11.2   Client–server architectures   244

            11.3   Distributed object architectures   249

            11.4   CORBA   252

            Key points   257
            Further reading   258
            Exercises   258

Chapter 12   Object-oriented design   260

            12.1   Objects and object classes   262

            12.2   An object-oriented design process   267

12.3 Design evolution   280

Key points   282
Further reading   282
Exercises   283

Chapter 13 **Real-time software design**   **285**

13.1 System design   287

13.2 Real-time executives   291

13.3 Monitoring and control systems   295

13.4 Data acquisition systems   300

Key points   303
Further reading   303
Exercises   304

Chapter 14 **Design with reuse**   **306**

14.1 Component-based development   310

14.2 Application families   318

14.3 Design patterns   322

Key points   325
Further reading   325
Exercises   326

Chapter 15 **User interface design**   **327**

15.1 User interface design principles   330

15.2 User interaction   332

15.3 Information presentation   334

15.4 User support   340

15.5 Interface evaluation   345

Key points   347
Further reading   348
Exercises   348

Part 4	Critical Systems	351

Chapter 16	Dependability	353
16.1	Critical systems	356
16.2	Availability and reliability	359
16.3	Safety	364
16.4	Security	367
	Key points	369
	Further reading	369
	Exercises	370

Chapter 17	Critical systems specification	371
17.1	Software reliability specification	373
17.2	Safety specification	379
17.3	Security specification	387
	Key points	389
	Further reading	389
	Exercises	390

Chapter 18	Critical systems development	392
18.1	Fault minimisation	393
18.2	Fault tolerance	400
18.3	Fault-tolerant architectures	410
18.4	Safe system design	413
	Key points	414
	Further reading	415
	Exercises	415

Part 5	Verification and Validation	417

Chapter 19	Verification and validation	419
19.1	Verification and validation planning	423
19.2	Software inspections	425

19.3 Automated static analysis   431

19.4 Cleanroom software development   434

Key points   437
Further reading   438
Exercises   438

Chapter 20 Software testing   **440**

20.1 Defect testing   442

20.2 Integration testing   452

20.3 Object-oriented testing   458

20.4 Testing workbenches   462

Key points   464
Further reading   465
Exercises   466

Chapter 21 Critical systems validation   **467**

21.1 Formal methods and critical systems   469

21.2 Reliability validation   470

21.3 Safety assurance   476

21.4 Security assessment   483

Key points   484
Further reading   484
Exercises   485

Part 6 Management   **487**

Chapter 22 Managing people   **489**

22.1 Limits to thinking   490

22.2 Group working   497

22.3 Choosing and keeping people   503

22.4   The People Capability Maturity Model   506

Key points   508
Further reading   509
Exercises   509

Chapter 23   Software cost estimation   511

23.1   Productivity   513

23.2   Estimation techniques   518

23.3   Algorithmic cost modelling   520

23.4   Project duration and staffing   531

Key points   533
Further reading   533
Exercises   534

Chapter 24   Quality management   535

24.1   Quality assurance and standards   539

24.2   Quality planning   544

24.3   Quality control   546

24.4   Software measurement and metrics   547

Key points   555
Further reading   555
Exercises   556

Chapter 25   Process improvement   557

25.1   Process and product quality   560

25.2   Process analysis and modelling   562

25.3   Process measurement   566

25.4   The SEI Process Capability Maturity Model   568

25.5   Process classification   573

Key points   576
Further reading   576
Exercises   577

Part 7	Evolution	579

Chapter 26	Legacy systems	581
	26.1 Legacy system structures	583
	26.2 Legacy system design	587
	26.3 Legacy system assessment	592
	Key points	598
	Further reading	599
	Exercises	599

Chapter 27	Software change	601
	27.1 Program evolution dynamics	603
	27.2 Software maintenance	605
	27.3 Architectural evolution	614
	Key points	620
	Further reading	620
	Exercises	621

Chapter 28	Software re-engineering	622
	28.1 Source code translation	626
	28.2 Reverse engineering	628
	28.3 Program structure improvement	629
	28.4 Program modularisation	632
	28.5 Data re-engineering	634
	Key points	638
	Further reading	639
	Exercises	639

Chapter 29	Configuration management	641
	29.1 Configuration management planning	644
	29.2 Change management	647

29.3   Version and release management   650

29.4   System building   655

29.5   CASE tools for configuration management   656

Key points   660
Further reading   661
Exercises   661

References   663
Index   679

Trademark Notice
The following are trademarks or registered trademarks of their respective companies:

Java, JavaBeans and Modula-2 are trademarks of Sun Microsystems, Inc.; Lotus Notes is a trademark of Lotus Development Corporation; Mac OS is a trademark of Apple Computer, Inc.; Microsoft, PowerPoint, Windows, Visual Basic and Visual C++ are trademarks of Microsoft Corporation; Unix is a trademark licensed through X/Open Company Ltd.

PART ONE

Overview

1 Introduction

Objectives

The objective of this chapter is to introduce the subject of software engineering. When you have read this chapter you will:

❑ understand what software engineering is and why it is important;

❑ know the answers to key questions which provide an introduction to software engineering;

❑ understand ethical and professional issues which are important for software engineers.

Contents

1.1 FAQs about software engineering

1.2 Professional and ethical responsibility

Virtually all countries now depend on complex computer-based systems. More and more products incorporate computers and controlling software in some form. The software in these systems represents a large and increasing proportion of the total system costs. Therefore, producing software in a cost-effective way is essential for the functioning of national and international economies.

Software engineering is an engineering discipline whose goal is the cost-effective development of software systems. Software is abstract and intangible. It is not constrained by materials, governed by physical laws or by manufacturing processes. In some ways, this simplifies software engineering as there are no physical limitations on the potential of software. In other ways, however, this lack of natural constraints means that software can easily become extremely complex and hence very difficult to understand.

Software engineering is still a relatively young discipline. The notion of 'software engineering' was first proposed in 1968 at a conference held to discuss what was then called the 'software crisis'. This software crisis resulted directly from the introduction of (at that time) powerful, third-generation computer hardware. Their power made hitherto unrealisable computer applications a feasible proposition. The resulting software was orders of magnitude larger and more complex than previous software systems.

Early experience in building these systems showed that an informal approach to software development was not good enough. Major projects were sometimes years late. They cost much more than originally predicted, were unreliable, difficult to maintain and performed poorly. Software development was in crisis. Hardware costs were tumbling whilst software costs were rising rapidly. New techniques and methods were needed to control the complexity inherent in large software systems.

These techniques have become part of software engineering and are now widely although not universally used. However, there are still problems in producing complex software which meets user expectations, is delivered on time and to budget. Many software projects still have problems and this has led to some commentators (Pressman, 1997) suggesting that software engineering is in a state of chronic affliction.

As our ability to produce software has increased so too has the complexity of the software systems required. New technologies resulting from the convergence of computers and communication systems place new demands on software engineers. For this reason and because many companies do not apply software engineering techniques effectively, we still have problems. Things are not as bad as the doomsayers suggest but there is clearly room for improvement.

I think that we have made tremendous progress since 1968 and that the development of software engineering has markedly improved our software. We have a much better understanding of the activities involved in software development. We have developed effective methods of software specification, design and implementation. New notations and tools reduce the effort required to produce large and complex systems.

Software engineers can be rightly proud of their achievements. Without complex software we would not have explored space, would not have the Internet and modern telecommunications, and all forms of travel would be more dangerous and expensive. Software engineering has contributed a great deal in its short lifetime and I am convinced that, as the discipline matures, its contributions in the 21st century will be even greater.

1.1   FAQs about software engineering

This section is designed to answer some fundamental questions about software engineering and also to give you some impression of my views of the discipline. The format that I have used here is the 'FAQ (Frequently Asked Questions) list'. This approach is commonly used in Internet newsgroups to provide newcomers with answers to frequently asked questions. I believe that it is a very effective way to give a succinct introduction to the subject of software engineering.

The questions which are answered in this section are shown in Figure 1.1.

1.1.1   What is software?

Many people equate the term *software* with computer programs. In fact, this is too restrictive a view. Software is not just the programs but also all associated documentation and configuration data which is needed to make these programs operate correctly. A software system usually consists of a number of separate programs, configuration files which are used to set up these programs, system documentation which describes the structure of the system and user documentation which explains how to use the system and, for software products, web sites for users to download recent product information.

Software engineers are concerned with developing software products, i.e. software which can be sold to a customer. There are two types of software product:

1. *Generic products*   These are stand-alone systems which are produced by a development organisation and sold on the open market to any customer who is able to buy them. Sometimes they are referred to as shrink-wrapped software. Examples of this type of product include databases, word processors, drawing packages and project management tools.

2. *Bespoke (or customised) products*   These are systems which are commissioned by a particular customer. The software is developed specially for that customer by a software contractor. Examples of this type of software include control systems for electronic devices, systems written to support a particular business process and air traffic control systems.

An important difference between these different types of software is that, in generic products, the organisation which develops the software controls the software

Question	Answer
What is software?	Computer programs and associated documentation. Software products may be developed for a particular customer or may be developed for a general market.
What is software engineering?	Software engineering is an engineering discipline which is concerned with all aspects of software production.
What is the difference between software engineering and computer science?	Computer science is concerned with theory and fundamentals; software engineering is concerned with the practicalities of developing and delivering useful software.
What is the difference between software engineering and system engineering?	System engineering is concerned with all aspects of computer-based systems development, including hardware, software and process engineering. Software engineering is part of this process.
What is a software process?	A set of activities whose goal is the development or evolution of software.
What is a software process model?	A simplified representation of a software process, presented from a specific perspective.
What are the costs of software engineering?	Roughly 60% of costs are development costs, 40% are testing costs. For custom software, evolution costs often exceed development costs.
What are software engineering methods?	Structured approaches to software development which include system models, notations, rules, design advice and process guidance.
What is CASE (Computer-Aided Software Engineering)?	Software systems which are intended to provide automated support for software process activities. CASE systems are often used for method support.
What are the attributes of good software?	The software should deliver the required functionality and performance to the user and should be maintainable, dependable and usable.
What are the key challenges facing software engineering?	Coping with legacy systems, coping with increasing diversity and coping with demands for reduced delivery times.

Figure 1.1 Frequently asked questions about software engineering

specification. For custom products, the specification is usually developed and controlled by the organisation that is buying the software. The software developers must work to that specification.

1.1.2   What is software engineering?

Software engineering is an engineering discipline which is concerned with all aspects of software production from the early stages of system specification through to maintaining the system after it has gone into use. In this definition, there are two key phrases:

1. 'engineering discipline'   Engineers make things work. They apply theories, methods and tools where these are appropriate but they use them selectively and always try to discover solutions to problems even when there are no applicable theories and methods to support them. Engineers also recognise that they must work to organisational and financial constraints, so they look for solutions within these constraints.

2. 'all aspects of software production'   Software engineering is not just concerned with the technical processes of software development but also with activities such as software project management and with the development of tools, methods and theories to support software production.

In general, software engineers adopt a systematic and organised approach to their work as this is often the most effective way to produce high-quality software. However, engineering is all about selecting the most appropriate method for a set of circumstances and a more creative, informal approach to development may be effective in some circumstances. Informal development is particularly appropriate for the development of web-based e-commerce systems which requires a blend of software and graphical design skills.

1.1.3   What is the difference between software engineering and computer science?

Essentially, computer science is concerned with the theories and methods which underlie computers and software systems whereas software engineering is concerned with the practical problems of producing software. Some knowledge of computer science is essential for software engineers in the same way that some knowledge of physics is essential for electrical engineers.

Ideally, all of software engineering should be underpinned by theories of computer science but in reality this is not the case. Software engineers must often use *ad hoc* approaches to develop the software. Elegant theories of computer science cannot always be applied to real, complex problems which require a software solution.

1.1.4   What is the difference between software engineering and system engineering?

System engineering or, more precisely, computer-based system engineering is concerned with all aspects of the development and evolution of complex systems where software plays a major role. System engineering is therefore concerned with hardware development, policy and process design and system deployment as well as software engineering. System engineers are involved in specifying the system, defining its overall architecture and then integrating the different parts to create the finished system. They are less concerned with the engineering of the system components (hardware, software, etc.).

System engineering is an older discipline than software engineering. People have been specifying and assembling complex industrial systems such as trains and chemical plants for more than 100 years. However, as the percentage of software in systems has increased, software engineering techniques such as use-case modelling, configuration management, etc. are being used in the systems engineering process. I discuss system engineering in more detail in Chapter 2.

1.1.5 What is a software process?

A software process is a set of activities and associated results which produce a software product. These activities are mostly carried out by software engineers. There are four fundamental process activities (covered later in the book) which are common to all software processes. These activities are:

1. *Software specification*   The functionality of the software and constraints on its operation must be defined.
2. *Software development*   The software to meet the specification must be produced.
3. *Software validation*   The software must be validated to ensure that it does what the customer wants.
4. *Software evolution*   The software must evolve to meet changing customer needs.

Different software processes organise these activities in different ways and are described at different levels of detail. The timing of the activities varies, as does the results of each activity. Different organisations may use different processes to produce the same type of product. However, some processes are more suitable than others for some types of application. If an inappropriate process is used, this will probably reduce the quality or the usefulness of the software product to be developed.

Software processes are discussed in more detail in Chapter 3 and the important topic of software process improvement is covered in Chapter 25.

1.1.6 What is a software process model?

A software process model is a simplified description of a software process which is presented from a particular perspective. Models, by their very nature, are simplifications, so a software process model is an abstraction of the actual process which is being described. Process models may include activities which are part of the software process, software products and the roles of people involved in software engineering. Some examples of the types of software process model which may be produced are:

1. *A workflow model*   This shows the sequence of activities in the process along with their inputs, outputs and dependencies. The activities in this model represent human actions.

2. *A data-flow or activity model*   This represents the process as a set of activit-
    ies each of which carries out some data transformation. It shows how the input
    to the process such as a specification is transformed to an output such as a design.
    The activities here may be at a lower level than activities in a workflow model.
    They may represent transformations carried out by people or by computers.

3. *A role/action model*   This represents the roles of the people involved in the
    software process and the activities for which they are responsible.

There are a number of different general models or paradigms of software
development:

1. *The waterfall approach*   This takes the above activities and represents them
    as separate process phases such as requirements specification, software design,
    implementation, testing and so on. After each stage is defined it is 'signed off'
    and development goes on to the following stage.

2. *Evolutionary development*   This approach interleaves the activities of speci-
    fication, development and validation. An initial system is rapidly developed
    from very abstract specifications. This is then refined with customer input to
    produce a system which satisfies the customer's needs. The system may then
    be delivered. Alternatively, it may be reimplemented using a more structured
    approach to produce a more robust and maintainable system.

3. *Formal transformation*   This approach is based on producing a formal
    mathematical system specification and transforming this specification, using
    mathematical methods, to a program. These transformations are 'correctness-
    preserving'. This means that you can be sure that the developed program meets
    its specification.

4. *System assembly from reusable components*   This technique assumes that parts
    of the system already exist. The system development process focuses on integra-
    ting these parts rather than developing them from scratch. I discuss software
    reuse in Chapter 14.

I return to these generic process models in Chapter 3.

1.1.7   What are the costs of software engineering?

There is no simple answer to this question as the precise distribution of costs across
the software process depends on the process used and the type of software which
is being developed. If we take the total cost of developing a complex software system as 100 cost units, the distribution of these cost units is likely to be something
like that shown in Figure 1.2.

This cost distribution holds where the costs of specification, design, implementation and integration are measured separately. Notice that system integration
and testing is the most expensive development activity. Figure 1.2 suggests that this

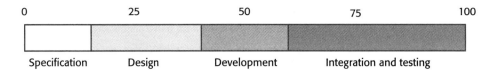

Figure 1.2
Development cost
distribution

is about 40 per cent of the total development costs but for some critical systems it is likely to be nearer 50 per cent of the total system costs.

If the software is developed using an evolutionary approach, there is no hard line between specification, design and development. Figure 1.2 would have to be modified for this type of development as shown in Figure 1.3. Specification costs are reduced because only a high-level specification is produced before development in this approach. Specification, design, implementation, integration and testing are carried out in parallel within a development activity. However, there is still a need for a separate system testing activity once the initial implementation is complete.

Figure 1.3 Costs
of evolutionary
development

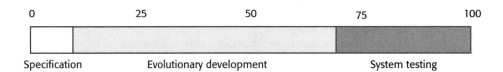

On top of development costs, costs are also incurred in changing the software after it has gone into use. For many software systems which have a long life-time, these costs are likely to exceed the development costs by a factor of 3 or 4 (Figure 1.4).

Figure 1.4
Evolution costs

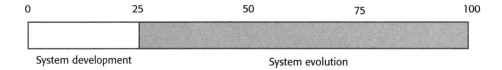

The above cost distribution holds for customised software which is specified by a customer and developed by a contractor. For software products which are (mostly) sold for PCs, the cost profile is likely to be different. These products are usually developed from an outline specification using an evolutionary develop-ment approach. Specification costs are relatively low. However, because they are intended for use on a range of different configurations, they must be extensively tested. Figure 1.5 shows the type of cost profile that might be expected for these products.

Figure 1.5 Product
development costs

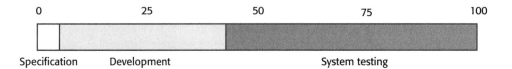

The evolution costs for generic software products are particularly hard to estimate. In many cases, there is little formal evolution of a product. Once a version of the product has been released, work starts on the next release and, for marketing reasons, this is likely to be presented as a new (but compatible) product rather than a modified version of a product which the user has already bought. Therefore, the evolution costs are not assessed separately as they are in customised software but are simply the development costs for the next version of the system.

The cost model for e-commerce web-based systems is likely to be different from both of these. These systems usually use off-the-shelf software for information management and have high user interface development costs. At the time of writing, these systems have only just come into use. I don't have any reliable figures on their development costs.

1.1.8   What are software engineering methods?

A software engineering method is a structured approach to software development whose aim is to facilitate the production of high-quality software in a cost-effective way. Methods such as Structured Analysis (DeMarco, 1978) and JSD (Jackson, 1983) were first developed in the 1970s. These methods attempted to identify the basic functional components of a system and function-oriented methods are still widely used. In the 1980s and 1990s, these function-oriented methods were supplemented by object-oriented methods such as those proposed by Booch (1994) and Rumbaugh (Rumbaugh *et al*., 1991). These different approaches have now been integrated into a single unified approach built around the Unified Modeling Language (UML) (Fowler and Scott, 1997; Booch *et al*., 1999; Rumbaugh *et al*., 1999a, 1999b).

Figure 1.6 Method components

All methods are based on the idea of developing models of a system which may be represented graphically and using these models as a system specification or design. Methods should include a number of different components (Figure 1.6).

Component	Description	Example
System model descriptions	Descriptions of the system models which should be developed and the notation used to define these models.	Object models, data-flow models, state machine models, etc.
Rules	Constraints which always apply to system models.	Every entity in a system model must have a unique name.
Recommendations	Heuristics which characterise good design practice in this method. Following these recommendations should lead to a well-organised system model.	No object should have more than seven sub-objects associated with it.
Process guidance	Descriptions of the activities which may be followed to develop the system models and the organisation of these activities.	Object attributes should be documented before defining the operations associated with an object.

There is no ideal method and different methods have different areas where they are applicable. For example, object-oriented methods are often appropriate for interactive systems but not for systems with stringent real-time requirements.

1.1.9 What is CASE?

The acronym CASE stands for Computer-Aided Software Engineering. It covers a wide range of different types of program which are used to support software process activities such as requirements analysis, system modelling, debugging and testing. All methods now come with associated CASE technology such as editors for the notations used in the method, analysis modules which check the system model according to the method rules and report generators to help create system documentation. The CASE tools may also include a code generator which automatically generates source code from the system model and some process guidance which gives advice to the software engineer on what to do next.

This type of CASE tool, aimed at supporting analysis and design, is sometimes called an upper-CASE tool because it supports early phases of the software process. By contrast, CASE tools which are designed to support implementation and testing such as debuggers, program analysis systems, test case generators and program editors are sometimes called lower-CASE tools.

1.1.10 What are the attributes of good software?

As well as the services which they provide, software products have a number of other associated attributes which reflect the quality of that software. These attributes are not directly concerned with what the software does. Rather, they reflect its behaviour while it is executing and the structure and organisation of the source program and associated documentation. Examples of these attributes (sometimes called non-functional attributes) are the software's response time to a user query and the understandability of the program code.

The specific set of attributes which you might expect from a software system obviously depends on its application. Therefore, a banking system must be secure, an interactive game must be responsive, a telephone switching system must be reliable, etc. These can be generalised into the set of attributes shown in Figure 1.7 which I believe are the essential characteristics of a well-designed software system.

The techniques discussed in this book focus on two of these attributes, namely maintainability and dependability. The majority of software engineering methods, tools and techniques are intended to help produce software with these characteristics. Software performance improvement is usually dependent on very specific domain knowledge and usability is a major, separate topic in its own right. However, I do discuss usability in Chapter 15.

Figure 1.7 Essential
attributes of good
software

Product characteristic	Description
Maintainability	Software should be written in such a way that it may evolve to meet the changing needs of customers. This is a critical attribute because software change is an inevitable consequence of a changing business environment.
Dependability	Software dependability has a range of characteristics, including reliability, security and safety. Dependable software should not cause physical or economic damage in the event of system failure.
Efficiency	Software should not make wasteful use of system resources such as memory and processor cycles. Efficiency therefore includes responsiveness, processing time, memory utilisation, etc.
Usability	Software must be usable, without undue effort, by the type of user for whom it is designed. This means that it should have an appropriate user interface and adequate documentation.

1.1.11   What are the key challenges facing software engineering?

Software engineering in the 21st century faces three key challenges:

1. *The legacy challenge*   The majority of large software systems which are in use today were developed many years ago yet they perform critical business functions. The legacy challenge is the challenge of maintaining and updating this software in such a way that excessive costs are avoided and essential business services continue to be delivered.

2. *The heterogeneity challenge*   Increasingly, systems are required to operate as distributed systems across networks that include different types of computer and with different kinds of support systems. The heterogeneity challenge is the challenge of developing techniques to build dependable software which is flexible enough to cope with this heterogeneity.

3. *The delivery challenge*   Many traditional software engineering techniques are time-consuming. The time they take is required to achieve software quality. However, businesses today must be responsive and change very rapidly. Their supporting software must change equally rapidly. The delivery challenge is the challenge of shortening delivery times for large and complex systems without compromising system quality.

Of course, these are not independent. For example, it may be necessary to make rapid changes to a legacy system to make it accessible across a network. To address these challenges we will need new tools and techniques as well as innovative ways of combining and using existing software engineering methods.

1.2 Professional and ethical responsibility

Like other engineers, software engineers must accept that their job involves wider responsibilities than simply the application of technical skills. Their work is carried out within a legal and social framework. Software engineering is obviously bounded by local, national and international laws. Software engineers must behave in an ethical and morally responsible way if they are to be respected as professionals.

It goes without saying that engineers should uphold normal standards of honesty and integrity. They should not use their skills and abilities to behave in a dishonest way or in a way that will bring disrepute to the software engineering profession. However, there are areas where standards of acceptable behaviour are not bounded by laws but by the more tenuous notion of professional responsibility. Some of these are:

1. *Confidentiality*   Engineers should normally respect the confidentiality of their employers or clients irrespective of whether or not a formal confidentiality agreement has been signed.

2. *Competence*   Engineers should not misrepresent their level of competence. They should not knowingly accept work which is outwith their competence.

3. *Intellectual property rights*   Engineers should be aware of local laws governing the use of intellectual property such as patents, copyright, etc. They should be careful to ensure that the intellectual property of employers and clients is protected.

4. *Computer misuse*   Software engineers should not use their technical skills to misuse other people's computers. Computer misuse ranges from relatively trivial (game playing on an employer's machine, say) to extremely serious (dissemination of viruses).

In this respect, professional societies and institutions have an important role to play. Organisations such as the ACM, the IEEE (Institute of Electrical and Electronic Engineers) and the British Computer Society publish a code of professional conduct or code of ethics. Members of these organisations undertake to follow that code when they sign up for membership. These codes of conduct are generally concerned with fundamental ethical behaviour.

The ACM and the IEEE have cooperated to produce a joint code of ethics and professional practice. This code exists in both a short form, shown in Figure 1.8, and a longer form (Gotterbarn *et al.*, 1999) which adds detail and substance to the shorter version. The rationale behind this code is summarised in the first two paragraphs of the longer form:

Computers have a central and growing role in commerce, industry, government, medicine, education, entertainment and society at large. Software engineers are

Software Engineering Code of Ethics and Professional Practice

ACM/IEEE-CS Joint Task Force on Software Engineering Ethics and Professional Practices

PREAMBLE
The short version of the code summarizes aspirations at a high level of the abstraction; the clauses that are included in the full version give examples and details of how these aspirations change the way we act as software engineering professionals. Without the aspirations, the details can become legalistic and tedious; without the details, the aspirations can become high sounding but empty; together, the aspirations and the details form a cohesive code.

Software engineers shall commit themselves to making the analysis, specification, design, development, testing and maintenance of software a beneficial and respected profession. In accordance with their commitment to the health, safety and welfare of the public, software engineers shall adhere to the following Eight Principles:

1. PUBLIC – Software engineers shall act consistently with the public interest.
2. CLIENT AND EMPLOYER – Software engineers shall act in a manner that is in the best interests of their client and employer consistent with the public interest.
3. PRODUCT – Software engineers shall ensure that their products and related modifications meet the highest professional standards possible.
4. JUDGMENT – Software engineers shall maintain integrity and independence in their professional judgment.
5. MANAGEMENT – Software engineering managers and leaders shall subscribe to and promote an ethical approach to the management of software development and maintenance.
6. PROFESSION – Software engineers shall advance the integrity and reputation of the profession consistent with the public interest.
7. COLLEAGUES – Software engineers shall be fair to and supportive of their colleagues.
8. SELF – Software engineers shall participate in lifelong learning regarding the practice of their profession and shall promote an ethical approach to the practice of the profession.

Figure 1.8 ACM/IEEE
Code of Ethics
(©IEEE/ACM 1999)

those who contribute by direct participation or by teaching, to the analysis, specification, design, development, certification, maintenance and testing of software systems. Because of their roles in developing software systems, software engineers have significant opportunities to do good or cause harm, to enable others to do good or cause harm, or to influence others to do good or cause harm. To ensure, as much as possible, that their efforts will be used for good, software engineers must commit themselves to making software engineering a beneficial and respected profession. In accordance with that commitment, software engineers shall adhere to the following Code of Ethics and Professional Practice.

The Code contains eight Principles related to the behaviour of and decisions made by professional software engineers, including practitioners, educators, managers, supervisors and policy makers, as well as trainees and students of the profession. The Principles identify the ethically responsible relationships in which individuals, groups, and organizations participate and the primary obligations within these relationships. The Clauses of each Principle are illustrations of some of the obligations included in these relationships. These obligations are founded in the software engineer's humanity, in special care owed to people affected by the work of software engineers, and the unique elements of the practice of software engineering. The Code prescribes these as obligations of anyone claiming to be or aspiring to be a software engineer.

In any situation where different people have different views and objectives you are likely to be faced with ethical dilemmas. For example, if you disagree, in principle, with the policies of more senior management in the company, how should you react? Clearly, this depends on the particular individuals and the nature of the disagreement. Is it best to argue a case for your position from within the organisation or to resign on principle? If you feel that there are problems with a software project, when do you reveal these to management? If you discuss these while they are just a suspicion, you may be over-reacting to a situation; if you leave it too late, it may be impossible to resolve the difficulties.

Such ethical dilemmas face all of us in our professional lives and, fortunately, in most cases they are either relatively minor or can be resolved without too much difficulty. Where they cannot be resolved, engineers are faced with, perhaps, another problem. The principled action may be to resign from their job but this may well affect others such as their partner or their children.

A particularly difficult situation for professional engineers arises when their employer acts in an unethical way. Say a company is responsible for developing a safety-critical system and because of time-pressure falsifies the safety validation records. Is the engineer's responsibility to maintain confidentiality or to alert the customer or publicise, in some way, that the delivered system may be unsafe?

The problem here is that there are no absolutes when it comes to safety. Although the system may not have been validated according to predefined criteria, these criteria may be too strict. The system may actually operate safely throughout its lifetime. It is also the case that, even when properly validated, the system may fail and cause an accident. Early disclosure of problems may result in damage to the employer and other employees; failure to disclose problems may result in damage to others.

You must make up your own mind in these matters. In this case, the potential for damage, the extent of the damage and the people affected by the damage should influence the decision. If the situation is very dangerous, it may be justified to publicise it using the national press (say). However, you should always try to resolve the situation while respecting the rights of your employer.

Another ethical issue is participation in the development of military and nuclear systems. Some people feel strongly about these issues and do not wish to participate in any systems development associated with military systems. Others will work on military systems but not on weapons systems. Yet others feel that national defence is an overriding principle and have no ethical objections to working on weapons systems. The appropriate ethical position here depends entirely on the views of the individuals who are involved.

In this situation it is important that both employers and employees should make their views known to each other in advance. Where an organisation is involved in military or nuclear work, they should be able to specify that employees must be willing to accept any work assignment. Equally, if employees are taken on and make clear that they do not wish to work on such systems, employers should not put pressure on them to do so at some later date.

The general area of ethics and professional responsibility is one which has received increasing attention over the past few years. It can be considered from a philosophical standpoint where the basic principles of ethics are considered and software engineering ethics are discussed with reference to these basic principles. This is the approach taken by Laudon (1995) and to a lesser extent by Huff and Martin (1995).

However, I find this approach rather abstract and difficult to relate to my everyday experience. I much prefer the more concrete approach embodied in codes of conduct and practice. I think that ethics are best discussed in a software engineering context and not as a subject in their own right. In this book, therefore, I do not include abstract ethical discussions but, where appropriate, include examples in the exercises which can be the basis of an ethical discussion.

KEY POINTS

▶ Software engineering is an engineering discipline which is concerned with all aspects of software production.

▶ Software products consist of developed programs and associated documentation. Essential product attributes are maintainability, dependability, efficiency and usability.

▶ The software process consists of activities which are involved in developing software products. Basic activities are software specification, development, validation and evolution.

▶ Methods are organised ways of producing software. They include suggestions for the process to be followed, the notations to be used, rules governing the system descriptions which are produced and design guidelines.

▶ CASE tools are software systems which are designed to support routine activities in the software process such as editing design diagrams, checking diagram consistency and keeping track of program tests which have been run.

▶ Software engineers have responsibilities to the engineering profession and society. They should not simply be concerned with technical issues.

▶ Professional societies publish codes of conduct which set out the standards of behaviour expected of their members.

FURTHER READING

Software Engineering: An Engineering Approach. A general text that includes a number of useful case studies. (J. F. Peters and W. Pedrycz, 2000, John Wiley and Sons.)

'Software Engineering Code of Ethics is approved'. An article that discusses the background to the development of the ACM/IEEE Code of Ethics and that includes both the short and long form of the Code. (D. Gotterbarn, K. Miller and S. Rogerson, *Comm. ACM,* October 1999.)

Software Engineering: A Practitioner's Approach. A general textbook that surveys a wide variety of software engineering topics. (R. S. Pressman, 1997, McGraw Hill.)

Ethics and Computing: Living Responsibly in a Computerized World. A good overview of the topic along with a number of more specialised papers. (K. W. Bowyer, 1996, IEEE Computer Society Press.)

Professional Issues in Software Engineering. This is an excellent book discussing legal and professional issues as well as ethics. (F. Bott, A. Coleman, J. Eaton and D. Rowland, 1995, UCL Press.)

'No silver bullet: Essence and accidents of software engineering'. In spite of its age, this paper is a good general introduction to the problems of software engineering. The essential message of the paper hasn't changed in the past 13 years. (F. P. Brooks, *IEEE Computer,* 20(4), April 1987.)

EXERCISES

1.1 By making reference to the distribution of software costs discussed in section 1.1.7, explain why it is appropriate to consider software to be more than the programs which can be executed by end-users of a system.

1.2 What are the four important attributes which all software products should have? Suggest four other attributes which may be significant.

1.3 What is the difference between a software process model and a software process? Suggest two ways in which a software process model might be helpful in identifying possible process improvements.

1.4 Explain why system testing costs are particularly high for generic software products which are sold to a very wide market.

1.5 Software engineering methods only became widely used when CASE technology became available to support them. Suggest five types of method support which can be provided by CASE tools.

1.6   Apart from the challenges of legacy systems, heterogeneity and rapid delivery, identify other problems and challenges that software engineering is likely to face in the 21st century.

1.7   Discuss whether professional engineers should be certified in the same way as doctors or lawyers.

1.8   For each of the clauses in the ACM/IEEE Code of Ethics shown in Figure 1.8, suggest an appropriate example that illustrates that clause.

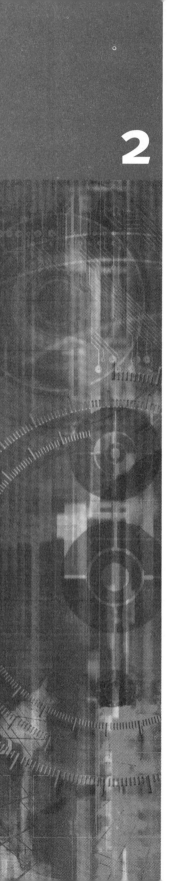

2 Computer-based system engineering

Objectives

The objective of this chapter is to introduce the concept of computer-based system engineering and to explain why knowledge of system engineering is important for software engineers. When you have read this chapter, you will:

❑ know why the software in a system is affected by broader system engineering issues;

❑ have been introduced to the concept of emergent system properties such as reliability, performance, safety and security;

❑ understand why the system's environment must be considered during the system design process;

❑ understand system engineering and system procurement processes.

Contents

2.1 Emergent system properties
2.2 Systems and their environment
2.3 System modelling
2.4 The system engineering process
2.5 System procurement

System engineering is the activity of specifying, designing, implementing, validating, deploying and maintaining systems *as a whole*. Systems engineers are not just concerned with software but with software, hardware and the system interactions with users and its environment. They must think about the services that the system provides, the constraints under which the system must be built and operated and the interactions of the system with its environment. Software engineers need an understanding of system engineering because problems of software engineering are often a result of system engineering decisions.

There are many possible definitions of a system from the very abstract to the concrete but a useful working definition is:

A system is a purposeful collection of interrelated components that work together to achieve some objective.

This general definition embraces a vast range of systems. For example, a very simple system such as a pen may only include three or four hardware components. By contrast, an air traffic control system is made up of thousands of hardware and software components plus human users who make decisions based on system information.

A characteristic of systems is that the properties and the behaviour of the system components are inextricably intermingled. The successful functioning of each system component depends on the functioning of some other components. Thus, software can only operate if the processor is operational. The processor can only carry out computations if the software system defining these computations has been successfully installed.

Systems are often hierarchical in that they include other systems. For example, a police command and control system may include a geographical information system to provide details of the location of incidents. These other systems are called *sub-systems*. A characteristic of sub-systems is that they can operate as independent systems in their own right. Therefore, the same geographical information system may be used in different systems. Its behaviour in a particular system, however, depends on its relationships with other sub-systems.

The complex relationships between the components in a system mean that the system is more than simply the sum of its parts. It has properties that are properties of the system as a whole. These *emergent properties* (Checkland, 1981) cannot be attributed to any specific part of the system. Rather, they emerge only when the system as a whole is considered. Some of these properties can be derived directly from the comparable properties of sub-systems but, more often, they result from complex sub-system interrelationships which cannot, in practice, be understood by analysing the individual system components.

Some examples of these emergent properties are:

1. *The overall weight of the system*   This is an example of an emergent property that can be computed from individual component properties.

2. *The reliability of the system*   This depends on the reliability of system components and the relationships between the components.

3. *The usability of a system*   This is a very complex property which is not simply dependent on the system hardware and software but also depends on the system operators and the environment where it is used.

In this book, I am concerned with computer-based systems which include hardware and software and which offer an interface, implemented in software, to human users. Software engineers should have some knowledge of computer-based system engineering (CBSE) (White *et al.*, 1993) because of the importance of software in these systems. For example, there were less than 10 megabytes of software in the US Apollo space programme to put a man on the moon in 1969 but there are about 100 megabytes of software in the US space station programme. Software engineering is therefore critical for the successful development of complex computer-based systems.

2.1 Emergent system properties

As discussed in the introduction to this chapter, the emergent properties of a system are attributes of the system as a whole. It is often difficult to predict the values of these emergent properties in advance. They can only be measured once the subsystems have been integrated to form the complete system.

There are two types of emergent properties:

1. Functional properties that appear when all the parts of a system work together to achieve some objective. For example, a bicycle has the functional property of being a transportation device once it has been assembled from its components.

2. Non-functional emergent properties such as reliability, performance, safety and security. These relate to the behaviour of the system in its operational environment. They are often critical for computer-based systems as failure to achieve some minimal defined level in these properties may make the system unusable. Some system functions may not be needed by all users so the system may be acceptable without them. However, a system that is unreliable or too slow is likely to be rejected by all its users.

To illustrate the complexity of emergent properties, consider system reliability. Reliability is a complex concept which must always be considered at the system rather than the individual component level. The components in a system are interdependent, so failures in one component can be propagated through the system and affect the operation of other components. System designers often cannot anticipate how the consequences of failures propagate through the system, so cannot make reliable estimates of reliability from data about the reliability of system components.

There are three closely related influences on the overall reliability of a system:

1. *Hardware reliability*   What is the probability of a hardware component failing and how long does it take to repair that component?

2. *Software reliability*   How likely is it that a software component will produce an incorrect output? Software failure is usually distinct from hardware failure in that software does not wear out. It can continue in operation even after an incorrect result has been produced. Software reliability is discussed in Chapters 16 and 17.

3. *Operator reliability*   How likely is it that the operator of a system will make an error?

All of these are closely linked. Hardware failure can cause spurious signals to be generated which are outside the range of inputs expected by software. The software can then behave unpredictably. Operator error is most likely in conditions of stress. These conditions arise when system failures are occurring. Operator errors may further stress the hardware, causing more failures and so on. Therefore, a situation can occur where a single sub-system failure that is recoverable can rapidly develop into a serious problem requiring a complete system shutdown.

Observed reliability depends on the context in which the system is used. As discussed already, the system environment cannot be specified in advance nor can the system designers place restrictions on that environment for operational systems. Different systems in an environment may react to problems in unpredictable ways, thus affecting the reliability of all of these systems. Therefore, even when the system has been integrated, it may be difficult to make accurate measurements of its reliability.

For example, say a system is designed to operate at normal room temperatures. To allow for variations and exceptional conditions, the electronic components of a system should be designed to operate within a certain range of temperature, say from 0 to 45 degrees. Outside this temperature range, the components will behave in an unpredictable way. Now assume that this system is installed close to an air conditioner. If this air conditioner fails and vents hot gas over the electronics these components and hence the whole system may then fail.

If this system had been installed elsewhere in that environment there would have been no problems. When the air conditioner worked normally there were no problems. However, because of the physical closeness of these machines, an unanticipated relationship existed between them that caused system failure.

Like reliability, other emergent properties such as performance or usability are difficult to assess but can be measured after the system is operational. Properties such as safety and security, however, pose different problems. Here, you are not simply concerned with an attribute that is related to the overall behaviour of the system but are concerned with behaviour that the system should *not* exhibit. A secure system is one which does not allow unauthorised access to its data but it is clearly impossible to predict all possible modes of access and explicitly forbid them. Therefore, it may only be possible to assess these properties by default. That is, you only know that a system is insecure when someone breaks into it.

2.2 Systems and their environment

Systems are not independent entities but exist in an environment. This environment affects the functioning and the performance of the system. Sometimes, the environment may be thought of as a system in its own right but, more generally, it consists of a number of other systems which interact with each other.

Figure 2.1 shows some of the systems that might be incorporated in an office building. The heating system, the power system, the lighting system, the plumbing system, the waste system and the security system are all sub-systems within the building which is itself a system. The building is located in a street that is in a town etc. The local environment of a system is the systems at the same level. The overall environment is composed of the local environment plus the environment of the containing system.

Consider the security system shown in the bottom left corner of Figure 2.1. The local environment of that security system is the other systems within the building. The overall environment includes all other systems outside the building in the street and the town as well as natural systems such as the weather system.

There are two main reasons why the environment of a system must be understood by systems engineers:

Figure 2.1 System hierarchies

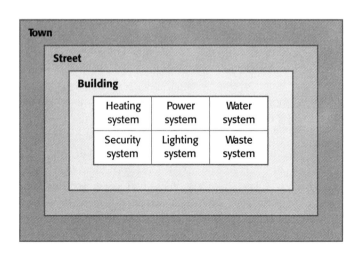

1. In many cases, the system is intended to make some changes in its environment. Therefore, a heating system changes its environment by increasing or decreasing its temperature. The correct functioning of the system can therefore only be assessed by the effects on the environment.

2. The functioning of a system can be affected by changes in its environment in ways which can be difficult to predict. For example, the electrical system in a building may be affected by environmental changes outside the building. Works in the street outside may cut a power cable and the electrical system is thus disabled. More subtly, a lightning storm can induce currents in the electrical system which affect its normal functioning.

As well as the physical environment shown in Figure 2.1, systems are also situated in an organisational environment. This includes policies and procedures that are themselves governed by wider political, economic, social and environmental issues. If the organisational environment is not properly understood, systems may not meet business needs and may be rejected by users and organisational managers.

Human and organisational factors deriving from the system's environment that affect the system design include:

1. *Process changes*   Does the system require changes to the work processes in the environment? If so, training will certainly be required. If changes are significant, or if they involve people losing their jobs, there is a danger that the system will be resisted by the users.

2. *Job changes*   Does the system de-skill the users in an environment or cause them to change the way they work? If so, they may actively resist the introduction of the system into the organisation. Designs that involve managers having to change their way of working to fit the computer system are often resented. The managers may feel that their status in the organisation is being reduced by the system.

3. *Organisational changes*   Does the system change the political power structure in an organisation? For example, if an organisation is dependent on a complex system, those who know how to operate the system have a great deal of political power.

These human, social and organisational factors are often critical in determining whether or not a system successfully meets its objectives. Unfortunately, predicting their effects on systems is very difficult for engineers who have little experience of social or cultural studies. To help understand the effects of systems on organisations, various methodologies have been developed such as Mumford's sociotechnics (Mumford, 1989) and Checkland's Soft Systems Methodology (Checkland, 1981; Checkland and Scholes, 1990). There have also been extensive sociological studies of the effects of computer-based systems on work (Ackroyd *et al.*, 1992).

Ideally, all relevant environmental knowledge should be included in the system specification so that it may be taken into account by the system designers. In reality, this is impossible. System designers must make environmental assumptions based on other comparable systems and on common sense. If they get these wrong, the system may malfunction in unpredictable ways. For example, if the designers of a system do not understand the notion of electromagnetic compatibility, then the system may malfunction when it is installed alongside other systems which emit electromagnetic radiation.

2.3 System modelling

As part of the system requirements and design activity, the system has to be modelled as a set of components and relationships between these components. These are normally illustrated graphically in a system architecture model that gives the reader an overview of the system organisation.

The system architecture is usually depicted as a block diagram showing the major sub-systems and the interconnections between these sub-systems. Each sub-system is represented by a rectangle in the block diagram and the existence of relationships between sub-systems is indicated by arrows joining these rectangles. The relationships indicated may include data flow, a 'uses'/'used by' relationship or some other type of dependency relationship.

This is illustrated in Figure 2.2 which shows the decomposition of an intruder alarm system into its principal components. The block diagram should be supplemented by brief descriptions of each sub-system as shown in Figure 2.3.

At this level of detail, the system is decomposed into sub-systems. Each sub-system can be represented in a similar way until the system is decomposed into

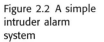

Figure 2.2 A simple intruder alarm system

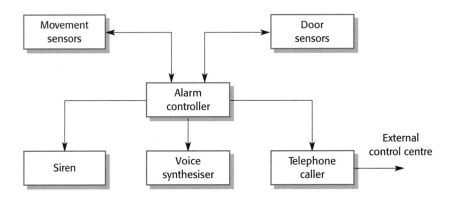

Figure 2.3
Sub-system
functionality in
the intruder
alarm system

Subsystem	Description
Movement sensors	Detects movement in the rooms monitored by the system
Door sensors	Detects door opening in the external doors of the building
Alarm controller	Controls the operation of the system
Siren	Emits an audible warning when an intruder is suspected
Voice synthesiser	Synthesises a voice message giving the location of the suspected intruder
Telephone caller	Makes external calls to notify security, the police, etc.

functional components. Functional components are components that, when viewed from the perspective of the sub-system, provide a single function. By contrast, a sub-system usually is multi-functional. Of course, when viewed from another perspective (say that of the component manufacturer), a functional component may itself be a system in its own right.

Historically, the system architecture model was used to identify hardware and software components which could be developed in parallel. However, this hardware/software distinction is becoming irrelevant. Almost all components now include some embedded computing capabilities. For example, a network linking machines will consist of physical cables plus repeaters and network gateways. The repeaters and the gateways include processors and software to drive these processors as well as specialised electronic components.

At the architectural level, it is now more appropriate to classify sub-systems according to their function before making decisions about hardware/software trade-offs. The decision whether a function should be provided in hardware or software may be governed by non-technical factors such as the availability of COTS components or the time available to develop the component.

Block diagrams may be used for all sizes of system. Figure 2.4 illustrates the architecture of a much larger system for air traffic control. There are several major sub-systems which are themselves large systems. Information flow between these sub-systems is shown by the arrowed lines connecting these systems.

2.3.1 Functional system components

As discussed in the previous section, a system architecture should be designed in terms of functional sub-systems without regard to whether these are hardware or software sub-systems. Rather, the functional components in a system may be classified under a number of different headings:

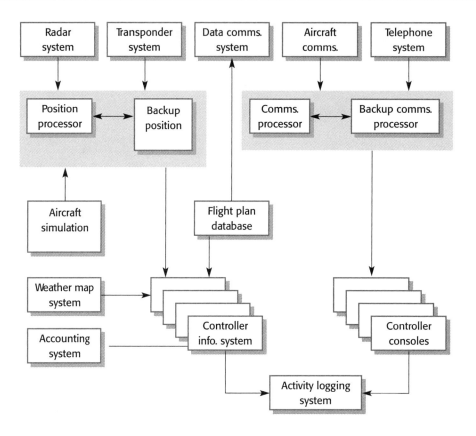

Figure 2.4 The architecture of an air traffic control system

1. *Sensor components* collect information from the system's environment. Examples of sensor components are radars in an air traffic control system, paper position sensors in a laser printer and a thermocouple in a furnace.

2. *Actuator components* cause some change in the systems environment. Examples of actuators are valves which open and close to increase or decrease the flow rate of liquid in a pipe, the flight surfaces on an aircraft which control the angle of flight and the paper feed mechanism on a laser printer which moves the paper across the scanning beam.

3. *Computation components* are components which, given some input, carry out some computations on that input and produce some output. An example of a computation component is a floating-point processor which carries out computations on real numbers.

4. *Communication components* are components whose function is to allow other system components to communicate with each other. An example of a communication component is an Ethernet linking different computers in a building.

5. *Coordination components* are system components whose function is to coordinate the operation of other components. An example of a coordination

Figure 2.5
Component types in
the intruder alarm
system

Component type	Components	Function
Sensor	Movement sensor, Door sensor	Detect movement in a protected space, detect protected door opening
Actuator	Siren	Audible warning of intrusion
Communication	Telephone caller	Call external control centre to issue warning of intrusion. Receive commands from control centre
Coordination	Alarm controller	Coordinate all system components. Act on commands from control panel and control centre
Interface	Voice synthesiser	Synthesise message giving location of intrusion

component is a scheduler in a real-time system. This decides when the different processes should be scheduled to run on a processor.

6. *Interface components* are components that transform the representation used by one system component into the representation used by another component. An example is a human interface component that takes some system model and displays it for the human operator. Another example is an analog–digital converter that converts an analog input into a digital output.

Figure 2.5 explains which of these different functional component types are used in the alarm system architecture illustrated in Figure 2.2.

Of course, there is no hard and fast division between the different component types. In the types of systems in which software engineers are likely to be involved, most components will include embedded software. Software will usually be used to control the overall system.

These component classifications are helpful when designing a system. Most systems include all of these types of component and you should explicitly identify each type of component from the requirements. If one or more component types is missing, this suggests that you may have left something out of your design.

2.4 The system engineering process

The phases of the system engineering process are shown in Figure 2.6. This process was an important influence on the 'waterfall' model of the software process which we discuss in Chapter 3.

Figure 2.6 The
system engineering
process

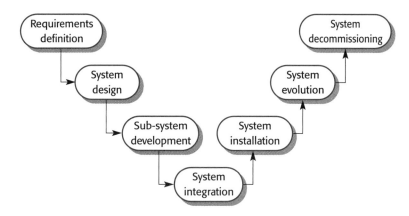

There are important distinctions between the system engineering process and the software development process:

1. *Interdisciplinary involvement*   Many different engineering disciplines may be involved in system engineering. There is immense scope for misunderstanding because of the different terminology used by different engineers.

2. *Reduced scope for rework during system development*   Once some system engineering decisions, such as the siting of radars in an ATC system, have been made they are very expensive to change. Reworking the system design to solve these problems is rarely possible. One reason why software has become so important in systems is that it allows for flexibility as changes can be made during the system development in response to new requirements.

System engineering is an interdisciplinary activity involving teams drawn from different backgrounds. System engineering teams are needed because of the wide knowledge required to consider all the implications of system design decisions. Consider an air traffic control (ATC) system that uses radars and other sensors to determine aircraft position (see Figure 2.4). Figure 2.7 shows some of the different disciplines that may be involved in the system engineering team.

For many systems, there are almost infinite possibilities for trade-offs between different types of sub-system. Different engineering disciplines must negotiate to decide how functionality should be provided. Often there is no 'correct' decision on how a system should be decomposed. Rather, there is a range of possible alternatives. The selection of one of these alternatives need not necessarily be made for technical reasons. Say one alternative in an air traffic control system is to build new radars rather than refit existing installations. If the civil engineers involved in this process do not have much other work, they may favour this alternative because it allows them to keep their jobs. They may then rationalise this choice using technical arguments.

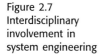
Figure 2.7
Interdisciplinary
involvement in
system engineering

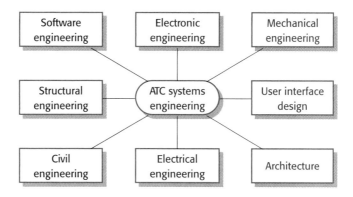

Because software is inherently flexible, many unexpected problems are left to software engineers to solve. Say the site of a radar is such that some image ghosting occurs. It is impractical to move the radar so some other way of removing this ghosting is required. The solution may be to enhance the image processing capabilities of the software to remove the ghost images. This may then require increased processor power in the system which may be difficult to provide.

Software engineers are often left with the problem of enhancing the software capabilities without increasing the hardware cost. Many so-called 'software failures' were not a consequence of inherent software problems. They were the result of trying to change the software to accommodate modified system engineering requirements. A good example of this was the failure of the Denver airport baggage system (Swartz, 1996).

2.4.1   System requirements definition

The system requirements definition activity is intended to discover the requirements for the system as a whole. As with software requirements analysis, the process involves consultations with system customers and end-users. This requirements definition phase usually concentrates on deriving three types of requirement:

1. *Abstract functional requirements* The basic functions that the system must provide are defined at an abstract level. Detailed functional requirements specification takes place at the sub-system level. For example, in the air traffic control system, this requirements activity would probably identify the need for a flight-plan database to store the flight plans of all aircraft entering the controlled airspace. However, the details of the database would not be specified unless they affected the requirements of other sub-systems.

2. *System properties* These are non-functional emergent system properties as discussed above. These may include properties such as availability, performance, safety, etc. These non-functional system properties affect the requirements for all sub-systems.

3. *Characteristics which the system must not exhibit* It is sometimes as important to specify what the system must not do as it is to specify what the system should do. For example, in an air traffic control system, it might be specified that the system should not present the controller with too much information.

An important part of the requirements definition phase is to establish a set of overall objectives which the system should meet. These should not necessarily be expressed in terms of the system's functionality but should define why the system is being procured for a particular environment.

To illustrate the distinction between these, consider a system for an office building to provide for fire protection and for intruder detection. A statement of objectives which is based around the system functionality might be:

To provide a fire and intruder alarm system for the building that will provide internal and external warning of fire or unauthorised intrusion.

This objective states explicitly that there needs to be an alarm system which provides some warnings of undesired events. Such a statement might be appropriate if there were already an existing alarm system which was to be replaced. By contrast, a broader statement of objectives might be:

To ensure that the normal functioning of the work carried out in the building is not seriously disrupted by events such as fire and unauthorised intrusion.

Stating the objective in this way both broadens and limits some design choices. It allows for intruder protection using sophisticated locking technology without any internal alarms. It may exclude the use of sprinklers for fire protection. These may affect the electrical systems in the building and seriously disrupt work which is going on.

A fundamental difficulty in establishing system requirements is that the problems which complex systems are usually built to help tackle are usually 'wicked problems' (Rittel and Webber, 1973). A 'wicked problem' is a problem which is so complex and where there are so many related entities that there is no definitive problem specification. The true nature of the problem only emerges as a solution is developed. An extreme example of a 'wicked problem' is earthquake planning. No one can accurately predict where the epicentre of an earthquake will be, what time it will occur, what effect it will have on the local environment, etc. We cannot therefore completely specify how to deal with a major earthquake. The problem can only be tackled after it has happened.

2.4.2 System design

System design (Figure 2.8) is concerned with how the system functionality is to be provided by the different components of the system. The activities involved in this process are:

Figure 2.8
The system
design process

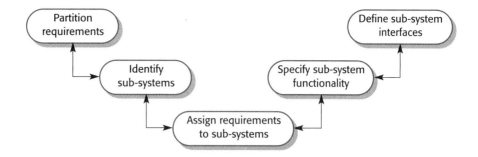

1. *Partition requirements* The requirements are analysed and collected into related groups. There are usually several possible partitioning options and a number of alternatives may be produced at this stage of the process.

2. *Identify sub-systems* Different sub-systems that can individually or collectively meet the requirements are identified. Groups of requirements are usually related to sub-systems, so this activity and requirements partitioning may be amalgamated. However, the sub-system identification may also be influenced by other organisational or environmental factors.

3. *Assign requirements to sub-systems* The requirements are assigned to sub-systems. In principle, this should be straightforward if the requirements partitioning is used to drive the sub-system identification. In practice, there is never a clean match between requirements partitions and identified sub-systems. Limitations of externally purchased sub-systems (COTS, see section 2.4.3) may mean that requirements have to be modified.

4. *Specify sub-system functionality* The specific functions provided by each sub-system are specified. This may be seen as part of the system design phase or, if the sub-system is a software system, part of the requirements specification activity for that system. Relationships between sub-systems should also be identified at this stage.

5. *Define sub-system interfaces* This involves defining the interfaces that are provided and required by each sub-system. Once these interfaces have been agreed, parallel development of the sub-systems becomes possible.

As the double-ended arrows in Figure 2.8 imply, there is a great deal of feedback and iteration from one stage to another in this design process. As problems and questions arise, rework of earlier stages is often necessary.

For almost all systems, there are many possible designs which may be developed. These cover a range of solutions with different combinations of hardware, software and human operations. The solution chosen for further development may be the most appropriate technical solution which meets the requirements. However, in many cases wider organisational and political influences influence the choice of solution. For example, if the system is a government system, it may prefer national rather than foreign suppliers even if the national product is technically inferior.

Sub-system development

During sub-system development, the sub-systems identified during system design are implemented. This may involve entering another system engineering process for individual sub-systems. Where a sub-system is a software system, a software process involving requirements, design, implementation, etc. may be started.

Occasionally, the development process will develop all sub-systems from scratch. More normally, however, some of the sub-systems are commercial, off-the-shelf (COTS) systems that are bought for integration into the system. It is usually much cheaper to buy existing products rather than develop special-purpose components. At this stage, the design activity may have to be re-entered to accommodate a bought-in component. COTS systems may not meet the requirements exactly but, if off-the-shelf products are available, it is usually worth the expense of rethinking the design.

Different sub-systems are usually developed in parallel. When problems are encountered which cut across sub-system boundaries, a system modification request must be made. Where systems involve extensive hardware engineering, making modifications after manufacturing has started is usually very expensive. Often 'work-arounds' which compensate for the problem must be found. These 'work-arounds' usually involve software changes because of the software's inherent flexibility. This leads to changes in the software requirements so, as I have discussed in Chapter 1, it is important to design software for change.

System integration

System integration involves taking independently developed sub-systems and putting them together to make up a complete system. Integration can be done using a 'big bang' approach where all the sub-systems are integrated at the same time. However, for both technical and managerial reasons, an incremental integration process where sub-systems are integrated one at a time is the best approach to adopt.

This incremental process is the most appropriate approach for two reasons:

1. It is usually impossible to schedule all the different sub-system developments so that all development is completed at the same time.

2. Incremental integration reduces the cost of error location. If many sub-systems are simultaneously integrated, an error that arises during testing may be located in any of these sub-systems. When a single sub-system is integrated with an already working system, errors which occur are probably in the newly integrated sub-system or in the interactions between the existing sub-systems and the new sub-system.

Sub-system faults that are a consequence of invalid assumptions about other sub-systems are often revealed during system integration. These may lead to disputes between the various contractors responsible for the different sub-systems. When problems are discovered in sub-system interaction, the different contractors may argue about who is responsible for the problem. Negotiations on how to solve the problems may take several weeks or months to resolve.

2.4.5   System installation

During system installation, the system is put into the environment in which it is intended to operate. While this may appear to be a simple process, many problems can arise which mean that the installation of a complex system can take months or even years.

Examples of these problems are:

1. The environment in which the system is to be installed is not the same as the environment assumed by the developers of the system. This is a common problem when software systems are installed. For example, the system may use functions provided by a specific version of the operating system. These may not be identical in the operating system version in the installation environment. When the system is installed, it may not work at all or may operate in a way that was not anticipated by its developers.

2. Potential users of the system may be hostile to its introduction. It may reduce their responsibility or the number of jobs in an organisation. People may therefore deliberately refuse to cooperate with the system installers. For example, they may refuse to participate in operator training or may deny access to information that is essential for system installation.

3. A new system may have to coexist with an existing system until the organisation is satisfied that the new system works properly. This causes particular installation problems if the systems are not completely independent but share some components. It may be impossible to install the new system without de-installing the old system. Trials of the new system can therefore only take place at times when the existing system is not used.

4. There may be physical installation problems. There may be difficulties fitting a new system into an existing building as there may not be enough room in existing ducts for network cables, air conditioning may be required, the furniture may not be large enough, etc. If the installation is to take place in a historic building, building modifications may be completely forbidden.

2.4.6   System operation

Once the system has been installed, it is put into operation. Operating the system may involve organising training sessions for operators and changing the normal work process to make effective use of the new system. Undetected problems may arise at this stage because the system specification may contain errors or omissions. While the system may perform to specification, its functions may not meet real operational needs. Consequently, the mode of use of the system may not be as anticipated by the system designers.

A problem that may emerge only after the system goes into operation is the problem of operating the new system with existing systems. There may be physical problems of incompatibility. It may be difficult to transfer data from one system to another. More subtle problems might be radically different user interfaces offered by different systems. Introducing the new system may increase the operator error rate for existing systems as operators mix up user interface commands.

2.4.7 System evolution

Large and complex systems have a very long lifetime. During their life, they have to evolve to correct errors in the original system requirements and meet new requirements which have emerged. The system's computers are likely to be replaced with new, faster machines. The organisation which uses the system may reorganise itself and hence use the system in a different way. The external environment of the system may change, thus forcing changes to the system.

System evolution, like software evolution (discussed in Part 7), is inherently costly for a number of reasons:

1. Proposed changes have to be analysed very carefully both from a business and a technical perspective. They must be approved by a range of people before being put into effect.

2. Because sub-systems are never completely independent, changes to one sub-system may adversely affect the performance or behaviour of other sub-systems. Consequent changes to these sub-systems may therefore be needed.

3. The reasons for original design decisions are often unrecorded. Those responsible for the system evolution have to work out why particular design decisions were made.

4. As systems age, their structure typically becomes corrupted by change so the costs of making further changes increases.

As society becomes increasingly dependent on systems of various types, the amount of effort devoted to evolution rather than new system development is increasing. These existing systems that must be retained are now sometimes called *legacy systems*. I discuss legacy systems in Chapter 26.

2.4.8 System decommissioning

System decommissioning means taking the system out of service after the end of its useful operational lifetime. Sometimes this is straightforward but some systems may contain materials which are potentially damaging to the environment. The system engineering activity should anticipate decommissioning and take the problems of disposing of the materials into account during the design phase. For example, the use of toxic chemicals might be confined to sealed modules which can be removed as a single unit and reprocessed.

As far as software is concerned there are, of course, no physical decommissioning problems. However, some software functionality may be incorporated in a system to assist with the decommissioning process. For example, software may be used to monitor the state of other system components. When the system is decommissioned, components which are not worn can therefore be identified and reused in other systems.

If the data in the system that is being decommissioned must be retained by the organisation, it must be converted for use by some other system. This can often involve significant costs as the data structure may be implicitly defined in the software itself. I cover some of these problems of data re-engineering in Chapter 28.

2.5 System procurement

The customers for complex computer-based systems are usually large organisations such as the military, government and emergency services. The system may be bought as a whole, may be bought as separate parts which are then integrated or may be specially designed and developed. For large systems, deciding which of these options to choose can take several months or years. The process of system procurement is concerned with making decisions about the best way for an organisation to acquire a system and deciding on the best suppliers of that system.

The procurement process is closely related to the systems engineering process. Some system specification and architectural design is done before these procurement decisions are made. There are two main reasons for this:

1. To buy or let a contract to design and build a system, a high-level specification of what that system should do must be completed.

2. It is almost always cheaper to buy a system than to design, manufacture and build it as a separate project. Some architectural design is necessary to identify those sub-systems that can be bought rather than specially designed and manufactured.

Large complex systems usually consist of a mixture of off-the-shelf components (COTS) and specially built components. One reason why more and more software is included in systems is that it allows more use of existing hardware components with the software acting as a 'glue' to make these different pieces of hardware work together effectively. The need to develop this 'glueware' is one reason why the savings from using off-the-shelf components are sometimes not as great as anticipated. I discuss the use of COTS systems in Chapter 14.

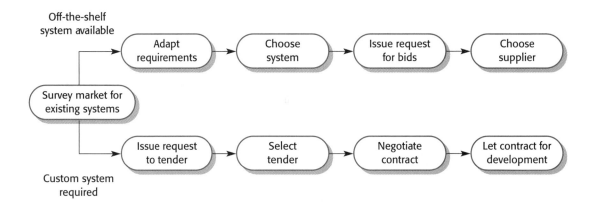

Figure 2.9 The
system procurement
process
Figure 2.9 shows the procurement process for both existing systems and systems which have to be specially designed. Some important points about the process shown in this diagram are:

1. Off-the-shelf components do not usually match requirements exactly, unless the requirements have been written with these components in mind. Therefore, choosing a system means finding the closest match between the system requirements and the facilities offered by off-the-shelf systems. The requirements then have to be modified. This can have knock-on effects on other sub-systems.

2. When a system is to be built specially, the specification of requirements acts as the basis of a contract for the system procurement. It is therefore a legal as well as a technical document.

3. After a contractor to build a system has been selected, there is a further contract negotiation period where further changes to the requirements may be agreed and issues such as the cost of change discussed.

Most hardware sub-systems and many software sub-systems such as database management systems are not developed specially when they are included in some larger system. Rather, existing sub-systems are used as they stand or are adapted for use in that system.

Very few single organisations have the capabilities to design, manufacture and test all the components of a large complex system. This supplier, who is usually called the principal contractor, may contract out the development of different sub-systems to a number of subcontractors (Figure 2.10). For large systems, such as air traffic control systems, a group of suppliers may form a consortium to bid for the contract. The consortium should include all of the capabilities required for this type of system so may include computer hardware suppliers, software developers, peripheral suppliers and suppliers of specialist equipment such as radars.

This contractor/subcontractor model minimises the number of organisations with which the procurer must deal. The subcontractors design and build parts of the system to a specification produced by the principal contractor. Once completed, these

Figure 2.10
The contractor/
subcontractor model

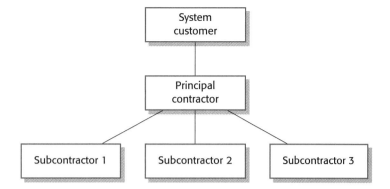

different parts are integrated by the principal contractor. They are then delivered to the customer buying the system. Depending on the contract, the procurer may allow the principal contractor a free choice of subcontractors or may require the principal contractor to choose subcontractors from an approved list.

KEY POINTS

▶ System engineering is a complex and difficult process which requires input from a range of engineering disciplines.

▶ The emergent properties of a system are properties that are characteristic of the system as a whole rather than of its component parts. They include properties such as performance, reliability, usability, safety and security. The success or failure of a system is often dependent on these emergent properties.

▶ System architectures are usually described using block diagrams showing the major sub-systems and their relationships.

▶ Types of functional system component include sensor components, actuator components, computation components, coordination components, communication components and interface components.

▶ The system engineering process includes specification, design, development, integration and testing. System integration, where sub-systems from different suppliers must be made to work together, is particularly critical.

▶ The system procurement process involves specifying the system, issuing a request for proposals, choosing a supplier and then letting a contract for the system. Usually, some parts of large computer-based systems are procured as commercial off-the-shelf (COTS) components.

FURTHER READING

Systems Engineering: Coping with Complexity. At the time of writing, this is the best available systems engineering book. It focuses on systems engineering processes with good chapters on requirements, architecture and project management. (R. Stevens, P. Brook, K. Jackson and S. Arnold, 1998, Prentice-Hall.)

'Airport 95: Automated baggage system'. An excellent and readable case study of what can go wrong with a systems engineering project and how software tends to get the blame for wider systems failures. (*ACM Software Engineering Notes*, 21, March 1996.)

'System engineering of computer-based systems'. This paper is a good overview of computer-based system engineering and calls for the establishment of a discipline of ECBS, i.e. the Engineering of Computer-based Systems. (S. White *et al., IEEE Computer*, **26**(11), November 1993.)

Systems Engineering: Principles and Practice of Computer-based Systems Engineering. Covers various aspects of CBSE, including the development process, project management and system design methods. (B. Thomé (ed.), 1993, John Wiley and Sons.)

EXERCISES

2.1 Explain why other systems within a system's environment can have unanticipated effects on the functioning of a system.

2.2 Modify Figure 2.8 to incorporate an explicit procurement activity once the sub-systems have been identified. Show, in your diagram, the feedback that results from the incorporation of this activity.

2.3 Explain why specifying a system to be used by emergency services for disaster management is an inherently wicked problem.

2.4 Suggest how the software systems used in a car can help with the decommissioning (scrapping) of the overall system.

2.5 Explain why it is important to produce an overall description of a system architecture at an early stage in the system specification process.

2.6 Figure 2.1 shows a range of systems in a building. The security system is an extended version of the system shown in Figure 2.2 that is intended to protect against intrusion and to detect fire. It incorporates smoke sensors, movement sensors and door sensors, video cameras, under computer control, located at various places in the building, an operator console where the system status is reported, and external communication facilities to call the appropriate services such as police, fire, etc. Draw a block diagram of a possible design for such a system.

2.7 A flood warning system is to be procured which will give early warning of possible flood dangers to sites that are threatened by floods. The system will include a set of sensors to monitor the rate of change of river levels, links to a meteorological system giving weather forecasts, links to the communication systems of emergency services (police, coastguard, etc.), video monitors installed at selected locations, and a control room equipped with operator consoles and video monitors.

Controllers can access database information and switch video displays. The system database includes information about the sensors, the location of sites at risk and the threat conditions for these sites (e.g. high tide, south-westerly winds), tide tables for coastal sites, the inventory and location of flood control equipment, contact details for emergency services, local radio stations, etc.

Draw a block diagram of a possible architecture for such a system. You should identify the principal sub-systems and the links between them.

2.8 Assuming that some system which has been ordered meets its specification, describe, using associated examples, three problems which might arise when it is installed in an organisation.

2.9 What are the arguments for and against considering system engineering as a profession in its own right such as electrical engineering or software engineering?

2.10 You are an engineer involved in the development of a financial system. During installation, you discover that this system will make a significant number of people redundant. The people in the environment deny you access to essential information to complete the system installation. To what extent should you, as a systems engineer, become involved in this? Is it your professional responsibility to complete the installation as contracted? Should you simply abandon the work until the procuring organisation has sorted out the problem?

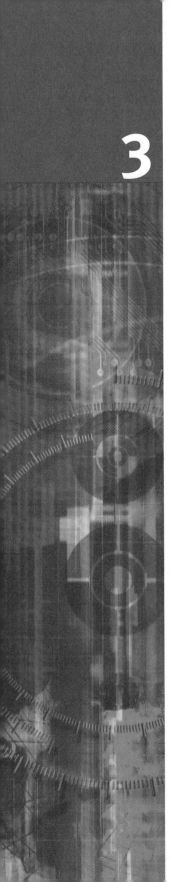

3 Software processes

Objectives

The objective of this chapter is to introduce you to the idea of a software process – a coherent set of activities for software production. When you have read this chapter you will:

❏ understand the concept of a software process and a software process model;

❏ understand a number of different software process models and when they might be used;

❏ understand, in outline, process models for software requirements engineering, software development, testing and evolution;

❏ have been introduced to CASE technology for software process support.

Contents

3.1   Software process models
3.2   Process iteration
3.3   Software specification
3.4   Software design and implementation
3.5   Software validation
3.6   Software evolution
3.7   Automated process support

As I suggested in Chapter 1, a software process is a set of activities and associated results which lead to the production of a software product. These may involve the development of software from scratch although it is increasingly the case that new software is developed by extending and modifying existing systems.

Software processes are complex and, like all intellectual processes, are reliant on human judgement. Because of the need for judgement and creativity, attempts to automate software processes have met with limited success. CASE tools (discussed in section 3.7) can support some process activities but there is no possibility, at least in the next few years, of more extensive automation where software takes over creative design from the engineers involved in the software process.

One reason why there is limited scope for process automation is the immense diversity of software processes. There is no ideal process and different organisations have developed completely different approaches to software development. Processes have evolved to exploit the capabilities of the people in an organisation and the specific characteristics of the systems which are being developed. Therefore, even within the same company, there may be many different processes used for software development.

Although there are many different software processes, there are fundamental activities which are common to all software processes. These are:

1. *Software specification*   The functionality of the software and constraints on its operation must be defined.
2. *Software design and implementation*   The software to meet the specification must be produced.
3. *Software validation*   The software must be validated to ensure that it does what the customer wants.
4. *Software evolution*   The software must evolve to meet changing customer needs.

I present an overview of these activities in this chapter and discuss them in much more detail in later parts of the book.

Although there is no 'ideal' software process, there is a lot of scope for improving the software process in many organisations. Processes may include outdated techniques or may not take advantage of the best practice in industrial software engineering. Indeed, many organisations still rely on *ad hoc* processes and do not take advantage of software engineering methods in their software development.

Software process improvement can be implemented in a number of different ways. It may come about through process standardisation where the diversity in software processes in an organisation is reduced. This leads to improved communication, reduction in training time and makes automated process support more economic. Standardisation is also an essential first step in introducing new software engineering methods and techniques and good software engineering practice. I return to the topic of software process improvement in Chapter 25.

3.1 Software process models

As discussed in Chapter 1, a software process model is an abstract representation of a software process. Each process model represents a process from a particular perspective so only provides partial information about that process. In this section, I introduce a number of very general process models (sometimes called process paradigms) and present these from an architectural perspective. That is, we see the framework of the process but not the details of specific activities.

These generic models are not definitive descriptions of software processes. Rather, they are useful abstractions which can be used to explain different approaches to software development. For many large systems, of course, there is no single software process that is used. Different processes are used to develop different parts of the system.

The process models that I discuss in this chapter are:

1. *The waterfall model* This takes the fundamental process activities of specification, development, validation and evolution and represents them as separate process phases such as requirements specification, software design, implementation, testing and so on.

2. *Evolutionary development* This approach interleaves the activities of specification, development and validation. An initial system is rapidly developed from abstract specifications. This is then refined with customer input to produce a system which satisfies the customer's needs.

3. *Formal systems development* This approach is based on producing a formal mathematical system specification and transforming this specification, using mathematical methods, to construct a program. Verification of system components is carried out by making mathematical arguments that they conform to their specification.

4. *Reuse-based development* This approach is based on the existence of a significant number of reusable components. The system development process focuses on integrating these components into a system rather than developing them from scratch.

Processes based on the waterfall model and evolutionary development are widely used for practical systems development. Formal system development has been successfully used in a number of projects (Mills *et al.*, 1987; Linger, 1994) but processes based on this model are still only used in a few organisations. Informal reuse is common in many processes but most organisations do not explicitly orient their software development processes around reuse. However, this approach is likely to be very influential in the 21st century as assembling systems from reusable components is essential for rapid software development. I discuss software reuse in Chapter 14.

3.1.1   The 'waterfall' model

The first published model of the software development process was derived from other engineering processes (Royce, 1970). This is illustrated in Figure 3.1. Because of the cascade from one phase to another, this model is known as the 'waterfall model' or software life cycle. The principal stages of the model map onto fundamental development activities:

1. *Requirements analysis and definition*   The system's services, constraints and goals are established by consultation with system users. They are then defined in detail and serve as a system specification.

2. *System and software design*   The systems design process partitions the requirements to either hardware or software systems. It establishes an overall system architecture. Software design involves identifying and describing the fundamental software system abstractions and their relationships.

3. *Implementation and unit testing*   During this stage, the software design is realised as a set of programs or program units. Unit testing involves verifying that each unit meets its specification.

4. *Integration and system testing*   The individual program units or programs are integrated and tested as a complete system to ensure that the software requirements have been met. After testing, the software system is delivered to the customer.

5. *Operation and maintenance*   Normally (although not necessarily) this is the longest life-cycle phase. The system is installed and put into practical use. Maintenance involves correcting errors which were not discovered in earlier stages of the life cycle, improving the implementation of system units and enhancing the system's services as new requirements are discovered.

Figure 3.1 The software life cycle

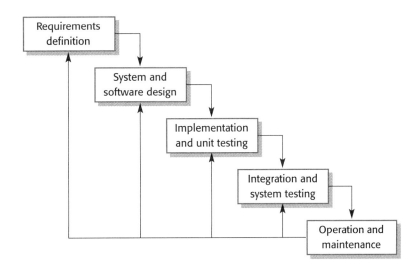

In principle, the result of each phase is one or more documents which are approved ('signed off'). The following phase should not start until the previous phase has finished. In practice, these stages overlap and feed information to each other. During design, problems with requirements are identified, during coding design problems are found and so on. The software process is not a simple linear model but involves a sequence of iterations of the development activities.

Because of the costs of producing and approving documents, iterations are costly and involve significant rework. Therefore, after a small number of iterations, it is normal to freeze parts of the development, such as the specification, and to continue with the later development stages. Problems are left for later resolution, ignored or are programmed around. This premature freezing of requirements may mean that the system won't do what the user wants. It may also lead to badly structured systems as design problems are circumvented by implementation tricks.

During the final life-cycle phase (operation and maintenance) the software is put into use. Errors and omissions in the original software requirements are discovered. Program and design errors emerge and the need for new functionality is identified. The system must therefore evolve to remain useful. Making these changes (software maintenance) may involve repeating some or all previous process stages.

The problem with the waterfall model is its inflexible partitioning of the project into these distinct stages. Commitments must be made at an early stage in the process and this means that it is difficult to respond to changing customer requirements. Therefore, the waterfall model should only be used when the requirements are well understood. However, the waterfall model reflects engineering practice. Consequently, software processes based on this approach are still used for software development, particularly when this is part of a larger systems engineering project.

3.1.2 Evolutionary development

Evolutionary development is based on the idea of developing an initial implementation, exposing this to user comment and refining this through many versions until an adequate system has been developed (Figure 3.2). Rather than have separate specification, development and validation activities, these are carried out concurrently with rapid feedback across these activities.

There are two types of evolutionary development:

1. *Exploratory development* where the objective of the process is to work with the customer to explore their requirements and deliver a final system. The development starts with the parts of the system which are understood. The system evolves by adding new features as they are proposed by the customer.

2. *Throw-away prototyping* where the objective of the evolutionary development process is to understand the customer's requirements and hence develop a better requirements definition for the system. The prototype concentrates on experimenting with those parts of the customer requirements which are poorly understood.

Figure 3.2
Evolutionary
development

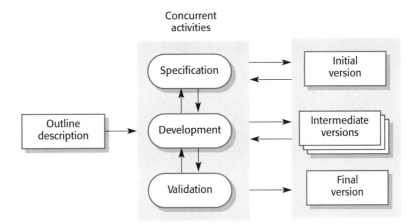

I cover evolutionary development processes and process support in Chapter 8 where various prototyping techniques are described.

An evolutionary approach to software development is often more effective than the waterfall approach in producing systems which meet the immediate needs of customers. The advantage of a software process which is based on an evolutionary approach is that the specification can be developed incrementally. As users develop a better understanding of their problem, this can be reflected in the software system. However, from an engineering and management perspective, it has three problems:

1. *The process is not visible*   Managers need regular deliverables to measure progress. If systems are developed quickly, it is not cost-effective to produce documents which reflect every version of the system.

2. *Systems are often poorly structured*   Continual change tends to corrupt the software structure. Incorporating software changes becomes increasingly difficult and costly.

3. *Special tools and techniques may be required*   These allow for rapid development but they may be incompatible with other tools or techniques and relatively few people may have the skills which are needed to use them.

For small systems (less than 100,000 lines of code) or for medium-sized systems (up to 500,000 lines of code) with a fairly short lifetime, I think that the evolutionary approach to development is the best approach. However, for large, long-lifetime systems, the problems of evolutionary development become particularly acute. For these systems, I recommend a mixed process that incorporates the best features of the waterfall and the evolutionary development models.

This may involve developing a throw-away prototype using an evolutionary approach to resolve uncertainties in the system specification. This system may then be reimplemented using a more structured approach. Parts of the system which are well understood can be specified and developed using a waterfall-based process. Other parts of the system, such as the user interface, which are difficult to specify in advance, should be developed using an exploratory programming approach.

3.1.3　Formal systems development

Formal systems development is an approach to software development which has something in common with the waterfall model but where the development process is based on formal mathematical transformation of a system specification to an executable program. This process is illustrated in Figure 3.3. For simplicity, I have left iteration out of this process model.

The critical distinctions between this approach and the waterfall model are:

1. The software requirements specification is refined into a detailed formal specification which is expressed in a mathematical notation.

2. The development processes of design, implementation and unit testing are replaced by a transformational development process where the formal specification is refined, through a series of transformations, into a program. This refinement process is illustrated in Figure 3.4.

In the transformation process, the formal mathematical representation of the system is systematically converted into a more detailed, but still mathematically correct, system representation. Each step adds detail until the formal specification is converted into an equivalent program. Transformations are sufficiently close that the effort of verifying the transformation is not excessive. It can therefore be

Figure 3.3
Formal systems
development

Figure 3.4 Formal
transformation

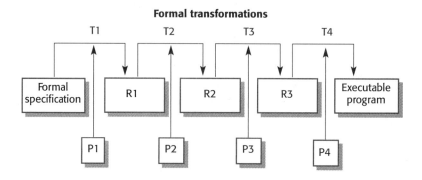

guaranteed, assuming there are no verification errors, that the program is a true implementation of the specification.

The advantage of the transformational approach compared to proving that a program meets its specification is that the distance between each transformation is less than the distance between a specification and a program. Program proofs are very long and impractical for large-scale systems. A transformational approach made up of a sequence of smaller steps is more tractable. However, choosing which transformation to apply is a skilled task and proving the correspondence of transformations is difficult.

The best known example of this formal development process is the Cleanroom process, which was originally developed by IBM (Mills *et al.*, 1987; Selby *et al.*, 1987; Linger, 1994; Prowell *et al.*, 1999). The Cleanroom process relies on incremental development of the software and each stage is developed and its correctness demonstrated using a formal approach. There is no testing for defects in the process and the system testing is focused on assessing the system's reliability. I discuss this process in Chapter 19.

Both the Cleanroom approach and another approach to formal development based on the B method (Wordsworth, 1996) have been applied successfully. There were few defects in the delivered system and the development costs were not significantly different from the costs of other approaches. This approach is particularly suited to the development of systems that have stringent safety, reliability or security requirements. The formal approach simplifies the production of a safety or security case which demonstrates to customers or certification bodies that the system does actually meet the safety or security requirements.

Outside of these specialised domains, processes based on formal transformations are not widely used. They require specialised expertise and, in reality, for the majority of systems this process does not offer significant cost or quality advantages over other approaches. The main reason for this is that system interaction is not amenable to formal specification and this takes up a very large part of the development effort for most software systems.

3.1.4 Reuse-oriented development

In the majority of software projects, there is some software reuse. This usually happens informally when people working on the project know of designs or code which is similar to that required. They look for these, modify them as required and incorporate them into their system. In the evolutionary approach, described in section 3.1.2, reuse is often seen as essential for rapid system development.

This informal reuse takes place irrespective of the generic process which is used. However, in the past few years, an approach to software development (component-based software engineering) which relies on reuse has emerged and is becoming increasingly widely used.

This reuse-oriented approach relies on a large base of reusable software components which can be accessed and some integrating framework for these components.

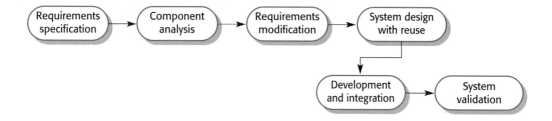

Figure 3.5
Reuse-oriented
development
Sometimes, these components are systems in their own right (COTS or Commercial Off-The-Shelf systems) that may be used to provide specific functionality such as text formatting, numeric calculation, etc. The generic process model for reuse-oriented development is shown in Figure 3.5.

While the initial requirements specification stage and the validation stage are comparable with other processes, the intermediate stages in a reuse-oriented process are different. These stages are:

1. *Component analysis*   Given the requirements specification, a search is made for components to implement that specification. Usually, there is not an exact match and the components which may be used provide only some of the functionality required.

2. *Requirements modification*   During this stage, the requirements are analysed using information about the components which have been discovered. They are then modified to reflect the available components. Where modifications are impossible, the component analysis activity may be re-entered to search for alternative solutions.

3. *System design with reuse*   During this phase, the framework of the system is designed or an existing framework is reused. The designers take into account the components which are reused and organise the framework to cater for this. Some new software may have to be designed if reusable components are not available.

4. *Development and integration*   Software which cannot be bought in is developed and the components and COTS systems are integrated to create the system. System integration, in this model, may be part of the development process rather than a separate activity.

The reuse-oriented model has the obvious advantage that it reduces the amount of software to be developed and so reduces cost and risks. It usually also leads to faster delivery of the software. However, requirements compromises are inevitable and this may lead to a system which does not meet the real needs of users. Furthermore, some control over the system evolution is lost as new versions of the reusable components are not under the control of the organisation using these components.

3.2 Process iteration

All of the above process models have advantages and disadvantages. For most large systems, there is a need to use different approaches for different parts of the system, so a hybrid model must be used. Furthermore, there is also a need to support process iteration where parts of the process are repeated as system requirements evolve. The system design and implementation work must be reworked to implement the changed requirements.

In this section, I discuss two hybrid models which support different approaches to development and which have been explicitly designed to support process iteration. These are:

1. incremental development where the software specification, design and implementation is broken down into a series of increments which are developed in turn;
2. spiral development where the development of the system spirals outwards from an initial outline through to the final developed system.

The essence of iterative processes is that the specification is developed in conjunction with the software. However, this conflicts with the procurement model of many organisations where the complete system specification is part of the contract for the system development. In the incremental approach, there is not a compete system specification until the final increment is specified. This requires a new form of contract which large customers such as government agencies may find difficult to accommodate.

3.2.1 Incremental development

The waterfall model of development requires customers for a system to commit to a set of requirements before design begins and the designer to commit to particular design strategies before implementation. Changes to the requirements during development require rework of the requirements, design and implementation. However, the advantages of the waterfall model are that it is a simple management model and its separation of design and implementation should lead to robust systems which are amenable to change.

By contrast, an evolutionary approach to development allows requirements and design decisions to be delayed but also leads to software which may be poorly structured and difficult to understand and maintain. Incremental development is an in-between approach which combines the advantages of both of these models.

The incremental approach to development (Figure 3.6) was suggested by Mills (Mills *et al.*, 1980) as a means of reducing rework in the development process and giving customers some opportunities to delay decisions on their detailed requirements until they had some experience with the system.

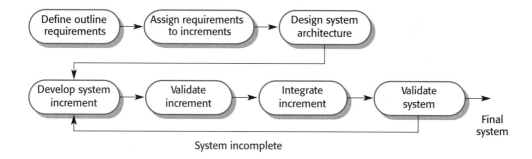

Figure 3.6
Incremental
development

In an incremental development process, customers identify, in outline, the services to be provided by the system. They identify which of the services are most important and which are least important to them. A number of delivery increments are then defined, with each increment providing a subset of the system functionality. The allocation of services to increments depends on the service priority. The highest priority services are delivered first to the customer.

Once the system increments have been identified, the requirements for the services to be delivered in the first increment are defined in detail and that increment is developed using the most appropriate development process. During that development, further requirements analysis for later increments can take place but requirements changes for the current increment are not accepted.

Once an increment is completed and delivered, customers can put it into service. This means that they take early delivery of part of the system functionality. They can experiment with the system which helps them clarify their requirements for later increments and for later versions of the current increment. As new increments are completed, they are integrated with existing increments so that the system functionality improves with each delivered increment. The common services may be implemented early in the process or may be implemented incrementally as functionality is required by an increment.

There is no need to use the same process for the development of each increment. Where the services in an increment have a well-defined specification, a waterfall model of development may be used for that increment. Where the specification is unclear, an evolutionary development model may be used.

This incremental development process has a number of advantages:

1. Customers do not have to wait until the entire system is delivered until they can gain value from it. The first increment satisfies their most critical requirements so the software can be immediately used.

2. Customers can use the early increments as a form of prototype and gain experience which informs the requirements for later system increments.

3. There is a lower risk of overall project failure. Although problems may be encountered in some increments, it is likely that some will be successfully delivered to the customer.

4. As the highest priority services are delivered first and later increments are integrated with them, it is inevitable that the most important system services receive the most testing. This means that customers are less likely to encounter software failures in the most important parts of the system.

However, there are some problems with incremental development. Increments should be relatively small (no more than 20,000 lines of code) and each increment should deliver some system functionality. It may therefore be difficult to map the customer's requirements onto increments of the right size. Furthermore, most systems require a set of basic facilities which are used by different parts of the system. As requirements are not defined in detail until an increment is to be implemented, it is difficult to identify common facilities that all increments require.

A recent evolution of this incremental approach called 'extreme programming' has been developed (Beck, 1999). This is based around the development and delivery of very small increments of functionality, customer involvement in the process, constant code improvement and egoless programming as discussed in Chapter 23. Beck's article includes several reports of the success of this approach but it is too early to say if this will become a mainstream approach to software development.

3.2.2   Spiral development

The spiral model of the software process (Figure 3.7) that was originally proposed by Boehm (1988) is now widely known. Rather than represent the software process as a sequence of activities with some backtracking from one activity to another, the process is represented as a spiral. Each loop in the spiral represents a phase of the software process. Thus, the innermost loop might be concerned with system feasibility, the next loop with system requirements definition, the next loop with system design and so on.

Each loop in the spiral is split into four sectors:

1. *Objective setting*   Specific objectives for that phase of the project are defined. Constraints on the process and the product are identified and a detailed management plan is drawn up. Project risks are identified. Alternative strategies, depending on these risks, may be planned.

2. *Risk assessment and reduction*   For each of the identified project risks, a detailed analysis is carried out. Steps are taken to reduce the risk. For example, if there is a risk that the requirements are inappropriate, a prototype system may be developed.

3. *Development and validation*   After risk evaluation, a development model for the system is then chosen. For example, if user interface risks are dominant, an appropriate development model might be evolutionary prototyping. If safety risks are the main consideration, development based on formal transformations may be the most appropriate and so on. The waterfall model may be the

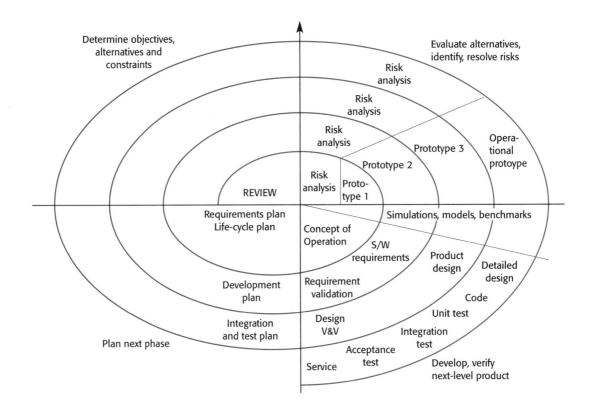

Figure 3.7 Boehm's
spiral model of the
software process
(© 1988 IEEE)

most appropriate development model if the main identified risk is sub-system integration.

4. *Planning*   The project is reviewed and a decision made whether to continue with a further loop of the spiral. If it is decided to continue, plans are drawn up for the next phase of the project.

The important distinction between the spiral model and other software process models is the explicit consideration of risk in the spiral model. Informally, risk is simply something which can go wrong. For example, if the intention is to use a new programming language, a risk is that the available compilers are unreliable or do not produce sufficiently efficient object code. Risks result in project problems such as schedule and cost overrun, so risk minimisation is a very important project management activity. In Chapter 4, which covers project management, I have included a detailed discussion of risk and risk management.

A cycle of the spiral begins by elaborating objectives such as performance, functionality, etc. Alternative ways of achieving these objectives and the constraints imposed on each of these alternatives are then enumerated. Each alternative is assessed against each objective. This usually results in the identification of sources of project risk.

The next step is to evaluate these risks by activities such as more detailed analysis, prototyping, simulation, etc. Once risks have been assessed, some development is carried out and this is followed by a planning activity for the next phase of the process.

There are no fixed phases such as specification or design in the spiral model. The spiral model encompasses other process models. Prototyping may be used in one spiral to resolve requirements uncertainties and hence reduce risk. This may be followed by a conventional waterfall development. Formal transformation may be used to develop those parts of the system with high security requirements.

3.3 Software specification

In this section and in the following three sections I discuss the basic activities of software specification, development, validation and evolution. The first of these activities, software specification, is intended to establish what services are required from the system and the constraints on the system's operation and development. This activity is now often called requirements engineering. Requirements engineering is a particularly critical stage of the software process as errors at this stage inevitably lead to later problems in the system design and implementation.

The requirements engineering process is shown in Figure 3.8. This process leads to the production of a requirements document which is the specification for the system. Requirements are usually presented at two levels of detail in this document. End-users and customers need a high-level statement of the requirements; system developers need a more detailed system specification.

Figure 3.8
The requirements
engineering process

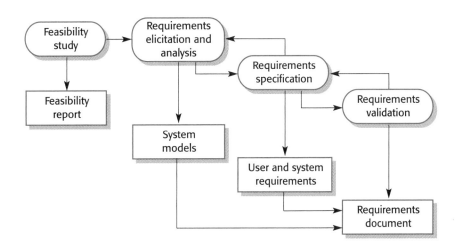

There are four main phases in the requirements engineering process:

1. *Feasibility study*   An estimate is made of whether the identified user needs may be satisfied using current software and hardware technologies. The study will decide if the proposed system will be cost-effective from a business point of view and if it can be developed given existing budgetary constraints. A feasibility study should be relatively cheap and quick. The result should inform the decision of whether to go ahead with a more detailed analysis.

2. *Requirements elicitation and analysis*   This is the process of deriving the system requirements through observation of existing systems, discussions with potential users and procurers, task analysis, etc. This may involve the development of one or more different system models and prototypes. These help the analyst understand the system to be specified.

3. *Requirements specification*   Requirements specification is the activity of translating the information gathered during the analysis activity into a document that defines a set of requirements. Two types of requirements may be included in this document. User requirements are abstract statements of the system requirements for the customer and end-user of the system; system requirements are a more detailed description of the functionality to be provided.

4. *Requirements validation*   This activity checks the requirements for realism, consistency and completeness. During this process, errors in the requirements document are inevitably discovered. It must then be modified to correct these problems.

Of course, the activities in the requirements process are not simply carried out in a strict sequence. Requirements analysis continues during definition and specification and new requirements come to light throughout the process. Therefore, the activities of analysis, definition and specification are interleaved.

3.4 Software design and implementation

The implementation stage of software development is the process of converting a system specification into an executable system. It always involves processes of software design and programming but, if an evolutionary approach to development is used, may also involve refinement of the software specification.

A software design is a description of the structure of the software to be implemented, the data which is part of the system, the interfaces between system components and, sometimes, the algorithms used. Designers do not arrive at a finished design immediately but develop the design iteratively through a number of

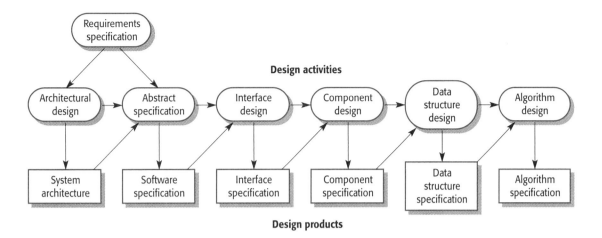

Design activities

Design products

Figure 3.9 A general
model of the design
process

different versions. The design process involves adding formality and detail as the design is developed, with constant backtracking to correct earlier designs.

The design process may involve developing several models of the system at different levels of abstraction. As a design is decomposed, errors and omissions in earlier stages are discovered. These feed back to allow earlier design models to be improved. Figure 3.9 is a model of this process which shows the design descriptions produced at different stages of design. This diagram suggests that the stages of the design process are sequential. In fact, design process activities are interleaved. Feedback from one stage to another and consequent design rework is inevitable in all design processes.

A specification for the next stage is the output of each design activity. This specification may be an abstract, formal specification that is produced to clarify the requirements or it may be a specification of how part of the system is to be realised. As the design process continues, these specifications become more detailed. The final results of the process are precise specifications of the algorithms and data structures to be implemented.

The specific design process activities are:

1. *Architectural design*   The sub-systems making up the system and their relationships are identified and documented. This important topic is covered in Chapter 10.

2. *Abstract specification*   For each sub-system, an abstract specification of its services and the constraints under which it must operate is produced.

3. *Interface design*   For each sub-system, its interface with other sub-systems is designed and documented. This interface specification must be unambiguous as it allows the sub-system to be used without knowledge of the sub-system operation. Formal specification methods as discussed in Chapter 9 may be used at this stage.

4. *Component design*   Services are allocated to different components and the interfaces of these components are designed.

5. *Data structure design*   The data structures used in the system implementation are designed in detail and specified.

6. *Algorithm design*   The algorithms used to provide services are designed in detail and specified.

This is a very general model of the design process and real, practical processes may adapt it in different ways. For example, the last two stages, data structure and algorithm design, may be part of design, or may be part of the implementation process. If there are objects available for reuse, this may constrain the architecture of the system and the interfaces of the system modules. It may mean that the number of components to be designed is significantly reduced. An exploratory approach to design may be used and the system interfaces may be designed after the data structures have been specified.

3.4.1   Design methods

In many software development projects, software design is still an *ad hoc* process. Starting from a set of requirements, usually in natural language, an informal design is prepared. Coding commences and the design is modified as the system is implemented. There is little or no formal change control or design management. When the implementation stage is complete, the design has usually changed so much from its initial specification that the original design document is an incorrect and incomplete description of the system.

A more methodical approach to software design is proposed by 'structured methods' which are sets of notations and guidelines for software design. Examples of structured methods include Structured Design (Constantine and Yourdon, 1979), Structured Systems Analysis (Gane and Sarson, 1979), Jackson System Development (Jackson, 1983) and various approaches to object-oriented design (Robinson, 1992; Booch, 1994; Rumbaugh *et al.*, 1991; Booch *et al.*, 1999; Rumbaugh *et al.*, 1999a, 1999b).

The use of structured methods normally involves producing graphical system models and results in large amounts of design documentation. CASE tools (see section 3.7) have been developed to support particular methods. Structured methods have been applied successfully in many large projects. They can deliver significant cost reductions because they use standard notations and ensure that standard design documentation is produced. No one method is demonstrably better or worse than other methods. The success or otherwise of methods often depends on their suitability for an application domain.

A structured method includes a design process model, notations to represent the design, report formats, rules and design guidelines. Although there are a large number of methods, they have much in common. Structured methods may support some or all of the following models of a system:

1. A data-flow model where the system is modelled using the data transformations which take place as it is processed.

2. An entity-relation model which is used to describe the basic entities in the design and the relations between them. Entity-relation models are the normal technique used to describe database structures.

3. A structural model where the system components and their interactions are documented.

4. Object-oriented methods include an inheritance model of the system, models of the static and dynamic relationships between objects and a model of how objects interact with each other when the system is executing.

Particular methods supplement these with other system models such as state transition diagrams, entity life histories that show how each entity is transformed as it is processed and so on. Most methods suggest that a centralised repository for system information or a data dictionary should be used. I discuss a number of these approaches to system modelling in Chapter 7.

In practice, the guidance given by the methods is informal, so different designers will develop different designs. These 'methods' are really standard notations and embodiments of good practice. By following these methods and applying the guidelines, a reasonable design should emerge. Designer creativity is still required to decide on the system decomposition and to ensure that the design adequately captures the system specification. Empirical studies of designers (Bansler and Bødker, 1993) have shown that they rarely follow methods slavishly. They pick and choose from the guidelines depending on local circumstances.

3.4.2 Programming and debugging

The development of a program to implement the system follows naturally from the system design processes. Although some classes of program, such as safety-critical systems, are designed in detail before any implementation begins, it is more normal for the later stages of design and program development to be interleaved. CASE tools may be used to generate a skeleton program from a design. This includes code to define and implement interfaces and, in many cases, the developer need only add details of the operation of each program component.

Programming is a personal activity and there is no general process which is usually followed. Some programmers will start with components that they understand, develop these and then move on to less well-understood components. Others will take the opposite approach, leaving familiar components till last because they know

Figure 3.10 The debugging process

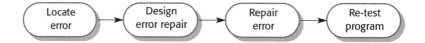

how to develop them. Some developers like to define data early in the process, then use this to drive the program development; others leave data unspecified for as long as possible.

Normally, programmers carry out some testing of the code they have developed. This often reveals program defects that must be removed from the program. This is called *debugging*. Defect testing and debugging are different processes. Testing establishes the existence of defects. Debugging is concerned with locating and correcting these defects.

Figure 3.10 illustrates a possible debugging process. Defects in the code must be located and the program modified to meet its requirements. Testing must then be repeated to ensure that the change has been made correctly. Thus the debugging process is part of both software development and software testing.

The debugger must generate hypotheses about the observable behaviour of the program, then test these hypotheses in the hope of finding the fault which caused the output anomaly. Testing the hypotheses may involve tracing the program code manually. It may require new test cases to localise the problem. Interactive debugging tools which show the intermediate values of program variables and a trace of the statements executed may be used to help the debugging process.

3.5 Software validation

Software validation or, more generally, verification and validation (V & V) is intended to show that a system conforms to its specification and that the system meets the expectations of the customer buying the system. It involves checking processes, such as inspections and reviews (see Chapter 19), at each stage of the software process from user requirements definition to program development. The majority of validation costs, however, are incurred after implementation when the operational system is tested (Chapter 20).

Except for small programs, systems should not be tested as a single, monolithic unit. Large systems are built out of sub-systems which are built out of modules which are composed of procedures and functions. The testing process should therefore proceed in stages where testing is carried out incrementally in conjunction with system implementation.

Figure 3.11 shows a five-stage testing process where system components are tested, the integrated system is tested and, finally, the system is tested with the customer's

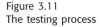
Figure 3.11
The testing process

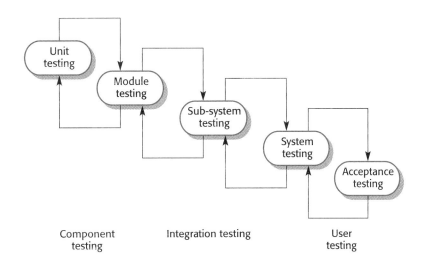

Component testing

Integration testing

User testing

data. Ideally, component defects are discovered early in the process and interface problems when the system is integrated. However, as defects are discovered the program must be debugged and this may require other stages in the testing process to be repeated. Errors in program components, say, may come to light during integration testing. The process is therefore an iterative one with information being fed back from later stages to earlier parts of the process.

The stages in the testing process are:

1. *Unit testing*   Individual components are tested to ensure that they operate correctly. Each component is tested independently, without other system components.

2. *Module testing*   A module is a collection of dependent components such as an object class, an abstract data type or some looser collection of procedures and functions. A module encapsulates related components, so can be tested without other system modules.

3. *Sub-system testing*   This phase involves testing collections of modules which have been integrated into sub-systems. The most common problems which arise in large software systems are interface mismatches. The sub-system test process should therefore concentrate on the detection of module interface errors by rigorously exercising these interfaces.

4. *System testing*   The sub-systems are integrated to make up the system. This process is concerned with finding errors that result from unanticipated interactions between sub-systems and sub-system interface problems. It is also concerned with validating that the system meets its functional and non-functional requirements and testing the emergent system properties.

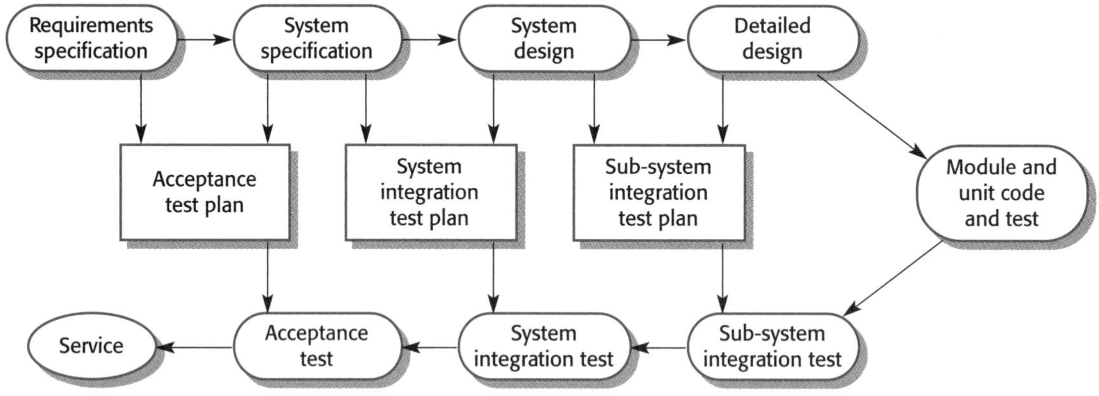

Figure 3.12 Testing
phases in the
software process

5. *Acceptance testing*   This is the final stage in the testing process before the system is accepted for operational use. The system is tested with data supplied by the system customer rather than simulated test data. Acceptance testing may reveal errors and omissions in the system requirements definition because the real data exercise the system in different ways from the test data. Acceptance testing may also reveal requirements problems where the system's facilities do not really meet the user's needs or the system performance is unacceptable.

Unit testing and module testing are usually the responsibility of the programmers developing the component. Programmers make up their own test data and incrementally test the code as it is developed. This is an economically sensible approach as the programmer knows the component best and is therefore the best person to generate test data. Unit testing is part of the implementation process and it is expected that a component conforming to its specification will be delivered as part of that process.

Later stages of testing involve integrating work from a number of programmers and must be planned in advance. An independent team of testers should work from pre-formulated test plans which are developed from the system specification and design. Figure 3.12 illustrates how test plans are the link between testing and development activities.

Acceptance testing is sometimes called *alpha testing*. Bespoke systems are developed for a single client. The alpha testing process continues until the system developer and the client agree that the delivered system is an acceptable implementation of the system requirements.

When a system is to be marketed as a software product, a testing process called *beta testing* is often used. Beta testing involves delivering a system to a number of potential customers who agree to use that system. They report problems to the system developers. This exposes the product to real use and detects errors which may not have been anticipated by the system builders. After this feedback, the system is modified and released either for further beta testing or for general sale.

3.6 Software evolution

The flexibility of software systems is one of the main reasons why more and more software is being incorporated in large, complex systems. Once a decision has been made to manufacture hardware, it is very expensive to make changes to the hardware design. For software, however, changes can be made at any time during or after the system development. These changes may be very expensive but still much cheaper than corresponding changes to system hardware.

Historically, there has always been a demarcation between the process of software development and the process of software evolution (software maintenance). Software development is considered to be a creative activity where a software system is developed from an initial concept through to a working system. Software maintenance is the process of changing that system once it has gone into use. Although the costs of 'maintenance' are often several times the initial development costs, maintenance processes are considered to be less challenging than original software development.

This demarcation is becoming increasingly irrelevant. Few software systems are now completely new systems and it makes much more sense to see development and maintenance as a continuum. Rather than two separate processes, it is more realistic to think of software engineering as an evolutionary process where software is continually changed over its lifetime in response to changing requirements and customer needs. This evolutionary process is illustrated in Figure 3.13.

Figure 3.13 System evolution

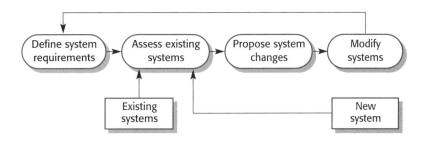

3.7 Automated process support

Computer-aided Software Engineering (CASE) is the name given to software that is used to support software process activities such as requirements engineering, design, program development and testing. CASE tools therefore include design editors, data dictionaries, compilers, debuggers, system building tools, etc.

CASE technology provides software process support by automating some process activities and by providing information about the software which is being developed. Examples of activities which can be automated using CASE include:

1. the development of graphical system models as part of the requirements specification or the software design;
2. understanding a design using a data dictionary which holds information about the entities and relations in a design;
3. the generation of user interfaces from a graphical interface description which is created interactively by the user;
4. program debugging through the provision of information about an executing program;
5. the automated translation of programs from an old version of a programming language such as COBOL to a more recent version.

CASE technology is now available for most routine activities in the software process. This has led to some improvements in software quality and productivity although these have been less than predicted by early advocates of CASE. They suggested that orders of magnitude improvement were likely if integrated CASE environments were used. In fact, the actual improvements which have been achieved are of the order of 40 per cent (Huff, 1992). Although this is significant, CASE has not revolutionised software engineering as was once predicted.

The improvements from the use of CASE are limited by two factors:

1. Software engineering is, essentially, a design activity based on creative thought. Existing CASE systems automate routine activities but attempts to harness artificial intelligence technology to provide support for design have not been successful.

2. In most organisations, software engineering is a team activity and software engineers spend quite a lot of time interacting with other team members. CASE technology does not provide much support for this.

Whether this situation will change in future is currently unclear. My view is that specific CASE products to support software design and software engineering teamwork are unlikely. However, generic design and cooperation support systems will be developed and adapted for use in the software process.

CASE technology is now mature and CASE tools and workbenches are available from a wide range of suppliers. However, rather than focus on any specific tools, I have simply presented an overview here with some discussion of specific support in related chapters of the book. In the book's web pages, I include links to more detailed material on CASE integration and links to CASE tool suppliers.

3.7.1   CASE classification

CASE classifications help us understand the different types of CASE tools and their role in supporting software process activities. There are various different ways of classifying CASE tools, each of which gives us a different perspective on these tools. In this section, I discuss CASE tools from three of these perspectives, namely:

1. *A functional perspective* where CASE tools are classified according to their specific function.

2. *A process perspective* where tools are classified according to the process activities which they support.

3. *An integration perspective* where CASE tools are classified according to how they are organised into integrated units which provide support for one or more process activities.

Figure 3.14 is a classification of CASE tools according to function. This table lists a number of different types of CASE tool and gives specific examples of each tool. This is not a complete list of CASE tools. Specialised tools such as tools to support reuse have not been included.

Figure 3.14
Functional
classification of
CASE tools

Tool type	Examples
Planning tools	PERT tools, estimation tools, spreadsheets
Editing tools	Text editors, diagram editors, word processors
Change management tools	Requirements traceability tools, change control systems
Configuration management tools	Version management systems, system building tools
Prototyping tools	Very high-level languages, user interface generators
Method-support tools	Design editors, data dictionaries, code generators
Language-processing tools	Compilers, interpreters
Program analysis tools	Cross-reference generators, static analysers, dynamic analysers
Testing tools	Test data generators, file comparators
Debugging tools	Interactive debugging systems
Documentation tools	Page layout programs, image editors
Re-engineering tools	Cross-reference systems, program re-structuring systems

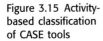

Figure 3.15 Activity-based classification of CASE tools

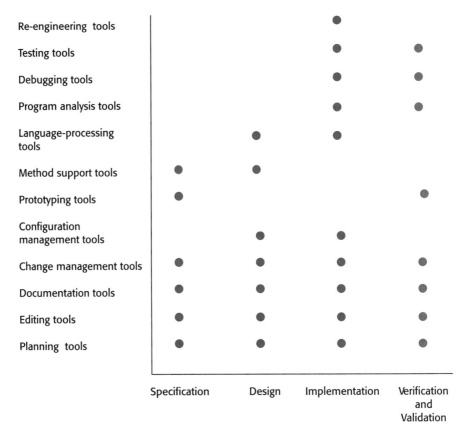

Figure 3.15 presents an alternative classification of CASE tools. It shows the process phases supported by a number of different types of CASE tool. Tools for planning and estimating, text editing, document preparation and configuration management may be used throughout the software process.

The breadth of support for the software process offered by CASE technology is another possible classification dimension. Fuggetta (1993) proposes that CASE systems should be classified into three categories:

1. *Tools* support individual process tasks such as checking the consistency of a design, compiling a program, comparing test results, etc. Tools may be general-purpose, stand-alone tools (e.g. a word-processor) or may be grouped into workbenches.

2. *Workbenches* support process phases or activities such as specification, design, etc. They normally consist of a set of tools with some greater or lesser degree of integration.

3. *Environments* support all or at least a substantial part of the software process. They normally include several different workbenches which are integrated in some way.

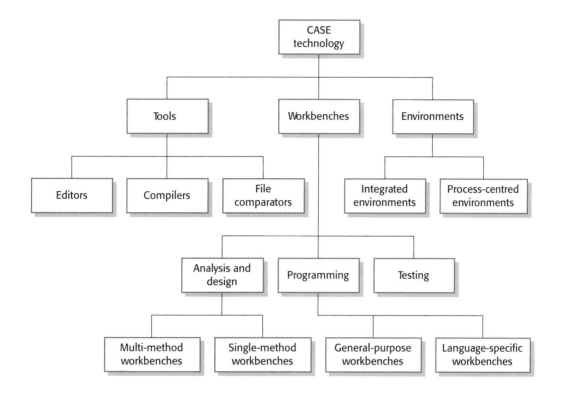

Figure 3.16 Tools, workbenches and environments

Figure 3.16 illustrates this classification and shows some examples of these different classes of CASE support. Of course, Figure 3.16 is simply an illustrative example; many types of tool and workbench have been left out of this diagram.

General-purpose tools are used at the discretion of the software engineer who makes decisions about when to apply them for process support. Workbenches, however, usually support some method which includes a process model and a set of rules/guidelines which apply to the software being developed. I have classified environments as integrated environments or process-centred environments. Integrated environments provide infrastructure support for data, control and presentation integration. Process-centred environments are more general. They include software process knowledge and a process engine which uses this process model to advise engineers on what tools or workbenches to apply and when they should be used.

In practice, the boundaries between these different classes are blurred. Tools may be sold as a single product but may embed support for different activities. For example, most word processors now provide a built-in diagram editor. CASE workbenches for design increasingly offer support for programming and testing so they are more akin to environments than specialised workbenches. It may therefore not always be easy to position a product using a classification. Nevertheless, it provides a useful first step to help understand the extent of process support which a tool is likely to provide.

KEY POINTS

▌ Software processes are the activities involved in producing a software system. Software process models are abstract representations of these processes.

▌ All software processes include software specification, software design and implementation, software validation and software evolution.

▌ Generic process models describe the organisation of software processes. Examples of generic models include the waterfall model, evolutionary development, formal systems development and reuse-oriented development.

▌ Iterative process models present the software process as a cycle of activities. The advantage of this approach is that it avoids premature commitments to a specification or design. Examples of iterative models include incremental development and the spiral model.

▌ Requirements engineering is the process of developing a software specification. It involves developing a specification which can be understood by users of the system and a more detailed specification for the system developers.

▌ Design and implementation processes are concerned with transforming a requirements specification into an executable software system. Systematic design methods may be used as part of this transformation.

▌ Software validation is the process of checking that the system conforms to its specification and that it meets the real needs of the users of the system.

▌ Software evolution is concerned with modifying existing software systems to meet new requirements. This is becoming the normal approach to software development for small and medium-sized systems.

▌ CASE technology provides automated support for software processes. CASE tools support individual process activities; CASE workbenches support a set of related activities; CASE environments support all or most software process activities.

FURTHER READING

'Embracing change with extreme programming'. An interesting overview of this new incremental process that has been designed for use in conjunction with object-oriented development. (K. Beck, *IEEE Computer*, 32(10), October 1999.)

Managing Software Quality and Business Risk. This is primarily a book about software management but it includes an excellent chapter (Chapter 4) on process models. (M. Ould, 1999, John Wiley and Sons Ltd.)

'Software process models'. I have written a more detailed description of software process models in the *Handbook of Computer Science and Engineering*. (A. Tucker (ed.), 1997, CRC Press.)

'A classification of CASE technology'. The classification scheme proposed in this article has been used here but Fuggetta goes into more detail and illustrates how a number of commercial products fit into this scheme. (A. Fuggetta, *IEEE Computer*, 26(12), December 1993.)

EXERCISES

3.1 Giving reasons for your answer based on the type of system being developed, suggest the most appropriate generic software process model which might be used as a basis for managing the development of the following systems:

- a system to control anti-lock braking in a car;
- a virtual reality system to support software maintenance;
- a university accounting system that replaces an existing system;
- an interactive system for railway passengers that finds train times from terminals installed in stations.

3.2 Explain why programs which are developed using evolutionary development are likely to be difficult to maintain.

3.3 Explain how both the waterfall model of the software process and the prototyping model can be accommodated in the spiral process model.

3.4 Suggest why it is important to make a distinction between developing the user requirements and developing the system requirements in the requirements engineering process.

3.5 Describe the main activities in the software design process and the outputs of these activities. Using an entity-relation diagram, show possible relationships between the outputs of these activities.

3.6 What are the five components of a design method? Take any method which you know and describe its components. Assess the completeness of the method which you have chosen.

3.7 Design a process model for running system tests and recording their results.

3.8 Explain why a software system that is used in a real-world environment must change or become progressively less useful.

3.9 Suggest how a CASE technology classification scheme may be helpful to managers responsible for CASE system procurement.

3.10 Survey the tool availability in your local development environment and classify the tools according to the parameters (function, activity, breadth of support) suggested here.

3.11 Historically, the introduction of technology has caused profound changes in the labour market and, temporarily at least, displaced people from jobs. Discuss whether the introduction of CASE technology is likely to have the same consequences for software engineers. If you don't think it will, explain why not. If you think that it will reduce job opportunities, is it ethical for the engineers affected to resist the introduction of this technology passively and actively?

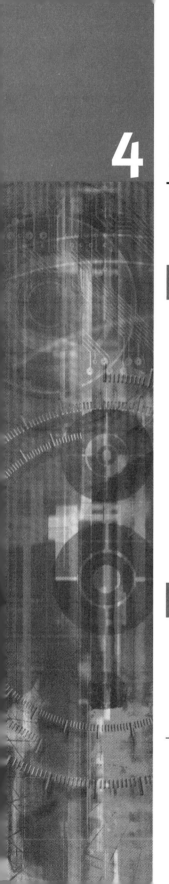

4 Project management

Objectives

The objective of this chapter is to give an overview of software project management. When you have read this chapter you will:

❏ understand the differences between software project management and other types of engineering project management;

❏ know the principal tasks of software project managers;

❏ understand why project planning is essential in all software projects;

❏ understand how graphical representations (bar charts and activity charts) are used by project managers to represent project schedules;

❏ understand the process of risk management and some of the risks which may arise in software projects.

Contents

4.1 Management activities
4.2 Project planning
4.3 Project scheduling
4.4 Risk management

The failure of many large software projects in the 1960s and early 1970s was the first indication of the difficulties of software management. Software was delivered late, was unreliable, cost several times the original estimates and often exhibited poor performance characteristics (Brooks, 1975). These projects did not fail because managers or programmers were incompetent. On the contrary, these large, challenging projects attracted people of above average ability. The fault lay in the approach to management that was used. Management techniques derived from other engineering disciplines were applied and these were ineffective for software development.

The need for management is an important distinction between professional software development and amateur programming. We need software project management because professional software engineering is always subject to budget and schedule constraints. These are set by the organisation developing the software. The software project manager's job is to ensure that the software project meets these constraints and delivers software which contributes to the business goals.

Software managers are responsible for planning and scheduling project development. They supervise the work to ensure that it is carried out to the required standards. They monitor progress to check that the development is on time and within budget. Good management cannot guarantee project success. However, bad management usually results in project failure. The software is delivered late, costs more than originally estimated and fails to meet its requirements.

Software managers do the same kind of job as other engineering project managers. However, software engineering is distinct from other types of engineering in a number of ways which can make software management particularly difficult. Some of the differences are:

1. *The product is intangible*   The manager of a shipbuilding project or of a civil engineering project can see the product being developed. If a schedule slips the effect on the product is visible. Parts of the structure are obviously unfinished. Software is intangible. It cannot be seen or touched. Software project managers cannot see progress. They rely on others to produce the documentation needed to review progress.

2. *There are no standard software processes*   We do not have a clear understanding of the relationships between the software process and product types. In engineering disciplines with a long history, the process is tried and tested. The engineering process for particular types of system, such as a bridge, is well understood. Our understanding of the software process has developed significantly in the past few years. However, we still cannot predict with certainty when a particular software process is likely to cause development problems.

3. *Large software projects are often 'one-off' projects*   Large software projects are usually different from previous projects. Managers, therefore, do have a large body of previous experience which can be used to reduce uncertainty in plans. Consequently, it is more difficult to anticipate problems. Furthermore, rapid technological changes in computers and communications outdate previous

experience. Lessons learned from that experience may not be transferable to new projects.

Because of these problems, it is not surprising that some software projects are late, over-budget and behind schedule. Software systems are often new and technically innovative. Engineering projects (such as new transport systems) which are innovative often also have schedule problems. Given the difficulties involved, it is perhaps remarkable that so many software projects are delivered on time and to budget!

Software project management is a huge topic and cannot be covered in a single chapter. Therefore, in this chapter, I simply introduce the subject and describe three important management activities, namely project planning, project scheduling and risk management. Later chapters (in Part 6) cover other aspects of software management, including managing people, software cost estimation and quality management.

4.1 Management activities

It is impossible to write a standard job description for a software manager. The job varies tremendously depending on the organisation and on the software product being developed. However, most managers take responsibility at some stage for some or all of the following activities:

* proposal writing
* project planning and scheduling
* project costing
* project monitoring and reviews
* personnel selection and evaluation
* report writing and presentations

The first stage in a software project may involve writing a proposal to carry out that project. The proposal describes the objectives of the project and how it will be carried out. It usually includes cost and schedule estimates. It may justify why the project contract should be awarded to a particular organisation or team.

Proposal writing is a critical task as the existence of many software organisations depends on having enough proposals accepted and contracts awarded. There can be no set guidelines for this task; proposal writing is a skill which is acquired by experience. Aron (1983) includes a discussion of this aspect of a project manager's job that is still relevant today.

Project planning is concerned with identifying the activities, milestones and deliverables produced by a project. A plan must then be drawn up to guide the development towards the project goals. Cost estimation is a related activity that is concerned with estimating the resources required to accomplish the project plan. I cover these in more detail later in this chapter and in Chapter 23.

Project monitoring is a continuing project activity. The manager must keep track of the progress of the project and compare actual and planned progress and costs. Although most organisations have formal mechanisms for monitoring, a skilled manager can often form a clear picture of what is going on by informal discussion with project staff.

Informal monitoring can often predict potential project problems as they may reveal difficulties as they occur. For example, daily discussions with project staff might reveal a particular problem in finding some software fault. Rather than waiting for a schedule slippage to be reported, the software manager might assign some expert to the problem or might decide that it should be programmed around.

During a project, it is normal to have a number of formal, project management reviews. They are concerned with reviewing overall progress and technical development of the project and considering the project's status against the aims of the organisation commissioning the software.

The development time for a large software project may be several years. During that time, organisational objectives are almost certain to change. These changes may mean that the software is no longer required or that the original project requirements are inappropriate. Management may decide to stop software development or to change the project to accommodate the changes to the organisation's objectives.

Project managers usually have to select people to work on their project. Ideally, skilled staff with appropriate experience will be available to work on the project. However, in most cases, managers have to settle for a less than ideal project team. The reasons for this are:

1. The project budget may not cover the use of highly paid staff. Less experienced, less well-paid staff may have to be used.

2. Staff with the appropriate experience may not be available either within an organisation or externally. It may be impossible to recruit new staff to the project. Within the organisation, the best people may already be allocated to other projects.

3. The organisation may wish to develop the skills of its employees. Inexperienced staff may be assigned to a project to learn and to gain experience.

The software manager has to work within these constraints when selecting project staff. However, problems are likely unless at least one project member has some experience of the type of system being developed. Without this experience, many simple mistakes are likely to be made. I discuss team building and staff selection in Chapter 22.

The project manager is usually responsible for reporting on the project to both the client and contractor organisations. Project managers must write concise, coherent documents which abstract critical information from detailed project reports. They must be able to present this information during progress reviews. Consequently, the ability to communicate effectively both orally and in writing is an essential skill for a project manager.

4.2 Project planning

Effective management of a software project depends on thoroughly planning the progress of the project. The project manager must anticipate problems which might arise and prepare tentative solutions to those problems. A plan, drawn up at the start of a project, should be used as the driver for the project. This initial plan should be the best possible plan given the available information. It evolves as the project progresses and better information becomes available.

A structure for a software development plan is described in section 4.2.1. As well as a project plan, managers may also have to draw up other types of plan. These are briefly described in Figure 4.1 and covered in more detail in the relevant chapter elsewhere in the book.

The pseudo-code shown in Figure 4.2 describes the project planning process for software development. It shows that planning is an iterative process which is only complete when the project itself is complete. As project information becomes available during the project, the plan must be regularly revised. The overall goals of the business are an important factor which must be considered when formulating the project plan. As these change, changes to the project plan are necessary.

The planning process starts with an assessment of the constraints (required delivery date, staff available, overall budget, etc.) affecting the project. This is carried out in conjunction with an estimation of project parameters such as its structure, size, and distribution of functions. The progress milestones and deliverables are then

Figure 4.1 Types of plan

Plan	Description
Quality plan	Describes the quality procedures and standards that will be used in a project. See Chapter 24.
Validation plan	Describes the approach, resources and schedule used for system validation. See Chapter 19.
Configuration management plan	Describes the configuration management procedures and structures to be used. See Chapter 29.
Maintenance plan	Predicts the maintenance requirements of the system, maintenance costs and effort required. See Chapter 27.
Staff development plan	Describes how the skills and experience of the project team members will be developed. See Chapter 22.

Figure 4.2 Project
planning

```
Establish the project constraints
Make initial assessments of the project parameters
Define project milestones and deliverables
while project has not been completed or cancelled loop
    Draw up project schedule
    Initiate activities according to schedule
    Wait ( for a while )
    Review project progress
    Revise estimates of project parameters
    Update the project schedule
    Renegotiate project constraints and deliverables
    if ( problems arise ) then
        Initiate technical review and possible revision
    end if
end loop
```

defined. The process then enters a loop. A schedule for the project is drawn up and the activities defined in the schedule are initiated or given permission to continue. After some time (usually about 2–3 weeks), progress is reviewed and discrepancies noted. Because initial estimates of project parameters are tentative, the plan will always need to be modified.

Project managers revise the assumptions about the project as more information becomes available. They replan the project schedule. If the project is delayed, they may have to renegotiate the project constraints and deliverables with the customer. If this renegotiation is unsuccessful and the schedule cannot be met, a project technical review may be held. The objective of this review is to find some alternative approach to development which falls within the project constraints and meets the schedule.

Of course, wise project managers do not assume that all will go well. Problems of some description nearly always arise during a project. The initial assumptions and scheduling should be pessimistic rather than optimistic. There should be sufficient contingency built into the plan that the project constraints and milestones need not be renegotiated every time round the planning loop.

4.2.1   The project plan

The project plan sets out the resources available to the project, the work breakdown and a schedule for carrying out the work. In some organisations, the project plan is a single document including all the different types of plan introduced above. In other cases, the project plan is solely concerned with the development process. References to other plans are included but the plans themselves are separate.

The plan structure which I describe here is for this latter type of plan. The details of the project plan vary depending on the type of project and organisation. However, most plans should include the following sections:

1. *Introduction*   This briefly describes the objectives of the project and sets out the constraints (e.g. budget, time, etc.) which affect the project management.

2. *Project organisation*   This describes the way in which the development team is organised, the people involved and their roles in the team.

3. *Risk analysis*   This describes possible project risks, the likelihood of these risks arising and the risk reduction strategies which are proposed. Risk management is covered in section 4.4.

4. *Hardware and software resource requirements*   This describes the hardware and the support software required to carry out the development. If hardware has to be bought, estimates of the prices and the delivery schedule should be included.

5. *Work breakdown*   This describes the breakdown of the project into activities and identifies the milestones and deliverables associated with each activity. Milestones and deliverables are discussed in section 4.2.2.

6. *Project schedule*   This describes the dependencies between activities, the estimated time required to reach each milestone and the allocation of people to activities.

7. *Monitoring and reporting mechanisms*   This describes the management reports which should be produced, when these should be produced and the project monitoring mechanisms used.

The project plan should be regularly revised during the project. Some parts, such as the project schedule, will change frequently; other parts will be more stable. A document organisation which allows for the straightforward replacement of sections should be used.

4.2.2   Milestones and deliverables

Managers need information. As software is intangible, this information can only be provided as documents that describe the state of the software being developed. Without this information, it is impossible to judge progress and cost estimates and schedules cannot be updated.

When planning a project, a series of *milestones* should be established where a milestone is an end-point of a software process activity. At each milestone, there should be a formal output, such as a report, that can be presented to management. Milestone reports need not be large documents. They may simply be a short report of achievements in a project activity. Milestones should represent the end of a distinct, logical stage in the project. Indefinite milestones such as 'Coding 80 per cent complete' which are impossible to validate are useless for project management.

A *deliverable* is a project result that is delivered to the customer. It is usually delivered at the end of some major project phase such as specification, design, etc.

ACTIVITIES

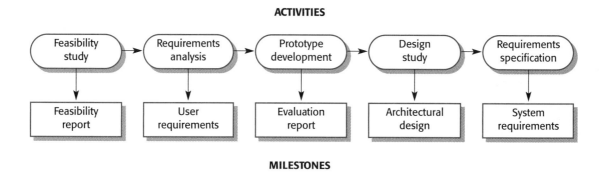

MILESTONES

Figure 4.3
Milestones in the
requirements process

Deliverables are usually milestones but milestones need not be deliverables. Milestones may be internal project results that are used by the project manager to check project progress but which are not delivered to the customer.

To establish milestones, the software process must be broken down into basic activities with associated outputs. For example, Figure 4.3 shows activities involved in requirements specification when prototyping is used to help validate requirements. The principal outputs for each activity (the project milestones) are shown. The project deliverables are the requirements definition and the requirements specification.

4.3 Project scheduling

Project scheduling is a particularly demanding task for software managers. Managers estimate the time and resources required to complete activities and organise them in a coherent sequence. Unless the project being scheduled is similar to a previous project, previous estimates are an uncertain basis for new project scheduling. Schedule estimation is further complicated by the fact that different projects may use different design methods and implementation languages.

If the project is technically advanced, initial estimates will almost certainly be optimistic even when managers try to consider all eventualities. In this respect, software scheduling is no different from scheduling any other type of large advanced project. New aircraft, bridges and even new models of cars are frequently late because of unanticipated problems. Schedules, therefore, must be continually updated as better progress information becomes available.

Project scheduling (Figure 4.4) involves separating the total work involved in a project into separate activities and judging the time required to complete these activities. Usually, some of these activities are carried out in parallel. Project schedulers must coordinate these parallel activities and organise the work so that the

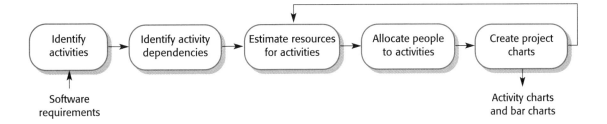

Figure 4.4
The project
scheduling process

workforce is used optimally. They must avoid a situation where the whole project is delayed because a critical task is unfinished.

Project activities should normally last at least a week. Finer subdivision means that a disproportionate amount of time must be spent on estimating and chart revision. It is also useful to set a maximum amount of time for any activity of about 8 to 10 weeks. If it takes longer than this, it should be subdivided for project planning and scheduling.

In estimating schedules, managers should not assume that every stage of the project will be problem free. Individuals working on a project may fall ill or may leave, hardware may break down and essential support software or hardware may be delivered late. If the project is new and technically advanced, certain parts of it may turn out to be more difficult and take longer than originally anticipated.

As well as calendar time, managers must also estimate the resources needed to complete each task. The principal resource is the human effort required. Other resources may be the disk space required on a server, the time required on specialised hardware, such as a simulator, and the travel budget required for project staff. I discuss estimation in more detail in Chapter 23.

A good rule of thumb is to estimate as if nothing will go wrong, then increase your estimate to cover anticipated problems. A further contingency factor to cover unanticipated problems may also be added to the estimate. This extra contingency factor depends on the type of project, the process parameters (deadline, standards, etc.) and the quality and experience of the software engineers working on the project. As a rule of thumb, I always add 30 per cent to my original estimate for anticipated problems then another 20 per cent to cover other things I hadn't thought of.

The project schedule is usually represented as a set of charts showing the work breakdown, activities dependencies and staff allocations. These are discussed in the following section. Software management tools, such as Microsoft Project, are now usually used to automate chart production.

4.3.1   Bar charts and activity networks

Bar charts and activity networks are graphical notations which are used to illustrate the project schedule. Bar charts show who is responsible for each activity and when the activity is scheduled to begin and end. Activity networks show the dependencies between the different activities making up a project. Bar charts and activity

Figure 4.5 Task
durations and
dependencies

Task	Duration (days)	Dependencies
T1	8	
T2	15	
T3	15	T1 (M1)
T4	10	
T5	10	T2, T4 (M2)
T6	5	T1, T2 (M3)
T7	20	T1 (M1)
T8	25	T4 (M5)
T9	15	T3, T6 (M4)
T10	15	T5, T7 (M7)
T11	7	T9 (M6)
T12	10	T11 (M8)

charts can be generated automatically from a database of project information using a project management tool.

Consider the set of activities shown in Figure 4.5. This table shows activities, their duration, and activity interdependencies. From Figure 4.5, you can see that Task T3 is dependent on Task T1. This means that T1 must be completed before T3 starts. For example, T1 might be the preparation of a component design and T3, the implementation of that design. Before implementation starts, the design should be complete.

Given dependency and estimated duration of activities, an activity network which shows activity sequences may be generated (Figure 4.6). It shows which activities can be carried out in parallel and which must be executed in sequence because of a dependency on an earlier activity. Activities are represented as rectangles. Milestones and project deliverables are shown with rounded corners. Dates in this diagram show the start date of the activity and are written in British style where the day precedes the month. You should read the network from left to right and from top to bottom.

In the project management tool used to produce this chart, all activities must end in milestones. An activity may start when its preceding milestone (which may depend on several activities) has been reached. Therefore, in the third column in Figure 4.5, I have also shown the corresponding milestone (e.g. M5) which is reached when the tasks in that column finish (see Figure 4.6).

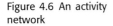
Figure 4.6 An activity network

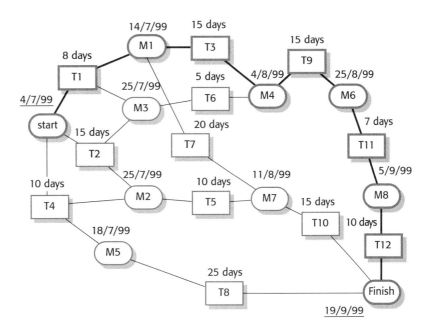

Before progress can be made from one milestone to another, all paths leading to it must be complete. For example, task T9, shown in Figure 4.6, cannot be started until tasks T3 and T6 are finished. The arrival at milestone M4 shows that these tasks have been completed.

The minimum time required to finish the project can be estimated by considering the longest path in the activity graph (the critical path). In this case, it is 11 weeks of elapsed time or 55 working days. In Figure 4.6 the critical path is shown as a sequence of emboldened boxes. The overall schedule of the project depends on the critical path. Any slippage in the completion of any critical activity causes project delays.

Delays in activities which do not lie on the critical path, however, need not cause an overall schedule slippage. So long as the delays do not extend these activities so much that the total time exceeds the critical path, the project schedule will not be affected. For example, if T8 is delayed, it may not affect the final completion date of the project as it does not lie on the critical path. The project bar chart (Figure 4.7) shows the extent of the possible delay as a shaded bar.

Managers also use activity networks when allocating project work. They can provide insights into activity dependencies which are not intuitively obvious. It may be possible to modify the system design so that the critical path is shortened. The project schedule may be shortened because of the reduced amount of time spent waiting for activities to finish.

Figure 4.7 is an alternative way of representing project schedule information. It is a bar chart (sometimes called a Gantt chart, after its inventor) showing a project calendar and the start and finish dates of activities.

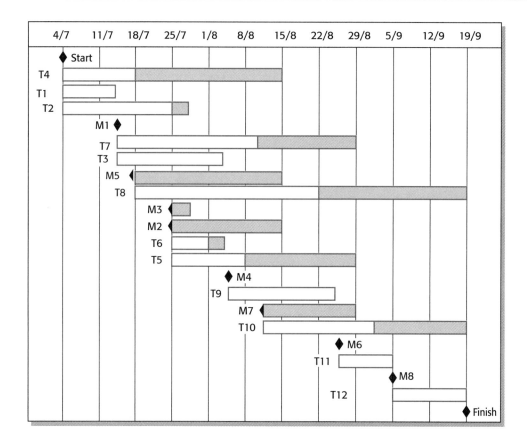

Figure 4.7 Activity bar chart

Some of the activities in Figure 4.7 are followed by a shaded bar whose length is computed by the scheduling tool. This shows that there is some flexibility in the completion date of these activities. If an activity does not complete on time, the critical path will not be affected until the end of the period marked by the shaded bar. Activities which lie on the critical path have no margin of error and they can be identified because they have no associated shaded bar.

As well as considering schedules, project managers must also consider resource allocation and, in particular, the allocation of staff to project activities. Figure 4.8 suggests an allocation of staff to the activities illustrated in Figure 4.7.

Figure 4.8 can also be processed by project management support tools and a bar chart generated which shows the time periods where staff are employed on the project (Figure 4.9). Staff don't have to be assigned to a project at all times. During intervening periods they may be on holiday, working on other projects, attending training courses or some other activity.

Large organisations usually employ a number of specialists who work on a project as required. This can cause scheduling problems. If one project is delayed while a specialist is working on it, this may have a knock-on effect on other projects. They may also be delayed because the specialist is not available.

Figure 4.8
Allocation of
people to activities

Task	Engineer
T1	Jane
T2	Anne
T3	Jane
T4	Fred
T5	Mary
T6	Anne
T7	Jim
T8	Fred
T9	Jane
T10	Anne
T11	Fred
T12	Fred

Figure 4.9 Staff
allocation vs time
chart

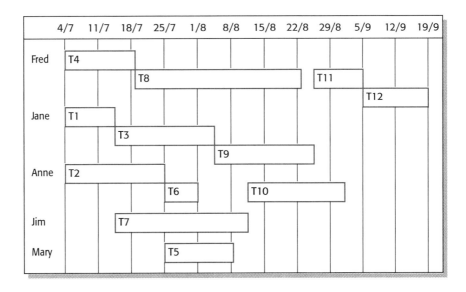

Inevitably, initial project schedules will be incorrect. As a project develops, estimates should be compared with actual elapsed time. This comparison can be used as a basis for revising the schedule for later parts of the project. When actual figures are known, the activity chart should be reviewed. Later project activities may then be reorganised to reduce the length of the critical path.

4.4 Risk management

An important task of a project manager is to anticipate risks which might affect the project schedule or the quality of the software being developed and to take action to avoid these risks. The results of the risk analysis should be documented in the project plan along with an analysis of the consequences of a risk occurring. Identifying risks and drawing up plans to minimise their effect on the project is called risk management (Hall, 1998; Ould, 1999).

Simplistically, you can think of a risk as a probability that some adverse circumstance will actually occur. Risks may threaten the project, the software that is being developed or the organisation. These categories of risk can be defined as follows:

1. *Project risks* are risks which affect the project schedule or resources.
2. *Product risks* are risks which affect the quality or performance of the software being developed.
3. *Business risks* are risks which affect the organisation developing or procuring the software.

Of course, this is not an exclusive classification. If an experienced programmer leaves a project this can be a project risk (because the delivery of the system may be delayed), a product risk (because a replacement may not be as experienced and so may make mistakes) and a business risk (because that experience is not available for bidding for future business).

Risk management is particularly important for software projects because of the inherent uncertainties which most projects face. These stem from loosely defined requirements, difficulties in estimating the time and resources required for software development, dependence on individual skills and requirements changes due to changes in customer needs. The project manager should anticipate risks, understand the impact of these risks on the project, the product and the business and take steps to avoid these risks. Contingency plans may be drawn up so that, if the risks do occur, immediate recovery action is possible.

The types of risk which may affect a project depend on the project and the organisational environment where the software is being developed. However, many risks are universal and I describe some of these in Figure 4.10.

Figure 4.10 Possible
software risks

Risk	Risk type	Description
Staff turnover	Project	Experienced staff will leave the project before it is finished.
Management change	Project	There will be a change of organisational management with different priorities.
Hardware unavailability	Project	Hardware which is essential for the project will not be delivered on schedule.
Requirements change	Project and product	There will be a larger number of changes to the requirements than anticipated.
Specification delays	Project and product	Specifications of essential interfaces are not available on schedule.
Size underestimate	Project and product	The size of the system has been underestimated.
CASE tool under-performance	Product	CASE tools which support the project do not perform as anticipated.
Technology change	Business	The underlying technology on which the system is built is superseded by new technology.
Product competition	Business	A competitive product is marketed before the system is completed.

The process of risk management is illustrated in Figure 4.11. It involves several
stages:

1. *Risk identification*   Possible project, product and business risks are identified.
2. *Risk analysis*   The likelihood and consequences of these risks are assessed.
3. *Risk planning*   Plans to address the risk either by avoiding it or minimising
   its effects on the project are drawn up.
4. *Risk monitoring*   The risk is constantly assessed and plans for risk mitigation
   are revised as more information about the risk becomes available.

Figure 4.11 The risk
management process

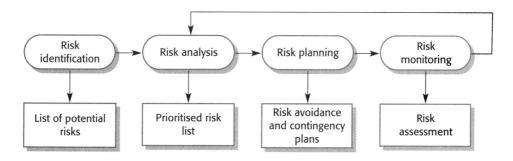

The risk management process, like all other project planning, is an iterative process which continues throughout the project. Once an initial set of plans are drawn up, the situation is monitored. As more information about the risks become available, they have to be re-analysed and new priorities established. The risk avoidance and contingency plans may be modified as new risk information emerges.

The results of the risk management process should be documented in a risk management plan. This should include a discussion of the risks faced by the project, an analysis of these risks and the plans which are required to manage these risks. Where appropriate, it may also include some results of the risk management, i.e. specific contingency plans to be activated if the risk occurs.

4.4.1 Risk identification

Risk identification is the first stage of risk management. It is concerned with discovering possible risks to the project. In principle, these should not be assessed or prioritised at this stage although, in practice, risks with very minor consequences or very low probability risks are not usually considered.

Risk identification may be carried out as a team process using a brainstorming approach or may simply be based on a manager's experience. To help the process, a list of possible risk types may be used. These types include:

1. *Technology risks*   Risks which derive from the software or hardware technologies which are being used as part of the system being developed.
2. *People risks*   Risks which are associated with the people in the development team.
3. *Organisational risks*   Risks which derive from the organisational environment where the software is being developed.
4. *Tools risks*   Risks which derive from the CASE tools and other support software used to develop the system.
5. *Requirements risks*   Risks which derive from changes to the customer requirements and the process of managing the requirements change.
6. *Estimation risks*   Risks which derive from the management estimates of the system characteristics and the resources required to build the system.

Figure 4.12 gives some examples of possible risks in each of these categories. The outcome of this process should be a long list of risks which could occur and which could affect the product, the process or the business.

4.4.2 Risk analysis

During the risk analysis process, each identified risk is considered in turn and a judgement made about the probability and the seriousness of the risk. There is no easy way to do this – it relies on the judgement and experience of the project

Figure 4.12 Risks
and risk types

Risk type	Possible risks
Technology	The database used in the system cannot process as many transactions per second as expected. Software components which should be reused contain defects which limit their functionality.
People	It is impossible to recruit staff with the skills required. Key staff are ill and unavailable at critical times. Required training for staff is not available.
Organisational	The organisation is restructured so that different management are responsible for the project. Organisational financial problems force reductions in the project budget.
Tools	The code generated by CASE tools is inefficient. CASE tools cannot be integrated.
Requirements	Changes to requirements which require major design rework are proposed. Customers fail to understand the impact of requirements changes.
Estimation	The time required to develop the software is underestimated. The rate of defect repair is underestimated. The size of the software is underestimated.

manager. These should not generally be precise numeric assessments but should be based around a number of bands:

1. The probability of the risk might be assessed as very low (<10%), low (10–25%), moderate (25–50%), high (50–75%) or very high (>75%).
2. The effects of the risk might be assessed as catastrophic, serious, tolerable or insignificant.

The results of this analysis process should then be tabulated with the table ordered according to seriousness of the risk. Figure 4.13 illustrates this for the risks identified in Figure 4.12. Obviously the assessment of probability and seriousness is arbitrary here. In practice, you need detailed information about the project, the process, the development team and the organisation to make this assessment.

Of course, both the probability and the assessment of the effects of a risk may change as more information about the risk becomes available and as risk management plans are implemented. Therefore, this table must be updated during each iteration of the risk process.

Once the risks have been analysed and ranked, a judgement must then be made about which are the most important risks which must be considered during the project. This judgement must depend on a combination of the probability of the risk

Figure 4.13 Risk
analysis

Risk	Probability	Effects
Organisational financial problems force reductions in the project budget.	Low	Catastrophic
It is impossible to recruit staff with the skills required for the project.	High	Catastrophic
Key staff are ill at critical times in the project.	Moderate	Serious
Software components which should be reused contain defects which limit their functionality.	Moderate	Serious
Changes to requirements which require major design rework are proposed.	Moderate	Serious
The organisation is restructured so that different management are responsible for the project.	High	Serious
The database used in the system cannot process as many transactions per second as expected.	Moderate	Serious
The time required to develop the software is underestimated.	High	Serious
CASE tools cannot be integrated.	High	Tolerable
Customers fail to understand the impact of requirements changes.	Moderate	Tolerable
Required training for staff is not available.	Moderate	Tolerable
The rate of defect repair is underestimated.	Moderate	Tolerable
The size of the software is underestimated.	High	Tolerable
The code generated by CASE tools is inefficient.	Moderate	Insignificant

arising and the effects of that risk. In general, all catastrophic risks should always be considered, as should all serious risks which have more than a moderate probability of occurrence.

Boehm (1988) recommends identify and monitoring the 'top 10' risks but I think this figure is rather arbitrary. The right number of risks to monitor must depend on the project. It might be five or it might be 15. However, the number of risks chosen for monitoring should be manageable. A very large number of risks would simply require too much information to be collected. From the risks identified in Figure 4.13, it is appropriate to consider all eight risks which have catastrophic or serious consequences.

Risk planning

The risk planning process considers each of the key risks which have been identified and identifies strategies to manage the risk. Again, there is no simple process which can be followed to establish risk management plans. It relies on the judgement and experience of the project manager. Figure 4.14 shows possible strategies which have been identified for the key risks from Figure 4.13.

These strategies fall into three categories:

1. *Avoidance strategies*   Following these strategies means that the probability that the risk will arise will be reduced. An example of a risk avoidance strategy is the strategy for dealing with defective components shown in Figure 4.14.

2. *Minimisation strategies*   Following these strategies means that the impact of the risk will be reduced. An example of a risk minimisation strategy is the strategy for staff illness shown in Figure 4.14.

3. *Contingency plans*   Following these strategies means that, if the worst happens, you are prepared for it and have a strategy in place to deal with it. An example of a contingency strategy is the strategy for organisational financial problems in Figure 4.14.

Figure 4.14 Risk management strategies

Risk	Strategy
Organisational financial problems	Prepare a briefing document for senior management showing how the project is making a very important contribution to the goals of the business.
Recruitment problems	Alert customer of potential difficulties and the possibility of delays, investigate buying-in components.
Staff illness	Reorganise team so that there is more overlap of work and people therefore understand each other's jobs.
Defective components	Replace potentially defective components with bought-in components of known reliability.
Requirements changes	Derive traceability information to assess requirements change impact, maximise information hiding in the design.
Organisational restructuring	Prepare a briefing document for senior management showing how the project is making a very important contribution to the goals of the business.
Database performance	Investigate the possibility of buying a higher-performance database.
Underestimated development time	Investigate buying-in components, investigate the use of a program generator.

Figure 4.15 Risk
factors

Risk type	Potential indicators
Technology	Late delivery of hardware or support software, many reported technology problems
People	Poor staff morale, poor relationships amongst team members, job availability
Organisational	Organisational gossip, lack of action by senior management
Tools	Reluctance by team members to use tools, complaints about CASE tools, demands for higher-powered workstations
Requirements	Many requirements change requests, customer complaints
Estimation	Failure to meet agreed schedule, failure to clear reported defects

4.4.4   Risk monitoring

Risk monitoring involves regularly assessing each of the identified risks to decide whether or not that risk is becoming more or less probable and whether the effects of the risk have changed. Of course, this cannot usually be observed directly, so you have to look at other factors which give you clues about the risk probability and its effects. These factors are obviously dependent on the types of risk. Figure 4.15 gives some examples of factors which may be helpful in assessing these risk types.

Risk monitoring should be a continuous process and, at every management progress review, each of the key risks should be considered separately and discussed by the meeting.

KEY POINTS

▶ Good software project management is essential if software engineering projects are to be developed on schedule and within budget.

▶ Software management is distinct from other engineering management. Software is intangible. Projects may be novel or innovative so there is no body of experience to guide their management. Software processes are not well understood.

▶ Software managers have diverse roles. Their most significant activities are project planning, estimating and scheduling. Planning and estimating are iterative processes.

They continue throughout a project. As more information becomes available, plans and schedules must be revised.

▶ A project milestone is a predictable outcome of an activity where some formal report of progress should be presented to management. Milestones should occur regularly throughout a software project. A deliverable is a milestone which is delivered to the project customer.

▶ Project scheduling involves the creation of various graphical representations of part of the project plan. These include activity charts showing the interrelationships of project activities and bar charts showing activity durations.

▶ Major project risks should be identified and assessed to establish their probability and consequences for the project. For risks which are probable and potentially serious, plans to avoid, manage or deal with that risk when it arises should be made. Risks should be explicitly discussed at each project progress meeting.

FURTHER READING

Managing Software Quality and Business Risk. Chapter 3 of this book is simply the best discussion of risk that I have seen anywhere. The book is oriented around risk and I think it is probably the best book on this topic that is available at the time of writing. (M. Ould, 1999, John Wiley and Sons.)

The Mythical Man Month. The problems of software management have been unchanged since the 1960s and this is one of the best books on the topic. An interesting and readable account of the management of one of the first very large software projects, the IBM OS/360 operating system. The second edition includes other classic papers by Brooks. (F. P. Brooks, 1975, Addison-Wesley.)

Assessment and Control of Software Risks. There are several books on risk management now available. This one is a particularly comprehensive discussion of the types of risk, why they arise and how to avoid them. (C. Jones, 1994, Prentice-Hall.)

Principles of Software Engineering Management. This is an idiosyncratic account of software management but it contains good advice. It is written in an easy-to-read way. (T. Gilb, 1988, Addison-Wesley.)

See Part 6 for other readings on management.

EXERCISES

4.1   Explain why the intangibility of software systems poses special problems for software project management.

4.2   Explain why the best programmers do not always make the best software managers. You may find it helpful to base your answer on the list of management activities given in section 4.1.

4.3   Explain why the process of project planning is an iterative one and why a plan must be continually reviewed during a software project.

4.4   Briefly explain the purpose of each of the sections in a software project plan.

4.5   What is the critical distinction between a milestone and a deliverable?

4.6   Figure 4.16 sets out a number of activities, durations and dependencies. Draw an activity chart and a bar chart showing the project schedule.

Figure 4.16 Task durations and dependencies

Task	Duration (days)	Dependencies
T1	10	
T2	15	T1
T3	10	T1, T2
T4	20	
T5	10	
T6	15	T3, T4
T7	20	T3
T8	35	T7
T9	15	T6
T10	5	T5, T9
T11	10	T9
T12	20	T10
T13	35	T3, T4
T14	10	T8, T9
T15	20	T12, T14
T16	10	T15

4.7 Figure 4.5 gives task durations for software project activities. Assume that a serious, unanticipated setback occurs and instead of taking 10 days, task T5 takes 40 days. Revise the activity network accordingly, highlighting the new critical path. Draw up new bar charts showing how the project might be reorganised.

4.8 Using reported instances of project problems in the literature, list management difficulties which occurred in these failed programming projects. (Start with Brooks's book, as suggested in Further Reading.)

4.9 In addition to the risks shown in Figure 4.12, identify six other possible risks which are likely to arise in software projects.

4.10 You are asked by your manager to deliver software to a schedule which you know can only be met by asking your project team to work unpaid overtime. All team members have young children. Discuss whether you should accept this demand from your manager and whether you should persuade your team to give their time to the organisation rather than their families. What factors might be significant in your decision?

4.11 As a programmer, you are offered promotion to project management but you feel that you can make a more effective contribution in a technical rather than a managerial role. Discuss whether you should accept the promotion.

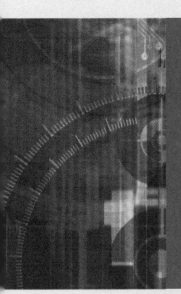

PART TWO

Requirements

5 Software requirements

Objectives

The objective of this chapter is to introduce software system requirements and to explain different ways of expressing these requirements. When you have read the chapter you will:

❑ understand the concepts of user requirements and system requirements and why these requirements may be expressed using different notations;

❑ understand the differences between functional and non-functional requirements;

❑ understand two techniques for describing system requirements, namely structured natural language and programming-language based descriptions;

❑ understand how requirements may be organised in a software requirements document.

Contents

5.1 Functional and non-functional requirements
5.2 User requirements
5.3 System requirements
5.4 The software requirements document

The problems that software engineers have to solve are often immensely complex. Understanding the nature of the problems can be very difficult, especially if the system is new. Consequently, it is difficult to establish exactly what the system should do. The descriptions of the services and constraints are the *requirements* for the system and the process of finding out, analysing, documenting and checking these services and constraints is called *requirements engineering*. In this chapter, I concentrate on the requirements themselves and how to describe them. The requirements engineering process was introduced in Chapter 3 and I discuss it in more detail in Chapter 6.

The term *requirement* is not used throughout the software industry in a consistent way. In some cases, a requirement is seen as a high-level, abstract statement of a service that the system should provide or a constraint on the system. At the other extreme, it is a detailed, mathematically formal definition of a system function. Davis (1993) explains why these differences exist.

> If a company wishes to let a contract for a large software development project, it must define its needs in a sufficiently abstract way that a solution is not pre-defined. The requirements must be written so that several contractors can bid for the contract, offering, perhaps, different ways of meeting the client organisation's needs. Once a contract has been awarded, the contractor must write a system definition for the client in more detail so that the client understands and can validate what the software will do. Both of these documents may be called the *requirements document* for the system.

Some of the problems that arise during the requirements engineering process are a result of failing to make a clear separation between these different levels of description. I make this separation by using the term *user requirements* to mean the high-level abstract requirements and *system requirements* to mean the detailed description of what the system should do. As well as these two levels of detail, a more detailed description (a software design specification) may be produced to bridge the requirements engineering and design activities. User requirements, system requirements and software design specification may be defined as follows:

1. *User requirements* are statements, in a natural language plus diagrams, of what services the system is expected to provide and the constraints under which it must operate.

2. *System requirements* set out the system services and constraints in detail. The system requirements document, which is sometimes called a functional specification, should be precise. It may serve as a contract between the system buyer and software developer.

3. *A software design specification* is an abstract description of the software design which is a basis for more detailed design and implementation. This specification adds further detail to the system requirements specification.

Figure 5.1 User and
system requirements

User requirement definition

> 1. The software must provide a means of representing and
>   accessing external files created by other tools.

System requirements specification

> 1.1 The user should be provided with facilities to define the type of
>   external files.
> 1.2 Each external file type may have an associated tool which may be
>   applied to the file.
> 1.3 Each external file type may be represented as a specific icon on
>   the user's display.
> 1.4 Facilities should be provided for the icon representing an
>   external file type to be defined by the user.
> 1.5 When a user selects an icon representing an external file, the
>   effect of that selection is to apply the tool associated with the type of
>   the external file to the file represented by the selected icon.

Figure 5.2 Readers
of different types of
specification

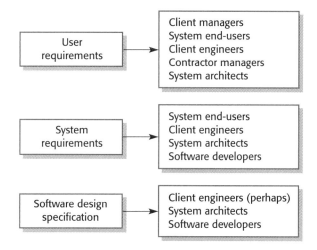

Different levels of system specification are useful because they communicate information about the system to different types of reader. Figure 5.1 illustrates the distinction between user and system requirements. It shows how a user requirement may be expanded into several system requirements.

The user requirements should be written for client and contractor managers who do not have a detailed technical knowledge of the system (Figure 5.2). The system requirements specification should be targeted at senior technical staff and project managers. Again, it will be used by staff from both the client and the contractor. System end-users may read both of these documents. Finally, the software design specification is an implementation-oriented document. It should be written for the software engineers who will develop the system.

5.1 Functional and non-functional requirements

Software system requirements are often classified as functional or non-functional requirements or as domain requirements:

1. *Functional requirements*   These are statements of services the system should provide, how the system should react to particular inputs and how the system should behave in particular situations. In some cases, the functional requirements may also explicitly state what the system should not do.

2. *Non-functional requirements*   These are constraints on the services or functions offered by the system. They include timing constraints, constraints on the development process, standards, etc.

3. *Domain requirements*   These are requirements that come from the application domain of the system and that reflect characteristics of that domain. They may be functional or non-functional requirements.

In reality, the distinction between these different types of requirement is not as clear cut as these simple definitions suggest. A user requirement concerned with security, say, may appear to be a non-functional requirement. However, when developed in more detail, it may lead to other requirements that are clearly functional such as the need to include user authorisation facilities in the system. Therefore, while it is helpful to classify requirements in this way when discussing them, you must remember that this is really an artificial distinction.

5.1.1 Functional requirements

The functional requirements for a system describe the functionality or services that the system is expected to provide. These depend on the type of software which is being developed, the expected users of the software and the type of system which is being developed. When expressed as user requirements, they are usually described in a fairly general way but functional system requirements describe the system function in detail, its inputs and outputs, exceptions, etc.

Functional requirements for a software system may be expressed in a number of different ways. Here are a number of functional requirements for a university library system (Kotonya and Sommerville, 1998) for students and faculty to order books and documents from other libraries:

1. The user shall be able to search either all of the initial set of databases or select a subset from it.
2. The system shall provide appropriate viewers for the user to read documents in the document store.

3. Every order shall be allocated a unique identifier (ORDER_ID) which the user shall be able to copy to the account's permanent storage area.

These are functional user requirements which define specific facilities which must be provided by the system. These have been taken from the user requirements document for the system and they illustrate that functional requirements may be written at different levels of detail (contrast requirements 1 and 3).

Many of the problems of software engineering stem from imprecision in the requirements specification. It is natural for a system developer to interpret an ambiguous requirement to simplify its implementation. Often, however, this is not what the customer wants. New requirements have to be established and changes made to the system. Of course, this delays system delivery and increases costs.

Consider the second example requirement for the library system in the above requirements list which refers to 'appropriate viewers' provided by the system. The library system can deliver documents in a range of formats and the intention of this requirement is that viewers for all of these formats should be available. However, it is worded ambiguously as it does not make clear that viewers for each document format should be provided. A developer under schedule pressure might simply provide a text viewer and claim that the requirement had been met.

In principle, the functional requirements specification of a system should be both complete and consistent. Completeness means that all services required by the user should be defined. Consistency means that requirements should not have contradictory definitions. In practice, for large, complex systems, it is practically impossible to achieve requirements consistency and completeness. The reason for this is partly because of the inherent system complexity and partly because different viewpoints (see Chapter 6) have inconsistent needs. These inconsistencies may not be obvious when the requirements are first specified. The problems only emerge after deeper analysis. As problems are discovered during reviews or in later life-cycle phases, the problems in requirements document must be corrected.

5.1.2   Non-functional requirements

Non-functional requirements, as the name suggests, are those requirements which are not directly concerned with the specific functions delivered by the system. They may relate to emergent system properties such as reliability, response time and store occupancy. Alternatively, they may define constraints on the system such as the capabilities of I/O devices and the data representations used in system interfaces.

Many non-functional requirements relate to the system as a whole rather than to individual system features. This means that they are often more critical than individual functional requirements. While failure to meet an individual functional requirement may degrade the system, failure to meet a non-functional system requirement may make the whole system unusable. For example, if an aircraft system does not meet its reliability requirements, it will not be certified as safe for

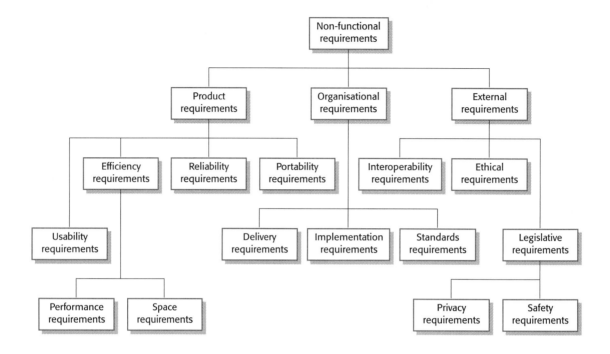

operation; if a real-time control system fails to meet its performance requirements, the control functions will not operate correctly.

However, non-functional requirements are not always concerned with the software system to be developed. Some non-functional requirements may constrain the process which may be used to develop the system. Examples of process requirements include a specification of the quality standards which must be used in the process, a specification that the design must be produced with a specified CASE toolset and a description of the process which should be followed.

Non-functional requirements arise through user needs, because of budget constraints, because of organisational policies, because of the need for interoperability with other software or hardware systems or because of external factors such as safety regulations, privacy legislation, etc. Figure 5.3 is a classification of the different types of non-functional requirements that may arise.

I have classified the different types of non-functional requirements shown in Figure 5.3 according to their derivation:

1. *Product requirements*   These are requirements that specify product behaviour. Examples include performance requirements on how fast the system must execute and how much memory it requires; reliability requirements that set out the acceptable failure rate; portability requirements and usability requirements.

2. *Organisational requirements*   These are derived from policies and procedures in the customer's and developer's organisation. Examples include process

standards which must be used; implementation requirements such as the programming language or design method used; and delivery requirements which specify when the product and its documentation are to be delivered.

3. *External requirements*   This broad heading covers all requirements which are derived from factors external to the system and its development process. These include interoperability requirements which define how the system interacts with systems in other organisations; legislative requirements which must be followed to ensure that the system operates within the law; and ethical requirements. Ethical requirements are requirements placed on a system to ensure that it will be acceptable to its users and the general public.

Figure 5.4 shows examples of product, organisational and external requirements. The product requirement relates to a programming support environment for the Ada language (an APSE). This restricts the freedom of the APSE designers in their choice of symbols used in the APSE user interface. It says nothing about the functionality of the APSE and clearly identifies a system constraint rather than a function. The organisational requirement specifies that the system must be developed according to a company standard process defined as XYZCo-SP-STAN-95. The external requirement is derived from the need for the system to conform to privacy legislation. It specifies that system operators should not have access to any data that they do not need.

A common problem with non-functional requirements is that they are sometimes difficult to verify. They may be written to reflect general goals of the customer such as ease of use, the ability of the system to recover from failure or rapid user response. These requirements cause problems for system developers as they leave scope for interpretation and subsequent dispute once the system is delivered. As an illustration of this problem, consider Figure 5.5. This shows a system goal relating to the usability of the system and how this can be expressed in a verifiable way as a non-functional requirement. This non-functional requirement can be verified by testing so you can check if the system has met the customer's goal.

Ideally, non-functional requirements should be expressed quantitatively using metrics that can be objectively tested. Figure 5.6 shows a number of possible metrics

Figure 5.4 Examples of non-functional requirements

Product requirement
4.C.8 It shall be possible for all necessary communication between the APSE and the user to be expressed in the standard Ada character set.

Organisational requirement
9.3.2 The system development process and deliverable documents shall conform to the process and deliverables defined in XYZCo-SP-STAN-95.

External requirement
7.6.5 The system shall not disclose any personal information about customers apart from their name and reference number to the operators of the system.

Figure 5.5 System
goals and verifiable
requirements

A system goal
The system should be easy to use by experienced controllers and should be
organised in such a way that user errors are minimised.

A verifiable non-functional requirement
Experienced controllers shall be able to use all the system functions after a total of
two hours' training. After this training, the average number of errors made by
experienced users shall not exceed two per day.

Figure 5.6 Metrics
for specifying
non-functional
requirements

Property	Measure
Speed	Processed transactions/second User/Event response time Screen refresh time
Size	K bytes Number of RAM chips
Ease of use	Training time Number of help frames
Reliability	Mean time to failure Probability of unavailability Rate of failure occurrence Availability
Robustness	Time to restart after failure Percentage of events causing failure Probability of data corruption on failure
Portability	Percentage of target-dependent statements Number of target systems

that may be used to specify non-functional system properties. Measurements can
be made during system testing to determine whether or not the system meets these
requirements.

In practice, quantitative requirements specification is often difficult. Customers
may not be able to translate their goals into quantitative requirements; for some goals,
such as maintainability goals, there are no metrics that can be used; the cost of
objectively verifying quantitative non-functional requirements may be very high.
Therefore, requirements documents will often include statements of goals mixed with
requirements. These goals may be useful to developers because they give some clues
to customer priorities. However, customers should be told that they are open to misinterpretation and cannot be objectively verified.

Non-functional requirements often conflict and interact with other system functional requirements. For example, it may be a requirement that the maximum store

occupied by a system should be 4 Mbytes because the entire system has to be fitted into read-only memory and installed on a spacecraft. A further requirement might be that the system should be written using Ada, a programming language that was designed for critical real-time software development. However, it may not be possible to compile an Ada program with the required functionality into less than 4 Mbytes. Some trade-off between these requirements must be made. An alternative development language may be used or increased memory added to the system.

In principle, functional and non-functional requirements should be differentiated in a requirements document. In practice, this is difficult. If the non-functional requirements are stated separately from the functional requirements, it is sometimes difficult to see the relationships between them. If stated with the functional requirements, it may be difficult to separate functional and non-functional considerations and to identify requirements which relate to the system as a whole. An appropriate balance must be found which depends on the type of system being specified. However, requirements that are clearly related to emergent system properties should be explicitly highlighted. This may be done either by putting them in a separate section of the requirements document or by distinguishing them, in some way, from other system requirements.

5.1.3   Domain requirements

Domain requirements are derived from the application domain of the system rather than from the specific needs of system users. They may be new functional requirements in their own right, constrain existing functional requirements or set out how particular computations must be carried out. Domain requirements are important because they often reflect fundamentals of the application domain. If these requirements are not satisfied, it may be impossible to make the system work satisfactorily.

To illustrate domain requirements, consider the following requirements from the library system:

1. There shall be a standard user interface to all databases which shall be based on the Z39.50 standard.

2. Because of copyright restrictions, some documents must be deleted immediately on arrival. Depending on the user's requirements, these documents will either be printed locally on the system server for manually forwarding to the user or routed to a network printer.

The first of these requirements is a constraint on a system functional requirement. It specifies that the user interface to the database must be implemented according to a specific library standard. The second requirement has been introduced because of copyright laws which apply to material used in libraries. It specifies that the

Figure 5.7 A domain
requirement from a
train protection
system

The deceleration of the train shall be computed as:

$$D_{train} = D_{control} + D_{gradient}$$

where $D_{gradient}$ is 9.81 ms^2 * compensated gradient/alpha and where the values of
9.81 ms^2/alpha are known for different types of train.

Figure 5.7 A domain requirement from a train protection system

system must include an automatic delete-on-print facility for some classes of
document.

To illustrate domain requirements that specify how a computation is carried out,
consider Figure 5.7 which has been taken from the specification of an automated
train protection system. This system automatically stops a train if it goes through
a red signal. This requirement states how the train deceleration is computed by the
system. It uses domain-specific terminology. To understand it, you need some understanding of the operation of railway systems and train characteristics.

The requirement for the train system illustrates the major problem with domain
requirements. They are expressed using language which is specific to the application domain and it is often difficult for software engineers to understand them. Domain
experts may leave information out of a requirement simply because it is so obvious to them. However, it may not be obvious to the developers of the system and
they may therefore implement the requirement in an unsatisfactory way.

5.2 User requirements

The user requirements for a system should describe the functional and non-
functional requirements so that they are understandable by system users who
don't have detailed technical knowledge. They should only specify the external
behaviour of the system and should avoid, as far as possible, system design characteristics. Consequently, the user requirements should not be defined using an implementation model. The user requirements must be written using natural language,
forms and simple intuitive diagrams.

However, various problems can arise when requirements are written in natural
language:

1. *Lack of clarity*   It is sometimes difficult to use language in a precise and unambiguous way without making the document wordy and difficult to read.
2. *Requirements confusion*   Functional requirements, non-functional requirements,
   system goals and design information may not be clearly distinguished.
3. *Requirements amalgamation*   Several different requirements may be expressed
   together as a single requirement.

Figure 5.8
A requirement on
a database for a
programming
environment

4.A.5 The database shall support the generation and control of configuration objects; that is, objects which are themselves groupings of other objects in the database. The configuration control facilities shall allow access to the objects in a version group by the use of an incomplete name.

Figure 5.9 A user
requirement for an
editor grid

2.6   Grid facilities To assist in the positioning of entities on a diagram, the user may turn on a grid in either centimetres or inches, via an option on the control panel. Initially, the grid is off. The grid may be turned on and off at any time during an editing session and can be toggled between inches and centimetres at any time. A grid option will be provided on the reduce-to-fit view but the number of grid lines shown will be reduced to avoid filling the smaller diagram with grid lines.

As an illustration of some of these problems, consider one of the requirements for an Ada programming environment shown in Figure 5.8.

This requirement includes both conceptual and detailed information. It expresses the concept that there should be configuration control facilities provided as an inherent part of the APSE. However, it also includes the detail that the configuration control facilities should allow access to the objects in a version group without specifying their complete name. This detail would have been better left to the system requirements specification.

It is good practice to separate user requirements from more detailed system requirements in a requirements document. Otherwise, non-technical readers of the user requirements may be overwhelmed by details which are really only relevant for technicians. Figure 5.9 illustrates this confusion. This example is taken from the requirements document for a CASE tool for editing software design models. The user may specify that a grid should be displayed so that entities may be accurately positioned in a diagram.

The first sentence mixes up three different kinds of requirement.

1. A conceptual, functional requirement states that the editing system should provide a grid. It presents a rationale for this.
2. A non-functional requirement giving detailed information about the grid units (centimetres or inches).
3. A non-functional user interface requirement which defines how that grid is switched on and off by the user.

The requirement in Figure 5.9 also gives some but not all initialisation information. It defines that the grid is initially off. However, it does not define its units when turned on. It provides some detailed information, namely that the user may toggle between units, but not the spacing between grid lines.

Figure 5.10
A definition of an
editor grid facility

2.6   Grid facilities

**2.6.1   The editor shall provide a grid facility where a matrix of horizontal and
vertical lines provide a background to the editor window.** This grid shall
be a passive grid where the alignment of entities is the user's responsibility.
Rationale: A grid helps the user to create a tidy diagram with well-spaced
entities. Although an active grid, where entities 'snap-to' grid lines can be
useful, the positioning is imprecise. The user is the best person to decide
where entities should be positioned.

Specification: ECLIPSE/WS/Tools/DE/FS Section 5.6

Figure 5.11 User
requirements for
node creation

3.5.1   Adding nodes to a design

**3.5.1.1   The editor shall provide a facility for users to add nodes of a specified
type to their design.**

3.5.1.2   The sequence of actions to add a node should be as follows:
1.   The user should select the type of node to be added.
2.   The user should move the cursor to the approximate node position in
the diagram and indicate that the node symbol should be added at that
point.
3.   The user should then drag the node symbol to its final position.
Rationale: The user is the best person to decide where to position a
node on the diagram. This approach gives the user direct control over
node type selection and positioning.

Specification: ECLIPSE/WS/Tools/DE/FS. Section 3.5.1

When user requirements include too much information, it constrains the freedom
of the system developer to provide innovative solutions to user problems and makes
the requirements difficult to understand. The user requirement should simply focus
on the key facilities to be provided. This is illustrated in Figure 5.10 where I have
rewritten the requirement for the editor grid to focus only on the essential system
features.

The rationale associated with the requirements is important. It helps the system
developers and maintainers to understand why the requirement has been included
and to assess the impact of requirements change. For example, in Figure 5.10, the
rationale recognises that an active grid where positioned objects automatically
'snap' to a grid line can be useful. However, it deliberately rejects this option in
favour of manual positioning. If a change to this is proposed at some later stage, it
is then clear that the use of a passive grid was deliberate rather than an implementation decision.

A further example of a more specific user requirement, which also defines part
of the editing system, is shown in Figure 5.11. This is a more detailed specification of a function. In this case, the definition includes a list of user actions. This is
sometimes necessary so that all functions can be provided in a consistent way.
Implementation details should not be included in this additional information.

Therefore, the definition does not set out how the cursor and the symbol are moved, or how the type is selected.

To minimise misunderstandings when writing user requirements, I recommend that you should follow some simple guidelines for writing requirements:

1.   Invent a standard format and ensure that all requirement definitions adhere to that format. Standardising the format means that omissions are less likely and makes requirements easier to check. The format I use includes emboldening the initial requirement, including a statement of rationale with each user requirement and a reference to the more detailed system requirement specification.

2.   Use language consistently. In particular, distinguish between mandatory and desirable requirements. It is usual practice to define mandatory requirements using 'shall' and desirable requirements using 'should' as can be seen in Figure 5.11. Therefore, it is mandatory that the system includes a facility to add nodes to a design. It is desirable that the sequence of actions should be as specified but this is not absolutely essential if there are good reasons why it can't be done in that way.

3.   Use text highlighting (bold and italic) to pick out key parts of the requirement.

4.   Avoid, as far as possible, the use of computer jargon. However, it will inevitably be the case that detailed technical terms which are used in the application domain of the system will be included in the user requirements.

5.3 System requirements

System requirements are more detailed descriptions of the user requirements. They may serve as the basis for a contract for the implementation of the system and should therefore be a complete and consistent specification of the whole system. They are used by software engineers as the starting point for the system design.

The system requirements specification may include different models of the system such as an object model or a data-flow model. I describe different models that may be used in the system requirements specification in Chapter 7.

In principle, the system requirements should state what the system should do and not how it should be implemented. However, at the level of detail required to specify the system completely, it is virtually impossible to exclude all design information. There are several reasons for this:

1.   An initial architecture of the system may be defined to help structure the requirements specification. The system requirements are organised according to the different sub-systems which make up the system.

2. In most cases, systems must interoperate with other existing systems. These constrain the design and these constraints generate requirements for the new system.

3. The use of a specific design (such as N-version programming to achieve reliability, discussed in Chapter 18) may be an external system requirement.

Natural language is often used to write system requirements specifications. However, as well as the problems identified in section 5.2, further problems with natural language can arise when it is used for more detailed specification:

1. Natural language understanding relies on the specification readers and writers using the same words for the same concept. This leads to misunderstandings because of the ambiguity of natural language. Jackson (1995) gives an excellent example of this when he discusses signs displayed by an escalator. These said 'Shoes must be worn' and 'Dogs must be carried'. I leave it to you to work out the conflicting interpretations of these phrases.

2. A natural language requirements specification is over-flexible. You can say the same thing in completely different ways. It is up to the reader to find out when requirements are the same and when they are distinct.

3. There is no easy way to modularise natural language requirements. It may be difficult to find all related requirements. To discover the consequence of a change, you may have to look at every requirement rather than just a group of related requirements.

Because of these problems, requirements specifications written in natural language are prone to misunderstandings. These are often not discovered until later phases of the software process and may then be very expensive to resolve.

There are various alternatives to the use of natural language which add structure to the specification and which help reduce ambiguity. These are shown in Figure 5.12.

Other approaches, such as specialised requirements languages (Teichrow and Hershey, 1977; Alford, 1977; Bell *et al.*, 1977; Alford, 1985), have also been developed but these are now rarely used. Davis (1990) summarises and compares some of these different approaches to requirements specification. In this chapter, I focus on the first two of these approaches, namely structured natural language and the use of design description languages.

5.3.1   Structured language specifications

Structured natural language is a restricted form of natural language for writing system requirements. The advantage of this approach is that it maintains most of the expressiveness and understandability of natural language but ensures that some degree

Figure 5.12
Notations for
requirements
specification

Notation	Description
Structured natural language	This approach depends on defining standard forms or templates to express the requirements specification.
Design description languages	This approach uses a language like a programming language but with more abstract features to specify the requirements by defining an operational model of the system.
Graphical notations	A graphical language, supplemented by text annotations, is used to define the functional requirements for the system. An early example of such a graphical language was SADT (Ross, 1977; Schoman and Ross, 1977). More recently, use-case descriptions (Jacobsen *et al.*, 1993) have been used. I discuss these in the following chapter.
Mathematical specifications	These are notations based on mathematical concepts such as finite-state machines or sets. These unambiguous specifications reduce the arguments between customer and contractor about system functionality. However, most customers don't understand formal specifications and are reluctant to accept them as a system contract. I discuss formal specification in Chapter 9.

of uniformity is imposed on the specification. Structured language notations may limit the terminology used and may use templates to specify system requirements. They may incorporate control constructs derived from programming languages and graphical highlighting to partition the specification.

A project which used structured natural language for specifying system requirements is described by Heninger (1980). Special-purpose forms were designed to describe the input, output and functions of an aircraft software system. The system requirements were specified using these forms.

To use a form-based approach to specifying system requirements, you must define one or more standard forms or templates to express the requirements. The specification may be structured around the objects manipulated by the system, the functions performed by the system or the events processed by the system. An example of such a form-based specification is shown in Figure 5.13. This is a more detailed definition of the Add node function for the design-editing system defined in Figure 5.11.

When a standard form is used for specifying functional requirements, the following information should be included:

1.   a description of the function or entity being specified;

2.   a description of its inputs and where these come from;

3.   a description of its outputs and where these go to;

4.   an indication of what other entities are used (the *requires* part);

Figure 5.13 System
requirements
specification using a
standard form

ECLIPSE/Workstation/Tools/DE/FS/3.5.1

Function   Add node

Description   Adds a node to an existing design. The user selects the type of node,
and its position. When added to the design, the node becomes the current selection.
The user chooses the node position by moving the cursor to the area where the
node is added.

Inputs   Node type, Node position, Design identifier.

Source   Node type and Node position are input by the user, Design identifier from
the database.

Outputs   Design identifier.

Destination   The design database. The design is committed to the database on
completion of the operation.

Requires   Design graph rooted at input design identifier.

Pre-condition   The design is open and displayed on the user's screen.

Post-condition   The design is unchanged apart from the addition of a node of the
specified type at the given position.

Side-effects   None

Definition: ECLIPSE/Workstation/Tools/DE/RD/3.5.1

5. if a functional approach is used, a pre-condition setting out what must be true
    before the function is called and a post-condition specifying what is true after
    the function is called;

6. a description of the side-effects (if any) of the operation.

Using formatted specifications removes some of the problems of natural language
specification in that there is less variability in the specification and requirements are
partitioned more effectively. However, some ambiguity may remain in the specification. Alternative methods which use more structured notations such as a PDL
(described below) go some way towards tackling the problem of specification
ambiguity. However, non-specialists usually find them harder to understand.

5.3.2   Requirements specification using a PDL

To counter the inherent ambiguities in natural language specification, it is possible
to describe requirements operationally using a program description language or PDL.
A PDL is a language derived from a programming language like Java or Ada. It
may contain additional, more abstract, constructs to increase its expressive power.
The advantage of using a PDL is that it may be checked syntactically and semantically by software tools. Requirements omissions and inconsistencies may be
inferred from the results of these checks.

Figure 5.14 A PDL
description of ATM
operation

```
class ATM {
    // declarations here
    public static void main (String args[]) throws InvalidCard {
        try {
            thisCard.read () ; // may throw InvalidCard exception
            pin = KeyPad.readPin () ; attempts = 1 ;
            while ( !thisCard.pin.equals (pin) & attempts < 4 )
                {   pin = KeyPad.readPin () ; attempts = attempts + 1 ;
                }
            if (!thisCard.pin.equals (pin))
                    throw new InvalidCard ("Bad PIN") ;
            thisBalance = thisCard.getBalance () ;
            do { Screen.prompt (" Please select a service ") ;
                service = Screen.touchKey () ;
                switch (service) {
                    case Services.withdrawalWithReceipt:
                            receiptRequired = true ;
                    case Services.withdrawalNoReceipt:
                            amount = KeyPad.readAmount () ;
                            if (amount > thisBalance)
                            {   Screen. printmsg ("Balance insufficient") ;
                                break ;
                            }
                            Dispenser.deliver (amount) ;
                            newbalance = thisBalance – amount ;
                            if (receiptRequired )
                                    Receipt.print (amount, newBalance) ;
                            break ;
                    // other service descriptions here
                    default: break ;
                }
            }
            while (service != Services.quit ) ;
            thisCard.returnToUser ("Please take your card") ;
        }
        catch (InvalidCard e )
        {   Screen.printmsg ("Invalid card or PIN") ;
        }
        // other exception handling here
    } //main ()
} //ATM
```

PDLs result in very detailed specifications and, sometimes, they are too close to the implementation for inclusion in a requirements document. However, I recommend their use in two situations:

1. When an operation is specified as a sequence of simpler actions and the order of execution is important. Descriptions of such sequences in natural language are sometimes confusing, particularly if nested conditionals and loops are involved. This is illustrated in Figure 5.14 which specifies part of the specification of an ATM. I have used Java as the PDL but have deliberately left out

parts of the description to save space. A complete Java description of the ATM can be downloaded from the book's web pages.

2. When hardware and software interfaces have to be specified. In many cases, the interfaces between sub-systems are defined in the system requirements specification. Using a PDL allows interface objects and types to be specified.

If the reader of the system requirements is familiar with the PDL used, specifying the requirements in this way can make them less ambiguous and easier to understand. If the PDL is based on the implementation language, there is a natural transition from requirements to design. The possibility of misinterpretation is reduced. Specifiers need not be trained in another description language.

There are disadvantages to this approach to requirements specification:

1. The language used to write the specification may not be sufficiently expressive to describe the system functionality.
2. The notation is only understandable to people who have some programming language knowledge.
3. The requirement may be taken as a design specification design rather than a model to help the user understand the system.

An effective way to use this approach to specification is to combine it with the use of structured natural language. A forms-based approach may be used to specify the overall system. A PDL may then be used to define control sequences or interfaces in more detail.

5.3.3 Interface specification

The vast majority of software systems must operate with other systems which have already been implemented and installed in an environment. If the new system and the existing systems must work together, the interfaces of existing systems must be precisely specified. These specifications should be defined early in the process and included (perhaps as an Appendix) in the requirements document.

There are three types of interface which may have to be defined:

1. Procedural interfaces where existing sub-systems offer a range of services which are accessed by calling interface procedures.

2. Data structures which are passed from one sub-system to another. A Java-based PDL may be used for this with the data structure being described using a class definition with attributes representing fields of the structure. However, I think entity-relationship diagrams (described in Chapter 7) are better for this type of description.

3. Representations of data (such as the ordering of bits) which have been established for an existing sub-system. Java does not support such detailed representation specification so I don't recommend the use of a Java-based PDL for this.

Figure 5.15 The Java
PDL description of a
print server interface

```
interface PrintServer {

// defines an abstract printer server
// requires: interface Printer, interface PrintDoc
// provides: initialize, print, displayPrintQueue, cancelPrintJob, switchPrinter

    void initialize ( Printer p ) ;
    void print ( Printer p, PrintDoc d ) ;
    void displayPrintQueue ( Printer p ) ;
    void cancelPrintJob (Printer p, PrintDoc d) ;
    void switchPrinter (Printer p1, Printer p2, PrintDoc d) ;
} //PrintServer
```

Formal notations, discussed in Chapter 9, allow interfaces to be defined in an unambiguous way but their specialised nature means that they are not understandable without special training. They are rarely used in practice for interface specification although, in my view, they are ideally suited for this purpose. Less formal, PDL interface descriptions are a compromise between comprehensibility and precision but are usually more precise than natural language interface specification.

Figure 5.15 is an example of a definition of the first of these interface types. In this case, the interface is the procedural interface offered by a print server. This manages a queue of requests to print files on different printers. Users may examine the queue associated with a printer and may remove their print jobs from that queue. They may also switch jobs from one printer to another.

The specification in Figure 5.15 is an abstract model of the print server without revealing any interface details. The functionality of the interface operations can be defined using structured natural language (Figure 5.10), using a Java-based PDL (Figure 5.14), or by using a formal notation as discussed in Chapter 9.

5.4 The software requirements document

The software requirements document (sometimes called the software requirements specification or SRS) is the official statement of what is required of the system developers. It should include both the user requirements for a system and a detailed specification of the system requirements. In some cases, the user and system requirements may be integrated into a single description. In other cases, the user requirements are defined in an introduction to the system requirements specification. If there are a large number of requirements, the detailed system requirements may be presented as separate documents.

The requirements document has a diverse set of users ranging from the senior management of the organisation who are paying for the system to the engineers responsible for developing the software. Figure 5.16, taken from (Kotonya and Sommerville, 1998), illustrates possible users of the document and how they use it.

Figure 5.16 Users of
a requirements
document

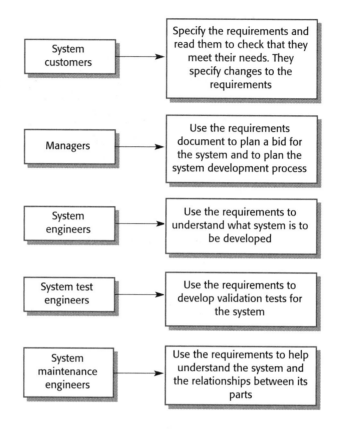

Heninger (1980) suggests that there are six requirements which a software
requirements document should satisfy:

- It should specify only external system behaviour.
- It should specify constraints on the implementation.
- It should be easy to change.
- It should serve as a reference tool for system maintainers.
- It should record forethought about the life cycle of the system.
- It should characterise acceptable responses to undesired events.

Although more than 20 years old, this is good advice. However, it is sometimes
difficult to specify systems in terms of what they will do (their external behaviour).
Inevitably, because of constraints from existing systems, the system design is constrained and this must be reflected in the requirements document. Other advice, such
as the need to record forethought about the system life cycle, is widely accepted
but not widely followed when writing requirements documents.

A number of different large organisations such as the US Department of Defense
and the IEEE have defined standards for requirements documents. Davis (1993) discusses some of these standards and compares their contents. The most widely known
standard is the IEEE/ANSI 830-1993 standard (IEEE, 1993). Thayer and Dorfman
(1997), in their excellent collection of articles on requirements engineering, include

a full specification of this standard. This IEEE standard suggests the following structure for requirements documents:

1. **Introduction**
   1.1   Purpose of the requirements document
   1.2   Scope of the product
   1.3   Definitions, acronyms and abbreviations
   1.4   References
   1.5   Overview of the remainder of the document

2. **General description**
   2.1   Product perspective
   2.2   Product functions
   2.3   User characteristics
   2.4   General constraints
   2.5   Assumptions and dependencies

3. **Specific requirements** covering functional, non-functional and interface
   requirements. This is obviously the most substantial part of the document but
   because of the wide variability in organisational practice, it is not appropriate
   to define a standard structure for this section. The requirements may document
   external interfaces, describe system functionality and performance, specify
   logical database requirements, design constraints, emergent system properties
   and quality characteristics.

4. **Appendices**

5. **Index**

Although the IEEE standard is not ideal, it contains a great deal of good advice
on how to write requirements and how to avoid problems. It is too general to be
an organisational standard in its own right. However, it can be tailored and adapted
to define a standard which is geared to the needs of a particular organisation. Figure 5.17 illustrates a possible organisation for a requirements document which is
based on the IEEE standard. However, I have extended this to include information
about predicted system evolution as recommended by Heninger.

Of course, the information which is included in a requirements document must
depend on the type of software being developed and the approach to development
which is used. If an evolutionary approach is adopted for a software product (say),
the requirements document will leave out many of the detailed chapters suggested
above. In this case, the designers and programmers use their judgement to decide
how to meet the outline user requirements for the system.

By contrast, when the software is part of a large system engineering project which
includes interacting hardware and software systems, it is often essential to define
the requirements to a fine level of detail. This means that the requirements documents are likely to be very long and they should include most of the chapters
shown in Figure 5.17. For long documents, it is particularly important to include a
comprehensive table of contents and document index so that readers can find the
information that they need.

Figure 5.17
The structure
of a requirements
document

Chapter	Description
Preface	This should define the expected readership of the document and describe its version history, including a rationale for the creation of a new version and a summary of the changes made in each version.
Introduction	This should describe the need for the system. It should briefly describe its functions and explain how it will work with other systems. It should describe how the system fits into the overall business or strategic objectives of the organisation commissioning the software.
Glossary	This should define the technical terms used in the document. You should not make assumptions about the experience or expertise of the reader.
User requirements definition	The services provided for the user and the non-functional system requirements should be described in this section. This description may use natural language, diagrams or other notations that are understandable by customers. Product and process standards which must be followed should be specified.
System architecture	This chapter should present a high-level overview of the anticipated system architecture showing the distribution of functions across system modules. Architectural components that are reused should be highlighted.
System requirements specification	This should describe the functional and non-functional requirements in more detail. If necessary, further detail may also be added to the non-functional requirements, e.g. interfaces to other systems may be defined.
System models	This should set out one or more system models showing the relationships between the system components and the system and its environment. These might be object models, data-flow models and semantic data models.
System evolution	This should describe the fundamental assumptions on which the system is based and anticipated changes due to hardware evolution, changing user needs, etc.
Appendices	These should provide detailed, specific information which is related to the application which is being developed. Examples of appendices that may be included are hardware and database descriptions. Hardware requirements define the minimal and optimal configurations for the system. Database requirements define the logical organisation of the data used by the system and the relationships between data.
Index	Several indexes to the document may be included. As well as a normal alphabetic index, there may be an index of diagrams, an index of functions, etc.

KEY POINTS

▶ Requirements for a software system set out what the system should do and define constraints on its operation and implementation.

▶ Functional requirements are statements of the services that the system must provide or are descriptions of how some computations must be carried out. Domain requirements are functional requirements that are derived from characteristics of the application domain.

▶ Non-functional requirements are product requirements which constrain the system being developed, process requirements which apply to the development process, and external requirements. They often relate to the emergent properties of the system so therefore apply to the system as a whole.

▶ User requirements are intended for use by people involved in using and procuring the system. They should be written using natural language, tables and diagrams so that they are understandable.

▶ System requirements are intended to communicate, in a precise way, the functions which the system must provide. To reduce ambiguity, they may be written in a structured language of some kind. This may be a structured form of natural language, a language based on a high-level programming language or a special language for requirements specification.

▶ The software requirements document is the agreed statement of the system requirements. It should be organised so that it can be used by both system customers and software developers.

FURTHER READING

Requirements Engineering: Processes and Techniques. This book covers all aspects of the requirements engineering process and discusses specific requirements specification techniques. (G. Kotonya and I. Sommerville, 1998 Wiley.)

Software Requirements Engineering. This is a collection of papers on requirements engineering that includes several relevant articles, including 'Recommended practice for software requirements specification'. This is a discussion of the IEEE standard for requirements documents. (R. H. Thayer and M. Dorfman (eds.), 1997, IEEE Computer Society Press.)

EXERCISES

5.1   Discuss the problems of using natural language for defining user and system requirements and show, using small examples, how structuring natural language into forms can help avoid some of these difficulties.

5.2   Discover ambiguities or omissions in the following statement of requirements for part of a ticket issuing system.

> An automated ticket issuing system sells rail tickets. Users select their destination, and input a credit card and a personal identification number. The rail ticket is issued and their credit card account charged with its cost. When the user presses the start button, a menu display of potential destinations is activated along with a message to the user to select a destination. Once a destination has been selected, users are requested to input their credit card. Its validity is checked and the user is then requested to input a personal identifier. When the credit transaction has been validated, the ticket is issued.

5.3   Rewrite the above description using the structured approach described in this chapter. Resolve the identified ambiguities in some appropriate way.

5.4   Write system requirements for the above system using a Java-based notation. You may make any reasonable assumptions about the system. Pay particular attention to specifying user errors.

5.5   Using the technique suggested here where natural language is presented in a standard way, write plausible user requirements for the following functions:
   • A unattended petrol (gas) pump system that includes a credit card reader. The customer swipes the card through the reader then specifies the amount of fuel required. The fuel is delivered and the customer's account debited.
   • The cash dispensing function in a bank auto-teller machine.
   • The spell checking and correcting function in a word processor.

5.6   Describe three different types of non-functional requirement which may be placed on a system. Give examples of each of these types of requirement.

5.7   Write a set of non-functional requirements for the ticket issuing system described above, setting out its expected reliability and its response time.

5.8   What are the requirements for a programming language so that it is suitable for defining interface specifications? Comment on the suitability of C, Java and Ada for this purpose.

5.9   Suggest how an engineer responsible for drawing up a system requirements specification might keep track of the relationships between functional and non-functional requirements.

5.10 You have taken a job with a software user who has contracted your previous employer to develop a system for them. You discover that your company's interpretation of the requirements is different from the interpretation taken by your previous employer. Discuss what you should do in such a situation. You know that the costs to your current employer will increase if the ambiguities are not resolved. You have also a responsibility of confidentiality to your previous employer.

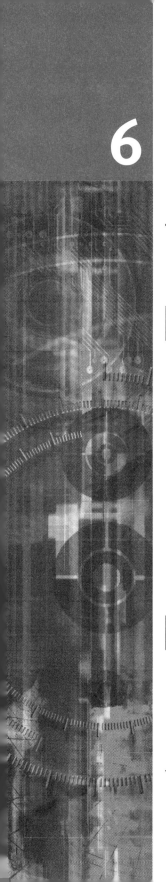

6 Requirements engineering processes

Objectives

The objective of this chapter is to describe a number of generic requirements engineering processes. When you have read this chapter, you will:

☐ understand the principal requirements engineering activities and their relationships;

☐ have been introduced to several techniques of requirements elicitation and analysis;

☐ understand the importance of requirements validation and how requirements reviews are used in this process;

☐ understand why requirements management is necessary and how it supports other requirements engineering activities.

Contents

6.1 Feasibility studies
6.2 Requirements elicitation and analysis
6.3 Requirements validation
6.4 Requirements management

Requirements engineering is a process that involves all of the activities required to create and maintain a system requirements document. There are four generic, high-level requirements engineering process activities. These are a system feasibility study, the elicitation and analysis of requirements, the specification of requirements and their documentation and, finally, the validation of these requirements. I cover all of these activities in this chapter apart from specification and documentation which I have already discussed in Chapter 5. Figure 6.1 illustrates the relationship between these activities. It also shows the documents produced at each stage of the requirements engineering (RE) process.

The requirements engineering activities shown in Figure 6.1 are concerned with the elicitation, documentation and checking of requirements. In virtually all systems, however, requirements change. The people involved develop a better understanding of what they want the software to do; the organisation buying the system changes; modifications are made to the system's hardware, software and organisational environment. Requirements management is an additional requirements engineering activity which is concerned with managing requirements change. This is covered in the final section of the chapter.

Some people consider requirements engineering to be the process of applying a structured method, such as object-oriented analysis (Rumbaugh *et al.*, 1991; Booch, 1994). This involves analysing the system and developing a set of graphical system models which then act as a system specification. The set of models describe the behaviour of the system and are annotated with additional information describing, for example, its required performance or reliability.

Although structured methods have a role to play in the requirements engineering process, there is much more to requirements engineering than is covered by these methods. They do not provide effective support for early RE process stages such as requirements elicitation. I therefore focus here on more general approaches to requirements engineering and I discuss structured analysis methods and system models in Chapter 7.

Figure 6.1
The requirements
engineering process

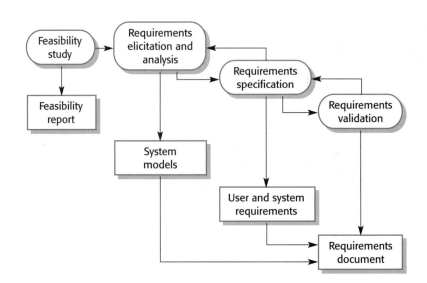

6.1 Feasibility studies

For all new systems, the requirements engineering process should start with a feasibility study. The input to the feasibility study is an outline description of the system and how it will be used within an organisation. The results of the feasibility study should be a report which recommends whether or not it is worth carrying on with the requirements engineering and system development process.

A feasibility study is a short, focused study which aims to answer a number of questions:

1. Does the system contribute to the overall objectives of the organisation?
2. Can the system be implemented using current technology and within given cost and schedule constraints?
3. Can the system be integrated with other systems which are already in place?

The issue of whether or not the system contributes to business objectives is critical. If a system does not support these objectives, it has no real value to the business. While this may seem obvious, many organisations develop systems which do not contribute to their objectives either because they don't have a clear statement of these objectives or because other political or organisation factors influence the system procurement.

Carrying out a feasibility study involves information assessment, information collection and report writing. The information assessment phase identifies the information which is required to answer the three questions set out above. Once the information has been identified, you should question information sources to discover the answers to these questions. Some examples of possible questions that may be put are:

1. How would the organisation cope if this system was not implemented?
2. What are the problems with current processes and how would a new system help alleviate these problems?
3. What direct contribution will the system make to the business objectives?
4. Can information be transferred to and from other organisational systems?
5. Does the system require technology which has not previously been used in the organisation?
6. What must be supported by the system and what need not be supported?

Information sources may include the managers of departments where the system will be used, software engineers who are familiar with the type of system that is proposed, technology experts, end-users of the system, etc. They should be interviewed during the feasibility study to collect the required information.

When the information is available, the feasibility study report is prepared. This should make a recommendation about whether or not the system development should continue. It may propose changes to the scope, budget and schedule of the system and suggest further high-level requirements for the system.

6.2 Requirements elicitation and analysis

After initial feasibility studies, the next stage of the requirements engineering process is requirements elicitation and analysis. In this activity, technical software development staff work with customers and system end-users to find out about the application domain, what services the system should provide, the required performance of the system, hardware constraints, and so on.

Requirements elicitation and analysis may involve a variety of different kinds of people in an organisation. The term *stakeholder* is used to refer to anyone who should have some direct or indirect influence on the system requirements. Stakeholders include end-users who will interact with the system and everyone else in an organisation who will be affected by it. Engineers who are developing or maintaining other related systems, business managers, domain experts, trade union representatives, and so on may also be system stakeholders.

Elicitation and analysis is a difficult process for a number of reasons:

1. Stakeholders often don't really know what they want from the computer system except in the most general terms; they may find it difficult to articulate what they want from the system; they may make unrealistic demands because they are unaware of the cost of their requests.

2. Stakeholders in a system naturally express requirements in their own terms and with implicit knowledge of their own work. Requirements engineers, without experience in the customer's domain, must understand these requirements.

3. Different stakeholders have different requirements and they may express these in different ways. Requirements engineers have to discover all potential sources of requirements and discover commonalities and conflict.

4. Political factors may influence the requirements of the system. These may come from managers who demand specific system requirements because these allow them to increase their influence in the organisation.

5. The economic and business environment in which the analysis takes place is dynamic. It inevitably changes during the analysis process. Hence the importance of particular requirements may change. New requirements may emerge from new stakeholders who were not originally consulted.

A generic process model of the elicitation and analysis process is shown in Figure 6.2. Each organisation will have its own version or instantiation of this general model depending on local factors such as the expertise of the staff, the type of system being developed, the standards used, etc.

The process activities are:

Figure 6.2
The requirements
elicitation and
analysis process

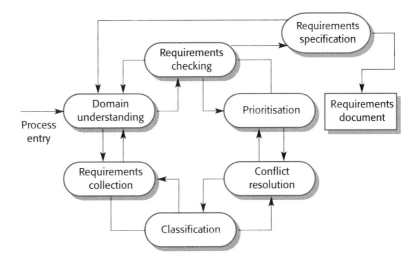

1. *Domain understanding* Analysts must develop their understanding of the application domain. For example, if a system for a supermarket is required, the analyst must find out how supermarkets operate.

2. *Requirements collection* This is the process of interacting with stakeholders in the system to discover their requirements. Obviously, domain understanding develops further during this activity.

3. *Classification* This activity takes the unstructured collection of requirements and organises them into coherent clusters.

4. *Conflict resolution* Inevitably, where multiple stakeholders are involved, requirements will conflict. This activity is concerned with finding and resolving these conflicts.

5. *Prioritisation* In any set of requirements some will be more important than others. This stage involves interaction with stakeholders to discover the most important requirements.

6. *Requirements checking* The requirements are checked to discover if they are complete, consistent and in accordance with what stakeholders really want from the system.

Figure 6.2 shows that requirements elicitation and analysis is an iterative process with continual feedback from each activity to other activities. The process cycle starts with domain understanding and ends with requirements checking. The analyst's understanding of the requirements improves with each round of the cycle.

In this section, I cover three techniques for requirements elicitation and analysis. These are viewpoint-oriented elicitation, scenarios and ethnography. Other techniques which may be used during this phase of the requirements engineering process include structured analysis methods, covered in Chapter 7, and prototyping, covered in Chapter 8. There is no perfect and universally applicable approach to requirements analysis and analysis. You normally have to use several of these approaches to develop a complete understanding and analysis of the requirements.

6.2.1 Viewpoint-oriented elicitation

For any medium-sized or large system, there are usually different types of end-user. Many stakeholders have some kind of interest in the system requirements. For example, system stakeholders for a bank auto-teller system (ATM) include:

1. *current bank customers* who receive services from the system;
2. *representatives from other banks* who have reciprocal agreements that allow each other's ATMs to be used;
3. *managers of bank branches* who obtain management information from the system;
4. *counter staff at bank branches* who are involved in the day-to-day running of the system, handling customer complaints, etc.;
5. *database administrators* who are responsible for integrating the system with the bank's customer database;
6. *bank security managers* who must ensure that the system will not pose a security hazard of some kind;
7. *the bank's marketing department* who are likely be interested in using the system as a means of marketing the bank;
8. *hardware and software maintenance engineers* who are responsible for maintaining and upgrading the hardware and software.

This list shows that for even a relatively simple system, there are many different *viewpoints* that should be considered. Different viewpoints on a problem see the problem in different ways. However, their perspectives are not completely independent but usually overlap so that they have common requirements.

Viewpoint-oriented approaches to requirements engineering recognise these different viewpoints and use them to structure and organise both the elicitation process and the requirements themselves. A key strength of viewpoint-oriented analysis is that it recognises the existence of multiple perspectives and provides a framework for discovering conflicts in the requirements proposed by different stakeholders.

Different methods have different ideas of what is meant by a 'viewpoint'. A viewpoint may be considered as:

1. *A data source or sink*   In this case, viewpoints are responsible for producing or consuming data. The analysis involves identifying all such viewpoints, identifying what data is produced or consumed and what processing is carried out. Methods such as SADT (Ross, 1977; Schoman and Ross, 1977) and CORE (Mullery, 1979), the first method to propose explicit viewpoints, use this type of viewpoint.

2. *A representation framework*   In this case, a viewpoint is considered to be a particular type of system model (Finkelstein *et al.*, 1990; Nuseibeh *et al.*, 1994). For example, different engineers might develop an entity-relational model, a state-machine model, etc. Each approach to analysis discovers different things about the system being analysed.

3. *A receiver of services*   In this case, viewpoints are external to the system and receive services from the system (Kotonya and Sommerville, 1992, 1996). Viewpoints may provide data for these services or control signals. The analysis involves examining the services received by different viewpoints, collecting these and resolving conflicts.

Each of these models of a viewpoint has different strengths and weaknesses. Viewpoints as data sources or sinks and viewpoints as representations are particularly valuable for discovering detailed conflicts between requirements (Easterbrook and Nuseibeh, 1996). However, they are less suited to structuring the requirements analysis process as there is no simple relationship between viewpoints and system stakeholders.

Interactive systems deliver services to end-users. Consequently, the most effective viewpoint-oriented approach for interactive systems analysis uses external viewpoints. These viewpoints interact with the system by receiving services from it and providing data and control signals to the system.

The advantages of this type of viewpoint are:

1. Viewpoints are external to the system so are a natural way to structure the requirements elicitation process.

2. It is relatively easy to decide if something is a valid viewpoint. Viewpoints must interact with the system in some way.

3. Viewpoints and services are a useful way of structuring non-functional requirements. Each service may have associated non-functional requirements. Multiple viewpoints allow the same service to have different non-functional requirements in different viewpoints.

The VORD (Viewpoint-Oriented Requirements Definition) method (Kotonya and Sommerville, 1996, 1998) has been designed as a service-oriented framework for requirements elicitation and analysis. The principal stages of the VORD method, shown in Figure 6.3, are:

1. Viewpoint identification, which involves discovering viewpoints that receive system services and identifying the specific services provided to each viewpoint.

2. Viewpoint structuring, which involves grouping related viewpoints into a hierarchy. Common services are provided at higher levels in the hierarchy and are inherited by lower-level viewpoints.

Figure 6.3
The VORD method

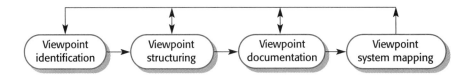

3.   Viewpoint documentation, which involves refining the description of the identified viewpoints and services.

4.   Viewpoint-system mapping, which involves identifying objects in an object-oriented design using service information which is encapsulated in viewpoints.

Viewpoint and service information in VORD is collected using standard forms. The forms used for viewpoint information (the viewpoint template) and service information (the service template) are shown in Figure 6.4. VORD also uses various diagrammatic notations, including viewpoint hierarchy diagrams (see example in Figure 6.8) and event scenarios (see example in Figure 6.10).

I illustrate the application of VORD by applying the first three steps in the analysis of requirements for a bank auto-teller (ATM) control system. Automated teller machines have an embedded software system to drive the machine hardware and to communicate with the bank's central account database.

The ATM accepts customer requests and delivers cash, account information, database updates, etc. Customers may withdraw and pay in cash, check their balance, transfer funds from one account to another, request an account statement, cheque book, etc. The machines provided by one bank may allow customers of other banks to use a subset (typically cash withdrawal and account balance querying) of their facilities.

The first step in viewpoint analysis is to identify possible viewpoints. As in all methods, this initial identification is probably the most difficult stage. One

Figure 6.4 Viewpoint and service template forms

Viewpoint template		Service template	
Reference:	The viewpoint name.	**Reference:**	The service name.
Attributes:	Attributes providing viewpoint information.	**Rationale:**	Reason why the service is provided.
Events:	A reference to a set of event scenarios describing how the system reacts to viewpoint events.	**Specification:**	Reference to a list of service specifications. These may be expressed in different notations.
Services:	A reference to a set of service descriptions.	**Viewpoints:**	List of viewpoint names receiving the service.
Sub-VPs:	The names of sub-viewpoints.	**Non-functional requirements:**	Reference to a set of non-functional requirements which constrain the service.
		Provider:	Reference to a list of system objects which provide the service.

Figure 6.5
Brainstorming
for viewpoint
identification

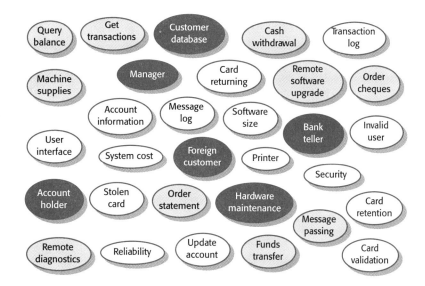

approach is a brainstorming approach where potential services and entities which interact with the system are identified. Stakeholders meet and suggest possible viewpoints which are written down in a bubble diagram as shown in Figure 6.5. In this diagram, potential viewpoints for an ATM system are shown in separate bubbles.

When brainstorming, you should try to identify potential viewpoints, system services, data inputs, non-functional requirements, control events and exceptions. At this stage of the analysis, you should not try to impose a structure on the diagram. Sources of information which may be used in creating this initial view of the system may be documents setting out the high-level goals of the system, knowledge of software engineers from previous projects or experience as bank customers. Interviews may be held with bank managers, counter staff, consultants, engineers and customers.

The next stage of the process is to identify viewpoints (shown as dark blue bubbles in Figure 6.5) and services (shown as shaded bubbles). The services should be allocated to viewpoints. Unallocated services can suggest viewpoints that have not been identified in the initial brainstorming session. For example, the 'Remote software upgrade' and 'Remote diagnostics' services in Figure 6.5 imply that there may be a need for a software maintenance viewpoint.

Figure 6.6 illustrates, for some of the viewpoints identified in Figure 6.5, the allocation of services. The same service may be allocated to several viewpoints.

As well as receiving services, viewpoints also provide inputs to these services. For example, auto-teller users must specify the amount of money they want when they withdraw cash. Viewpoints also provide control information to determine if and when services are delivered.

During this early stage of the process, this data and control information is simply identified by name. Figure 6.7 shows this control information for the account holder viewpoint whose services are identified in Figure 6.6. Control information is

Figure 6.6 Viewpoint service information

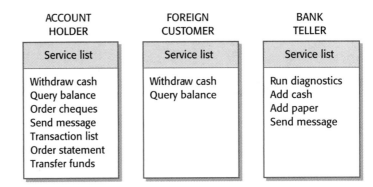

Figure 6.7 Viewpoint data and control information

ACCOUNT HOLDER	Control input	Data input
	Start transaction	Card details
	Cancel transaction	PIN
	End transaction	Amount required
	Select service	Message

provided through buttons on the machine; data through the user's card or the machine keyboard.

The viewpoint information is used to fill in viewpoint template forms and to organise the viewpoints into an inheritance hierarchy. To show viewpoint commonalities and to reuse viewpoint information, the inheritance hierarchy factors out viewpoints which provide common services. Services, data and control information are inherited by sub-viewpoints.

Figure 6.8 shows part of the viewpoint hierarchy for the ATM system. To avoid clutter, I have shown only the services associated with two viewpoints and I have left out a number of bank staff viewpoints. As services are inherited down the viewpoint hierarchy, the general services associated with the 'Customer' viewpoint (Query balance and Withdraw cash) are inherited by 'Account holder' and 'Foreign customer'.

The next process stage is to discover more detailed information about the services provided, the data which they require and how these are controlled. Requirements are elicited from the stakeholders associated with each viewpoint. The service needs of each different viewpoint are discussed with either end-users or with viewpoint experts if the viewpoint is another automated system. Figure 6.9 shows an example of a completed viewpoint template for the customer viewpoint and a template for the cash withdrawal service.

Notice that one of the fields in the viewpoint template is used to refer to event scenarios which describe how the system behaves in response to various events. These event scenarios are discussed in the following section.

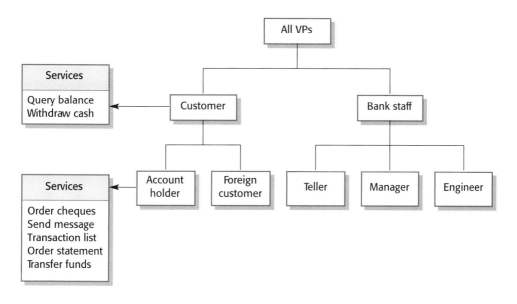

Figure 6.8
Viewpoint hierarchy

Viewpoint and service templates and event scenarios are developed for all identified viewpoints and services. The information may then be cross-checked to discover errors in the analysis and requirements conflicts. As this generates a great deal of information, VORD, like other analysis methods, is only practically usable with CASE tool support. A free set of CASE tools for VORD is available and can be downloaded through the book's web pages.

Figure 6.9 Customer
viewpoint and cash
withdrawal
descriptions

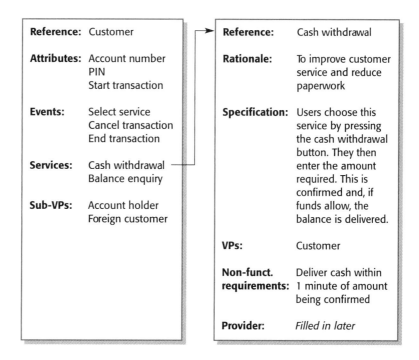

Scenarios

People usually find it easier to relate to real-life examples rather than abstract descriptions. They can understand and criticise a scenario of how they might interact with a software system. Requirements engineers can use the information gained from this discussion to formulate the actual system requirements.

Scenarios can be particularly useful for adding detail to an outline requirements description. They are descriptions of example interaction sessions. Each scenario covers one or a small number of possible interactions. Different forms of scenarios have been developed and they provide different types of information at different levels of detail about the system.

The scenario starts with an outline of the interaction and, during elicitation, details are added to create a complete description of that interaction. At its most general, a scenario may include:

1. a system state description at the beginning of the scenario;
2. a description of the normal flow of events in the scenario;
3. a description of what can go wrong and how this is handled;
4. information about other activities which might be going on at the same time;
5. a description of the state of the system after completion of the scenario.

Scenario-based elicitation can be carried out informally where the requirements engineer works with stakeholders to identify scenarios and to capture details of these scenarios. Alternatively, a more structured approach such as event scenarios or use-cases may be used.

Event scenarios

Event scenarios are used in VORD to document the system behaviour when presented with specific events. Each distinct interaction event such as inserting a card into an ATM or selecting an ATM service may be documented with a separate event scenario. Event scenarios include a description of data flows and the actions of the system and document the exceptions which can arise. To illustrate event scenarios, consider Figure 6.10 which shows the scenario to a 'Start transaction' event. This is initiated by a customer inserting his or her card into the machine. This is a more abstract description than the Java-PDL description given in Chapter 5.

The diagrammatic conventions used in event scenarios are:

1. Data provided from a viewpoint or delivered to a viewpoint is shown in ellipses.
2. Control information enters and leaves at the top of each box.
3. Data leaves from the right of each box. If it is not enclosed, this means that it is internal to the system.
4. Exceptions are shown at the bottom of the box. Where there are several possible exceptions, these are enclosed in a box as shown on the left of Figure 6.10.
5. The name of the next expected event after completion of the scenario is shown in a shaded box.

Figure 6.10 Event
scenario – Start
transaction

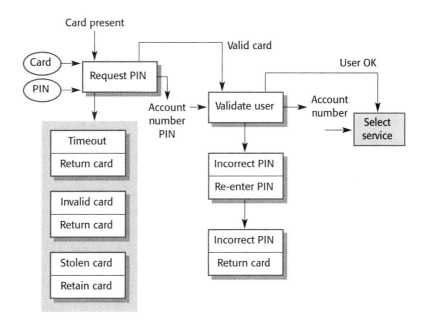

Figure 6.10 shows that when a card is entered, the customer's personal identi-fication number (PIN) is requested. The customer inputs his or her card (the card must be present to trigger the request) and PIN. If the card is a valid card which can be processed by the machine, control can move to the next stage.

In the first stage, there are three possible exceptions:

1. *Timeout*   The customer may fail to enter a PIN within the allowed time limit. The card is returned.
2. *Invalid card*   The card is not recognised and is returned.
3. *Stolen card*   The card is recognised as a stolen card and is retained by the machine.

Each exception may be defined in more detail by constructing a separate data and control analysis diagram showing how that exception occurs. Alternatively, the general diagram may be annotated with extra information that explains when exceptions occur and the actions that should be taken.

The 'Validate user' stage checks that the PIN is associated with the customer's account number in which case it can trigger the next stage (Select service) with the 'User OK' event. The account number is also output from this stage. Possible excep-tions are the input of an incorrect PIN in which case the PIN is requested again. The diagram shows that this repeated request can also have an exception. If an incor-rect PIN is again input, the card is returned.

Use-cases

Use-cases are a scenario-based technique for requirements elicitation which were first introduced in the Objectory method (Jacobson *et al.*, 1993). They have now

Figure 6.11
A lending use-case

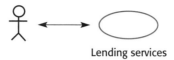

Lending services

become a fundamental feature of the UML notation for describing object-oriented system models. In their simplest form, a use-case identifies the actors involved in an interaction and names the type of interaction. This is illustrated in Figure 6.11 which describes a Library-services use-case where a user can borrow or return a book from a library.

Figure 6.11 illustrates the essentials of the use-case notation. Actors in the process are represented as stick figures and each class of interaction is represented as a named ellipse. The set of use-cases represents all of the possible interactions that will be represented in the system requirements. This is illustrated in Figure 6.12 which develops the library example and shows other use-cases in that environment.

There is sometimes confusion about whether or not a use-case is a scenario on its own or, as suggested by Fowler (Fowler and Scott, 1997), a use-case encapsulates a set of scenarios where each scenario is a single thread through the use-case. In this case, there would be a scenario for the normal interaction plus scenarios for each possible exception.

Within the UML, sequence diagrams may be used to add information to a use-case. These sequence diagrams show the actors involved in the interaction, the objects within the system with which they interact and the operations which are associated with these objects. As an illustration of this, Figure 6.13 shows the interactions involved in acquiring and cataloguing a book for the library.

Figure 6.13 illustrates that there are two objects of classes Library Item and Catalog involved in the Catalogue Management use case. The sequence of actions is from top to bottom and the labels on the arrows between the actors and objects indicate the names of operations. Therefore, when a book is bought, the *New* operation is enacted on Catalog and the *Acquire* operation on Item. Once the book is available, the *Catalog item* operation is enacted on Item.

Figure 6.12
Library use-cases

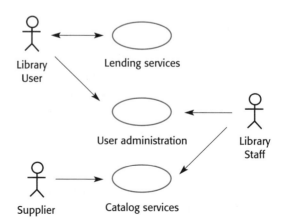

Figure 6.13
Sequence diagram
for catalogue
management

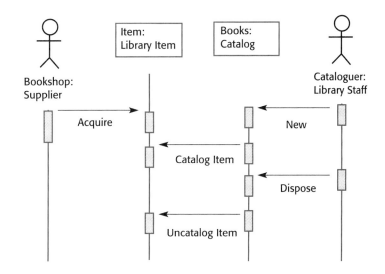

The UML is a *de facto* standard for object-oriented modelling so use-cases and use-case based elicitation are increasingly used for requirements elicitation. I discuss other aspects of the UML in Chapter 7 which covers system modelling and in Chapter 12 which covers object-oriented design.

6.2.3   Ethnography

Software systems do not exist in isolation. They are used in a social and organisational context and software system requirements may be derived or constrained by that context. Satisfying these social and organisational requirements is often critical for the success of the system. One reason why many software systems are delivered but never used is that they do not take proper account of the importance of this type of system requirement.

Ethnography is an observational technique that can be used to understand social and organisational requirements. An analyst immerses himself or herself in the working environment where the system will be used. The day-to-day work is observed and notes made of the actual tasks in which participants are involved. The value of ethnography is that it helps discover implicit system requirements which reflect the actual rather than the formal processes in which people are involved.

People often find it very difficult to articulate details of their work because it is second nature to them. They understand their own work but may not understand its relationship to other work in the organisation. Social and organisational factors which affect the work but which are not obvious to individuals may only become clear when noticed by an unbiased observer.

Suchman (1983) used ethnography to study office work and found that the actual work practices were far richer, more complex and more dynamic than the simple models assumed by office automation systems. The difference between the assumed and the actual work was the most important reason why these office systems had no significant effect on productivity. Other ethnographic studies for system requirements understanding have included work on air traffic control (Bentley *et al.*, 1992; Hughes *et al.*, 1992), underground railway control rooms (Heath and Luff, 1991), financial systems (Hughes *et al.*, 1994) and various design activities (Pycock and Bowers, 1996; Button and Sharrock, 1997).

Ethnography is particularly effective at discovering two types of requirements:

1.   Requirements that are derived from the way in which people actually work rather than the way in which process definitions say they ought to work. For example, air traffic controllers may switch off an aircraft conflict alert system which detects aircraft with intersecting flight paths even though normal control procedures specify that it should be used. Their control strategy is designed to ensure that these aircraft are moved apart before problems occur and they find that the conflict alert alarm distracts them from their work.

2.   Requirements that are derived from cooperation and awareness of other people's activities. For example, air traffic controllers may use an awareness of other controllers' work to predict the number of aircraft which will be entering their control sector. They then modify their control strategies depending on that predicted workload. Therefore, an automated ATC system should allow controllers in a sector to have some visibility of the work in adjacent sectors.

Ethnography may be combined with prototyping (Figure 6.14). The ethnography informs the development of the prototype so that fewer prototype refinement cycles are required. Furthermore, the prototyping focuses the ethnography by identifying problems and questions which can then be discussed with the ethnographer. He or she should then look for the answers to these questions during the next phase of the system study (Sommerville *et al.*, 1993).

Ethnographic studies can reveal critical process details which are often missed by other requirements elicitation techniques. However, because of its focus on the end-user, this approach is not appropriate for discovering organisational or domain requirements. It cannot always identify new features which should be added to a system. Ethnography is not, therefore, a complete approach to elicitation and it should be used with other approaches such as use-case analysis.

Figure 6.14
Ethnography and
prototyping for
requirements
analysis

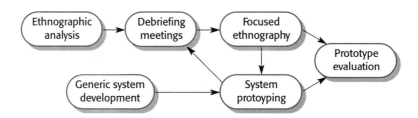

6.3 Requirements validation

Requirements validation is concerned with showing that the requirements actually define the system which the customer wants. It has much in common with analysis as it is concerned with finding problems with the requirements. However, they are distinct processes since validation should be concerned with a complete draft of the requirements document whereas analysis involves working with incomplete requirements.

Requirements validation is important because errors in a requirements document can lead to extensive rework costs when they are subsequently discovered during development or after the system is in service. The cost of making a system change resulting from a requirements problem is much greater than repairing design or coding errors. The reason for this is that a change to the requirements usually means that the system design and implementation must also be changed and that the system must be re-tested.

During the requirements validation process, different types of checks should be carried out on the requirements in the requirements document. These checks include:

1. *Validity checks*   A user may think that a system is needed to perform certain functions. However, further thought and analysis may identify additional or different functions that are required. Systems have diverse users with different needs and any set of requirements is inevitably a compromise across the user community.

2. *Consistency checks*   Requirements in the document should not conflict. That is, there should not be contradictory constraints or different descriptions of the same system function.

3. *Completeness checks*   The requirements document should include requirements which define all functions and constraints intended by the system user.

4. *Realism checks*   Using knowledge of existing technology, the requirements should be checked to ensure that they can actually be implemented. These checks should also take account of the budget and schedule for the system development.

5. *Verifiability*   To reduce the potential for dispute between customer and contractor, system requirements should always be written so that they are verifiable. This means that a set of checks can be designed which can demonstrate that the delivered system meets that requirement.

There are a number of requirements validation techniques which can be used in conjunction or individually:

1. *Requirements reviews*   The requirements are analysed systematically by a team of reviewers. This process is discussed in the following section.

Figure 6.15
Automated
consistency checking
of requirements

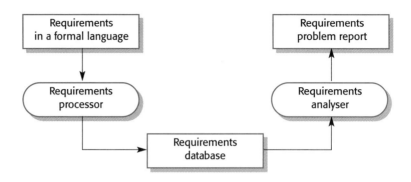

2. *Prototyping*   In this approach to validation, an executable model of the system is demonstrated to end-users and customers. They can experiment with this model to see if it meets their real needs. I discuss prototyping techniques in Chapter 8.

3. *Test-case generation*   Requirements should, ideally, be testable. If the tests for the requirements are devised as part of the validation process, this often reveals requirements problems. If a test is difficult or impossible to design, this usually means that the requirements will be difficult to implement and should be reconsidered.

4. *Automated consistency analysis*   If the requirements are expressed as a system model in a structured or formal notation then CASE tools may be used to check the consistency of the model. This is illustrated in Figure 6.15. To check the consistency, the CASE tool must build a requirements database and then, using the rules of the method or notation, check all of the requirements in this database. A requirements analyser produces a report of inconsistencies which it has discovered.

The difficulties of requirements validation should not be under-estimated. Demonstrating that a set of requirements meets a user's needs is difficult. Users must picture the system in operation and imagine how that system would fit into their work. It is hard for skilled computer professionals to perform this type of abstract analysis and even harder for system users. As a result, requirements validation rarely discovers all requirements problems and changes to correct omissions and misunderstandings after the requirements document has been agreed are inevitable.

6.3.1   Requirements reviews

A requirements review is a manual process which involves multiple readers from both client and contractor staff checking the requirements document for anomalies and omissions. The review process may be managed in the same way as program inspections (see Chapter 19). Alternatively, it may be organised on a larger scale with many participants involved in checking different parts of the document.

Requirements reviews can be informal or formal. Informal reviews simply involve contractors discussing requirements with as many system stakeholders as possible. It is surprising how often communication between system developers and stakeholders ends after elicitation and there is no confirmation that the documented requirements are what the stakeholders really said they wanted. Many problems can be detected simply by talking about the system to stakeholders before making a commitment to a formal review.

In a formal requirements review, the development team should 'walk' the client through the system requirements, explaining the implications of each requirement. The review team should check each requirement for consistency and should check the requirements as a whole for completeness. Reviewers may also check for:

1. *Verifiability*   Is the requirement as stated realistically testable?

2. *Comprehensibility*   Is the requirement properly understood by the procurers or end-users of the system?

3. *Traceability*   Is the origin of the requirement clearly stated? You may have to go back to the source of the requirement to assess the impact of a change. Traceability is important as it allows the impact of change on the rest of the system to be assessed. I discuss it in more detail in the following section.

4. *Adaptability*   Is the requirement adaptable? That is, can the requirement be changed without large-scale effects on other system requirements?

Conflicts, contradictions, errors and omissions in the requirements should be pointed out during the review and formally recorded. It is then up to the users, the system procurer and the system developer to negotiate a solution to these identified problems.

6.4 Requirements management

The requirements for large software systems are always changing. One reason for this is that these systems are usually developed to address 'wicked' problems (as discussed in Chapter 2). Because the problem cannot be fully defined, the software requirements are bound to be incomplete. During the software process, the developer's understanding of the problem is constantly changing and these changes feed back to the requirements.

Furthermore, large software systems are usually required to improve upon the *status quo*. The existing system may be a manual system or an out-of-date computer system. Although difficulties with the current system may be known, it is hard to anticipate what effects the 'improved' system will have on the organisation. Once end-users have experience of a system, new requirements emerge for the following reasons:

1. Large systems usually have a diverse user community. Different users have different requirements and priorities. These may be conflicting or contradictory. The final system requirements are inevitably a compromise between them and, with experience, it is often discovered that the balance of support given to different users needs to be changed.

2. The people who pay for a system and the users of a system are rarely the same people. System customers impose requirements because of organisational and budgetary constraints. These may conflict with end-user requirements.

3. The business and technical environment of the system changes and these must be reflected in the system itself. New hardware may be introduced, it may be necessary to interface the system with other systems, business priorities may change with consequent changes in the system support which is needed and new legislation and regulations may be introduced which must be implemented by the system. Non-functional requirements are particularly affected by changes in hardware technology.

Requirements management is the process of understanding and controlling changes to system requirements. The process of requirements management is carried out in conjunction with other requirements engineering processes. Planning starts at the same time as initial requirements elicitation and active requirements management should start as soon as a draft version of the requirements document is available.

I discuss each of these activities below. Before going on to this description, however, I discuss why requirements inevitably change and explain why some types of requirements are more susceptible to change than others.

6.4.1   Enduring and volatile requirements

Developing software requirements focuses attention on software capabilities, business objectives and other business systems. As the requirements definition is developed, a better understanding of users' needs is achieved. This feeds information back to the user which causes the requirements to be changed (Figure 6.16). It may take several years to specify and develop a large system. Over that time, the system's environment and the business objectives will almost certainly change. The requirements must therefore evolve to reflect this.

From an evolution perspective, requirements fall into two classes:

1. *Enduring requirements*   These are relatively stable requirements which derive from the core activity of the organisation and which relate directly to the domain

Figure 6.16
Requirements
evolution

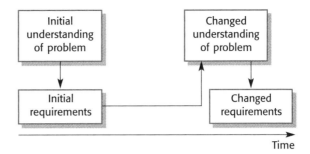

of the system. For example, in a hospital there will always be requirements concerned with patients, doctors, nurses, treatments, etc. These requirements may be derived from domain models that show the entities and relations which characterise an application domain (Prieto-Díaz and Arango, 1991; Easterbrook, 1993).

2. *Volatile requirements*   These are requirements which are likely to change during the system development or after the system has been put into operation. Examples of volatile requirements are requirements resulting from government health-care policies.

Harker *et al.* (1993) have suggested that volatile requirements fall into five classes. However, I think that two of their classes are closely related. I prefer a classification as shown in Figure 6.17.

Figure 6.17
Classification of
volatile requirements

Requirement Type	Description
Mutable requirements	Requirements which change because of changes to the environment in which the organisation is operating. For example, in hospital systems, the funding of patient care may change and thus require different treatment information to be collected.
Emergent requirements	Requirements which emerge as the customer's understanding of the system develops during the system development. The design process may reveal new emergent requirements.
Consequential requirements	Requirements which result from the introduction of the computer system. Introducing the computer system may change the organisation's processes and open up new ways of working which generate new system requirements.
Compatibility requirements	Requirements which depend on the particular systems or business processes within an organisation. As these change, the compatibility requirements on the commissioned or delivered system may also have to evolve.

6.4.2   Requirements management planning

Planning is an essential first stage in the requirements management process. Requirements management is very expensive and, for each project, the planning stage establishes the level of requirements management detail which is required. During the requirements management stage, you have to decide on:

1. *Requirements identification*   Each requirement must be uniquely identified so that it can be cross-referenced by other requirements and so that it may be used in traceability assessments.

2. *A change management process*   This is the set of activities which assess the impact and cost of changes. I discuss it in more detail in the following section.

3. *Traceability policies*   These policies define the relationships between requirements and between the requirements and the system design that should be recorded and how these records should be maintained.

4. *CASE tool support*   Requirements management involves the processing of large amounts of information about the requirements. Tools which may be used range from specialist requirements management system to spreadsheets and simple database systems.

There are many relationships between requirements and other requirements and between the requirements and the system design. There are also links between requirements and the underlying reasons why these requirements were proposed. When changes are proposed, you have to trace the impact of these changes on other requirements and the system design. Traceability is an overall property of a requirements specification which reflects the ease of finding related requirements.

There are three types of traceability information which may be maintained:

1. *Source traceability information* links the requirements to the stakeholders who proposed the requirements and to the rationale for these requirements. When a change is proposed, this information is used to discover the stakeholders so that they can be consulted about the change.

2. *Requirements traceability information* links dependent requirements within the requirements document. This information is used to assess how many requirements are likely to be affected by a proposed change and the extent of consequential requirements changes which may be necessary.

3. *Design traceability information* links the requirements to the design modules where these requirements are implemented. This information is used to assess the impact of proposed requirements changes on the system design and implementation.

Traceability information is often represented using traceability matrices which relate requirements to stakeholders, each other or design modules. If we consider

Figure 6.18
A traceability matrix

Req. id	1.1	1.2	1.3	2.1	2.2	2.3	3.1	3.2
1.1		U	R					
1.2			U			R		U
1.3	R			R				
2.1			R		U			U
2.2								U
2.3		R		U				
3.1								R
3.2							R	

traceability matrices which link requirements to other requirements, each requirement is represented by both a row and a column in the matrix. Where a dependency between requirements exist, this is recorded in the cell at the row/column intersection.

This is illustrated in Figure 6.18 which shows a simple traceability matrix which records the dependencies between requirements. A U in the row/column intersection illustrates that the requirement in the row uses the facilities specified in the requirement named in the column; an R means that there is some other weaker relationship between the requirements. For example, they may both define the requirements for parts of the same sub-system.

Traceability matrices may be used when a small number of requirements have to be managed but they become very unwieldy and expensive to maintain for large systems with many requirements. For these systems, you have to capture traceability information in a requirements database where each requirement is explicitly linked to related requirements. The impact of changes can then be assessed by using the database browsing facilities. Alternatively, it may be possible to generate the traceability matrices automatically.

Requirements management needs some automated support and the CASE tools used should be chosen during the planning phase. Tool support is required for:

1. *Requirements storage*   The requirements should be maintained in a secure, managed data store which is accessible to everyone involved in the requirements engineering process.

2. *Change management*   The process of change management (Figure 6.19) is simplified if active tool support is available.

3. *Traceability management*   As discussed above, tool support for traceability allows related requirements to be discovered. Some tools are available which use

natural language processing techniques to help discover possible relationships between the requirements.

For small systems, it may not be necessary to use specialised requirements management tools. The requirements management process may be supported using the facilities available in word processors, spreadsheets and PC databases. However, for larger systems, more specialised tool support is required. I have included links to information about requirements management tools such as DOORS and Requisite Pro in the book's web pages.

6.4.3   Requirements change management

Requirements change management (Figure 6.19) should be applied to all proposed changes to the requirements. The advantage of using a formal process for change management is that all change proposals are treated consistently and that changes to the requirements document are made in a controlled way. There are three principal stages to a change management process:

1. *Problem analysis and change specification*   The process starts with an identified requirements problem or, sometimes, with a specific change proposal. During this stage, the problem or the change proposal is analysed to check that it valid. A more specific requirements change proposal may then be made.

2. *Change analysis and costing*   The effect of the proposed change is assessed using traceability information and general knowledge of the system requirements. The cost of making the change is estimated both in terms of modifications to the requirements document and, if appropriate, to the system design and implementation. Once this analysis is completed, a decision is made whether or not to proceed with the requirements change.

3. *Change implementation*   The requirements document and, where necessary, the system design and implementation is modified. The requirements document should be organised so that changes can be accommodated without extensive rewriting. As with programs, changeability in documents is achieved by minimising external references and making the document sections as modular as possible.

Figure 6.19
Requirements
change management

If a requirements change to a system is urgently required, there is always a temptation to make that change to the system and then retrospectively modify

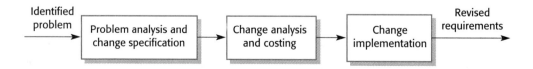

the requirements document. This almost inevitably leads to the requirements specification and the system implementation getting out of step. Once system changes have been made, requirements document changes may be forgotten or made in a way that is not consistent with the system changes.

KEY POINTS

▶ The requirements engineering process includes a feasibility study, requirements elicitation and analysis, requirements specification, requirements validation and requirements management.

▶ Requirements analysis is an iterative process which involves domain understanding, requirements collection, classification, structuring, prioritisation and validation.

▶ Different stakeholders in the system have different requirements. All complex systems should therefore be analysed from a number of different viewpoints. Viewpoints may be sources or sinks of data, different system representations or entities which are outside the system and receive services from it.

▶ Social and organisational factors have a strong influence on system requirements and may determine whether or not the software is actually used.

▶ Requirements validation is the process of checking the requirements for validity, consistency, completeness, realism and verifiability. Requirements reviews and prototyping are the principal techniques used for requirements validation.

▶ Business, organisational and technical changes inevitably lead to changes to the requirements for a software system. Requirements management is the process of managing and controlling these changes.

▶ The requirements management process includes management planning where policies and procedures for requirements management are specified and change management where changes are analysed and their impact assessed.

FURTHER READING

Mastering the Requirements Process. A readable book that is intended for practising requirements engineers. It gives specific guidance on developing an effective requirements engineering process. (S. Robertson and J. Robertson, 1999, Addison Wesley Longman.)

Requirements Engineering: Processes and Techniques. This book includes a more detailed look at the activities in the requirements engineering process and discusses the VORD method and its application. (G. Kotonya and I. Sommerville, 1998, John Wiley and Sons.)

Software Requirements: Objects, Functions and States. This book has a reasonable chapter on analysis in general and includes a good survey of methods of requirements analysis. However, it does not cover approaches to analysis based on multiple viewpoints. (A. M. Davis, 1993, Prentice-Hall.)

Exploring Requirements: Quality before Design. An excellent, very readable book that gives practical advice on the realities of requirements engineering. (D. C. Gause and G. M. Weinberg, 1989, Dorset House.)

EXERCISES

6.1   Suggest who might be stakeholders in a university student records system. Explain why it is almost inevitable that the requirements of different stakeholders will conflict in some ways.

6.2   A software system is to be developed to automate a library catalogue. This system will contain information about all the books in a library and will be usable by library staff and by book borrowers and readers. The system should support catalogue browsing, querying, and should provide facilities allowing users to send messages to library staff reserving a book which is on loan. Identify the principal viewpoints which might be taken into account in the specification of this system and show their relationships using a viewpoint hierarchy diagram.

6.3   For three of the viewpoints identified in the library cataloguing system, suggest services which might be provided to that viewpoint, data which the viewpoint might provide and events which control the delivery of these services.

6.4   For the services identified in Exercise 6.3, identify what might be the most important non-functional constraints.

6.5   Using your own knowledge of how an ATM is used, develop a set of use-cases that could be used to derive the requirements for an ATM system.

6.6   Discuss an example of a type of system where social and political factors might strongly influence the system requirements. Explain why these factors are important in your example.

6.7   Who should be involved in a requirements review? Draw a process model showing how a requirements review might be organised.

6.8   Why do traceability matrices become difficult to manage when there are many system requirements? Design a requirements structuring mechanism, based on viewpoints, which might help reduce the scale of this problem.

6.9   When emergency changes have to be made to systems, the system software may have to be modified before changes to the requirements have been approved. Suggest a model of a process for making these modifications which ensures that the requirements document and the system implementation do not become inconsistent.

6.10 Your company uses a standard analysis method which is normally applied in all requirements analyses. In your work, you find that this method cannot represent social factors which are significant in the system you are analysing. You point this out to your manager who makes clear that the standard should be followed. Discuss what you should do in such a situation.

7 System models

Objectives

The aim of this chapter is to introduce a number of different types of system model which may be developed during the requirements engineering process. When you have read the chapter, you will:

❑ understand why it is important to model the context of a system;

❑ understand the concepts of behavioural modelling, data modelling and object modelling;

❑ have been introduced to some of the notations defined in the Unified Modeling Language (UML) and how these notations may be used to develop different types of system model;

❑ understand how CASE workbenches support system modelling.

Contents

7.1   Context models
7.2   Behavioural models
7.3   Data models
7.4   Object models
7.5   CASE workbenches

User requirements must be written in natural language because they have to be understood by people who are not technical experts. However, more detailed system requirements may be expressed in a more technical way. One widely used technique is to document the system specification as a set of system models. These models are graphical representations that describe the problem to be solved and the system that is to be developed. Because of the graphical representations used, models are often more understandable than detailed natural language descriptions of the system requirements. They are also an important bridge between the analysis and design processes.

Models may be used in the analysis process to develop an understanding of the existing system that is to be replaced or improved or to specify the required system. They can be used to represent the system from different perspectives:

1. an external perspective where the context or environment of the system is modelled;
2. a behavioural perspective where the behaviour of the system is modelled;
3. a structural perspective where the architecture of the system or the structure of the data processed by the system is modelled.

I cover these three perspectives in this chapter and also discuss object modelling which combines, to some extent, behavioural and structural modelling.

Structured methods such as structured systems analysis (DeMarco, 1978) and object-oriented analysis (Rumbaugh *et al.*, 1991; Booch, 1994) provide a framework for detailed system modelling as part of requirements elicitation and analysis. Most structured methods have their own preferred set of system models. They usually define a process which may be used to derive these models and a set of rules and guidelines which apply to the models. Standard documentation is produced for the system. CASE tools (discussed in section 7.5) are usually available for method support. These tools include model editors, automate system documentation and provide some model checking capabilities.

However, structured analysis methods suffer from a number of weaknesses:

1. They do not provide effective support for understanding or modelling non-functional system requirements.

2. They are indiscriminate in that they do not usually include guidelines to help users decide whether or not a method is appropriate for a particular problem. Nor do they normally include advice on how they may be adapted for use in a particular environment.

3. They often produce too much documentation. The essence of the system requirements may be hidden by the mass of detail which is included.

4. The models that are produced are very detailed and users often find them difficult to understand. These users therefore cannot really check the realism of these models.

In practice, requirements engineers don't have to restrict themselves to the models proposed in any particular method. For example, object-oriented methods do not usually suggest that data-flow models should be developed. However, in my experience, such models are sometimes useful as part of an object-oriented analysis process. They often reflect the end-user's understanding of the system. They may also contribute directly to object identification (the data which flows) and the identification of operations on these objects.

The most important aspect of a system model is that it leaves out detail. A system model is an abstraction of the system being studied rather than an alternative representation of that system. Ideally, a *representation* of a system should maintain all the information about the entity being represented. An *abstraction* deliberately simplifies and picks out the most salient characteristics. For example, in the unlikely event of this book being summarised in the *Reader's Digest*, the presentation there would be an abstraction of the key points. If it was translated from English into Italian, this would be an alternative representation. The translator's intention would be to maintain all the information as it is presented in English.

Different types of system model are based on different approaches to abstraction. A data-flow model (for example) concentrates on the flow of data and the functional transformations on that data. It leaves out details of the data structures. By contrast, an entity-relation model is intended to document the system data and its relationships without concern for the functions in the system.

Examples of the different types of system model which might be produced during the analysis process are:

1. *A data-processing model*   Data-flow diagrams show how data is processed at different stages in the system.
2. *A composition model*   Entity-relation diagrams show how entities in the system are composed of other entities.
3. *An architectural model*   Architectural models show the principal sub-systems which make up a system.
4. *A classification model*   Object class/inheritance diagrams show how entities have common characteristics.
5. *A stimulus-response model*   State transition diagrams show how the system reacts to internal and external events.

All these types of model are covered in this chapter. Wherever possible, I use notations from the Unified Modeling Language (UML) which is emerging as a standard modelling language, particularly for object-oriented modelling (Booch *et al.*, 1999; Rumbaugh *et al.*, 1999a). Where UML does not include appropriate notations, I use simple intuitive notations for model description.

7.1 Context models

At an early stage in the requirements elicitation and analysis process you should decide on the boundaries of the system. This involves working with system stakeholders to distinguish what is the system and what is the system's environment. You should make these decisions early in the process to limit the system costs and the time needed for analysis.

In some cases, the boundary between a system and its environment is relatively clear. For example, where an automated system is replacing an existing manual or computerised system, the environment of the new system is usually the same as the existing system's environment. In other cases, there is more flexibility. You decide on the boundary between the system and its environment during the requirements engineering process.

For example, the environment of a CASE toolset may include an existing database whose services are used by the system or the toolset may define its own internal database. Given that a database already exists, the positioning of the boundary between these systems may be a difficult technical and managerial problem. It is only possible to make a decision about what is and what is not part of the system after you have done some analysis.

The definition of a system context is not a value-free judgement. Social and organisational concerns may mean that the position of a system boundary may be determined by non-technical factors. For example, a system boundary may be positioned so that the analysis process can all be carried out on one site; it may be chosen so that a particularly difficult manager need not be consulted; it may be positioned so that the system cost is increased and the system development division must therefore expand to design and implement the system.

Once some decisions on the boundaries of the system have been made, part of the analysis activity is the definition of that context and the dependencies that a system has on its environment. Normally, producing a simple architectural model is the first step in this activity.

This is illustrated in Figure 7.1. This is an architectural model which illustrates the structure of the information system that includes a bank auto-teller network. High-level architectural models are usually expressed as simple block diagrams where each sub-system is represented by a named rectangle and lines indicate that there are some associations between sub-systems.

Figure 7.1
The context of
the ATM system

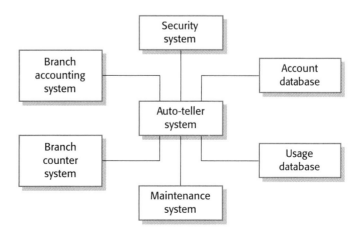

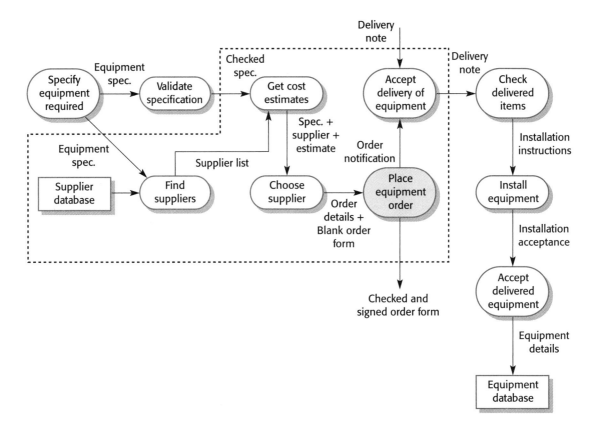

Figure 7.2 Process model of equipment procurement

From Figure 7.1 we see that each auto-teller machine is connected to an account database, a local branch accounting system, a security system and a system to support machine maintenance. The system is also connected to a usage database which monitors how the network of ATMs is used and to a local branch counter system. This counter system provides services such as backup and printing. These, therefore, need not be included in the auto-teller itself.

Architectural models describe the environment of a system. However, they do not show the relationships between the other systems in the environment and the system that is being specified. External systems might produce data for or consume data from the system. They might share data with the system, they might be connected directly, through a network, or not connected at all. They might be physically co-located or located in separate buildings. All of these relations might affect the requirements of the system being defined and must be taken into account.

Therefore, simple architectural models are normally supplemented by other models such as process models which show the process activities supported by the system and data-flow models (described in the following section) that show how data is transferred between the system and other systems in its environment.

Figure 7.2 illustrates a process model for the process of procuring equipment in an organisation. This involves specifying the equipment required, finding and choosing suppliers, ordering the equipment, taking delivery of the equipment and testing it after delivery. When specifying computer support for this process you have to decide which of these activities will actually be supported. The other activities are outside the boundary of the system. In Figure 7.2, the dotted line encloses the activities that are within the system boundary.

7.2 Behavioural models

Behavioural models are used to describe the overall behaviour of the system. I discuss two types of behavioural model, namely data-flow models which model the data processing in the system and state machine models which model how the system reacts to events. These models may be used separately or together, depending on the type of system which is being developed.

Most business systems are primarily driven by data. They are controlled by the data inputs to the system with relatively little external event processing. A data-flow model may be all that is needed to represent the behaviour of these systems. By contrast, real-time systems are often event-driven with minimal data processing. A state machine model (discussed in section 7.2.2) is the most effective way to represent their behaviour. Other classes of system may be both data- and event-driven so both types of model should be developed.

7.2.1   Data-flow models

Data-flow models are an intuitive way of showing how data is processed by a system. At the analysis level, they should be used to model the way in which data is processed in the existing system. The notation used in these models represents functional processing, data stores and data movements between functions. The use of data-flow models for analysis became widespread after the publication of DeMarco's book (1978) on structured systems analysis. They are an intrinsic part of methods that have been developed from this work.

Data-flow models are used to show how data flows through a sequence of processing steps. The data is transformed at each step before moving on to the next stage. These processing steps or transformations are program functions when data-flow diagrams are used to document a software design. However, in an analysis model, the processing may be carried out by people or computers.

A data-flow model is illustrated in Figure 7.3 which shows the steps involved in processing an order for goods (such as computer equipment) in an organisation. This particular model describes the data processing in the 'Place equipment order' activity in the overall process model shown in Figure 7.2. The model shows how the order for the goods moves from process to process. It also shows the data stores that are involved in this process.

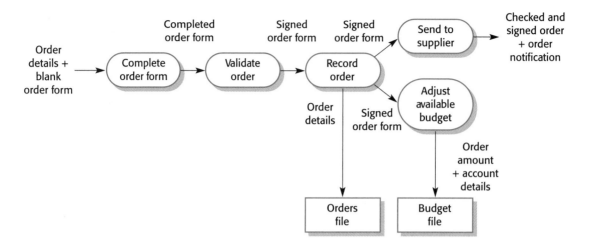

Figure 7.3 Data-flow
diagram of order
processing

In the notation that I use to describe data-flow diagrams in Figure 7.3, rounded rectangles represent processing steps, arrows annotated with the data name represent flows and rectangles represent data stores or data sources.

Data-flow models are valuable because tracking and documenting how the data associated with a particular process moves through the system helps analysts understand what is going on. Data-flow diagrams have the advantage that, unlike some other modelling notations, they are simple and intuitive. It is often possible to explain them to potential system users who can therefore participate in validating the analysis.

In principle, the development of models such as data-flow models should be a 'top-down' process. In this example, this would imply that the overall procurement process should be analysed first. The analysis of sub-processes such as ordering should then be carried out. In practice, analysis is never like that. Information about the system is normally acquired about several different levels at the same time. Lower-level models may be developed first, then abstracted to create a more general model.

Data-flow models show a functional perspective where each transformation represents a single function. As well as describing processing within a system, it is sometimes useful to use data-flow descriptions to illustrate the context of the system. The data-flow model can show how different systems and sub-systems exchange information. These sub-systems need not be single functions. For example, one sub-system might be a storage server with a fairly complex interface. Figure 7.4 shows an example of a data-flow diagram used in this way. In this example, the rounded rectangles represent sub-systems.

7.2.2   State machine models

State machine models are used to model the behaviour of a system in response to internal or external events. The state machine model shows system states and events which cause transitions from one state to another. It does not show the flow of data within the system. This type of model is particularly useful for modelling real-time systems because these systems are often driven by stimuli from the system's

Figure 7.4 Data-flow
diagram of a CASE
toolset

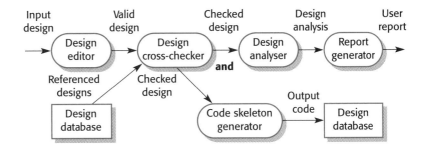

Figure 7.4 Data-flow diagram of a CASE toolset

environment. For example, the real-time alarm system discussed in Chapter 13 responds to stimuli from movement sensors, door opening sensors, etc.

State machine models are an integral part of real-time design methods such as that proposed by Ward and Mellor (1985) and Harel (1987, 1988). Harel's method uses a notation called *Statecharts* and these were the basis for the state machine modelling notation in the UML.

A state machine model of a system assumes that, at any time, the system is in one of a number of possible states. When a stimulus is received, this may trigger a transition to a different state. For example, a system controlling a valve may move from a state 'Valve open' to a state 'Valve closed' when an operator command (the stimulus) is received.

Figure 7.5 State machine model of a simple microwave oven

This approach to system modelling is illustrated in Figure 7.5. This diagram shows a state machine model of a simple microwave oven equipped with buttons to set

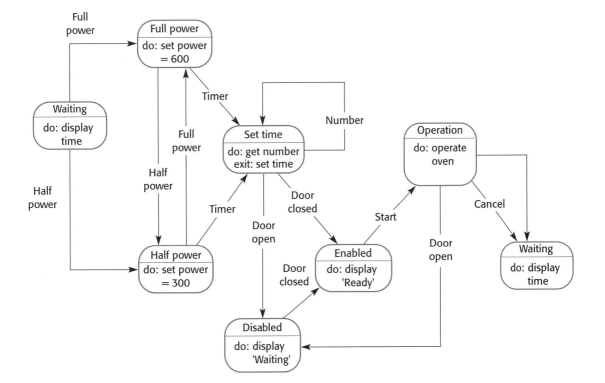

the power and the timer and to start the system. Real microwave ovens are actually much more complex than the system described here. However, this model includes the essential features of the system. To simplify the model, I have assumed that the sequence of actions in using the microwave is:

1. Select the power level (either half-power or full-power).
2. Input the cooking time.
3. Press start and the food is cooked for the given time.

For safety reasons, the oven should not operate when the door is open and, on completion of cooking, a buzzer is sounded. The oven has a very simple alphanumeric display which is used to display various alerts and warning messages.

Figure 7.6
Microwave oven
state and stimulus
description

State	Description
Waiting	The oven is waiting for input. The display shows the current time.
Half power	The oven power is set to 300 watts. The display shows 'Half power'.
Full power	The oven power is set to 600 watts. The display shows 'Full power'.
Set time	The cooking time is set to the user's input value. The display shows the cooking time selected and is updated as the time is set.
Disabled	Oven operation is disabled for safety. Interior oven light is on. Display shows 'Not ready'.
Enabled	Oven operation is enabled. Interior oven light is off. Display shows 'Ready to cook'.
Operation	Oven in operation. Interior oven light is on. Display shows the timer countdown. On completion of cooking, the buzzer is sounded for 5 seconds. Oven light is on. Display shows 'Cooking complete' while buzzer is sounding.

Stimulus	Description
Half power	The user has pressed the half power button
Full power	The user has pressed the full power button
Timer	The user has pressed one of the timer buttons
Number	The user has pressed a numeric key
Door open	The oven door switch is not closed
Door closed	The oven door switch is closed
Start	The user has pressed the start button
Cancel	The user has pressed the cancel button

The UML notation that I use to describe state machine models is designed for modelling the behaviour of objects. However, it is a general-purpose notation that can be used for any type of state machine modelling. The rounded rectangles in a model represent system states. They include a brief description (following 'do') of the actions taken in that state. The labelled arrows represent stimuli which force a transition from one state to another.

Therefore, from Figure 7.5, we can see that the system responds initially to either the full-power or the half-power button. Users can change their minds after selecting one of these and select the alternative. The time is set and then, so long as the door is closed, the start button is enabled. Pushing this button starts the oven operation and cooking takes place for the specified time.

The UML notation lets you indicate the activity which takes place in a state. However, in a detailed system specification you have to provide more detail about both the stimuli and the system states (Figure 7.6). This information may be maintained in a data dictionary as discussed later in this section.

The problem with the state machine approach is that the number of possible states increases rapidly. For large system models, therefore, some structuring of these state models is necessary. One way to do this is by using the notion of a superstate which encapsulates a number of separate states. This superstate looks like a single state on a high-level model but is then expanded in more detail on a separate diagram. To illustrate this concept, consider the Operation state in Figure 7.5. This is a superstate which can be expanded as illustrated in Figure 7.7.

The Operation state includes a number of sub-states. It shows that operation starts with a status check and if any problems are discovered then an alarm is indicated and operation is disabled. Cooking involves running the microwave generator for the specified time and, on completion, a buzzer is sounded. If the door is opened during operation, the system moves to the disabled state as shown in Figure 7.5.

Figure 7.7
Microwave oven
operation

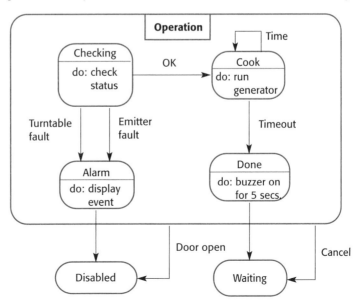

7.3 Data models

Most large software systems make use of a large database of information. In some cases, this database exists independently of the software system. In others, it is created for the system being developed. An important part of systems modelling is to define the logical form of the data processed by the system.

The most widely used data modelling technique is entity–relation–attribute modelling (ERA modelling) which shows the data entities, their associated attributes and the relations between these entities. This approach to modelling was first proposed in the mid-1970s by Chen (1976) with several variants developed since then (Codd, 1979; Hammer and McLeod, 1981; Hull and King, 1987). However, all of these have the same basic form.

The UML does not include a specific notation for this type of data modelling as it assumes an object-oriented development process and models data using objects and their relationships. However, you can think of entities as simplified object classes (they have no operations) and you can use UML class models with named associations between the classes as data models. Although the resultant data models are not 'good' UML, this is outweighed by the convenience of using a standard notation.

Data models are often used in conjunction with data-flow models to describe the structure of the information which is being processed. I have illustrated this by including a data model of a software design (Figure 7.8). Such a design could be processed by the various components of the CASE toolset shown in Figure 7.4.

Designs are directed graphs. They consist of a set of nodes of different types connected by links representing the relationships between design nodes. There is a screen representation of this graph which is a design diagram and a corresponding database representation. The editing system performs a mapping from the database representation to the screen representation every time it draws a diagram. The information produced by the editor for other design analysis tools should include the logical representation of the design graph. However, these analysis tools are not interested in the details of the physical screen representation. They process the entities, their logical attributes (such as their names) and their relationships.

Figure 7.8 shows that a design has attributes whose values are the design name, a design description, a creation date (C-date) and a modification date (M-date). The design is composed of a set of nodes and a set of links. Nodes have associated links between them. Nodes and links have name and type attributes. They may have a set of associated labels that store other descriptive information. Each label has an associated icon and text.

Entity-relationship models have been widely used in database design. The relational database schemas derived from these models are naturally in third normal form which is a desirable characteristic (Barker, 1989). Because of the explicit typing and the recognition of sub- and super-types, it is also straightforward to implement these models using object-oriented databases.

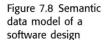
Figure 7.8 Semantic
data model of a
software design

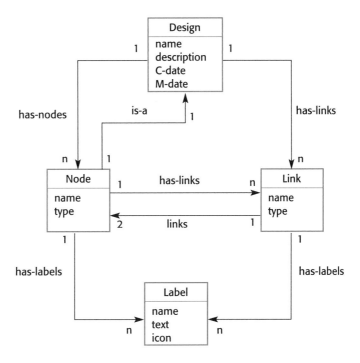

Like all graphical models, ERA models lack detail and they should be supplemented with more detailed descriptions of the entities, relationships and attributes included in the model. These more detailed descriptions can be collected in a repository or data dictionary. Data dictionaries are generally useful when developing system models and may be used to manage all information from all types of system model.

A data dictionary is, simplistically, an alphabetic list of the names which are included in the different models of a system. As well as the name, the dictionary should include an associated description of the named entity and, if the name represents a composite object, there may be a description of the composition. Other information such as the date of creation, the creator, and the representation of the entity may also be included depending on the type of model which is being developed.

The advantages of using a data dictionary are:

1. It is a mechanism for name management. Many different people may have to invent names for entities and relationships when developing a large system model. These names should be used consistently and should not clash. The data dictionary software can check for name uniqueness and tell requirements analysts of name duplications.

2. It serves as a store of organisational information that can link analysis, design, implementation and evolution. As the system is developed, information is taken to inform the development. New information is added to it. All information about an entity is in one place.

Figure 7.9 Examples
of data dictionary
entries

Name	Description	Type	Date
has-labels	1:N relation between entities of type Node or Link and entities of type Label.	Relation	5.10.1998
Label	Holds structured or unstructured information about nodes or links. Labels are represented by an icon (which can be a transparent box) and associated text.	Entity	8.12.1998
Link	A 1:1 relation between design entities represented as nodes. Links are typed and may be named.	Relation	8.12.1998
name (label)	Each label has a name which identifies the type of label. The name must be unique within the set of label types used in a design.	Attribute	8.12.1998
name (node)	Each node has a name which must be unique within a design. The name may be up to 64 characters long.	Attribute	15.11.1998

All system names whether they be names of entities, types, relations, attributes or services should be entered in the dictionary. Support software should be available to create, maintain and interrogate the dictionary. This software might be integrated with other tools so that dictionary creation is partially automated. Most CASE tools which support system modelling also include support for data dictionaries.

An example of data dictionary entries is shown in Figure 7.9. I have used names taken from the semantic data model of a design shown in Figure 7.8. I have simplified the presentation of this example by leaving out some names and by shortening the associated information. A more complete data dictionary entry would include links to the representation of the information (e.g. a type declaration) and reverse links to where the name is used.

7.4 Object models

An object-oriented approach to the whole software development is now commonly used, particularly for interactive systems development. This means expressing the systems requirements using an object model, designing using objects and developing the system in an object-oriented programming language such as Java or C++.

Object models developed during requirements analysis may be used to represent both system data and its processing. In this respect, they combine some of the uses of data-flow and semantic data models. They are also useful for showing how entities in the system may be classified and composed of other entities.

For some classes of system, object models are natural ways of reflecting the real-world entities that are manipulated by the system. This is particularly true when the system processes information about concrete entities such as cars, aircraft, books, etc. which have clearly identifiable attributes. More abstract, higher-level entities, such as the concept of a library, a medical record system or a word processor, are harder to model as object classes. They do not necessarily have a simple interface consisting of independent attributes and operations.

Object models developed during requirements analysis certainly simplify the transition to object-oriented design and programming. However, I have found that end-users of a system often find object models unnatural and difficult to understand. They often prefer to adopt a more functional, data-processing view. Therefore, it is sometimes helpful to supplement object models with data-flow models that show the end-to-end data processing in the system.

An object class is an abstraction over a set of objects which identifies common attributes (as in a semantic data model) and the services or operations which are provided by each object. Objects are executable entities with the attributes and services of the object class. Objects are instantiations of the object class and many different objects may be created from a class. Generally, the models developed using analysis focus on object classes and their relationships.

Models of systems which are developed during requirements analysis should model real-world entities using object classes. They should not include details of the individual objects in the system. Various types of object models can be produced showing how object classes are related to each other, how objects are aggregated to form other objects, how objects interact with other objects and so on. All of these can add to our understanding of a system which is being specified.

The analysis process for identifying objects and object classes is recognised as one of the most difficult areas of object-oriented development. Object identification is basically the same for analysis and design. The methods of object identification covered in Chapter 12, which discusses object-oriented design, may be used. I concentrate here on some of the object models which might be generated during the analysis process.

Various methods of object-oriented analysis were proposed in the 1990s (Booch, 1994; Coad and Yourdon, 1990; Rumbaugh et al., 1991). These methods have a great deal in common and three of the key developers (Booch, Rumbaugh and Jacobson) decided to integrate their approaches to produce a unified method (Rumbaugh et al., 1999b). The Unified Modeling Language (UML) used in this unified method has become an effective standard for object modelling. UML includes notations for different types of system model. We have already seen use-case models and sequence diagrams in Chapter 5 and state machine models earlier in this chapter.

An object class in UML as illustrated in the examples in Figure 7.10 is represented as a vertically oriented rectangle with three sections:

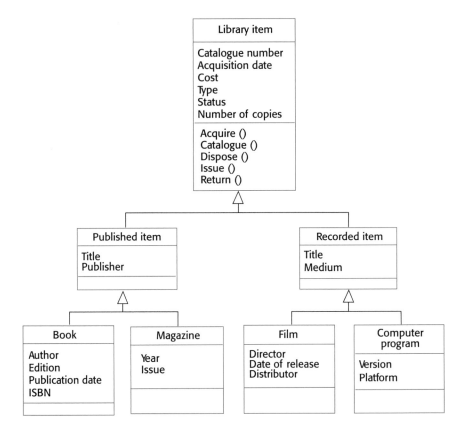

Figure 7.10 Part of a
class hierarchy for a
library system

1. The name of the object class is in the top section.
2. The class attributes are in the middle section.
3. The operations associated with the object class are in the lower section of the
    rectangle.

I don't have space to cover all of the UML so I focus here on object models for
showing how objects can be classified and inherit attributes and operations from
other objects, aggregation models which show how objects are composed and simple
behavioural models which show object interactions.

7.4.1   Inheritance models

Object-oriented modelling involves identifying the classes of object which are
important in the domain being studied. These are then organised into a taxonomy.
A taxonomy is a classification scheme which shows how an object class is related
to other classes through common attributes and services.

To display this taxonomy, the classes are organised into an inheritance hierarchy
where the most general object classes are presented at the top of the hierarchy. More

Figure 7.11 User
class hierarchy

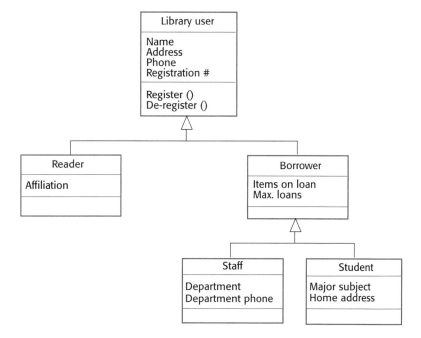

specialised objects inherit their attributes and services. These specialised objects may have their own attributes and services.

Figure 7.10 illustrates part of a simplified class hierarchy for a library system model. This hierarchy gives information about the items held in the library. The library holds various types of item such as books, music, recordings of films, magazines, newspapers, etc. In Figure 7.10, the most general item is at the top of the tree and has a set of attributes and services which are common to all library items. These are inherited by the classes Published item and Recorded item which add their own attributes which are then inherited by lower-level items.

Figure 7.11 is an example of another inheritance hierarchy which might be part of a library model. In this case, the users of a library are shown. There are two classes of user: those who are allowed to borrow books and those who may only read books in the library without taking them away.

In the UML notation, inheritance is shown 'upwards' rather than 'downwards' as it is in some other object-oriented notations. That is, the arrowhead (shown as a triangle) points from the classes which inherit attributes and operations to the superclass. Rather than use the term inheritance, the UML refers to the generalisation relationship.

The design of class hierarchies is not easy. One advantage of developing such models is that the analyst needs to understand, in detail, the domain in which the system is to be installed. As an example of the subtlety of the problems which arise in practice, consider the library item hierarchy. It would seem that the attribute 'Title' could be held in the most general item, then inherited by lower-level items.

Figure 7.12 Multiple
inheritance

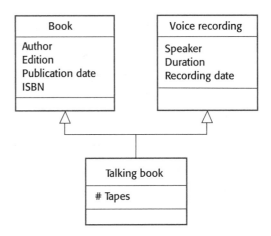

However, while everything in a library must have some kind of identifier or
registration number, it does not follow that everything must have a title. For
example, a library may hold the personal papers of a retired politician. Many of
these items may not be explicitly titled. These will be classified using some other
class (not shown here) which has a different set of attributes.

Figures 7.10 and 7.11 show class inheritance hierarchies where every object class
inherits its attributes and operations from a single parent class. Multiple inheritance
models may also be constructed where a class has several parents. Its inherited attributes
and services are a conjunction of those inherited from each superclass. Figure 7.12
shows an example of a multiple inheritance model which may also be part of the
library model.

The main problem with multiple inheritance is designing an inheritance graph
where objects do not inherit unnecessary attributes. Other problems include the
difficulty of reorganising the inheritance graph when changes are required and resolving name clashes where two or more superclasses have attributes with the same name
but different meanings. At the system modelling level, such clashes are relatively
easy to resolve by manually altering the object model. They cause more problems
in object-oriented programming.

7.4.2 Object aggregation

As well as acquiring attributes and services through an inheritance relationship
with other objects, some objects are made up of other objects. That is, an object is
an aggregate of a set of other objects. The classes representing these objects may
be modelled using an object aggregation model as shown in Figure 7.13. In this
example, I have modelled a library item which is a study pack for a university
course. This study pack includes lecture notes, exercises, sample solutions, copies
of transparencies used in lectures, and videotapes.

The UML notation for aggregation is to represent the composition by including
a diamond shape on the source of the link. Therefore, Figure 7.13 can be read as

Figure 7.13 An
aggregate object
representing a
course

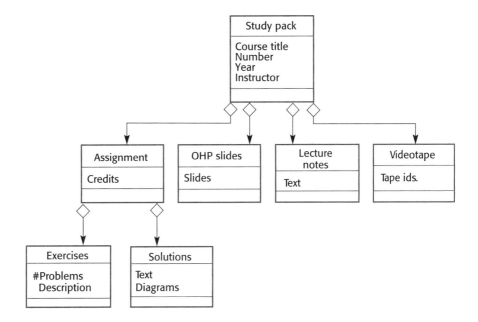

'A study pack is composed of one of more assignments, OHP slide packages, lecture notes and videotapes'.

7.4.3   Object behaviour modelling

To model the behaviour of objects, we have to show how the operations provided by the objects are used. In the UML, behaviours are modelled using scenarios which are based on use-cases as discussed in Chapter 6. We have already seen an example of behaviour modelling in Chapter 6 where Figure 6.13 illustrates the management of a library catalogue. As well as sequence diagrams, the UML also includes collaboration diagrams which show the sequence of messages exchanged by objects. These are similar to sequence diagrams and I do not cover them here.

I illustrate how sequence diagrams may be used for behaviour modelling by describing a scenario where users withdraw items from the library in electronic form. For example, imagine a situation where the study packs shown in Figure 7.13 could be maintained electronically and downloaded to the student's computer.

Figure 7.14 shows a sequence diagram with objects along the top of the diagram. Operations are indicated by labelled arrows and the sequence of operations is from top to bottom. In this scenario, the library user accesses the catalogue to see if the item required is available electronically and, if so, requests the electronic issue of that item. For copyright reasons, this must be licensed so there is a transaction between the item and the user where the licence is agreed. The item to be issued is then sent to a network server object for compression before being sent to the library user.

Figure 7.14 The
issue of electronic
items

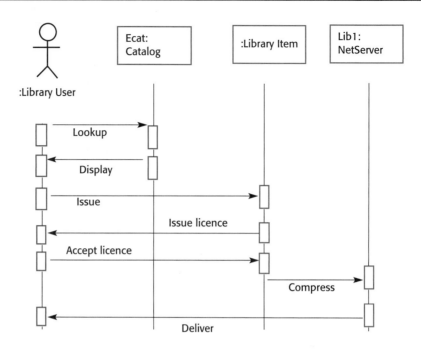

7.5 CASE workbenches

A CASE workbench is a set of tools that supports a particular phase of the software process such as design, implementation or testing. The advantage of grouping CASE tools into a workbench is that tools can work together to provide more comprehensive support than is possible with a single tool. Common services can be implemented and called by all other tools. Workbench tools may be integrated either through shared files, a shared repository or shared data structures.

Analysis and design workbenches are designed to support system modelling during the analysis and design stages of the software process. These workbenches support the creation, editing and analysis of the graphical notations used in structured methods. Analysis and design workbenches may support a specific design or analysis method, such as object-oriented analysis and design. Alternatively, they may be more general diagram editing systems with knowledge of the diagram types that are used in several methods. Method-oriented workbenches incorporate method rules and guidelines. Some automatic checking of the diagrams is therefore possible.

Figure 7.15 shows the tools which may be included in an analysis and design workbench. These tools are normally integrated through a shared repository whose structure is proprietary to the workbench vendor. Analysis and design workbenches

Figure 7.15
An analysis and
design workbench

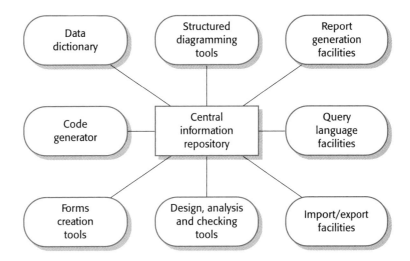

are therefore usually closed environments. It is difficult for users to add their own tools or to modify the tools that are provided.

The analysis and design workbench illustrated in Figure 7.15 includes:

1. *Diagram editors* to create data-flow diagrams, object hierarchies, entity-relationship diagrams, etc. These editors are not just drawing tools but are aware of the types of entities in the diagram. They capture information about these entities and save this information in the central repository.

2. *Design analysis and checking tools* which process the design and report on errors and anomalies. These may be integrated with the editing system so that user errors are trapped at an early stage in the process.

3. *Repository query languages* which allow the designer to find designs and associated design information in the repository.

4. *A data dictionary* which maintains information about the entities used in a system design.

5. *Report definition and generation tools* which take information from the central store and automatically generate system documentation.

6. *Forms definition tools* which allow screen and document formats to be specified.

7. *Import/export facilities* which allow the interchange of information from the central repository with other development tools.

8. *Code generators* which generate code or code skeletons automatically from the design captured in the central store.

In some cases, it is possible to generate a program or a program fragment from the information provided in the system model. The code generators which are included in analysis and design workbenches may generate code in a language such as Java, C++ or C. As models exclude low-level details, the code generator in a design workbench may not be able to generate the complete system. Some hand-coding is usually necessary to complete the generated program.

Some analysis and design workbenches are intended to support methods that are geared to the development of business system applications. The development platform and the application platform are the same so a database system such as Sybase or Oracle is used to implement the shared tool repository. These workbenches include most of the facilities of a 4GL programming environment so, instead of generating a conventional programming language from a design, they may generate a 4GL database language.

KEY POINTS

▶ A model is an abstract view of a system which ignores some system details. Complementary system models can be developed which present different information about the system.

▶ Context models show how the system being modelled is positioned in an environment with other systems and processes. Architectural models, process models and data-flow models may be used as context models.

▶ Data-flow diagrams may be used to model the data processing carried out by a system. The system is modelled as a set of data transformations with functions acting on the data.

▶ State machine models are used to model a system's behaviour in response to internal or external events.

▶ Semantic data models describe the logical structure of the data which is imported to and exported by the system. These models show system entities, their attributes and the relationships in which they participate. They may be supplemented with data dictionaries that provide a more detailed description of the data.

▶ Object models describe the logical system entities and their classification and aggregation. They combine a data model with a processing model. Possible object models which may be developed include inheritance models, aggregation models and behavioural models.

▶ CASE workbenches support the development of system models by providing model editing, checking, reporting and documentation tools.

FURTHER READING

Structured Analysis and System Specification. This was perhaps the first and is certainly the best known description of data-flow modelling. This topic is also covered in many more modern books but they have not necessarily improved on the original. (T. DeMarco, 1978, Yourdon Press.)

Software Requirements: Objects, Functions and States. This book focuses on system modelling in the requirements engineering process. The coverage of system modelling is its major strength. (A. M. Davis, 1993, Prentice-Hall.)

The Unified Modeling Language User Guide. This is one of a series of three books by the same authors who were the inventors of UML and the Unified Method. This and companion texts by the same authors are the definitive UML textbooks. (G. Booch, J. Rumbaugh, I. Jacobson, 1998, Addison-Wesley.)

EXERCISES

7.1 Draw a context model for a patient information system in a hospital. You may make any reasonable assumptions about the other hospital systems which are available but your model must include a patient admissions system and an image storage system for X-rays.

7.2 Based on your experience with a bank ATM, draw a data-flow diagram modelling the data processing involved when a customer withdraws cash from the machine.

7.3 Model the data processing which might take place in an electronic mail system. You should model the mail-sending and mail-receiving processing separately.

7.4 Draw state machine models of the control software for:

- an automatic washing machine which has different programs for different types of clothes;

- the software for a compact disc player;

- a telephone answering machine which records incoming messages and displays the number of accepted messages on an LED display. The system should allow the telephone owner to dial in, type a sequence of numbers (identified as tones) and have the recorded messages replayed over the phone.

7.5 Extend the model of a software design shown in Figure 7.8 to include physical layout information. Nodes may be represented by composite symbols which are a combination of simpler symbols such as rectangle, line, etc. and are displayed at a particular coordinate. Links are made up of a number of line segments which may be solid or dotted lines. Text is displayed in a specified font. The name associated with a node, link or label is positioned inside or near to the named item.

7.6   Model the object classes which might be used in an electronic mail system. If you have tried Exercise 7.3, describe the similarities and differences between the data processing model and the object model.

7.7   Using an entity-relation approach, describe a possible data model for the library cataloguing system described in this chapter. Assume that the items in the library are those modelled in Figure 7.10.

7.8   Develop an object model including a class hierarchy diagram and an aggregation diagram showing the principal components of a personal computer system and its system software.

7.9   Develop a sequence diagram showing the interactions involved when a student registers for a course in a university. Courses may have a limited number of places so the registration process must include checks that places are available. Assume that the student accesses an electronic course catalogue to find out about available courses.

7.10 Describe three modelling activities that may be supported by a CASE workbench for some analysis method. Suggest three activities that cannot readily be automated.

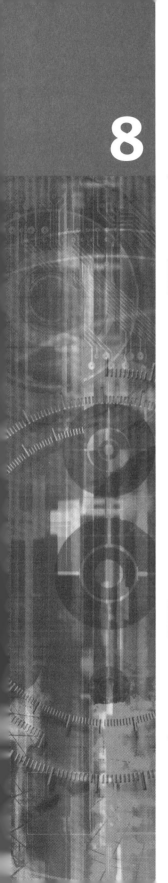

8 Software prototyping

Objectives

The aims of this chapter are to explain how software prototyping is used in the software process and to describe different approaches to prototype development. When you have read this chapter, you will:

❏ understand the role of prototyping in different types of development project;

❏ understand the difference between evolutionary and throw-away prototyping;

❏ have been introduced to three different techniques of prototype development, namely very high-level language development, database programming and application and component reuse;

❏ understand why prototyping is the only viable technique for user interface design and development.

Contents

8.1 Prototyping in the software process
8.2 Rapid prototyping techniques
8.3 User interface prototyping

Software customers and end-users usually find it very difficult to express their real requirements. It is almost impossible to predict how a system will affect working practices, how it will interact with other systems and what user operations should be automated. Careful requirements analysis along with systematic reviews of the requirements help to reduce the uncertainty about what the system should do. However, there is no real substitute for trying out a requirement before agreeing to it. This is possible if a system prototype is available.

A prototype is an initial version of a software system which is used to demonstrate concepts, try out design options and, generally, to find out more about the problem and its possible solutions. Rapid development of the prototype is essential so that costs are controlled and users can experiment with the prototype early in the software process.

A software prototype supports two requirements engineering process activities:

1. *Requirements elicitation*   System prototypes allow users to experiment to see how the system supports their work. They get new ideas for requirements and can find areas of strength and weakness in the software. They may then propose new system requirements.

2. *Requirements validation*   The prototype may reveal errors and omissions in the requirements which have been proposed. A function described in a specification may seem useful and well defined. However, when that function is used with others, users often find that their initial view was incorrect or incomplete. The system specification may then be modified to reflect their changed understanding of the requirements.

Prototyping can be used as a risk analysis and reduction technique (see Chapter 4). A significant risk in software development is requirements errors and omissions. The costs of fixing requirements errors at later stages in the process can be very high. Experiments have shown (Boehm *et al.*, 1984) that prototyping reduces the number of problems with the requirements specification. Furthermore, the overall development costs may be lower if a prototype is developed.

Prototyping is therefore part of the requirements engineering process. However, the distinction between prototyping as a separate activity and mainstream software development has blurred over the past few years. Many systems are now developed using an evolutionary approach where an initial version is created quickly and modified to produce a final system. An iterative process model such as incremental development (discussed in Chapter 3) may be used in conjunction with a language designed for rapid application development. Therefore, the techniques used for developing a prototype for requirements validation may also be used for developing the software system itself. I discuss this in section 8.1.

As well as allowing users to improve the requirements specification, developing a system prototype may have other benefits:

1. Misunderstandings between software developers and users may be identified as the system functions are demonstrated.

2. Software development staff may find incomplete and/or inconsistent requirements as the prototype is developed.
3. A working, albeit limited, system is available quickly to demonstrate the feasibility and usefulness of the application to management.
4. The prototype may be used as a basis for writing the specification for a production-quality system.

Developing a prototype usually leads to improvements in the specification of the system. Once a prototype is available, it can also be used for other purposes (Ince and Hekmatpour, 1987):

1. *User training*   A prototype system can be used for training users before the final system has been delivered.

2. *System testing*   Prototypes can run 'back-to-back' tests. The same test cases are submitted to the prototype and to the system under test. If both systems give the same result, the test case has not detected a fault. If the results differ, it may mean that there is a system fault and the reasons for the difference should be investigated.

In a study of 39 different prototyping projects, Gordon and Bieman (1995) found that the benefits of using prototyping in the software process were:

1. improved system usability;
2. a closer match of the system to the user needs;
3. improved design quality;
4. improved maintainability;
5. reduced development effort.

Their study therefore suggests that the improvements in usability and better user requirements which stem from using a prototype do not necessarily mean an overall increase in system development costs. Prototyping usually increases costs in the early stages of the software process but reduces later costs. The main reason for this is that rework during development is avoided as customers request fewer system changes. However, they found that a negative consequence of prototyping was that overall system performance is sometimes degraded as inefficient prototype code is reused.

A process model for prototype development is shown in Figure 8.1. The objectives of prototyping should be made explicit from the start of the process. These may be to develop a system to prototype the user interface, to develop a system to validate functional system requirements or to develop a system to demonstrate the feasibility of the application to management. The same prototype cannot meet all objectives. If objectives are left implicit, management or end-users may misunderstand the function of the prototype. Consequently, they may not get the benefits that they expected from the prototype development.

Figure 8.1 The process of prototype development

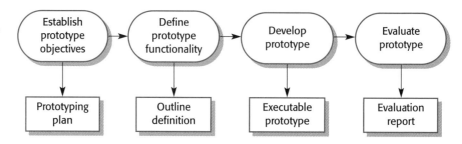

The next stage in the process to is decide what to put into and, perhaps more importantly, what to leave out of the prototype system. To reduce prototyping costs and accelerate the delivery schedule, you may leave some functionality out of the prototype. You may decide to relax non-functional requirements such as response time and memory utilisation. Error handling and management may be ignored or may be rudimentary unless the objective of the prototype is to establish a user interface. Standards of reliability and program quality may be reduced.

The final stage of the process is prototype evaluation. Ince and Hekmatpour suggest that this is the most important stage of prototyping. Provision must be made during this stage for user training and the prototype objectives should be used to derive a plan for evaluation. Users need time to become comfortable with a new system and to settle into a normal pattern of usage. Once they are using the system normally, they then discover requirements errors and omissions.

8.1 Prototyping in the software process

As I have already discussed, it is difficult for end-users to anticipate how they will use new software systems to support their everyday work. If these systems are large and complex, it is probably impossible to make this assessment before the system is built and put into use.

One way of tackling this difficulty is to use an evolutionary approach to systems development. This means giving the user a system which is incomplete and then modifying and augmenting it as the user requirements become clear. Alternatively, a deliberate decision might be made to build a 'throw-away' prototype to help requirements analysis and validation. After evaluation, the prototype is discarded and a production-quality system built. Figure 8.2 illustrates both of these approaches to prototype development.

Evolutionary prototyping starts with a relatively simple system which implements the most important user requirements. This is augmented and changed as new requirements are discovered. Ultimately, it becomes the system which is required. There is no detailed system specification and, in many cases, there may not be a formal

Figure 8.2
Evolutionary and
throw-away
prototyping

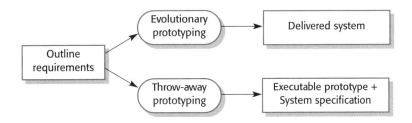

requirements document. Evolutionary prototyping is now the normal technique used for web-site development and e-commerce applications.

By contrast, the throw-away prototyping approach is intended to help refine and clarify the system specification. The prototype is written, evaluated and modified. The prototype evaluation informs the development of the detailed system specification which is included in the system requirements document. Once the specification has been written the prototype is no longer useful and is thrown away.

There is an important difference between the objectives of evolutionary and throw-away programming:

1. The objective of evolutionary prototyping is to deliver a working system to end-users. This means that you should normally start with the user requirements which are best understood and which have the highest priority. Lower priority and vaguer requirements are implemented when and if they are demanded by the users.

2. The objective of throw-away prototyping is to validate or derive the system requirements. You should start with those requirements that are not well understood because you need to find out more about them. Requirements that are straightforward may never need to be prototyped.

Another important distinction between these approaches is in the management of the quality of the systems. Throw-away prototypes have, by definition, a very short lifetime. It must be possible to change them rapidly during development but long-term maintainability is not required. Poor performance and reliability may be acceptable in a throw-away prototype so long as it fulfils its principal function of helping with the understanding of requirements.

By contrast, prototypes which evolve into the final system should be developed to the same organisational quality standards as any other software. They should have a robust structure so that they are maintainable for many years. They should be reliable and efficient and they should conform to relevant organisational standards.

8.1.1   Evolutionary prototyping

Evolutionary prototyping is based on the idea of developing an initial implementation, exposing this to user comment and refining this through many stages until an adequate system has been developed (Figure 8.3). This approach to development

Figure 8.3
Evolutionary
prototyping

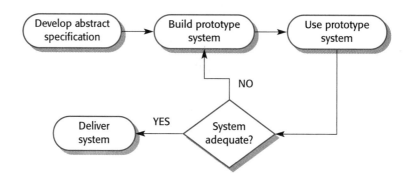

was used initially for those systems (such as AI systems) which are difficult or impossible to specify. However, it has now become a mainstream technique of software development. Evolutionary prototyping is part of or has much in common with techniques of rapid application development (RAD) and Joint Application Development (JAD) (Millington and Stapleton, 1995; Wood and Silver, 1995; Stapleton, 1997).

There are two main advantages to adopting this approach to software development:

1. *Accelerated delivery of the system* As I discussed in the introduction to the book, the pace of business change means that it is essential that software support is made available quickly. In some cases, rapid delivery and usability is more important than details of functionality or long-term software maintainability.

2. *User engagement with the system* The involvement of users with the development process does not just mean that the system is more likely to meet their requirements. It also means that the end-users of the system have made a commitment to it and are likely to want to make it work.

There are differences in detail between the particular methods of rapid software development but they all share some fundamental characteristics:

1. The processes of specification, design and implementation are interleaved. There is no detailed system specification and the design documentation produced usually depends on the tools used to implement the system. The user requirements document only defines the most important characteristics of the system.

2. The system is developed in a series of increments. End-users and other system stakeholders are involved in designing and evaluating each increment. They may propose changes to the software and new requirements which should be implemented in a later version of the system.

3. Techniques for rapid system development are used (see section 8.2). These may include CASE tools and fourth-generation languages.

4. System user interfaces are usually developed using an interactive development system (see section 8.3) which allows the interface design to be created quickly by drawing and placing icons on the interface.

Evolutionary prototyping and specification-based approaches to software development differ in their view of verification and validation. Verification is the process of checking that a program conforms to its specification. As there is no detailed specification for the prototype, verification is therefore impossible.

Validation should demonstrate that the program is suitable for its intended purpose rather than its conformance to a specification. This is also difficult without a detailed specification as there is no explicit statement of purpose. The end-users involved in the process may be happy with the system, but other stakeholders may feel excluded and unsatisfied that the system meets their purposes.

Verification and validation of a system which has been developed using evolutionary prototyping can only therefore check if the system is adequate, that is, if it is good enough for its intended purpose. Adequacy, of course, is not readily measurable and only subjective judgements of a program's adequacy can be made. This does not invalidate its usefulness; human performance cannot be guaranteed to be correct but we are satisfied if performance is adequate for the task in hand. However, as I discuss below, this does cause problems where systems are developed for customers by an external software development contractor.

There are three main problems with evolutionary prototyping which are particularly important when large, long-lifetime systems are to be developed:

1. *Management problems*   Software management structures for large systems are set up to deal with a software process model that generates regular deliverables to assess progress. Prototypes evolve so quickly that it is not cost-effective to produce a great deal of system documentation. Furthermore, rapid prototype development may require unfamiliar technologies to be used. Managers may find it difficult to use existing staff because they lack these skills.

2. *Maintenance problems*   Continual change tends to corrupt the structure of the prototype system. This means that anyone apart from the original developers is likely to find it difficult to understand. Furthermore, if specialised technology is used to support rapid prototype development this may become obsolete. Therefore, finding people who have the required knowledge to maintain the system may be difficult.

3. *Contractual problems*   The normal contractual model between a customer and a software developer is based around a system specification. When there is no such specification, it may be difficult to design a contract for the system development. Customers may be unhappy with a contract which simply pays developers for the time spent on the project as this can lead to function creep and budget overruns; developers are unlikely to accept a fixed-price contract as they cannot control the changes requested by the end-users.

Figure 8.4
An incremental
development process

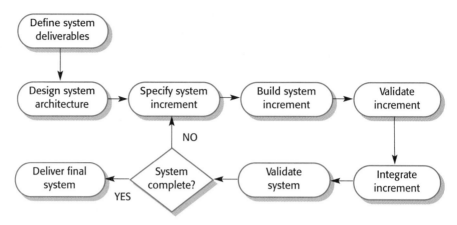

These difficulties mean that customers must be realistic about the use of evolutionary prototyping as a development technique. It allows small and medium-sized systems to be developed and delivered rapidly. System development costs may be reduced and usability is improved. If users are involved in the development, it is likely to be appropriate for their real needs. However, organisations who use this approach must accept that the lifetime of the system will be relatively short. As maintenance problems increase, the system will have to be replaced or completely rewritten. For large systems which may involve a number of different subcontractors, the management problems of evolutionary prototyping become intractable. Where prototypes are developed for parts of these systems, they should be throwaway prototypes.

Incremental development (Figure 8.4) avoids some of the problems of constant change which characterise evolutionary prototyping. An overall system architecture is established early in the process to act as a framework. System components are incrementally developed and delivered within this framework. Once these have been validated and delivered, neither the framework nor the components are changed unless errors are discovered. User feedback from delivered components, however, can influence the design of components scheduled for later delivery.

Incremental development is more manageable than evolutionary prototyping as the normal software process standards are followed. Plans and documentation must be produced for each system increment. It allows some user feedback early in the process and limits system errors as the development team are not concerned with interactions between quite different parts of the software system. Once an increment has been delivered, its interfaces are frozen. Later increments must adapt to these interfaces and can be tested against them.

8.1.2   Throw-away prototyping

A software process model based on an initial throw-away prototyping stage is illustrated in Figure 8.5. This approach extends the requirements analysis process with

Figure 8.5
A software process
with throw-away
prototyping

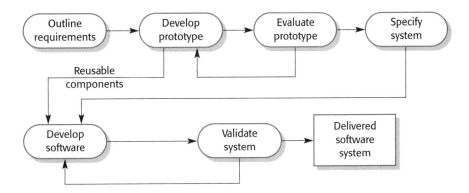

the intention of reducing overall life-cycle costs. The principal function of the prototype is to clarify requirements and provide additional information for managers to assess process risks. After evaluation, the prototype is thrown away. It is not used as a basis for further system development.

This approach to system prototyping is commonly used for hardware systems. The prototype is used to check the design before expensive commitments to manufacturing the system have been made. An electronic system prototype may be developed using off-the-shelf components before investment is made in special-purpose integrated circuits to implement the production version of the system.

However, a throw-away software prototype is not normally used for design validation but to help develop the system requirements. The prototype design is often quite different from that of the final system. The system must be developed as quickly as possible so that users can feed back their prototype experience to the development of the system specification. Functionality may be stripped from the throw-away prototype where these functions are well understood, quality standards may be relaxed and performance criteria ignored. The prototype development language will often be different from the final system implementation language.

The process model in Figure 8.5 assumes that the prototype is developed from an outline system specification, delivered for experiment and modified until the client is satisfied with its functionality. At this stage, a phased software process model is entered, a specification is derived from the prototype and the system reimplemented in a final production version. Components from the prototype may be reused in the production-quality system so development costs may be reduced.

Rather than derive a specification from the prototype, it is sometimes suggested that the system specification should be the prototype implementation itself. The instruction to the software contractor should simply be 'write a system like this one'. There are several problems with this approach:

1. Important features may have been left out of the prototype to simplify rapid implementation. In fact, it may not be possible to prototype some of the most important parts of the system such as safety-critical functions.

2. An implementation has no legal standing as a contract between customer and contractor.

3. Non-functional requirements such as those concerning reliability, robustness and safety cannot be adequately tested in a prototype implementation.

A general problem with developing an executable, throw-away prototype is that the mode of use of the prototype may not correspond with how the final delivered system is used. The tester of the prototype may be particularly interested in the system and may not be typical of system users. The training time during prototype evaluation may be insufficient. If the prototype is slow, the evaluators may adjust their way of working and avoid those system features which have slow response times. When provided with better response in the final system, they may use it in a different way.

Developers are sometimes pressurised by managers to deliver throw-away prototypes for use, particularly when there are delays in delivering the final version of the software. However, this is usually unwise for the following reasons:

1. It may be impossible to tune the prototype to meet non-functional requirements such as performance, security, robustness and reliability requirements which were ignored during prototype development.

2. Rapid change during development inevitably means that the prototype is undocumented. The only design specification is the prototype code. This is not good enough for long-term maintenance.

3. The changes made during prototype development will probably have degraded the system structure. The system will be difficult and expensive to maintain.

4. Organisational quality standards are normally relaxed for prototype development.

Throw-away prototypes do not have to be executable software prototypes to be useful in the requirements engineering process. Paper-based mock-ups of the system user interface (Rettig, 1994) have been shown to be effective in helping users refine an interface design and work through usage scenarios. These are very cheap to develop and can be constructed in a few days. An extension of this technique is a 'Wizard of Oz' prototype where only the user interface is developed. Users interact with this interface but their requests are passed to a person who interprets them and outputs the appropriate response. These approaches to prototyping are discussed in Sommerville and Sawyer (1997).

8.2 Rapid prototyping techniques

Rapid prototyping techniques are development techniques which emphasise speed of delivery rather than other system characteristics such as performance, maintainability or reliability. There are three rapid development techniques that are practical for developing industrial-strength prototypes:

1. dynamic high-level language development;
2. database programming;
3. component and application assembly.

For convenience, I describe these techniques in separate sections. In practice, however, they are often all used in the development of a system prototype. For example, a database programming language may be used to extract data for processing with the detailed processing executed using reusable components. The system user interface may be defined using visual programming. Luqi (1992) describes how such a mixed approach was used to create a prototype of a command and control system.

Prototype development is now usually supported through a set of tools which includes support for at least two of these techniques. For example, the Smalltalk VisualWorks system supports a very high-level language and provides many reusable components which may be included in applications. Lotus Notes includes support for database programming using a very high-level language and reusable components which may be linked to database operations.

Most prototyping systems now support a visual programming approach where some or all of the prototype is developed interactively. Rather than write a sequential program, the prototype developer manipulates graphical icons representing functions, data or user interface components and associates processing scripts with these icons. An executable program is generated automatically from the visual representation of the system. This simplifies program development and reduces prototyping costs. I discuss visual programming in more detail in section 8.2.3 which covers component and application reuse.

8.2.1   Dynamic high-level language development

Dynamic high-level languages are programming languages which include powerful run-time data management facilities. These simplify program development because they reduce many problems of storage allocation and management. The language system includes facilities which normally have to be built from more primitive constructs in languages like Ada or C. Examples of very high-level languages are Lisp (based on list structures), Prolog (based on logic) and Smalltalk (based on objects).

Until relatively recently, very high-level dynamic languages were not widely used for large system development because they need a large run-time support system. This run-time support increases the storage needs and reduces the execution speeds of programs written in the language. However, the increasing power and reducing cost of computer hardware have made these factors less important.

This means that, for many business applications, these languages can replace imperative programming languages such as C, COBOL and Ada. Java is clearly a

Language	Type	Application domain
Smalltalk	Object-oriented	Interactive systems
Java	Object-oriented	Interactive systems
Prolog	Logic	Symbolic processing
Lisp	List-based	Symbolic processing

mainstream development language with its roots in C++ yet it incorporates many of the features of Smalltalk such as platform independence and automatic storage management. Java provides many of the advantages of very high-level languages with the rigour and the opportunities for performance optimisation offered by conventional third-generation languages. Many reusable Java components are available so it is clearly a very suitable language for evolutionary prototyping.

Figure 8.6 shows the dynamic languages that are most commonly used for prototype development. When choosing a prototyping language, you should ask a number of questions:

1. *What is the application domain of the problem?* As shown in Figure 8.6, different languages are best suited to different application domains. If you want to prototype applications which involve natural language processing (say), a language such as Lisp or Prolog is more suitable than Java or Smalltalk.

2. *What user interaction is required?* Different languages provide different levels of support for user interaction. Some languages, such as Smalltalk and Java, are well integrated with web browsers while others, such as Prolog, are best suited to text-based interfaces.

3. *What support environment is provided with the language?* Mature support environments with many tools and easy access to reusable components simplify the prototype development process.

Dynamic high-level languages may be used in combination to create a system prototype. Different parts of the system may be programmed in different languages and a communication framework established between the parts. Zave (1989) describes this approach to development in the prototyping of a telephone network system. Four different languages were used: Prolog for database prototyping, Awk (Aho *et al.*, 1988) for billing, CSP (Hoare, 1985) for protocol specification and PAISLey (Zave and Schell, 1986) for performance simulation.

There is never an ideal language for prototyping large systems as different parts of the system are so diverse. The advantage of a mixed-language approach is that the most appropriate language for a logical part of the application can be chosen, thus speeding up prototype development. The disadvantage is that it may be difficult to establish a communication framework which will allow multiple languages to communicate. The entities used in the different languages are very diverse. Consequently, lengthy code sections may be needed to translate an entity from one language to another.

8.2.2   Database programming

Evolutionary development is now a standard technique for implementing small and medium-sized applications in the business systems domain. The majority of business applications involve manipulating data from a database and producing outputs which involve organising and formatting that data.

To support the development of these applications, all commercial database management systems now support database programming. Database programming is carried out using a specialised language which embeds knowledge of the database and which includes operations that are geared to database manipulation. The language's supporting environment provides tools to support user interface definition, numeric computation and report generation. The term *fourth-generation language* (4GL) is used to refer to both the database programming language and its supporting environment.

Fourth-generation languages are successful because there is a great deal of commonality across data processing applications. In essence, these applications are concerned with updating a database and producing reports from the information in the database. Standard forms are used for input and output. 4GLs are geared towards producing interactive applications which rely on abstracting information from an organisational database, presenting it to end-users on their terminal or workstation and then updating the database with changes made by users. The user interface usually consists of a set of standard forms or a spreadsheet.

The tools which are included in a 4GL environment (Figure 8.7) are:

1. A database query language which is now usually SQL (Date and Darwen, 1997). This may be input directly or generated automatically from forms filled in by an end-user.

Figure 8.7
Fourth-generation
language
components

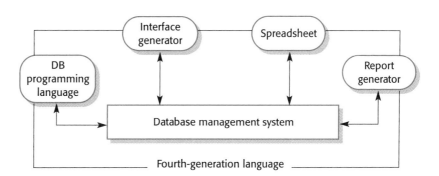

2. An interface generator which is used to create forms for data input and display.

3. A spreadsheet for the analysis and manipulation of numeric information.

4. A report generator which is used to define and create reports from information in the database.

Most business applications rely on structured forms for input and output so 4GLs provide powerful facilities for screen definition and report generation. Screens are often defined as a series of linked forms (in one application we studied, there were 137 different form definitions) so the screen generation system must provide for:

1. *interactive form definition* where the developer defines the fields to be displayed and how these are to be organised;
2. *form linking* where the developer can specify that particular inputs cause further forms to be displayed;
3. *field verification* where the developer defines allowed ranges for values input to form fields.

Most 4GLs now support the development of database interfaces based on World Wide Web browsers. These allow the database to be accessed from anywhere with a valid Internet connection. This reduces training costs and software costs and allows external users to have access to a database. However, the inherent limitations of web browsers and Internet protocols mean that this approach may be unsuitable for systems where very fast, interactive responses are required.

4GL-based development can be used either for evolutionary prototyping or in conjunction with a method-based analysis where system models are used to generate the prototype system. The structure which CASE tools impose on the application and the associated documentation mean that evolutionary prototypes developed using this approach should be more maintainable than manually developed systems. The CASE tools may generate SQL or may generate code in a lower-level language such as COBOL. Forte (1992) describes a number of tools of this type in a brief survey of fourth-generation languages.

While 4GLs are very suitable for prototype development, there are some disadvantages in using them for production systems. Programs written in a 4GL are usually slower than similar programs in conventional programming languages and usually require much more memory. For example, I was involved in an experiment where rewriting a 4GL program in C++ resulted in a 50 per cent reduction in memory requirements. The C program also ran 10 times faster than the 4GL system.

Although they clearly reduce systems development costs, the effect of 4GLs on overall life-cycle costs for large data processing systems is not yet clear. Programs tend to be unstructured and difficult to maintain and 4GLs are not standardised. Post-delivery costs may therefore be high. Particular problems can arise when 4GL systems have to be re-engineered. There is no standardisation or uniformity across fourth-generation languages. This means that users may have to rewrite programs because the language in which they were originally written is obsolete.

8.2.3   Component and application assembly

The time needed to develop a system can be reduced if many parts of that system can be reused rather than designed and implemented. Prototypes can be constructed quickly if you have a set of reusable components and some mechanism to compose these components into systems. The composition mechanism must include control facilities and a mechanism for component communications. This approach is illustrated in Figure 8.8.

Prototyping with reusable components involves developing a system specification by taking account of what reusable components are available. This may mean that some requirements compromises may be have to be made. The functionality of the available components may not be a precise fit for the user requirements. However, user requirements are often fairly flexible so, in most cases, this approach can be used for prototype development.

Prototype development with reuse can be supported at two levels:

1. The application level where entire application systems are integrated with the prototype so that their functionality can be shared. For example, if the prototype requires a text processing capability, this can be provided by integrating a standard word processing system. Applications, such as Microsoft Office applications, support application linking.

2. The component level where individual components are integrated within a standard framework to implement the system. This standard framework can be a scripting language which is designed for evolutionary development such as Visual Basic, TCL/TK (Ousterhout, 1994), Python (Lutz, 1996) or Perl (Wall *et al.*, 1996). Alternatively, it can be a more general component integration framework based on CORBA, DCOM or JavaBeans (Sessions, 1997; Orfali and Harkey, 1998; Pope, 1998).

Application reuse gives access to all of the functionality of an application. If the application also provides scripting or tailoring facilities (e.g. Excel macros) these may be used to develop some prototype functionality. A compound document metaphor is helpful to understand this approach to prototype development. The data processed by the prototype system is organised into a compound document that acts as a container for several different objects. These objects contain different types of data (such

Figure 8.8
Reusable component
composition

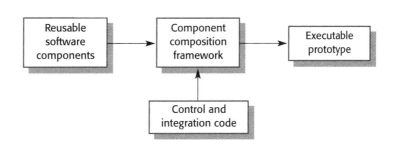

Figure 8.9
Application linking

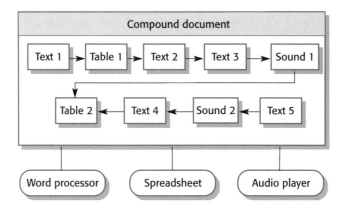

as a table, a diagram, a form) that can be processed by different applications. Objects are linked and typed so that accessing an object results in the associated application being initiated.

Figure 8.9 illustrates the notion of a prototype system being made up of an compound document that includes text elements, spreadsheet elements and sound files. Text elements are processed by the word processor, tables by the spreadsheet application and the sound files by an audio player. When a system user accesses an object of a particular type, the associated application is called to provide user functionality. For example, when objects of type sound are accessed, the audio player is called to process these objects.

To illustrate the type of prototype which might be developed using this approach, consider the process of requirements management discussed in Chapter 6. A requirements management support system needs a way of capturing requirements, storing these requirements, producing reports, discovering requirements relationships and managing these relationships as traceability tables. This could be prototyped by linking a database (to store requirements), a word processor (to capture requirements and format reports), a spreadsheet (to manage traceability tables) and specially written code to find relationships between the requirements.

The main advantage of this approach is that a lot of prototype functionality can be implemented quickly at a very low cost. If the prototype users are already familiar with the applications making up the prototype, then they do not have to learn how to use new features. However, if they do not know how to use the applications, learning may be difficult, especially as they may be confused by application functionality which isn't necessary. There may be performance problems with the prototype because of the need to switch from one application system to another. This depends on the operating system support which is provided. The most widely used support for this approach is Microsoft's object linking and embedding (OLE) (Sessions, 1997) mechanism.

It is not always possible or sensible to reuse whole applications. Development with reuse relies on finer-grain reusable components. These may be functions or objects which carry out particular operations such as sorting, searching, displaying, etc. The

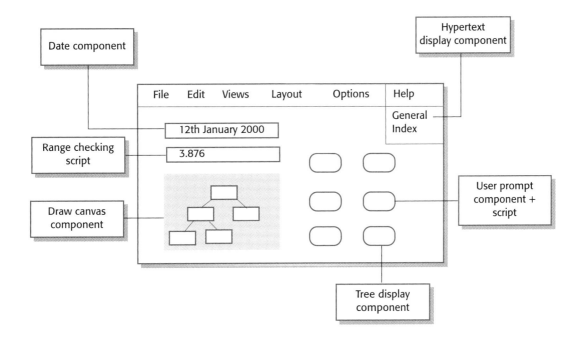

Figure 8.10 Visual programming with reuse

prototype system is developed by defining an overall control structure and then integrating the components with that structure. If components which carry out the required function are not available, special-purpose code is developed and, if appropriate, made available for future reuse.

Visual development systems such as Visual Basic support this reuse-based approach to application development. Application programmers build the system interactively by defining the interface in terms of screens, fields, buttons and menus. These are named, and processing scripts are associated with individual parts of the interface (e.g. a button named 'Simulate'). These scripts may be calls to reusable components, special-purpose code or a mixture of both of these.

I illustrate this approach in Figure 8.10 which shows an application screen including menus along the top, input fields (the white fields on the left of the display), output fields (the shaded field on the left of the display) and buttons which are the rounded rectangles on the right of the display. When these entities are positioned on the display by the prototype construction system, the developer defines which reusable component should be associated with them or writes a program fragment to carry out the required processing. In Figure 8.10, I show the components associated with some of the display elements.

Visual Basic is an example of a family of languages called scripting languages (Ousterhout, 1998). Scripting languages are typeless high-level languages that are designed to integrate components to create systems. An early example of a scripting language was the Unix shell (Bourne, 1978) and, since its development, a number of other more powerful scripting languages have been created (Ousterhout, 1994; Lutz, 1996; Wall *et al.*, 1996). Scripting languages include control structures and graphical toolkits and Ousterhout (1998) illustrates that they radically reduce the time required for system development.

This approach to system development allows for the rapid development of relatively small and simple applications which can be built by one person or a small team of people. For larger systems which must be developed by larger teams it is more difficult to organise. There is no explicit system architecture and there are often complex dependencies between different parts of the system. These cause difficulties when changes are required. It is also limited to a specific set of interaction objects and thus it may be difficult to implement non-standard user interfaces. More general component-based development around an architectural framework, as discussed in Chapter 14, is more appropriate for large systems.

8.3 User interface prototyping

Graphical user interfaces have now become the norm for interactive systems. The effort involved in specifying, designing and implementing a user interface represents a significant part of application development costs. As discussed in Chapter 15, designers should not impose their view of an acceptable user interface on users. The user must take part in the interface design process. This realisation led to an approach to design called user-centred design (Norman and Draper, 1986) that depends on interface prototyping and user involvement throughout the interface design process.

From a software engineering point of view, prototyping is an essential part of the user interface design process. Because of the dynamic nature of user interfaces, textual descriptions and diagrams are not good enough for expressing the user interface requirements. Therefore, evolutionary prototyping with end-user involvement is the only sensible way to develop graphical user interfaces for software systems.

Interface generators are graphical screen design systems where interface components such as menus, fields, icons and buttons are selected from a menu and positioned on an interface. As I have already discussed, systems of this type are an essential part of a database programming system and Visual Basic (discussed above) has based its standard development technique around such a system. Shneiderman (1998) discusses a number of these systems. Interface generators create a well-structured program generated from an interface specification. The iterations which are an inherent part of evolutionary development do not degrade the software structure and reimplementation is not required.

Millions of people now have access to World Wide Web browsers. These support a page definition language (HTML) which has been extended from a simple text mark-up language to a comprehensive notation for user interface specification. Buttons, fields, forms and tables may be included in web pages as well as multimedia objects giving access to sounds, video and virtual reality displays.

Processing scripts may be associated with user interface objects with processing carried out either on the web client or centrally on the web server.

Because of the widespread availability of web browsers and the power of HTML and its associated processing capabilities, more and more user interfaces are being built as web-based interfaces. As I discuss in Chapter 26, which covers legacy systems, these interfaces are not simply confined to new systems. Web-based interfaces are replacing forms-based interfaces for a wide range of legacy systems.

Web-based user interfaces may be prototyped by using a standard web-site editor which is, essentially, a user interface builder. Entities on the web page are defined and positioned and actions are associated with them either using built-in HTML capabilities (e.g. link to another page) or by using Java or CGI scripts.

KEY POINTS

▶ A system prototype can be developed to give end-users a concrete impression of the system capabilities. The prototype may therefore help in establishing and validating system requirements.

▶ As pressure grows for the rapid delivery of software, prototyping is becoming increasingly used as the standard development technique for small and medium-sized systems, especially in the business domain.

▶ 'Throw-away' prototyping involves developing a prototype to understand the system requirements. In evolutionary prototyping, a prototype evolves through several versions to the final system.

▶ When implementing a throw-away prototype, you first develop the parts of the system you understand least; in an evolutionary prototype, you develop the parts of the system you understand best.

▶ Rapid development is important for prototype systems. To deliver a prototype quickly, you may have to leave out some system functionality or relax non-functional constraints such as response speed and reliability.

▶ Prototyping techniques include the use of very high-level languages, database programming and prototype construction from reusable components. Many prototyping environments support a visual programming approach to development.

▶ User interfaces should always be developed using prototyping as it is not possible to specify these effectively using a static model. Users should be involved in the evaluation and evolution of the prototype.

FURTHER READING

'Scripting: Higher-level programming for the 21st century'. An overview of scripting languages by the inventor of TCL/TK who discusses the advantages of this approach for rapid application development. (J. K. Ousterhout, *IEEE Computer,* March 1998.)

'Rapid prototyping: Lessons learned'. This is a good summary of the advantages and disadvantages of rapid prototyping of software. It is based on an empirical survey of a number of different types of software system. (V. Scott Gordon and J. Bielman, *IEEE Software,* January 1995.)

'Twenty-two tips for a happier, healthier prototype'. Mostly sound advice on prototyping presented from the perspective of a user interface designer. (James Rudd and Scott Isensee, *ACM Interactions* 1.1, January 1994.)

EXERCISES

8.1 You have been asked to investigate the feasibility of prototyping in the software development process in your organisation. Write a report for your manager discussing the classes of project where prototyping should be used and setting out the expected costs and benefits from using prototyping.

8.2 Explain why, for large systems development, it is recommended that prototypes should be 'throw-away' prototypes.

8.3 What features of languages like Smalltalk and Lisp contribute to their support of rapid prototyping?

8.4 Under what circumstances would you recommend that prototyping should be used as a means of validating system requirements?

8.5 Suggest difficulties that might arise when prototyping real-time embedded computer systems.

8.6 A software manager is involved in a project development of a software design support system that supports the translation of software requirements to a formal software specification. Comment on the advantages and disadvantages of the following development strategies:

(a) Develop a throw-away prototype using a prototyping language such as Smalltalk. Evaluate this prototype and then review requirements. Develop the final system using C.

(b) Develop the system from the existing requirements using Java and then modify it to adapt to any changed user requirements.

(c)   Develop the system using evolutionary prototyping using a prototyping language such as Smalltalk. Modify the system according to the user's requests and deliver the modified prototype.

8.7   Discuss prototyping using reusable components and suggest problems which may arise using this approach. What is the most effective way to specify reusable components?

8.8   What are the advantages and disadvantages of using Microsoft's OLE mechanism for rapid application development?

8.9   You have been asked by a charity to prototype a system that keeps track of all donations they have received. This system has to maintain the names and addresses of donors, their particular interests, the amount donated, and when it was donated. If the donation is over a certain amount, the donor may attach conditions to the donation (e.g. it must be spent on a particular project) and the system must keep track of these donations and how they were spent. Discuss how you would prototype this system bearing in mind that the charity has a mixture of paid workers and volunteers. Many of the volunteers are retirees who have had little or no computer experience.

8.10 You have developed a throw-away prototype system for a client who is very happy with it. However, she suggests that there is no need to develop another system but that you should deliver the prototype and offers an excellent price for the system. You know that there may be future problems with maintaining the system. Discuss how you might respond to this customer.

9 Formal specification

Objectives

The principal objective of this chapter is to introduce formal specification techniques that can be used to add detail to a system requirements specification. When you have read this chapter, you will:

❑ understand why formal specification techniques help discover problems in system requirements;

❑ understand the use of algebraic techniques of formal specification to define interface specifications;

❑ understand how formal, model-based formal techniques may be used for behavioural specification.

Contents

9.1 Formal specification in the software process
9.2 Interface specification
9.3 Behavioural specification

In 'traditional' engineering disciplines such as electrical and civil engineering, progress has usually involved the development of better mathematical techniques. The engineering industry has had no difficulty accepting the need for mathematical analysis and in incorporating mathematical analysis into its processes. Mathematical analysis is a routine part of the process of developing and validating a product design.

However, software engineering has not followed the same path. Although there has now been more than 25 years of research into the use of mathematical techniques in the software process, these techniques have had a limited impact. So-called 'formal methods' of software development are not widely used in industrial software development. Most software development companies do not consider it cost-effective to apply them in their software processes.

The term 'formal methods' includes a number of different activities, including formal system specification, specification analysis and proof, transformational development (discussed in Chapter 3) and program verification. All of these activities are dependent on a formal specification of the software. A formal software specification is a specification expressed in a language whose vocabulary, syntax and semantics are formally defined. This need for a formal definition means that the specification languages must be based on mathematical concepts whose properties have been investigated and are well understood. The branch of mathematics which is used is called discrete mathematics and the mathematical concepts are drawn from set theory, logic and algebra.

In the 1980s, formal specification and more general formal methods were seen by many researchers as the most likely route to dramatic improvements in software quality. They argued that the rigour and detailed analysis that are an essential part of formal methods would lead to programs with fewer errors and which were more suited to user's needs. They predicted that, by the 21st century, a large proportion of software would be developed using formal methods.

Clearly, this prediction has not been fulfilled. There are a number of reasons for this:

1. *Successful software engineering*   The use of software engineering methods such as structured methods, configuration management, information hiding, etc. in the design and development processes has resulted in improvements in software quality. This contradicts predictions that program proofs are essential for quality improvement.

2. *Market changes*   In the 1980s, software quality was seen as the key software engineering problem. However, since then, the key issue for many classes of software development is not quality but time-to-market. Software must be developed quickly and customers are often willing to accept software with some faults if rapid delivery can be achieved. Techniques for rapid software development do not interface well with formal specifications. Of course, quality is an important factor but it must be achieved in the context of rapid delivery.

3. *Limited scope of formal methods*   Formal methods are not, in general, well suited to specifying user interfaces and user interaction. As the user interface

component has become a greater and greater part of many systems, any benefits gained from the use of formal methods are limited.

4. *Limited scalability of formal methods*   Formal methods do not scale up well. Successful projects which have used these techniques have limited their use to relatively small critical kernel systems. This problem has been exacerbated by the lack of tool support for these techniques.

These factors mean that the risks of adopting formal methods on most software projects outweigh the possible benefits from their use. The costs and problems of introducing formal methods into software processes are very high. However, formal specification is an excellent way of discovering specification errors and presenting the system specification in an unambiguous way. All successful projects which have used formal methods have reported fewer errors in the delivered software.

Therefore, in systems where failure must be avoided, the use of formal methods can be justified and is likely to be cost-effective. The use of formal methods is increasing in the specialised area of critical systems development where emergent system properties such as safety, reliability and security are very important. These critical systems, as discussed in Part 4, have very high validation costs and the costs of system failure are large and are increasing. Formal methods are being used because they can reduce these costs.

Critical systems where formal methods have been applied successfully include an air traffic control information system (Hall, 1996), railway signalling systems (Dehbonei and Mejia, 1995), spacecraft systems (Easterbrook *et al.*, 1998) and medical control systems (Jacky, 1995; Jacky *et al.*, 1997). They have also been used for software tool specification (Neil *et al.*, 1998), the specification of part of IBM's CICS system (Wordsworth, 1991) and a real-time system kernel (Spivey, 1990). The Cleanroom method of software development (Mills *et al.*, 1987; Linger, 1994; Prowell *et al.*, 1999), which I discuss in Chapter 19, relies on formally based arguments that code conforms to its specification. In the UK, the use of formal methods is mandated by the Ministry of Defence for safety-critical systems (MOD, 1995).

9.1 Formal specification in the software process

In the discussion of the requirements engineering process in Chapter 6, I suggested that there were three levels of software specification which may be developed. These are user requirements, system requirements and a software design specification. The user requirements are the most abstract specification and the software design specification is the most detailed. In general, formal mathematical specifications lie somewhere between system requirements and software design specifications. They do not include implementation detail but should present a complete mathematical model of the system.

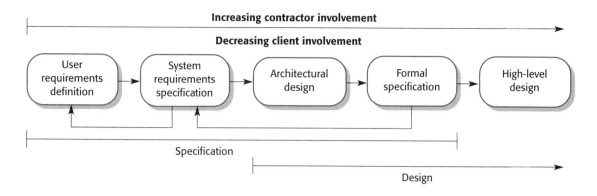

Figure 9.1
Specification
and design

The involvement of the client for the software decreases and the involvement of the contractor increases as the specification is developed. In the early stages of the process, it is essential that the specification is 'customer-oriented'. It should be written so that it is understandable to the client and should make as few assumptions as possible about the software design. However, the final stage of the process, which is the construction of a complete, consistent and precise specification, is principally intended for the software contractor. It serves as a basis for the system implementation. This precise specification may be a formal specification.

Figure 9.1 shows the stages of software specification and its interface with the design process. The specification stages shown in Figure 9.1 are not independent nor are they necessarily developed in the sequence shown. Figure 9.2 shows that specification and design activities may be carried out in parallel streams. There is a two-way relation between each stage in the process. Information is fed from the specification to the design process and vice versa.

As a specification is developed in detail, the specifier's understanding of that specification increases. Creating a formal specification forces a detailed systems analysis that usually reveals errors and inconsistencies in the informal requirements specification. This error detection is the most potent argument for developing a formal specification (Hall, 1990). Requirements problems which remain undetected until later stages of the software process are usually expensive to correct.

Depending on the process used, specification problems discovered during formal analysis might influence changes to the requirements specification if this has not

Figure 9.2 Formal
specification in the
software process

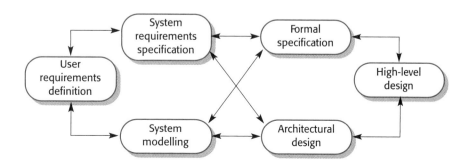

Figure 9.3 Software
development costs
with formal
specification

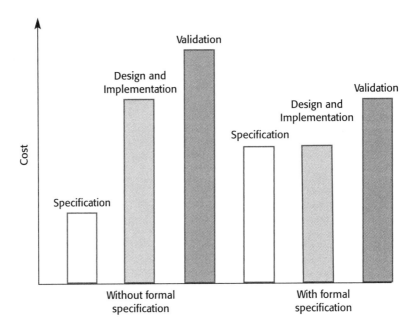

already been agreed. If the requirements specification has been accepted as the basis of a contract, the problems which have been discovered should be raised with the customer for resolution before starting on the system design.

Developing and analysing a formal specification front-loads software development costs. Figure 9.3 shows how software process costs are affected by the use of formal specification. When a conventional process is used, validation costs are about 50 per cent of development costs and implementation and design costs are about twice the costs of specification. With formal specification, specification and implementation costs are comparable and system validation costs are significantly reduced. As the development of the formal specification discovers requirements problems, rework to correct these problems after the system has been designed is avoided.

There are two approaches to formal specification that have been used to write detailed specifications for non-trivial software systems. These are:

1. an algebraic approach where the system is described in terms of operations and their relationships;

2. a model-based approach where a model of the system is built using mathematical constructs such as sets and sequences and the system operations are defined by how they modify the system state.

Different languages in these families have been developed to specify sequential and concurrent systems. Figure 9.4 shows examples of the languages in each of these classes. In this chapter, I introduce both of these techniques. The examples here

Figure 9.4 Formal
specification
languages

	Sequential	Concurrent
Algebraic	Larch (Guttag *et al.*, 1985, 1993) OBJ (Futatsugi *et al.*, 1985)	Lotos (Bolognesi and Brinksma, 1987)
Model-based	Z (Spivey, 1992) VDM (Jones, 1980) B (Wordsworth, 1996)	CSP (Hoare, 1985) Petri Nets (Peterson, 1981)

give you an impression how formal specification results in a precise, detailed
specification but I don't discuss specification language details or specification techniques. You can download a more detailed description of both of these techniques
from the book's website.

9.2 Interface specification

Large systems are usually decomposed into sub-systems that are developed independently. Sub-systems make use of other sub-systems, so an essential part of the
specification process is to define sub-system interfaces. Once the interfaces are agreed
and defined, the sub-systems can be developed independently.

Sub-system interfaces are often defined as a set of abstract data types or objects
(Figure 9.5). These describe the data and operations that can be accessed through
the sub-system interface. A sub-system interface specification can therefore be produced by combining the specifications of the components which make up the sub-
system interface.

Precise sub-system interface specifications are important because sub-system
developers must write code that uses the services of other sub-systems before these
have been implemented. The interface specification provides information for
sub-system developers so that they know what services will be available in other
sub-systems and how these can be accessed. Clear and unambiguous sub-system

Figure 9.5
Sub-system interface
objects

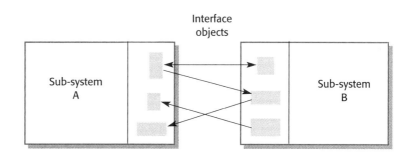

Figure 9.6
The structure
of an algebraic
specification

```
< SPECIFICATION NAME >

sort < name >
imports < LIST OF SPECIFICATION NAMES >
──────────────────────────────────────────
Informal description of the sort and its operations
──────────────────────────────────────────
Operation signatures setting out the names and the types of
the parameters to the operations defined over the sort
──────────────────────────────────────────
Axioms defining the operations over the sort
```

interface specifications reduce the chances of misunderstandings between a sub-system providing some service and the sub-systems using that service.

The algebraic approach was originally designed for the definition of abstract data type interfaces. In an abstract data type, the type is defined by specifying the type operations rather than the type representation. Therefore, it is very similar to an object class. The algebraic method of formal specification defines the abstract data type in terms of the relationships between the type operations.

Guttag (1977) first discussed this approach in the specification of abstract data types. Cohen *et al.* (1986) show how the technique can be extended to complete system specification using an example of a document retrieval system. Liskov and Guttag (1986) also cover the algebraic specification of abstract data types. LARCH (Guttag *et al.*, 1993) is probably the best known language for algebraic specification.

The structure of an object specification is shown in Figure 9.6. The body of the specification has four components:

- An introduction that declares the sort (the type name) of the entity being specified. A sort is the name of a set of objects. It is usually implemented as a type. The introduction may also include an imports declaration where the names of specifications defining other sorts are declared. Importing a specification makes these sorts available for use.

- A description part where the operations are described informally. This makes the formal specification easier to understand. The formal specification complements this description by providing an unambiguous syntax and semantics for the type operations.

- The signature part defines the syntax of the interface to the object class or abstract data type. The names of the operations that are defined, the number and sorts of their parameters and the sorts of operation results are described in the signature.

- The axioms part defines the semantics of the operations by defining a set of axioms which characterise the behaviour of the abstract data type. These axioms relate the operations used to construct entities of the defined sort with operations used to inspect its values.

The process of developing a formal specification of a sub-system interface should include the following activities:

1. *Specification structuring*   Organise the informal interface specification into a set of abstract data types or object classes. You should informally define the operations associated with each class.

2. *Specification naming*   Establish a name for each abstract type specification, decide whether or not they require generic parameters and decide on names for the sorts identified.

3. *Operation selection*   Choose a set of operations for each specification based on the identified interface functionality. You should include operations to create instances of the sort, to modify the value of instances and to inspect the instance values. You may have to add functions to those initially identified in the informal interface definition.

4. *Informal operation specification*   Write an informal specification of each operation. This should describe how the operations affect the defined sort.

5. *Syntax definition*   Define the syntax of the operations and the parameters to each operation. This is the signature part of the formal specification. Update the informal specification at this stage if necessary.

6. *Axiom definition*   Define the semantics of the operations by describing what conditions are always true for different operation combinations.

To explain the technique of algebraic specification, I will specify a simple data structure (a linked list) with a limited number of operations associated with it. This is illustrated in Figure 9.7.

Figure 9.7 A simple
list specification

LIST (Elem)

sort List
imports INTEGER

Defines a list where elements are added at the end and removed from the front. The operations are Create, which brings an empty list into existence, Cons, which creates a new list with an added member, Length, which evaluates the list size, Head, which evaluates the front element of the list, and Tail, which creates a list by removing the head from its input list. Undefined represents an undefined value of type Elem.

Create → List
Cons (List, Elem) → List
Head (List) → Elem
Length (List) → Integer
Tail (List) → List

Head (Create) = Undefined **exception** (empty list)
Head (Cons (L, v)) = **if** L = Create **then** v **else** Head (L)
Length (Create) = 0
Length (Cons (L, v)) = Length (L) + 1
Tail (Create) = Create
Tail (Cons (L, v)) = **if** L = Create **then** Create **else** Cons (Tail (L), v)

To develop the example of the list specification, assume that the first stage, namely specification structuring, has been carried out and that the need for a list has been identified. The name of the specification and the name of the sort can be the same although it is useful to distinguish between these by using some convention. I use upper case for the specification name (LIST) and lower case with an initial capital for the sort name (List). As lists are collections of other types, the specification has a generic parameter (Elem). The type Elem can represent an integer, a string, a list, etc.

In general, for each abstract data type, the required operations must include an operation to bring instances of the type into existence (Create) and to construct the type from its elements (Cons). In the case of lists, there should be an operation to evaluate the first list element (Head), an operation which returns the list created by removing the first element (Tail) and an operation to count the number of list elements (Length).

To define the syntax of each of these operations, you must decide which parameters are required for the operation and the results of the operation. In general, input parameters are either the sort being defined (List) or the generic sort. Results of operations may be either of those sorts or some other sort such as Integer or Boolean. In the list example, the Length operation returns an integer. An imports declaration declaring that the specification of integer is used should therefore be included in the specification.

The axioms that define the semantics of an abstract data type are written using the operations defined in the signature part. They specify the semantics by setting out what is always true about the behaviour of entities with that abstract type.

Operations on an abstract data type usually fall into two classes:

1. *Constructor operations* which create or modify entities of the sort defined in the specification. Typically, these are given names such as Create, Update, Add or, in this case, Cons meaning construct.

2. *Inspection operations* which evaluate attributes of the sort defined in the specification. Typically, these are given names which correspond to attribute names or names such as Eval, Get, etc.

A good rule of thumb for writing an algebraic specification is to establish the constructor operations and write down an axiom for each inspection operation over each constructor. This suggests that if there are m constructor operations and n inspection operations there should be m * n axioms defined.

However, the constructor operations associated with an abstract type may not all be primitive constructors. It may be possible to define them using other constructors and inspection operations. If a constructor operation can be defined using other constructors, it is only necessary to define the inspection operations using the primitive constructors.

In the list specification, the constructor operations are Create, Cons and Tail which build lists. The inspection operations are Head and Length which are used to discover list attributes. The Tail operation, however, is not a primitive constructor. There is therefore no need to define axioms over the Tail operation for Head and Length operations but Tail must be defined using the primitive constructors.

Evaluating the head of an empty list results in an undefined value. The specifications of Head and Tail show that Head evaluates the front of the list and Tail evaluates to the input list with its head removed. The specification of Head states that the head of a list created using Cons is either the value added to the list (if the initial list is empty) or is the same as the head of the initial list parameter to Cons. Adding an element to a list does not affect its head unless the list is empty.

Recursion is commonly used when writing algebraic specifications. The value of the Tail operation is the list which is formed by taking the input list and removing its head. The definition of Tail shows how recursion is used in constructing algebraic specifications. The operation is defined on empty lists then recursively on non-empty lists with the recursion terminating when the empty list results.

It is sometimes easier to understand recursive specifications by developing a short example. Say we have a list [5, 7] where 5 is the front of the list and 7 the end of the list. The operation Cons ([5, 7], 9) should return a list [5, 7, 9] and a Tail operation applied to this should return the list [7, 9]. The sequence of equations which results from substituting the parameters in the above specification with these values is:

```
Tail ([5, 7, 9]) =
    Tail (Cons ([5, 7], 9)) =
    Cons (Tail ([5, 7]), 9) =
    Cons (Tail (Cons ([5], 7)), 9) =
    Cons (Cons (Tail ([5]), 7), 9) =
        Cons (Cons (Tail (Cons ([], 5)), 7), 9) =
        Cons (Cons ([Create], 7), 9) =
    Cons ([7], 9) =
        [7, 9]
```

The systematic rewriting of the axiom for Tail illustrates that it does indeed produce the anticipated result. The axiom for Head can be verified in a similar way.

Now let us look at how this technique may be used in a critical system. Assume that, in an air traffic control system, an object has been designed to represent a controlled sector of airspace. Each controlled sector may include a number of aircraft each of which has a different aircraft identifier. For safety reasons, all aircraft must be separated by at least 300 metres in height. The system warns the controller if an attempt is made to position an aircraft so that this constraint is breached.

To simplify the description, I have only defined a limited number of operations on the sector object. In a practical system, there are likely to be many more operations and more complex safety conditions related to the horizontal separation of the aircraft. The critical operations on the object are:

1. *Enter*   This operation adds an aircraft (represented by an identifier) to the airspace at a specified height. There must not be other aircraft at that height or within 300 metres of it.

2. *Leave*   This operation removes the specified aircraft from the controlled sector. This operation is used when the aircraft moves to an adjacent sector.

3. *Move*   This operation moves an aircraft from one height to another. Again, the safety constraint that vertical separation of aircraft must be at least 300 metres is checked.

4. *Lookup*   Given an aircraft identifier, this operation returns the current height of that aircraft in the sector.

It makes it easier to specify these operations, if some other interface operations are defined. These are:

1. *Create*   This is a standard operation for an abstract data type. It causes an empty instance of the type to be created. In this case, it represents a sector that has no aircraft in it.

2. *Put*   This is a simpler version of the *Enter* operation. It simply adds an aircraft to the sector without any associated constraint checking.

3. *In-space*   Given an aircraft call sign, this Boolean operation returns true if the aircraft is in the controlled sector, false otherwise.

4. *Occupied*   Given a height, this Boolean operation returns true if there is an aircraft within 300 metres of that height, false otherwise.

The advantage of defining these simpler operations is that you can then use them as building blocks to define the more complex operations on the **Sector** sort. The algebraic specification of this sort is shown in Figure 9.8.

Essentially, the basic constructor operations are **Create** and **Put** and I use these in the specification of the other operations. **Occupied** and **In-space** are checking operations that are defined using **Create** and **Put** and are then used in other specifications. I don't have space to explain all operations in detail here but I will discuss two of them (**Occupied** and **Move**). With this information, you should be able to understand the specification of the other operations.

1. The specification of **Occupied** states that in an empty airspace (**Create**) a level is always vacant. When applied to an airspace which has been populated using a **Put** operation, **Occupied** checks if the specified height is within 300 metres of the height of the aircraft added to the sector by the **Put** operation. If so, the height is already occupied so the value of **Occupied** is true. If not, the operation checks the sector recursively. You can think of this check being carried out on the last aircraft put into the sector. If the height is not within range of the height of that aircraft, the operation then checks against the previous aircraft which has been put into the sector and so on. Eventually, if there are no aircraft within range of the specified height, the check is carried out against an empty sector so returns false.

Figure 9.8 The
specification of a
controlled sector

```
SECTOR
   sort Sector
   imports INTEGER, BOOLEAN

   Enter - adds an aircraft to the sector if safety conditions are satisfed
   Leave - removes an aircraft from the sector
   Move - moves an aircraft from one height to another if safe to do so
   Lookup - Finds the height of an aircraft in the sector

   Create - creates an empty sector
   Put - adds an aircraft to a sector with no constraint checks
   In-space - checks if an aircraft is already in a sector
   Occupied - checks if a specified height is available

   Enter (Sector, Call-sign, Height)  → Sector
   Leave (Sector, Call-sign)  → Sector
   Move (Sector, Call-sign, Height)  → Sector
   Lookup (Sector, Call-sign) → Height

   Create  → Sector
   Put (Sector, Call-sign, Height)  → Sector
   In-space (Sector, Call-sign)  → Boolean
   Occupied (Sector, Height)  → Boolean

   Enter (S, CS, H) =
       if      In-space (S, CS )  then  S exception (Aircraft already in sector)
       elsif   Occupied (S, H) then S exception (Height conflict)
       else    Put (S, CS, H)

   Leave (Create, CS) = Create exception (Aircraft not in sector)
   Leave (Put (S, CS1, H1), CS) =
       if CS = CS1 then S else Put (Leave (S, CS), CS1, H1)

   Move (S, CS, H) =
       if      S = Create then Create  exception (No aircraft in sector)
       elsif   not In-space (S, CS) then S  exception (Aircraft not in sector)
       elsif   Occupied (S, H) then S exception (Height conflict)
       else    Put (Leave (S, CS), CS, H)

   -- NO-HEIGHT is a constant indicating that a valid height cannot be returned

   Lookup (Create, CS) =  NO-HEIGHT  exception (Aircraft not in sector)
   Lookup (Put (S, CS1, H1), CS) =
       if CS = CS1  then H1 else Lookup (S, CS)

   Occupied (Create, H) = false
   Occupied (Put (S, CS1, H1), H) =
       if    (H1 > H and H1 - H ≤ 300) or (H > H1 and H - H1 ≤ 300)  then true
       else   Occupied (S, H)

   In-space (Create, CS) = false
   In-space (Put (S, CS1, H1), CS ) =
       if CS = CS1 then true else In-space (S, CS)
```

2. The specification of Move states that, if a Move operation is applied to an empty
    airspace (**Create**), the airspace is unchanged and an exception is raised to indic-
    ate that the specified aircraft is not in the airspace. When applied to an airspace
    which is populated using Put, the operation first checks (using In-space) if the
    aircraft is in the sector. If not, an exception is raised. If it is in the sector, it
    then checks that the specified height is available (using Occupied), raising an
    exception if there is already an aircraft at that height. If the space is available,
    the Move operation is equivalent to the specified aircraft leaving the airspace
    and being put into the sector at the new height.

9.3 Behavioural specification

The simple algebraic techniques described in the previous section are particularly suited to describing interfaces where the object operations are independent of the object state. That is, the results of applying an operation should not depend on the results of previous operations. Where this condition does not hold, algebraic techniques can become cumbersome. Furthermore, I think that algebraic descriptions of system behaviour are often artificial and difficult to understand.

An alternative approach to formal specification that has been more widely used in industrial projects is model-based specification. Model-based specification is an approach to formal specification where the system specification is expressed as a system state model. System operations are specified by defining how they affect the state of the system model. Hence, the behaviour of the system may be defined.

Mature notations for developing model-based specifications are VDM (Jones, 1980; Jones, 1986), B (Wordsworth, 1996) and Z (Hayes, 1987; Spivey, 1992). I use Z (pronounced Zed, not Zee) here. In Z, systems are modelled using sets and relations between sets. However, Z has augmented these mathematical concepts with constructs that specifically support software specification.

In an introduction to model-based specification, I can only give an overview of how a specification can be developed. A complete description of the Z notation would be longer than this chapter. Rather, I present some small examples to illustrate the technique and introduce notation as it is required. A full description of the Z notation is given in textbooks such as those by Diller (1994), Woodcock (Woodcock and Davies, 1996) and Jacky (1997).

Formal specifications can be difficult and tedious to read, especially when they are presented as large mathematical formulae. Understandably, this has inhibited many software engineers from investigating their potential in systems development. The designers of Z have paid particular attention to this problem. Specifications are presented as informal text supplemented with formal descriptions. The formal description is included as small, easy to read chunks (called schemas) which are distinguished from associated text using graphical highlighting. Schemas are used to introduce state variables and to define constraints and operations on the state. Schema operations include schema composition, schema renaming and schema hiding. These operations allow schemas to be manipulated. They are a powerful mechanism for system specification.

To be most effective, a formal specification must be supplemented by supporting, informal description. The Z schema presentation has been designed so that it stands out from surrounding text (Figure 9.9).

The schema signature defines the entities which make up the state of the system and the schema predicate sets out conditions which must always be true for these entities. Where a schema defines an operation, the predicate may set out pre- and post-conditions. The difference between these pre- and post-conditions defines the action specified in the operation schema.

Figure 9.9
The structure of
a Z schema

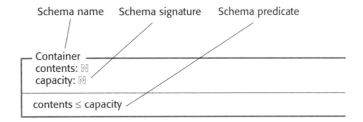

Figure 9.10 A block
diagram of an insulin
pump

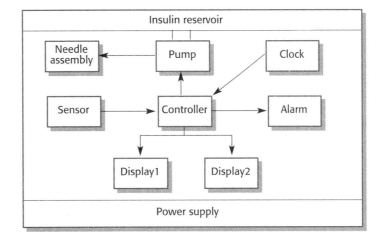

To illustrate the use of Z in the specification of a critical system, I use a simplified example of an insulin pump system used by diabetics. Diabetics cannot metabolise glucose naturally and require injections of genetically engineered insulin, a hormone which is essential for glucose metabolism. This system monitors the blood glucose level of diabetics and automatically injects insulin as required. I also use this example in Part 4 where I cover the development of critical systems.

Figure 9.10 illustrates the structure of this insulin pump. The blood glucose is monitored at regular intervals and, if it is increasing, insulin is injected to bring down the glucose level.

1. *Needle assembly*   Connected to pump. Component used to deliver insulin into the diabetic's body.

2. *Sensor*   Measures the level of glucose in the user's blood. The input from the sensor is represented by **reading?** in the formal specification.

3. *Pump*   Pumps insulin from a reservoir to the needle assembly. The value representing the number of increments of insulin to be administered is represented by **dose** in the formal specification.

4. *Controller*   Controls the entire system. Has on/off switch plus an override button plus a button to set the amount to be delivered. For simplicity, I haven't modelled this override capability in the formal description.

Figure 9.11 Insulin
pump schema

```
┌─ Insulin_pump ────────────────────────────────
│ reading? : ℕ
│ dose, cumulative_dose: ℕ
│ r0, r1, r2: ℕ      // used to record the last 3 readings taken
│ capacity: ℕ
│ alarm!: {off, on}
│ pump!: ℕ
│ display1!, display2!: STRING
├───────────────────────────────────────────────
│ dose ≤ capacity ∧ dose ≤ 5 ∧ cumulative_dose ≤ 50
│ capacity ≥ 40  ⇒  display1! = " "
│ capacity ≤ 39 ∧ capacity ≥ 10 ⇒  display1! = "Insulin low"
│ capacity ≤ 9 ⇒  alarm! = on ∧ display1! = "Insulin very low"
│ r2 = reading?
└───────────────────────────────────────────────
```

5. *Alarm*   Sounded if there is some problem. The value sent to the alarm is represented by alarm! in the following specification.

6. *Displays*   There are two displays. One shows the last measured blood sugar reading, the other displays status messages. These displays are represented by display1! and display2! in the formal specification.

7. *Clock*   Provides the controller with the current time.

Even for a small system like the insulin pump, the formal specification is fairly long. Although the basic operation of the system is simple, there are many possible alarm conditions that have to be considered. Therefore, I include only some of the principal schemas of the specification here and explain what they mean.

The basic schema which models the state of the insulin pump is shown in Figure 9.11. We can see here how the two basic parts of the schema are used. In the top part, names and types are declared and in the bottom part of the schema some conditions which are always true are set out.

The state is modelled using a number of state variables. By convention, names in Z which are followed by a ? are used to represent inputs and names which are followed by a ! represent outputs. However, these are simply naming conventions and the variables represented are treated in exactly the same way as any other state variables. The names declared in the schema are:

1. reading?   This is a natural number (i.e. a non-negative integer) that represents the reading from the blood glucose sensor. This is an input value.

2. dose, cumulative_dose   These are also natural numbers representing the dose of insulin to be delivered and the cumulative dose of insulin delivered over some period of time.

3. r0, r1, r2   These represent the last three readings and are used to compute the rate of change of blood glucose.

4. capacity   A natural number representing the capacity of the insulin reservoir in the pump.

5. alarm!   This output represents the alarm on the machine which signals some exceptional condition.

6. pump!   This is a natural number representing the control signals sent to the physical pump assembly. This is an output value.

7. display1!, display2!   These output values of type string represent two text displays on the insulin pump. One display (display1) is used to display text messages, the other (display2) is used to show the dose of insulin delivered.

The schema predicate defines invariants that are always true with an implicit 'and' between each line of the predicate. Conditions over the system state which are always true for the insulin pump are:

1. The dose must be less than or equal to the capacity. That is, it is impossible to deliver more insulin than is in the reservoir.

2. No single dose may be greater than 5 units of insulin and the total dose delivered in a time period must not exceed 50 units of insulin. These are safety conditions which I discuss in Chapter 17.

3. display1! shows a message indicating the status of the insulin reservoir. You can think of the Z phrase <logical expression 1> $\Rightarrow$ <logical expression 2> as being the same as **if** <logical expression 1> **then** <logical expression 2>. If the reservoir holds 40 units or more, then the display is blank, if between 10 and 40 units, then a warning is displayed, if less than 10 units, then an alarm is sounded and a more urgent warning is displayed.

The insulin pump operates by checking the blood glucose every 10 minutes and (simplistically) insulin is delivered if the rate of change of blood glucose is increasing. The amount of insulin to be delivered is computed as shown in Figure 9.12 which shows the DOSAGE schema. If the rate of change is static, a fixed amount of insulin is delivered. You can see from this schema that there are various different situations that affect the dose delivered. The details of these are not really relevant here.

I don't model the temporal behaviour of the system (i.e. the fact that the glucose sensor is checked every 10 minutes) using Z. Although this is certainly possible, it is rather clumsy and, in my view, an informal description actually communicates the specification more concisely than a formal specification.

Figure 9.12 illustrates a commonly used feature of Z, namely the delta schema. If a schema name is included in the declarations part, this is equivalent to including all the names declared in that schema in the declaration and the conditions are included in the predicate part. They are conjoined (anded) with the predicates that are declared in the DOSAGE schema. If the schema name is preceded by a Δ, this introduces a new set of values whose names are the same as those declared in the included schema but which are 'decorated' with a prime (') symbol. These primed values represent the values of the associated state variables after an operation.

Figure 9.12
DOSAGE schema

```
┌─ DOSAGE ──────────────────────────────────
│ ΔInsulin_Pump
├───────────────────────────────────────────
│ (
│ dose = 0 ∧
│     (
│             (( r1 ≥ r0) ∧ ( r2 = r1)) ∨
│             (( r1 > r0) ∧  (r2 ≤ r1)) ∨
│             (( r1 < r0) ∧  ((r1-r2) > (r0-r1)))
│     ) ∨
│ dose = 4 ∧
│     (
│             (( r1 ≤ r0) ∧ (r2=r1))  ∨
│             (( r1 < r0) ∧ ((r1-r2) ≤ (r0-r1)))
│     ) ∨
│ dose =(r2 - r1) * 4 ∧
│     (
│             (( r1 ≤ r0) ∧  (r2 > r1)) ∨
│             (( r1 > r0) ∧  ((r2 - r1) ≥ (r1 - r0)))
│     )
│ )
│ capacity' = capacity - dose
│ cumulative_dose' = cumulative_dose + dose
│ r0' = r1 ∧  r1' = r2
```

Figure 9.13
Output schemas

```
┌─ DISPLAY ─────────────────────────────────
│ ΔInsulin_Pump
├───────────────────────────────────────────
│ display2!' = Nat_to_string (dose) ∧
│ (reading? < 3 ⇒ display1!' = "Sugar low" ∨
│ reading? > 30 ⇒ display1!' = "Sugar high" ∨
│ reading? ≥ 3 and reading? ≤ 30 ⇒ display1!' = "OK")
```

```
┌─ ALARM ───────────────────────────────────
│ ΔInsulin_Pump
├───────────────────────────────────────────
│ ( reading? < 3 ∨ reading? > 30 ) ⇒ alarm!' = on ∨
│ ( reading? ≥  3 ∧ reading? ≤ 30 ) ⇒ alarm!' = off
```

Therefore, if an operation modifies a value val (say), the value after the operation is referred to as val'. The delta schema in DOSAGE therefore introduces the names capacity', cumulative_dose', etc.

The schemas modelling the outputs of the insulin pump device are shown in Figure 9.13. These model the machine displays and the built-in alarm. Again a delta schema is used to introduce the decorated variable names although, in this case, only the output variables are referenced. The DISPLAY schema states that display2! shows the dose which has been computed (Nat_to_string is a conversion function) and that display1! either shows a warning message or 'OK'. The ALARM schema sets out the conditions when the alarm is activated. It is switched on if the blood glucose reading is too low (less than 3) or too high (more than 30).

The predicates in all of the Z schemas must be consistent. That is, there should not be a statement made in one schema which contradicts the predicate in another schema. When there are inconsistencies, these often indicate specification problems and various mathematical techniques may be applied to a Z specification for inconsistency analysis. I won't go into these here. However, by examining the four Z schemas, we can see an inconsistency which I have deliberately introduced but which could plausibly be introduced by accident in a real specification.

In the overall Insulin_pump schema, it is stated that display1! should show the state of the insulin reservoir. However, the DISPLAY schema states that this display should show a different type of warning message or should indicate that the blood glucose level is within acceptable bounds. There is a conflict here. What therefore should be shown on this display? This has to be resolved by discussing the problem with medical experts and potential users of the system.

Highlighting problems which must be resolved is one of the main advantages of using a formal specification. With an informal specification, it is much easier to overlook these conflicts and they must be resolved at a later stage of the development process.

KEY POINTS

▶ Methods of formal system specification complement informal specification techniques. They may be used to refine a detailed but informal system requirements specification. They therefore help bridge the gap between requirements and design.

▶ Formal specifications are precise and unambiguous. They remove areas of doubt in a specification and avoid some of the problems of language misinterpretation. However, non-specialists may find formal specifications difficult to understand.

▶ The principal value of using formal methods in the software process is that it forces an analysis of the system requirements at an early stage. Correcting errors at this stage is cheaper than modifying a delivered system.

▶ Formal specification techniques are most applicable in the development of critical systems where safety, reliability and security are particularly important. They may also be used to specify standards.

▶ Algebraic techniques of formal specification are particularly suited to specifying interfaces where the interface is defined as a set of object classes or abstract data types. These techniques conceal the system state and specify the system in terms of relationships between the interface operations.

▶ Model-based techniques model the system using mathematical constructs such as sets and functions. They may expose the system state and this simplifies some types of behavioural specification.

FURTHER READING

IEEE Transactions on Software Engineering, January 1998. This issue of the journal includes a special section on the practical uses of formal methods in software engineering. It includes papers on both Z and LARCH.

'Formal methods: Promises and problems'. This article is a realistic discussion of the potential gains from using formal methods and the difficulties of integrating the use of formal methods into practical software development. (Luqi and J. Goguen, *IEEE Software,* 14(1), January 1997.)

'Strategies for incorporating formal specifications in software development'. In this article, the authors classify different approaches to formal specification. They suggest that the lack of methodological and tool support is a significant factor in the non-use of formal methods. (M. D. Fraser, K. Kumar and V. Vaishnavi, *Comm. ACM*, 37(10), October 1994.)

'A specifier's introduction to formal methods'. Although this is now more than 10 years old, fundamental specification techniques have not changed significantly. This is a good introductory article which describes the principles of formal specification and introduces a number of different approaches. (J. M. Wing, *IEEE Computer*, 23(9), September 1990.)

EXERCISES

9.1 Suggest why the architectural design of a system should precede the development of a formal specification.

9.2 You have been given the task of 'selling' formal specification techniques to a software development organisation. Outline how you would go about explaining the advantages of formal specifications to sceptical, practising software engineers.

9.3 Explain why it is particularly important to define sub-system interfaces in a precise way and why algebraic specification is particularly appropriate for sub-system interface specification.

9.4 An abstract data type representing a stack has the following operations associated with it:

New: Bring a stack into existence
Push: Add an element to the top of the stack
Top: Evaluate the element on top of the stack
Retract: Remove the top element from the stack and return the modified stack
Empty: True if there are no elements on the stack

Define this abstract data type using an algebraic specification.

9.5 In the example of a controlled airspace sector, the safety condition is that aircraft may not be within 300 m of height in the same sector. Modify the specification shown in Figure 9.8 to allow aircraft to occupy the same height in the sector so long as they are separated by at least 8 km of horizontal difference. You may ignore aircraft in adjacent sectors. *Hint*: You have to modify the constructor operations so that they include the aircraft position as well as its height. You also have to define an operation that, given two positions, returns the separation between them.

9.6 Bank teller machines rely on using information on the user's card giving the bank identifier, the account number and the user's personal identifier. They also derive account information from a central database and update that database on completion of a transaction. Using your knowledge of ATM operation, write Z schemas defining the state of the system, card validation (where the user's identifier is checked) and cash withdrawal.

9.7 Modify the Insulin_pump schema shown in Figure 9.11 and the DOSAGE schema shown in Figure 9.12 so that the system user may override the computed dose and specify the dose to be delivered. The safety conditions specified in the Insulin_pump schema should still hold. The fact that the system is operating in override mode should be indicated on a display.

9.8 You are a systems engineer and you are asked to suggest the best way to develop the safety-critical software for a heart pacemaker. You suggest formally specifying the system but your suggestion is rejected by your manager. You think his reasons are weak and based on prejudice. Is it ethical to develop the system using methods that you think are inadequate?

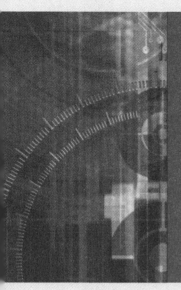

PART THREE

Design

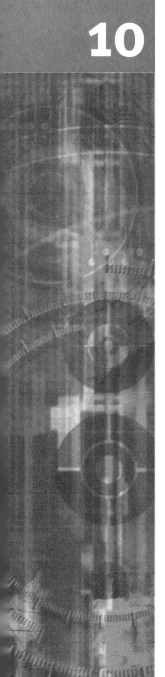

10 Architectural design

Objectives

The objective of this chapter is to introduce the concepts of software architecture and architectural design. When you have read the chapter, you will

❑ understand why the architectural design of software is important;

❑ understand that different models may be required to document a system architecture;

❑ have been introduced to a number of different types of software architecture covering system structure, control and modular decomposition;

❑ understand how domain-specific architectural models may be used as a basis for product-line architectures and to compare architectural implementations.

Contents

10.1 System structuring

10.2 Control models

10.3 Modular decomposition

10.4 Domain-specific architectures

Large systems are always decomposed into sub-systems that provide some related set of services. The initial design process of identifying these sub-systems and establishing a framework for sub-system control and communication is called *architectural design* and the output of this design process is a description of the *software architecture*.

The overall structure of the design process was discussed in section 3.4. In Figure 3.9, I presented a model of the design process where architectural design is the first stage in that process and represents a critical link between the design and requirements engineering processes. Ideally, a specification should not include any design information. In practice, this is unrealistic except for very small systems. Architectural decomposition is necessary to structure and organise the specification. A good example of this was introduced in Figure 2.4 which shows the architecture of an air traffic control system. The architectural model is often the starting point for the specification of the various parts of the system.

The architectural design process is concerned with establishing a basic structural framework for a system. It involves identifying the major components of the system and the communications between these components. Bass *et al.* (1998) discuss three advantages of explicitly designing and documenting a software architecture:

1. *Stakeholder communication*   The architecture is a high-level presentation of the system that may be used as a focus for discussion by a range of different stakeholders.

2. *System analysis*   Making the system architecture explicit at an early stage in the system development means that some analysis may be carried out. Architectural design decisions have a profound effect on whether or not the system can meet critical requirements such as performance, reliability and maintainability.

3. *Large-scale reuse*   A system architecture is a compact, manageable description of how a system is organised and how the components interoperate. The architecture can be transferred across systems with similar requirements and so can support large-scale software reuse. It may be possible to develop product-line architectures where the same architecture is used across a range of related systems. I discuss this in section 10.4 and in Chapter 14.

Different designers approach the architectural design process in different ways. The process used depends on application knowledge and on the skill and intuition of the system architect. However, the following activities are common to all architectural design processes:

1. *System structuring*   The system is structured into a number of principal sub-systems where a sub-system is an independent software unit. Communications between sub-systems are identified. This is covered in section 10.1.

2. *Control modelling*   A general model of the control relationships between the parts of the system is established. This is covered in section 10.2.

3. *Modular decomposition*   Each identified sub-system is decomposed into modules. The architect must decide on the types of module and their interconnections. This is covered in section 10.3.

These activities are usually interleaved rather than carried out in sequence. During any of these processes, you may have to develop the design in more detail to find out if architectural design decisions allow the system to meet its requirements.

There is no clear distinction between sub-systems and modules but I find it useful to think of them as follows:

1. *A sub-system* is a system in its own right whose operation does not depend on the services provided by other sub-systems. Sub-systems are composed of modules and have defined interfaces which are used for communication with other sub-systems.

2. *A module* is normally a system component that provides one or more services to other modules. It makes use of services provided by other modules. It is not normally considered to be an independent system. Modules are usually composed from a number of other, simpler system components.

The output of the architectural design process is an architectural design document. This consists of a number of graphical representations of the system models along with associated descriptive text. It should describe how the system is structured into sub-systems and how each sub-system is structured into modules. The different graphical models of the system present different perspectives on the architecture. Architectural models that may be developed may include:

1. A static structural model that shows the sub-systems or components that are to be developed as separate units.
2. A dynamic process model that shows how the system is organised into processes at run-time. This may be different from the static model.
3. An interface model that defines the services offered by each sub-system through their public interface.
4. Relationship models that show relationships such as data flow between the sub-systems.

A number of researchers have proposed the use of architectural description languages (ADLs) to describe system architectures. Bass *et al.* (1998) describe the main features of these languages. The basic elements of ADLs are components and connectors and they include rules and guidelines for well-formed architectures. However, like all specialised languages, they suffer from the disadvantage that they can only be understood by language experts – they are inaccessible to domain and application specialists. This makes them difficult to analyse from a practical perspective. I therefore think it likely they will only be used in a small number of applications. Rather, informal models and notations such as the UML will mostly be used for architectural description.

Architectural design may be based on a particular architectural model or style (Garlan and Shaw, 1993). An awareness of these models, their applications, strengths and weaknesses is important. I describe several different structural models, control models and decomposition models in this chapter.

However, the architectures of most large systems do not conform to a single model. Different parts of the system may be designed using different architectural models. Furthermore, in some cases, the system architecture may be a composite architecture. This is created by combining different architectural models. Designers must find the most appropriate model, then modify it according to the problem requirements. An example of this is shown in section 10.4 in the discussion of compiler architecture where a repository model is combined with a data-flow model.

The system architecture affects the performance, robustness, distributability and maintainability of a system. The particular style and structure chosen for an application may therefore depend on the non-functional system requirements:

1. *Performance* If performance is a critical requirement, this suggests that the architecture should be designed to localise critical operations within a small number of sub-systems with as little communication as possible between these sub-systems. This may mean using relatively large-grain rather than fine-grain components to reduce component communications.

2. *Security* If security is a critical requirement, this suggests that a layered structure for the architecture should be used with the most critical assets protected in the innermost layers and with a high level of security validation applied to these layers.

3. *Safety* If safety is a critical requirement, this suggests that the architecture should be designed so that safety-related operations are all located either in a single sub-system or in a small number of sub-systems. This reduces the costs and problems of safety validation and makes it possible to provide related protection systems.

4. *Availability* If availability is a critical requirement, this suggests that the architecture should be designed to include redundant components so that it is possible to replace and update components without stopping the system. Fault-tolerant system architectures for high-availability systems are covered in Chapter 18.

5. *Maintainability* If maintainability is a critical requirement, this suggests that the system architecture should be designed using fine-grain, self-contained components that may readily be changed. Producers of data should be separated from consumers and shared data structures should be avoided.

Obviously there is potential conflict between some of these architectures. For example, performance is improved by using large-grain components and maintainability by using fine-grain components. If both of these are important system requirements, some compromise solution must be found. As discussed above, this can sometimes be achieved by using different architectural styles for different parts of the system.

10.1 System structuring

The first phase of the architectural design activity is usually concerned with decomposing a system into a set of interacting sub-systems. At its most abstract level, an architectural design may be depicted as a block diagram where each box in the diagram represents a sub-system. Boxes within boxes indicate that the sub-system has itself been decomposed to sub-systems. Arrows mean that data and/or control is passed from sub-system to sub-system in the direction of the arrows. An architectural block diagram presents an overview of the system structure. It is generally understandable to the various engineers who may be involved in the system development process.

Figure 10.1 is a structural model of the architecture for a packing robot system. This robotic system can pack different kinds of object. It uses a vision sub-system to pick out objects on a conveyor, identifies the type of object and selects the right kind of packaging. It then moves objects from the delivery conveyor to be packaged. Packaged objects are placed on another conveyor. Other examples of architectural designs at this level are shown in Figures 2.2 and 2.4.

Figure 10.1 Block diagram of a packing robot control system

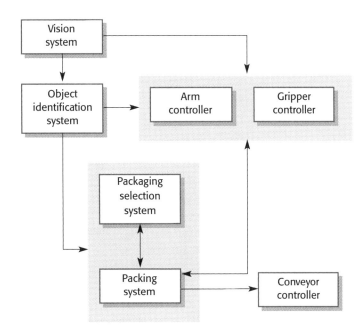

Bass *et al.* (1998) claim that simple box and line diagrams are not useful architectural representations as they do not show the nature of the relationships between system components nor their externally visible properties. From a software designer's perspective, this is absolutely correct. However, this type of model is effective for communication with system stakeholders and for project planning. As it is not cluttered with detail, stakeholders can relate to it and understand an abstract view of the system. It identifies the key sub-systems that are independently developed so managers can start assigning people to plan the development of these systems. Box and line diagrams should certainly not be the only architectural representation that is used; however, I think that they are one of a number of useful architectural models.

More specific models of the structure may be developed which show how sub-systems share data, how they are distributed and how they interface with each other. I discuss three of these standard models, namely a repository model, a client–server model and an abstract machine model in this section.

10.1.1 The repository model

Sub-systems making up a system must exchange information so that they can work together effectively. There are two fundamental ways in which this can be done.

1. All shared data is held in a central database that can be accessed by all sub-systems. A system model based on a shared database is sometimes called a *repository model*.

2. Each sub-system maintains its own database. Data is interchanged with other sub-systems by passing messages to them.

The majority of systems which use large amounts of data are organised around a shared database or repository. This model is therefore suited to applications where data is generated by one sub-system and used by another. Examples of this type of system include command and control systems, management information systems, CAD systems and CASE toolsets.

Figure 10.2 is an example of a CASE toolset architecture based on a shared repository. The first shared repository for CASE tools was probably developed in the early 1970s by a UK company called ICL to support their operating system development (McGuffin *et al.*, 1979). This model became more widely known when Buxton (1980) made proposals for the Stoneman environment to support the development of systems written in Ada. Since then, many CASE toolsets have been developed around a shared repository.

The advantages and disadvantages of a shared repository are as follows:

1. It is an efficient way to share large amounts of data. There is no need to transmit data explicitly from one sub-system to another.

Figure 10.2 The architecture of an integrated CASE toolset

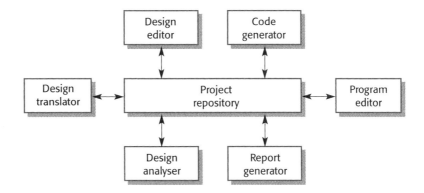

2. However, sub-systems must agree on the repository data model. Inevitably, this is a compromise between the specific needs of each tool. Performance may be adversely affected by this compromise. It may be difficult or impossible to integrate new sub-systems if their data models do not fit the agreed schema.

3. Sub-systems which produce data need not be concerned with how that data is used by other sub-systems.

4. However, evolution may be difficult as a large volume of information is generated according to an agreed data model. Translating this to a new model will certainly be expensive; it may be difficult or even impossible.

5. Activities such as backup, security, access control and recovery from error are centralised. They are the responsibility of the repository manager. Tools can focus on their principal function rather than be concerned with these issues.

6. However, different sub-systems may have different requirements for security, recovery and backup policies. The repository model forces the same policy on all sub-systems.

7. The model of sharing is visible through the repository schema. It is straightforward to integrate new tools given that they are compatible with the agreed data model.

8. However, it may be difficult to distribute the repository over a number of machines. Although it is possible to distribute a logically centralised repository, there may be problems with data redundancy and inconsistency.

In the above model, the repository is passive and control is the responsibility of the sub-systems using the repository. An alternative approach has been derived for AI systems that use a 'blackboard' model which triggers sub-systems when particular data becomes available. This is appropriate when the form of the repository data is less well structured. Decisions about which tool to activate can only be made when the data has been analysed. This model is discussed by Nii (1986).

The client–server model

The client–server architectural model is a distributed system model which shows how data and processing are distributed across a range of processors. The major components of this model are:

1. A set of stand-alone servers which offer services to other sub-systems. Examples of servers are print servers which offer printing services, file servers which offer file management services and a compile server which offers programming language compilation services.

2. A set of clients that call on the services offered by servers. These are normally sub-systems in their own right. There may be several instances of a client program executing concurrently.

3. A network which allows the clients to access these services. In principle, this is not really necessary as both the clients and the servers could run on a single machine. In practice, however, this model would not be used in such a situation.

Clients may have to know the names of the available servers and the services that they provide. However, servers need not know either the identity of clients or how many clients there are. Clients access the services provided by a server through remote procedure calls.

An example of a system built around a client–server model is shown in Figure 10.3. This is a multi-user hypertext system to provide a film and photograph library. In this system, there are several servers which manage and display the different types of media. Video frames need to be transmitted quickly and in synchrony but at relatively low resolution. They may be compressed in a store. Still pictures, however, must be sent at a high resolution. The catalogue must be able to deal with

Figure 10.3
The architecture of a film and picture library system

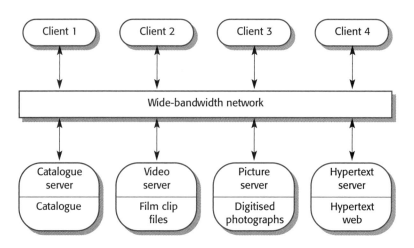

a variety of queries and provide links into the hypertext information systems. The client program is simply an integrated user interface to these services.

The client–server approach can be used to implement a repository-based system where the repository is provided as a system server. Sub-systems accessing the repository are clients. Normally, however, each sub-system manages its own data. Servers and clients exchange data for processing. This can result in performance problems when large amounts of data are exchanged. However, as faster networks are developed, this problem is becoming less significant.

The most important advantage of the client–server model is that it is a distributed architecture. Effective use can be made of networked systems with many distributed processors. It is easy to add a new server and integrate it with the rest of the system or to upgrade servers transparently without affecting other parts of the system. I discuss distributed architectures, including client–server architectures and distributed object architectures, in more detail in Chapter 11.

However, changes to existing clients and servers may be required to gain the full benefits of integrating a new server. There is no shared data model and sub-systems usually organise their data in different ways. This means that specific data models may be established for each server which allow its performance to be optimised. The lack of a shared reference model for data may mean that it is difficult to anticipate problems in integrating data from a new server. Each server must take responsibility for data management activities such as backup and recovery.

10.1.3 The abstract machine model

The abstract machine model of an architecture (sometimes called a layered model) models the interfacing of sub-systems. It organises a system into a series of layers each of which provides a set of services. Each layer defines an *abstract machine* whose machine language (the services provided by the layer) is used to implement the next level of abstract machine. For example, a common way to implement a language is to define an ideal 'language machine' and compile the language into code for this machine. A further translation step then converts this abstract machine code to real machine code.

A well-known example of this approach is the OSI reference model of network protocols (Zimmermann, 1980) which is discussed in section 10.4. Another influential example was proposed by Buxton (1980) who suggested a three-layer model for an Ada Programming Support Environment (APSE). Figure 10.4 has something in common with this and shows how a version management system might be integrated using this abstract machine approach.

The version management system relies on managing versions of objects and provides general configuration management facilities as discussed in Chapter 29. To support these configuration management facilities, it uses an object management system which provides information storage and management services for objects. This system uses a database system to provide basic data storage and services such as transaction management, rollback and recovery, and access control. The

Figure 10.4 Abstract
machine model of a
version management
system

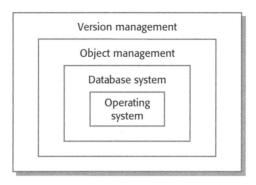

database management uses the underlying operating system facilities and filestore
in its implementation.

The layered approach supports the incremental development of systems. As a
layer is developed, some of the services provided by that layer may be made available to users. This architecture is also changeable and portable. If its interface is
preserved, a layer can be replaced by another layer. When layer interfaces change,
only the adjacent layer is affected. As layered systems localise machine dependencies in inner layers, they can be implemented on other computers relatively cheaply.
Only the inner, machine-dependent layers need be reimplemented.

A disadvantage of the layered approach is that structuring systems in this way
can be difficult. Basic facilities, such as file management, which are required by all
abstract machines, may be provided by inner layers. Services required by the user
may therefore require access to an abstract machine that is several levels beneath
the outermost layer. This subverts the model as an outer layer is no longer simply
dependent on its immediate predecessor.

Performance can also be a problem because of the multiple levels of command
interpretation which are sometimes required. If there are many layers, some overhead is always associated with layer management. To avoid these problems, applications may have to communicate directly with inner layers rather than use the facilities
provided in the abstract machine.

10.2 Control models

The models for structuring a system are concerned with how a system is decomposed into sub-systems. To work as a system, sub-systems must be controlled so
that their services are delivered to the right place at the right time. Structural models do not (and should not) include control information. Rather, the architect should
organise the sub-systems according to some control model which supplements the

structure model which is used. Control models at the architectural level are concerned with the control flow between sub-systems.

Two general approaches to control can be identified:

1. *Centralised control*   One sub-system has overall responsibility for control and starts and stops other sub-systems. It may also devolve control to another sub-system but will expect to have this control responsibility returned to it.

2. *Event-based control*   Rather than control information being embedded in a sub-system, each sub-system can respond to externally generated events. These events might come from other sub-systems or from the environment of the system.

Control models supplement structural models. All the above structural models may be realised using centralised or event-based control.

10.2.1   Centralised control

In a centralised control model, one sub-system is designated as the system controller and has responsibility for managing the execution of other sub-systems. Centralised control models fall into two classes depending on whether the controlled sub-systems execute sequentially or in parallel.

1. *The call–return model*   This is the familiar top-down subroutine model where control starts at the top of a subroutine hierarchy and, through subroutine calls, passes to lower levels in the tree. The subroutine model is only applicable to sequential systems.

2. *The manager model*   This is applicable to concurrent systems. One system component is designated as a system manager and controls the starting, stopping and coordination of other system processes. A process is a sub-system or module which can execute in parallel with other processes. A form of this model may also be applied in sequential systems where a management routine calls particular sub-systems depending on the values of some state variables. This is usually implemented as a case statement.

The call–return model is illustrated in Figure 10.5. The main program can call Routines 1, 2 and 3, Routine 1 can call Routines 1.1 or 1.2, Routine 3 can call Routines 3.1 or 3.2, etc. This is a model of the program dynamics. It is *not* a structural model; there is no need for Routine 1.1, for example, to be part of Routine 1.

This familiar model is embedded in programming languages such as Ada, Pascal and C. Control passes from a higher-level routine in the hierarchy to a lower-level routine. It then returns to the point where the routine was called. The currently executing subroutine has responsibility for control and can either call other routines or return control to its parent. It is poor programming style to return to some other point in the program.

Figure 10.5 The
call–return model
of control

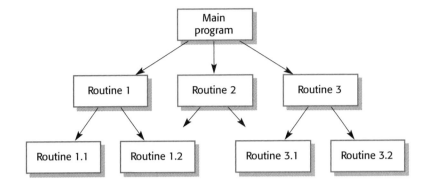

This call–return model may be used at the module level to control functions or objects. Subroutines in a programming language that are called by other subroutines are naturally functional. However, in many object-oriented systems, operations on objects (methods) are implemented as procedures or functions. For example, when a Java object requests a service from another object, it does so by calling an associated method.

The rigid and restricted nature of this model is both a strength and a weakness. It is a strength because it is relatively simple to analyse control flows and work out how the system will respond to particular inputs. It is a weakness because, as I discuss in Chapter 18, exceptions to normal operation are awkward to handle.

Figure 10.6 is an illustration of a centralised management model of control for a concurrent system. This model is often used in 'soft' real-time systems which do not have very tight time constraints. The central controller manages the execution of a set of processes associated with sensors and actuators. The building monitoring system discussed in Chapter 13 follows this model of control.

Figure 10.6
A centralised
control model for
a real-time system

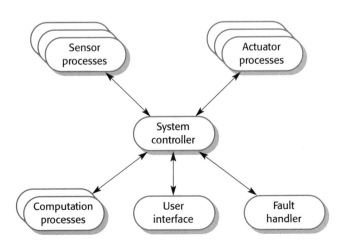

The system controller process decides when processes should be started or stopped depending on system state variables. It checks if other processes have produced information to be processed or to pass information to them for processing. The controller usually loops continuously, polling sensors and other processes for events or state changes. For this reason, this model is sometimes called an event-loop model.

10.2.2   Event-driven systems

In centralised control models, control decisions are usually determined by the values of some system state variables. By contrast, event-driven control models are driven by externally generated events. The term *event* in this context does not just mean a binary signal. It may be a signal which can take a range of values. The distinction between an event and a simple input is that the timing of the event is outside the control of the process which handles that event. A sub-system may need to access state information to handle these events but this state information does not usually determine the flow of control.

There are a variety of different types of event-driven systems which may be developed. These include spreadsheets where changing the value of a cell causes other cells to be modified, rule-based production systems as used in AI where a condition becoming true causes an action to be triggered, and active objects where changing a value of an object's attribute triggers some actions. Garlan *et al.* (1992) discuss these different types of system.

In this section, I discuss two event-driven control models:

1. *Broadcast models*   In these models, an event is, in principle, broadcast to all sub-systems. Any sub-system which can handle that event responds to it.

2. *Interrupt-driven models*   These are exclusively used in real-time systems where external interrupts are detected by an interrupt handler. They are then passed to some other component for processing.

Broadcast models are effective in integrating sub-systems distributed across different computers on a network. Interrupt-driven models are used in real-time systems with stringent timing requirements.

In a broadcast model (Figure 10.7), sub-systems register an interest in specific events. When these events occur, control is transferred to the sub-system which can handle the event. The distinction between this model and the centralised model shown in Figure 10.6 is that the control policy is not embedded in the event and message handler. Sub-systems decide which events they require and the event and message handler ensures that these events are sent to them.

All events could be broadcast to all sub-systems but this imposes a great deal of processing overhead. More often, the event and message handler maintains a register of sub-systems and the events of interest to them. Sub-systems generate

Figure 10.7
A control model
based on selective
broadcasting

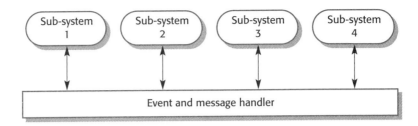

events indicating, perhaps, that some data is available for processing. The event handler detects the events, consults the event register and passes the event to those sub-systems which have declared an interest.

The event handler also usually supports point-to-point communication. A sub-system can explicitly send a message to another sub-system. There have been a number of variations of this model such as the Field environment (Reiss, 1990) and Hewlett-Packard's Softbench (Fromme and Walker, 1993). Both of these have been used to control tool interactions in software engineering environments. Object request brokers, discussed in Chapter 11, also support this model of control for distributed object communications.

The advantage of this broadcast approach is that evolution is relatively simple. A new sub-system to handle particular classes of events can be integrated by registering its events with the event handler. Any sub-system can activate any other sub-system without knowing its name or location. The sub-systems can be implemented on distributed machines. This distribution is transparent to other sub-systems.

The disadvantage of this model is that sub-systems don't know if or when events will be handled. When a sub-system generates an event it does not know which other sub-systems have registered an interest in that event. It is quite possible for different sub-systems to register for the same events. This may cause conflicts when the results of handling the event are made available.

Real-time systems that require externally generated events to be handled very quickly must be event-driven. For example, if a real-time system is used to control the safety systems in a car, it must detect a possible crash and, perhaps, inflate an airbag before the driver's head hits the steering wheel. To provide this rapid response to events, you have to use interrupt-driven control.

An interrupt-driven control model is illustrated in Figure 10.8. There are a known number of interrupt types with a handler defined for each type. Each type of interrupt is associated with the memory location where its handler's address is stored. When an interrupt of a particular type is received, a hardware switch causes control to be transferred immediately to its handler. This interrupt handler may then start or stop other processes in response to the event signalled by the interrupt.

This model should only be used in hard real-time systems where immediate response to some event is necessary. It may be combined with the centralised management model. The central manager handles the normal running of the system with interrupt-based control for emergencies.

Figure 10.8
An interrupt-driven
control model

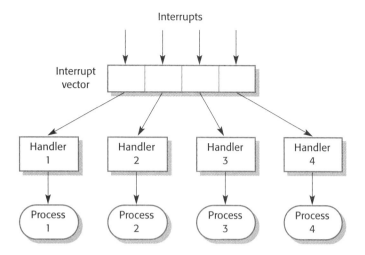

The advantage of this approach to control is that it allows very fast responses to events to be implemented. Its disadvantages are that it is complex to program and difficult to validate. It may be impossible to replicate patterns of interrupt timing during the system testing process. It can be difficult to change systems developed using this model if the number of interrupts is limited by the hardware. Once this limit is reached, no other types of event can be handled. This limitation can sometimes be circumvented by mapping several types of event onto a single interrupt, then leaving the handler to work out which event has occurred. However, this may be an impractical approach if a very fast response to the interrupt is required.

10.3 Modular decomposition

After a structural architecture has been designed, the next stage of the architectural design process is the decomposition of sub-systems into modules. There is not a rigid distinction between system decomposition and modular decomposition. The models discussed in section 10.1 could be applied at this level. However, the components in modules are usually smaller than sub-systems and this allows alternative decomposition models to be used.

I consider two models which may be used when decomposing a sub-system into modules:

1. *An object-oriented model* The system is decomposed into a set of communicating objects.

2. *A data-flow model*   The system is decomposed into functional modules which accept input data and transform it, in some way, to output data. This is also called a pipeline approach.

In the object-oriented model, modules are objects with private state and defined operations on that state. In the data-flow model, modules are functional transformations. In both cases, modules may be implemented as sequential components or as processes.

Designers should avoid, if possible, making premature decisions about concurrency. The advantage of avoiding a concurrent system design is that sequential programs are easier to design, implement, verify and test than parallel systems. Time dependencies between processes are hard to formalise, control and verify. It is best to decompose systems into modules, then decide during implementation whether these need to execute in sequence or in parallel.

10.3.1   Object models

An object-oriented model of a system architecture structures the system into a set of loosely coupled objects with well-defined interfaces. Objects call on the services offered by other objects. I have already introduced object models in Chapter 7 and I discuss them in more detail in Chapter 12.

Figure 10.9 is an example of an object-oriented architectural model of an invoice processing system. This system can issue invoices to customers, receive payments, issue receipts for these payments and reminders for unpaid invoices. I use the UML notation introduced in Chapter 7 where object classes have names and a set of associated attributes. Operations, if any, are defined in the lower part of the rounded rectangle representing the object. Dashed arrows indicate that an object uses the attributes or services provided by another object.

Figure 10.9
An object model
of an invoice
processing system

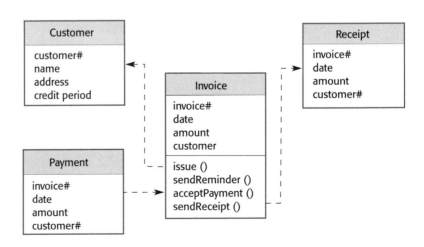

An object-oriented decomposition is concerned with object classes, their attributes and operations. When implemented, objects are created from these classes and some control model is used to coordinate object operations – in this particular example, the 'Invoice' class which has various associated operations which implement the system functionality. This class makes use of other classes representing customers, payments and receipts.

The advantages of the object-oriented approach are well known. Because objects are loosely coupled, the implementation of objects can be modified without affecting other objects. Objects are often representations of real-world entities so the structure of the system is readily understandable. Because these real-world entities are used in different systems, objects can be reused. Object-oriented programming languages have been developed which provide direct implementations of architectural components.

However, the object-oriented approach does have disadvantages. To use services, objects must explicitly reference the name and the interface of other objects. If an interface change is required to satisfy proposed system changes, the effect of that change on all users of the changed object must be evaluated. While objects may map cleanly to small-scale real-world entities, more complex entities are sometimes difficult to represent as objects.

10.3.2   Data-flow models

In a data-flow model, functional transformations process their inputs and produce outputs. Data flows from one to another and is transformed as it moves through the sequence. Each processing step is implemented as a transform. Input data flows through these transforms until converted to output. The transformations may execute sequentially or in parallel. The data can be processed by each transform item by item or in a single batch.

When the transformations are represented as separate processes, this model is sometimes called the pipe and filter model after the terminology used in the Unix system. The Unix system provides pipes which act as data conduits and a set of commands which are functional transformations. Systems which conform to this model can be implemented by combining Unix commands using pipes and the control facilities of the Unix shell. The term 'filter' is used because a transformation 'filters out' the data it can process from its input data stream.

Variants of this data-flow model have been in use since computers were first used for automatic data processing. When transformations are sequential with data processed in batches, this architectural model is a batch sequential model. This is a common architecture for some classes of data processing systems such as billing systems which generate large numbers of output reports that are derived from simple computations on a large number of input records.

An example of this type of system architecture is shown in Figure 10.10. An organisation has issued invoices to customers. Once a week, payments which have

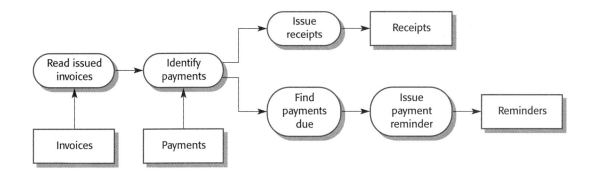

Figure 10.10
A data-flow model
of an invoice
processing system

been made are reconciled with the invoices. For those invoices that have been paid, a receipt is issued. For those invoices that have not been paid within the allowed payment time, a reminder is issued.

This is a model of only part of the invoice processing system; alternative transformations would be used for the issue of invoices. Notice the difference between this and its object-oriented equivalent discussed in the previous section. The object model is more abstract as it does not include information about the sequence of operations.

The advantages of this architecture are:

1. It supports the reuse of transformations.
2. It is intuitive in that many people think of their work in terms of input and output processing.
3. Evolving the system by adding new transformations is usually straightforward.
4. It is simple to implement either as a concurrent or a sequential system.

The principal disadvantage of the model stems from the need for a common format for data transfer which can be recognised by all transformations. Each transformation must either agree with its communicating transformations on the format of the data which will be processed, or a standard format for all data communicated must be imposed. The latter approach is the only feasible approach when transformations are stand-alone and reusable. In Unix, the standard format is simply a character sequence. Each transformation must parse its input and unparse its output to the agreed form. This increases system overhead and may mean that it is impossible to integrate transformations that use incompatible data formats.

Interactive systems are difficult to write using the data-flow model because of the need for a stream of data to be processed. While simple textual input and output can be modelled in this way, graphical user interfaces have more complex I/O formats and control which is based on events such as mouse clicks or menu selections. It is difficult to translate this into a form compatible with the data-flow model.

10.4 Domain-specific architectures

The above architectural models are general models. They can be applied to many different classes of application. As well as these general models, architectural models which are specific to a particular application domain may also be used. Although instances of these systems differ in detail, the common architectural structure can be reused when developing new systems. These architectural models are called *domain-specific architectures*.

There are two types of domain-specific architectural model:

1. *Generic models* which are abstractions from a number of real systems. They encapsulate the principal characteristics of these systems. For example, in real-time systems, there might be generic architectural models of different system types such as data collection systems, monitoring systems, etc.

2. *Reference models* which are more abstract and describe a larger class of systems. They are a way of informing designers about the general structure of that class of system. For example, Rockwell and Gera (1993) have proposed a reference model for software factories.

There is not, of course, a rigid distinction between these different types of model. Generic models can also sometimes serve as reference models. I make a distinction between them here because generic models may be reused directly in a design. Reference models are normally used to communicate domain concepts and compare possible architectures.

This reflects the derivation of these models. Generic models are usually derived 'bottom-up' from existing systems whereas reference models are derived 'top-down'. They are abstract system representations. Reference models do not necessarily reflect the actual architecture of existing systems in the domain.

10.4.1 Generic models

Perhaps the best known example of a generic architectural model is a compiler model. Thousands of compilers have been written. It is now generally agreed that compilers should include the following modules:

1. A lexical analyser which takes input language tokens and converts them to some internal form.
2. A symbol table, built by the lexical analyser, which holds information about the names and types used in the program.
3. A syntax analyser which checks the syntax of the language being compiled. It uses a defined grammar of the language and builds a syntax tree.

Figure 10.11
A data-flow model
of a compiler

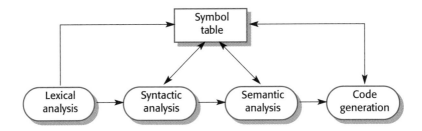

4. A syntax tree which is an internal structure representing the program being compiled.
5. A semantic analyser which uses information from the syntax tree and the symbol table to check the semantic correctness of the input program.
6. A code generator which 'walks' the syntax tree and generates machine code.

Other components might also be included which transform the syntax tree to improve efficiency and remove redundancy from the generated machine code.

The components which make up a compiler can be organised according to different architectural models. As Garlan and Shaw point out (1993), compilers can be implemented using a composite model. A data-flow architecture may be used, with the symbol table acting as a repository for shared data. The phases of lexical, syntactic and semantic analysis are organised sequentially as shown in Figure 10.11.

This model is still widely used. It is effective in batch environments where programs are compiled and executed without user interaction. However, it is less effective when the compiler is to be integrated with other language processing tools such as a structured editing system, an interactive debugger, a program prettyprinter, etc. The generic system components can then be organised in a repository-based model as shown in Figure 10.12.

Figure 10.12
The repository
model of a language
processing system

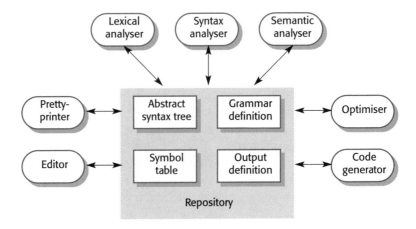

In this model of a compiler, the symbol table and syntax tree act as a central information repository. Tools or tool fragments communicate through it. Other information such as the grammar definition and the definition of the output format for the program have been taken out of the tools and into the repository.

There are, in practice, a very large number of domain-specific architectural models. Some further examples of generic process architectures for real-time systems are illustrated in Chapter 13.

However, relatively few generic, domain-specific models are publicly available. Organisations which develop these models see them as valuable intellectual property which they need for future system development. They often represent the architecture of a product line where related products are implemented using the same basic architecture. For example, printer drivers for printers with different capabilities (speed, paper options, etc.) may all use the same fundamental architecture. I discuss product-line architectures in Chapter 14.

10.4.2 Reference architectures

Generic architectural models reflect the architecture of existing systems. In contrast, reference models are usually derived from a study of the application domain. They represent an idealised architecture which includes all the features that systems might incorporate.

Reference architectures may be used as a basis for system implementation. This was the intention behind the OSI reference model (Zimmermann, 1980) for open systems interconnection. The model was intended as a standard. If a system conformed to the model, it should be able to communicate with other conformant systems. Thus, a stock control system in a supermarket which followed the OSI model could exchange data directly with the supplier's ordering system.

However, reference models should not normally be considered as a route to implementation. Rather, their principal function is to serve as a means of comparing different systems in a domain. A reference model provides a vocabulary for comparison. It acts as a standard, against which systems can be evaluated.

The OSI model is a seven-layer model for open systems interconnection. The model is illustrated in Figure 10.13. The exact functions of the different layers are not important here. In essence, the lower layers are concerned with physical interconnection, the middle layers with data transfer and the upper layers with the transfer of semantically meaningful application information such as standardised documents, etc.

The designers of the OSI model had the very practical objective of defining a standard so that conformant systems could communicate with each other. Each layer should only depend on the layer beneath it. As technology developed, a layer could be transparently reimplemented without affecting the systems using other layers.

In practice, however, the problems of the layered approach to architectural modelling have compromised this objective. Because of the vast differences between networks, simple interconnection may be impossible. Although the functional

Figure 10.13
The OSI reference
model architecture

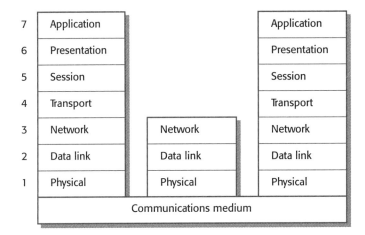

characteristics of each layer are well defined, the non-functional characteristics are not defined. System developers have to implement their own higher-level facilities and skip layers in the model. Alternatively, they have to design non-standard features to improve system performance.

Consequently, the transparent replacement of a layer in the model is hardly ever possible. However, this does not negate the usefulness of the model as it provides a basis for the abstract structuring and the systematic implementation of communications between systems.

Other reference models which have been proposed include a model for CASE environments (ECMA, 1991) and a model for software factories (Rockwell and Gera, 1993). Some design patterns (Gamma *et al.*, 1995) may also be considered as reference architectures. These are discussed in Chapter 14.

KEY POINTS

▶ The software architecture is the fundamental framework for structuring the system. Different architectural models such as a structural model, a control model and a decomposition model may be developed during architectural design.

▶ Large systems rarely conform to a single architectural model. They are heterogeneous and incorporate different models at different levels of abstraction.

▶ System decomposition models include repository models, client–server models and abstract machine models. Repository models share data through a common store. Client–server models usually distribute data. Abstract machine models are layered, with each layer implemented using the facilities provided by its foundation layer.

▶ Control models include centralised control and event models. In centralised models, control decisions are made depending on the system state; in event models external events control the system.

▶ Modular decomposition models include data-flow and object models. Data-flow models are functional whereas object models are based on loosely coupled entities that maintain their own state and operations.

▶ Domain-specific architectural models are abstractions over an application domain. Domain-specific models may be generic models which are constructed bottom-up from existing systems or reference models which are idealised, abstract models of the domain.

FURTHER READING

Software architecture is a hot topic and there are a large number of books available. Books that I have found useful are:

Software Architecture in Practice. This is a practical discussion of software architectures that does not oversell the approach and that provides a clear business rationale why architectures are important. (L. Bass, P. Clements and R. Kazman, 1998, Addison-Wesley.)

Systems Engineering: Coping with Complexity. Chapter 4 of this book on systems engineering discusses the architectural design of systems rather than simply software. This is a refreshingly different perspective. (R. Stevens, P. Brook, K. Jackson and S. Arnold, 1998, Prentice-Hall.)

Software Architecture: Perspectives on an Emerging Discipline. This was the first book on software architecture and has a good discussion on different architectural styles. (M. Shaw and D. Garlan, 1996, Prentice-Hall.)

EXERCISES

10.1 Explain why it may be necessary to design the system architecture before the specifications are written.

10.2 Construct a table showing the advantages and disadvantages of the different structural models discussed in this chapter.

10.3 Giving reasons for your answer, suggest an appropriate structural model for the following systems:

- an automated ticket issuing system used by passengers at a railway station;
- a computer-controlled video conferencing system which allows video, audio and computer data to be visible to several participants at the same time;
- a robot floor cleaner which is intended to clean relatively clear spaces such as corridors. The cleaner must be able to sense walls and other obstructions.

10.4 Design an architecture for the above systems based on your choice of model. Make reasonable assumptions about the system requirements.

10.5 Explain why a call–return model of control is not usually suitable for real-time systems which control some process.

10.6 Giving reasons for your answer, suggest an appropriate control model for the following systems:

- a batch processing system which takes information about hours worked and pay rates and prints salary slips and bank credit transfer information;
- a set of software tools which are produced by different vendors but which must work together;
- a television controller which responds to signals from a remote control unit.

10.7 Discuss their advantages and disadvantages as far as distributability is concerned of the data-flow model and the object model. Assume that both single machine and distributed versions of an application are required.

10.8 You are given two integrated CASE toolsets and are asked to compare them. Explain how you could use a reference model for CASE (Brown *et al.*, 1992) to make this comparison.

10.9 Should there be a separate profession of 'software architect' whose role is to work independently with a customer to design a software architecture? This would then be implemented by some software company. What might be the difficulties of establishing such a profession?

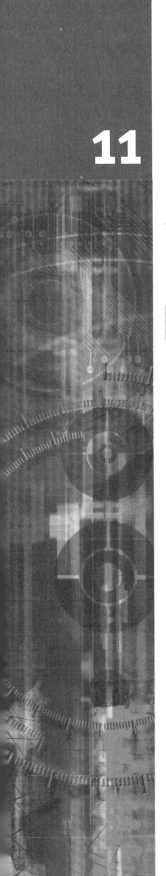

11 Distributed systems architectures

Objectives

The objective of this chapter is to describe, in more detail, the architectures of distributed software systems. When you have read this chapter, you will:

❏ understand the main advantages and disadvantages of distributed systems architectures;

❏ understand different approaches to the development of client–server architectures;

❏ understand the differences between client–server and distributed object architectures;

❏ understand the concept of an object request broker and the principles underlying the CORBA standards.

Contents

11.1   Multiprocessor architectures
11.2   Client–server architectures
11.3   Distributed object architectures
11.4   CORBA

Virtually all large computer-based systems are now distributed systems. A distributed system is a system where the information processing is distributed over several computers rather than confined to a single machine. Obviously, the engineering of distributed systems has a great deal in common with the engineering of any other software but there are specific issues that have to be taken into account when designing this type of system. I have already introduced some of these issues in the introduction to client–server architectures in Chapter 10 and I cover them in more detail here.

Software engineers must be aware of these design issues because distributed systems are so widely used. Until relatively recently, most large systems were centralised systems that ran on a single mainframe with terminals attached to it. These terminals had little or no processing capability, so all information processing was the responsibility of the mainframe computer. Designers did not have to think about issues of distributed processing. Now, there are three major types of system:

1. Personal systems that are not distributed and that are designed to run on a personal computer or workstation. Examples of this type of system include word processors, spreadsheets, graphics systems, etc.

2. Embedded systems that run on a single processor or on an integrated group of processors. Examples of this type of system include control systems for domestic devices, instrument management systems, etc.

3. Distributed systems where the system software runs on a loosely integrated group of cooperating processors linked by a network. Examples of such systems include bank ATM systems, booking systems, groupware systems, etc.

Currently, there are fairly distinct boundaries between these types of system but these boundaries are likely to blur in future. As high-speed wireless networking becomes widely available, it will be possible to dynamically integrate products with embedded systems such as electronic organisers with more general systems.

Coulouris *et al.* (1994) identify six important characteristics of distributed systems:

1. *Resource sharing*   A distributed system allows the sharing of hardware and software resources such as disks, printers, files, compilers, etc. that are associated with different computers on a network. Obviously, resource sharing is also possible on multi-user systems but in this case all resources must be provided and managed by a central computer.

2. *Openness*   The openness of a system is the extent to which it can be extended by adding new non-proprietary resources to it. Distributed systems are open systems that normally include hardware and software from different vendors.

3. *Concurrency*   In a distributed system, several processes may operate at the same time on different computers on the network. These processes may (but need not) communicate with each other during their normal operation.

4. *Scalability*   In principle at least, distributed systems are scalable in that the capabilities of the system can be increased by adding new resources to cope with new demands on the system. In practice, scalability may be limited by the network linking the individual computers in the system. If many new computers are added then the network capacity may be inadequate.

5. *Fault tolerance*   The availability of several computers and the potential for replicating information mean that distributed systems can be tolerant of some hardware and software failures (see Chapter 18). In most distributed systems, a degraded service can be provided when failures occur; complete loss of service tends to occur only when there is a network failure.

6. *Transparency*   Transparency is the concealment from the user of the distributed nature of the system. A system design goal may be that users have completely transparent access to resources and have no need to know anything about the distribution of the system. However, in many cases giving the users some knowledge of the system organisation allows them to make better use of the resources.

Of course, distributed systems do have some disadvantages:

*   *Complexity*   Distributed systems are more complex than centralised systems. This makes it more difficult to understand their emergent properties and to test these systems. For example, rather than the performance of the system being dependent on the execution speed of one processor, it depends on the network bandwidth and the speed of the different processors on the network. Moving resources from one part of the system to another can radically affect the system's performance.

*   *Security*   The system may be accessed from several different computers and the traffic on the network may be subject to eavesdropping. This makes it more difficult to manage the security in a distributed system.

*   *Manageability*   The different computers in a system may be of different types and may run different versions of the operating system. Faults in one machine may propagate to other machines with unexpected consequences. These mean that more effort is required to manage and maintain the system in operation.

*   *Unpredictability*   As all users of the WWW know, distributed systems are unpredictable in their response. The response depends on the overall load on the system, its organisation and the network load. As all of these may change over a short time, the time taken to respond to a user request may vary dramatically from one request to another.

As well as discussing the advantages and disadvantages of distributed systems, Coulouris *et al.* (1994) identify the critical design issues for distributed systems. These are shown in Figure 11.1. I focus in this chapter on distributed software

Figure 11.1 Issues in
distributed systems
design

Design issue	Description
Resource identification	The resources in a distributed system are spread across different computers and a naming scheme has to be devised so that users can discover and refer to the resources that they need. An example of such a naming scheme is the URL (Uniform Resource Locator) that is used to identify WWW pages. If a meaningful and universally understood identification scheme is not used then many of these resources will be inaccessible to system users.
Communications	The universal availability of the Internet and the efficient implementation of Internet TCP/IP communication protocols means that, for most distributed systems, these are the most effective way for the computers to communicate. However, where there are specific requirements for performance, reliability, etc. alternative approaches to communications may be used.
Quality of service	The quality of service offered by a system reflects its performance, availability and reliability. It is affected by a number of factors such as the allocation of processes to processes in the system, the distribution of resources across the system, the network and the system hardware and the adaptability of the system.
Software architectures	The software architecture describes how the application functionality is distributed over a number of logical components and how these components are distributed across processors. Choosing the right architecture for an application is essential to achieve the desired quality of service.

architectures as I think that this is most relevant to software engineering. Specialised books on distributed systems cover these other topics.

The challenge for distributed systems designers is to design the software and hardware to provide desirable distributed system characteristics and, at the same time, minimise the problems that are inherent in these systems. To do so, you need to understand the advantages and disadvantages of different distributed systems architectures. I cover two generic types of distributed systems architecture here:

1. *Client–server architectures* In this approach, the system may be thought of as a set of services that are provided to clients that make use of these services. Servers and clients are treated differently in these systems.

2. *Distributed object architectures* In this case, there is no distinction between servers and clients and the system may be thought of as a set of interacting objects whose location is irrelevant. There is no distinction between a service provider and a user of these services.

The different components in a distributed system may be implemented in different programming languages and may execute on completely different types of processor. Models of data, information representation and protocols for communication may all be different. A distributed system therefore requires some software that can manage these diverse parts, ensure that they can communicate and exchange data. The term *middleware* is used to refer to this software – it sits in the middle between the different distributed components of the system.

Bernstein (1996) summarises different types of middleware that are available to support distributed computing. Middleware is general-purpose software that is usually bought off-the-shelf rather than written specially by application developers. Examples of middleware are software for managing communications with databases, transaction managers, data converters, communication controllers, etc. I describe distributed systems frameworks, a very important class of middleware, later in this chapter.

Distributed systems are usually developed using an object-oriented approach. These systems are made up of loosely integrated, independent parts each of which may interact directly with users or with other parts of the system. Parts of the system may have to respond to independent events. Software objects reflect these characteristics so are a natural abstraction for distributed systems components. If you are not familiar with the concept of objects, I recommend that you read Chapter 12 and then come back to this chapter.

11.1 Multiprocessor architectures

The simplest model of a distributed system is a multiprocessor system where the system consists of a number of different processes that may (but need not) execute on separate processors. This model is common in large real-time systems. As I discuss in Chapter 13, these systems collect information, make decisions using this information, then send signals to actuators that modify the system's environment.

Logically, the processes concerned with information collection, decision making and actuator control could all run on a single processor under the control of a scheduler. Using multiple processors improves the performance and resilience of the system. The distribution of processes to processors may be pre-determined (this is common in critical systems) or may be under the control of a despatcher that decides which process to allocate to each processor.

An example of this type of system is shown in Figure 11.2. This is a simplified model of a traffic control system. A set of distributed sensors collect information on the traffic flow and process this locally before sending it to a control room. Operators make decisions using this information and give instructions to a separate traffic light control process. In this example, there are separate logical processes for managing the sensors, the control room and the traffic lights. These logical processes may be single processes or a group of processes. In this example, they run on separate processors.

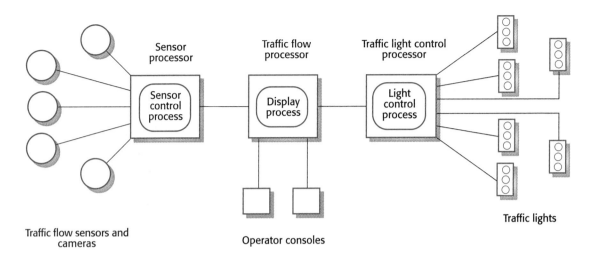

Figure 11.2
A multiprocessor
traffic control system

Software systems composed of multiple processes are not necessarily distributed systems. If more than one processor is available then distribution can be implemented but the system designers need not always consider distribution issues during the design process. The design approach for this type of system is essentially that for real-time systems as discussed in Chapter 13.

11.2 Client–server architectures

Figure 11.3 A client–
server system

I have already introduced the concept of client–server architectures in Chapter 10. In a client–server architecture, an application is modelled as a set of services that are provided by servers and a set of clients that use these services (Orfali and

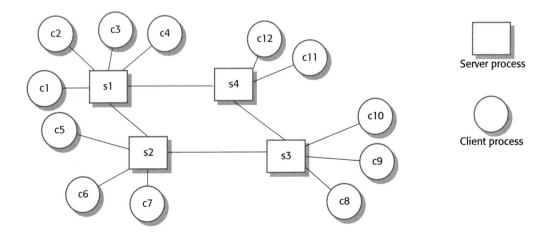

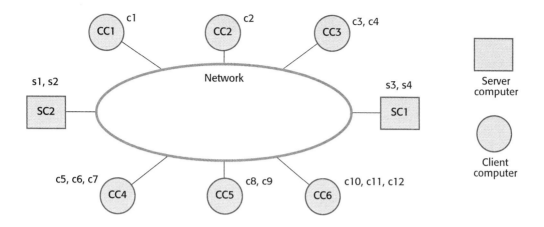

Figure 11.4
Computers in a
client–server network

Harkey, 1998). Clients need to be aware of the servers that are available but usually do not know of the existence of other clients. Clients and servers are different processes, as shown in Figure 11.3 which is a logical model of a distributed client–server architecture.

There is not necessarily a 1:1 mapping between processes and processors in the system. Figure 11.4 shows the physical architecture of a system with six client computers and two server computers. These can run the client and server processes shown in Figure 11.3. In general, when I talk of clients and servers I mean these logical processes rather than the physical computers on which these processes execute.

The design of client–server systems should reflect the logical structure of the application that is being developed. One way to look at an application is illustrated in Figure 11.5 which shows an application structured into three layers. The presentation layer is concerned with presenting information to the user and with all user interaction. The application processing layer is concerned with implementing the logic of the application and the data management layer is concerned with all database operations. In centralised systems these need not be clearly separated. However, when you are designing a distributed system, you should make a clear

Figure 11.5
Application layers

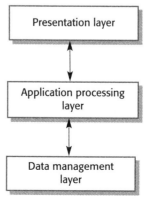

Figure 11.6 Thin
and fat clients

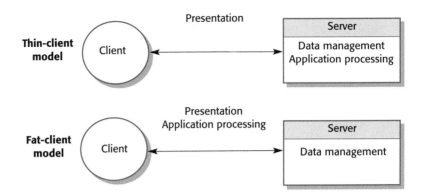

Figure 11.6 Thin
and fat clients

distinction between them as it then becomes possible to distribute each layer to a
different computer.

The simplest client–server architecture is called a two-tier client–server architecture where an application is organised as a server (or multiple identical servers)
and a set of clients. As illustrated in Figure 11.6, two-tier client–server architectures
can take two forms:

1. *Thin-client model*   In a thin-client model, all of the application processing and
   data management is carried out on the server. The client is simply responsible
   for running the presentation software.

2. *Fat-client model*   In this model, the server is only responsible for data management. The software on the client implements the application logic and the
   interactions with the system user.

A thin-client, two-tier architecture is the simplest approach to use when centralised
legacy systems (see Chapter 26) are evolved to a client–server architecture. The user
interface for these systems is migrated to PCs and the application itself acts as a
server and handles all application processing and data management. A thin-client
model may also be implemented when the clients are simple network devices rather
than PCs or workstations. The network device runs an Internet browser and the user
interface implemented through that system.

A major disadvantage of the thin-client model is that it places a heavy processing load on both the server and the network. The server is responsible for all computation and this may involve the generation of significant network traffic between
the client and the server. There is a lot of processing power available in modern
PCs and this is largely unused in the thin-client approach.

By contrast, the fat-client model makes use of this available processing power
and distributes both the application logic processing and the presentation to the client.
The server is essentially a transaction server that manages all database transactions.
A well-known example of this type of architecture is banking ATM systems where
the ATM is the client and the server is a mainframe running the customer account
database.

Figure 11.7
A client–server
ATM system

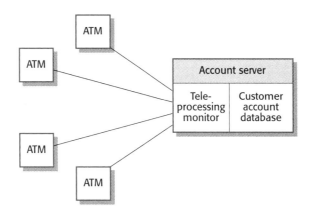

This ATM network system is illustrated in Figure 11.7. Notice that the ATMs do not connect directly to the customer database but connect to a teleprocessing monitor. A teleprocessing (TP) monitor is a middleware system that organises communications with remote clients and serialises client transactions for processing by the database. Using serial transactions means that the system can recover from faults without corrupting the system data.

While the fat-client model distributes processing more effectively than a thin-client model, system management is more complex. Application functionality is spread across many different computers. When the application software has to be changed, this involves reinstallation on every client computer. This can be a major cost if there are hundreds of clients in the system.

The advent of Java and downloadable applets has allowed the development of a client–server model that is somewhere between the thin-client and the fat-client model. Some of the application processing software may be downloaded to the client as Java applets, thus relieving the load on the server. The user interface is built using a web browser that can run Java applets. However, web browsers from different suppliers and even different versions of web browsers from the same supplier do not always display in the same way. Earlier versions on older computers may not be able to run Java. Therefore, you should only use this approach when you are confident that all system users have compatible, Java-enabled browsers.

The essential problem with a two-tier client–server approach is that the three logical layers – presentation, application processing, data management – must be mapped onto two computer systems. There may be either problems with scalability and performance if the thin-client model is chosen or problems of system management if the fat-client model is used. To avoid these problems, an alternative approach is to use a three-tier client–server architecture (Figure 11.8). In this architecture, the presentation, the application processing and the data management are logically separate processes.

A three-tier client–server software architecture does not necessarily mean that there are three computer systems connected to the network. A single server computer can run both the application processing and the application data management

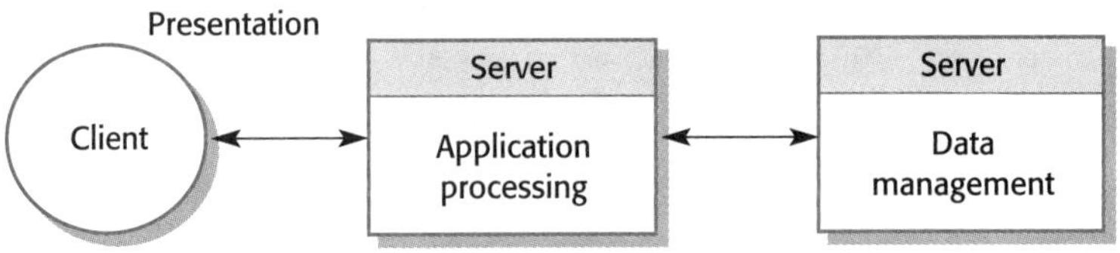

Figure 11.8 A three-tier client–server architecture

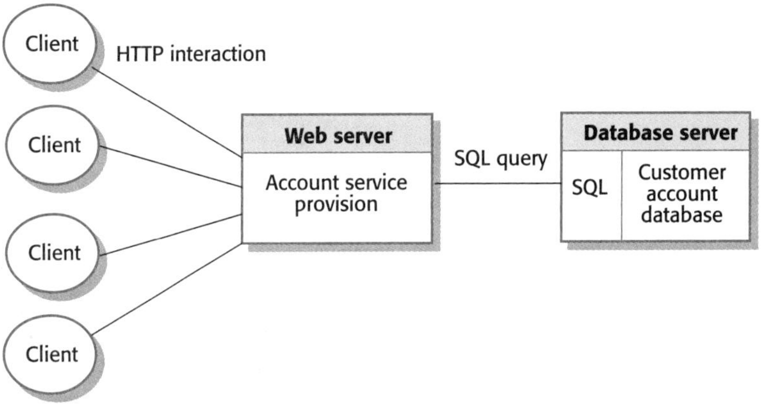

Figure 11.9
The distribution architecture of an Internet banking system

as separate, logical servers. However, if demands rise, it is relatively straightforward to separate the application processing and the data management and execute these on separate processors.

An Internet banking system is an example of the type of system that may be implemented using a three-tier client–server architecture. The bank's customer database (usually hosted on a mainframe computer) provides data management services, a web server provides the application services such as facilities to transfer cash, generate statements, pay bills, etc. and the user's own computer with an Internet browser is the client. This is illustrated in Figure 11.9. This system is scalable as it is relatively easy to add new web servers as the number of customers increase.

The use of a three-tier architecture in this case allows the information transfer between the web server and the database server to be optimised. The communications between these systems do not have to be based on the Internet standards but can use faster, lower-level communications protocols. Efficient middleware that supports database queries in SQL (Structured Query Language) is used to handle information retrieval from the database.

In some cases, it is appropriate to extend the three-tier client–server model to a multi-tier variant where additional servers are added to the system. Multi-tier systems may be used where applications need to access and use data from different databases. In this case, an integration server is positioned between the application server and the database servers that are accessed. The integration server collects the distributed data and presents it to the application as if it was available in a single database.

Three-tier client–server architectures and multi-tier variants that distribute the application processing across several servers are inherently more scalable than two-tier architectures. Network traffic is reduced in contrast with thin-client two-tier architectures.

Architecture	Applications
Two-tier C/S architecture with thin clients	Legacy system applications where separating application processing and data management is impractical Computationally intensive applications such as compilers with little or no data management Data-intensive applications (browsing and querying) with little or no application processing
Two-tier C/S architecture with fat clients	Applications where application processing is provided by COTS (e.g. Microsoft Excel) on the client Applications where computationally intensive processing of data (e.g. data visualisation) is required Applications with relatively stable end-user functionality used in an environment with well-established system management
Three-tier or multi-tier C/S architecture	Large-scale applications with hundreds or thousands of clients Applications where both the data and the application are volatile Applications where data from multiple sources are integrated

Figure 11.10
Use of different
client–server
architectures

The application processing is the most volatile part of the system and it can be easily updated because it is centrally located. Processing, in some cases, may be distributed between the application logic and the data management servers, thus leading to more rapid response to client requests.

Designers of client–server architectures must take a number of factors into account when choosing the most appropriate architecture. Situations where the client–server architectures that I have discussed are likely to be appropriate are shown in Figure 11.10.

11.3 Distributed object architectures

In the client–server model of a distributed system, clients and servers are different. Clients receive services from servers and not from other clients; servers may act as clients by receiving services from other servers but they do not request services from clients; clients must know the services that are offered by specific servers and must know how to contact these servers. This model works well for many types of application. However, it limits the flexibility of system designers in that they must decide where services are to be provided. They must also plan for scalability and so provide some means for the load on servers to be distributed as more clients are added to the system.

A more general approach to distributed system design is to remove the distinction between client and server and to design the system architecture as a distributed object architecture. In a distributed object architecture (Figure 11.11) the fundamental system components are objects that provide an interface to a set of services that

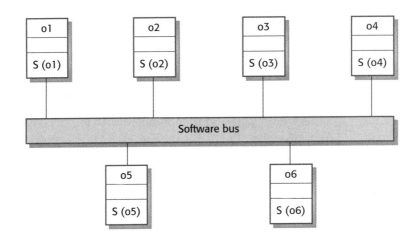

Figure 11.11
Distributed object
architecture

they provide. Other objects call on these services with no logical distinction between a client (a receiver of a service) and a server (a provider of a service).

Objects may be distributed across a number of computers on a network and communicate through middleware. By analogy with a hardware bus that allows different cards to be plugged into it and supports communication between hardware devices, this middleware may be thought of as a software bus. It provides a set of services that allow objects to communicate and to be added and removed from the system. This middleware is called an object request broker. Its role is to provide a seamless interface between objects. I discuss object request brokers in section 11.4.

The advantages of this model of a distributed system architecture are:

- It allows the system designer to delay decisions on where and how services should be provided. Service-providing objects may execute on any node of the network. Therefore, the distinction between fat- and thin-client models becomes irrelevant as there is no need to decide in advance where application logic objects are located.

- It is a very open system architecture that allows new resources to be added to it as required. As I discuss in the following section, software bus standards have been developed and implemented that allow objects written in different programming languages to communicate and to provide services to each other.

- The system is flexible and scalable. Different instances of the system with the same service provided by different objects or by replicated objects can be created to cope with different system loads. New objects can be added as the load on the system increases without disrupting other system objects.

- It is possible to reconfigure the system dynamically with objects migrating across the network as required. This may be important where there are fluctuating patterns of demand on services. A service-providing object can migrate to the same processor as service-requesting objects, thus improving the performance of the system.

A distributed object architecture can be used in two ways in system design:

1. As a logical model that allows you to structure and organise the system. In this case, you think about how to provide application functionality solely in terms of services and combinations of services. You then work out how to provide these services using a number of distributed objects. At this level, the objects that you design are usually large-grain objects (sometimes called business objects) that provide domain-specific services. For example, in a retail application there may be business objects concerned with stock control, customer communications, goods ordering, etc. This logical model can, of course, then be realised as an implementation model.

2. As a flexible approach to the implementation of client–server systems. In this case, the logical model of the system is a client–server model but both clients and servers are realised as distributed objects communicating through a software bus. This makes it possible to change the system easily, for example, from a two-tier to a multi-tier system. In this case, the server or the client may not be implemented as a single distributed object but may consist of a number of smaller objects that each provide specialised services.

An example of a type of system where a distributed object architecture might be appropriate is a data mining system that looks for relationships between the data that is stored in a number of different databases (Figure 11.12). An example of a data mining application might be where a retail business has different types of shop (say food stores and hardware stores) and they try to find relationships between the purchases of different types of food and different types of hardware. For instance, people who buy baby food may also buy particular types of wallpaper. With this knowledge, the business can then specifically target baby-food customers with combined offers.

Figure 11.12
The distribution
architecture of a
data mining system

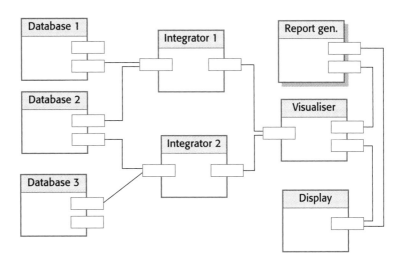

In this example, each database can be encapsulated as a distributed object with an interface that provides read-only access to its data. Integrator objects are each concerned with specific types of relationship and they collect information from all of the databases to try to deduce the relationships. There might be an integrator object that is concerned with seasonal variations in goods sold and another that is concerned with relationships between different types of goods.

Visualiser objects interact with integrator objects to produce a visualisation or a report on the relationships that have been discovered. Because of the large volumes of data that are handled, visualiser objects will normally use graphical presentations of the relationships that have been discovered. I discuss graphical information presentation in Chapter 15.

A distributed object architecture rather than a client–server architecture is appropriate for this type of application, for three reasons:

1. Unlike a bank ATM system (say), the logical model of the system is not one of service provision where there are distinguished data management services.

2. It allows the number of databases that are accessed to be increased without disrupting the system. Each database is simply another distributed object. The database objects can provide a simplified interface that controls access to the data. The databases that are accessed may reside on different machines.

3. It allows new types of relationship to be mined by adding new integrator objects. Parts of the business that are interested in specific relationships can extend the system by adding integrator objects that operate on their computers without requiring knowledge of any other integrators that are used elsewhere.

The major disadvantage of distributed object architectures is that they are more complex to design than client–server systems. Client–server systems appear to be a fairly natural way to think about systems. They reflect many human transactions where people request and receive services from other people who specialise in providing these services. It is more difficult to think about more general service provision and we do not yet have a great deal of experience with the design and development of large-grain business objects.

11.4 CORBA

As I indicated in the previous section, the implementation of a distributed object architecture requires middleware (object request brokers) to handle communications between the distributed objects. In principle, the objects in the system may be implemented using different programming languages, may run on different platforms and their names need not be known to all other objects in the system. The middleware 'glue' therefore has to do a lot of work to ensure seamless object communications.

At the time of writing, there are two principal standards for middleware to support distributed object computing:

1. *CORBA (Common Object Request Broker Architecture)*   CORBA is a set of standards for middleware that has been defined by the Object Management Group (OMG). The OMG is a consortium of companies, including major players such as Sun, Hewlett-Packard and IBM. The CORBA standards define a generic machine-independent approach to distributed object computing. A number of implementations of this standard by different vendors have been developed. CORBA implementations are available for Unix and Microsoft operating systems.

2. *DCOM (Distributed Component Object Model)*   DCOM is a standard that has been developed and implemented by Microsoft and that is integrated with Microsoft's operating system. Its model of distributed computing is less general than the CORBA model and DCOM offers more limited support for interoperability. At the time of writing, use of DCOM is limited to Microsoft operating systems.

I focus on CORBA here because it is the more general model. I also think it likely that CORBA, DCOM and other approaches such as Java's RMI (Remote Method Invocation) will converge and this convergence will be based on the CORBA standards. There is no need for more than one standard in this area and different standards hinder long-term progress.

The CORBA standards have been defined by the Object Management Group (OMG) which is made up of over 500 companies to promote object-oriented development. The role of the OMG is to define standards for object-oriented development but not to provide specific implementations of these standards. The defined standards are publicly available free of charge from the OMG's web site. The OMG is not just concerned with CORBA but has defined a wide range of other standards including UML (Rumbaugh *et al.*, 1999a) and common business objects. I have included a link to these standards from the book's web pages.

The OMG's vision of a distributed application is shown in Figure 11.13 which I have adapted from Siegel's diagram of the Object Management Architecture (Siegel, 1998). This proposes that a distributed application should be made up of a number of components:

1. Application objects that are designed and implemented for this application.

2. Standard objects that are defined by the OMG for a specific domain. At the time of writing, a number of task forces have been set up to define domain object standards in finance/insurance, electronic commerce, healthcare, and a number of other areas.

3. Fundamental CORBA services that provide basic distributed computing services such as directories, security management, etc.

4. Horizontal CORBA facilities such as user interface facilities, system management facilities, etc. The term horizontal facilities suggests that these facilities

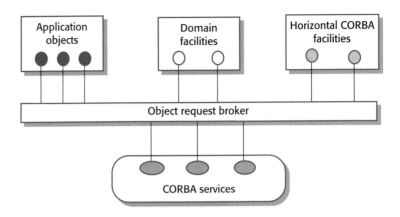

Figure 11.13
The structure of
a CORBA-based
distributed
application

are common to many application domains and the facilities are therefore used in many different applications.

The CORBA standards cover all aspects of this vision. There are four major elements to these standards:

1. An object model for application objects where a CORBA object is an encapsulation of state with a well-defined, language-neutral interface described in an IDL (Interface Definition Language).

2. An object request broker (ORB) that manages requests for object services. The ORB locates the object providing the service, prepares it for the request, sends the service request and returns the results to the requester.

3. A set of object services that are general services likely to be required by many distributed applications. Examples of services are directory services, transaction services and persistence services.

4. A set of common components built on top of these basic services that may be required by applications. These may be vertical domain-specific components or horizontal, general-purpose components that are used by many applications. I discuss components in Chapter 14.

The CORBA object model considers an object to be an encapsulation of attributes and services as is normal for objects. However, CORBA objects must have a separate interface definition that defines the public attributes and operations of the object. CORBA object interfaces are defined using a standard, language-independent interface definition language (IDL). If an object wishes to use services provided by another object then it accesses these services through the IDL interface. CORBA objects have a unique identifier called an Interoperable Object Reference (IOR). This IOR is used when one object requests services from another.

The object request broker knows about the objects that are requesting services and their interfaces. The ORB handles the communication between the objects. The

Figure 11.14 Object
communications
through an ORB

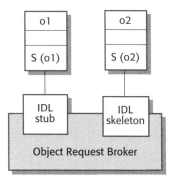

communicating objects do not need to know the location of other objects, nor do they need to know anything about their implementation. As the IDL interface insulates the objects from the ORB, it is possible to change the object implementation in a completely transparent way. The object location can change between invocations and this is transparent to other objects in the system.

This is illustrated in Figure 11.14 which illustrates how two objects o1 and o2 may communicate through an ORB. The calling object (o1) has an associated IDL stub that defines the interface of the object that is providing the required service. The implementor of o1 embeds calls to this stub in his or her object implementation when a service is required. The IDL is a superset of C++ so it is very easy to access this stub if you are programming in C++ and fairly easy in C or Java. Language mappings to IDL have also been defined for other languages such as Ada and COBOL. In these cases, tool support is usually required to support the link to the IDL.

The object that is providing the service has an associated IDL skeleton that links the interface to the implementation of the services. Simplistically, when a service is called through the interface, the IDL skeleton translates this into a call to the service in whatever implementation language has been used. When the method or procedure has been executed, the IDL skeleton translates the results into IDL so that they can be accessed by the calling object. Where an object both provides services to other objects and uses services that are provided elsewhere, it needs both an IDL skeleton and IDL stubs. An IDL stub is required for every object that is used.

Object request brokers are not usually implemented as separate processes but are a framework (see Chapter 14) that can be linked with object implementations. Therefore, in a distributed system, each computer that is running distributed objects will have its own object request broker. This will handle all local invocations of objects. However, when a request is made to a service that is to be provided by a remote object, this requires inter-ORB communications.

This situation is illustrated in Figure 11.15. In this example, if object o1 or o2 requests a service from o3 or o4, this requires the associated ORBs to communicate. A CORBA implementation supports ORB-to-ORB communication by providing all ORBs access to all IDL interface definitions and by implementing the OMG's standard Generic Inter-ORB Protocol (GIOP). This protocol defines standard messages that ORBs can exchange to implement remote object invocation and

Figure 11.15
Inter-ORB
communications

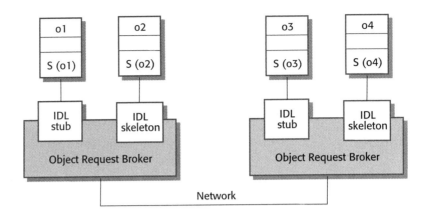

information transfer. When combined with lower-level Internet TCP/IP protocols, the GIOP allows ORBs to communicate across the Internet.

The CORBA initiative has been under way since the 1980s and the early versions of CORBA were simply concerned with supporting distributed objects. However, as the standards have evolved they have become more extensive. As well as a mechanism for distributed object communications, the CORBA standards now define some standard services that may be provided to support distributed object oriented applications.

You can think of CORBA services as those facilities that are likely to be required by many distributed systems. The standards define approximately 15 common services. Some examples of these generic services are:

1. Naming and trading services that allow objects to refer to and discover other objects on the network. The naming service is a directory service that allows objects to be named. Other objects may discover the IOR of objects that they wish to use through the naming service. This is like the white pages of a phone directory. Objects using the service have to know the registered names of other objects. The trading services are like the yellow pages. Objects can find out what other objects have registered with the trader service and can access the specification of these objects.

2. Notification services that allow objects to notify other objects that some event has occurred. Objects may register their interest in a particular event with the service and, when that event occurs, they are automatically notified. For example, say the system includes a print spooler that queues documents to be printed and a number of printer objects. The print spooler registers that it is interested in an 'end of printing' event from a printer object. The notification service informs it when printing is complete and it can then schedule the next document on that printer.

3. Transaction services that support atomic transactions and rollback on failure. Transactions are a fault-tolerance facility (see Chapter 18) that support recovery

from errors during an update operation. If an object update operation fails then the object state can be rolled back to its state before the update was started.

It is intended that the CORBA standards should include interface definitions for a wide range of components that may be used by distributed application builders. These may be vertical components or horizontal components. Vertical components are components that are specific to an application domain. As I have already discussed, various task forces from different industry sectors have been set up to define these components. Horizontal components are general-purpose components such as user interface components. A task force is also responsible for developing these specifications.

At the time of writing, these component specifications are still under development and have not yet been agreed. In my view, this is likely to be the weakest area of the CORBA standards and it may be several years before standard component specifications and implementations are available.

KEY POINTS

▶ Virtually all new large systems are now distributed systems where the system software runs on a loosely integrated group of networked processors.

▶ Distributed systems can support resource sharing, openness, concurrency, scalability, fault tolerance and transparency.

▶ Client–server systems are distributed systems where the system is modelled as a set of services that are provided by servers to client processes.

▶ In a client–server system, the user interface always runs on a client and data management is always provided by a shared server. Application functionality may be implemented on the client computer or on the server.

▶ In a distributed object architecture, there is no distinction between clients and servers. Objects provide general services that may be called on by other objects. This approach may be used for implementing client–server systems.

▶ Distributed object systems require middleware to handle object communications and to allow objects to be added to and removed from the system. Conceptually, you can think of this middleware as a software bus that objects plug into.

▶ The CORBA standards are a set of standards for middleware that supports distributed object architectures. They include object model definitions, definitions of an object request broker and common service definitions. Various implementations of the CORBA standards are available.

FURTHER READING

Communications of the ACM, October 1998. This special issue includes a number of articles, written for non-specialised readers, on CORBA. I particularly recommend the introductory article by Siegel.

Client–server Programming with Java and CORBA. A how-to guide on developing distributed client–server systems. It focuses on developing these systems in Java and discusses Java's approach to remote method invocation and its relationships with CORBA. (R. Orfali and D. Harkey, 1998, John Wiley and Sons.)

'Frameworks for component-based client–server computing'. This review discusses client–server architectures and both CORBA and DCOM and how they may be used as a basis for implementing client–server systems. (S. M. Lewandowski, *Computer Surveys*, 30(1), March 1998.)

'Middleware: A model for distributed systems services'. This is an excellent overview paper that summarises the role of middleware in distributed systems and discusses the range of middleware services that may be provided. (P. A. Bernstein, *Comm. ACM*, 39(2), February 1996.)

EXERCISES

11.1 Explain why distributed systems are inherently more scalable than centralised systems. What are the likely limits on the scalability of the system?

11.2 What is the fundamental difference between a fat-client and a thin-client approach to client–server systems development? Explain why the use of Java as an implementation language blurs the distinction between these approaches.

11.3 It is proposed to develop a system for stock information where dealers can access information about companies and can evaluate various investment scenarios using a simulation system. Different dealers use this simulation in different ways according to their experience and the type of stocks that they are dealing with. Suggest a client–server architecture for this system that shows where functionality is located. Justify the client–server system model that you have chosen.

11.4 By making reference to the application model shown in Figure 11.5, discuss possible problems that might arise when converting a 1980s mainframe legacy system for insurance policy processing to a client–server architecture.

11.5 Distributed systems based on a client–server model have been developed since the 1980s but it is only recently that system architectures based on distributed objects have been implemented. Suggest three reasons why this should be the case.

11.6   Explain why the use of distributed objects with an object request broker simplifies the implementation of scalable client–server systems. Illustrate your answer with an example.

11.7   How is the CORBA IDL used to support communications between objects that have been implemented in different programming languages? Explain why this approach may cause performance problems if there are radical differences between the languages used for object implementation.

11.8   What are the basic facilities that must be provided by an object request broker?

11.9   It could be argued that developing CORBA standards for horizontal and vertical components is anti-competitive. If these are developed and adopted, it inhibits the development of better components by smaller companies. Discuss the general role of standardisation in supporting and restricting competition in the software market.

12 Object-oriented design

Objectives

The objective of this chapter is to introduce an approach to software design where the design is structured as interacting objects. When you have read this chapter, you will:

❏ understand how a software design may be represented as a set of interacting objects that manage their own state and operations;

❏ know the most important activities in a general object-oriented design process;

❏ understand different models that may be used to document an object-oriented design;

❏ have been introduced to the representation of these models in the Unified Modeling Language (UML).

Contents

12.1 Objects and object classes
12.2 An object-oriented design process
12.3 Design evolution

Object-oriented design is a design strategy where system designers think in terms of 'things' instead of operations or functions. The executing system is made up of interacting objects that maintain their own local state and provide operations on that state information (Figure 12.1). They hide information about the representation of the state and hence limit access to it. An object-oriented design process involves designing the object classes and the relationships between these classes. When the design is realised as an executing program, the required objects are created dynamically using the class definitions.

Object-oriented design is part of *object-oriented development* where an object-oriented strategy is used throughout the development process:

- *Object-oriented analysis* is concerned with developing an object-oriented model of the application domain. The identified objects reflect entities and operations that are associated with the problem to be solved.

- *Object-oriented design* is concerned with developing an object-oriented model of a software system to implement the identified requirements. The objects in an object-oriented design are related to the solution to the problem that is being solved. There may be close relationships between some problem objects and some solution objects but the designer inevitably has to add new objects and to transform problem objects to implement the solution.

- *Object-oriented programming* is concerned with realising a software design using an object-oriented programming language. An object-oriented programming language, such as Java, supports the direct implementation of objects and provides facilities to define object classes.

The transition between these stages of development should be a seamless one with the same notation used at each stage. Moving to the next stage involves refining the previous stage by adding detail to existing object classes and devising new classes to provide additional functionality. As information is concealed within objects, detailed design decisions about the representation of data can be delayed until the system is implemented. In some cases, decisions on the distribution of objects and whether or not objects can be sequential or concurrent may also be delayed. This means that software designers are not constrained by details of the system implementation. They can devise designs that can be adapted to different execution environments.

Figure 12.1 A system made up of interacting objects

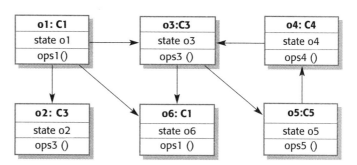

Object-oriented systems should be maintainable as the objects are independent. They may be understood and modified as stand-alone entities. Changing the implementation of an object or adding services should not affect other system objects. Because objects are associated with things, there is often a clear mapping between real-world entities (such as hardware components) and their controlling objects in the system. This improves the understandability and hence the maintainability of the design.

Objects are potentially reusable components because they are independent encapsulations of state and operations. Designs can be developed using objects that have been created in previous designs. This reduces design, programming and validation costs. It may also lead to the use of standard objects (hence improving design understandability) and reduces the risks involved in software development. However, as I discuss in Chapter 14, reuse is sometimes best implemented using collections of objects (components or frameworks) rather than individual objects.

Several object-oriented design methods have been proposed (Coad and Yourdon, 1990; Robinson, 1992; Jacobson et al., 1993; Booch, 1994; Graham, 1994). A unification of the notations used in these methods has been defined (UML) along with an associated design process (Rumbaugh et al., 1999b). I don't describe any particular design method here but I discuss generic object-oriented concepts and design activities in section 12.2. I use the UML notation throughout the chapter.

12.1 Objects and object classes

The terms 'object' and 'object-oriented' are now widely used. They are applied to different types of entity, design methods, systems and programming languages. However, there is a general acceptance that an object is an encapsulation of information and this is reflected in my definition of an object and an object class:

An object is an entity that has a state and a defined set of operations which operate on that state. The state is represented as a set of object attributes. The operations associated with the object provide services to other objects (clients) which request these services when some computation is required.

Objects are created according to an object class definition. An object class definition serves as a template for creating objects. It includes declarations of all the attributes and operations which should be associated with an object of that class.

The notation that I use here for object classes is that defined in the UML. An object class is represented as a named rectangle with two sections. The object attributes are listed in the top section. The operations that are associated with the object are set out in the bottom section. Figure 12.2 illustrates this notation using an object class which models an employee in an organisation. In the UML, the term

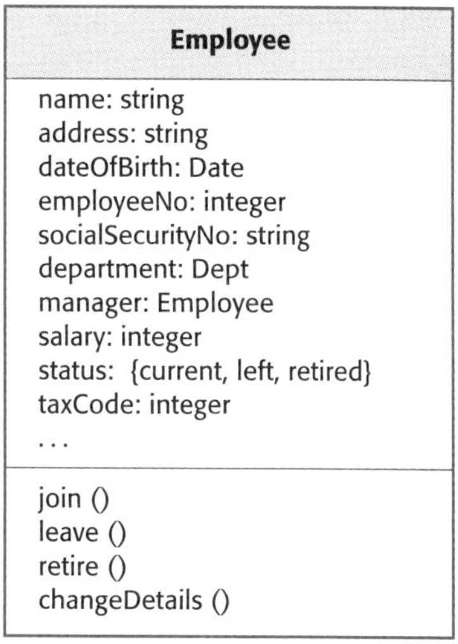

Figure 12.2 An
employee object

Employee
name: string address: string dateOfBirth: Date employeeNo: integer socialSecurityNo: string department: Dept manager: Employee salary: integer status: {current, left, retired} taxCode: integer . . .
join () leave () retire () changeDetails ()

'operation' is the specification of an action; the term 'method' is used to refer to the implementation of the operation.

The class Employee defines a number of attributes that hold information about employees, including their name and address, social security number, tax code, etc. The ellipsis (. . .) indicates that there are more attributes associated with the class that are not shown here. Operations associated with the object are join (called when an employee joins the organisation), leave (called when an employee leaves the organisation), retire (called when the employee becomes a pensioner of the organisation) and changeDetails (called when some employee information needs to be modified).

Objects communicate by requesting services (calling methods) from other objects and, if necessary, by exchanging the information required for service provision. The copies of information needed to execute the service and the results of service execution are passed as parameters. Some examples of this style of communication are:

```
// Call a method associated with a buffer object that returns the next value
// in the buffer
v = circularBuffer.Get ();
// Call the method associated with a thermostat object that sets the
// temperature to be maintained
thermostat.setTemp (20);
```

In some distributed systems, object communications are implemented directly as text messages which objects exchange. The receiving object parses the message, identifies the service and the associated data and carries out the requested service. However, when the objects coexist in the same program, method calls are implemented in the same way as procedure or function calls in a language such as C or Ada.

When service requests are implemented in this way, communication between objects is synchronous. That is, the calling object waits for the service request to be completed. However, if objects are implemented as concurrent processes or threads the object communication may be asynchronous. The calling object may continue in operation while the requested service is executing. I explain how objects may be implemented as concurrent processes later in this section.

As I discussed in Chapter 7, where I described a number of possible object models, object classes can be arranged in a generalisation or inheritance hierarchy that shows the relationship between general and more specific object classes. The more specific object class is completely consistent with the general object class but includes further information. In the UML, generalisation is indicated by an arrow that points to the parent class. In object-oriented programming languages, generalisation is usually implemented using the inheritance mechanism. The child class inherits attributes and operations from the parent class.

Figure 12.3 shows an example of such a hierarchy where different classes of employee are shown. Classes lower down the hierarchy have the same attributes and operations as their parent classes but may add new attributes and operations or modify some of those from their parent classes. This means that there is one-way interchangeability. If the name of a parent class is used in a model, this means that the object in the system may be defined as either of that class or of any of its descendants.

The class Manager in Figure 12.3 has all of the attributes and operations of the class Employee but has, in addition, two new attributes that record the budgets controlled by the manager and the date that the manager was appointed to a particular management role. Similarly, the class Programmer adds new attributes that define the project that the programmer is working on and the programming language skills

Figure 12.3
A generalisation
hierarchy

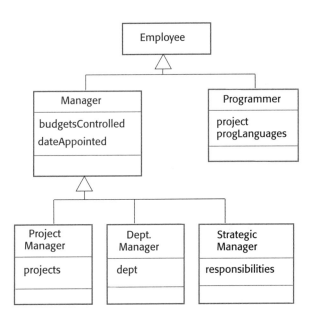

Figure 12.4 An
association model

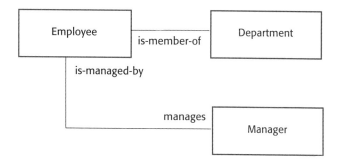

that he or she has. Objects of class **Manager** or **Programmer** may therefore be used
anywhere where an object of class **Employee** is required.

Objects that are members of an object class participate in relationships with
other objects. These relationships may be modelled by describing the associations
between the object classes. In the UML, associations are denoted by a line between
the object classes that may optionally be annotated with information about the association. This is illustrated in Figure 12.4 which shows the association between objects
of class **Employee** and objects of class **Department** and between objects of class
Employee and objects of class **Manager**.

Association is a very general relationship and is often used in the UML to indicate that either an attribute of an object is an associated object or the implementation of an object method relies on the associated object. However, in principle at
least, any kind of association is possible. One of the most common associations is
aggregation which illustrates how objects may be composed of other objects. See
Chapter 7 for a discussion of this type of association.

12.1.1 Concurrent objects

Conceptually, an object requests a service from another object by sending a 'service request' message to that object. There is no requirement for serial execution
where one object waits for completion of a requested service. Consequently, the
general model of object interaction allows objects to execute concurrently as parallel processes. These objects may execute on the same computer or as distributed
objects on different machines.

In practice, most object-oriented programming languages have as their default a
serial execution model where requests for object services are implemented in the
same way as function calls. Therefore, when an object called theList is created from
a normal object class, you write in Java:

```
theList.append (17)
```

This calls the **append** method associated with **theList** object to add the element
17 to **theList** and execution of the calling object is suspended until the append

operation has been completed. However, Java includes a very simple mechanism (threads) that lets you create objects that execute concurrently. It is therefore easy to take an object-oriented design and produce an implementation where the objects are concurrent processes.

There are two kinds of concurrent object implementation:

1. *Servers* where the object is realised as a parallel process with methods corresponding to the defined object operations. Methods start up in response to an external message and may execute in parallel with methods associated with other objects. When they have completed their operation, the object suspends itself and waits for further requests for service.

2. *Active objects* where the state of the object may be changed by internal operations executing within the object itself. The process representing the object continually executes these operations so never suspends itself.

Servers are most useful in a distributed environment where the calling object and the called object execute on different computers. The response time for the service that is requested is unpredictable so, wherever possible, you should design the system so that the object that has requested a service does not have to wait for that service to be completed. They can also be used in a single machine where a service takes some time to complete (e.g. printing a document) and the service may be requested by several different objects.

Active objects are used when an object needs to update its own state at specified intervals. This is common in real-time systems where objects are associated with

Figure 12.5
Implementation of
an active object
using Java threads

```
class Transponder extends Thread {

        Position currentPosition ;
        Coords c1, c2 ;
        Satellite sat1, sat2 ;
        Navigator theNavigator ;

        public Position givePosition ()
        {
              return currentPosition ;
        }
        public void run ()
        {
            while (true)
            {
                  c1 = sat1.position () ;
                  c2 = sat2.position () ;
                  currentPosition = theNavigator.compute (c1, c2) ;
            }

        }
} //Transponder
```

hardware devices that collect information about the system's environment. The object's methods allow other objects access to the state information.

Figure 12.5 shows how an active object may be defined and implemented in Java. This object class represents a transponder on an aircraft. The transponder keeps track of the aircraft's position using a satellite navigation system. It can respond to messages from air traffic control computers. It provides the current aircraft position in response to a request to the givePosition method.

This object is implemented as a thread where a continuous loop in the run method includes code to compute the aircraft's position using signals from satellites. Threads are created in Java by using the built-in Thread class as a parent class in a class declaration. Threads must include a method called run and this is started by the Java run-time system when objects that are defined as threads are created. This is shown in Figure 12.5.

12.2 An object-oriented design process

In this section, I illustrate the process of object-oriented design by developing an example design for the control software that is embedded in an automated weather station. As I discussed in the introduction, there are several methods of object-oriented design with no definitive 'best' method or design process. The process that I cover here is a general one that incorporates activities that are common to most OOD processes. In this respect, it is comparable to the proposed UML process (Rumbaugh *et al.*, 1999b) but I have significantly simplified this process for presentation here.

The general process that I use here for object-oriented design has a number of stages:

1. Understand and define the context and the modes of use of the system
2. Design the system architecture
3. Identify the principal objects in the system
4. Develop design models
5. Specify object interfaces

I have deliberately not illustrated this as a simple process diagram as that would imply that there was a neat sequence of activities in this process. In fact, all of the above activities can be thought of as interleaved activities that influence each other. Objects are identified and the interfaces fully or partially specified as the architecture of the system is defined. As object models are produced, these individual object definitions may be refined and this may mean changes to the system architecture.

I discuss these as separate stages in the design process later in this section. However, you should not assume from this that design is a simple, well-structured process.

In reality, you develop a design by proposing solutions and refining these solutions as information becomes available. You inevitably have to backtrack and retry when problems arise. Sometimes you explore options in detail to see if they work; at other times you ignore details until late in the process.

I illustrate these process activities by developing an example of an object-oriented design. The example that I use to illustrate object-oriented design is part of a system for creating weather maps using automatically collected meteorological data. The detailed requirements for such a weather mapping system would take up many pages. However, an overall system architecture can be developed from a relatively brief system description:

> A weather mapping system is required to generate weather maps on a regular basis using data collected from remote, unattended weather stations and other data sources such as weather observers, balloons and satellites. Weather stations transmit their data to the area computer in response to a request from that machine.

> The area computer system validates the collected data and integrates the data from different sources. The integrated data is archived and, using data from this archive and a digitised map database, a set of local weather maps is created. Maps may be printed for distribution on a special-purpose map printer or may be displayed in a number of different formats.

This description shows that part of the overall system is concerned with collecting data, part with integrating the data from different sources, part with archiving that data and part with creating weather maps. Figure 12.6 illustrates a possible system architecture that can be derived from this description. This is a layered architecture (discussed in Chapter 10) that reflects the different stages of processing in the system, namely data collection, data integration, data archiving and map generation.

Figure 12.6 Layered architecture for weather mapping system

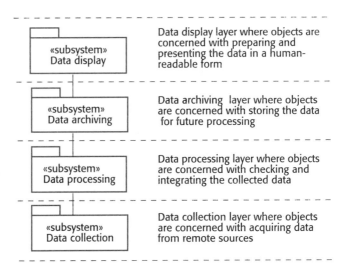

«subsystem»
Data display

Data display layer where objects are concerned with preparing and presenting the data in a human-readable form

«subsystem»
Data archiving

Data archiving layer where objects are concerned with storing the data for future processing

«subsystem»
Data processing

Data processing layer where objects are concerned with checking and integrating the collected data

«subsystem»
Data collection

Data collection layer where objects are concerned with acquiring data from remote sources

Figure 12.7
Sub-systems in
the weather
mapping system

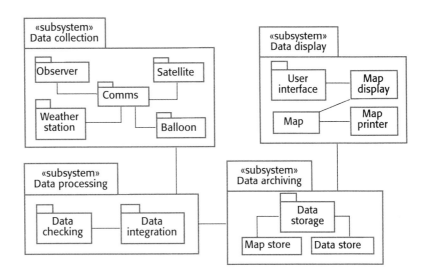

A layered architecture is appropriate in this case because each stage relies only on the processing of the previous stage for its operation.

In Figure 12.6, I have shown the different layers and have included the layer name in a UML package symbol that has been denoted as a sub-system. A UML package represents a collection of objects and other packages. I have used it here to show that each layer includes a number of other components.

In Figure 12.7 I have expanded on this abstract architectural model by showing the components of the sub-systems. Again, these are very abstract and they have been derived from the information in the description of the system. I continue the design example by focusing on the weather station sub-system that is part of the data collection layer.

12.2.1   System context and models of use

The first stage in any software design process is to develop an understanding of the relationships between the software that is being designed and its external environment. Developing this understanding helps you decide how to provide the required system functionality and how to structure the system so that it can communicate effectively with its environment.

The system context and the model of system use represent two complementary models of the relationships between a system and its environment:

1. The system context is a static model that describes the other systems in that environment.
2. The model of the system use is a dynamic model that describes how the system actually interacts with its environment.

Figure 12.8
Use-cases for the
weather station

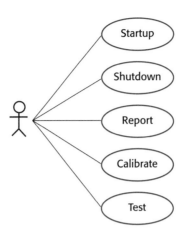

The context model of a system may be represented using associations (see Figure 12.4) where, essentially, a simple block diagram of the overall system architecture is produced. This can be expanded by representing a sub-system model using UML packages as shown in Figure 12.7. This illustrates that the context of the weather station system is within a sub-system concerned with data collection. It also shows other sub-systems that make up the weather mapping system.

When you model the interactions of a system with its environment you should use an abstract approach that does not include too much detail of these interactions. The approach that is proposed in the UML is to develop a use-case model where each use-case represents an interaction with the system. In use-case models (also discussed in Chapter 6), each possible interaction is named in an ellipse and the external entity involved in the interaction is represented by a stick figure. In the case of the weather station system, this external entity is not a human but the data processing system for the weather data.

A use-case model for the weather station is shown in Figure 12.8. This shows that weather station interacts with external entities for startup and shutdown, for reporting the weather data that has been collected and for instrument testing and calibration.

Each of these use cases can be described using a simple natural language description. This helps designers identify objects in the system and gives them an understanding of what the system is intended to do. I use a stylised form of this description that clearly identifies what information is exchanged, how the interaction is initiated etc. This is shown in Figure 12.9 where I have described the Report use case from Figure 12.8.

Of course, you can use any technique for describing use-cases so long as the description is short and easily understandable. You need to develop descriptions for each of the use-cases that are shown in the model.

The use-case description helps to identify objects and operations in the system. From the description of the Report use-case, it is obvious that objects representing the instruments that collect weather data will be required, as will an object representing the summary of the weather data. Operations to request weather data and to send weather data are required.

Figure 12.9 Report
use-case description

System	Weather station
Use-case	Report
Actors	Weather data collection system, Weather station
Data	The weather station sends a summary of the weather data that has been collected from the instruments in the collection period to the weather data collection system. The data sent are the maximum, minimum and average ground and air temperatures, the maximum, minimum and average air pressures, the maximum, minimum and average wind speeds, the total rainfall and the wind direction as sampled at five-minute intervals.
Stimulus	The weather data collection system establishes a modem link with the weather station and requests transmission of the data.
Response	The summarised data is sent to the weather data collection system.
Comments	Weather stations are usually asked to report once per hour but this frequency may differ from one station to another and may be modified in future.

12.2.2   Architectural design

Once the interactions between the software system that is being designed and the system's environment have been defined, you can use this information as a basis for designing the system architecture. Of course, you need to combine this with your general knowledge of principles of architectural design and with more detailed domain knowledge.

The automated weather station is a relatively simple system and its architecture can again be represented as a layered model. I have illustrated this in Figure 12.10 as three UML packages within the more general Weather station package. Notice how I have used UML annotations (text in boxes with a folded corner) to provide additional information here.

The three layers in the weather station software are:

1. the interface layer which is concerned with all communications with other parts of the system and with providing the external interfaces of the system;

2. the data collection layer which is concerned with managing the collection of data from the instruments and with summarising the weather data before transmission to the mapping system;

3. the instruments layer which is an encapsulation of all of the instruments that are used to collect raw data about the weather conditions.

Figure 12.10
The weather
station architecture

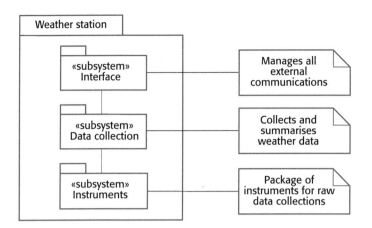

In general, you should try to decompose a system so that architectures are as simple as possible. A good rule of thumb is that there should not be more than seven fundamental entities included in an architectural model. Each of these entities can be described separately but, of course, you may choose to reveal the structure of the entities as I have done in Figure 12.7.

12.2.3   Object identification

By this stage in the design process, you will already have formulated some ideas about the essential objects in the system that you are designing. In the weather station system, it is clear that the instruments are objects and you need at least one object at each of the architectural levels. This reflects a general principle that objects tend to emerge during the design process. However, you usually also have to look for and document other objects that may be relevant.

Although I have headed this section *object* identification, in practice this process is actually concerned with identifying *object classes*. The design is described in terms of these classes. Inevitably, you have to refine the object classes that you initially identify and revisit this stage of the process as you develop a deeper understanding of the design.

There have been various proposals made about how to identify object classes:

1. Use a grammatical analysis of a natural language description of a system. Objects and attributes are nouns, operations or services are verbs (Abbott, 1983). This approach has been embodied in the HOOD method for object-oriented design (Robinson, 1992) which has been widely used in the European aerospace industry.

2. Use tangible entities (things) in the application domain such as aircraft, roles such as manager, events such as request, interactions such as meetings, locations such as offices, organisational units such as companies, etc. (Shlaer and

Mellor, 1988; Coad and Yourdon, 1990; Wirfs-Brock *et al.*, 1990). Support this by identifying storage structures (abstract data structures) in the solution domain that might be required to support these objects.

3. Use a behavioural approach where the designer first understands the overall behaviour of the system. The various behaviours are assigned to different parts of the system and an understanding is derived of who initiates and participates in these behaviours. Participants who play significant roles are recognised as objects (Rubin and Goldberg, 1992).

4. Use a scenario-based analysis where various scenarios of system use are identified and analysed in turn. As each scenario is analysed, the team responsible for the analysis must identify the required objects, attributes and operations. A method of analysis called CRC cards where analysts and designers take on the role of objects is effective in supporting this scenario-based approach (Beck and Cunningham, 1989).

These approaches help you get started with object identification. In practice, many different sources of knowledge have to be used to discover objects and object classes. Objects and operations that are initially identified from the informal system description can be a starting point for the design. Further information from application domain knowledge or scenario analysis may then be used to refine and extend the initial objects. This information may be collected from requirements documents, from discussions with users and from an analysis of existing systems.

I have used a hybrid approach here to identify the weather station objects. I don't have space to describe all the objects but I have shown five object classes in Figure 12.11. The Ground thermometer, Anemometer and Barometer represent

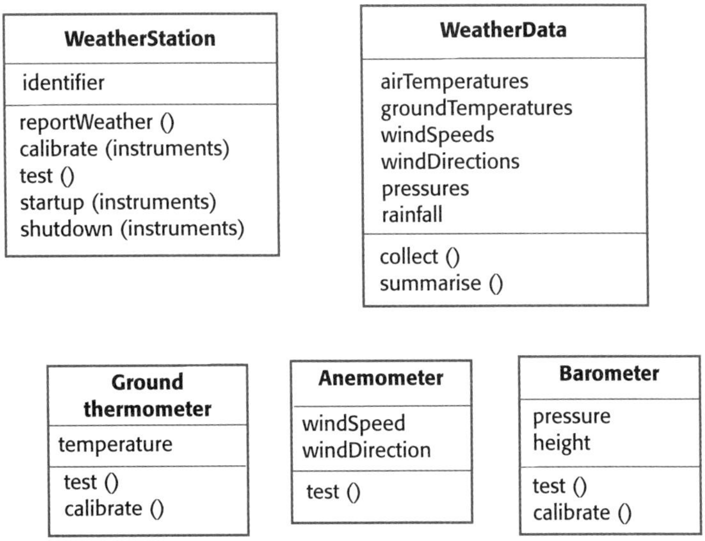

Figure 12.11
Examples of object classes in the weather station system

application domain objects and the WeatherStation and WeatherData objects have been identified from the system description and the scenario (use-case) description.

These objects are related to the different levels in the system architecture.

1. The WeatherStation object class provides the basic interface of the weather station with its environment. Its operations therefore reflect the interactions shown in Figure 12.8. In this case, I use a single object class to encapsulate all of these interactions but, in other designs, it may be more appropriate to use several classes to provide the system interface.

2. The WeatherData object class encapsulates the summarised data from the different instruments in the weather station. Its associated operations are concerned with collecting and summarising the data that is required.

3. The GroundThermometer, Anemometer and Barometer object classes are directly related to instruments in the system. They reflect tangible hardware entities in the system and the operations are concerned with controlling that hardware.

At this stage in the design process, knowledge of the application domain may be used to identify further objects and services. In this case, we know that weather stations are often located in remote places. They include various instruments which sometimes go wrong. Instrument failures should be reported automatically. This implies that attributes and operations to check the correct functioning of the instruments are necessary. Obviously, there are many remote weather stations. You therefore need some way of identifying the data collected from each station, so each weather station should have its own identifier.

I have decided not to make the objects associated with each instrument active objects. The collect operation in WeatherData calls on instrument objects to make readings when required. Active objects include their own control and, in this case, it would mean that each instrument would decide when to make readings. However, the disadvantage of this is that, if a decision was made to change the timing of the data collection or if different weather stations collected data differently, new object classes would have to be introduced. By making the instrument objects make readings on request, any changes to collection strategy can be easily implemented without changing the objects associated with the instruments.

12.2.4 Design models

Design models show the objects or object classes in a system and, where appropriate, different kinds of relationships between these entities. Design models essentially are the design. They are the bridge between the requirements for the system and the system implementation. This means that there are conflicting requirements on these models. They have to be abstract so that unnecessary detail doesn't hide the relationships between them and the system requirements. However, they also have to include enough detail for programmers to make implementation decisions.

In general, you get round this conflict by developing different models at different levels of detail. Where there are close links between requirements engineers, designers and programmers, abstract models may be all that is required. Specific design decisions may be made as the system is implemented. When the links between system specifiers, designers and programmers are indirect (e.g. where a system is being designed in one part of an organisation but implemented elsewhere), more detailed models may be required.

An important step in the design process, therefore, is to decide which design models you need and the level of detail of these models. This also depends on the type of system that is being developed. A sequential data processing system will be designed in a different way from an embedded real-time system and different design models will therefore be used. There are very few systems where all models are necessary and minimising the number of models that are produced reduces the costs of the design and the time required to complete the design process.

There are two types of design models that should normally be produced to describe an object-oriented design. These are:

1. Static models that describe the static structure of the system in terms of the system object classes and their relationships. Important relationships that may be documented at this stage are generalisation relationships, uses/used-by relationships and composition relationships.

2. Dynamic models that describe the dynamic structure of the system and that show the interactions between the system objects (not the object classes). Interactions that may be documented include the sequence of service requests made by objects and the way in which the state of the system is related to these object interactions.

The UML provides for a large number of possible static and dynamic models that may be produced to document a design. Booch *et al.* (1999) propose nine different types of diagram to represent these models. I don't have space to go into all of these and not all are appropriate for the weather station example. The models that I will discuss in this section are:

1. Sub-system models that show logical groupings of objects into coherent subsystems. These are represented using a form of class diagram where each subsystem is shown as a package. Sub-system models are static models.

2. Sequence models that show the sequence of object interactions. These are represented using a UML sequence or a collaboration diagram. Sequence models are dynamic models.

3. State machine models that show how individual objects change their state in response to events. These are represented in the UML using statechart diagrams. State machine models are dynamic models.

**Figure 12.12
Weather station
packages**

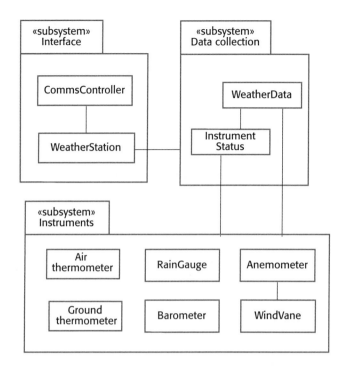

I have already discussed other types of model that may be developed earlier in this chapter and in other chapters. Use-case models show interactions with the system (Figure 12.8, Figures 6.12 and 6.13), object models describe the object classes (Figure 12.2), generalisation or inheritance models (Figures 7.10, 7.11 and 7.12) show how classes may be generalisations of other classes and aggregation models (Figure 7.13) show how collections of objects are related.

A sub-system model is, in my view, one of the most helpful static models as it shows how the design may be organised into logically related groups of objects. We have already seen examples of this type of model in Figure 12.7 which showed the sub-systems in the weather mapping system. In the UML, packages are encapsulation constructs and do not reflect directly on entities in the system that is developed. However, they may be reflected in structuring constructs such as Java libraries.

Figure 12.12 shows the objects in the sub-systems in the weather station. I also show some associations in this model. For example, the **CommsController** object is associated with the **WeatherStation** object and the **WeatherStation** object is associated with the **Data collection** package. This means that this object is associated with one or more objects in this package. A package model plus an object class model should describe the logical groupings in the system.

One of the most useful and understandable dynamic models that may be produced is a sequence model that documents, for each mode of interaction, the sequence of object interactions that take place. In a sequence model:

Figure 12.13
Sequence of
operations – data
collection

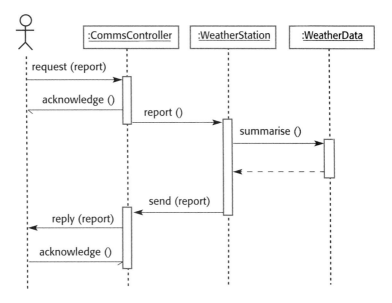

1. The objects involved in the interaction are arranged horizontally with a vertical line linked to each object.

2. Time is represented vertically so that time progresses down the dashed vertical lines. Therefore, the sequence of operations can be read easily from the model.

3. Interactions between objects are represented by labelled arrows linking the vertical lines. These are *not* data flows but represent messages or events that are fundamental to the interaction.

4. The thin rectangle on the object lifeline represents the time when the object is the controlling object in the system. An object takes over control at the top of this rectangle and relinquishes control to another object at the bottom of the rectangle. If there is a hierarchy of calls, control is not relinquished until the last return to the initial method call has been completed.

This is illustrated in Figure 12.13 which shows the sequence of interactions when the external mapping system requests the data from the weather station. This diagram may be read as follows:

1. An object that is an instance of CommsController (:CommsController) receives a request from its environment to send a weather report. It acknowledges receipt of this request. The half-arrowhead indicates that the message sender does not expect a reply.

2. This object sends a message to an object that is an instance of WeatherStation to create a weather report. The instance of CommsController then suspends itself (its control box ends). The style of arrowhead used indicates that the

CommsController object instance and the WeatherStation object instance are objects that may execute concurrently.

3. The object that is an instance of WeatherStation sends a message to a WeatherData object to summarise the weather data. In this case, the different style of arrowhead used indicates that the instance of WeatherStation waits for a reply.

4. This summary is computed and control returns to the WeatherStation object. The dotted arrow indicates a return of control.

5. This object sends a message to CommsController requesting it to transfer the data to the remote system. The WeatherStation object then suspends itself.

6. The CommsController object sends the summarised data to the remote system, receives an acknowledgement and then suspends itself waiting for the next request.

From the sequence diagram we can see that the CommsController object and the WeatherStation object are actually concurrent processes where execution can be suspended and resumed. Essentially, the CommsController object instance listens for messages from the external system, decodes these messages and initiates weather station operations.

When documenting a design, you should produce a sequence diagram for each significant interaction. If you have developed a use-case model then there should be a sequence diagram for each use-case that you have identified.

Sequence diagrams are used to model the combined behaviour of a group of objects but you may also want to summarise the behaviour of a single object in response to the different messages that it can process. To do this, you can use a state machine model that shows how the object instance changes state depending on the messages that it receives. The UML uses statecharts, initially invented by Harel (1987) to describe state machine models.

Figure 12.14 is a statechart for the WeatherStation object that shows how it responds to requests for various services.

You can read this diagram as follows:

1. If the object state is 'Shutdown' then it can only respond to a startup () message. It then moves into a state where it is waiting for further messages. The unlabelled arrow with the black blob indicates that the 'Shutdown' state is the initial state.

2. In the 'Waiting' state, the system expects further messages. If a shutdown () message is received, the object returns to the shutdown state.

3. If a reportWeather () message is received, the system moves to a summarising state then, when the summary is complete, to a transmitting state where the information is transmitted through the CommsController. It then returns to a waiting state.

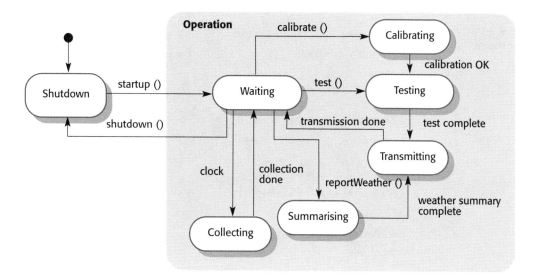

Figure 12.14
State diagram for
WeatherStation

4. If a calibrate () message is received, the system moves to a calibrating state, then a testing state, then a transmitting state before returning to the waiting state. If a test () message is received, the system moves directly to the testing state.

5. If a signal from the clock is received, the system moves to a collecting state where it is collecting data from the instruments. Each instrument is instructed in turn to collect its data.

It is not usually necessary to produce a statechart for all of the objects that you have defined. Many of the objects in a system are relatively simple objects and a state machine model would not help implementors to understand these objects.

Object interface specification

An important part of any design process is the specification of the interfaces between the different components in the design. You need to specify interfaces so that objects and other components can be designed in parallel. Once an interface has been specified, the developers of other objects may assume that interface will be implemented.

Designers should avoid interface representation information in their interface design. Rather the representation should be hidden and object operations provided to access and update the data. If the representation is hidden, it can be changed without affecting the objects that use these attributes. This leads to a design which is inherently more maintainable. For example, an array representation of a stack may be changed to a list representation without affecting other objects which use the stack. By contrast, it often makes sense to expose the attributes in a static design model as this is the most compact way of illustrating essential characteristics of the objects.

Figure 12.15 Java
description of
weather station
interface

```
interface WeatherStation {

    public void WeatherStation () ;

    public void startup () ;
    public void startup (Instrument i) ;

    public void shutdown () ;
    public void shutdown (Instrument i) ;

    public void reportWeather () ;

    public void test () ;
    public void test ( Instrument i ) ;

    public void calibrate ( Instrument i) ;

    public int getID () ;

} //WeatherStation
```

There is not necessarily a simple 1:1 relationship between objects and interfaces. The same object may have several interfaces that are each viewpoints on the methods that it provides. This is supported directly in Java where interfaces are declared separately from objects and objects 'implement' interfaces. Equally, a group of objects may all be accessed through a single interface.

Object interface design is concerned with specifying the detail of the interface to an object or to a group of objects. This means defining the signatures and semantics of the services that are provided by the object or by a group of objects. Interfaces can be specified in the UML using the same notation as in a class diagram. However, there is no attribute section and the UML stereotype <<interface>> should be included in the name part.

An alternative approach that I prefer is to use a programming language to define the interface. This is illustrated in Figure 12.15 which shows the interface specification in Java of the weather station. As interfaces become more complex, this approach becomes more effective because the syntax checking facilities in the compiler may be used to discover errors and inconsistencies in the interface description. The Java description can show that some methods can take different numbers of parameters. Therefore, the **shutdown** method can either be applied to the station as a whole if it has no parameters or can shut down a single instrument.

12.3 Design evolution

An important advantage of an object-oriented approach to design is that it simplifies the problem of making changes to the design. The reason for this is that object state representation does not influence the design. Changing the internal details of an object is unlikely to affect any other system objects. Furthermore, because objects are loosely coupled, it is usually straightforward to introduce new objects without significant effects on the rest of the system.

To illustrate the robustness of the object-oriented approach, assume that pollution monitoring capabilities are to be added to each weather station. This involves adding an air quality meter to compute the amount of various pollutants in the atmosphere. The pollution readings are transmitted at the same time as the weather data. To modify the design, the following changes must be made:

1. An object class called **Air quality** should be introduced as part of **WeatherStation** at the same level as **WeatherData**.

2. An operation **reportAirQuality** should be added to **WeatherStation** to send the pollution information to the central computer. The weather station control software must be modified so that pollution readings are automatically collected when requested by the top-level **WeatherStation** object.

3. Objects representing the types of pollution monitoring instruments should be added. In this case, levels of nitrous oxide, smoke and benzene can be measured.

Figure 12.16 shows **WeatherStation** and the new objects added to the system. Apart from at the highest level of the system (**WeatherStation**) no software changes are required in the original objects in the weather station. The addition of pollution data collection does not affect weather data collection in any way.

Figure 12.16 New objects to support pollution monitoring

WeatherStation
identifier
reportWeather ()   reportAirQuality ()   calibrate (instruments)   test ()   startup (instruments)   shutdown (instruments)

Air quality
NOData   smokeData   benzeneData
collect ()   summarise ()

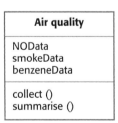

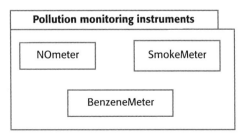

Pollution monitoring instruments
NOmeter   SmokeMeter   BenzeneMeter

KEY POINTS

▶ Object-oriented design is a means of designing software so that the fundamental components in the design represent objects with their own private state and operations rather than functions.

▶ An object should have constructor and inspection operations allowing its state to be inspected and modified. The object provides services (operations using state information) to other objects. Objects are created at run-time using a specification in an object class definition.

▶ Objects may be implemented sequentially or concurrently. A concurrent object may be a passive object whose state is only changed through its interface or an active object that can change its own state without outside intervention.

▶ The Unified Modeling Language (UML) has been designed to provide a range of different notations that can be used to document an object-oriented design.

▶ The process of object-oriented design includes activities to design the system architecture, identify objects in the system, describe the design using different object models and document the object interfaces.

▶ A range of different models may be produced during an object-oriented design process. These include static models (class models, generalisation models, association models) and dynamic models (sequence models, state machine models).

▶ Object interfaces must be defined precisely so that they can be used by other objects. A programming language such as Java may be used to document object interfaces.

▶ An important advantage of object-oriented design is that it simplifies the evolution of the system.

FURTHER READING

Comm. ACM, October 1999. This special issue includes a number of articles on the practical use of the UML for design. The article by Bell and Schmidt on using a design case study is particularly recommended.

Using UML: Software Engineering with Objects and Components. A nice, easy-to-read introduction to object-oriented design using UML. (R. Pooley and P. Stevens, 1999, Addison Wesley Longman.)

The Unified Modeling Language User Guide. The definitive text on UML and its use for describing object-oriented designs. There are two other associated texts – one is a UML reference manual, the other proposes an object-oriented development process. (G. Booch, I. Jacobson and J. Rumbaugh, 1999, Addison-Wesley.)

EXERCISES

12.1 Explain why adopting an approach to design that is based on loosely coupled objects that hide information about their representation should lead to a design which may be readily modified.

12.2 Using examples, explain the difference between an object and an object class.

12.3 Under what circumstances might it be appropriate to develop a design where objects execute concurrently?

12.4 Using the UML graphical notation for object classes, design the following object classes identifying attributes and operations. Use your own experience to decide on the attributes and operations that should be associated with these objects:

- a telephone;
- a printer for a personal computer;
- a personal stereo system;
- a bank account;
- a library catalogue.

12.5 Develop the design of the weather station design in detail by proposing interface descriptions of the objects shown in Figure 12.11. This may be expressed in Java, in C++, or in the UML.

12.6 Develop the design of the weather station to show the interaction between the data collection sub-system and the instruments that collect weather data. Use sequence charts to show this interaction.

12.7 Identify possible objects in the following systems and develop an object-oriented design for them. You may make any reasonable assumptions about the systems when deriving the design.

- A group diary and time management system is intended to support the timetabling of meetings and appointments across a group of co-workers. When an appointment is to be made which involves a number of people, the system finds a common slot in each of their diaries and arranges the appointment for that time. If no common slots are available, it interacts with the users to rearrange their personal diaries to make room for the appointment.

- A petrol (gas) station is to be set up for fully automated operation. Drivers swipe their credit card through a reader connected to the pump, the card is verified by communication with a credit company computer and a fuel limit established. The driver may then take the fuel required. When fuel delivery is complete and the pump hose is returned to its holster, the driver's credit card account is debited with the cost of the fuel taken. The credit card is returned after debiting. If the card is invalid, it is returned by the pump before fuel is dispensed.

12.8   Write precise interface definitions in Java or C++ for the objects you have defined in Exercise 12.7.

12.9   Draw a sequence diagram showing the interactions of objects in a group diary system when a group of people arrange a meeting.

12.10 Draw a statechart showing the possible state changes in one or more of the objects that you have defined in Exercise 12.7.

13 Real-time software design

Objectives

The objectives of this chapter are to introduce techniques that are used in the design of real-time systems and to describe some generic real-time system architectures. When you have read this chapter, you will:

❑ understand the concept of a real-time system and why real-time systems are usually implemented as a set of concurrent processes;

❑ have been introduced to a design process for real-time systems;

❑ understand the role of a real-time executive;

❑ understand common process architectures for monitoring and control systems and data acquisition systems.

Contents

13.1 System design
13.2 Real-time executives
13.3 Monitoring and control systems
13.4 Data acquisition systems

Computers are used to control a wide range of systems ranging from simple domestic machines to entire manufacturing plants. These computers interact directly with hardware devices. The software in these systems is an embedded real-time system that must react to events generated by the hardware and issue control signals in response to these events. It is *embedded* in some larger hardware system and must respond, in *real time*, to events from the system's environment.

Real-time systems are different from other types of software system. Their correct functioning is dependent on the system responding to events within a given (usually short) time interval. I define a real-time system as follows:

> A real-time system is a software system where the correct functioning of the system depends on the results produced by the system and the time at which these results are produced. A 'soft' real-time system is a system whose operation is *degraded* if results are not produced according to the specified timing requirements. A 'hard' real-time system is a system whose operation is *incorrect* if results are not produced according to the timing specification.

One way of looking at a real-time system is as a stimulus/response system. Given a particular input stimulus, the system must produce some corresponding response. The behaviour of a real-time system can therefore be defined by listing stimuli that are received by the system, the associated responses and the time at which the response must be produced.

Stimuli fall into two classes:

1. *Periodic stimuli* These occur at predictable time intervals. For example, the system may examine a sensor every 50 milliseconds and take action (respond) depending on that sensor value (the stimulus).

2. *Aperiodic stimuli* These occur irregularly. They are usually signalled using the computer's interrupt mechanism. An example of such a stimulus would be an interrupt indicating that an I/O transfer was complete and that data was available in a buffer.

Periodic stimuli in a real-time system are usually generated by sensors associated with the system. These provide information about the state of the system's environment. The responses are directed to a set of actuators that control some hardware unit that then influences the system's environment. Aperiodic stimuli may be generated either by the actuators or by sensors. They often indicate some exceptional condition, such as a hardware failure, which must be handled by the system. This sensor–system–actuator model of an embedded real-time system is illustrated in Figure 13.1.

A real-time system has to respond to stimuli that occur at different times. Its architecture must therefore be organised so that control is transferred to the appropriate handler for that stimulus as soon as it is received. This is impractical in sequential programs. Real-time systems are, therefore, normally designed as a set

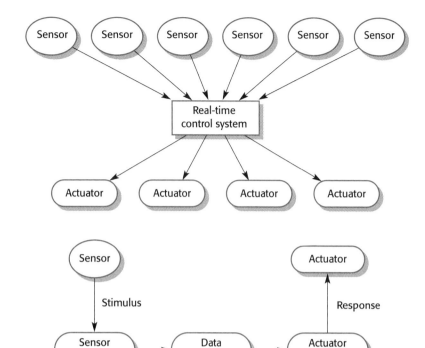

Figure 13.1 General model of a real-time system

Figure 13.2 Sensor/actuator control processes

of concurrent, cooperating processes. Part of the real-time system (the real-time executive) is dedicated to managing these processes.

The generality of this stimulus/response model of a real-time system leads to the generic architectural model where there are three types of process (see Figure 13.2). For each type of sensor, there is a sensor management process; computational processes compute the required response for the stimuli received by the system; actuator control processes manage actuator operation. This model allows data to be collected quickly from the sensor (before the next input becomes available) and allows processing and the associated actuator response to be carried out later.

13.1 System design

As discussed in Chapter 2, part of the system design process involves deciding which system capabilities are to be implemented in software and which in hardware. Timing constraints or other requirements may mean that some system functions, such as signal processing, have to be implemented using specially designed hardware. The system design process may therefore involve the design of special-purpose hardware as well as real-time software design.

Hardware components deliver much better performance than the equivalent software. System processing bottlenecks can be identified and replaced by hardware, thus avoiding expensive software optimisation. Providing performance in hardware means that the software design can be structured for adaptability and that performance considerations can take second place.

Decisions on hardware/software partitioning should, if possible, be left until as late as possible in the design process. This implies that the system architecture should be made up of stand-alone components which can be implemented in either hardware or software. Fortunately, building a design in this way is exactly the aim of the designer trying to design a maintainable system. A good system design process should therefore result in a system which can be implemented in either hardware or software.

The design process for real-time systems differs from other software design processes because the system response times must be considered early in the process. Events (the stimuli) rather than objects or functions should be central to the design process. There are several stages in this design process:

1. Identify the stimuli that the system must process and the associated responses.

2. For each stimulus and associated response, identify the timing constraints which apply to both stimulus and response processing.

3. Aggregate the stimulus and response processing into a number of concurrent processes. A good general model for the system architecture is to associate a process with each class of stimulus and response as shown in Figure 13.2.

4. For each stimulus and response, design algorithms to carry out the required computations. Algorithm designs often have to be developed relatively early in the design process to give an indication of the amount of processing required and the time required to complete that processing.

5. Design a scheduling system which will ensure that processes are started in time to meet their deadlines.

6. Integrate the system under the control of a real-time executive.

Naturally, this is an iterative process. Once a process architecture has been established and a scheduling policy decided, extensive assessments and simulations are needed to check that the system will meet its timing constraints. This analysis may reveal that the system will not perform adequately. The process architecture, the scheduling policy, the executive or all of these may then have to be redesigned to improve the performance of the system.

Analysing the timing of a real-time system is difficult. Because of unpredictable nature of aperiodic stimuli, the designers must make some assumptions as to the probability of these stimuli occurring (and therefore requiring service) at any particular time. These assumptions may be incorrect and system performance after delivery may not be adequate. Dasarthy (1985) and Burns (1991) discuss general issues of timing validation. Gomaa's book (1993) includes a good discussion of methods for performance analysis.

Processes in a real-time system must be coordinated. Process coordination mechanisms ensure mutual exclusion to shared resources. When one process is modifying a shared resource, other processes should not be able to change that resource. Mechanisms for ensuring mutual exclusion include semaphores (Dijkstra, 1968b), monitors (Hoare, 1974) and critical regions (Brinch-Hansen, 1973). I do not cover these mechanisms here as they are well documented in operating system texts (Tanenbaum and Woodhull, 1997; Silberschaltz and Galvin, 1998).

Because real-time systems must meet their timing constraints, it may not be practical to use design strategies for hard real-time systems that involve additional implementation overhead. For example, object-oriented design involves hiding data representations and accessing attribute values through operations defined with the object. This involves an inevitable overhead and consequent loss of performance.

13.1.1   Real-time system modelling

Real-time systems have to respond to events occurring at irregular intervals. These events (or stimuli) often cause the system to move to a different state. For this reason, state machine modelling, described in Chapter 7, may be used as a way of describing a real-time system.

A state model of a system assumes that, at any time, the system is in one of a number of possible states. When a stimulus is received, this may cause a transition to a different state. For example, a system controlling a valve may move from a state 'Valve open' to a state 'Valve closed' when an operator command (the stimulus) is received.

I illustrate this approach to system modelling using the model of a simple microwave oven that I introduced in Chapter 7. Figure 13.3 shows a state machine model of a simple microwave oven equipped with buttons to set the power and the timer and to start the system. The rounded rectangles represent system states and the arrowed labels represent stimuli which force a transition from one state to another. The names chosen in the state machine diagram are descriptive and the associated information indicates actions taken by the system actuators or information that is displayed.

You can trace the operation of the oven by reading the model from left to right. In the initial state (Waiting), the user may select either full-power or half-power. The next state is entered when the user presses the timer button and sets the time. Operation may then be enabled when the oven door is closed and the food is cooked in the Operation state. Finally, when cooking is complete, the oven returns to the Waiting state.

State machine models are a good, language-independent way of representing the design of a real-time system. For this reason, they are an integral part of real-time design methods (Ward and Mellor, 1985; Harel, 1987, 1988). Harel's method, which is based on a notation called *Statecharts*, has addressed the problem of the inherent

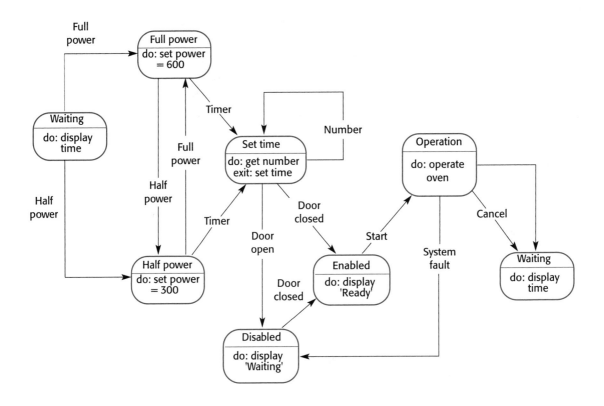

Figure 13.3 State machine model of a microwave oven

complexity of state machine models. Statecharts structure state models so that groups of state can be considered as a single entity. The notation also allows concurrent systems to be represented as state models. State models are also supported in the Unified Modeling Language (Rumbaugh *et al.*, 1999a) and I use the UML notation here.

13.1.2 Real-time programming

The programming language used for implementing a real-time system may also influence the design. Hard real-time systems are still sometimes programmed in assembly language so that tight deadlines can be met. Systems-level languages, such as C, that allow efficient code to be generated may also be used.

The advantage of using a low-level systems programming language like C is that it allows the development of very efficient programs. However, the language does not include any constructs to support concurrency or the management of shared resources. It relies on operating system or executive facilities and, hence, there is increased scope for programming error. Programs are also often more difficult to understand.

Ada was originally designed for embedded systems implementation and has features such as tasking, exceptions and representation clauses. Its *rendezvous* capability is a good general-purpose mechanism for task synchronisation (Burns and Wellings, 1990; Barnes, 1994). Unfortunately, the original version of Ada (Ada 83) was unsuitable for hard real-time systems implementation. It was impossible to specify task deadlines, there is no inbuilt exception if a deadline is not met and a strict first-in, first-out policy for servicing a queue of task entries is imposed. A revision of the 1983 Ada standard (Barnes, 1998) addressed some of these issues. The revised version of the language provided protected types that allowed for the easier implementation of protected, shared data structures and more control over task scheduling and timing. These have improved Ada as a real-time programming language but they still do not provide sufficient control for hard real-time systems.

The initial versions of Java (then called Oak) were designed for writing small-scale embedded systems such as those in domestic appliance controllers. The Java designers have therefore included some support for concurrent processes in the form of concurrent objects (threads) and synchronised methods. However, as these systems do not have strict timing constraints, Java does not include facilities to control the scheduling of threads or to specify that threads should run at particular times.

Java, therefore, is not suitable for programming hard-real time systems or systems where processes have strict deadlines. The fundamental problems with Java as a real-time programming language are:

1. It is not possible to specify the time at which threads should execute.
2. Garbage collection is uncontrollable – it may be started at any time. Therefore, the timing behaviour of threads is unpredictable.
3. It is not possible to discover the sizes of queue associated with shared resources.
4. The implementation of the Java Virtual Machine varies from one computer to another, so the same program can have different timing behaviours.
5. The language does not allow for detailed run-time space or processor analysis.

At the time of writing, work is under way to address some of these problems and to define a real-time version of Java (Nilsen, 1998). However, it is not clear how this can be separated from the implementation of the underlying Java Virtual Machine. There is therefore an inevitable conflict between language portability and real-time characteristics.

13.2 Real-time executives

A real-time executive is analogous to an operating system in a general-purpose computer. It manages processes and resource allocation in a real-time system.

Figure 13.4
Components of a
real-time executive

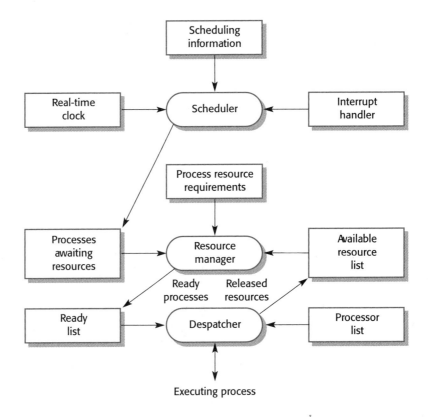

Figure 13.4
Components of a
real-time executive

It starts and stops appropriate processes so that stimuli can be handled and allocates memory and processor resources. It does not, however, usually include more complex operating system facilities such as file management.

Baker and Scallon (1986) present a good discussion of the facilities required in real-time executives. Cooling (1991) also covers this topic and briefly discusses commercial real-time executive products. Although there are several real-time executive products available, the specialised requirements of many real-time systems often require that the executive has to be designed as part of the system.

The components of an executive (Figure 13.4) depend on the size and complexity of the real-time system being developed. Normally, for all except the simplest systems, they will include:

1. *A real-time clock*   This provides information to schedule processes periodically.
2. *An interrupt handler*   This manages aperiodic requests for service.
3. *A scheduler*   This component is responsible for examining the processes which can be executed and choosing one of these for execution.
4. *A resource manager*   Given a process which is scheduled for execution, the resource manager allocates appropriate memory and processor resources.
5. *A despatcher*   This component is responsible for starting the execution of a process.

Systems that provide a continuous service, such as telecommunication and monitoring systems with high reliability requirements, may also include further executive capabilities:

- *A configuration manager*   This is responsible for the dynamic reconfiguration (Kramer and Magee, 1985) of the system's hardware. Hardware modules may be taken out of service and the system upgraded by adding new hardware without shutting down the system.

- *A fault manager*   This component is responsible for detecting hardware and software faults and taking appropriate action to recover from these faults. Principles of fault tolerance and recovery are discussed in Chapter 18.

Stimuli processed by a real-time system usually have different levels of priority. For some stimuli, such as those associated with certain exceptional events, it is essential that their processing should be completed within the specified time limits. Other processes may be safely delayed if a more critical process requires service. Consequently, the executive for a real-time system has to be able to manage at least two priority levels for system processes:

1. *Interrupt level*   This is the highest priority level. It is allocated to processes which need a very fast response. One of these processes will be the real-time clock process.

2. *Clock level*   This level of priority is allocated to periodic processes.

There may be a further priority level allocated to background processes (such as a self-checking process) which do not need to meet real-time deadlines. These processes are scheduled for execution when processor capacity is available.

Within each of these priority levels, different classes of process may be allocated different priorities. For example, there may be several interrupt lines. An interrupt from a very fast device may have to pre-empt processing of an interrupt from a slower device to avoid information loss. The allocation of process priorities so that all processes are serviced in time usually requires extensive analysis and simulation.

13.2.1   Process management

Process management in a real-time executive is concerned with managing the set of concurrent processes that are part of the real-time system. The process manager has to choose a process for execution, allocate memory and processor resources to that process and start its execution on a processor.

Periodic processes are processes which must be executed at pre-specified time intervals for data acquisition and actuator control. The executive uses its real-time clock to determine when a process is to be executed. In most real-time systems,

Figure 13.5
Real-time executive
actions required
to start a process

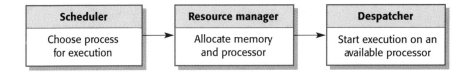

there will be several classes of periodic process. These will have different periods (the time between process executions), execution times and deadlines (the time by which processing must be complete). The executive must choose the appropriate process for execution at any one time.

The real-time clock is configured to 'tick' periodically where a 'tick' period might typically be a few milliseconds. The clock 'tick' initiates an interrupt-level process which then schedules the process manager for periodic processes. The interrupt-level process is not normally responsible for managing periodic processes because interrupt processing must be completed as quickly as possible.

The actions taken by the executive for periodic process management are shown in Figure 13.5. The list of periodic processes is examined by the scheduler which selects a process to be executed. The choice depends on the process priority, the process periods, the expected execution times and the deadlines of the ready processes. Sometimes, two processes with different deadlines should be executed at the same clock tick. In such a situation, one must be delayed so long as its deadline can still be met.

When an interrupt is detected by the executive, this indicates that some service is required. The computer's interrupt mechanism causes control to transfer to a predetermined memory location that contains an instruction to jump to an interrupt service routine. Interrupt service routines must be simple, short and have fast execution times. While the interrupt is being serviced, other interrupts are disabled and will be ignored by the system. To make the probability of information loss as low as possible, the time spent in this state must be minimised.

The service routine should disable further interrupts to avoid being interrupted itself. It should discover the cause of the interrupt and initiate, with a high priority, a process to handle the stimulus causing the interrupt. In some high-speed data acquisition systems, the interrupt handler saves the data which the interrupt signalled was available in a buffer for later processing. Interrupts are then enabled again and control is returned to the executive.

At any one time, there may be several processes, with different priorities, which should be executed. It is up to the scheduler to decide the order of execution. Effective scheduling is essential if the real-time requirements for a system are to be satisfied. There are two fundamental scheduling strategies:

1. *Non pre-emptive scheduling* Once a process has been scheduled for execution it runs to completion or until it is blocked for some reason such as waiting for input. This causes problems when there are processes with different priorities and a high-priority process has to wait for a low-priority process to finish.

2. *Pre-emptive scheduling*   The execution of an executing process may be stopped if a higher-priority processes requires service. The higher-priority process pre-empts the execution of the lower-priority process and is allocated to a processor.

Within these strategies, different scheduling algorithms have been developed. These include round-robin scheduling where each process is executed in turn, rate monotonic scheduling where the process with the shortest period is given priority and shortest deadline first scheduling (Burns and Wellings, 1997). Each of these has different advantages and disadvantages but I do not have space to cover these here.

Information about the process to be executed is passed to the resource manager. The resource manager allocates memory and, in a multiprocessor system, a processor to this process. The process is then placed on the 'ready list', a list of processes which are ready for execution. When a processor finishes executing a process and becomes available, the despatcher is invoked. It scans the ready list to find a process which can be executed on the available processor and starts its execution.

13.3 Monitoring and control systems

There are a number of fairly standard system classes of real-time system such as monitoring systems, data acquisition systems, command and control systems, etc. Each of these system types has a characteristic process architecture so, when a system is developed, its architecture can usually be derived from one of these standard types. Therefore, rather than discuss general design issues, I illustrate real-time systems design using these generic models.

Monitoring and control systems are an important class of real-time system. They check sensors providing information about the system's environment and take actions depending on the sensor reading. Monitoring systems take action when some exceptional sensor value is detected. Control systems continuously control hardware actuators depending on the value of associated sensors.

Consider the following example:

A burglar alarm system is to be implemented for a building. This uses several different types of sensor. These include movement detectors in individual rooms, window sensors on ground floor windows which detect if a window has been broken, and door sensors which detect door opening on corridor doors. There are 50 window sensors, 30 door sensors and 200 movement detectors in the system.

When a sensor detects the presence of an intruder, the system automatically calls the local police and, using a voice synthesiser, reports the location of the alarm. It switches on lights in the rooms around the active sensor and sets off an audible alarm. The alarm system is normally powered by mains power but is equipped with a battery backup. Power loss is detected using a separate power circuit monitor that monitors the mains voltage. It interrupts the alarm system when a voltage drop is detected.

This system is a 'soft' real-time system which does not have stringent timing requirements. The sensors do not need to detect high-speed events so they need only be polled twice per second.

The design process starts by identifying the aperiodic stimuli which the system receives and the associated responses. I have simplified the design by ignoring stimuli generated by system self-checking procedures and external stimuli generated to test the system or to switch it off in the event of a false alarm. This means that there are only two classes of stimulus which must be processed:

1. *Power failure*   This is generated by the circuit monitor. The required response is to switch the circuit to backup power by signalling an electronic power switching device.

2. *Intruder alarm*   This is a stimulus generated by one of the system sensors. The response to this stimulus is to compute the room number of the active sensor, set up a call to the police, initiate the voice synthesiser to manage the call, and switch on the audible intruder alarm and the building lights in the area.

Figure 13.6
Stimulus/response
timing requirements

Stimulus/Response	Timing requirements
Power fail interrupt	The switch to backup power must be completed within a deadline of 50 ms.
Door alarm	Each door alarm should be polled twice per second.
Window alarm	Each window alarm should be polled twice per second.
Movement detector	Each movement detector should be polled twice per second.
Audible alarm	The audible alarm should be switched on within $\frac{1}{2}$ second of an alarm being raised by a sensor.
Lights switch	The lights should be switched on within $\frac{1}{2}$ second of an alarm being raised by a sensor.
Communications	The call to the police should be started within 2 seconds of an alarm being raised by a sensor.
Voice synthesiser	A synthesised message should be available within 4 seconds of an alarm being raised by a sensor.

The next step in the design process is to consider the timing constraints associated with each stimulus and associated response. These timing constraints are shown in Figure 13.6. In this diagram, the different classes of sensor that can generate an alarm stimulus have been listed separately as these have different timing requirements.

Allocation of the system functions to concurrent processes is the next design stage. There are three different types of sensor which must be polled periodically, so each of these sensor types has an associated process. There is an interrupt-driven system to handle power failure and switching, a communications system, a voice synthesiser, an audible alarm system and a light switching system to switch on lights around the sensor. Each of these systems is controlled by an independent process. This suggests the system architecture shown in Figure 13.7.

In the notation used in Figure 13.7, annotated arrows joining processes indicate data flows between processes with the annotation indicating the type of data flow. The arrow associated with each process on the top right indicates control. The arrows on a periodic process use solid lines with the minimum number of times a process should be executed per second as an annotation.

Figure 13.7
Process architecture
of the burglar
alarm system

The rate of period scheduling is determined by the number of sensors and the timing requirements of the system. For example, there are 30 door sensors which

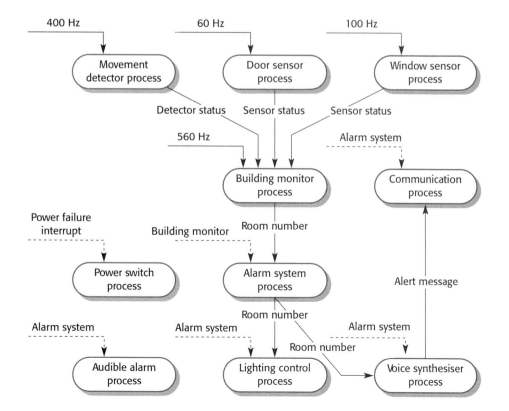

Figure 13.8 Java
implementation of
the building monitor
process

```java
// See http://www.software-engin.com/ for links to the complete Java code for this
// example

class BuildingMonitor extends Thread {

    BuildingSensor win, door, move ;

    Siren     siren = new Siren () ;
    Lights   lights = new Lights () ;
    Synthesizer synthesizer = new Synthesizer () ;
    DoorSensors doors = new DoorSensors (30) ;
    WindowSensors windows = new WindowSensors (50) ;
    MovementSensors movements = new MovementSensors (200) ;
    PowerMonitor pm = new PowerMonitor () ;

    BuildingMonitor()
    {
        // initialise all the sensors and start the processes
        siren.start () ; lights.start () ;
        synthesizer.start () ; windows.start () ;
        doors.start () ; movements.start () ; pm.start () ;
    }

    public void run ()
    {
        int room = 0 ;
        while (true)
        {
            // poll the movement sensors at least twice per second (400 Hz)
            move = movements.getVal () ;
            // poll the window sensors at least twice/second (100 Hz)
            win = windows.getVal () ;
            // poll the door sensors at least twice per second (60 Hz)
            door = doors.getVal () ;
            if (move.sensorVal == 1 | door.sensorVal == 1 | win.sensorVal == 1)
                {
                    // a sensor has indicated an intruder
                    if (move.sensorVal == 1)  room = move.room ;
                    if (door.sensorVal == 1)  room = door.room ;
                    if (win.sensorVal == 1)   room = win.room ;

                    lights.on (room) ; siren.on () ; synthesizer.on (room) ;
                    break ;
                }
        }
        lights.shutdown () ; siren.shutdown () ; synthesizer.shutdown () ;
        windows.shutdown () ; doors.shutdown () ; movements.shutdown () ;

    } // run
} //BuildingMonitor
```

must be interrogated twice per second. This means that the associated door sensor process must run 60 times per second (60 Hz). Similarly, the movement detector process must run 400 times per second.

Aperiodic processes have dashed lines on the control arrows. The lines are annotated with the event that causes the process to be scheduled. The control information on the actuator processes (i.e. the audible alarm controller, the lighting controller, etc.) indicates that they are started by an explicit command from the Alarm system process. All processes need not receive data from other processes. For example, the process responsible for managing a power failure has no need for data from elsewhere in the system.

These processes may be implemented in Java using threads. Figure 13.8 shows the Java code that implements the BuildingMonitor process which polls the system sensors. If these signal an intruder, the software activates the associated alarm system. It is assumed in this design that the timing requirements (included as comments) can be met. As I discussed earlier, Java 2.0 does not include facilities to allow thread execution frequency to be specified.

As this system does not have strict timing requirements, it is possible to implement it in Java. Of course, there is no way to guarantee in Java 2.0 that the timing specifications will be met. In this example, all sensors are polled the same number of times. This would not cause practical problems in such a system.

Once the system process architecture has been established, algorithms for stimulus processing and response generation should be designed. As discussed in section 13.1, this detailed design stage is necessary early in the design process to ensure that the system can meet its specified timing constraints. If the associated algorithms are complex, changes to the timing constraints may be required. Unless signal processing is required, real-time system algorithms are often very simple. They only require a memory location to be checked, some simple computations to be carried out or a signal to be despatched. This is the case with the burglar alarm system so I have left out the algorithm design stage.

The final step in the design process is to design a scheduling system which ensures that a process will always be scheduled to meet its deadlines. In this example, deadlines are not tight. Process priorities should be organised so that all sensor polling processes have the same priority. The process for handling a power failure should be a higher-priority interrupt-level process. The priorities of the processes managing the alarm system should be the same as the sensor processes. If the system was implemented in Java then the Java run-time system would manage process scheduling.

The burglar alarm system is a monitoring system rather than a control system as it does not include actuators which are directly affected by sensor values. An example of a control system is a building heating control system. This system monitors temperature sensors in different rooms in the building and switches a heater unit off and on depending on the actual temperature and the temperature set on the room thermostat. The thermostat also controls the switching of the furnace in the system.

Figure 13.9
Process architecture
of a temperature
control system

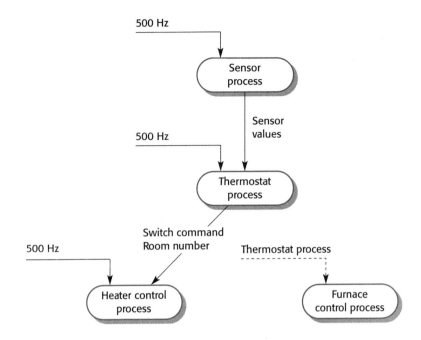

The process architecture of this system is shown in Figure 13.9. It is clear that its general form is similar to the burglar alarm system. Further development of this example is left as an exercise for the reader.

13.4 Data acquisition systems

Data acquisition systems are another class of real-time system that are usually based on a generic architectural model. These systems collect data from sensors for subsequent processing and analysis.

To illustrate this class of system, consider the system model shown in Figure 13.10. This represents a system which collects data from sensors monitoring the neutron flux in a nuclear reactor. The sensor data is placed in a buffer from which it is extracted and processed and the average flux level is displayed on an operator's display.

Each sensor has an associated process that converts the analogue input flux level into a digital signal. It passes this flux level, with the sensor identifier, to the sensor data buffer. The process responsible for data processing takes the data

Figure 13.10 The architecture of a fiux monitoring system

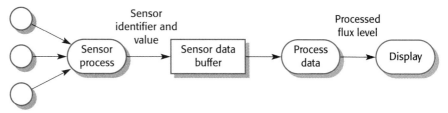

Figure 13.11 A ring buffer for data acquisition

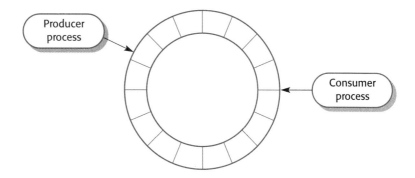

from this buffer, processes it and passes it to a display process for output on an operator console.

In real-time systems that involve data acquisition and processing, the execution speeds and periods of the acquisition process and the processing process may be out of step. When significant processing is required, the data acquisition may go faster than the data processing. If only simple computations need be carried out, the processing may be faster than the data acquisition.

To smooth out these speed differences, most data acquisition systems buffer input data using a circular or ring buffer. The process producing the data (the producer) adds information to this buffer and the process using the data (the consumer) takes information from the buffer (Figure 13.11).

Obviously, mutual exclusion must be implemented to prevent the producer and consumer processes accessing the same element in the buffer at the same time. The system must also ensure that the producer does not try to add information to a full buffer and the consumer does not take information from an empty buffer.

In Figure 13.12 I show a possible implementation of the data buffer as a Java object. The values in the buffer are of type **SensorRecord** and there are two operations that are defined, namely **get** and **put**. The **get** operation takes an item from the buffer and the **put** operation adds an item to the buffer. The constructor for the buffer sets the size when objects of type **CircularBuffer** are declared.

Figure 13.12 A Java
implementation of a
ring buffer

```
class CircularBuffer
{
    int bufsize ;
    SensorRecord [] store ;
    int numberOfEntries = 0 ;
    int front = 0, back = 0 ;

    CircularBuffer (int n) {
        bufsize = n ;
        store = new SensorRecord [bufsize] ;
    } // CircularBuffer

    synchronized void put (SensorRecord rec ) throws InterruptedException
    {
        if ( numberOfEntries == bufsize)
            wait () ;
        store [back] = new SensorRecord (rec.sensorId, rec.sensorVal) ;
        back = back + 1 ;
        if (back == bufsize)
            back = 0 ;
        numberOfEntries = numberOfEntries + 1 ;
        notify () ;
    } // put

    synchronized SensorRecord get () throws InterruptedException
    {
        SensorRecord result = new SensorRecord (-1, -1) ;
        if (numberOfEntries == 0)
                wait () ;
        result = store [front] ;
        front = front + 1 ;
        if (front == bufsize)
            front = 0 ;
        numberOfEntries = numberOfEntries - 1 ;
        notify () ;
        return result ;
    } // get
} // CircularBuffer
```

The synchronized modifier associated with the get and put methods indicates that
these methods should not operate concurrently. When one of these methods is invoked,
the run-time system obtains a lock on the object instance to ensure that the other
method cannot be invoked at the same time and thus manipulate the same entry in
the buffer. The wait and notify method invocations within these methods ensure that
entries cannot be put into a full buffer or taken from an empty buffer. The wait
method causes the invoking thread to suspend itself until another thread tells it to
stop waiting by calling the notify method. When wait is called, the lock on the protected object is released. The notify method wakes up one of the threads that is waiting and causes it to restart execution.

KEY POINTS

▶ A real-time system is a software system that must respond to events in real time. Its correctness does not just depend on the results it produces but also on the time when these results are produced.

▶ A general model for real-time systems architecture involves associating a process with each class of sensor and actuator device. Other coordination processes may also be required.

▶ The architectural design of a real-time system usually involves organising the system as a set of interacting, concurrent processes.

▶ A real-time executive is responsible for process and resource management. It always includes a scheduler which is the component responsible for deciding which process should be scheduled for executing. Scheduling decisions are made using process priorities.

▶ Monitoring and control systems periodically poll a set of sensors which capture information from the system's environment. They take actions, depending on the sensor readings, by issuing commands to actuators.

▶ Data acquisition systems are usually organised according to a producer–consumer model. The producer process puts the data into a circular buffer where it is consumed by the consumer process. The buffer is also implemented as a process so that conflicts between the producer and consumer are eliminated.

▶ Although Java has facilities for supporting concurrency, it is not suitable for the development of time-critical real-time systems. It lacks facilities to control execution and it is impossible to analyse the timing behaviour of Java programs.

FURTHER READING

Doing Hard Time: Developing Real-time Systems with UML, Objects Frameworks and Patterns. This book discusses how object-oriented techniques can be used in the design of real-time systems. As hardware speeds increase, this is becoming an increasingly viable approach to real-time systems design. (B. P. Douglass, 1999, Addison-Wesley.)

'Adding real-time capabilities to Java'. A good description of why Java is not suited to real-time systems development. (K. Nilsen, *Comm. ACM,* 41(6), June 1998.)

Real-time Systems and Programming Languages, 2nd edition. An excellent and comprehensive text that provides broad coverage of all aspects of real-time systems. (A. Burns and A. Wellings, 1997, Addison-Wesley.)

Advances in Real-time Systems. This is an excellent IEEE tutorial volume that covers various aspects of real-time systems design and implementation. Some of the chapters assume that the reader is familiar with the subject area but others are good introductions. (J. A. Stankovic and K. Ramamritham, 1993, IEEE Press.)

EXERCISES

13.1 Using examples, explain why real-time systems usually have to be implemented using concurrent processes.

13.2 Explain why an object-oriented approach to software development may not be suitable for real-time systems.

13.3 Draw state machine models of the control software for the following systems:

- An automatic washing machine which has different programs for different types of clothes.

- The software for a compact disc player.

- A telephone answering machine which records incoming messages and displays the number of accepted messages on an LED display. The system should allow the telephone owner to dial in, type a sequence of numbers (identified as tones) and have the recorded messages replayed over the phone.

- A drinks vending machine which can dispense coffee with and without milk and sugar. The user deposits a coin and makes his or her selection by pressing a button on the machine. This causes a cup with powdered coffee to be output. The user places this cup under a tap, presses another button and hot water is dispensed.

13.4 Using the real-time system design techniques discussed in this chapter, redesign the weather station data collection system covered in Chapter 12 as a stimulus/response system.

13.5 Design a process architecture for an environmental monitoring system which collects data from a set of air quality sensors situated around a city. There are 5000 sensors organised into 100 neighbourhoods. Each sensor must be interrogated 4 times per second. When more than 30 per cent of the sensors in a particular neighbourhood indicate that the air quality is below an acceptable level, local warning lights are activated. All sensors return the readings to a central computer which generates/reports every 15 minutes on the air quality in the city.

13.6 Discuss the strengths and weaknesses of Java as a programming language for real-time systems.

Figure 13.13 Train
protection system
description

- The system acquires information on the speed limit of a segment from a trackside transmitter which continually broadcasts the segment identifier and its speed limit. The same transmitter also broadcasts information on the status of the signal controlling that track segment. The time required to broadcast track segment and signal information is 50 milliseconds.
- The train can receive information from the trackside transmitter when it is within 10 m of a transmitter.
- The maximum train speed is 180 kph.
- Sensors on the train provide information about the current train speed (updated every 250 milliseconds) and the train brake status (updated every 100 milliseconds).
- If the train speed exceeds the current segment speed limit by more than 5 kph, a warning is sounded in the driver's cabin. If the train speed exceeds the current segment speed limit by more than 10 kph, the train's brakes are automatically applied until the speed falls to the segment speed limit. Train brakes should be applied within 100 milliseconds of the time when the excessive train speed has been detected.
- If the train enters a track segment which is signalled with a red light, the train protection system applies the train brakes and reduces the speed to zero. Train brakes should be applied within 100 milliseconds of the time when the red light signal is received.
- The system continually updates a status display in the driver's cabin.

13.7 A train protection system automatically applies the brakes of a train if the speed limit for a segment of track is exceeded or if the train enters a track segment which is currently signalled with a red light (i.e. the segment should not be entered). Details are shown in Figure 13.13. Identify the stimuli that must be processed by the on-board train control system and the associated responses to these stimuli.

13.8 Suggest a possible process architecture for this system.

13.9 If a periodic process in the on-board train protection system is used to collect data from the trackside transmitter, how often must it be scheduled to ensure that the system is guaranteed to collect information from the transmitter? Explain how you arrived at your answer.

13.10 You are asked to work on a real-time development project for a military application but have no previous experience of projects in that domain. Discuss what you, as a professional software engineer, should do before starting work on the project.

14 Design with reuse

Objectives

The objective of this chapter is to explain how the reuse of existing software may be incorporated into the systems design process. When you have read this chapter, you will:

❑ understand the benefits of reusing software components and some of the problems of reuse that can arise;

❑ understand different types of component that may be reused and design processes for reuse;

❑ have been introduced to the notion of application families and understand how application families are an effective way to reuse software;

❑ understand how patterns are high-level abstractions that promote design reuse in object-oriented development.

Contents

14.1 Component-based development
14.2 Application families
14.3 Design patterns

The design process in most engineering disciplines is based on component reuse. Mechanical or electrical engineers do not specify a design where every component has to be manufactured specially. They base their design on components that have been tried and tested in other systems. These components are not just small components such as flanges and valves but include major sub-systems such as engines, condensers or turbines.

It is now generally accepted that we need a comparable approach for software development. Software should be considered as an asset and reuse of these assets is essential to increase the return on their development costs. Demands for lower software production and maintenance costs, faster delivery of systems and increased quality can only be met by widespread and systematic software reuse.

To achieve software reuse, it must be considered during the software design or requirements engineering process. Opportunistic reuse is possible during programming when components are discovered that happen to fit a requirement. However, *systematic* reuse requires a design process that considers how existing designs may be reused and that explicitly organises the design around available software components.

Reuse-based software engineering is an approach to development which tries to maximise the reuse of existing software. The software units that are reused may be of radically different sizes. For example:

1. *Application system reuse* The whole of an application system may be reused either by incorporating it without change into other systems (COTS product reuse, section 14.1.2) or by developing application families that may run on different platforms or may be specialised to the needs of particular customers (application families, section 14.2).

2. *Component reuse* Components of an application ranging in size from subsystems to single objects may be reused. For example, a pattern-matching system developed as part of a text processing system may be reused in a database management system. This is covered in section 14.3.

3. *Function reuse* Software components which implement a single function, such as a mathematical function, may be reused. This form of reuse, based around standard libraries, has been common for the past 40 years.

Application system reuse has been widely practised for many years as software companies implement their systems across a range of machines and tailor them for different environments. Function reuse is also well established through standard libraries of reusable functions such as graphics and mathematical libraries. However, although there has been interest in component reuse since the early 1980s, it is only in the past few years that it has become accepted as a practical approach to software systems development.

An obvious advantage of software reuse is that overall development costs should be reduced. Fewer software components need be specified, designed, implemented and validated. However, cost reduction is only one potential advantage of reuse. There are a number of other advantages to reusing software assets, as shown in Figure 14.1.

Benefit	Explanation
Increased reliability	Reused components that have been exercised in working systems should be more reliable than new components. They have been tried and tested in a variety of different environments. Design and implementation faults are discovered and eliminated in the initial use of the components, thus reducing the number of failures when the component is reused.
Reduced process risk	If a component exists, there is less uncertainty in the costs of reusing that component than in the costs of development. This is an important factor for project management as it reduces the uncertainties in project cost estimation. This is particularly true when relatively large components such as sub-systems are reused.
Effective use of specialists	Instead of application specialists doing the same work on different projects, these specialists can develop reusable components which encapsulate their knowledge.
Standards compliance	Some standards, such as user interface standards, can be implemented as a set of standard components. For example, reusable components may be developed to implement menus in a user interface. All applications present the same menu formats to users. The use of standard user interfaces improves reliability as users are less likely to make mistakes when presented with a familiar interface.
Accelerated development	Bringing a system to market as early as possible is often more important than overall development costs. Reusing components speeds up system production because both development and validation time should be reduced.

Figure 14.1 Benefits of software reuse

There are three critical requirements for software design and development with reuse:

1. It must be possible to find appropriate reusable components. Organisations need a base of properly catalogued and documented reusable components. It must be easy to find components in this catalogue if they exist.

2. The reuser of the components must be confident that the components will behave as specified and will be reliable. Ideally, all components in an organisation's catalogue should be certified to confirm that they have reached some quality standards. In practice, this is unrealistic and people in a company learn informally about reliable components.

3. The components must have associated documentation to help the reuser understand them and adapt them to a new application. The documentation should include information about where components have been reused and any reuse problems which have been found.

The successful use of Visual Basic and Visual C++ with components and Java with JavaBeans has demonstrated the value of reuse. Component-based software

Problem	Explanation
Increased maintenance costs	If component source code is not available then maintenance costs may be increased, as the reused elements of the system may become increasingly incompatible with system changes.
Lack of tool support	CASE toolsets do not support development with reuse. It may be difficult or impossible to integrate these tools with a component library system. The software process assumed by these tools may not take reuse into account.
Not-invented-here syndrome	Some software engineers sometimes prefer to rewrite components as they believe that they can improve on the reusable component. This is partly to do with trust and partly to do with the fact that writing original software is seen as more challenging than reusing other people's software.
Maintaining a component library	Populating a component library and ensuring that software developers can use this library can be expensive. Our current techniques for classifying, cataloguing and retrieving software components are immature.
Finding and adapting reusable components	Software components have to be discovered in a library, understood and, sometimes, adapted to work in a new environment. Engineers must be reasonably confident of finding a component in the library before they will routinely include a component search as part of their normal development process.

Figure 14.2
Problems with reuse

engineering (Szyperski, 1998) is becoming widely accepted as a cost-effective approach to software development.

However, there are some costs and problems associated with reuse (Figure 14.2). These may inhibit the introduction of reuse and may mean that the reductions in overall development cost through reuse may be less than anticipated.

These difficulties mean that systematic reuse does not just happen but must be planned and introduced through an organisation-wide reuse programme. This has been recognised for many years in Japan (Matsumoto, 1984) where reuse is an integral part of the Japanese 'factory' approach to software development (Cusamano, 1989). Companies such as Hewlett-Packard have also been very successful in their reuse programmes (Griss and Wosser, 1995) and their experience has been incorporated in a general book by Jacobson *et al.* (1997).

An alternative to the component-oriented view of reuse is the generator view. In this approach to reuse, reusable knowledge is captured in a program generator system which can be programmed in a domain-oriented language. The application description specifies, in an abstract way, which reusable components are to be used, how they are to be combined and their parameterisation. Using this information, an operational software system can be generated (Figure 14.3).

Generator-based reuse is only possible when domain abstractions and their mapping to executable code can be identified. A domain-specific language (such as a 4GL) is then used to compose and control the domain abstractions. Areas where this has been successful include:

Figure 14.3
Generator-based
reuse

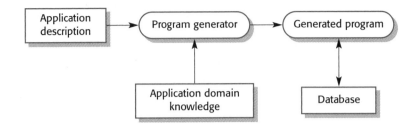

1. *Application generators for business data processing*   The input to these may be a 4GL or may be completely interactive where the user defines screens and processing actions. The output is a program in a language such as COBOL or SQL.

2. *Parser generators for language processing*   The generator input is a grammar describing the language to be parsed and the output is a language parser.

3. *Code generators in CASE tools*   The input to these generators is a software design and the output is a program implementing the designed system.

Generator-based reuse is cost-effective but depends on identifying stereotypical domain abstractions. This has been possible in the above areas and, to a lesser extent, in areas such as command and control systems (O'Connor *et al.*, 1994). Its prime advantage is that it is easier for end-users to develop programs using generators compared to other component-based approaches to reuse. However, the need for a deep understanding of application domain concepts and domain models has limited the applicability of this technique.

14.1 Component-based development

Component-based development or component-based software engineering emerged in the late 1990s as a reuse-based approach to software systems development. Its motivation was frustration that object-oriented development had not led to extensive reuse as originally suggested. Single object classes were too detailed and specific and had to be bound with an application either at compile-time or when the system was linked. Detailed knowledge of the classes were required to use them and this usually meant that source code had to be available. This presented difficult problems for marketing components. In spite of early optimistic predictions, no significant market for individual objects has ever developed.

Components are more abstract than object classes and can be considered to be stand-alone service providers. When a system needs some service, it calls on

Figure 14.4
Component
interfaces

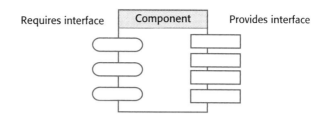

a component to provide that service without caring about where that component is executing or the programming language used to develop the component. For example, a very simple component could be a single mathematical function that computes the square root of a number. When a program requires a square root computation, it calls on that component to provide it. At the other end of the scale, a system that needs to carry out some arithmetic computations could call on a spreadsheet component that provides a calculation service.

Viewing a component as a service provider emphasises two critical characteristics of a reusable component:

1. The component is an independent executable entity. Source code is not available so that the component is not compiled with other system components.

2. Components publish their interface and all interactions are through that interface. The component interface is expressed in terms of parameterised operations and its internal state is never exposed.

Components are defined by their interfaces and, in the most general cases, can be thought of as having two related interfaces as shown in Figure 14.4:

• A *provides* interface that defines the services provided by the component

• A *requires* interface that specifies what services must be available from the system that is using the component. If these are not provided then the component will not work.

For example, consider a component that provides printing services as illustrated in Figure 14.5. In this case, the services that are provided are services to print a document, to discover the state of the queue associated with a particular printer, to register and unregister a printer with the printing services component, to move a print job from one printer to another and to remove a job from a print queue. The requirements for this component are that the underlying platform should provide a service called GetPDFile to retrieve the printer description file for a printer type and a service called PrinterInt that transfers commands to a specified printer.

Components may exist at different levels of abstraction, from a simple library subroutine to an entire application such as Microsoft Excel. Meyer (1999) identifies five distinct levels of abstraction:

Figure 14.5
A printing services
component

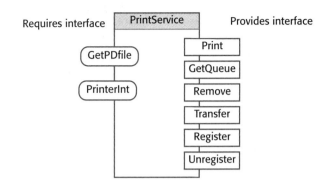

1. *Functional abstraction*   The component implements a single function such as a mathematical function. In essence, the *provides* interface is the function itself.

2. *Casual groupings*   The component is a collection of loosely related entities that might be data declarations, functions, etc. The *provides* interface consists of the names of all of the entities in the grouping.

3. *Data abstractions*   The component represents a data abstraction or class in an object-oriented language. The *provides* interface consists of operations to create, modify and access the data abstraction.

4. *Cluster abstractions*   The component is a group of related classes that work together. These are sometimes called frameworks. The *provides* interface is the composition of all of the provides interfaces of the objects that make up the framework. I discuss frameworks in section 14.1.1.

5. *System abstraction*   The component is an entire self-contained system. Reusing system-level abstractions is sometimes called COTS product reuse. The *provides* interface is the so-called API (Application Programming Interface) that is defined to allow programs to access the system commands and operations. I discuss COTS product reuse in section 14.1.2.

Component-oriented development can be integrated into a systems development process by incorporating a specific reuse activity as shown in Figure 14.6. The system designer completes a high-level design and specifications of the components of that design. These specifications are used to find components to reuse. These may be incorporated at the architectural level or at more detailed design levels.

Although this approach can result in significant reuse, it contrasts with the approach adopted in other engineering disciplines where reusability drives the design process. Rather than design then search for reusable components, engineers first search for

Figure 14.6
An opportunistic
reuse process

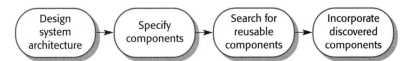

Figure 14.7
Development
with reuse

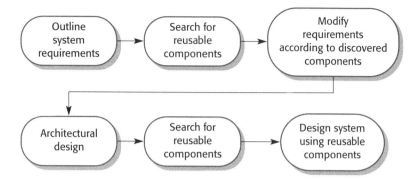

reusable components. They base their design on the components that are available (Figure 14.7).

In reuse-driven development, the system requirements are modified according to the reusable components available. The design is also based around existing components. Of course, this means that there may have to be requirements compromises. The design may be less efficient than a special-purpose design. However, the lower costs of development, more rapid system delivery and increased system reliability should compensate for this.

The process of implementing the system using components is usually either a prototyping process or an incremental development process. A standard programming language such as Java may be used with components in a library referenced from the program. Alternatively (and more commonly) a scripting language that is specifically designed for integrating reusable components is used to support rapid program development.

The first scripting language that was proposed for reusable component integration was the Unix shell (Bourne, 1978). Since then, a number of scripting languages, such as Visual Basic and TCL/TK, have been developed. Ousterhout (1998) discusses the benefits of scripting languages, including their typeless nature and the fact that they are interpreted rather than compiled.

As I discussed in Chapter 8 (Software Prototyping), users of Visual Basic construct applications visually by defining the interface by selecting types of interface component such as menus, text input fields, check boxes, etc. and positioning them on the screen. Individual components or component sequences that carry out some computation may then be associated with the interface entities.

Perhaps the main difficulty with component-based development is the problem of maintenance and evolution. Typically, the source code of components is not available and, as application requirements change, it may be impossible to change the components to reflect these requirements. The option of changing requirements at this stage to fit available components is not usually possible as the application is already in use. Additional work is therefore required to reuse components and, over time, this leads to increased maintenance costs. However, given that component-based development allows for faster delivery of software, organisations may be willing to accept these longer-term costs.

14.1.1   Application frameworks

The early proponents of object-oriented development suggested that objects were the most appropriate abstraction for reuse. However, as I explained in the previous section, objects are often too fine-grain and are specialised to a particular application. Instead, it has become clear that reuse is best supported in an object-oriented development process through larger-grain abstractions called frameworks.

Frameworks (or application frameworks) are a sub-system design made up of a collection of abstract and concrete classes and the interface between them (Wirfs-Brock and Johnson, 1990). Particular details of the application sub-system are implemented by adding components and by providing concrete implementations of abstract classes in the framework. Frameworks are rarely applications in their own right. Applications are normally constructed by integrating a number of frameworks.

Fayad and Schmidt (1997) have identified three classes of framework:

1. *System infrastructure frameworks*   These frameworks support the development of system infrastructures such as communications, user interfaces and compilers (Schmidt, 1997).

2. *Middleware integration frameworks*   These consist of a set of standards and associated object classes that support component communication and information exchange. Examples of this type of framework include CORBA, Microsoft's COM and DCOM and Java Beans (Orfali and Harkey, 1998). I have already described this type of framework in Chapter 11 where I covered distributed object architectures.

3. *Enterprise application frameworks*   These are concerned with specific application domains such as telecommunications or financial systems (Baumer *et al.*, 1997). These embed application domain knowledge and support the development of end-user applications. These frameworks are related to application families whose structure I discuss in section 14.2. However, they are usually more abstract and thus allow a wider range of applications to be created.

As the name suggests, a framework is a generic structure that can be extended to create a more specific sub-system or application. Extending the framework may involve adding concrete classes that inherit operations from abstract classes in the framework. In addition, call-backs may be defined. These are methods that are called in response to events that are recognised by the framework.

At the time of writing, the best developed frameworks are system infrastructure frameworks, especially those concerned with graphical user interfaces. Enterprise application frameworks are starting to emerge (Codenie *et al.*, 1997) but we are still trying to understand the most effective structures and organisations for these frameworks.

One of the best known and widely used frameworks for GUI design is the Model-View-Controller framework (Figure 14.8). This was originally proposed in the 1980s as an approach to GUI design that allowed for multiple presentations of

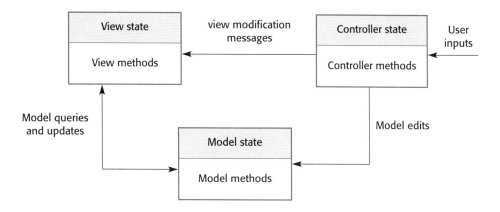

Figure 14.8
The Model-View-
Controller framework
an object and separate styles of interaction with each of these presentations. The MVC framework supports the presentation of data in different ways (see Figure 14.13) and separate interaction with each of these presentations. When the data is modified through one of the presentations, all of the other presentations are updated.

Frameworks are often instantiations of a number of patterns as discussed in section 14.2. For example, the MVC framework includes the Observer pattern which is described in Figure 14.12, the Strategy pattern which is concerned with updating the model, the Composite pattern and a number of others that are discussed by Gamma *et al.* (1995).

Applications that are constructed using frameworks can be the basis for further reuse through the concept of application families as discussed in section 14.3. Because these applications are constructed using a framework, modifying family members to create new family members is simplified.

The fundamental problem with frameworks is their inherent complexity and the time it takes to learn to use them. Several months may be required to completely understand a framework so it is likely that, in large organisations, some software engineers will become framework specialists. There is no doubt that this is an effective approach to reuse but the high cost of introduction limits its widespread use.

14.1.2   COTS product reuse

The term COTS (Commercial-Off-The-Shelf) products can, in principle, apply to any component that is offered by a third-party vendor. However, it is more normally used to refer to system software products. Hence we refer to COTS systems or sometimes just COTS (Commercial Off-the-shelf Systems). I normally prefer to talk about COTS systems. As the functionality offered by these systems is much wider than that of more specialised components, the potential payoff through reuse is increased.

Of course, some types of COTS system have been reused for many years. Database systems are perhaps the best example of this. Very few developers would consider implementing their own database management system. However, until fairly recently, there were only a few large systems such as database management systems and teleprocessing monitors that were routinely reused.

New approaches to system design that allow program access to system functions now mean that creating large systems, such as e-commerce systems, by integrating a range of COTS systems should always be considered as a serious design option. Because of the functionality that these systems offer, it is possible to reduce costs and delivery times by orders of magnitude compared to the development of new software. Furthermore, risks may be reduced as the product is already available and managers can see if it meets their requirements.

In principle, using a large-scale COTS system is the same as using any other more specific component. You have to understand the system interfaces and use them exclusively to communicate with the component; you have to trade off specific requirements against rapid development and reuse; you have to design a system architecture that allows the COTS systems to operate together.

However, the fact that these products are usually large systems in their own right and are often sold as separate stand-alone systems introduces additional problems. Boehm (1999) discusses four problems with COTS system integration:

1. *Lack of control over functionality and performance*   Although the published interface of a product may appear to offer the required facilities, these may not be properly implemented or may perform poorly. The product may have hidden operations that interfere with its operation. Fixing these problems may be a priority for the COTS product integrator but may not be of real concern to the product vendor. Users may simply have to find work-arounds to problems if they wish to reuse the COTS product.

2. *Problems with COTS system interoperability*   It is sometimes difficult to get COTS products to work together because each product embeds different assumptions about how it will be used. Garlan *et al.* (1995) reported on their experience of trying to integrate four COTS products and found that three of these products were event-based but each used a different model of events and assumed that it had exclusive access to the event queue. As a consequence, the project required five times as much effort as originally predicted and the schedule was two years rather than the predicted six months.

3. *No control over system evolution*   Vendors of COTS products make their own decisions on system changes in response to market pressures. For PC products, in particular, new versions are often produced very frequently and may not be compatible with all previous versions. New versions may have additional unwanted functionality and previous versions may become unavailable and unsupported.

4. *Support from COTS vendors*   The level of support that is available from COTS vendors varies widely. Because these are off-the-shelf systems, vendor support is particularly important when problems arise because developers do

not have access to the source code and detailed documentation of the system. While vendors may commit to providing support, changing market and economic circumstances may make it difficult for them to deliver this commitment. For example, a COTS system vendor may decide to discontinue a product because of limited demand or may be taken over by another company that does not wish to support all of its current products.

Of course, it is unlikely that all of these problems will arise in every case but my guess is that at least one of them should be expected in most COTS integration projects. Consequently, the cost and schedule benefits from COTS reuse are likely to be less than they might appear from an initial optimistic analysis.

Furthermore, Boehm (1999) reckons that, in many cases, the cost of system maintenance and evolution may be greater when COTS products are used. All of the above difficulties are life-cycle problems and they don't just affect the initial development of the system. As the people involved in the system maintenance become more remote from the original system developers, the more likely it is that real difficulties will arise with the integrated COTS products.

In spite of these problems, the benefits of COTS product reuse are very significant because these systems offer so much functionality to the reuser. Months and sometimes years of implementation effort can be saved if an existing system is reused and system development times drastically reduced. Given that rapid system delivery is the key requirement for many systems, this form of reuse is likely to become more and more widely practised.

14.1.3 Component development for reuse

The ideal component development process should be an experience-based process where reusable components are specially constructed from existing components that have already been reused in an opportunistic way. By using knowledge of reuse problems and component adaptations required to support reuse, a more generic and hence more reusable version of the component can be created.

There are various component characteristics that lead to reusability:

1. The component should reflect stable domain abstractions. Stable domain abstractions are fundamental concepts in the application domain that change slowly. For example, in a banking system, domain abstractions might be accounts, account holders, statements, etc. In a hospital management system, domain abstractions might be patients, treatments, nurses, etc.

2. The component should hide the way in which its state is represented and should provide operations that allow the state to be accessed and updated. For example, in a component that represents a bank account, there should be operations to query the balance of the account, change the account balance, record transactions on the account, etc.

3. The component should be as independent as possible. Ideally, a component should be stand-alone so that it does not need any other components to operate. In practice, this is only possible for very simple components, and more complex components will inevitably have some dependencies on other components. It is best to minimise these, especially if they are dependencies on components, such as operating system functions, that may change.

4. All exceptions should be part of the component interface. Components should not handle exceptions themselves as different applications will have different requirements for exception handling. Rather, the component should define what exceptions can arise and should publish these as part of the interface. For example, a simple component implementing a stack data structure should detect and publish stack overflow and stack underflow exceptions.

In many existing systems there are large segments of code that implement domain abstractions but cannot be used directly as components. The reason for this is that they are not packaged according to the model in Figure 14.4 with clearly defined *requires* and *provides* interfaces. To make these components reusable, it is usually necessary to construct a wrapper. The wrapper hides the complexity of the underlying code and provides an interface for external components to access services that are provided.

There is an inevitable trade-off between reusability and usability of a component. To make the component reusable implies providing a very general interface with operations that cater for different ways in which the component may be used. To make the component usable implies providing a simple, minimal interface that is easy to understand. Reusability adds complexity and hence reduces component understandability. It is therefore more difficult for engineers to decide when and how to reuse that component. Designers of reusable components must therefore find a compromise between generality and understandability.

14.2 Application families

One of the most effective approaches to reuse is based around the notion of application families. An application family or product line is a related set of applications that has a common domain-specific architecture as discussed in Chapter 10. However, each specific application is specialised in some way. The common core of the application family is reused each time that a new application is required. The new development may involve writing some additional components and adapting some of the components in the application to meet new demands.

There are various types of specialisation of an application family that may be developed:

Figure 14.9
A generic resource
management system

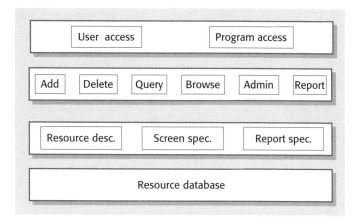

1. *Platform specialisation* where different versions of the application are developed for different platforms. For example, versions of the application may exist for Windows NT, Solaris and Linux platforms. In this case, the functionality of the application is normally unchanged; only those components that interface with the hardware and operating system are modified.

2. *Configuration specialisation* where different versions of the application are created to handle different peripheral devices. For example, a system for the emergency services may exist in different versions depending on the type of radio system used. In this case, the functionality may vary to reflect the functionality of the peripherals, and components that interface with peripherals must be modified.

3. *Functional specialisation* where different versions of the application are created for customers with different requirements. For example, a library automation system may be modified depending on whether it is used in a public library, a reference library or a university library. In this case, components that implement functionality may be modified and new components added to the system.

To illustrate this approach to reuse, consider Figure 14.9 which illustrates the architecture of a system for inventory management. Inventory management systems are used by organisations to keep track of their assets. Therefore, a power utility might have an inventory management system that tracks all fixed installations and the equipment installed at these installations. A university might have an inventory management system to keep track of the equipment used in its teaching labs.

Inventory management systems obviously vary depending on the type of resources that are being managed and the information that is required for each resource. For example, the power utility system will not need to have a facility that allows resource locations to be changed – the nature of this system is that these are fixed. The university inventory system, however, must be able to change the location of equipment as it is moved from one lab to another.

Nevertheless, these systems must provide a core of facilities such as the ability to add a resource to the inventory, the ability to remove a resource from the inventory, the ability to query and browse the inventory and the ability to create reports. It is therefore possible to design the architecture of inventory management systems in such a way that it becomes a family of applications with each instance of the system supporting different types of resources.

To allow significant reuse in such situations, the system architecture must be designed to separate the essential facilities of the system from the detailed information about the resources that are to be managed and the user access to such information. In Figure 14.9, this is achieved by using a layered architecture where a specific layer includes descriptions of the resources, the screens to be displayed and the reports to be produced. The higher layers of the system use these descriptions in their operation and do not include 'hard-wired' information about the resources. Different inventory management applications may be produced by modifying this description layer.

Of course, this type of tailoring may be achieved in object-oriented systems by specifying an abstract resource object and then using the inheritance facilities to specialise this depending on the type of resource that is being managed. This would probably lead to a rather different architecture from that shown in Figure 14.9. However, for this type of system, object-oriented development may not be appropriate. When applications rely on large databases with millions of records but relatively few types of logical entity, an object-oriented system is likely to be significantly less efficient than a system built around a relational database. At the time of writing, commercial object-oriented databases are still relatively slow and are not suited to supporting hundreds of transactions per second.

As well as developing new members of the application family by developing new resource descriptions, it is also possible to add new functionality to the system by including new modules in the system layers. To illustrate this, I have adapted the resource management system in Figure 14.9 to create a library system (Figure 14.10).

Figure 14.10
A library system

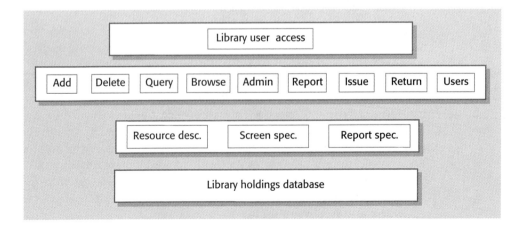

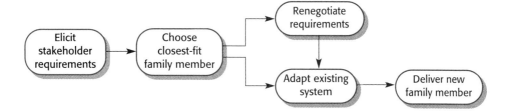

Figure 14.11
Family member
development

This involves adding new facilities to issue and return resources and to allow users to be registered with the system. These are shown on the right in Figure 14.10. As program access is not required in this case, the top level of the system need only support user access to the resources.

In general, developing applications by adapting a generic version of the application means that a very high proportion of the application code is reused. Furthermore, application experience is often transferable from one system to another so that when software engineers join a development team, their learning process is shortened. Testing is simplified because tests for large parts of the application may also be reused and the overall development time for the application is reduced.

Figure 14.11 shows the steps involved in adapting an application family to create a new application. The details of the process are likely to differ radically depending on the application domain and the system's organisational environment. The steps involved in the generic process are:

1. *Elicit stakeholder requirements*   This may be based on a normal requirements engineering process. However, as a system already exists, it will normally involve demonstrating and experimenting with that system and expressing the requirements as modifications that are required.

2. *Choose closest-fit family member*   The requirements are analysed and the family member that is the closest fit to these is chosen for modification. This need not be the system that was demonstrated.

3. *Renegotiate requirements*   As more details of the changes required to the existing system emerge and the project is planned, there may be some requirements renegotiation to minimise the changes that are needed.

4. *Adapt existing system*   New modules are developed for the existing system and existing system modules are adapted to meet the new requirements.

5. *Deliver new family member*   The new member of the application family is delivered to the customer. At this stage, you should document its key features so that it may be used as a basis for other system developments in the future.

When you create a new member of an application family you may have to find a compromise between reusing as much of the generic application as possible and satisfying detailed stakeholder requirements. The more detailed the system requirements, the less likely that the existing components will meet these requirements. However, if stakeholders are willing to be flexible and to limit the system modifications that are required, the system can usually be delivered more quickly and at a lower cost.

With some exceptions, application families usually emerge from existing applications. That is, an organisation develops an application and then, when a new application is required, uses this as a basis for the new application. Further demands for new applications cause the process to continue. However, as change tends to corrupt application structure, at some stage a specific decision to design a generic application family is made. This design is based on reusing the knowledge that has been gained from developing the initial set of applications.

14.3 Design patterns

When you try to reuse executable components you are inevitably constrained by detailed design decisions that have been made by the implementors of these components. These range from the particular algorithms that have been used to implement the components to the objects and types in the component interfaces. If these design decisions conflict with your particular requirements then reusing the component is either impossible or introduces significant inefficiencies into your system.

One way round this is to reuse more abstract designs that do not include implementation detail. These are then implemented specifically to fit your application requirements. The first instances of this approach to reuse came in the documentation and publication of fundamental algorithms (Knuth, 1971) and, later, in the documentation of abstract data types such as stacks, trees and lists (Booch, 1987). More recently, this approach to reuse has been embodied in the notion of design patterns.

Design patterns (Gamma *et al.*, 1995) were derived from ideas put forward by Christopher Alexander (Alexander *et al.*, 1977), who suggested that there were certain patterns of building design that were common and that were inherently pleasing and effective. The 'pattern' is a description of the problem and the essence of its solution so that the solution may be reused in different settings. The pattern is not a detailed specification. Rather, you can think of it as a description of accumulated wisdom and experience. It is a well-tried solution to a common problem. In this respect, patterns may be used during analysis to develop system models as well as during the design process.

In software design, design patterns have been inevitably associated with object-oriented design. They often rely on object characteristics such as inheritance and polymorphism to provide generality. However, the general principle is one that is equally applicable to all approaches to software design.

Gamma *et al.* (1995) define the four essential elements of a design patterns:

1. A name that is a meaningful reference to the pattern.

2. A description of the problem area that explains when the pattern may be applied.

3. A solution description that describes the different parts of the design solution, their relationships and responsibilities. This is not a concrete design description. It is a template for a design solution that can be instantiated in different ways. This is often expressed graphically and shows the relationships between the objects and object classes in the solution.

4. A statement of the consequences – the results and trade-offs – of applying the pattern. This is used to help designers understand whether or not a pattern can be effectively applied in a particular situation.

These essential elements of a pattern description may themselves be further decomposed. For example Gamma *et al.* (1995) break down the problem description into *motivation* – a description of why the pattern is useful, and *applicability* – a description of situations where the pattern may be used. Under the description of the solution, they describe the pattern structure, participants, collaborations and implementation.

To illustrate pattern description I have described one of the most commonly used patterns suggested by Gamma *et al.*, namely the Observer pattern (Figure 14.12). This pattern is used when different presentations of an object's state are required.

Figure 14.12
Description of the
Observer pattern

Pattern name: Observer

Description: Separates the display of the state of an object from the object itself and allows alternative displays to be provided. When the object state changes, all displays are automatically notified and updated to reflect the change.

Problem description: In many situations, it is necessary to provide multiple displays of some state information such as a graphical display and a tabular display. Not all of these may be known when the information is specified. All alternative presentations may support interaction and, when the state is changed, all displays must be updated.

This pattern may be used in all situations where more than one display format for state information may be required and where it is not necessary for the object that maintains the state information to know about the specific display formats used.

Solution description: The structure of the pattern is shown in Figure 14.14. This defines two abstract objects – Subject and Observer, and two concrete objects – ConcreteSubject and ConcreteObject, which inherit the attributes of the related abstract objects. The state to be displayed is maintained in ConcreteSubject which also inherits operations from Subject allowing it to add and remove Observers and to issue a notification when the state has changed.

The ConcreteObserver maintains a copy of the state of ConcreteSubject and implements the Update () interface of Observer which allows these copies to be kept in step. The ConcreteObserver automatically displays its state – this is not normally an interface operation.

Consequences: The subject only knows the abstract Observer and does not know details of the concrete class. Therefore there is minimal coupling between these objects. Because of this lack of knowledge, optimisations that enhance display performance are impractical. Changes to the subject may cause a set of linked updates to observers to be generated, some of which may not be necessary.

Figure 14.13
Multiple displays

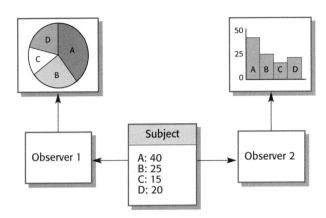

It separates the object that must be displayed and the different forms of presentation. This is illustrated in Figure 14.13 which shows two graphical presentations of the same data set. In my description, I use the four essential description elements and supplement these with a brief statement of what the pattern can do.

Graphical representations are normally used to illustrate the object classes that are used in patterns and their relationships. Figure 14.14 is the representation in UML of the Observer pattern.

The use of patterns is a very effective form of reuse but, in my opinion, they have a high cost of introduction into design processes and they can only be used effectively by experienced programmers. The reason for the high cost of introduction is that patterns are complex. To use them effectively, a designer has to know and understand many patterns in detail. This is unlike an executable component where only the interfaces need be understood. Obviously, developing this understanding takes some time.

Patterns are only suitable for use by experienced programmers because they can recognise generic situations where a pattern can be applied. Inexperienced programmers, even if they have read the pattern books, will always find it hard to decide if a pattern should be reused or if they need a special-purpose solution.

Figure 14.14 The
Observer pattern

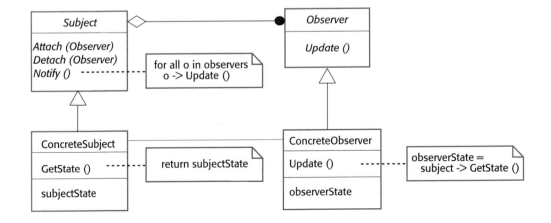

KEY POINTS

▶ Design with reuse involves designing the software around existing examples of good design and making use of software components where these are available.

▶ The advantages of software reuse are lower costs, faster software development and lower risks. System reliability is increased and specialists can be used more effectively by concentrating their expertise on the design of reusable components.

▶ Component-based development relies on using 'black-box' components with clearly defined 'requires' and 'provides' interfaces. Types of component that may be reused include functions, data abstractions, frameworks and complete application systems.

▶ COTS product reuse is concerned with the reuse of large-scale, off-the-shelf systems. These provide a lot of functionality and their reuse can radically reduce costs and development time.

▶ Software components that have been designed for reuse should be independent, should reflect stable domain abstractions, should provide access to state through interface operations and should not handle exceptions themselves.

▶ Application families are related applications that are developed from one or more base applications. A generic system is adapted and specialised to meet specific requirements for functionality, target platform or operational configuration.

▶ Design patterns are high-level abstractions that document successful design solutions. They are fundamental to design reuse in object-oriented development. A pattern description should include a pattern name, a problem and solution description, and a statement of the results and trade-offs of using the pattern.

FURTHER READING

Component Software: Beyond Object-oriented Programming. At the time of writing, this is the only available book on component-based development, although I expect that others will appear in the near future. It is quite a good description of the approach but is not really accessible unless you have some background in object-oriented development. (C. Szyperski, 1999, Addison Wesley Longman.)

Software Reuse: Architecture, Process and Organisation for Business Success. A comprehensive discussion of reuse with a particular emphasis on organisational issues and integrating reuse with an object-oriented development process. (I. Jacobson, M. Griss and P. Jonsson, 1997, Addison-Wesley.)

Design Patterns: Elements of Reusable Object-oriented Software. This is the original software patterns handbook that introduced the notion of software patterns to a wide community. (E. Gamma, R. Helm, R. Johnson and J. Vlissides, 1995, Addison-Wesley.)

EXERCISES

14.1   What are the major technical and non-technical factors which hinder software reuse? From your own experience, do you reuse much software? If not, why not?

14.2   Explain why the savings in cost from reusing existing software is not simply proportional to the size of the components that are reused.

14.3   Give four circumstances where you might recommend against software reuse.

14.4   Suggest possible requires and provides interfaces for the following components:

- A component implementing a bank account.
- A component implementing a language-independent keyboard. Keyboards in different countries have different key organisations and different character sets.
- A component that implements version management facilities as discussed in Chapter 29.

14.5   What is the difference between an application framework and a COTS product as far as reuse is concerned? Why is it sometimes easier to reuse a COTS product than an application framework?

14.6   Using the example of the weather station system described in Chapter 12, suggest an architecture for a family of applications that are concerned with remote monitoring and data collection.

14.7   Using the example of an inventory management family shown in Figure 14.9, suggest operations that have to be added or changed to support the reordering of inventory items when the level falls below some specified number.

14.8   Why are patterns an effective form of design reuse? What are the disadvantages to this approach to reuse?

14.9   The reuse of software raises a number of copyright and intellectual property issues. If a customer pays a software contractor to develop some system, who has the right to reuse the developed code? Does the software contractor have the right to use that code as a basis for a generic component? What payment mechanisms might be used to reimburse providers of reusable components? Discuss these issues and other ethical issues associated with the reuse of software.

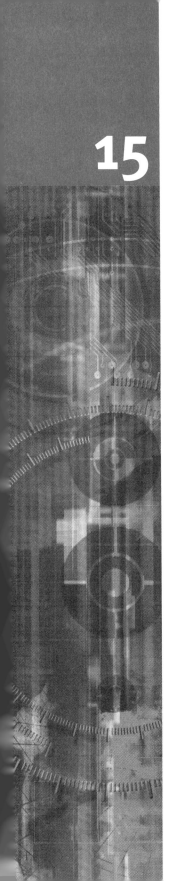

15 User interface design

Objectives

The objective of this chapter is to introduce some aspects of user interface design that are important for software engineers. When you have read this chapter, you will:

❏ understand general design principles that should be followed by engineers responsible for user interface design;

❏ be aware of five different styles of interaction with a software system;

❏ have been introduced to different styles of information presentation and know when graphical presentation of information is appropriate;

❏ understand some fundamentals of the design of the user support that is embedded in software;

❏ understand usability attributes and simple approaches to system evaluation.

Contents

15.1 User interface design principles
15.2 User interaction
15.3 Information presentation
15.4 User support
15.5 Interface evaluation

Computer system design encompasses a spectrum of activities from hardware design to user interface design. While specialists are often employed for hardware design, very few organisations employ specialist interface designers. Therefore, software engineers must often take responsibility for user interface design as well as for the design of the software to implement that interface. Human factors specialists may assist with this process in large organisations; in smaller companies such specialists are rarely used.

Good user interface design is critical to the success of a system. An interface that is difficult to use will, at best, result in a high level of user errors. At worst, users will simply refuse to use the software system irrespective of its functionality. If information is presented in a confusing or misleading way, users may misunderstand the meaning of information. They may initiate a sequence of actions that corrupt data or even cause catastrophic system failure.

When the first edition of this book was published in 1982, the standard interaction device was a 'dumb' alphanumeric terminal with green or blue characters displayed on a black background. User interfaces had to be textual or form-based. Almost all computer users now have a personal computer. These provide a graphical user interface (GUI) that supports a high-resolution colour display and interaction using a mouse as well as a keyboard.

Although text-based interfaces are still widely used, especially in legacy systems, computer users now expect application systems to have some form of graphical user interface. Figure 15.1 shows the principal characteristics of this type of interface.

The advantages of GUIs are:

1. They are relatively easy to learn and use. Users with no computing experience can learn to use the interface after a brief training session.

2. The user has multiple screens (windows) for system interaction. Switching from one task to another is possible without losing sight of information generated during the first task.

Figure 15.1
The characteristics
of graphical user
interfaces

Characteristic	Description
Windows	Multiple windows allow different information to be displayed simultaneously on the user's screen.
Icons	Icons represent different types of information. On some systems, icons represent files; on others, icons represent processes.
Menus	Commands are selected from a menu rather than typed in a command language.
Pointing	A pointing device such as a mouse is used for selecting choices from a menu or indicating items of interest in a window.
Graphics	Graphical elements can be mixed with text on the same display.

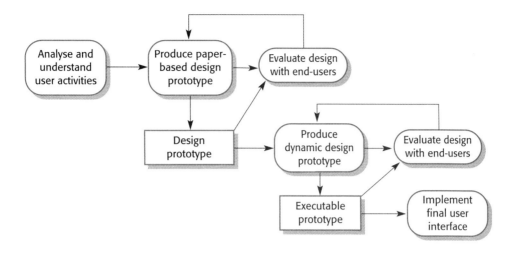

Figure 15.2
The user interface
design process

3. Fast, full-screen interaction is possible with immediate access to anywhere on the screen.

The objective of this chapter is to sensitise software engineers to some of the key issues underlying user interface design. Software designers and programmers are often competent users of the technology, such as Java's Swing classes (Eckstein *et al.*, 1998) or HTML (Musciano and Kennedy, 1998), that is fundamental to user interface implementation. All too often, however, they do not use this technology in an appropriate way and create user interfaces that are inelegant, inappropriate and hard to use.

I focus, therefore, on giving some advice on the design of end-user facilities rather than the design of the software that implements these facilities. Because of space limitations, I only consider graphical interfaces. I do not cover interfaces that require special (perhaps very simple) displays such as mobile phones, video recorders, televisions, copiers and fax machines. Naturally, I can only introduce the topic here and I recommend texts such as those by Shneiderman (1998), Dix *et al.* (1998) and Preece *et al.* (1994) for more information on this topic.

Figure 15.2 illustrates the iterative process of user interface design. As I discuss in Chapter 8, exploratory development is the most effective approach to interface design. This prototyping process may start with simple paper-based interface mock-ups before going on to develop screen-based designs that simulate user interaction. A user-centred approach (Norman and Draper, 1986) should be used, with end-users of the system playing an active part in the design process. In some cases, the user's role is an evaluation one; in others, they participate as full members of the design team (Kyng, 1988; Greenbaum and Kyng, 1991).

A critical UI design activity is the analyses of the user activities that are to be supported by the computer system. Without an understanding of what the user wants to do with the computer system, there is no realistic prospect of designing an effect-ive user interface. To develop this understanding, you may use techniques such as task analysis (Diaper, 1989), ethnographic studies as discussed in Chapter 6 (Suchman, 1983; Hughes *et al.*, 1997), user interviews and observations or, commonly, a mixture of all of these.

15.1 User interface design principles

User interface designers must take into account the physical and mental capabilities of the people who use software. People have a limited short-term memory (see Chapter 22) and they make mistakes, especially when they have to handle too much information or are under stress. They have a diverse range of physical capabilities. You have to take all of these into account when designing user interfaces.

Human capabilities are the basis for the design principles shown in Figure 15.3. These are general principles which are applicable to all user interface designs and should normally be instantiated as more detailed design guidelines for specific organisations or types of system. A longer list of more specific user interface design guidelines is given by Shneiderman (1998).

The principle of user familiarity suggests that users should not be forced to adapt to an interface because it is convenient to implement. The interface should use terms familiar to the user and the objects manipulated by the system should be directly related to the user's environment. For example, if a system is designed for use by air traffic controllers, the objects manipulated should be aircraft, flight paths, beacons, etc. Associated operations might be increase or reduce aircraft speed, adjust

Figure 15.3 User interface design principles

Principle	Description
User familiarity	The interface should use terms and concepts which are drawn from the experience of the people who will make most use of the system.
Consistency	The interface should be consistent in that, wherever possible, comparable operations should be activated in the same way.
Minimal surprise	Users should never be surprised by the behaviour of a system.
Recoverability	The interface should include mechanisms to allow users to recover from errors.
User guidance	The interface should provide meaningful feedback when errors occur and provide context-sensitive user help facilities.
User diversity	The interface should provide appropriate interaction facilities for different types of system user.

heading and change height. The underlying implementation of the interface in terms of files and data structures should be hidden from the end-user.

The principle of user interface consistency means that system commands and menus should have the same format, parameters should be passed to all commands in the same way, and command punctuation should be similar. Consistent interfaces reduce user learning time. Knowledge learnt in one command or application is applicable in other parts of the system.

Interface consistency across sub-systems is also important. As far as possible, commands with similar meanings in different sub-systems should be expressed in the same way. Errors are often caused when the same keyboard command, such as 'Control-k' or 'Control-b' means different things in different systems. For example, in the word processor that I used to write this book, 'Control-b' means embolden text but in the graphics program that I used to create diagrams, 'Control-b' means move the selected object behind another object. I make mistakes when using them together and often try to embolden text in a diagram using the key combination. This causes the text to disappear and can be very confusing. Windowing system standards usually define command key shortcuts and should be followed to help avoid this type of error.

This level of consistency is low-level consistency. Interface designers should always try to achieve this in a user interface. Consistency at a higher level is also some-times desirable. For example, it may be appropriate to support the same operations (such as print, copy, etc.) on all types of system entities. However, Grudin (1989) points out that complete consistency is neither possible or desirable. It may be sensible to implement deletion from a desktop by dragging entities into a trashcan. It would be unnatural to delete text in a word processor in this way.

The principle of minimal surprise is appropriate because users get very irritated when a system behaves in an unexpected way. As a system is used, users build a mental model of how the system works. If an action in one context causes a particular type of change, it is reasonable to expect that the same action in a dif-ferent context will cause a comparable change. If something completely different happens, the user is both surprised and confused. Interface designers must there-fore ensure that comparable actions have comparable effects.

The principle of recoverability is important because users inevitably make mistakes when using a system. The interface design can minimise these mistakes (e.g. using menus means that typing mistakes are avoided) but mistakes can never be completely eliminated. User interfaces should contain facilities allowing users to recover from their mistakes. These can be of two kinds:

1. *Confirmation of destructive actions*   If users specify an action which is poten-tially destructive, they should be asked to confirm that this is really what they want before any information is destroyed.

2. *The provision of an undo facility*   Undo restores the system to a state before the action occurred. Multiple levels of undo are useful as users don't always recognise immediately that a mistake has been made.

A related principle is the principle of user assistance. Interfaces should have built-in user assistance or help facilities. These should be integrated with the system and should provide different levels of help and advice. Levels should range from basic information on getting started with the system to a full description of system facilities. Help facilities, as discussed in section 15.4, should be structured and users should not be overwhelmed with information when they ask for help.

The principle of user diversity recognises that, for many interactive systems, there may be different types of users. Some users will be casual users who interact occasionally with the system while others may be 'power users' who use the system for several hours each day. Casual users need interfaces that provide guidance whereas power users require shortcuts that allow them to interact as quickly as possible. Furthermore, users may suffer from different types of disability and, if possible, the interface should be adaptable to cope with these. Therefore, it may be necessary to provide facilities to display enlarged text, to replace sound with text, to produce very large buttons and so on.

The principle of recognising user diversity can conflict with the other interface design principles because some types of user may prefer to have very rapid interaction rather than, for example, user interface consistency. Similarly, the level of user guidance required can be radically different for different types of user and it may be impossible to develop support that is suitable for all types of user. The interface designer must inevitably make compromises depending on the actual users of the system.

15.2 User interaction

The designer of a user interface to a computer is faced with two key issues. How can information from the user be provided to the computer system and how can information from the computer system be presented to the user? A coherent user interface must integrate user interaction and information presentation.

User interaction is the focus of this section, with information presentation covered in section 15.3. User interaction means issuing commands and associated data to the computer system. On early computers, the only way to do this was through a command-line interface where a special-purpose language was used to communicate with the machine. However, this approach was only usable by experts and a number of other approaches have evolved that are easier to use. Shneiderman (1998) has classified these different forms of interaction into five primary styles:

1. *Direct manipulation* where the user interacts directly with objects on the screen. For example, to delete a file, a user may drag it to a trashcan.

2. *Menu selection* where a user selects a command from a list of possibilities (a menu). It is often the case that another screen object is selected at the same

Interaction style	Main advantages	Main disadvantages	Application examples
Direct manipulation	Fast and intuitive interaction Easy to learn	May be hard to implement Only suitable where there is a visual metaphor for tasks and objects	Video games CAD systems
Menu selection	Avoids user error Little typing required	Slow for experienced users Can become complex if many menu options	Most general-purpose systems
Form fill-in	Simple data entry Easy to learn	Takes up a lot of screen space	Stock control Personal loan processing
Command language	Powerful and flexible	Hard to learn Poor error management	Operating systems Library information retrieval systems
Natural language	Accessible to casual users Easily extended	Requires more typing Natural language understanding systems are unreliable	Timetable systems WWW information retrieval systems

Figure 15.4
Advantages and
disadvantages of
interaction styles

time and the command operates on that object. In this approach, to delete a file, the user selects the file, then selects the delete command.

3. *Form fill-in* where a user fills in the fields of a form. Some fields may have associated menus and the form may have action 'buttons' that, when pressed, cause some action to be initiated. It would be artificial to delete a file using a form-based interface. It would involve filling in the name of the file, then 'pressing' a delete button.

4. *Command language* where the user issues a special command and associated parameters to instruct the system what to do. To delete a file, the user issues a delete command with the filename as a parameter.

5. *Natural language* where the user issues a command in natural language. To delete a file, the user might therefore type 'delete the file named xxx'.

Each of these different styles of interaction has advantages and disadvantages and are best suited to different types of application and users (Shneiderman, 1998). Figure 15.4 shows the main advantages and disadvantages of these styles and suggests types of application where they might be used.

Of course, these interaction styles may be mixed and several different styles are used in the same application. For example, Microsoft Windows supports direct manipulation of the iconic representation of files and directories, menu-based command selection and, for some commands such as configuration commands, the user must fill in a special-purpose form that is presented to them.

User interfaces on the World Wide Web are based on the support provided by HTML (the page description language used for web pages) along with languages

Figure 15.5 Multiple
user interfaces

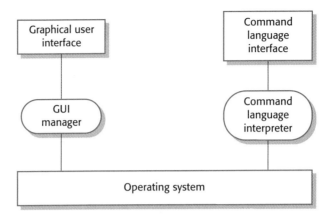

such as Java that can associate programs with components on a page. As these
web-based interfaces are often designed for casual users, they mostly use forms-
based interfaces. It is possible to construct direct manipulation interfaces on the web
but, at the time of writing, this is still a complex programming task.

In principle, it should be possible to separate the interaction style from the underlying entities that are manipulated through the user interface. This was the basis
of the Seeheim model (Pfaff and ten Hagen, 1985) of user interface management.
In this model, the presentation of information, the dialogue management and the
application are separate. In reality, this model is an ideal one rather than a practical one but it is certainly possible to have separate interfaces for different classes
of users (casual users and experienced users, say) that interact with the same underlying system. This is illustrated in Figure 15.5 which shows a command language
interface and a graphical interface to an underlying operating system such as Linux.

This separation of presentation, interaction and the entities that are involved in
the user interface is also fundamental to the Model-View-Controller approach that
I discuss in the next section. This is comparable to the Seeheim model but is used
to implement the user interface to objects rather than entire applications.

15.3 Information presentation

All interactive systems have to provide some way of presenting information to
users. The information presentation may simply be a direct representation of the
input information (e.g. text in a word processor) or it may present the information
graphically. It is good system design practice to keep the software required for
information presentation separate from the information itself. To some extent, this
contradicts object-oriented philosophy which suggests that operations on data

Figure 15.6
Information
presentation

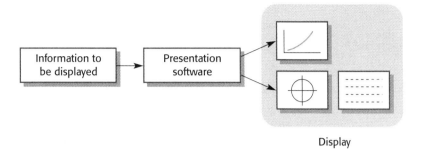

Display

should be defined with the data itself. However, this presupposes that the designer of the objects always knows the best way to present information; this is definitely not always true. It is often difficult to know the best way to present data when it is being defined and object structures should not 'hard-wire' presentation operations.

By separating the presentation system from the data, the representation on the user's screen can be changed without having to change the underlying computational system. This is illustrated in Figure 15.6.

The MVC approach (Figure 15.7), first made widely available in Smalltalk (Goldberg and Robson, 1983), is an effective way to support multiple presentations of data. Users can interact with each presentation using a style that is appropriate to it. The data to be displayed is encapsulated in a model object. Each model object may have a number of separate view objects associated with it where each view is a different display representation of the model. I have already illustrated this in the previous chapter where I discussed the MVC approach as an object-oriented framework.

Each view has an associated controller object that handles user input and device interaction. Therefore, a model that represents numeric data may have a view that represents the data as a histogram and a view that presents the data as a table. The model may be edited by changing the values in the table or by lengthening or shortening the bars in the histogram. I have illustrated this in Chapter 14 (Figure 14.13) where I discussed the use of the Observer pattern in implementing the MVC framework.

Figure 15.7
The MVC model of
user interaction

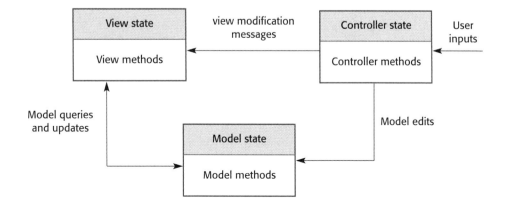

Finding the best presentation of information needs knowledge of the background of the users of the information and the way in which they use the system. In deciding how to present information, the designer must take a number of factors into account:

1. Is the user interested in precise information or in the relationships between different data values?
2. How quickly do the information values change? Should the change in a value be indicated immediately to the user?
3. Must the user take some action in response to a change in information?
4. Does the user need to interact with the displayed information via a direct manipulation interface?
5. Is the information to be displayed textual or numeric? Are relative values of information items important?

Information that does not change during a session may be presented either graphically or as text depending on the application. Textual presentation takes up less screen space but cannot be read 'at a glance'. Information that does not change should be distinguished from dynamic information by using a different presentation style. For example, all static information could be presented in a particular font, or could be highlighted using a particular colour or could always have an associated icon.

Information should be represented as text when precise numeric information is required and the information changes relatively slowly. If the data changes quickly or if the relationships between data are significant, graphical presentation should usually be used.

For example, consider a system which records and summarises the sales figures for a company on a monthly basis. Figure 15.8 illustrates how the same information can be presented as text or in a graphical form.

Managers studying sales figures are usually more interested in trends or anomalous figures rather than precise values. Graphical presentation of this information, as a histogram, makes the anomalous figures in March and May stand out from the others. Figure 15.8 also illustrates how textual presentation takes less space than a graphical representation of the same information.

Dynamically varying numeric information is usually best presented graphically using an analogue representation. Constantly changing digital displays are confusing as precise information is difficult to assimilate quickly. The graphical display can be supplemented if necessary with a precise digital display. Different ways of presenting dynamic numeric information are shown in Figure 15.9.

Continuous analogue displays give the viewer some sense of relative value. In Figure 15.10, the values of temperature and pressure are approximately the same. However, the graphical display shows that temperature is close to its maximum value whereas pressure has not reached 25 per cent of its maximum. With only a digital value, the viewer needs to know the maximum values. They must mentally compute the relative state of the reading. The extra thinking time required can lead to

Figure 15.8
Alternative
information
presentations

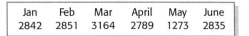

Jan	Feb	Mar	April	May	June
2842	2851	3164	2789	1273	2835

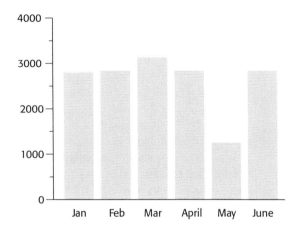

Figure 15.9 Methods
of presenting
dynamically varying
numeric information

Dial with needle   Pie chart   Thermometer   Horizontal bar

Figure 15.10
Graphical
information display
showing relative
values

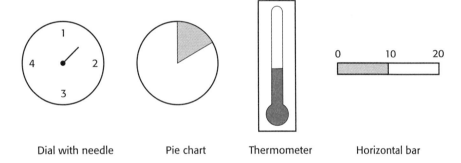

human errors in stressful situations when problems occur and operator displays may be showing abnormal readings.

When precise alphanumeric information is presented, graphics can be used to pick out the information from its background. Rather than presenting a line of information, it can be displayed in a box or indicated using an icon (Figure 15.11). The box displaying the message overlays the current screen display. The user's attention is immediately drawn to it.

Graphical highlighting may also be used to draw the user's attention to changes to parts of the display. However, if these changes occur rapidly, graphical

Figure 15.11
Textual highlighting
of alphanumeric
information

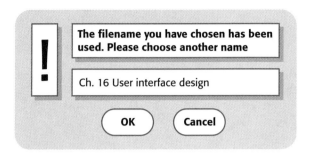

highlighting should not be used as rapid changes may cause the display to appear to flash. This distracts and irritates users.

When large amounts of information have to be presented, abstract visualisations that link related data items may be used. This can expose relationships that are not obvious from the raw data. User interface designers should be aware of the possibilities of visualisation, especially when the system user interface must represent physical entities. Examples of data visualisations are:

1. Weather information, gathered from a number of sources, is shown as a weather map with isobars, weather fronts, etc.
2. The state of a telephone network is displayed graphically as a linked set of nodes in a network management centre.
3. The state of a chemical plant is visualised by showing pressures and temperatures in a linked set of tanks and pipes.
4. A model of a molecule is displayed and manipulated in three dimensions using a virtual reality system.
5. A set of web pages is displayed as a hyperbolic tree (Lamping *et al.*, 1995).

Shneiderman (1998) includes a good overview of different approaches to visualisation and identifies different classes of visualisation that may be used. These include visualising data using 2-D and 3-D presentations and as trees or networks. Most of these are concerned with the display of large amounts of information managed on a computer. However, the most common use of visualisation in user interfaces is to represent some physical structure such as the molecular structure of a new drug, the links in a telecommunications network, etc. Three-dimensional presentations that may use special virtual reality equipment are particularly effective in product visualisations. Direct manipulation of these visualisations is a very effective way to interact with the data.

15.3.1   Colour in interface design

All interactive systems, apart from specialised, small-screen systems, support colour displays and user interfaces make use of colour in different ways. In some systems (such as word processors) it is simply used for highlighting; in others (such as CAD systems) it is used to show different layers in a design.

Colour can improve user interfaces by helping users understand and manage complexity. However, it is easy to misuse colour and to create user interfaces that are visually unattractive and error-prone. As a general principle, user interface designers should be conservative in their use of colour in user displays. Shneiderman (1998) gives 14 key guidelines for the effective use of colour in user interfaces. The most important of these are:

1. *Limit the number of colours used and be conservative how these are used*   You should not use more than four or five separate colours in a window and no more than seven in a system interface. Colour should be used selectively and consistently. You should not use it simply to brighten up an interface.

2. *Use colour change to show a change in system status*   If a display changes colour, this should mean that a significant event has occurred. Thus, in a fuel gauge, a change of colour may indicate that fuel is running low. Colour highlighting is particularly important in complex displays where hundreds of distinct entities may be displayed.

3. *Use colour coding to support the task which users are trying to perform*   If they have to identify anomalous instances, highlight these instances; if similarities are also to be discovered, highlight these using a different colour.

4. *Use colour coding in a thoughtful and consistent way*   If one part of a system displays error messages in red (say), all other parts should do likewise. Red should not be used for anything else. If it is, the user may interpret the red display as an error message. You should be aware that some classes of user may have assumptions about the meaning of particular colours.

5. *Be careful about colour pairings*   Because of the physiology of the eye, people cannot focus on red and blue simultaneously. Eyestrain is a likely consequence of a red on blue display. Other colour combinations may also be visually disturbing or difficult to read.

The two most common errors made by designers when incorporating colour in a user interface are to associate meanings with particular colours and to use too many colours in a display.

Colour should not be used to represent meaning, for two reasons. About 10 per cent of men are colour-blind and may misinterpret the meaning. Human colour perceptions are different and there are different conventions in different professions about the meaning of particular colours. Users with different backgrounds may unconsciously interpret the same colour in different ways. For example, to a driver red usually means *danger*. However, to a chemist, red means *hot*.

If too many colours are used or if the colours are too bright, the display may be confusing. The mass of colour may disturb the user (in the same way that some abstract paintings cannot be viewed comfortably for a long time) and cause visual fatigue. User confusion is also possible if colours are used inconsistently.

15.4 User support

A design principle suggested in the first section of this chapter was that user interfaces should always provide some form of online help system. Help systems are one facet of a general part of user interface design, namely the provision of user guidance which covers three areas:

• the messages produced by the system in response to user actions;
• the online help system;
• the documentation provided with the system.

The design of useful and informative information for users should be taken seriously and should be subject to the same quality process as designs or programs. Managers must allow sufficient time and effort for message design and it may be appropriate to involve professional writers and graphic artists in the process. When designing error messages or help text, the factors shown in Figure 15.12 should be taken into account.

15.4.1 Error messages

The first impression that users may have of a software system is the system error messages. Inexperienced users may start work, make an initial error and immedi-

Figure 15.12 Design factors in message wording

Factor	Description
Context	The user guidance system should be aware of what the user is doing and should adjust the output message to the current context.
Experience	As users become familiar with a system they become irritated by long, 'meaningful' messages. However, beginners find it difficult to understand short terse statements of the problem. The user guidance system should provide both types of message and allow the user to control message conciseness.
Skill level	Messages should be tailored to the users' skills as well as their experience. Messages for the different classes of user may be expressed in different ways depending on the terminology which is familiar to the reader.
Style	Messages should be positive rather than negative. They should use the active rather than the passive mode of address. They should never be insulting or try to be funny.
Culture	Wherever possible, the designer of messages should be familiar with the culture of the country where the system is sold. There are distinct cultural differences between Europe, Asia and America. A suitable message for one culture might be unacceptable in another.

Figure 15.13
Nurse input of a
patient's name

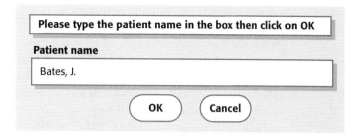

> **Please type the patient name in the box then click on OK**
>
> **Patient name**
>
> Bates, J.
>
> (OK)   (Cancel)

ately have to understand the resulting error message. This can be difficult enough for skilled software engineers. It is often impossible for inexperienced or casual system users.

The background and experience of users should be anticipated when designing error messages. For example, say a system user is a nurse in an intensive-care ward in a hospital. Patient monitoring is carried out by a computer system. To view a patient's current state (heart rate, temperature, etc.), the system user selects 'display' from a menu and inputs the patient's name in the box as shown in Figure 15.13.

In this case, say the patient's name was Pates rather than Bates so that the name input by the nurse could not be recognised. The system generates an error message. Error messages should always be polite, concise, consistent and constructive. They must not be abusive and should not have associated beeps or other noises which might embarrass the user. Wherever possible, the message should suggest how the error might be corrected. The error message should be linked to a context-sensitive online help system.

Figure 15.14 shows examples of good and bad error messages. The left-hand message is badly designed. It is negative (it accuses the user of making an error), it is not tailored to the user's skill and experience level and it does not take context information into account. It does not suggest how the situation might be rectified. It uses system-specific terms (patient-id) rather than user-oriented language. The right-hand message is better. It is positive, implying that the problem is a system rather than a user problem. It identifies the problem in the nurse's terms, and offers an easy way to correct the mistake by pressing a single button. The help system is available if required.

Figure 15.14 System
and user-oriented
error messages

System-oriented error message

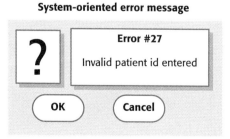

> **?**
>
> **Error #27**
>
> Invalid patient id entered
>
> (OK)   (Cancel)

User-oriented error message

> **Patient J. Bates is not registered**
>
> Click on Patients for a list of registered patients
> Click on Retry to re-input a patient name
> Click on Help for more information
>
> (Patients) (Help) (Retry) (Cancel)

Help system design

When users are presented with an error message they do not understand, they turn to the help system for information. This is an example of *help!* meaning 'help, I'm in trouble'. Another form of help request is *help?* which means 'help, I want information'. Different system facilities and message structures may be needed to provide these different types of help.

Help systems should provide a number of different user entry points (Figure 15.15). These should allow the user to enter the help system at the top of the message hierarchy and browse for information. Alternatively, they may enter the help system to get an explanation of an error message or may request an explanation of a particular application command.

All comprehensive help systems have a complex network structure where each frame of help information may refer to several other information frames. The structure of this network is usually hierarchical with cross-links as shown in Figure 15.15. General information is held at the top of the hierarchy, detailed information at the bottom.

Problems can arise with help systems when users enter the network after making a mistake and then navigate around the network. Within a short time, they can become hopelessly lost. They must abandon the session and start again at some known point in the network.

Displaying help information in multiple windows can help alleviate this situation. Figure 15.16 shows a screen display where there are three help windows.

Figure 15.15 Entry points to a help system

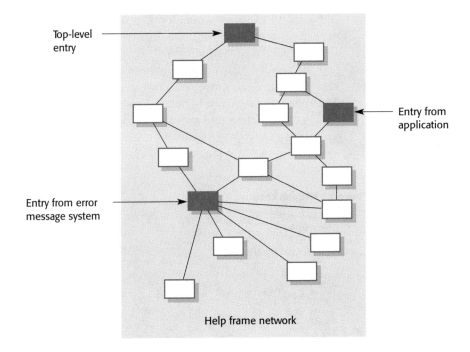

Top-level entry

Entry from application

Entry from error message system

Help frame network

Figure 15.16 Help
system windows

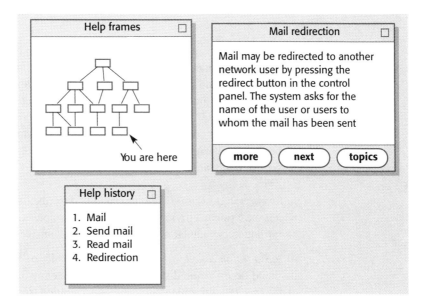

However, screen space is always limited and the designer must be aware that displaying extra windows may obscure other information which is important.

The text in a help system should be prepared with the help of application specialists. The help frame should not simply be a reproduction of the user manual as people read paper and screens in different ways. The text itself, its layout and style have to be carefully signed to ensure that it is readable in a relatively small window. In Figure 15.16, the help frame ('Mail redirection') is relatively short. You should not overwhelm the user with information in any one frame. Three buttons are provided in the help frame to request more information, to move on to the next help frame and to call up a list of topics on which help is available.

The 'history' window shows the frames which have already been visited. It should be possible to return to these frames by picking an item from this list. The navigation window is a graphical 'map' of the help system network. The current position in this map should be highlighted by using colour, shading or, in this case, by annotation.

Users should be able to move to another frame by selecting it from the frame being read, by selecting a frame in the 'history window' to reread or to retrace their steps or by selecting a node in the network 'map' to move to that node.

Help systems may be implemented as a set of linked World Wide Web pages or by using a generic hypertext system that can be integrated with applications. The hierarchy may be easily traversed by selecting parts of a message that are highlighted as links. World Wide Web systems have the advantage that they are easy to implement and do not require any special software. However, it can be difficult to link these to the application to provide context-sensitive help.

15.4.3 ## User documentation

User documentation is not strictly part of user interface design but it is good practice to design the online help support in conjunction with paper documentation. The system manuals should provide more detailed information than the online help and should be designed so that it can be used by different classes of system end-user.

To cater for these different classes of user and different levels of user expertise, there are at least five documents (or perhaps chapters in a single document) which should be delivered with a software system (Figure 15.17).

These documents are:

1. *A functional description* which should describe, very briefly, the services which the system provides. Users should be able to read this document with an introductory manual and decide if the system is what they need.

2. *An installation document* should provide details of how to install the system. It should describe the disks on which the system is supplied, the files on these disks and the minimal hardware configuration required. It should include installation instructions and details of how to set up configuration-dependent files.

3. *An introductory manual* which should present an informal introduction to the system, describing its 'normal' usage. It should describe how to get started and how end-users might make use of the common system facilities. It should be liberally illustrated with examples. It should include information on how to recover from mistakes and restart useful work. Carroll (1992) suggests that focusing on error recovery and minimising the information that users have to read by eliminating redundancy is an effective way to organise introductory manuals.

Figure 15.17
Types of document
produced to support
users

4. *A reference manual* should describe the system facilities and their usage, provide a list of error messages and possible causes and describe how to recover from detected errors.

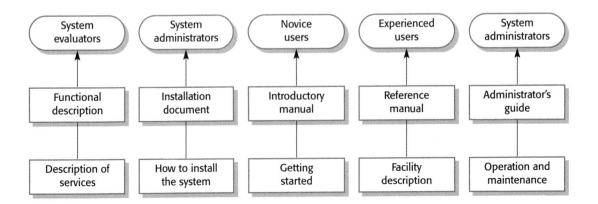

5. *An administrator's manual* may be provided for some types of system. This should describe the messages generated when the system interacts with other systems and how to react to these messages. If system hardware is involved, it might explain how to recognise and repair hardware-related problems, how to connect new peripherals, etc.

As well as manuals, other, easy-to-use documentation might be provided. A quick reference card listing available system facilities and how to use them is particularly convenient for experienced system users.

15.5 Interface evaluation

Interface evaluation is the process of assessing the usability of an interface and checking that it meets user requirements. Therefore, it should be part of the normal verification and validation process for software systems. Neilsen (1993) in his book on usability engineering includes a good chapter on this topic.

Ideally, an evaluation should be conducted against a usability specification based on usability attributes as shown in Figure 15.18. Metrics for these usability attributes can be devised. For example, a learnability metric might state that an operator who is familiar with the work supported should be able to use 80 per cent of the system functionality after a three-hour training session. However, it is more common to specify usability (if it is specified at all) qualitatively rather than using metrics. Interface designers therefore have to use their judgement and experience in the interface evaluation.

Systematic evaluation of a user interface design can be an expensive process involving cognitive scientists and graphics designers. It may involve designing and carrying out a statistically significant number of experiments with typical users in

Figure 15.18
Usability attributes

Attribute	Description
Learnability	How long does it take a new user to become productive with the system?
Speed of operation	How well does the system response match the user's work practice?
Robustness	How tolerant is the system of user error?
Recoverability	How good is the system at recovering from user errors?
Adaptability	How closely is the system tied to a single model of work?

specially constructed laboratories fitted with monitoring equipment. A user interface evaluation of this kind is economically unrealistic for systems developed by small organisations with limited resources.

There are a number of simpler, less expensive techniques of user interface evaluation which can identify particular user interface design deficiencies:

1. questionnaires which collect information about what users thought of the interface;
2. observation of users at work with the system and 'thinking aloud' about how they are trying to use the system to accomplish some task;
3. video 'snapshots' of typical system use;
4. the inclusion in the software of code which collects information about the most-used facilities and the most common errors.

Surveying users by using a questionnaire is a relatively cheap way of evaluating an interface. The questions should be precise rather than general. It is no use asking questions like 'Please comment on the usability of the interface' as the responses will probably vary so much that no common trend will emerge. Rather, specific questions such as 'Please rate the understandability of the error messages on a scale from 1 to 5. A rating of 1 means very clear and 5 means incomprehensible' are better. They are both easier to answer and more likely to provide useful information to improve the interface.

Users should be asked to rate their own experience and background when filling in the questionnaire. This allows the designer to find out if users from any particular background have problems with the interface. Questionnaires can even be used before any executable system is available if a paper mock-up of the interface is constructed and evaluated.

Observation-based evaluation simply involves watching users as they use a system, looking at the facilities used, the errors made, etc. This can be supplemented by 'think aloud' sessions where users talk about what they are trying to achieve, how they understand the system and how they are trying to use the system to accomplish their objectives.

Relatively low-cost video equipment means that direct observation can be supported by recording user sessions for later analysis. Complete video analysis is expensive and requires a specially equipped evaluation suite with several cameras focused on the user and on the screen. However, video recording of selected user operations can be helpful to detect problems. Other evaluation methods must be used to find out which operations cause user difficulties.

Analysis of recordings allows the designer to find out if the interface requires too much hand movement (a problem with some systems is that users must regularly move their hands from keyboard to mouse) and to see if unnatural eye movements are necessary. An interface which requires many shifts of focus may mean that the user makes more errors and misses parts of the display.

Instrumenting code to collect usage statistics allows interfaces to be improved in a number of ways. The most common operations can be detected. The interface can be reorganised so that these are the fastest to select. For example, if pop-up or pull-down menus are used, the most frequent operations should be at the top of the menu and destructive operations towards the bottom. Code instrumentation also allows error-prone commands to be detected and modified.

Finally, a means of easy user response can be provided by equipping each program with a 'gripe' command which the user can use to pass messages to the tool maintainer. This makes users feel that their views are being considered. The interface designer and other engineers can gain rapid feedback about individual problems.

None of these relatively simple approaches to user interface evaluation is foolproof and they are unlikely to detect all user interface problems. However, the techniques can be used with a group of volunteers before a system is released without a large outlay of resources. Many of the worst problems of the user interface design can then be discovered and corrected.

 KEY POINTS

▶ The interface design process should be user-centred. An interface should interact with users in their terms, should be logical and consistent and should include facilities to help users with the system and to recover from their mistakes.

▶ Styles of interaction with a software system include direct manipulation, menu systems, form fill-in, command languages and natural language.

▶ Graphical information display should be used when it is intended to present trends and approximate values. Digital display should only be used when precision is required.

▶ Colour should be used sparingly and consistently in user interfaces. Designers should take account of the fact that a significant number of people are colour-blind.

▶ User help systems should provide two kinds of help: Help! which is 'help, I'm in trouble' and Help? which is 'help, I need information'.

▶ Error messages should not suggest that the user is to blame. They should offer suggestions on how to repair the error and provide a link to a help system.

▶ User documentation should include beginner's and reference manuals. Separate documents for system administrators should be provided.

▶ The system specification should include, wherever possible, quantitative values for usability attributes and the evaluation process should check the system against these requirements.

FURTHER READING

Human-Computer Interaction, 2nd edition. A good general text whose strengths are a focus on design issues and cooperative work. (A. Dix, J. Finlay, G. Abowd and R. Beale, 1998, Prentice-Hall.)

Designing the User Interface. This is the latest revision of what was probably the first textbook in this area. An excellent, wide-ranging book. (B. Shneiderman, 1998, Addison-Wesley.)

Developing User Interfaces. This book focuses on the implementation rather than on the design of user interfaces. It is therefore a good complement to other texts that concentrate on interface design. (D. Olsen, 1998, Morgan Kaufmann.)

EXERCISES

15.1 I suggested in section 15.1 that the objects manipulated by users should be drawn from their domain rather than a computer domain. Suggest appropriate objects for the following types of user and system:

- a warehouse assistant using an automated parts catalogue;
- an airline pilot using an aircraft safety monitoring system;
- a manager manipulating a financial database;
- a policeman using a patrol car control system.

15.2 Suggest situations where it is unwise or impossible to provide a consistent user interface.

15.3 What factors have to be taken into account when designing a menu-based interface for 'walk-up' systems such as bank ATM machines? Write a critical commentary on the interface of an ATM that you use.

15.4 Suggest ways in which the user interface to an e-commerce system such as an online bookstore or music retailer might be adapted for users who are physically challenged with some form of visual impairment or problems with muscular control.

15.5 Discuss the advantages of graphical information display and suggest four applications where it would be more appropriate to use graphical rather than digital displays of numeric information.

15.6 What are the guidelines which should be followed when using colour in a user interface? Suggest how colour might be used more effectively in the interface of an application system that you use.

15.7 Write a short set of guidelines for designers of user guidance systems.

15.8 Consider the error messages produced by MS-Windows, Unix, MacOS or some other operating system. Suggest how these might be improved.

15.9 Design a questionnaire to gather information about the user interface of some tool (such as a word processor) with which you are familiar. If possible, distribute this questionnaire to a number of users and try to evaluate the results. What do these tell you about the user interface design?

15.10 Discuss whether it is ethical to instrument software without telling end-users that their work is being monitored.

15.11 What ethical issues might user interface designers face when trying to reconcile the needs of end-users of a system with the needs of the organisation which is paying for the system to be developed?

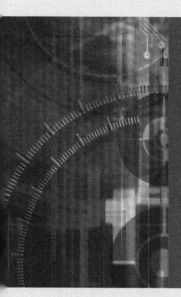

PART FOUR

Critical Systems

16 Dependability

Objectives

The objective of this chapter is to introduce the notion of dependability and its importance to critical systems. When you have read this chapter, you will:

❑ understand four dimensions of dependability, namely availability, reliability, safety and security;

❑ have been introduced to the notion of critical systems where system failure can have severe human or economic consequences;

❑ understand that to achieve dependability you need to avoid mistakes during the development of a system, detect and remove errors when the system is in use and limit the damage caused by operational failures.

Contents

16.1 Critical systems
16.2 Availability and reliability
16.3 Safety
16.4 Security

All of us are familiar with the problems of computer system failures. For no obvious reason, computer systems sometimes crash and fail to deliver the services that have been requested. Programs running on these computers may not operate as expected and, occasionally, may corrupt the data that is managed by the system. We have learned to live with these failures and few of us completely trust the personal computers that we normally use.

The dependability of a computer system is a property of the system that equates to its trustworthiness. Trustworthiness essentially means the degree of user confidence that the system will operate as they expect and that the system will not 'fail' in normal use. This property cannot be expressed numerically but we use relative terms such as 'not dependable', 'very dependable' and 'ultra-dependable' to reflect different degrees of trust that we might have in a system.

Trustworthiness and usefulness are not, of course, the same thing. The word processor that I used to write this book is not, in my opinion, a very dependable system but it is very useful. However, to reflect my lack of trust in the system I frequently save my work and keep multiple backup copies of it. Therefore, I compensate for the lack of system dependability by actions that limit the damage that might result from system failure.

There are four principal dimensions to dependability as shown in Figure 16.1:

1. *Availability* Informally, the availability of a system is the probability that it will be up and running and able to deliver useful services at any given time.

2. *Reliability* Informally, the reliability of a system is the probability, over a given period of time, that the system will correctly deliver services as expected by the user.

3. *Safety* Informally, the safety of a system is a judgement of how likely it is that the system will cause damage to people or its environment.

Figure 16.1
Dimensions of
dependability

4. *Security* Informally, the security of a system is a judgement of how likely it is that the system can resist accidental or deliberate intrusion.

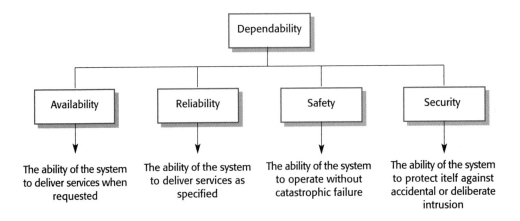

Figure 16.2
Cost/dependability
curve

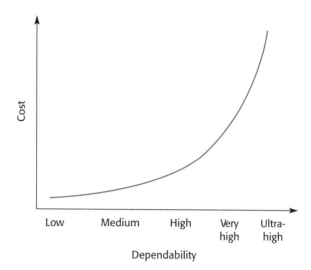

As I discuss in Chapter 17, availability and dependability are, essentially, probabilities and therefore can be expressed quantitatively. Safety and security are judgements that are made on the basis of evidence about the system. These are rarely expressed as numerical values but may be expressed in terms of integrity levels. Therefore, the safety of a level 1 system is less than the safety of a level 2 system that is less than the safety of a level 3 system and so on.

Because of additional design, implementation and validation overheads, increasing the dependability of a system can dramatically increase development costs. Figure 16.2 shows the relationship between costs and incremental improvements in dependability. This graph holds for all aspects of dependability – reliability, availability, safety and security. Because of the exponential nature of this cost/dependability curve, it is not possible to prove that a system is 100 per cent dependable as the costs of dependability assurance would then be infinite.

It is generally true that high levels of dependability can only be achieved at the expense of system performance. Dependable software includes extra, often redundant, code to perform the necessary checking for exceptional system states and to recover from system faults. This reduces system performance and increases the amount of store required by the software. However, there are a number of reasons why dependability is usually a more important attribute than performance:

1. *Systems that are unreliable, unsafe or insecure are often unused*   If a system is not trusted by its users, they will often refuse to use it. Furthermore, they may also refuse to use products from the same company as the untrustworthy system as they believe that these may also be untrustworthy.

2. *System failure costs may be enormous*   For some applications, such as a reactor control system or an aircraft navigation system, the cost of system failure is orders of magnitude greater than the cost of the control system.

3. *It is difficult to retrofit dependability*   It is usually possible to tune an ineffi-cient system because most execution time is spent in small program sections. A system that can't be trusted is more difficult to improve as untrustworthi-ness tends to be distributed throughout the system.

4. *It is often possible to compensate for lack of system performance*   Users can sometimes adjust their work to cope with a poorly performing system. A lack of dependability, by contrast, usually surprises the user. Untrustworthy software may violate system and user data without warning and may fail with serious consequences that only manifest themselves at a later date.

5. *Untrustworthy systems may cause information loss*   Data is very expensive to collect and maintain; it may sometimes be worth more than the computer sys-tem on which it is processed. A great deal of effort and money may have to be spent duplicating valuable data to guard against data corruption.

The dependability of the software product is influenced by the software process used to develop that product. A repeatable process which is oriented towards defect avoidance is likely to develop a dependable system. However, there is not a sim-ple relationship between product and process quality. Conforming to a particular process does not allow any quantitative product quality assessment to be made. The relationships between process and product quality are discussed in Chapters 24 and 25 which cover quality management and process improvement.

16.1 Critical systems

The failure of many software-controlled systems causes inconvenience but no ser-ious, long-term damage. However, there are some systems where failures can result in significant economic losses, physical damage or threats to human life. These sys-tems are usually called *critical systems*. Dependability is an essential attribute of critical systems and all aspects of dependability (availability, reliability, safety and security) may be important. Achieving a high level of dependability is usually the most important requirement for critical systems.

There are three main types of critical system:

1. *Safety-critical systems*   A system whose failure may result in injury, loss of life or major environmental damage. An example of a safety-critical system is a control system for a chemical manufacturing plant.

2. *Mission-critical systems*   A system whose failure may result in the failure of some goal-directed activity. An example of a mission-critical system is a navigational system for a spacecraft.

3. *Business-critical systems*   A system whose failure may result in the failure of the business using that system. An example of a business-critical system is a customer account system in a bank.

The costs of failure of a critical system are often very high. These costs include the direct failure costs which may require the system to be replaced and indirect costs such as the costs of litigation and lost business that may result if the system is unavailable. The high potential cost of failure means that the trustworthiness of development techniques and processes is usually more important than the costs of applying these techniques.

Consequently, critical systems are usually developed using well-tried techniques rather than newer techniques that have not been subject to extensive practical experience. It is only relatively recently, for example, that object-oriented techniques have been used for critical systems development and many critical systems development projects are still based on a function-oriented design.

However, software engineering techniques that are not normally cost-effective may be used for critical systems development; for example, the use of formal specification and formal verification of a program against its specification. One reason why this is used is that it helps reduce the amount of testing required. For critical systems, the costs of verification and validation are usually very high and may consume more than 50 per cent of the total system development costs.

Although this book focuses on software engineering and these chapters concentrate on software issues, dependability is really a systems concept. When considering dependability in critical systems, there are three types of system 'component' that are prone to failure:

1. system hardware that may fail because of mistakes in its design, because components fail as a result of manufacturing errors or because hardware components have come to an end of their natural life;

2. system software that may fail because of mistakes in its specification, design or implementation;

3. human operators of the system that may fail to operate the system correctly.

Therefore, if your goal is to improve the dependability of a system, you have to consider all of these aspects and their interactions. I illustrate this in some of the examples that are developed in the other chapters in this part of the book.

16.1.1 A simple safety-critical system

To illustrate the chapters on critical systems, I use an example of a simple safety-critical medical system. This is an insulin delivery system for the control of diabetes. I hope that most readers will have general knowledge of this condition and its treatment. I have already introduced this system in Chapter 9 and formally specified part of its functionality.

Figure 16.3 Insulin
pump structure

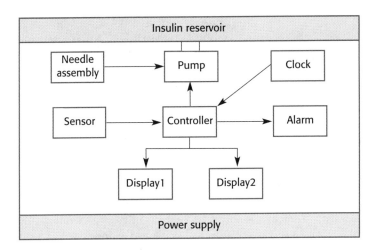

Diabetes is a relatively common condition where the human body is unable to produce sufficient quantities of a hormone called insulin. Insulin metabolises glucose in the blood. The conventional treatment of diabetes involves regular injections of genetically engineered insulin.

The problem with this treatment is that the level of insulin in the blood does not depend on the blood glucose level but is a function of the time when the insulin injection was taken. This can lead to very low levels of blood glucose (if there is too much insulin) or very high levels of blood sugar (if there is too little insulin). Low blood sugar is, in the short term, a more serious condition as it can result in temporary brain malfunctioning and, ultimately, unconsciousness and death. In the long term, continual high levels of blood sugar can lead to eye damage, kidney damage, and heart problems.

Current advances in developing miniaturised sensors have meant that it is now possible to develop automated insulin delivery systems. These monitor blood sugar levels and deliver an appropriate dose of insulin when required. Insulin delivery systems like this already exist for the treatment of hospital patients. In future, it may be possible for many diabetics to have such systems permanently attached to their bodies.

An insulin delivery system might work by using a micro-sensor embedded in the patient to measure some blood parameter which is proportional to the sugar level. This is then sent to the pump controller. This controller computes the sugar level, judges how much insulin is required and sends signals to a miniaturised pump to deliver the insulin via a permanently attached needle. Insulin delivery systems are likely to be software controlled. Figure 16.3 shows the components and organisation of the insulin pump. Figure 16.4 is a data-flow model that illustrates how an input blood sugar level is transformed to a sequence of pump control commands.

Three dimensions of dependability apply to this insulin delivery system:

1. *Availability* It is important that the system should be available to deliver insulin when required.

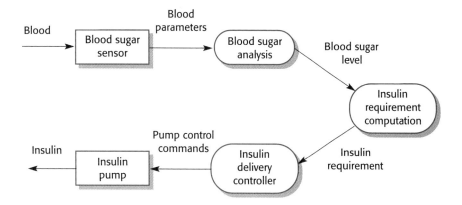

Figure 16.4 Data-flow model of the insulin pump

2. *Reliability*   It is important that the system performs reliably and delivers the correct amount of insulin to counter the current level of blood sugar.

3. *Safety*   Failure of the system could, in principle, cause excessive doses of insulin to be delivered and this would threaten the life of the user. It is important that this class of system failures should not occur.

I explain in later chapters how these dependability dimensions can be specified and validated.

16.2 Availability and reliability

In this section I discuss two closely related dimensions of dependability, namely availability and reliability. The availability of a system is the probability that it will be able to deliver services to its users when requested to do so. The reliability is the probability that system services will be delivered as specified. Obviously, reliability subsumes availability because if a specified service is not delivered then the system is obviously not behaving according to its specification.

However, it is useful to distinguish between these characteristics because the requirements for availability and reliability may be different. For example, some systems can tolerate relatively frequent failures so long as they can recover quickly from these failures. They therefore have relatively low reliability requirements. The same systems, however, may have high availability requirements because of users' expectations of continuous service.

A good example of such a system is a telephone exchange switch. Users expect a dial tone when they pick up a phone so the system has high availability requirements. However, if a system fault causes a connection to fail, this is often recoverable. Exchange switches usually include repair facilities that can reset the system and retry the connection attempt. This can be done very quickly and the phone user may not even notice that a failure has occurred. Therefore, availability rather than reliability is the key dependability requirement in such a situation.

A further distinction between these characteristics is that availability does not simply depend on the system itself but also the time that is required to repair faults that make the system unavailable. Therefore, if system A fails once per year and system B fails once per month then A is more reliable then B. However, if system A takes three days to restart whereas system B takes 10 minutes to restart then the availability of B over the year is considerably greater than that of A. Users would probably prefer system B to system A.

System reliability and availability may be defined more precisely as follows:

1. *Reliability*   The probability of failure-free operation over a specified time in a given environment for a specific purpose.
2. *Availability*   The probability that a system, at a point in time, will be operational and able to deliver the requested services.

These are careful definitions of these terms and one of the practical problems in developing reliable systems is that our intuitive notions of reliability and availability are often sometimes broader than these limited definitions. The definition of reliability states that the environment in which the system is used and the purpose for which it is used must be taken into account when considering its reliability. Therefore, measurements of reliability in one environment are not necessarily transferable to another environment where the system is used in a different way.

For example, the reliability of a software system may be measured in an office environment where most users are uninterested in the operation of the software. They follow the instructions for its use and do not try to experiment with the system. In a university environment, the reliability may be quite different. Here, students explore the boundaries of the system and may use the system in unexpected ways. These may result in system failures that did not occur in the more constrained office environment.

Human perceptions and patterns of use are also significant. For example, consider a situation where a car has a fault in its windscreen wiper system that results in the intermittent failure of the wipers to operate correctly in heavy rain. The reliability of that system as perceived by a driver depends on where the driver lives and uses the car. A driver in Seattle (wet climate) will probably be more affected by this failure than a driver in Las Vegas (dry climate). The Seattle driver's perception will be that the system is unreliable whereas the driver in Las Vegas may never notice the problem.

A further difficulty with these definitions is that they do not take into account the severity of failure or the consequences of unavailability. People, naturally, are more concerned about system failures that have serious consequences and their perception of system reliability is influenced by these consequences. For example, a car engine that cuts out immediately after starting but inevitably operates correctly after restarting is irritating. However, it does not affect the normal operation of the

Figure 16.5
Reliability
terminology

Term	Description
System failure	An event that occurs at some point in time when the system does not deliver a service as expected by its users.
System error	Erroneous system behaviour where the behaviour of the system does not conform to its specification.
System fault	An incorrect system state, i.e. a system state that is unexpected by the designers of the system.
Human error or mistake	Human behaviour that results in the introduction of faults into a system.

car and many drivers would not think that it was unreliable. By contrast, most drivers will think that an engine which cuts out while driving at high speed once per month (say) is unreliable.

A strict definition of reliability relates the system implementation to its specification. That is, the system is behaving reliably if its behaviour is consistent with that defined in the specification. However, a common cause of perceived unreliability is that the system specification does not match the expectations of the system users. Unfortunately, many specifications are incomplete or incorrect and it is left to software engineers to interpret how the system should behave. As they are not domain experts, they may not, therefore, implement the behaviour that users expect.

Reliability and availability are usually considered to be the most important dimensions of dependability. If a system is unreliable, it is difficult to ensure system safety or security as they may be compromised by system failures. If a system is unavailable, the consequent economic losses can be very high. Unreliable software results in high costs for end-users. Developers of unreliable systems may acquire a bad reputation for quality and lose future business opportunities.

Reliability is compromised by system failures. These may be a failure to provide a service, a failure to deliver a service as specified or the delivery of a service in such a way that it is unsafe or insecure. Some of these failures are a consequence of specification errors or failures in associated systems such as a telecommunications system. However, many failures are a consequence of erroneous system behaviour that derives from faults in the system. When discussing reliability, it is helpful to distinguish between the terms fault, error and failure. I have defined these terms in Figure 16.5.

System faults do not necessarily result in system errors as the faulty state may be transient and it may be corrected before erroneous behaviour occurs. System errors do not necessarily result in system failures as the behaviour may also be transient and have no observable effect or the system may include protection that ensures that the erroneous behaviour is discovered and corrected before the system services are affected.

Figure 16.6 A system
as an input/output
mapping

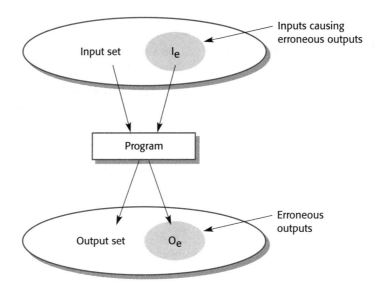

This distinction between the different terms shown in Figure 16.5 is helpful because
it helps us identify three complementary approaches that may be used to improve
the reliability of a system:

1. *Fault avoidance*   Development techniques are used that either minimise the
   possibility of mistakes and/or trap mistakes before these result in the introduction
   of system faults. Examples of such techniques include avoiding error-prone programming language constructs such as pointers and the use of static analysis
   to detect program anomalies as discussed in Chapter 19.

2. *Fault detection and removal*   The use of verification and validation techniques
   that increase the chances that faults will be detected and removed before the
   system is used. Systematic system testing and debugging is an example of a
   fault detection technique.

3. *Fault tolerance*   The use of techniques that ensure that faults in a system do
   not result in system errors or that ensure that system errors do not result in system failures. The incorporation of self-checking facilities in a system and the
   use of redundant system modules are examples of fault tolerance techniques.

The development of fault-tolerant systems is covered in Chapter 18 where I also
briefly discuss some techniques for fault avoidance. Process-based approaches to
fault avoidance are covered in Chapter 24. Fault detection is discussed in Chapters 19 and 20.

Software faults cause software failures when the faulty code is executed with a
set of inputs which expose the software fault. The code works properly for most
inputs. Figure 16.6, derived from Littlewood (1990), shows a software system as
a mapping of an input to an output set. A program has many possible inputs (for

Figure 16.7 Software
usage patterns

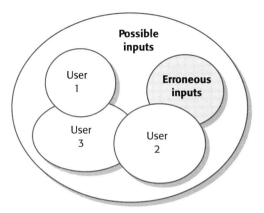

simplicity, combinations and sequences of inputs are considered as a single input). The program responds to these inputs by producing an output or a set of outputs.

Some of these inputs (shown in the shaded ellipse in Figure 16.6) cause system failures where erroneous outputs are generated by the program. The software reliability is related to the probability that, in a particular execution of the program, the system input will be a member of the set of inputs which cause an erroneous output.

There is a complex relationship between observed system reliability and the number of latent software faults. Mills *et al.* (1987) point out that not all software faults are equally likely to cause software failure. Usually, there are a number of members of I_e which are more likely to be selected than others. If these inputs do not cause the faulty parts of the software to be executed, there will be no failures. The reliability of the program, therefore, mostly depends on the number of inputs causing erroneous outputs during normal use of the system. Faults that only occur in exceptional situations have little effect on the system's reliability.

Reliability is related to the probability of an error occurring in operational use. Removing software faults from parts of the system which are rarely used makes little real difference to the perceived reliability. Mills *et al.* found that, in their software, removing 60 per cent of product defects led to only a 3 per cent reliability improvement. This was confirmed in a separate study of errors in IBM software products. Adams (1984) noted that many defects in the products were only likely to cause failures after hundreds or thousands of months of product usage.

Therefore, a program may contain known faults but may still be seen as reliable by its users. They may never select an erroneous input so program failures never arise. Furthermore, experienced users often 'work around' software faults which are known to cause failures. They deliberately avoid using system features which they know can cause problems for them. Repairing the faults in these features may make no practical difference to the reliability as seen by these users.

Each user of a system uses it in different ways. Faults which affect the reliability of the system for one user may never be revealed under a different mode of working (Figure 16.7). In Figure 16.7, the set of erroneous inputs corresponding to the shaded ellipse in Figure 16.6 is shaded. The set of inputs produced by User 2 intersects with this erroneous input set. User 2 will therefore experience some system failures. User 1 and User 3, however, never use inputs from the erroneous set. For them, the software will always be reliable.

16.3 Safety

The safety of a system is a system attribute that reflects the system's ability to operate, normally or abnormally, without threatening people or the environment. Where safety is an essential attribute of a critical system, the system is a safety-critical system. Examples of safety-critical systems are control and monitoring systems in aircraft, process control systems in chemical and pharmaceutical plants and automobile control systems.

Hardware control of safety-critical systems is simpler to implement and analyse than software control. However, we are now building systems of such complexity that they cannot be controlled by hardware alone. Some software control is essential because of the need to manage large numbers of sensors and actuators with complex control laws. An example of such complexity is found in advanced military aircraft which are aerodynamically unstable. They require continual software-controlled adjustment of their flight surfaces to ensure that they do not crash.

Safety-critical software falls into two classes:

1. *Primary, safety-critical software*   This is software which is embedded as a controller in a system. Malfunctioning of such software can cause a hardware malfunction which results in human injury or environmental damage. I focus on this type of software.

2. *Secondary safety-critical software*   This is software which can indirectly result in injury. Examples of such systems are computer-aided engineering design systems whose malfunctioning might result in a design fault in the object being designed. This fault may pose a threat to humans if the designed system malfunctions. Another example of a secondary safety-critical system is a medical database holding details of drugs administered to patients. Errors in this system might result in an incorrect drug dosage being administered.

System reliability and system safety are related but distinct dependability attributes. Of course, a safety-critical system should be reliable in that it should conform to its specification and operate without failures. It may incorporate fault-tolerant features so that it can provide continuous service even if faults occur. However, fault-tolerant systems are not necessarily safe. The software may still malfunction and cause system behaviour which results in an accident.

Apart from the fact that we can never be 100 per cent certain that a software system is fault-free and fault-tolerant, there are several other reasons why software systems that are reliable are not necessarily safe:

1. The specification may be incomplete in that it does not describe the required behaviour of the system in some critical situations. A high percentage of system malfunctions (Boehm *et al.*, 1975; Endres, 1975; Nakajo and Kume, 1991; Lutz, 1993) are the result of specification rather than design errors. In a study of errors in embedded systems, Lutz concludes:

    > . . . difficulties with requirements are the key root cause of the safety-related software errors which have persisted until integration and system testing

2. Hardware malfunctions may cause the system to behave in an unpredictable way and may present the software with an unanticipated environment. When components are close to failure they may behave erratically and generate signals that are outside the ranges that can be handled by the software.

3. The operator of the system may generate inputs that are not individually incorrect but which, in particular situations, can lead to a system malfunction. An anecdotal example of this is where a mechanic instructed the utility management software on an aircraft to raise the undercarriage. The software carried out the mechanic's instruction in spite of the fact that the plane was on the ground!

A specialised vocabulary has evolved to discuss safety-critical systems and it is important to understand the specific terms used. In Figure 16.8 I show some definitions that I have adapted from terms initially defined by Leveson (1985).

The key to assuring safety is to ensure either that accidents do not occur or that the consequences of an accident are minimal. This can be achieved in three complementary ways:

1. *Hazard avoidance*   The system is designed so that hazards are avoided. For example, a cutting system that requires the operator to press two separate buttons at the same time to operate the machine avoids the hazard of the operator's hands being in the blade pathway.

2. *Hazard detection and removal*   The system is designed so that hazards are detected and removed before they result in an accident. For example, a chemical plant system may detect excessive pressure and open a relief valve to reduce these pressures before an explosion occurs.

3. *Damage limitation*   The system may include protection features that minimise the damage that may result from an accident. For example, an aircraft engine normally includes automatic fire extinguishers. If a fire occurs, it can often be controlled before it poses a threat to the passengers or crew.

Figure 16.8 Safety
terminology

Term	Definition
Accident (or mishap)	An unplanned event or sequence of events which results in human death or injury, damage to property or to the environment. A computer-controlled machine injuring its operator is an example of an accident.
Hazard	A condition with the potential for causing or contributing to an accident. A failure of the sensor that detects an obstacle in front of a machine is an example of a hazard.
Damage	A measure of the loss resulting from a mishap. Damage can range from many people killed as a result of an accident to minor injury or property damage.
Hazard severity	An assessment of the worst possible damage which could result from a particular hazard. Hazard severity can range from catastrophic where many people are killed to minor where only minor damage results.
Hazard probability	The probability of the events occurring which create a hazard. Probability values tend to be arbitrary but range from *probable* (say 1/100 chance of a hazard occurring) to implausible (no conceivable situations are likely where the hazard could occur).
Risk	This is a measure of the probability that the system will cause an accident. The risk is assessed by considering the hazard probability, the hazard severity and the probability that a hazard will result in an accident.

Accidents generally occur when several things go wrong at the same time. An analysis of serious accidents (Perrow, 1984) suggested that they were almost all due to a combination of malfunctions rather than single failures. The unanticipated combination led to interactions which resulted in system failure. Perrow also suggests that it is impossible to anticipate all possible combinations of system malfunction and that accidents are an inevitable part of using complex systems. Software tends to increase system complexity so using software control *may* increase the probability of system accidents.

This does not mean that software control invariably increases the risk associated with a system. Software control and monitoring can improve the safety of systems. Software-controlled systems can monitor a wider range of conditions than electromechanical systems. They can be adapted relatively easily. They involve the use of computer hardware which has very high inherent reliability and which is physically small and lightweight. Software-controlled systems can provide sophisticated safety interlocks. They can support control strategies which reduce the amount of time people need to spend in hazardous environments.

16.4 Security

The security of a system is an assessment of the extent that the system protects itself from external attacks that may be accidental or deliberate. Examples of attacks might be viruses, unauthorised use of system services, unauthorised modification of the system or its data, etc. Security is important for all critical systems. Without a reasonable level of security, the availability, reliability and safety of the system may be compromised if external attacks cause some damage to the system.

The reason for this is that all methods for assuring availability, reliability and security rely on the fact that the operational system is the same as the system that was originally installed. If this installed system has been compromised in some way (for example, if the software has been modified to include a virus) then the arguments for reliability and safety that were originally made can no longer hold. The system software may be corrupted and may behave in an unpredictable way.

Conversely, errors in the development of a system can lead to security loopholes. If a system does not respond to unexpected inputs or if array bounds are not checked then attackers can exploit these weaknesses to gain access to the system. One major security incident (the Internet worm) (Spafford, 1989) took advantage of the fact that programs in C do not include array bound checking to overwrite part of memory with code that allowed unauthorised access to the system.

Of course, there are some types of critical system where security is the most important dimension of system dependability. Military systems, systems for electronic commerce and systems that involve the processing and interchange of confidential information must be designed so that they achieve a high level of security. If an airline reservation system (say) is unavailable, this causes inconvenience and some delays in issuing tickets. However, if the system is insecure and can accept fake bookings then the airline that owns the system can lose a great deal of money as a result of this problem.

There are three types of damage that may be caused through external attack:

1. *Denial of service*   The system may be forced into a state where its normal services become unavailable. This, obviously, then affects the availability of the system.

2. *Corruption of programs or data*   The software components of the system may be altered in an unauthorised way. This may affect the system's behaviour and hence its reliability and safety. If damage is severe, the availability of the system may be affected.

3. *Disclosure of confidential information*   The information managed by the system may be confidential and the external attack may expose this to unauthorised people. Depending on the type of data, this could affect the safety of the system and may allow later attacks that affect the system availability or reliability.

Figure 16.9 Security
terminology

Term	Definition
Exposure	Possible loss or harm in a computing system.
Vulnerability	A weakness in a computer-based system that may be exploited to cause loss or harm.
Attack	An exploitation of a system vulnerability.
Threats	Circumstances that have potential to cause loss or harm.
Control	A protective measure that reduces a system vulnerability.

As with other aspects of dependability, there is a specialised terminology associated with security. Some important terms, as discussed by Pfleeger (1997), are defined in Figure 16.9.

There is a clear analogy here with some of the terminology of safety so that an exposure is analogous to an accident and a vulnerability is analogous to a hazard. Therefore there are comparable approaches that may be used to assure the security of a system:

1. *Vulnerability avoidance* The system is designed so that vulnerabilities do not occur. For example, if a system is not connected to an external public network then there is no possibility of an attack from members of the public.

2. *Attack detection and neutralisation* The system is designed to detect vulnerabilities and remove them before they result in an exposure. An example of vulnerability detection and removal is the use of a virus checker that analyses incoming files for viruses and modifies these files to remove the virus.

3. *Exposure limitation* The consequences of a successful attack are minimised. Examples of exposure limitation are regular system backups and a configuration management policy that allows damaged software to be re-created.

Security has become increasingly important as more and more systems are connected to the Internet. Internet connections provide additional system functionality (e.g. a customer may be able to access his or her bank account directly) but also means that the system can be attacked by people with hostile intentions. The Internet also means that details of specific system vulnerabilities may be easily disseminated so that more people may be able to attack the system.

A related, very important attribute for Internet-based systems is survivability (Ellison *et al.*, 1999a). Survivability is the ability of a system to continue to deliver service while it is under attack and, potentially, while part of the system is disabled. Survivability is clearly related to both security and availability. Work on survivability focuses on identifying key system components and ensuring that they can deliver a minimal service (Ellison *et al.*, 1999b). Three strategies are used to enhance survivability, namely resistance to attack, attack recognition and recovery from the damage caused by an attack. I do not have space to cover this topic here but have included some links from the book's web pages to information on survivability research.

KEY POINTS

▶ The dependability of a computer system is a property of the system that reflects the user's degree of trust in the system. The most important dimensions of dependability are availability, reliability, safety and security.

▶ A critical system is a system where failures can result in significant economic losses, physical damage or threats to human life. Three important classes of critical system are safety-critical systems, mission-critical systems and business-critical systems.

▶ The availability of a system is the probability that it will be able to deliver services to its users when requested to do so and the reliability is the probability that system services will be delivered as specified.

▶ Reliability and availability are usually considered to be the most important dimensions of dependability. If a system is unreliable, it is difficult to ensure system safety or security as they may be compromised by system failures.

▶ Reliability is related to the probability of an error occurring in operational use. A program may contain known faults but may still be seen as reliable by its users. They may never use features of the system that are affected by these faults.

▶ The safety of a system is a system attribute that reflects the system's ability to operate, normally or abnormally, without threatening people or the environment. Where safety is an essential attribute of a critical system, the system is a safety-critical system.

▶ Security is important for all critical systems. Without a reasonable level of security, the availability, reliability and safety of the system may be compromised if external attacks cause some damage to the system.

FURTHER READING

'Survivability: Protecting your critical systems'. An accessible introduction to the topic of survivability and why it is important. (R. Ellison *et al.*, *IEEE Internet Computing*, Nov./Dec. 1999.)

Computer Security. This book is an excellent introduction to the area of computer security. It covers basic principles, practice, distributed systems security and security theory. (D. Gollmann, 1999, John Wiley and Sons.)

Handbook of Software Reliability Engineering. This book is a detailed discussion of software reliability from both a practical and a theoretical stand-point. (M. R. Lyu, 1996, McGraw-Hill.)

Computer-related Risks. This is a collection drawn from the Internet Risks Forum of incidents that have occurred in automated systems. It shows how much can actually go wrong in safety-related systems. (P. G. Neumann, 1995, Addison-Wesley.)

EXERCISES

16.1 What are the most important dimensions of system dependability? Why is it the case that the cost of assuring dependability is exponential?

16.2 Suggest six reasons why dependability is important in critical systems.

16.3 Using an example, explain the difficulties of describing what software reliability means.

16.4 Assess the reliability of some software system which you use regularly by keeping a log of system failures and observed faults. Write a user's handbook which describes how to make effective use of the system in the presence of these faults.

16.5 Identify six consumer products which may contain, or which may contain in future, safety-critical software systems.

16.6 Explain why ensuring system reliability is not a guarantee of system safety.

16.7 In a medical system that is designed to deliver radiation to treat tumours, suggest one hazard that may arise and propose one software feature that may be used to ensure that the identified hazard does not result in an accident.

16.8 Explain why there is a close relationship between system availability and system security.

16.9 In computer security terms, explain the differences between an attack and a threat.

16.10 Is it ethical for an engineer to agree to deliver a software system with known faults to a customer? Does it make any different if the customer is told of the existence of these faults in advance? Would it be reasonable to make claims about the reliability of the software in such circumstances?

16.11 Assume you were part of a team which developed software for a chemical plant which went wrong and caused a serious pollution incident. Your boss is interviewed on television and states that there are no faults in the software and that the problems must be due to poor operational procedures. You are approached by a newspaper for your opinion. Discuss how you should handle such an interview.

17 Critical systems specification

Objectives

The objective of this chapter is to explain how to specify functional and non-functional dependability requirements. When you have read this chapter, you will:

❑ have been introduced to a number of metrics for reliability specification and will understand how these metrics may be used to specify reliability requirements;

❑ understand how safety requirements for critical systems may be derived from an analysis of hazards and risks;

❑ understand the similarities between the processes for specifying safety and security requirements.

Contents

17.1 Software reliability specification
17.2 Safety specification
17.3 Security specification

I have discussed requirements processes and techniques for the development of system specifications in Chapters 5–9. This chapter supplements these chapters with a discussion of particular issues that arise in the specification of critical systems. Because of the high potential costs of system failure, it is important to ensure that the specification for critical systems is high quality and accurately reflects the real needs of users of the system.

The need for dependability in critical systems generates both functional and non-functional system requirements:

1. System functional requirements may be generated to define error checking and recovery facilities and features that provide protection against system failures.

2. Non-functional requirements may be generated to define the required reliability and availability of the system.

In addition to these requirements, safety and security considerations can generate a further type of requirement that is difficult to classify as a functional or a non-functional requirement. These are perhaps best described as the 'shall not' requirements. By contrast with normal functional requirements that define what the system shall do, 'shall not' requirements define system behaviour that is unacceptable. Examples of 'shall not' requirements are:

The system shall not allow users to modify access permissions on any files that they have not created (security)

The system shall not allow reverse thrust mode to be selected when the aircraft is in flight (safety)

The system shall not allow the simultaneous activation of more than three alarm signals (safety)

These 'shall not' requirements are sometimes decomposed into more specific software functional requirements. Alternatively, implementation decisions may be deferred until the system is designed.

The user requirements for critical systems will always be specified using natural language and system models. However, as I discuss in Chapter 9, formal specification and associated verification are most likely to be cost-effective in critical systems development (Hall, 1996; Wordsworth, 1996). Formal specifications are not just a basis for a verification of the design and implementation. They are the most precise way of specifying systems, so reduce the scope for misunderstanding. Furthermore, constructing a formal specification forces a detailed analysis of the requirements and this is an effective way of discovering problems in the specification.

17.1 Software reliability specification

Reliability is a complex concept which should always be considered at the system rather than the individual component level. Because the components in a system are interdependent, a failure in one component can be propagated through the system and affect the operation of other components. In a computer-based system, you have to consider three dimensions when specifying the overall system reliability:

1. *Hardware reliability*   What is the probability of a hardware component failing and how long does it take to repair that component?

2. *Software reliability*   How likely is it that a software component will produce an incorrect output? Software failures are different from hardware failures in that software does not wear out. It can continue operating correctly after an incorrect result has been produced.

3. *Operator reliability*   How likely is it that the operator of a system will make an error?

All of these are closely linked. Hardware failure can cause spurious signals to be generated that are outside the range of inputs expected by software. The software can then behave unpredictably. Unexpected system behaviour may confuse the operator and may result in operator stress. Operator error is most likely in conditions of stress. The operator may then act incorrectly and supply inputs that are inappropriate for the current failure situation. These inputs further confuse the system and more errors are generated. Therefore, a situation can occur where a single sub-system failure that is recoverable can rapidly develop into a serious problem requiring a complete system shutdown.

Software reliability engineering (Lyu, 1996) is a specialised sub-discipline of systems engineering that is concerned with making overall judgements on system reliability. It takes into account the probabilities of failure of different components in a system and how these are combined to affect the overall reliability of a system. Simplistically, if a system depends on component A and component B with failure probabilities of P_A and P_B, then the overall probability of system failure P_S is:

$$P_S = P_A + P_B$$

As the number of dependent components increases, the overall probability of system failure increases. If there are very many critical components in a system then these individual components must be very reliable to ensure that P_S is relatively low. To increase reliability, components may be replicated as discussed in Chapter 18. A number of identical components work together and the component group is operational so long as any one component works correctly. This means (simplistically again) that if the probability of failure of a component is P_A and if all failures are independent then the overall failure probability P_S of a group of n identical replicated components is computed by multiplying the probability of failure of each component:

$$P_S = P_A^n$$

Systems reliability should be specified as a non-functional requirement that is expressed quantitatively using one of the metrics discussed in the next section. To meet the non-functional reliability requirements, it may be necessary to specify additional functional and design requirements on the system that specify how failures may be avoided or tolerated. Examples of these reliability requirements are:

1. A predefined range for all values that are input by the operator shall be defined and the system shall check that all operator inputs fall within this predefined range.
2. As part of the initialisation process, the system shall check all disks for bad blocks.
3. N-version programming shall be used to implement the braking control system.
4. The system must be implemented in a safe subset of Ada and checked using static analysis (see Chapter 19).

There are no simple rules that may be used to derive functional reliability requirements. In organisations that develop critical systems, there is usually organisational knowledge about possible reliability requirements and how these impact the actual reliability of a system. These organisations may specialise in specific types of system such as railway control systems, so the reliability requirements, once derived, are reused across a range of systems.

17.1.1   Reliability metrics

Reliability metrics were first devised for hardware components. Hardware component failure is inevitable due to physical factors such as mechanical abrasion, electrical heating, etc. Components have some average lifetime and this is reflected in the most widely used hardware reliability metric, 'Mean Time to Failure' (MTTF). The MTTF is the mean time for which a component is expected to be operational. Once a hardware component fails then the failure is usually permanent, so the 'Mean Time to Repair' (MTTR) which reflects the time taken to repair or replace the component is also significant.

However, these hardware metrics are not always applicable for software reliability specification because of the differing nature of software and hardware failures. Software component failures are often transient rather than permanent. They only manifest themselves with some inputs. If the data is undamaged, the system can often continue in operation after a failure has occurred.

Metrics which have been used for specifying software reliability and availability are shown in Figure 17.1. The choice of which metric should be used depends

Figure 17.1
Reliability metrics

Metric	Explanation
POFOD Probability of failure on demand	The likelihood that the system will fail when a service request is made. A POFOD of 0.001 means that one out of a thousand service requests may result in failure.
ROCOF Rate of failure occurrence	The frequency of occurrence with which unexpected behaviour is likely to occur. A ROCOF of 2/100 means that two failures are likely to occur in each 100 operational time units. This metric is sometimes called the failure intensity.
MTTF Mean time to failure	The average time between observed system failures. An MTTF of 500 means that one failure can be expected every 500 time units.
AVAIL Availability	The probability that the system is available for use at a given time. Availability of 0.998 means that in every 1000 time units, the system is likely to be available for 998 of these.

on the type of system to which it applies and the requirements of the application domain. Some examples of the types of system where these different metrics may be used are:

1. *Probability of failure on demand*   This metric is most appropriate for systems where services are demanded at unpredictable or at relatively long time intervals and where there are serious consequences if the service is not delivered. It might be used to specify protection systems such as the reliability of a pressure relief system in a chemical plant or an emergency shutdown system in a power plant.

2. *Rate of occurrence of failures*   This metric should be used where regular demands are made on system services and where it is important that these services are correctly delivered. It might be used in the specification of a bank teller system that processes customer transactions or in an hotel reservation system.

3. *Mean time to failure*   This metric should be used in systems where there are long transactions, i.e. where people use the system for a long time. The mean time to failure should be longer than the average length of transaction. Examples of systems where this metric may be used are word processor systems or CAD systems.

4. *Availability*   This metric should be used in non-stop systems where users expect the system to deliver a continuous service. Examples of such systems are telephone switching systems and railway signalling systems.

There are three kinds of measurement which can be made when assessing the reliability of a system:

1. The number of system failures given a number of requests for system services. This is used to measure the POFOD.
2. The time (or number of transactions) between system failures. This is used to measure ROCOF and MTTF.
3. The elapsed repair or restart time when a system failure occurs. Given that the system must be continuously available, this is used to measure AVAIL.

Time units which may be used in these metrics are calendar time, processor time or may be some discrete unit such as number of transactions. In systems that spend much of their time waiting to respond to a service request, such as telephone switching systems, the time unit that should be used is processor time. Basing reliability on calendar time would give an optimistic figure.

Calendar time is an appropriate time unit to use for systems which are in continuous operation. For example, monitoring systems, such as alarm systems, and other types of process control systems fall into this category. Systems which process transactions such as bank ATMs or airline reservation systems have variable loads placed on them depending on the time of day. In these cases, the unit of 'time' used should be the number of transactions, i.e. the ROCOF would be number of failed transactions per N thousand transactions.

17.1.2 Non-functional reliability requirements

In many system requirements documents, reliability requirements are not carefully specified. The reliability specifications are subjective and unmeasurable. For example, statements such as 'The software shall be reliable under normal conditions of use' are meaningless. Quasi-quantitative statements such as 'The software shall exhibit no more than N faults/1000 lines' are equally useless. It is impossible to measure the number of faults/1000 lines of code as you can't tell when all faults have been discovered. Furthermore, the statement means nothing in terms of the dynamic behaviour of the system. It is software failures not software faults that affect the reliability of a system.

The types of failure that can occur are system specific and the consequences of a system failure depend on the nature of that failure. When writing a reliability specification, the specifier should identify different types of failure and consider whether these should be treated differently in the specification. Examples of different types of failure are shown in Figure 17.2. Obviously, combinations of these such as a failure which is transient, recoverable and corrupting can occur.

Most large systems are composed of several sub-systems with different reliability requirements. Because very highly reliable software is expensive, it is usually sensible to assess the reliability requirements of each sub-system separately rather than impose the same reliability requirement on all sub-systems. This avoids placing unnecessarily high demands for reliability on those sub-systems where it is unnecessary.

The steps involved in establishing a reliability specification are:

Figure 17.2 Failure
classification

Failure class	Description
Transient	Occurs only with certain inputs
Permanent	Occurs with all inputs
Recoverable	System can recover without operator intervention
Unrecoverable	Operator intervention needed to recover from failure
Non-corrupting	Failure does not corrupt system state or data
Corrupting	Failure corrupts system state or data

1. For each identified sub-system, identify the different types of system failure which may occur and analyse the consequences of these failures.

2. From the system failure analysis, partition failures into appropriate classes. A reasonable starting point is to use the failure types shown in Figure 17.2.

3. For each failure class identified, define the reliability requirement using an appropriate reliability metric. It is not necessary to use the same metric for different classes of failure. If a failure requires some intervention to recover from it, the probability of that failure occurring on demand might be the most appropriate metric. When automatic recovery is possible and the effect of the failure is user inconvenience, ROCOF might be more appropriate.

4. Where appropriate, identify functional reliability requirements that define system functionality to reduce the probability of critical failures.

As an example of a reliability specification, consider the reliability requirements for a bank auto-teller machine (ATM). Assume that each machine in the network is used about 300 times per day. The lifetime of the system hardware is eight years and the software is normally upgraded every two years. Therefore, during the lifetime of a software release, each machine will handle about 200,000 transactions. A bank has 1000 machines in its network. This means that there are 300,000 transactions on the central database per day (say 100 million per year).

Failures fall into two broad classes: those that affect a single machine in the network and those that affect the database and therefore all ATMs in the network. Clearly, the latter type of failure is less acceptable than those failures which are local to an ATM.

Figure 17.3 shows possible failure classes and possible reliability specifications for different types of system failure. The reliability requirements state that it is acceptable for a permanent failure to occur in a machine roughly once per three years. This means that, on average, one machine in the banking network might be affected each day. By contrast, faults which simply mean that a transaction has to be aborted

Figure 17.3
Reliability
specification for
an ATM

Failure class	Example	Reliability metric
Permanent, non-corrupting	The system fails to operate with any card which is input. Software must be restarted to correct failure.	ROCOF 1 occurrence/1000 days
Transient, non-corrupting	The magnetic stripe data cannot be read on an undamaged card which is input.	ROCOF 1 in 1000 transactions
Transient, corrupting	A pattern of transactions across the network causes database corruption.	Unquantifiable! Should never happen in the lifetime of the system

and the user must start again can occur relatively frequently. Their only effect is to cause minor user inconvenience.

Ideally, faults that corrupt the database should never occur in the lifetime of the software. Therefore, the reliability requirement which might be placed on this is that the probability of a corrupting failure occurring when a demand is made is less than 1 in 200 million transactions. That is, in the lifetime of an ATM software release, there should never be an error which causes database corruption.

However, a reliability requirement like this cannot actually be tested. Say each transaction takes 1 second of machine time and a simulator can be built for the ATM network. Simulating the transactions which take place in a single day across the network will take 300,000 seconds. This is approximately 3.5 days. Clearly this period could be reduced by reducing the transaction time and using multiple simulators but it is still very difficult to test the system to validate the reliability specification.

It is impossible to validate qualitative requirements which demand a very high level of reliability. For example, say a system was intended for use in a safety-critical application, so it should never fail over the total lifetime of the system. Assume that 1000 copies of the system are to be installed and the system is 'executed' 1000 times per second. The projected lifetime of the system is 10 years. The total estimated number of system executions is therefore approximately $3 * 10^{14}$. There is no point in specifying that the rate of occurrence of failure should be $1/10^{15}$ executions (this allows for some safety factor) as you cannot test the system for long enough to validate this level of reliability.

As a further example of reliability specification, consider the insulin pump system that was introduced in Chapter 16. This system delivers insulin a number of times per day and the user's blood glucose is monitored several times per hour. Because the use of the system is intermittent and failure consequences are serious, the most appropriate reliability metric is POFOD (Probability of Failure on Demand).

As I discuss in the following section, failure to deliver insulin does not have immediate safety implications so commercial factors rather than safety factors govern the level of reliability required. Service costs are high because users need a very fast repair and replacement service. It is in the manufacturer's interest to limit the number of permanent failures that require repair.

Again, two types of failure can be identified:

1. Transient failures that can be repaired by user actions such as resetting or recalibrating the machine. For these types of failure, a relatively low value of POFOD (say 0.002) may be acceptable. This means that one failure may occur in every 500 demands made on the machine. This is approximately once every 3.5 days.

2. Permanent failures that require the machine to be repaired by the manufacturer. The probability of this type of failure should be much lower. Roughly once a year is the minimum figure, so POFOD should be no more than 0.00002.

The cost of developing and validating a system reliability specification can be very high. Organisations must be realistic about whether these costs are worthwhile. They are clearly justified in systems where reliable operation is critical, such as telephone switching systems, or where system failure may result in large economic losses. They are probably not justified for many types of business or scientific system. These usually have relatively modest reliability requirements as the costs of failure are simply processing delays and it is straightforward and relatively inexpensive to recover from these.

17.2 Safety specification

Safe operation is the required characteristic of a safety-related software system. This means that you must consider, during the requirements engineering process, potential hazards that might arise. Each hazard should be assessed for the risk it poses and the specification may either describe how the software should behave to minimise the risk or might require that the hazard should never arise.

The process of safety specification and assurance is part of an overall 'safety life cycle' that is illustrated in Figure 17.4. Figure 17.4 is a simplified form of Redmill's presentation of the safety life cycle (Redmill, 1998) as proposed in an international standard for safety management IEC 61508 (IEC, 1998). As you can see from Figure 17.4, this standard covers all aspects of safety management from initial scope definition through planning and system development to system decommissioning.

The first stages of the IEC standard 61508 safety life cycle define the scope of the system, assess the potential system hazards and estimate the risk they pose. This is followed by safety requirements specification and the allocation of these safety requirements to different sub-systems. The development activity involves planning

Figure 17.4 The IEC
61508 safety life
cycle

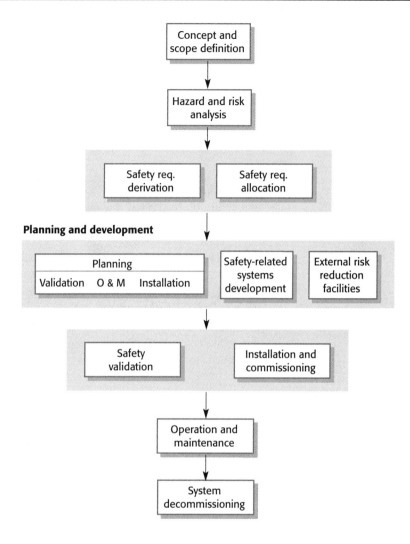

Figure 17.4 The IEC 61508 safety life cycle

and implementation. The safety-critical system itself is designed and implemented, as are related external systems that may provide additional protection. In parallel with this, the safety validation, the installation and the operation and maintenance of the system are planned.

Safety management does not stop on delivery of the system. After delivery, the system must be installed as planned so that the hazard analysis remains valid. Safety validation is then carried out before the system is put into use. Safety must also be managed during the operation and (particularly) the maintenance of the system. Many safety-related systems problems arise because of a poor maintenance process, so it is particularly important that the system is designed for maintainability. Finally, safety considerations that may apply during decommissioning (e.g. disposal of hazardous material in circuit boards) should also be taken into account.

17.2.1   Hazard and risk analysis

Hazard and risk analysis involves analysing the system and its operational environment. Its objective is to discover potential hazards that might arise in that environment, the root causes of these hazards and the risks associated with them. This is a complex and difficult process which requires lateral thinking and input from many different sources of expertise. It should be undertaken by experienced engineers in conjunction with domain experts and professional safety advisers. Group working techniques such as brainstorming may be used to identify hazards. Hazards may also be identified because one of the analysts involved has direct experience of some previous incident which resulted in a hazard.

Figure 17.5 shows the iterative process of hazard and risk analysis:

1. *Hazard identification*   Potential hazards which might arise are identified. These are dependent on the environment in which the system is to be used.

2. *Risk analysis and hazard classification*   The hazards are considered separately. Those which are potentially serious and not implausible are selected for further analysis. At this stage, some hazards may be eliminated simply because they are very unlikely ever to arise (e.g. simultaneous lightning strike and earthquake).

3. *Hazard decomposition*   Each hazard is analysed individually to discover potential causes of that hazard. Techniques such as fault-tree analysis (discussed later in this section) may be used.

4. *Risk reduction assessment*   Proposals for ways in which the identified risks may be reduced or eliminated are made. These are input to a more detailed safety requirements specification activity as shown in the safety life cycle model (Figure 17.4).

For large systems, hazard and risk analysis is usually structured into a number of phases (Leveson, 1986). These include:

- preliminary hazard analysis where major risks are identified;
- more detailed system and sub-system hazard analysis;
- software hazard analysis where the risks of software failure are considered;
- operational hazard analysis which is concerned with the system user interface and risks that arise from operator errors.

Figure 17.5 Hazard and risk analysis

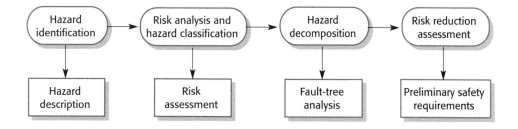

These analyses identify hazards and associate a risk with each hazard. This involves estimating the probability that the hazard will arise, estimating the probability that the hazard will cause a mishap and estimating the likely severity of that mishap. Engineering judgement is used to make these risk assessments.

The process of hazard analysis generally involves considering different classes of hazard such as physical hazards, electrical hazards, biological hazards, radiation hazards (where appropriate), hazards due to service failure and so on. Each of these classes is then analysed in detail to discover associated hazards.

For the insulin delivery system, introduced above, the hazards and their associated classes are:

1. insulin overdose (service failure);
2. insulin underdose (service failure);
3. power failure due to exhausted battery (electrical);
4. machine interferes electrically with other medical equipment such as a heart pacemaker (electrical);
5. poor sensor and actuator contact caused by incorrect fitting (physical);
6. parts of machine break off in patient's body (physical);
7. infection caused by introduction of machine (biological);
8. allergic reaction to the materials or insulin used in the machine (biological).

The risks associated with these hazards are covered in section 17.2.3. Because this is a small system, multiple phases of hazard analysis are not necessary. Many safety-critical systems, however, are very large (e.g. a chemical plant) and hazard analysis is a long, complex and expensive process.

17.2.2   Fault-tree analysis

For each identified hazard, a detailed analysis should be carried out to discover the conditions which might cause that hazard. Hazard analysis techniques can be either deductive or inductive. Deductive techniques, which tend to be easier to use, start with the hazard and work from that to the possible system failure; inductive techniques start with a proposed system failure and identify which hazards might arise. Wherever possible, both inductive and deductive techniques should be used for hazard analysis.

There are various techniques which have been proposed as possible approaches to such analyses. These include reviews and checklists, and more formal techniques such as Petri net analysis (Peterson, 1981), formal logic (Jahanian and Mok, 1986) and fault-tree analysis (Leveson and Harvey, 1983).

I cover fault-tree analysis here. This is a widely used hazard analysis technique which is relatively easy to understand without specialist domain knowledge. Fault-tree analysis involves identifying the undesired event and working backwards from that event to discover the possible causes of the hazard. The hazard is at the root of the tree and the leaves represent potential causes of the hazard.

Figure 17.6 Fault
tree for insulin
delivery system

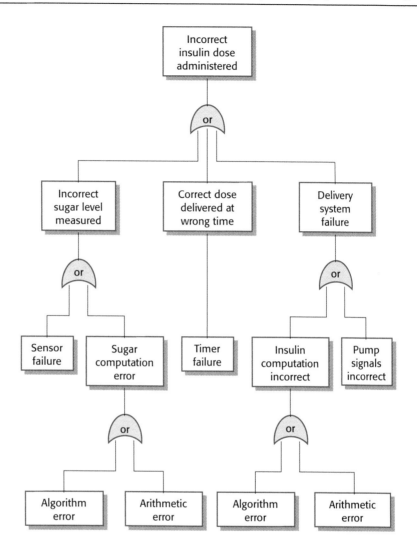

Software-related hazards are normally concerned with failure to deliver a system service or with the failure of monitoring systems. Monitoring systems may detect potentially hazardous conditions such as power failures.

Figure 17.6 is the fault tree which can be identified for the possible software-related hazards in the insulin delivery system. Insulin underdose and insulin overdose really represent a single hazard, namely 'incorrect insulin dose administered' and a single fault tree can be drawn. Of course, when specifying how the software should react to hazards, the distinction between an insulin underdose or overdose must be taken into account.

The fault tree in Figure 17.6 is incomplete. Only potential software faults have been fully decomposed. Hardware faults such as low battery power causing a sensor failure are not shown. At this level, further analysis is not possible. However, as a design and implementation is developed more detailed fault tree analyses should be carried out. Leveson and Harvey (1983) and Leveson (1985) show how fault trees can be developed throughout the software design down to the individual programming language statement level.

17.2.3 Risk assessment

The process of risk assessment begins after all hazards have been identified. Risk assessment considers the severity of each hazard, the probability that it will arise and the probability that an accident will result from the hazard. For each hazard, the outcome of the risk assessment process is a statement of acceptability. This classifies the acceptability of the hazard as follows:

1. *Intolerable*   The system must be designed in such a way that either the hazard cannot arise or, if it does arise, it will not result in an accident.

2. *As low as reasonably practical (ALARP)*   The system must be designed so that the probability of an accident arising because of the hazard is minimised, subject to other considerations such as cost, delivery, etc.

3. *Acceptable*   While the system designers should take all possible steps to reduce the probability of this hazard arising, these should not increase costs, delivery time or other non-functional system attributes.

Figure 17.7 (Brazendale and Bell, 1994) shows these three regions. The shape of the diagram reflects the costs of ensuring hazards do not result in accidents. The cost of system design to cope with the hazard is a function of the width of the triangle. The highest costs are incurred by hazards at the top of the diagram, the lowest costs by hazards at the apex of the triangle.

Figure 17.7
Levels of risk

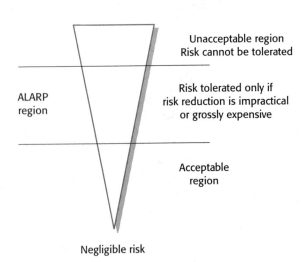

Unacceptable region
Risk cannot be tolerated

ALARP region

Risk tolerated only if
risk reduction is impractical
or grossly expensive

Acceptable region

Negligible risk

Figure 17.8
Risk analysis of
identified hazards

Identified hazard	Hazard probability	Hazard severity	Estimated risk	Acceptability
1. Insulin overdose	Medium	High	High	Intolerable
2. Insulin underdose	Medium	Low	Low	Acceptable
3. Power failure	High	Low	Low	Acceptable
4. Machine incorrectly fitted	High	High	High	Intolerable
5. Machine breaks in patient	Low	High	Medium	ALARP
6. Machine causes infection	Medium	Medium	Medium	ALARP
7. Electrical interference	Low	High	Medium	ALARP
8. Allergic reaction	Low	Low	Low	Acceptable

The boundaries between the regions in Figure 17.7 are not fixed for any particular class of system. Rather, they tend to be pushed downwards with time due to public expectations of safety and political considerations. Although the financial costs of accepting hazards and paying for any resulting accidents may be less than the costs of accident prevention, public opinion may mean that the additional costs must be accepted. For example, it may be cheaper for a company to clean up pollution on the rare occasion it occurs rather than install systems for pollution prevention. This may have been acceptable in the 1960s and 1970s but it is not likely to be publicly or politically acceptable now. The boundary between the intolerable region and the ALARP region has moved downwards so that hazards that may have been accepted in the past are now intolerable.

The risk assessment process involves estimating the hazard probability and the hazard severity. This is usually very difficult to do in an exact way and generally depends on making engineering judgements. Probabilities and severities are assigned using relative terms such as 'probable', 'unlikely' and 'rare', and 'high', 'medium' and 'low'. Previous system experience may allow some numeric value to be associated with these terms. However, because accidents are relatively uncommon, it is usually very difficult to validate the accuracy of this value.

Figure 17.8 shows a risk classification for the hazards identified in the previous section for the insulin delivery system. As I am not a physician, the estimates in that table are for illustration only. Notice that an insulin overdose is potentially more serious than an insulin underdose in the short term.

Hazards 3–8 are not software related so I don't discuss them further here. To counter these hazards, the machine should have built-in self-checking software which should monitor the system state and warn of some of these hazards. The warning will often allow the hazard to be detected before it causes an accident. Examples of hazards which might be detected are power failure and incorrect placement of machine. The monitoring software is, of course, safety-related as failure to detect a hazard could result in an accident.

17.2.4 Risk reduction

Once potential hazards and their causes have been identified, the system specification should be formulated so that these hazards are unlikely to result in an accident. In Chapter 16, I identified three possible strategies that may be used:

1. *Hazard avoidance*   The system is designed so that the hazard cannot arise.
2. *Hazard detection and removal*   The system is designed so that hazards are detected and neutralised before they result in an accident.
3. *Damage limitation*   The system is designed so that the consequences of an accident are minimised.

Normally, the designers of safety-critical systems use a combination of these approaches. For example, intolerable hazards may be handled by reducing their probability as far as possible and adding a protection system should the hazard arise.

In an insulin delivery system, a 'safe state' is a shutdown state where no insulin is injected. Over a short period this will not pose a threat to the diabetic's health. If the potential software problems identified in Figure 17.6 are considered, the following 'solutions' might be developed:

1. *Arithmetic error*   This arises when some arithmetic computation causes a representation failure. The specification must identify all possible arithmetic errors which may occur. These depend on the algorithm used. The specification might state that an exception handler must be included for each identified arithmetic error. The specification should set out the action to be taken for each of these errors if they arise. A safe action is to shut down the delivery system and activate a warning alarm.

2. *Algorithmic error*   This is a more difficult situation as no definite anomalous situation can be detected. It might be detected by comparing the required insulin dose computed with the previously delivered dose. If it is much higher, this may mean that the amount has been computed wrongly. The system may also keep track of the dose sequence. After a number of above average doses have been delivered, a warning may be issued and further dosage limited.

Fault trees are also used to identify potential hardware problems. It may provide insights into requirements for software to detect and, perhaps, correct these problems. For example, insulin doses are not administered at a very high frequency, no more than two or three times per hour and sometimes less than this. There is, therefore, available processor capacity in the system to run diagnostic and self-checking programs. Hardware errors such as sensor, pump or timer errors can be discovered and warnings issued before they have a serious effect on the patient.

Figure 17.9
Examples of safety
requirements for an
insulin pump

SR1: The system shall not deliver a single dose of insulin that is greater than a specified maximum dose for a system user.

SR2: The system shall not deliver a daily cumulative dose of insulin that is greater than a specified maximum for a system user.

SR3: The system shall include a hardware diagnostic facility that shall be executed at least 4 times per hour.

SR4: The system shall include an exception handler for all of the exceptions that are identified in Table 3.

SR5: The audible alarm shall be sounded when any hardware anomaly is discovered and a diagnostic message as defined in Table 4 should be displayed.

Some of the resulting safety requirements for the insulin pump system are shown in Figure 17.9. These are user requirements and, naturally, they would be expressed in more detail in a final system specification. In these requirements, the references to Tables 3 and 4 relate to tables that would be included in the requirements document.

17.3 Security specification

The specification of security requirements for systems has something in common with safety requirements. It is impractical to specify them quantitatively and security requirements are often 'shall not' requirements that define unacceptable system behaviour rather than required system functionality. However, there are important differences between these types of requirements:

1. The notion of a safety life cycle that covers all aspects of safety management is well developed. The area of security specification and management is immature and there is no accepted equivalent of a security life cycle.

2. The set of security threats faced by systems is fairly generic. All systems must protect themselves against intrusion, denial of service, etc. By contrast, hazards in safety-critical systems are normally domain specific.

3. Security techniques and technologies such as encryption and authentication devices are fairly mature. However, much security technology has been developed for specialised systems (such as military or financial systems) and there are problems in transferring it to more general use. Software safety techniques are still the subject of research.

The conventional (non-computerised) approach to security analysis is based around the assets to be protected and their value to an organisation. Therefore, a

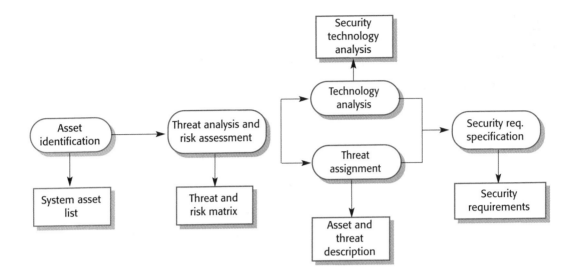

Figure 17.10
Security specification bank will provide high security in an area where large amounts of money are stored compared to other public areas (say) where the potential losses are limited. The same approach can be used for specifying security for computer-based systems. A possible security specification process is shown in Figure 17.10.

The stages in this process are:

1. *Asset identification and evaluation* The assets (data and programs) and their required degree of protection are identified. Note that the degree of required protection depends on the asset value, so that a password file (say) is normally more valuable than a set of public web pages as a successful attack on the password file has serious system-wide consequences.

2. *Threat analysis and risk assessment* Possible security threats are identified and the risks associated with each of these threats are estimated.

3. *Threat assignment* Identified threats are related to the assets so that, for each identified asset, there is a list of associated threats.

4. *Technology analysis* Available security technologies and their applicability against the identified threats are assessed.

5. *Security requirements specification* The security requirements are specified. Where appropriate, these will explicitly identify the security technologies that may be used to protect against different threats to the system.

Security specification and security management are currently important research areas. Standards for security management are under development (ISO/IEC, 1998) and it is likely that these will be agreed in the next few years.

KEY POINTS

▶ Reliability requirements should be defined quantitatively in the system requirements specification.

▶ There are several different reliability metrics such as probability of failure on demand, rate of occurrence of failure, mean time to failure and availability. The most appropriate metric for a specific system depends on the type of system and application domain. Different metrics may be used for different sub-systems.

▶ Non-functional reliability specifications can lead to functional system requirements that define system features whose function is to reduce the number of system failures and hence increase reliability.

▶ Hazard analysis is a key activity in the safety specification process. It involves identifying hazardous conditions which can compromise system safety. System requirements are then generated to ensure that these hazards do not arise or, if they occur, they do not result in an accident.

▶ Risk analysis is the process of assessing the likelihood that a hazard will result in an accident. Risk analysis identifies critical hazards which must be avoided in the system and classifying risks according to their seriousness.

▶ To specify security requirements, you should identify the assets that are to be protected and define how security techniques and technology should be used to protect these assets.

FURTHER READING

'Requirements definition for survivable network systems'. Discusses the problems of defining requirements for survivable systems where survivability relates to both availability and security. (R. C. Linger, N. R. Mead and H. F. Lipson, *Proc. ICRE'98*, IEEE Press.)

Requirements Engineering: A Good Practice Guide. This book includes a section on the specification of critical systems and a discussion of the use of formal methods in critical systems specification. (I. Sommerville and P. Sawyer, 1997, John Wiley and Sons.)

Safeware: System Safety and Computers. This is a thorough discussion of all aspects of safety-critical systems. It is particularly strong in its description of hazard analysis and the derivation of requirements from this. (N. Leveson, 1995, Addison-Wesley.)

EXERCISES

17.1 Why is it sometimes inappropriate to use hardware reliability metrics in estimating software systems reliability? Illustrate your answer with an example.

17.2 Suggest appropriate reliability metrics for the following classes of software system. Give reasons for your choice of metric. Predict the usage of these systems and suggest appropriate values for the reliability metrics:

- a system which monitors patients in a hospital intensive care unit;
- a word processor;
- an automated vending machine control system;
- a system to control braking in a car;
- a system to control a refrigeration unit;
- a management report generator.

17.3 You are responsible for writing the specification for a software system that controls a network of EPOS (electronic point of sale) terminals in a store. The system accepts bar code information from a terminal, queries a product database and returns the item name and its price to the terminal for display. The system must be continuously available during the store's opening hours.

Giving reasons for your choice, choose appropriate reliability metrics for specifying the reliability of such a system and write a plausible reliability specification that takes into account the fact that some faults are more serious than others.

17.4 Suggest four functional requirements that might be generated for this store system to help improve system reliability.

17.5 Explain why the boundaries in the risk triangle shown in Figure 17.7 are liable to change with time and with changing social attitudes.

17.6 In the insulin pump system, the user has to change the needle and insulin supply at regular intervals and may also change the maximum single dose and the maximum daily dose that may be administered. Suggest three user errors that might occur and propose safety requirements that would avoid these errors resulting in an accident.

17.7 A safety-critical software system for treating cancer patients has two principal components:

- A radiation therapy machine that delivers controlled doses of radiation to tumour sites. This machine is controlled by an embedded software system.

- A treatment database which includes details of the treatment given to each patient. Treatment requirements are entered in this database and are automatically downloaded to the radiation therapy machine.

Identify three hazards that may arise in this system. For each hazard, suggest a defensive requirement which will reduce the probability that these hazards will result in an accident. Explain why your suggested defence is likely to reduce the risk associated with the hazard.

17.8   Suggest how fault-tree analysis could be modified for use in security specification. Threats in a security-critical system are analogous to hazards in a safety-critical system.

17.9   Should software engineers working on the specification and development of safety-related systems be professionally certified in some way?

18 Critical systems development

Objectives

The objective of this chapter is to introduce implementation techniques that are used in the development of critical systems. When you have read this chapter you will:

- ❑ understand software development techniques that help avoid introducing faults into a software system;

- ❑ understand the concept of software fault tolerance and how defensive programming may be used to support fault tolerance;

- ❑ understand how exception handling facilities in a programming language may be used in the implementation of fault-tolerant systems;

- ❑ have been introduced to N-version programming and recovery blocks – two different approaches to implementing fault-tolerant architectures.

Contents

18.1 Fault minimisation
18.2 Fault tolerance
18.3 Fault-tolerant architectures
18.4 Safe system design

Improved software engineering techniques, better programming languages and better quality management have led to very significant improvements in dependability for most software. However, for critical systems, such as those which control unattended machinery, telecommunications switches or aircraft engines, additional care is needed to achieve high levels of dependability. In these cases, special programming techniques may be used to ensure that the system is safe, secure and reliable.

There are two complementary approaches that may be used when the goal is to develop dependable software:

1. *Fault avoidance*   The design and implementation process for the system should use approaches to software development that minimise human error and that help discover system faults before the system is put into use.

2. *Fault tolerance*   The system should be designed in such a way that faults or unexpected system behaviour during system execution are detected and managed in such a way that system failure does not occur.

Sometimes, a third approach, fault detection, is suggested but I think that this is subsumed under fault avoidance and fault tolerance. Faults that are detected before delivery are avoided in the operational system; faults that are detected during execution are part of fault tolerance.

Fault avoidance means avoiding faults in systems that are delivered to customers. We can do this in two ways: by the use of programming techniques that minimise the number of faults introduced into systems (fault minimisation); and by using static and dynamic validation techniques that discover these faults and allow them to be corrected before system delivery (fault detection). In this chapter I cover fault minimisation and fault tolerance, with a number of verification and validation techniques aimed at fault detection covered in Chapters 19–21.

18.1 Fault minimisation

A good software process should have the objective of developing *fault-free software*. Fault-free software is software which exactly conforms to its specification. However, this does not necessarily mean that the software will always behave as expected by its users. There may be errors in the specification that are reflected in the software or the users may misunderstand or misuse the software system. Software that is fault-free is not, therefore, necessarily free of failures. However, minimising software faults does have a significant impact on the number of system failures and should always be a goal of critical systems development.

There are a number of requirements for the development of fault-free software:

1. There must be a precise (preferably formal) system specification that defines the system to be implemented.

2. The organisation developing the system must have an organisational quality culture where quality is the driver of the software process. In general, programmers should expect to write bug-free programs.

3. An approach to software design and implementation based on information hiding and encapsulation should be used. Object-oriented languages such as Java obviously satisfy this condition. The development of programs that are designed for readability and understandability should be encouraged.

4. A strongly typed programming language such as Java or Ada must be used for development. In a language with strong typing, many programming errors can be detected by the language compiler.

5. The use of some programming constructs that are potentially error-prone should be avoided wherever possible. I discuss these constructs in the next section.

6. A development process should be defined and developers trained in the application of this process. Quality managers should check process conformance.

Achieving fault-free software is very difficult if low-level programming languages with limited type checking such as C are used for program development. There are two reasons for this:

1. These languages include constructs such as pointers that we know from experience are error-prone. Irrespective of how much care a programmer takes, it is still possible to introduce program faults that are very difficult to detect.

2. The nature of these languages is such that they lead to a terse programming style. This makes the programs more difficult to read and understand and so it is therefore less likely that readers of a program will spot errors that have occurred.

Of course, the advantage of using these low-level languages is that their constructs are less abstract and so it is possible to write very efficient programs. In some cases, high performance is essential and cannot be achieved in any other way. In those circumstances, more effort must be devoted to testing and error detection if a high level of dependability is required.

I believe that our software engineering techniques are such that fault-free software is achievable but economically impracticable. It is extremely difficult and expensive to achieve this goal. The cost of finding and removing remaining faults tends to rise exponentially (Figure 18.1) during validation. As the software becomes more reliable, more and more testing is required to find fewer and fewer faults.

Consequently, software development organisations either explicitly or implicitly accept that their software will contain some residual faults. The level of faults depends on the type of system. Shrink-wrapped products have a relatively high level of faults

Figure 18.1 The increasing costs of residual fault removal

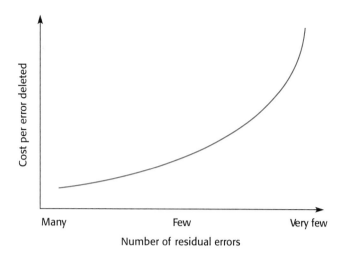

(although they are much better than they were 10 years ago) whereas critical systems usually have a much lower fault density.

The rationale for accepting faults is that if and when the system fails, it is cheaper to pay for the consequences of failure rather than discover and remove the faults before system delivery. This is a fairly common practice amongst vendors of software products for personal computers. However, as I have discussed in Chapter 16, the decision to release faulty software is not simply an economic decision. The social and political acceptability of system failure must also be taken into account.

18.1.1   Error avoidance

Faults in programs and therefore many program failures are often a consequence of human errors. Programmers make mistakes because they lose track of all of the relationships between the state variables. They write program statements that result in unexpected behaviour and system state changes. People will always make mistakes but it became clear in the late 1960s that some approaches to programming were more error-prone than others.

Dijkstra (1968a) recognised that the goto statement was an inherently error-prone programming construct. It made it difficult to localise state changes. This observation led to the development of so-called *structured programming*. Structured programming means programming without using goto statements, programming using only while loops and if statements as control constructs and designing using a top-down approach. The adoption of structured programming was an important milestone in the development of software engineering because it was the first step away from an undisciplined approach to software development.

Apart from unconditional branches (goto statements), there are several other programming language constructs and programming techniques which are inherently error-prone. Faults are less likely to be introduced into programs if the use of these constructs is minimised. These include:

1. *Floating-point numbers*   Floating-point numbers are inherently imprecise. They present a particular problem when they are compared because representation imprecision may lead to invalid comparisons. For example, 3.00000000 may sometimes be represented as 2.99999999 and sometimes as 3.00000001. A comparison would show these to be unequal. Fixed-point numbers where a number is represented to a given number of decimal places are safer as exact comparisons are possible.

2. *Pointers*   Pointers are low-level constructs that hold addresses that refer directly to areas of the machine memory. They are dangerous because errors in their use can be devastating, because they allow 'aliasing' as discussed below and because they make bound checking of arrays and other structures harder to implement. Buffer overflow where an attacker deliberately constructs a program to write memory beyond the end of a buffer is a known security vulnerability.

3. *Dynamic memory allocation*   Program memory may be allocated at run-time rather than compile-time. The danger with this is that the memory may not be de-allocated so that the system eventually runs out of available memory. This can be a very subtle type of error to detect as the system may run successfully for a long time before the problem occurs.

4. *Parallelism*   Parallelism is dangerous because of the difficulties of predicting the subtle effects of timing interactions between parallel processes. Timing problems cannot usually be detected by program inspection and the peculiar combination of circumstances which cause a timing problem may not occur during system testing. Parallelism may be unavoidable but its use should be carefully controlled to minimise inter-process dependencies. Programming language facilities such as Ada tasks or Java threads help manage parallelism so that some programming errors are avoided.

5. *Recursion*   Recursion is the situation where a procedure or method calls itself or calls another procedure which then calls the original calling procedure. Its use can result in concise programs but it can be difficult to follow the logic of recursive programs. Programming errors are therefore more difficult to detect. Errors in using recursion may result in the allocation of all the system's memory as temporary stack variables are created.

6. *Interrupts*   Interrupts are a means of forcing control to transfer to a section of code irrespective of the code currently executing. The dangers of this are obvious as the interrupt may cause a critical operation to be terminated.

7. *Inheritance*   Inheritance in object-oriented programming languages supports reuse and problem decomposition but it does mean that the code associated with an object is not all in one place. This makes it more difficult to understand the behaviour of the object. Hence, it is more likely that programming errors will be missed. Furthermore, inheritance when combined with dynamic binding can cause timing problems at run-time. At different times, different instances of a

specific method could be called and different amounts of time will be spent searching for the correct method instance.

8. *Aliasing*   This occurs when different names are used to refer to the same entity in a program. It is easy for program readers to miss statements that change the entity when they have several names to consider.

9. *Default input processing*   Some systems provide a default for input processing irrespective of the input that is presented to the system. This is a security loophole as an attacker may exploit this by presenting the program with unexpected inputs that are not rejected by the system.

Some standards for safety-critical systems development completely prohibit the use of these constructs. However, this extreme position is not normally practical. All of these constructs and techniques are useful but they must be used with care. Wherever possible, their potentially dangerous effects should be controlled by using them within abstract data types or objects. These act as natural 'firewalls' limiting the damage caused if errors occur.

The designers of Java have recognised some of the problems of error-prone constructs. The language does not have a facility for arbitrary transfers of control (a goto statement), it has built-in garbage collection so has no need of dynamic memory allocation and does not support pointers. However, Java's numeric representation is such that overflow is not detected by the run-time system and failures due to floating-point errors are still possible.

18.1.2   Information hiding

A security principle which is adopted by military organisations is the 'need to know' principle. Only those individuals who need to know a particular piece of information to carry out their duties are given that information. Information which is not directly relevant to their work is withheld.

When programming, an analogous principle should be adopted to control access to system data. Program components should be allowed access only to data that they need for their implementation. Access to other data should be denied by concealing it using the scope rules of the programming language. If information hiding is used, hidden information cannot be corrupted by program components that are not supposed to use it. If the interface remains the same, the data representation may be changed without affecting other components in the system.

Information hiding is much simpler in Java than in older programming languages such as C or Pascal. These languages do not have encapsulation constructs such as object classes and so details of the implementation of data structures cannot be protected. Other parts of the program can access the structure directly. This can lead to unexpected side-effects when changes are made.

It is generally good practice when programming in an object-oriented language to provide methods that access and update attribute values rather than allow other

Figure 18.2 A queue
specification using a
Java interface
declaration

```
interface Queue {

    public void put (Object o) ;
    public void remove (Object o) ;
    public int size () ;

} //Queue
```

Figure 18.3 A Signal
declaration in Java

```
class Signal {

    static public final int red = 1 ;
    static public final int amber = 2 ;
    static public final int green = 3 ;

    public int sigState ;
}
```

objects to access these attributes directly. This means that the representation of the attribute can be changed without reference to the other objects that use the attribute. It is particularly important that this approach is used for data structures and other complex attributes.

Java's interface definition construct means that it is possible to use this approach and to declare the interface to an object without reference to its implementation. This is illustrated in Figure 18.2. Users of objects of type Queue can put objects onto the queue, remove them from the queue and query the size of the queue. However, in the class that implements this interface, the actual implementation of the queue should be concealed by declaring the attributes and methods to be private to that object class.

A related type of information hiding is illustrated in Figure 18.3. In situations where a limited set of values may be assigned to some variable, these values should be declared as constants. Languages such as C++ support enumerated types but in Java this must be implemented by associating these constraints with the class declaration. For example, consider a signalling system that supports red, amber and green lights and that is being implemented in Java. A Signal type should be defined that includes constant declarations reflecting these colours. It is therefore possible to refer to Signal.red, Signal.green, etc. This avoids the accidental assignment of incorrect values to variables of type Signal.

18.1.3   Reliable software processes

To develop software with a minimal number of faults it is essential to have a software development process that is well defined, repeatable and that includes a spectrum of verification and validation activities. A well-defined process is a process that has been standardised and documented. A repeatable process is one that does not rely on individual interpretation and judgement. Rather, irrespective of the people involved in the process, the organisation can be confident that the process will be successful. I discuss the importance of processes, in general, and process improvement in Chapter 25.

The process should include a well-planned, comprehensive testing process as well as other activities whose aim is fault detection. Validation activities that are geared to fault minimisation include:

1. *Requirements inspections*   As discussed in Chapter 6, these are intended to discover problems with the system specification. A high proportion of faults in delivered software result from requirements errors. If these can be discovered and eliminated from the specification then this class of faults will be minimised.

2. *Requirements management*   Requirements management, discussed in Chapter 6, is concerned with keeping track of changes to requirements and tracing these through to the design and implementation. Many errors in delivered systems are a result of failure to ensure that a requirements change has actually been included in the design and implementation of the system.

3. *Model checking*   Model checking involves the automatic analysis of system models by CASE tools that check that these models have both internal consistency and external consistency. Internal consistency means that a single model is consistent; external consistency means that different models of the system (e.g. a state model and an object model) are consistent.

4. *Design and code inspections*   As I discuss in Chapter 19, design and code inspections are often based on checklists of common faults and are intended to discover and remove these faults before system testing.

5. *Static analysis*   Static analysis is an automated technique of program analysis where the program is analysed in detail to find potentially erroneous conditions. I discuss this in Chapter 19.

6. *Test planning and management*   A comprehensive set of tests for the system should be designed and the testing process itself should be carefully managed to ensure complete test coverage and traceability between the system tests and the system requirements and design. I discuss testing in Chapter 20.

Effective configuration management is essential for all of the documentation associated with a critical system. As discussed in Chapter 29, configuration management is concerned with keeping track of the different versions of a system and its components. Errors in systems sometimes result from the integration of the wrong component or the wrong version of a component.

18.2 Fault tolerance

A fault-tolerant system is a system that can continue in operation after some system faults have manifested themselves. The goal of fault tolerance is to ensure that system faults do not result in system failure. Fault tolerance is needed in situations where system failure could cause some catastrophic accident or where a loss of system operation would cause large economic losses. For example, the computers in an aircraft must carry on working until the aircraft has landed; the computers in an air traffic control system must be continuously available while planes are in the air.

You might think that fault-tolerance facilities do not have to be included in a system that has been developed using techniques that minimise faults. If there are no faults in the system, there would not seem to be any chance of system failure. However, 'fault-free' does not mean 'failure-free'. It can only mean that the program corresponds to its specification. The specification may contain errors or omissions and may be based on incorrect assumptions about the system's environment. And, of course, we can never conclusively demonstrate that a system is completely fault-free. In systems that have the highest reliability and availability requirements, explicit support for fault tolerance may therefore be required.

There are four aspects to fault tolerance:

1. *Fault detection*   The system must detect that a particular state combination has occurred and could lead to a system failure.

2. *Damage assessment*   The parts of the system state which have been affected by the fault must be detected.

3. *Fault recovery*   The system must restore its state to a known 'safe' state. This may be achieved by correcting the damaged state (forward error recovery) or by restoring the system to a known 'safe' state (backward error recovery).

4. *Fault repair*   This involves modifying the system so that the fault does not recur. In many cases, software faults manifest themselves as transient states. They are due to a peculiar combination of system inputs. No repair is necessary as normal processing can resume immediately after fault recovery. This is an important distinction between hardware and software faults.

There are two complementary approaches that may be used to implement fault tolerance in software:

1. *Defensive programming* is an approach to program development where programmers assume that there may be undetected faults or inconsistencies in their programs. Redundant code is incorporated to check the system state after modifications and to ensure that the state change is consistent. If inconsistencies are detected, the state change is retracted or the state is restored to a known correct state.

2. *Fault-tolerant architectures* are hardware and software system architectures that provide explicit support for fault tolerance. They include hardware and software redundancy and incorporate a fault tolerance controller that detects problems and supports fault recovery. I discuss this approach to fault tolerance in section 18.3.

Defensive programming is a technique that can be used in any system. Essentially, you have to add extra checking and error recovery facilities to programs even in situations where it appears that errors are unlikely to occur. However, before I go on to discuss this technique, I describe exception handling, an essential facility for supporting fault tolerance.

18.2.1   Exception handling

When an error of some kind or an unexpected event occurs during the execution of a program, this is called an *exception*. Examples of exceptions might be a system power failure, an attempt to access a non-existent data item, numeric overflow and underflow, etc. Exceptions may be caused by hardware or software conditions. When an exception occurs, it must be managed by the system. This can be done within the program itself or may involve transferring control to a system exception handling mechanism.

In programming languages such as C, if statements must be used to detect the exception and to transfer control to the exception handling code. There are two problems with this approach:

1. Different exceptions may occur at different points in the program and the same exception may occur at different places. This means that a large number of explicit exception checks have to be included in the program. This increases the program size and complexity and makes it more difficult to understand. There is an increased probability of programmers making errors and program readers failing to spot these errors when checking the program.

2. When an exception occurs in a sequence of nested function or procedure calls, there is no easy way to transmit it from one function to another. Control is passed down through a sequence of procedures. When an exception occurs, this control structure has to be unwound. Consider the situation in Figure 18.4 where function A calls function B which calls function C. If an exception occurs during the execution of C this may be so serious that execution of B cannot continue. Function B has to return immediately to function A which must also be informed that B has terminated abnormally and that an exception has occurred. Again, a lot of extra code may have to be added to the program to manage the exceptions.

If the programming language includes constructs that support exception handling then you do not need extra conditional statements to check for exceptions. Rather,

Figure 18.4
Exception return
in embedded
function call

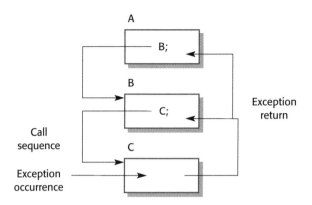

the programming language supports a special built-in type (often called **Exception**) and different exceptions may be declared to be of this type. When an exceptional situation occurs, the exception is signalled and the programming language run-time system transfers control to an exception handler. This is a code section that states exception names and appropriate actions to handle each exception.

Explicit exception handling facilities are provided in Ada, C++ and Java. In Java, new types of exception may be declared by extending the built-in **Exception** class. Exceptions are signalled in Java using a **throw** statement. The handler of an exception is indicated by the keyword **catch** and this is followed by a block of code that can handle the exception.

Figure 18.5 illustrates the use of exceptions in Java. This example is part of the software for the insulin pump introduced in Chapter 16. It is a sensor controller that reads a blood glucose value from a sensor. The first declaration in Figure 18.5 shows how exceptions in Java are declared. The built-in object class called **Exception** is extended and the constructor method defines the code to be implemented when the exception is thrown. In this case, an alarm is activated.

The **Sensor** class provides a single method called **readVal** that includes a **throw** statement in its declaration. This means that a **SensorFailureException** may be thrown from within the method but that the calling method is expected to provide a handler for **SensorFailureException**. The **try** keyword indicates that an exception may be thrown in the following block of code. The exception **SensorFailureException** is thrown if a value of less than zero is returned when the sensor is checked. **DeviceIO.readInteger** can throw an exception called **deviceIOException**, so a handler for this must be included following the **catch** keyword. In this case, the handler simply throws a sensor failure exception to indicate that the calling object should handle the exception.

The exception handling facilities in a programming language need not just be used for system fault management. They can also be used to handle error conditions that can be anticipated although they should normally only occur rarely. I have illustrated this in Figure 18.6. This Java class is an implementation of a temperature controller on a food freezer. The required temperature may be set between −18 and −40 degrees Celsius.

Figure 18.5
Exceptions in Java

```java
class SensorFailureException extends Exception {

    SensorFailureException (String msg) {
        super (msg) ;
        Alarm.activate (msg) ;
    }
} // SensorFailureException

class Sensor {

    int readVal () throws SensorFailureException {

    try {
        int theValue = DeviceIO.readInteger () ;
        if (theValue < 0)
            throw new SensorFailureException ("Sensor failure") ;
        return theValue ;
    }
    catch (deviceIOException e)
        {
            throw new SensorFailureException (" Sensor read error ") ;
        }
    }    // readVal
} // Sensor
```

Frozen food may start to defrost and bacteria become active at temperatures over −18 degrees. The control system maintains this temperature by switching a refrigerant pump on and off depending on the value of a temperature sensor. If the required temperature cannot be maintained, the controller sets off an alarm.

In the Java implementation, the temperature of the freezer is discovered by interrogating an object called tempSensor and the required temperature by inspecting an object called tempDial. A pump object (Pump) responds to signals to switch its state. Once the pump has been switched on, the system waits for some time (by calling Thread.sleep) for the temperature to fall. If it has not fallen sufficiently an exception called FreezerTooHotException is thrown.

The exception handler (located at the end of the code) catches this exception and activates the Alarm object. A handler is also included for the built-in exception InterruptedException that can be thrown by Thread.sleep. This logs the exception, then rethrows it for handling by the main method.

18.2.2   Fault detection

Programming languages such as Java and Ada have a strict type system. This allows many errors which cause state corruption and system failure to be detected at compile-time. The compiler can detect those problems which breach the strict type rules of the language. Compiler checking is obviously limited to static values but the compiler can also automatically generate code that performs run-time checks

Figure 18.6
Exceptions in a
freezer temperature
controller

```
class FreezerController {

    Sensor tempSensor = new Sensor () ;
    Dial tempDial = new Dial () ;
    float freezerTemp = tempSensor.readVal () ;
    final float dangerTemp = (float) -18.0 ;
    final long coolingTime = (long) 200000.0 ;

    public void run ( ) throws InterruptedException {
    try {
        Pump.switchIt (Pump.on) ;
        do {
            if (freezerTemp > tempDial.setting ())
                if (Pump.status == Pump.off)
                {
                    Pump.switchIt (Pump.on) ;
                    Thread.sleep (coolingTime) ;
                }
            else
                if (Pump.status == Pump.on)
                    Pump.switchIt (Pump.off) ;

            if (freezerTemp > dangerTemp)
                throw new FreezerTooHotException () ;
            freezerTemp = tempSensor.readVal () ;

        } while (true) ;

    } // try block
    catch (FreezerTooHotException f)
    {   Alarm.activate ( ) ; }
    catch (InterruptedException e)
    {
        System.out.println ("Thread exception") ;
        throw new InterruptedException ( ) ;
    }
    } //run
} // FreezerController
```

on, for example, assignment to arrays. These ensure that the array index is not out of the range of the array and that the assignment is to a legal array member.

The first stage of fault tolerance is to detect that a fault (an erroneous system state) either has occurred or will occur unless some action is taken immediately. Normally, an exception is then thrown to a section of code in the program that can manage the detected fault.

There are two types of fault detection:

1. *Preventative fault detection* In this case, the fault detection mechanism is initiated before a state change is committed. If a potentially erroneous state is detected then the state change is not made. Generally, the fault detection system throws an exception that indicates the type of the discovered fault.

Figure 18.7
PositiveEven number
class in Java

```
class PositiveEvenInteger {
    int val = 0 ;
    PositiveEvenInteger (int n) throws NumericException
    {
        if (n < 0 | n%2 == 1)
            throw new NumericException () ;
        else
            val = n ;
    }// PositiveEvenInteger
    public void assign (int n) throws NumericException
    {
        if (n < 0 | n%2 == 1)
            throw new NumericException () ;
        else
            val = n ;
    } // assign
    int toInteger ()
    {
        return val ;
    } //to Integer
    boolean equals (PositiveEvenInteger n)
    {
        return (val == n.val) ;
    } // equals
} //PositiveEven
```

2. *Retrospective fault detection*   In this case, the fault detection mechanism is initiated after the system state has been changed to check if a fault has occurred. If a fault is discovered, an exception is signalled and a repair mechanism is used to recover from the fault.

Preventative fault detection is often implemented by defining constraints that apply to the system state and checking these constraints when a new state is computed. This is simplified when the state is partitioned into a set of objects. Constraints that apply to individual objects may be defined and checked automatically when object methods that may change the state are initiated. This is illustrated in Figure 18.7 which is a Java class that implements a positive even number type.

In this case, the state constraint is that only integers that are positive and are even numbers may be assigned. If an attempt is made to assign a value that violates this constraint, an exception (NumericException) is thrown and signalled to the calling method. Notice that the exception is not handled within the PositiveEvenInteger class. Exception handling should always be the responsibility of the calling method as it knows the most appropriate exception action to take.

Preventative fault detection largely avoids the problems of damage repair as the system state will always be valid. However, it involves significant overhead in that every operation that modifies the state must check the constraint before the state change is committed. In some classes of system where performance is important or where it is relatively straightforward to repair a damaged state, retrospective fault detection may be used. Furthermore, if the state correctness constraint applies to the relationships between objects, this cannot be implemented by checking a constraint on an individual object.

Retrospective fault detection always involves checking a state constraint but, in this case, the state as a whole is examined and a checking function applied to individual state variables or across several state variables. Individual checking functions can be associated in Java by using the following interface:

```
interface CheckableObject {
    public boolean check () ;
}
```

Objects to be checked are instantiations of an object class that implements this interface and so each object has an associated check function. Each object class implements its own check function which defines the particular constraints that apply to objects of that class. When the state as a whole is checked, dynamic binding is used to ensure that the check function that is appropriate for the class of object that is being checked is applied. We can see an example of this in Figure 18.8 where the check function checks that the elements of an array satisfy some constraint.

Retrospective fault detection applied to more than one state variable is illustrated later in Figure 18.9. In this example, the fault detection check is applied to consecutive elements of an array and checks that the array is ordered.

18.2.3   Damage assessment

Damage assessment involves analysing the system state to gauge the extent of the state corruption. In many cases, it can be avoided by checking for fault occurrence before finally committing a change of state. If a fault is detected, the state change is not accepted so that no damage is caused. However, damage assessment may be needed when a state commitment cannot be avoided or when a fault arises because an invalid sequence of individually correct state changes results in an incorrect system state.

The role of the damage assessment procedures is not to recover from the fault but to assess what parts of the state space have been affected by the fault. Damage can only be assessed if it is possible to apply some 'validity function' which checks if the state is consistent. If inconsistencies are found, these are highlighted or signalled in some way.

In Figure 18.8, I have illustrated how damage assessment may be implemented in Java. I assume that the data structure called RobustArray is a collection of objects of type CheckableObject. The class that implements the CheckableObject type must

Figure 18.8 An array
class with damage
assessment

```
class RobustArray {

    // Checks that all the objects in an array of objects
    // conform to some defined constraint

    boolean [] checkState ;
    CheckableObject [] theRobustArray ;

    RobustArray (CheckableObject [] theArray)
    {
        checkState = new boolean [theArray.length] ;
        theRobustArray = theArray ;
    } //RobustArray

    public void assessDamage () throws ArrayDamagedException
    {
        boolean hasBeenDamaged = false ;

        for (int i = 0 ; i < this.theRobustArray.length ; i ++)
        {
            if (! theRobustArray [i].check ())
                {
                    checkState [i] = true ;
                    hasBeenDamaged = true ;
                }
            else
                checkState [i] = false ;
        }
        if (hasBeenDamaged)
            throw new ArrayDamagedException () ;
    } //assessDamage

} // RobustArray
```

include a method called check that can test if the value of the object satisfies some
constraint. It makes sense for this checking method to be associated with this object
rather than the RobustArray object as the details of the check depend on the use of
the type CheckableObject.

The assessDamage method in the RobustArray class examines every element of
the array and checks that its state is correct. If one of more elements of the array
do not meet the state constraints that are defined in the Check function then the elements that are damaged are recorded in the checkState array. An exception called
ArrayDamagedException is then thrown. A handler for this exception that manages
the damage must be included in the calling method. This can use the information in checkState to decide what to do.

Other techniques that can be used for fault detection and damage assessment
are dependent on the system state representation and on the application. Possible
methods are:

1. The use of checksums in data exchange and check digits in numeric data.
2. The use of redundant links in data structures which contain pointers.
3. The use of watchdog timers in concurrent systems.

Coding checks (Fujiwara and Pradhan, 1990) can be used when data is exchanged where a checksum is associated with numeric data. A checksum is a value that is computed by applying some mathematical function to the data. The function used should give a unique value for the packet of data which is exchanged. This checksum is computed by the sender which applies the checksum function to the data and appends that function value to the data. The receiver applies the same function the data and compares the checksum values. If these differ, some data corruption has occurred. This can also be used to detect security intrusions and deliberate corruption of data. The corrupted data will have a different checksum so the fact that the corruption has occurred can be detected.

When linked data structures are used, the representation can be made redundant by including backward references. That is, for every reference from A to B, there exists a comparable reference from B to A. You can also keep count of the number of elements in the structure. Checking can determine whether or not backward and forward references are consistent (they should refer to each other) and whether or not the stored size and the computed structure size are the same.

When processes must react within a specific time period, a watch-dog timer may be installed. A watch-dog timer is a timer which must be reset by the executing process after its action is complete. It is started at the same time as a process and times the process execution. It may be interrogated by a controller at regular intervals. If, for some reason, the process fails to terminate, the watch-dog timer is not reset. The controller can therefore detect that a problem has arisen and take action to force process termination.

18.2.4 Fault recovery

Fault recovery is the process of modifying the state space of the system so that the effects of the fault are minimised. The system can continue in operation, perhaps in some degraded form. Forward recovery involves trying to correct the damaged system state. Backward recovery restores the system state to a known 'correct' state.

Forward error recovery is sometimes application specific with domain knowledge used to compute possible state corrections. However, where the state information includes built-in redundancy, forward error recovery strategies may sometimes be used. There are two general situations where forward error recovery can be applied:

1. *When coded data is corrupted* The use of coding techniques which add redundancy to the data allows errors to be corrected as well as detected.

2. *When linked structures are corrupted* If forward and backward pointers are included in the data structure, the structure can be re-created if enough pointers remain uncorrupted. This technique is frequently used for file system and database repair.

Backward error recovery is a simpler technique that restores the state to a known safe state after an error has been detected. Most database systems include backward

Figure 18.9 Safe
sort procedure with
backward error
recovery

```
class SafeSort {

    static void sort ( int [] intarray, int order ) throws SortError
    {
        int [] copy = new int [intarray.length];

        // copy the input array

        for (int i = 0 ; i < intarray.length ; i++)
            copy [i] = intarray [i] ;
        try {
            Sort.bubblesort (intarray, intarray.length, order) ;
            if (order == Sort.ascending)
                for (int i = 0 ; i <= intarray.length-2 ; i++)
                    if (intarray [i] > intarray [i+1])
                        throw new SortError () ;
            else
                for (int i = 0 ; i <= intarray.length-2 ; i++)
                    if (intarray [i+1] > intarray [i])
                        throw new SortError () ;
        } // try block
        catch (SortError e )
        {
            for (int i = 0 ; i < intarray.length ; i++)
                intarray [i] = copy [i] ;
            throw new SortError ("Array not sorted") ;
        } //catch
    } // sort
} // SafeSort
```

error recovery. When a user initiates a database computation a *transaction* is initiated. Changes made during that transaction are not immediately incorporated in the database. The database is only updated after the transaction is finished and no problems are detected. If the transaction fails, the database is not updated.

Transactions allow error recovery because they do not commit changes to the database until they have completed. However, they do not permit recovery from state changes that are valid but incorrect. Checkpointing is a technique that can recover from this situation. The system state is duplicated periodically. When a problem is discovered, a correct state may be restored from one of these copies.

As an example of how backward recovery can be implemented using exceptions, consider the Java class SafeSort shown in Figure 18.9 which includes code for error detection and backward recovery.

The method copies the array before the sort operation. In this example, I use a bubble sort for simplicity but obviously any sorting algorithm may be used. If there is an error in the sorting algorithm and the array is not properly sorted, this is detected by explicit checks on the order of the elements in the array. If the array is not properly sorted, a SortError exception is thrown. The exception handler does not try to repair the problem but restores the original value of the array and rethrows SortError to indicate to the calling method that the sort has not been successful. It is the calling method's responsibility to recover from the error.

18.3 Fault-tolerant architectures

Defensive programming is an effective technique for implementing fault tolerance. It is relatively simple and does not normally involve adding much complexity to the system. However, it cannot cope effectively with system faults that arise from interactions between the hardware and the software. Furthermore, misunderstandings of the requirements may mean that both the system code and the associated defence are incorrect. For the most critical systems, particularly those with stringent availability requirements, a specific system architecture designed to support fault tolerance may be required. Examples of systems that use this approach to fault tolerance are systems in aircraft that must be in operation throughout the duration of the flight, telecommunication systems and critical command and control systems.

There has been a need for many years to build fault-tolerant hardware. The most commonly used hardware fault-tolerant technique is based around the notion of triple-modular redundancy (TMR). The hardware unit is replicated three (or sometimes more) times. The output from each unit is compared. If one of the units fails and does not produce the same output as the other units, its output is ignored. A fault manager may try to repair the faulty unit automatically but if this is impossible, the system is automatically reconfigured to take the unit out of service. The system then continues to function with two working units (Figure 18.10).

This approach to fault tolerance relies on most hardware failures being the result of component failures rather than design faults. The components are therefore likely

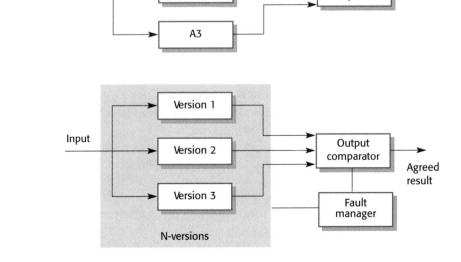

Figure 18.10
Triple-modular
redundancy to cope
with hardware failure

Figure 18.11
N-version
programming

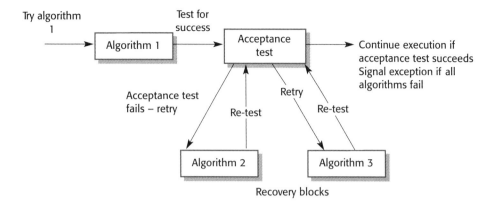

Figure 18.12
Recovery blocks

to fail independently. It assumes that, when fully operational, all hardware units perform to specification. There is therefore a low probability of simultaneous component failure in all hardware units.

Of course, the components could all have a common design fault and thus all produce the same (wrong) answer. The chances of this can be reduced by using hardware units which have a common specification but which are designed and built by different manufacturers. It is assumed that the probability of different teams making the same design or manufacturing error is small.

If the availability and reliability requirements for a system are such that fault-tolerant hardware is necessary, then software fault tolerance is also required. There have been two comparable approaches to the provision of software fault tolerance (Figures 18.11 and 18.12). Both have been derived from the hardware model where redundant components (or perhaps redundant systems) are included and faulty components may be taken out of service.

These two approaches to software fault tolerance are:

1. *N-version programming* Using a common specification, the software system is implemented in a number of different versions by different teams. These versions are executed in parallel on separate computers. Their outputs are compared using a voting system and inconsistent outputs or outputs that are not produced in time are rejected. At least three versions of the system should be available so that two versions should be consistent in the event of a single failure. This is the most commonly used approach to software fault tolerance. It has been used in railway signalling systems, in aircraft systems and in reactor protection systems. Avizienis (1985, 1995) describes this approach.

2. *Recovery blocks* In this approach, each program component includes a test to check if the component has executed successfully. It also includes alternative code which allows the system to back-up and repeat the computation if the test detects a failure. The implementations are deliberately different interpretations of the same specification. They are executed in sequence rather than in

parallel so replicated hardware is not required. In N-version programming, the implementations may be different but it is not uncommon for different development teams to choose the same algorithms to implement the specification. Randell (1975) and Randell and Xu (1995) describe the recovery block method.

Both of these approaches are based on the notion of design and implementation diversity. When diverse approaches are used to implement the same specification, it is a reasonable assumption that different versions of the software will not include the same faults so common failures are unlikely. Diversity can be achieved in a number of ways:

1. By including requirements that different approaches to design should be used. For example, one team may be required to produce an object-oriented design and another team may produce a function-oriented design.

2. By including requirements that the implementations should be written in different programming languages. For example, in a three-version system, Ada, C++ and Java could be used to write the software versions.

3. By requiring the use of different tools and development environments for the system.

4. By explicitly requiring different algorithms to be used in some parts of the implementation. However, this limits the freedom of the design team and may be difficult to reconcile with system performance requirements.

Each team should work with a separate specification (the V-spec) that has been derived from the system requirements specification (Avizienis, 1995). As well as specifying the functionality of the system, the V-spec should define where to generate system outputs for comparison. The development teams for each version should work in isolation to reduce the likelihood of them developing common misunderstanding about the system.

Design diversity certainly increases the overall reliability of the system. However, a number of experiments have suggested that the assumption that different design teams do not make the same mistakes may not always be valid (Knight and Leveson, 1986; Brilliant *et al.*, 1990; Leveson, 1995). Different development teams may make the same mistakes because of common misinterpretations of the specification or because they independently arrive at the same algorithms to solve the problem. Recovery blocks reduce the probability of common errors because different algorithms are used for each recovery block.

The weakness of both these approaches to fault tolerance is that they are based on the assumption that the specification is correct. They do not tolerate specification errors. In many cases, however, the specification is incorrect or incomplete so that the system behaves in an unexpected way. One way to reduce the possibility of common specification errors is to develop the V-specs for the system independently and to define these in different languages. Therefore, one development team might work from a formal specification, another from a state-based system model and the third from a natural language specification. This helps avoid some errors of specification interpretation but does not get round the problem of specification errors.

The provision of software fault tolerance requires the software to be executed under the control of a fault-tolerant controller which will ensure that the steps involved in tolerating a fault are executed. This controller examines the outputs and compares them. If they differ, some recovery actions may be initiated. Laprie *et al.* (1995) describe fault tolerant systems architectures. Interested readers should follow up the further reading for more information on this topic.

18.4 Safe system design

As a general rule, the design for safety-critical software should be based around information hiding and software simplicity. Those parts of the system that are safety-critical should be isolated from other parts of the system. This may be achieved through the use of data and control abstraction or may be achieved using physical separation. The safety-critical software may execute on a separate computer with minimal communication links to other parts of the system.

Safety-critical software should be as simple as possible. Potentially error-prone language features, discussed earlier in the chapter, should be avoided wherever possible. They may even be disallowed by standards for safety-critical systems development. In some cases, it may be a requirement that the system is developed in a language subset that has excluded unsafe features. Such subsets have been developed for Modula-2, Ada and Pascal and it is likely that a safe subset of Java will be developed. These subsets exclude language features that are not properly defined and features that are inherently unsafe such as real numbers, pointers, etc.

Fault-tolerant software should only be used in safety-critical systems when there is no safe state and the safety of the system depends on its availability. These techniques increase complexity, so making the software harder to validate. As I discussed in the previous section, research has demonstrated that the arguments for reliability through diversity (N-version programming) are not always valid. When developing software from the same specification, different teams made the same mistakes. Software redundancy did not give the theoretically predicted increase in system reliability. Furthermore, if the specification is incorrect, all versions will include the common specification errors.

This does not mean that N-version programming is useless. It may reduce the absolute number of failures in the system. While admitting that common faults were present in the different system versions, Bishop *et al.* (1986) found that the number of system failures was reduced. N-version programming gives increased confidence but not absolute confidence in the system reliability.

Rather than use N-version programming which increases system complexity, an alternative is to keep the system as simple as possible and devote a lot of resources to system validation. Keeping software simple reduces the probability that errors will be introduced. It also means that the very high costs of safety validation are reduced. Only a relatively small amount of software is safety-related.

Parnas *et al.* (1990) support this approach. They suggest that safety can best be assured by minimising and isolating safety-critical code components and by using the simplest possible techniques for writing safety-critical code sections. Validation should be based on a combination of thorough testing, reviews based on mathematical specifications and a certified development process.

KEY POINTS

▶ Dependability in a program can be achieved by avoiding the introduction of faults and by including fault tolerance facilities that allow the system to remain operational after a fault has caused a system failure.

▶ Some programming constructs and techniques such as goto statements, pointers, recursion, inheritance and floating-point numbers are inherently error-prone. These should not be used when developing dependable systems.

▶ The use of a well-defined, repeatable process is essential if faults in a system are to be minimised. The process should include verification and validation activities at all stages from requirements definition through to system implementation.

▶ Software which is fault tolerant can continue in execution in spite of faults which cause system failures.

▶ There are four aspects of program fault tolerance, namely failure detection, damage assessment, fault recovery and fault repair.

▶ Defensive programming is a programming technique which involves incorporating checks for faults and fault recovery code in the program. Faults are detected before they cause a system failure.

▶ The exception handling facilities provided in languages such as Java and C++ are used to support defensive programming. They avoid duplication of code and localise error handling in a program.

▶ N-version programming and recovery blocks are alternative approaches to fault-tolerant architectures where redundant copies of the hardware and software are maintained. Both rely on design diversity and the use of a fault-tolerance controller to coordinate the execution of redundant program units.

FURTHER READING

Software Fault Tolerance. This collection includes several articles discussing recovery blocks and N-version programming. It also includes a good article on fault-tolerant system architectures. (M. R. Lyu (ed.), 1995, John Wiley and Sons.)

EXERCISES

18.1 Explain why inheritance is a potentially error-prone construct and why its use should be minimised when developing critical systems in an object-oriented language.

18.2 Given that recursion is an inherently error-prone construct, design an object class to implement binary trees that does not use recursion in its implementation.

18.3 Describe three techniques of defensive programming that may be used to reduce the probability that a software fault leads to a system failure.

18.4 Briefly describe forward and backward fault recovery strategies. Why is backward fault recovery used more often than forward fault recovery? Give two examples of classes of system where backward fault recovery may be used.

18.5 What pre-conditions must hold before forward error recovery can be implemented in a fault-tolerant system? Is forward error recovery possible in interactive systems?

18.6 Design an abstract data type or object class called RobustList which implements forward error recovery in a linked list. You should include operations to check the list for corruption and to rebuild the list if corruption has occurred. Assume that you can check corruption by maintaining forward and backward references to and from adjacent members of the list.

18.7 Suggest circumstances where it is appropriate to use a fault-tolerant architecture when implementing a software-based control system and explain why this approach is required.

18.8 It has been suggested that the control software for a radiation therapy machine (used to treat patients with cancer) should be implemented using N-version programming. Comment on whether or not you think this is a good suggestion.

18.9 Give two reasons why all the different system versions in an N-version system may all fail in a similar way.

18.10 Discuss the problems of developing and maintaining 'non-stop' systems such as telephone exchange software. How might exceptions be used in the development of such systems?

18.11 Using the techniques discussed here to produce safe software obviously involves considerable extra costs. What extra costs can be justified if 100 lives will be saved over the 15-year lifetime of a system? Would the same costs be justified if 10 lives were saved? How much is a life worth? Does the earning capability of the people affected make a difference to this judgement?

PART FIVE

Verification and Validation

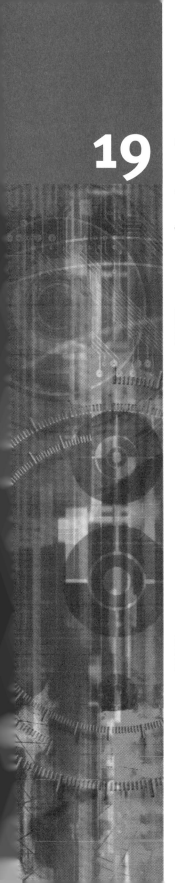

19 Verification and validation

Objectives

The objective of this chapter is to introduce software verification and validation with a particular focus on static verification techniques. When you have read this chapter, you will:

❏ understand the distinctions between software verification and software validation;

❏ have been introduced to program inspections as a method of discovering defects in programs;

❏ understand why static analysis of programs is an important verification technique;

❏ understand the Cleanroom method of program development and why it can be effective.

Contents

19.1 Verification and validation planning
19.2 Software inspections
19.3 Automated static analysis
19.4 Cleanroom software development

Verification and validation (V & V) is the name given to the checking and analysis processes that ensure that software conforms to its specification and meets the needs of the customers who are paying for that software. Verification and validation is a whole life-cycle process. It starts with requirements reviews and continues through design reviews and code inspections to product testing. There should be V & V activities at each stage of the software process. These activities check that the results of process activities are as specified.

Verification and validation are not the same thing although they are easily confused. The difference between them is succinctly expressed by Boehm (1979):

- 'Validation: Are we building the right product?'
- 'Verification: Are we building the product right?'

These definitions tell us that the role of verification involves checking that the software conforms to its specification. You should check that the system meets its specified functional and non-functional requirements. Validation, however, is a more general process. You should ensure that the software meets the expectations of the customer. It goes beyond checking conformance of the system to its specification to showing that the software does what the customer expects as distinct from what has been specified.

As discussed in Chapter 6, early validation of the system requirements is very important. It is easy to make errors and omissions in the system's requirements and, in such cases, the final software will probably not meet its customer's expectations. However, in reality, requirements validation is unlikely to discover all requirements problems. Some flaws and deficiencies in the requirements can sometimes only be discovered when the system implementation is complete.

Within the V & V process, two techniques of system checking and analysis may be used:

1. *Software inspections* analyse and check system representations such as the requirements document, design diagrams and the program source code. They may be applied at all stages of the process. Inspections may be supplemented by some automatic analysis of the source text of a system or associated documents. Software inspections and automated analyses are static V & V techniques as they do not require the system to be executed.

2. *Software testing* involves executing an implementation of the software with test data and examining the outputs of the software and its operational behaviour to check that it is performing as required. Testing is a dynamic technique of verification and validation because it works with an executable representation of the system.

Figure 19.1 shows the place of software inspections and testing in the software process. The arrows indicate the stages in the process where the techniques may be used. Therefore, software inspections can be used at all stages of the software process. Testing, however, can only be used when a prototype or an executable program is available.

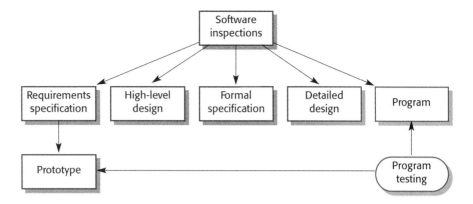

Inspection techniques include program inspections, automated source code analysis and formal verification. However, static techniques can only check the correspondence between a program and its specification (verification); they cannot demonstrate that the software is operationally useful. Nor can they check non-functional characteristics of the software such as its performance and reliability. Therefore, some testing is always required to validate a software system.

Although software inspections are now widely used, program testing is still the predominant verification and validation technique. Testing involves exercising the program using data like the real data processed by the program. The existence of program defects or inadequacies is inferred by examining the outputs of the program and looking for anomalies. Testing may be carried out during the implementation phase to verify that the software behaves as intended by its designer and after the implementation is complete.

There are two distinct types of testing that may be used at different stages in the software process:

1. *Defect testing* is intended to find inconsistencies between a program and its specification. These inconsistencies are usually due to program faults or defects. The tests are designed to reveal the presence of defects in the system rather than to simulate its operational use. I cover this type of testing in Chapter 20.

2. *Statistical testing* is used to test the program's performance and reliability and to check how it works under operational conditions. Tests are designed to reflect the actual user inputs and their frequency. After running the tests, an estimate of the operational reliability of the system can be made by counting the number of observed system failures. Program performance may be judged by measuring the execution time and the response time of the system as it processes the statistical test data. I discuss statistical testing and reliability estimation in Chapter 21.

Of course, there is not a hard and fast boundary between these approaches to testing. During defect testing, testers will get an intuitive feel for the software's reliability; during statistical testing, it is likely that some defects will be discovered.

The ultimate goal of the verification and validation process is to establish confidence that the software system is 'fit for purpose'. This does not mean that the program must be completely free of defects. Rather, it means that the system must be good enough for its intended use. The level of required confidence depends on the system's purpose, the expectations of the system users and the current marketing environment for the system:

1. *Software function* The level of confidence required is dependent on how critical the software is to an organisation. For example, the level of confidence required for software that is used to control a safety-critical system is very much higher than that required for a prototype software system that has been developed to demonstrate some new ideas.

2. *User expectations* It is a sad reflection on the software industry that many users have low expectations of their software and are not surprised when it fails during use. They are willing to accept these system failures when the benefits of use outweigh the disadvantages. However, user tolerance of system failures has been decreasing since the 1990s. It is now less acceptable to deliver unreliable systems, so software companies must devote more effort to verification and validation.

3. *Marketing environment* When a system is marketed, the sellers of the system must take into account competing programs, the price that customers are willing to pay for a system and the required schedule for delivering that system. Where a company has few competitors, it may decide to release a program before it has been fully tested and debugged because they want to be the first into the market. Where customers are not willing to pay high prices for software, they may be willing to tolerate more software faults. All of these factors must be considered when deciding how much effort should be spent on the V & V process.

During software verification and validation, defects in the program are normally discovered and the program must then be modified to correct these defects. This *debugging process* is often integrated with other verification and validation activities. However, testing (or, more generally, verification and validation) and debugging are different processes that do not have to be integrated:

1. Verification and validation is a process that establishes the existence of defects in a software system.
2. Debugging is a process (Figure 19.2) that locates and corrects these defects.

There is no simple method for program debugging. Skilled debuggers look for patterns in the test output where the defect is exhibited and use knowledge of the type of defect, the output pattern, the programming language and the programming process to locate the defect. Process knowledge is important. Debuggers know of common programmer errors (such as failing to increment a counter) and match these

Figure 19.2 The
debugging process

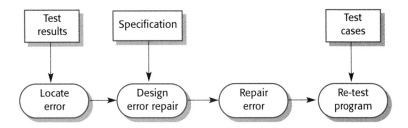

against the observed patterns. Characteristic programming language errors, such as
pointer misdirection in C, may also be considered.

Locating the faults in a program is not always a simple process as the fault need
not necessarily be close to the point where the program failed. To locate a program
fault, the programmer responsible for debugging may have to design additional program tests that repeat the original fault and that help discover the source of the fault
in the program. Manual tracing of the program, simulating execution, may be necessary. In some cases, debugging tools that collect information about the program's
execution may be helpful.

Interactive debugging tools are generally part of a suite of language support tools
that are integrated with a compilation system. They provide a specialised run-time
environment for the program that allows access to the compiler symbol table and,
from there, to the values of program variables. Users can often control execution
by 'stepping' their way through the program statement by statement. After each statement has been executed, the values of variables can be examined and potential errors
discovered.

After a defect in the program has been discovered, it must be corrected and the
system should then be revalidated. This may involve reinspecting the program or
repeating previous test runs (regression testing). Regression testing is used to check
that the changes made to a program have not introduced new faults into the system. Experience has shown that a relatively high proportion of 'fault repairs' are
either incomplete repairs or introduce new faults into the program.

In principle during regression testing, all tests should be repeated after every defect
repair; in practice, this is too expensive. As part of the test plan, dependencies between
parts of the system and the tests associated with each part should be identified. That
is, there should be traceability from the test cases to the program features that are
tested. If this traceability is documented, you may then run a subset of the entire
test data set to check the modified component and its dependants.

19.1 Verification and validation planning

Verification and validation is an expensive process. For some large systems, such
as real-time systems with complex non-functional constraints, half the system

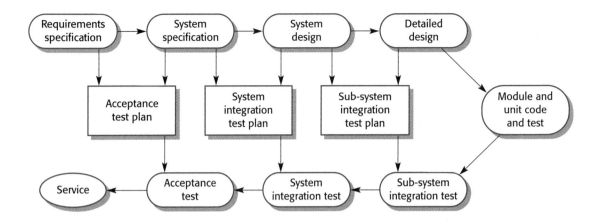

Figure 19.3
Test plans as a
link between
development and
testing

development budget may be spent on V & V. Careful planning is needed to get the most out of inspections and testing and to control the costs of the verification and validation process.

The planning of validation and verification of a software system should start early in the development process. The model of software development shown in Figure 19.3 shows how test plans should be derived from the system specification and design. This is sometimes called the V-model (turn Figure 19.3 on end to see the V). This diagram also shows how the verification and validation activity is broken down into a number of stages with each phase driven by tests that have been defined to check the conformance of the program with its design and specification.

The V & V planning process should decide on the balance between static and dynamic approaches to verification and validation, draw up standards and procedures for software inspections and testing, establish checklists to drive program inspections (see section 19.2) and define the software test plan. The relative effort devoted to inspections and testing depends on the type of system being developed and the organisational expertise. The more critical a system, the more effort should be devoted to static verification techniques.

Test planning is concerned with setting out standards for the testing process rather than describing product tests. Test plans are not just management documents. They are also intended for software engineers involved in designing and carrying out system tests. They allow technical staff to get an overall picture of the system tests and to place their own work in this context. Test plans also provide information to staff who are responsible for ensuring that appropriate hardware and software resources are available to the testing team.

The major components of a test plan are shown in Figure 19.4. This plan should include significant amounts of contingency so that slippages in design and implementation can be accommodated and staff allocated to testing can be deployed in other activities. A good description of test plans and their relation to more general quality plans is given in Frewin and Hatton (1986).

Figure 19.4
The structure of a
software test plan

The testing process
A description of the major phases of the testing process. These might be as
described earlier in this chapter.

Requirements traceability
Users are most interested in the system meeting its requirements and testing should
be planned so that all requirements are individually tested.

Tested items
The products of the software process which are to be tested should be specified.

Testing schedule
An overall testing schedule and resource allocation for this schedule. This, obviously,
is linked to the more general project development schedule.

Test recording procedures
It is not enough simply to run tests. The results of the tests must be systematically
recorded. It must be possible to audit the testing process to check that it been
carried out correctly.

Hardware and software requirements
This section should set out software tools required and estimated hardware
utilisation.

Constraints
Constraints affecting the testing process such as staff shortages should be anticipated
in this section.

Like other plans, the test plan is not a static document. It should be revised regularly as testing is an activity that is dependent on implementation being complete. If part of a system is incomplete, it cannot be delivered for integration testing as discussed in the following chapter. The plan must therefore be revised to redeploy the testers to some other activity.

19.2 Software inspections

Systematic program testing requires a large number of tests to be developed, executed and examined. This means that the process is time-consuming and expensive. Each test run tends to discover a single program fault or, at best, only a few faults. The reason for this is that failures resulting from system faults often cause system data corruption. Consequently, it can be difficult to tell if output anomalies are a result of a new fault or are a side-effect of an existing fault.

Software inspections do not require the program to be executed so may be used as a verification technique before programs are implemented. During an inspection, you examine the source representation of a system. This could be a system model, a specification or high-level language code. You use knowledge of the system to be developed and the semantics of the source representation to discover errors. Each error can be considered in isolation without being concerned about how it will affect the behaviour of the system. Error interactions are not significant and an entire component can be verified in a single session.

Inspections have proved to be an effective technique of error detection. Errors can be found more cheaply through inspection than by extensive program testing. This was demonstrated in an experiment by Basili and Selby (1987) who empirically compared the effectiveness of inspections and testing. They found that static code reviewing was more effective and less expensive than defect testing in discovering program faults. Gilb and Graham (1993) have also found this to be true.

Fagan (1986) reported that more than 60 per cent of the errors in a program can be detected using informal program inspections. Mills *et al.* (1987) suggest that a more formal approach, using mathematical verification, can detect more than 90 per cent of the errors in a program. This technique is used in the Cleanroom process which I describe in section 19.3. The inspection process can also consider other quality attributes such as compliance with standards, portability and maintainability. These quality attributes are discussed in Chapter 24.

There are two reasons why reviews and inspections are usually more effective than testing for discovering defects in components and sub-systems:

1. Many different defects may be detected in a single inspection session. The problem with testing is that it can often detect only one error per test because defects can cause the program to crash or interfere with the symptoms of other program defects.

2. They reuse domain and programming language knowledge. In essence, the reviewers are likely to have seen the types of error that commonly occur in particular programming languages and in particular types of application. They can therefore focus on these error types during the analysis.

This does not mean that inspections should completely replace system testing. Rather, they should be used as an initial verification process to find most program defects. Inspections of the software can check conformance with a specification but they cannot validate dynamic behaviour. Furthermore, it is often impractical to inspect a complete system that is integrated from a number of different sub-systems. Testing is the only possible V & V technique at the system level. Testing is also necessary for reliability assessment, performance analysis, user interface validation and to check that the software requirements are what the user really wants.

Reviews and testing are not competing V & V techniques. They have their own advantages and disadvantages and should be used together in the verification and validation process. Indeed, Gilb and Graham (1993) suggest that one of the most effective uses of reviews is to review the test cases for a system. Reviews can discover problems with these tests and can help design more effective ways to test the system.

It is sometimes difficult to introduce inspections into traditional software development organisations. Software engineers with experience of program testing may be reluctant to accept that these techniques can be more effective than testing for defect detection. Managers may be suspicious of these techniques because they require additional costs during design and development and they may not wish to take the risk that there will not be corresponding savings during program testing. Inspections inevitably 'front-load' software V & V costs and only result in cost savings after the development teams become experienced in their use.

I discuss software inspections in this chapter by describing program inspections where the program source code is inspected for defects. However, software inspections may be applied to any documents produced during the software process. Comparable inspection techniques can be applied to requirements specifications, detailed design definitions, data structure designs, test plans and user documentation.

19.2.1 Program inspections

Program inspections are reviews whose objective is program defect detection. The notion of a formalised inspection process was first developed at IBM in the 1970s and is described by Fagan (1976, 1986). It is now a widely used method of program verification. From Fagan's original method, a number of alternative approaches to inspection have been developed (Gilb and Graham, 1993). However, these are all based on Fagan's original notion that a team with members from different backgrounds should make a careful, line-by-line review of the program source code.

The key difference between program inspections and other types of quality review is that the principal goal of inspections is defect detection rather than to consider broader design issues. Defects may be either logical errors, anomalies in the code that might indicate an erroneous condition or non-compliance with organisational or project standards. By contrast, other types of review may be more concerned with schedule, costs, progress against defined milestones or assessing whether or not the software is likely to meet organisational goals.

The process of inspection is a formal one carried out by a small team of at least four people. Team members systematically analyse the code and point out possible defects. In Fagan's original proposals, he suggested roles such as author, reader, tester and moderator. The reader reads the code aloud to the inspection team, the tester inspects the code from a testing perspective and the moderator organises the process.

As organisations have gained experience with inspection, other proposals for team roles have emerged. In a discussion of how inspection was successfully introduced in Hewlett-Packard's development process, Grady and Van Slack (1994) suggest six roles as shown in Figure 19.5. Different roles may be adopted by the same person, so the team size may vary from one inspection to another.

Grady and Van Slack report that there is not always a need for a reader role. In this respect, they have modified the process from that originally proposed by Fagan,

Figure 19.5 Roles
in the inspection
process

Role	Description
Author or owner	The programmer or designer responsible for producing the program or document. Responsible for fixing defects discovered during the inspection process.
Inspector	Finds errors, omissions and inconsistencies in programs and documents. May also identify broader issues which are outside the scope of the inspection team.
Reader	Paraphrases the code or document at an inspection meeting.
Scribe	Records the results of the inspection meeting.
Chairman or moderator	Manages the process and facilitates the inspection. Reports process results to the chief moderator.
Chief moderator	Responsible for inspection process improvements, checklist updating, standards development, etc.

where an integral part of the process involved reading the program aloud. Gilb and Graham (1993) also do not think that a reader is needed. They suggest that inspectors should be selected to reflect different viewpoints such as testing, end-user, quality management, etc.

Before a program inspection begins, it is essential that:

1. There is a precise specification of the code to be inspected. It is impossible to inspect a component at the level of detail required to detect defects without a complete specification.

2. The members of the inspection team are familiar with the organisational standards.

3. There is an up-to-date, syntactically correct version of the code available. There is no point in inspecting code which is 'almost complete' even if a delay causes schedule disruption.

A very general inspection process is shown in Figure 19.6. This is adapted as required by organisations using program inspections.

The moderator is responsible for inspection planning. This involves selecting an inspection team, organising a meeting room and ensuring that the material to be inspected and its specifications are complete. The program to be inspected is presented to the inspection team during the overview stage where the author of the code describes what the program is intended to do. This is followed by a period of individual preparation. Each inspection team member studies the specification and the program and looks for defects in the code.

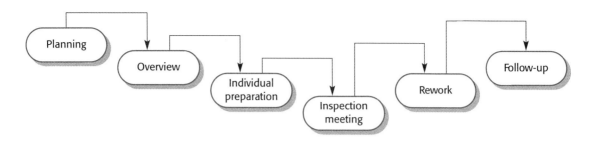

Figure 19.6 The
inspection process

The inspection itself should be relatively short (no more than two hours) and should be exclusively concerned with identifying defects, anomalies and non-compliance with standards. The inspection team should not suggest how these defects should be corrected nor recommend changes to other components.

Following inspection, the program is modified by its author to correct the identified problems. In the follow-up stage, the moderator must decide whether a reinspection of the code is required. Alternatively, he or she may decide that a complete reinspection is not required and that the defects have been successfully fixed. The document is then approved by the moderator for release.

The inspection process should always be driven by a checklist of common programmer errors. This should be established by discussion with experienced staff and regularly updated as more experience is gained of the inspection process. Different checklists should be prepared for different programming languages.

This checklist varies according to programming language because of the different levels of checking provided by the language compiler. For example, an Ada compiler checks that functions have the correct number of parameters, a C compiler does not. Possible checks which might be made during the inspection process are shown in Figure 19.7. Gilb and Graham (1993) emphasise that each organisation should develop its own inspection checklist. This should be based on local standards and practices and should be updated as new types of defects are found.

As an organisation gains experience of the inspection process, it can use the results of that process as a means of process improvement. An analysis of defects found during the inspection process can be made. The inspection team and the authors of the code which was inspected can suggest reasons why these defects occurred. Wherever possible, the process should then be modified to eliminate the reasons for defects so they will not recur in future systems.

Gilb and Graham report that a number of organisations have abandoned unit testing in favour of inspections. They have found that program inspections are so effective at finding errors that the costs of unit testing are not justifiable. As I discuss later in the chapter, software inspections have replaced unit testing in the Cleanroom software development process.

The amount of code which can be inspected in a given time depends on the experience of the inspection team, the programming language and the application domain. When the inspection process was measured in IBM, Fagan made the following observations:

Fault class	Inspection check
Data faults	Are all program variables initialised before their values are used? Have all constants been named? Should the upper bound of arrays be equal to the size of the array or Size −1? If character strings are used, is a delimiter explicitly assigned? Is there any possibility of buffer overflow?
Control faults	For each conditional statement, is the condition correct? Is each loop certain to terminate? Are compound statements correctly bracketed? In case statements, are all possible cases accounted for? If a break is required after each case in case statements, has it been included?
Input/output faults	Are all input variables used? Are all output variables assigned a value before they are output? Can unexpected inputs cause corruption?
Interface faults	Do all function and method calls have the correct number of parameters? Do formal and actual parameter types match? Are the parameters in the right order? If components access shared memory, do they have the same model of the shared memory structure?
Storage management faults	If a linked structure is modified, have all links been correctly reassigned? If dynamic storage is used, has space been allocated correctly? Is space explicitly de-allocated after it is no longer required?
Exception management faults	Have all possible error conditions been taken into account?

Figure 19.7
Inspection checks

1. About 500 source code statements per hour can be considered during the overview stage.
2. During individual preparation, about 125 source code statements per hour can be examined.
3. From 90 to 125 statements per hour can be inspected during the meeting.

These figures are confirmed by data collected by AT & T (Barnard and Price, 1994) where measurements of the inspection process showed comparable values.

Fagan suggests that the maximum time spent on an inspection should be about two hours as the efficiency of the defect detection process falls off after that time. Inspection should therefore be a frequent process, carried out on relatively small software components, during program development.

With four people involved in an inspection team, the cost of inspecting 100 lines of code is roughly equivalent to one person-day of effort. This assumes that the inspection itself takes about an hour and that each team member spends 1–2 hours in preparing for the inspection. Testing costs are very variable and depend on the number of faults in the program. However, the effort required for the program inspection is probably less than half the effort that would be required for equivalent defect testing.

The introduction of assessment has implications for project management and sensitive management is important if inspection is to be accepted by software development teams. Inspections are a public process of error detection compared with the more private testing process and, inevitably, mistakes that are made by individuals are revealed to the whole programming team.

Managers must ensure that there is a clear separation between inspections and personnel appraisals. Inspection results that reveal errors should never be used in career assessments of engineers. Inspection team leaders must be carefully trained to manage the process and to develop a culture where support is provided when errors are discovered and there is no notion of blame associated with these errors.

19.3 Automated static analysis

Static program analysers are software tools which scan the source text of a program and detect possible faults and anomalies. They do not require the program to be executed. Rather, they parse the program text and thus recognise the different types of statement in the program. They can then detect whether or not statements are well formed, make inferences about the control flow in the program and, in many cases, compute the set of all possible values for program data. They complement the error detection facilities provided by the language compiler.

The intention of automatic static analysis is to draw the verifier's attention to anomalies in the program such as variables that are used without initialisation, variables which are unused, data whose value could go out of range, etc. Some of the checks which can be detected by static analysis are shown in Figure 19.8. While these are not necessarily erroneous conditions, it is often the case that many of these anomalies are a result of programming errors or omissions. Automated static analysis is best used with software inspections. It provides additional information for the inspection team.

The stages involved in static analysis include:

1. *Control flow analysis*   This stage identifies and highlights loops with multiple exit or entry points and unreachable code. Unreachable code is code that is surrounded by unconditional goto statements or which is in a branch of a conditional statement where the guarding condition can never be true.

2. *Data use analysis*   This stage highlights how variables in the program are used. It detects variables that are used without previous initialisation, variables that are written twice without an intervening assignment and variables that are declared but never used. Data use analysis also discovers ineffective tests where the test

Figure 19.8
Automated static
analysis checks

Fault class	Static analysis check
Data faults	Variables used before initialisation Variables declared but never used Variables assigned twice but never used between assignments Possible array bound violations Undeclared variables
Control faults	Unreachable code Unconditional branches into loops
Input/output faults	Variables output twice with no intervening assignment
Interface faults	Parameter type mismatches Parameter number mismatches Non-usage of the results of functions Uncalled functions and procedures
Storage management faults	Unassigned pointers Pointer arithmetic

condition is redundant. Redundant conditions are conditions whose value never changes – they are either always true or always false.

3. *Interface analysis*   This analysis checks the consistency of routine and procedure declarations and their use. It is unnecessary if a strongly typed language like Java is used for implementation as the compiler carries out these checks. Interface analysis can detect type errors in weakly typed languages like FORTRAN and C. Interface analysis can also detect functions and procedures which are declared and never called or function results that are never used.

4. *Information flow analysis*   This phase of the analysis identifies the dependencies between input variables and output variables. While it does not detect anomalies, the derivation of the values used in the program are explicitly listed. Erroneous derivations should therefore be easier to detect during a code inspection or review. Information flow analysis can also show the conditions that affect a variable's value.

5. *Path analysis*   This phase of semantic analysis identifies all possible paths through the program and sets out the statements executed in that path. It essentially unravels the program's control and allows each possible predicate to be analysed individually.

Information flow analysis and path analysis generate an immense amount of information. This information does not highlight anomalous conditions but simply presents the program from a different viewpoint. Because of the large amount of information generated, these phases of static analysis are sometimes left out of the process. Only the early phases, which detect anomalous conditions directly, are used.

Figure 19.9 LINT
static analysis

```
138% more lint_ex.c

#include <stdio.h>
printarray (Anarray)
  int Anarray ;
{
  printf("%d",Anarray) ;
}
main ()
{
  int Anarray[5] ; int i ; char c ;
  printarray (Anarray, i, c) ;
  printarray (Anarray) ;
}

139% cc lint_ex.c
140% lint lint_ex.c

lint_ex.c(10): warning: c may be used before set
lint_ex.c(10): warning: i may be used before set
printarray: variable # of args. lint_ex.c(4) :: lint_ex.c(10)
printarray, arg. 1 used inconsistently lint_ex.c(4) :: lint_ex.c(10)
printarray, arg. 1 used inconsistently lint_ex.c(4) :: lint_ex.c(11)
printf returns value which is always ignored
```

Static analysers are particularly valuable when a programming language like C is used. C does not have strict type rules and the checking which the C compiler can do is limited. Therefore, there is a great deal of scope for programmer errors which can be automatically discovered by the analysis tool. This is particularly import-ant when C (and to a lesser extent C++) is used for critical systems development. In this case, static analysis can significantly reduce testing costs.

Unix and Linux systems include a static analyser called LINT for C programs. LINT provides static checking which is equivalent to that provided by the compiler in a strongly typed language such as Java. An example of the output produced by LINT is shown in Figure 19.9. In this transcript of a Unix terminal session, com-mands are shown in italics. The first command lists the (nonsensical) program. It defines a function with one parameter called printarray, then calls this function with three parameters. Variables i and c are declared but are never assigned values. The value returned by the function is never used.

The line numbered 139 shows the C compilation of this program with no errors reported by the C compiler. This is followed by a call of the LINT static analyser which detects and reports program errors.

The static analyser shows that the scalar variables c and i have been used but not initialised and that printarray has been called with a different number of argu-ments than are declared. It also identifies the inconsistent use of the first argument in printarray and the fact that the function value is never used.

Tool-based analysis cannot replace inspections as there are some types of error that static analysers cannot detect. For example, they can detect uninitialised variables but they cannot detect initialisations that are incorrect. In weakly typed languages like C, static analysers can detect functions that have the wrong numbers and types of arguments but they cannot detect situations where an incorrect argument of the correct type has been passed to a function.

There is no doubt that, for languages like C, static analysis is an effective technique for discovering program errors. However, with modern programming languages like Java, the language designers have removed some error-prone language features. All variables must be initialised, there are no goto statements so unreachable code is less likely to be created accidentally and storage management is automatic. This approach of error avoidance rather than error detection is more effective in improving program reliability. Therefore, automatic static analysis may not be cost-effective for Java programs.

19.4 Cleanroom software development

Cleanroom software development (Mills *et al.*, 1987; Cobb and Mills, 1990; Linger, 1994; Prowell *et al.*, 1999) is a software development philosophy that is based on avoiding software defects by using a rigorous inspection process. The objective of this approach to software development is zero-defect software. The name 'Cleanroom' was derived by analogy with semiconductor fabrication units. In these units (cleanrooms) defects are avoided by manufacturing in an ultra-clean atmosphere. I discuss it in this chapter because it has replaced the unit testing of system components by inspections to check the consistency of these components with their specifications.

A model of the Cleanroom process, adapted from the description given by Linger (1994), is shown in Figure 19.10.

The Cleanroom approach to software development is based on five key characteristics:

Figure 19.10
The Cleanroom
development process

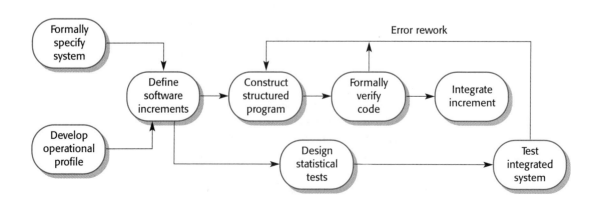

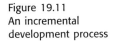

Figure 19.11
An incremental
development process

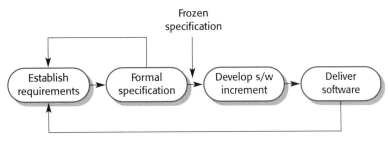

1. *Formal specification*   The software to be developed is formally specified. A state-transition model which shows system responses to stimuli is used to express the specification.

2. *Incremental development*   The software is partitioned into increments which are developed and validated separately using the Cleanroom process. These increments are specified, with customer input, at an early stage in the process.

3. *Structured programming*   Only a limited number of control and data abstraction constructs are used. The program development process is a process of stepwise refinement of the specification. A limited number of constructs are used and the aim is to apply correctness-preserving transformations (discussed in Chapter 3) to the specification to create the program code.

4. *Static verification*   The developed software is statically verified using rigorous software inspections. There is no unit or module testing process for code components.

5. *Statistical testing of the system*   The integrated software increment is tested statistically, as discussed in Chapter 21, to determine its reliability. These statistical tests are based on an operational profile which is developed in parallel with the system specification as shown in Figure 19.10.

Incremental development, shown in Figure 19.11 and discussed earlier in Chapter 3, involves producing and delivering the software in discrete increments. An increment can be executed by user commands and is a useful, limited, system in its own right. Users feed back reports of the system and propose changes that are required. Incremental development is important because it minimises the disruption caused to the development process by customer-requested requirements changes.

When a specification is specified as a single unit, customer requirements changes (which are inevitable) disrupt the specification and development process. The specification and design must be continually reworked. With incremental development, the specification for the increment is frozen although change requests for the rest of the system are accepted. The software increment is delivered on completion.

The approach to incremental development in the Cleanroom process is to deliver critical customer functionality in early increments. Less important system functions are included in later increments. The customer therefore has the opportunity of trying these critical increments before the whole system has been delivered. If requirements problems are discovered, the customer feeds back this information to the development team and requests a new release of the increment.

This means that the most important customer functions receive the most validation. As new increments are developed, they are combined with the existing increments and the integrated system is tested. Therefore, existing increments are re-tested with new test cases as new system increments are added.

The Cleanroom process is designed to support rigorous program inspection. A state-based system model is produced to serve as a system specification and this is refined through a series of different system models to an executable program. The approach used for development is based on well-defined transformations that attempt to preserve the correctness at each transformation to a more detailed representation. This general approach to development is discussed in Chapter 3. Program inspections are supplemented by rigorous mathematical arguments which demonstrate that the output of the transformation is consistent with its input.

The mathematical arguments used in the Cleanroom process are weaker than formal mathematical proofs. Formal mathematical proofs that a program is correct with respect to its specification are very expensive to develop. They depend on using knowledge of the formal semantics of the programming language to construct theories that relate the program and its formal specification. These theories must then be proven mathematically, often with the assistance of large and complex theorem-prover programs. Because of their high cost and the specialist skills that are needed, proofs are usually only developed for the most safety-critical or security-critical applications.

There are three teams involved when the Cleanroom process is used for large system development:

1. *The specification team*   This group is responsible for developing and maintaining the system specification. Customer-oriented specifications (requirements definition) and mathematical specifications for verification are produced by this team. In some cases, when the specification is complete, the specification team will also take responsibility for development.

2. *The development team*   This team has the responsibility of developing and verifying the software. The software is not executed during the development process. A structured, formal approach to verification based on inspection of code supplemented with correctness arguments is used.

3. *The certification team*   This team is responsible for developing a set of statistical tests to exercise the software after it has been developed. These tests are based on the formal specification. Test case development is carried out in parallel with software development. The test cases are used to certify the software reliability. Reliability growth models, discussed in Chapter 21, may be used to decide when to stop testing.

Use of the Cleanroom approach has resulted in software with very few errors and does not seem to be any more expensive than conventional development. Cobb and Mills (1990) discuss several successful Cleanroom development projects which had a uniformly low failure rate in delivered systems. The costs of these projects were comparable with other projects which used conventional development techniques.

Static verification is cost-effective in the Cleanroom process. The vast majority of defects are discovered before execution and are not introduced into the developed software. Linger (1994) reports that, on average, only 2.3 defects per thousand lines of source code were discovered during testing for Cleanroom projects. Overall development costs are not increased because less effort is required to test and repair the developed software.

Selby *et al.* (1987), using students as developers, compared Cleanroom development with conventional techniques. They found that most teams could successfully use the Cleanroom method. The programs produced were of higher quality than those developed using traditional techniques – the source code had more comments and a simpler structure. More of the Cleanroom teams met the development schedule.

Cleanroom development works when practised by skilled and committed engineers. However, use of the method has been confined to technologically advanced organisations and its adoption has been relatively slow. Reports of the success of the Cleanroom approach in industry have mostly, though not exclusively, come from its developers. We don't know if this process can be transferred effectively to other types of software development organisation. These organisations usually have fewer, less committed and less skilled engineers. Transferring the Cleanroom approach to these organisations still remains a challenge.

KEY POINTS

▶ Verification and validation are not the same thing. Verification is intended to show that a program meets its specification. Validation is intended to show that the program does what the user requires.

▶ Test plans should include a description of the items to be tested, the testing schedule, the procedures for managing the testing process, the hardware and software requirements and any testing problems which are likely to arise.

▶ Static verification techniques involve examination and analysis of the program source code to detect errors. They should be used with program testing as part of the V & V process.

▶ Program inspections are effective in finding program errors. The aim of an inspection is to locate faults. The inspection process should be driven by a fault checklist.

▶ Program code is systematically checked by a small team. Team members include a team leader or moderator, the author of the code, a reader who presents the code during the inspection and a tester who considers the code from a testing perspective.

▶ Static analysers are software tools which process program source code and draw attention to anomalies such as unused code sections and uninitialised variables. These anomalies may be the result of faults in the code.

▶ Cleanroom software development is an approach to software development that relies on static techniques for program verification and statistical testing for system reliability certification. It has been successful in producing systems which have a high level of reliability.

FURTHER READING

Cleanroom Software Engineering: Technology and Process. A fairly new book on the Cleanroom approach that has sections on the basics of the technique, the process and a practical case study. (S. J. Powell, C. J. Trammell, R. C. Linger, J. H. Poore, 1999, Addison Wesley Longman.)

Software Inspection. A very thorough book which covers program inspections as a defect detection technique in detail. It tends to be rather wordy at times but the case studies are particularly useful for illustrating the practice of inspection. (T. Gilb and D. Graham, 1993, Addison-Wesley.)

'Using Inspections to Investigate Program Correctness'. This article discusses how a mathematically based but not completely formal inspection process is effective in discovering program errors. (R. N. Britcher, *IEEE Computer*, 21(11), November 1988.)

EXERCISES

19.1 Discuss the differences between verification and validation and explain why validation is a particularly difficult process.

19.2 Explain why it is not necessary for a program to be completely free of defects before it is delivered to its customers. To what extent can testing be used to validate that the program is fit for its purpose?

19.3   Explain why program inspections are an effective technique for discovering errors in a program. What types of error are unlikely to be discovered through inspections?

19.4   Explain why an organisation with a competitive, elitist culture would probably find it difficult to introduce program inspections as a V & V technique.

19.5   Using your knowledge of Java, C++, C or some other programming language, derive a checklist of common errors (not syntax errors) which could not be detected by a compiler but which might be detected in a program inspection.

19.6   Produce a list of conditions which could be detected by a static analyser for Java, Ada or C++. Comment on this list compared to the list given in Figure 19.7.

19.7   Read the published papers on Cleanroom development and write a management report highlighting the advantages, costs and risks of adopting this approach to software development.

19.8   A manager decides to use the reports of program inspections as an input to the staff appraisal process. These reports show who made and who discovered program errors. Is this ethical managerial behaviour? Would it be ethical if the staff were informed in advance that this would happen? What difference might it make to the inspection process?

19.9   One approach which is commonly adopted to system testing is to test the system until the testing budget is exhausted and then deliver the system to customers. Discuss the ethics of this approach.

20 Software testing

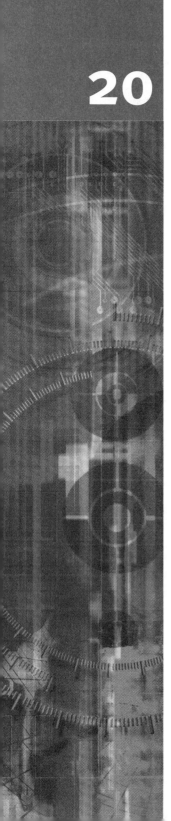

Objectives

The objective of this chapter is to introduce techniques that may be used to test programs to discover program faults. When you have read the chapter, you will:

❑ understand a number of testing techniques that are used to discover program faults;

❑ have been introduced to guidelines that support the testing of component interfaces;

❑ understand specific approaches to component testing and integration testing for object-oriented systems;

❑ understand the principles of operation of CASE tool support for testing.

Contents

20.1 Defect testing
20.2 Integration testing
20.3 Object-oriented testing
20.4 Testing workbenches

In Chapter 3, I discussed a general testing process that started with the testing of individual program units such as functions or objects. These were then integrated into sub-systems and systems and the interactions of these units were tested. Finally, after completion of the system, the customer may carry out a series of acceptance tests to check that the system performs as specified.

A more abstract view of this testing process is shown in Figure 20.1. The component testing stage is concerned with testing the functioning of clearly identifiable components. These may be functions or groups of methods collected together into a module or objects. During integration testing, these components are integrated to form sub-systems or the complete system. At this stage, testing should focus on interactions between the components and on the functionality and performance of the system as a whole. Inevitably, however, defects in components that have been missed during earlier testing are discovered during integration testing.

As part of the V & V planning process, managers have to make decisions on who should be responsible for the different stages of testing. For most systems, programmers take responsibility for testing their own code (modules or objects). Once this is completed, the work is handed over to an integration team who integrate the modules from different developers, build the software and test the system as a whole. However, for critical systems, a more formal process may be used where independent testers are responsible for all stages of the testing process. Tests are developed separately and detailed records are maintained.

When testing critical systems, a detailed specification of each software component is used by the independent team to derive the tests for the system. However, in most other cases, testing is a more intuitive process as there is not time to write detailed specifications of every part of a software system. Rather, the interfaces of the major system components are specified and individual programmers and programming teams take the responsibility for the design, development and testing of these components. Testing is usually based on an intuitive understanding of how these components should operate.

Integration testing, however, must be based on a written system specification. This can be a detailed system requirements specification as discussed in Chapter 5 or it can be a user-oriented specification of the features that should be implemented in the system. A separate team is always responsible for integration testing. As discussed in Chapter 3, they use the user and system requirements documents to develop detailed integration testing plans (see Figure 3.12).

Books on testing, such as those by Beizer (1990), Kit (1995) and Perry (1995), are based on practical experience where systems are developed using a functional model. They do not specifically address the testing of object-oriented systems. From

Figure 20.1
Testing phases

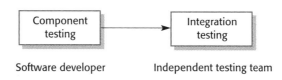

a testing perspective, object-oriented systems differ from function-oriented systems in two fundamental ways:

1. In function-oriented systems, there is a fairly clear distinction between basic program units (functions) and collections of these program units (modules). In object-oriented systems, there is no such distinction. Objects may be simple entities such as a list or complex entities such as the weather station object described in Chapter 12 which includes a number of other objects.

2. There is often no clear hierarchy of objects as is commonly found in function-oriented systems. The integration strategies such as top-down or bottom-up integration that are discussed in section 20.2 are often inappropriate.

These differences mean that the boundary between component testing and integration testing is blurred for object-oriented systems. It is a continuation of the seamless object-oriented development process where objects are the basic structure used at all stages of the software process. While many testing techniques are independent of the system design, some techniques have been developed that are specifically geared to testing object-oriented systems. I discuss approaches to object-oriented testing in section 20.3.

20.1 Defect testing

The goal of defect testing is to expose latent defects in a software system before the system is delivered. This contrasts with validation testing which is intended to demonstrate that a system meets its specification. Validation testing requires the system to perform correctly using given acceptance test cases. A successful defect test is a test which causes the system to perform *incorrectly* and hence exposes a defect. This emphasises an important fact about testing. It demonstrates *the presence*, not the absence, of program faults.

A general model of the defect testing process is shown in Figure 20.2. Test cases are specifications of the inputs to the test and the expected output from the system plus a statement of what is being tested. Test data are the inputs which have been devised to test the system. Test data can sometimes be generated automatically. Automatic test case generation is impossible because the test output cannot be predicted.

Exhaustive testing, where every possible program execution sequence is tested, is impractical. Testing, therefore, has to be based on a subset of possible test cases. Organisations should develop policies for choosing this subset rather than leave this to the development team. These policies might be based on general testing policies

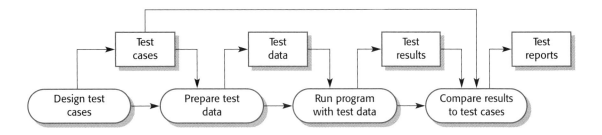

Figure 20.2
The defect
testing process

such as a policy that all program statements should be executed at least once. Alternatively, the testing policies may be based on experience of system usage and may focus on testing the features of the operational system. For example:

1. All system functions that are accessed through menus should be tested.
2. Combinations of functions (e.g. text formatting) that are accessed through the same menu must be tested.
3. Where user input is provided, all functions must be tested with both correct and incorrect input.

It is clear from experience with major software products such as word processors or spreadsheets that comparable guidelines have been used during product testing. Unusual combinations of functionality can result in errors but the most commonly used functions usually work correctly.

20.1.1 Black-box testing

Functional or black-box testing is an approach to testing where the tests are derived from the program or component specification. The system is a 'black box' whose behaviour can only be determined by studying its inputs and the related outputs. Another name for this is *functional testing* because the tester is only concerned with the functionality and not the implementation of the software.

Figure 20.3 illustrates the model of a system which is assumed in black-box testing. This approach is equally applicable to systems that are organised as functions or as objects. The tester presents inputs to the component or the system and examines the corresponding outputs. If the outputs are not those predicted then the test has *successfully* detected a problem with the software.

The key problem for the defect tester is to select inputs that have a high probability of being members of the set I_e. In many cases, the selection of these test cases is based on the previous experience of test engineers. They use domain knowledge to identify test cases which are likely to reveal defects. However, the systematic approach to test data selection discussed in the next section may also be used to supplement this heuristic knowledge.

Figure 20.3
Black-box testing

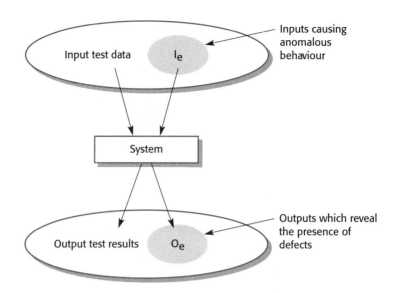

20.1.2 Equivalence partitioning

The input data to a program usually fall into a number of different classes. These have common characteristics, e.g. positive numbers, negative numbers, strings without blanks, etc. Programs normally behave in a comparable way for all members of a class. Because of this equivalent behaviour, these classes are sometimes called equivalence partitions or domains (Beizer, 1990). One systematic approach to defect testing is based on identifying all equivalence partitions which must be handled by a program. Test cases are designed so that the inputs or outputs lie within these partitions.

In Figure 20.4, each equivalence partition is shown as an ellipse. Input equivalence partitions are sets of data where all of the set members should be processed in an equivalent way. Output equivalence partitions are program outputs that have common characteristics so can be considered as a distinct class. You also identify partitions where the inputs are outside the other partitions that you have chosen. These test if the program handles invalid input correctly. Valid and invalid inputs also form equivalence partitions.

Once you have identified a set of partitions, you then choose test cases from each of these partitions. A good guideline to follow for test case selection is to choose test cases on the boundaries of the partitions plus cases close to the mid-point of the partition. The rationale for this guideline is that designers and programmers tend to consider typical values of inputs when developing a system. These are tested by choosing the mid-point of the partition. Boundary values are often atypical (e.g. zero may behave differently from other non-negative numbers) so are overlooked by developers. Program errors often occur when processing these atypical values.

The equivalence partitions may be identified by using the program specification or user documentation and by the tester using experience to predict which classes

Figure 20.4
Equivalence
partitioning

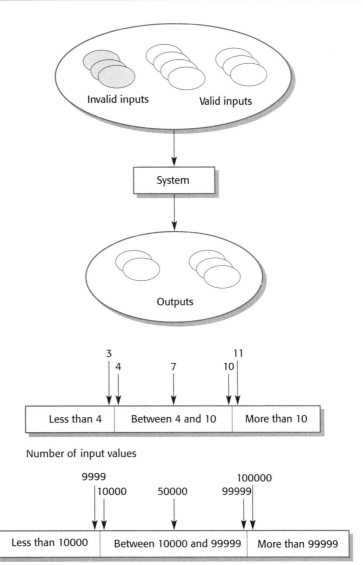

Figure 20.5
Equivalence
partitions

of input value are likely to detect errors. For example, say a program specification states that the program accepts 4 to 10 inputs which are five-digit integers greater than 10,000. Figure 20.5 shows the identified equivalence partitions for this situation and possible test input data values.

To illustrate the derivation of test cases, I use the specification of a simplified example (a search routine) that searches a sequence of elements for a given element (the key). It returns the position of that element in the sequence. The specification of this routine, using pre- and post-conditions, is shown in Figure 20.6. The pre-condition states that the search routine has not been designed to work with empty sequences. The post-condition states that the variable Found is set if the key

Figure 20.6 The
specification of a
search routine

procedure Search (Key : ELEM ; T: SEQ of ELEM ;
Found : **in out** BOOLEAN; L: **in out** ELEM_INDEX) ;

Pre-condition
-- the sequence has at least one element
T'FIRST <= T'LAST
Post-condition
-- the element is found and is referenced by L
(Found **and** T (L) = Key)
or
-- the element is not in the sequence
(**not** Found **and**
not (**exists** i, T'FIRST >= i <= T'LAST, T (i) = Key))

element is in the sequence. The position of the key element is indicated by the index
L. The index is undefined if the element is not in the sequence.

From this specification, two obvious equivalence partitions can be identified:

• inputs where the key element is a member of the sequence (**Found = true**);
• inputs where the key element is not a sequence member (**Found = false**).

As well as deriving equivalence partitions from the system specification, there
are various testing guidelines that can also be used. Some examples of these testing guidelines which apply to sequences are:

1. Test software with sequences that have only a single value. Programmers natur-
    ally think of sequences as made up of several values and sometimes they embed
    this assumption in their programs. Consequently, the program may not work
    properly when presented with a single-value sequence.

2. Use different sequences of different sizes in different tests. This decreases the
    chances that a program with defects will accidentally produce a correct output
    because of some accidental characteristics of the input.

3. Derive tests so that the first, middle and last elements of the sequence are accessed.
    This approach reveals problems at partition boundaries.

Using these guidelines, two further equivalence partitions of the input array can
be identified:

• The input sequence has a single value.
• The number of elements in the input sequence is greater than 1.

These partitions must be combined with the previously identified equivalence
partitions, giving the equivalence partitions summarised in Figure 20.7.

A set of possible test cases based on these partitions is also shown in Figure 20.7.
If the key element is not in the sequence, the value of L is undefined ('??'). The
guideline that different sequences of different sizes should be used has been applied
in these test cases.

Figure 20.7
Equivalence
partitions for search
routine

Array	Element
Single value	In sequence
Single value	Not in sequence
More than 1 value	First element in sequence
More than 1 value	Last element in sequence
More than 1 value	Middle element in sequence
More than 1 value	Not in sequence

Input sequence (T)	Key (Key)	Output (Found, L)
17	17	true, 1
17	0	false, ??
17, 29, 21, 23	17	true, 1
41, 18, 9, 31, 30, 16, 45	45	true, 7
17, 18, 21, 23, 29, 41, 38	23	true, 4
21, 23, 29, 33, 38	25	false, ??

The set of input values used to test the search routine is not exhaustive. The routine may fail if the input sequence happens to include the elements 1, 2, 3 and 4. However, it is reasonable to assume that if the test fails to detect defects when one member of a class is processed, no other members of that class will identify defects. Of course, defects may still exist. Some equivalence partitions may not have been identified, errors may have been made in equivalence partition identification or the test data may have been incorrectly prepared.

I have deliberately left out tests that are designed to present the system with parameters in the wrong order, of the wrong type, etc. This type of error is best detected using program inspection or automated static analysis. Similarly, the tests do not check for unexpected corruption of data outside the component. It does not make sense for black-box tests to check such corruption. Code inspection, as discussed in Chapter 19, can reveal whether this kind of problem is likely to arise.

20.1.3 Structural testing

Structural testing (Figure 20.8) is an approach to testing where the tests are derived from knowledge of the software's structure and implementation. This approach is

Figure 20.8
Structural testing

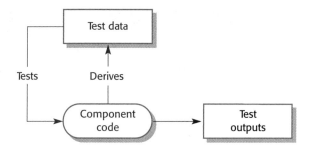

Figure 20.9 Java
implementation of a
binary search routine

```
class BinSearch {

// This is an encapsulation of a binary search function that takes an array of
// ordered objects and a key and returns an object with 2 attributes, namely
// index - the value of the array index
// found - a boolean indicating whether or not the key is in the array
// An object is returned because it is not possible in Java to pass basic types by
// reference to a function and so return two values
// The key is -1 if the element is not found

    public static void search ( int key, int [] elemArray, Result r )
    {
        int bottom = 0 ;
        int top = elemArray.length - 1 ;
        int mid ;
        r.found = false ; r.index = -1 ;
        while ( bottom <= top )
        {
            mid = (top + bottom) / 2 ;
            if (elemArray [mid] == key)
            {
                r.index = mid ;
                r.found = true ;
                return ;
            } // if part
            else
            {
                if (elemArray [mid] < key)
                    bottom = mid + 1 ;
                else
                    top = mid - 1 ;
            }
        } //while loop
    } // search
} //BinSearch
```

sometimes called 'white-box' testing , 'glass-box' testing or 'clear-box' testing to
distinguish it from black-box testing.

Structural testing is usually applied to relatively small program units such as subroutines or the operations associated with an object. As the name implies, the tester

Figure 20.10
Binary search
equivalence classes

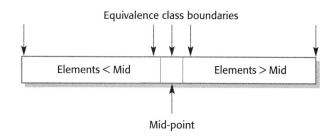

can analyse the code and use knowledge about the structure of a component to derive test data. The analysis of the code can be used to find how many test cases are needed to guarantee that all of the statements in the program or component are executed at least once during the testing process.

Knowledge of the algorithm used to implement some function can be used to identify further equivalence partitions. To illustrate this, I have instantiated the search routine specification (Figure 20.6) as a binary search routine (Figure 20.9). Of course, this has stricter pre-conditions. The sequence is implemented as an array, that array must be ordered and the value of the lower bound of the array must be less than the value of the upper bound.

By examining the code of the search routine, we can see that binary searching involves splitting the search space into three parts. Each of these parts makes up an equivalence partition (Figure 20.10). Test cases where the key lies at the boundaries of each of these partitions should be chosen to exercise the code.

The test cases shown in Figure 20.7 must therefore be modified so that the input array is arranged in ascending order. Further cases based on knowledge of the algorithm used should be added to the test set. These are elements which are adjacent to the mid-point of the array. Figure 20.11 shows a set of test cases for the binary search routine.

Figure 20.11 Test cases for search routine

Input array (T)	Key (Key)	Output (Found, L)
17	17	true, 1
17	0	false, ??
17, 21, 23, 29	17	true, 1
9, 16, 18, 30, 31, 41, 45	45	true, 7
17, 18, 21, 23, 29, 38, 41	23	true, 4
17, 18, 21, 23, 29, 33, 38	21	true, 3
12, 18, 21, 23, 32	23	true, 4
21, 23, 29, 33, 38	25	false, ??

Path testing

Path testing is a structural testing strategy whose objective is to exercise every independent execution path through a component or program. If every independent path is executed then all statements in the component must have been executed at least once. Furthermore, all conditional statements are tested for both true and false cases. In an object-oriented development process, path testing may be used when testing methods associated with objects.

The number of paths through a program is usually proportional to its size. As modules are integrated into systems, it becomes unfeasible to use structural testing techniques. Path testing techniques are therefore mostly used at the unit testing and module testing stages of the testing process.

Path testing does not test all possible combinations of all paths through the program. For any components apart from very trivial ones without loops, this is an impossible objective. There are an infinite number of possible path combinations in programs with loops. Defects which manifest themselves when particular path combinations arise may still be present even although all program statements have been executed at least once.

The starting point for path testing is a program flow graph. This is a skeletal model of all paths through the program. A flow graph consists of nodes representing decisions and edges showing flow of control. The flow graph is constructed by replacing program control statements by equivalent diagrams. If there are no goto statements in a program, it is a simple process to derive its flow graph. Sequential statements (assignments, procedure calls and I/O statements) can be ignored in the flow graph construction. Each branch in a conditional statement (if-then-else or case) is shown as a separate path and loops are indicated by an arrow looping back to the loop condition node. Loops and conditional branches are illustrated in the flow graph for the binary search routine (Figure 20.12).

The objective of structural testing is to ensure that each independent program path is executed at least once. An independent program path is one which traverses at least one new edge in the flow graph. In program terms, this means exercising one or more new conditions. Both the true and false branches of all conditions must be executed.

The flow graph for the binary search procedure is shown in Figure 20.12. By tracing the flow, therefore, we see that the independent paths through the binary search flow graph are:

1, 2, 3, 8, 9
1, 2, 3, 4, 6, 7, 2
1, 2, 3, 4, 5, 7, 2
1, 2, 3, 4, 6, 7, 2, 8, 9

If all of these paths are executed we can be sure that:

1.   every statement in the method has been executed at least once, and
2.   every branch has been exercised for true and false conditions.

Figure 20.12 Flow graph for a binary search routine

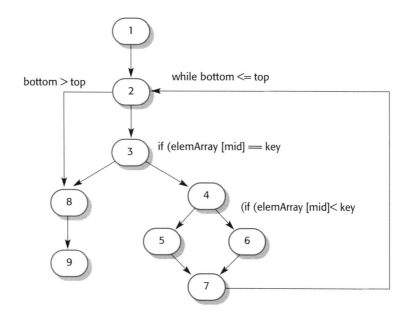

The number of independent paths in a program can be discovered by computing the cyclomatic complexity (McCabe, 1976) of the program flow graph. The cyclomatic complexity, CC, of any connected graph G may be computed according to the following formula:

CC (G) = Number (edges) − Number (nodes) + 2

For programs without goto statements, the value of the cyclomatic complexity is one more than the number of conditions in the program. In a compound condition with more than one test you should count each test. Thus, if there are six if-statements and a while loop, with all conditional expressions simple, the cyclomatic complexity is 8. If a conditional expression is a compound expression with two logical operators ('and' or 'or') the cyclomatic complexity is 10. The cyclomatic complexity of the binary search routine (Figure 20.10) is 4.

After discovering the number of independent paths through the code by computing the cyclomatic complexity, the next step is to design test cases to execute each of these paths. The minimum number of test cases required to test all program paths is equal to the cyclomatic complexity.

Test case design is straightforward in the case of the binary search routine. However, when programs have a complex branching structure, it may be difficult to predict how any particular test case will be processed. In these cases, a dynamic program analyser can be used to discover the program's execution profile.

Dynamic program analysers are testing tools that work in conjunction with compilers. During compilation, additional object code instructions are added to the generated code. These count the number of times each program statement has been executed. After the program has been run, an execution profile can be printed which shows which parts of the program have and have not been executed using particular test cases. This execution profile therefore reveals untested program sections.

20.2 Integration testing

Once individual program components have been tested, they must be integrated to create a partial or complete system. This integration process involves building the system (see Chapter 29) and testing the resultant system for problems that arise from component interactions. Integration tests should be developed from the system specification and integration testing should begin as soon as usable versions of some of the system components are available.

The main difficulty that arises in integration testing is localising errors that are discovered during the process. There are complex interactions between the system components and, when an anomalous output is discovered, it may be hard to find the source of the error. To make it easier to locate errors, you should always use an incremental approach to system integration and testing. Initially, you should integrate a minimal system configuration and test this system. You then add components to this minimal configuration and test after each added increment.

In the example shown in Figure 20.13, test sequences T1, T2 and T3 are first run on a system composed of module A and module B (the minimal system). If these reveal defects, these are corrected. Module C is integrated and tests T1, T2 and T3 are repeated to ensure that there have not been unexpected interactions with A and B. If problems arise in these tests, this probably means that they are due to interactions with the new module. The source of the problem is localised, thus

Figure 20.13
Incremental
integration testing

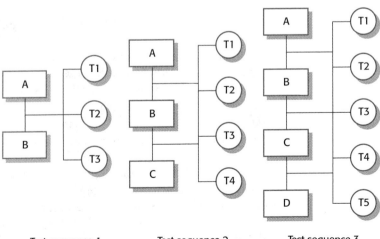

Test sequence 1   Test sequence 2   Test sequence 3

simplifying defect location and repair. Test sequence T4 is also run on the system. Finally, module D is integrated and tested using existing and new tests (T5).

Of course, reality is rarely as simple as this model suggests. The implementation of system features may be spread across a number of components. Testing a new feature may therefore require several different components to be integrated. The testing may reveal errors in the interactions between these individual components and other parts of the system. Repairing errors may be difficult because it affects the whole group of components that implement the system feature. Furthermore, when a new component is integrated and tested, this can change the pattern of previous, already tested, component interactions. Errors may be revealed that were not exposed in the tests of the simpler configuration.

20.2.1   Top-down and bottom-up testing

Top-down and bottom-up test strategies (Figure 20.14) reflect different approaches to system integration. In top-down integration, the high-level components of a system are integrated and tested before their design and implementation has been

Figure 20.14
Top-down and
bottom-up
integration testing

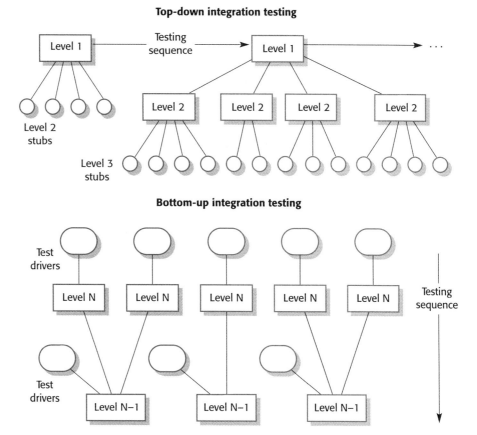

completed. In bottom-up integration, low-level components are integrated and tested before the higher-level components have been developed.

Top-down testing is an integral part of a top-down development process where the development process starts with high-level components and works down the component hierarchy. The program is represented as a single abstract component with sub-components represented by stubs. Stubs have the same interface as the component but very limited functionality. After the top-level component has been programmed and tested, its sub-components are implemented and tested in the same way. This process continues until the bottom-level components are implemented. The whole system has then been completely tested.

By contrast, bottom-up testing involves integrating and testing the modules at the lower levels in the hierarchy, and then working up the hierarchy of modules until the final module is tested. This approach does not require the architectural design of the system to be complete so it can start at an early stage in the development process. It may be used where the system reuses and modifies components from other systems.

Top-down and bottom-up integration testing can be compared under four headings:

1. *Architectural validation*   Top-down testing is more likely to discover errors in the system architecture and high-level design at an early stage in the development process. As these are usually structural errors, early detection means that they can be corrected without undue costs. With bottom-up testing, the high-level design is not validated until a late stage in the process.

2. *System demonstration*   With top-down development a limited, working system is available at an early stage in the development. This is an important psychological boost to those involved in the system development. It demonstrates the feasibility of the system to management. Validation can begin early in the testing process as a demonstrable system can be made available to users. However, if the system is constructed from reusable components, it may also be possible to produce some kind of demonstration using a bottom-up approach.

3. *Test implementation*   Strict top-down testing is difficult to implement because program stubs simulating lower levels of the system must be produced. These program stubs may either be a simplified version of the component required or may request the tester to input an appropriate value or to simulate the action of the component. When using bottom-up testing, you have to write test drivers to exercise the lower-level components. These test drivers simulate the components' environment and call the component that is to be tested.

4. *Test observation*   Both bottom-up and top-down testing can have problems with test observation. In many systems, the higher levels of the system that are implemented first in a top-down process do not generate output but, to test these levels, they must be forced to do so. The tester must create an artificial environment to generate the test results. With bottom-up testing, it may also be

necessary to create an artificial environment (the test drivers) so that the execution of the lower-level components can be observed.

In reality, systems are usually developed and tested using a mixture of top-down and bottom-up approaches. Different development schedules for different parts of the system mean that the integration and testing team must work with whatever components are available. Therefore, a mixture of stubs and test drivers must inevitably be developed during the integration testing process.

20.2.2   Interface testing

Interface testing takes place when modules or sub-systems are integrated to create larger systems. Each module or sub-system has a defined interface which is called by other program components. The objective of interface testing is to detect faults which may have been introduced into the system because of interface errors or invalid assumptions about interfaces.

Figure 20.15 illustrates interface testing. The arrows to the box boundary mean that the test cases are not applied to the individual components but to the sub-system created by combining these components.

This form of testing is particularly important for object-oriented development, particularly when objects and object classes are reused. Objects are essentially defined by their interfaces and may be reused in combination with different objects in different systems. Interface errors cannot be detected by testing the individual objects. The errors are a result of the interaction between objects rather than the isolated behaviour of a single object.

There are different types of interface between program components and, consequently, different types of interface error that can occur:

Figure 20.15
Interface testing

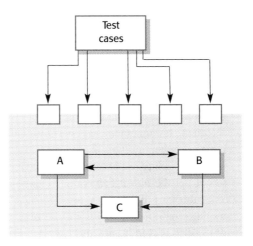

1. *Parameter interfaces* These are interfaces where data or sometimes function references are passed from one component to another.

2. *Shared memory interfaces* These are interfaces where a block of memory is shared between sub-systems. Data is placed in the memory by one sub-system and retrieved from there by other sub-systems.

3. *Procedural interfaces* These are interfaces where one sub-system encapsulates a set of procedures which can be called by other sub-systems. Objects and abstract data types have this form of interface.

4. *Message passing interfaces* These are interfaces where one sub-system requests a service from another sub-system by passing a message to it. A return message includes the results of executing the service. Some object-oriented systems have this form of interface, as do client–server systems.

Interface errors are one of the most common forms of error in complex systems (Lutz, 1993). These errors fall into three classes:

- *Interface misuse* A calling component calls some other component and makes an error in the use of its interface. This type of error is particularly common with parameter interfaces where parameters may be of the wrong type, may be passed in the wrong order or the wrong number of parameters may be passed.

- *Interface misunderstanding* A calling component misunderstands the specification of the interface of the called component and makes assumptions about the behaviour of the called component. The called component does not behave as expected and this causes unexpected behaviour in the calling component. For example, a binary search routine may be called with an unordered array to be searched. The search would then fail.

- *Timing errors* These occur in real-time systems which use a shared memory or a message passing interface. The producer of data and the consumer of data may operate at different speeds. Unless particular care is taken in the interface design, the consumer can access out-of-date information because the producer of the information has not updated the shared interface information.

Testing for interface defects is difficult because some interface faults may only manifest themselves under unusual conditions. For example, say an object implements a queue as a fixed-length data structure. A calling object may assume that the queue is implemented as an infinite data structure and may not check for queue overflow when an item is entered. This condition can only be detected during testing by designing test cases which force the queue to overflow and cause that overflow to corrupt the object behaviour in some detectable way.

A further problem may arise because of interactions between faults in different modules or objects. Faults in one object may only be detected when some other object behaves in an unexpected way. For example, an object may call some other object to receive some service and may assume that the response is correct. If there has been a misunderstanding about the value computed, the returned value may be valid but incorrect. This will only manifest itself when some later computation goes wrong.

Some general guidelines for interface testing are:

1. Examine the code to be tested and explicitly list each call to an external component. Design a set of tests where the values of the parameters to the external components are at the extreme ends of their ranges. These extreme values are most likely to reveal interface inconsistencies.

2. Where pointers are passed across an interface, always test the interface with null pointer parameters.

3. Where a component is called through a procedural interface, design tests which should cause the component to fail. Differing failure assumptions are one of the most common specification misunderstandings.

4. Use stress testing, as discussed in the following section, in message passing systems. Design tests which generate many more messages than are likely to occur in practice. Timing problems may be revealed in this way.

5. Where several components interact through shared memory, design tests which vary the order in which these components are activated. These tests may reveal implicit assumptions made by the programmer about the order in which the shared data is produced and consumed.

Static techniques are often more cost-effective than testing for discovering interface errors. A strongly typed language such as Java allows many interface errors to be trapped by the compiler. Where a weaker language, such as C, is used, a static analyser such as LINT (see Chapter 19) can detect interface errors. Program inspections can concentrate on component interfaces and questions about the assumed interface behaviour can be asked during the inspection process.

20.2.3 Stress testing

Once a system has been completely integrated it is possible to test the system for emergent properties (see Chapter 2) such as performance and reliability. Performance tests have to be designed to ensure that the system can process its intended load. This usually involves planning a series of tests where the load is steadily increased until the system performance becomes unacceptable.

Some classes of system are designed to handle a specified load. For example, a transaction processing system may be designed to process up to 100 transactions per second; an operating system may be designed to handle up to 200 separate terminals. Stress testing continues these tests beyond the maximum design load of the system until the system fails. This type of testing has two functions:

1. It tests the failure behaviour of the system. Circumstances may arise through an unexpected combination of events where the load placed on the system exceeds the maximum anticipated load. In these circumstances, it is important that system failure should not cause data corruption or unexpected loss of user services. Stress testing checks that overloading the system causes it to 'fail-soft' rather than collapse under its load.

2. It stresses the system and may cause defects to come to light which would not normally manifest themselves. Although it can be argued that these defects are unlikely to cause system failures in normal usage, there may be unusual combinations of normal circumstances which the stress testing replicates.

Stress testing is particularly relevant to distributed systems based on a network of processors. These systems often exhibit severe degradation when they are heavily loaded. The network becomes swamped with coordination data which the different processes must exchange so the processes become slower and slower as they wait for the required data from other processes.

20.3 Object-oriented testing

In Figure 20.1, I suggested that there were two fundamental activities in the testing process. These are component testing where system components are tested individually and integration testing where collections of components are integrated into sub-systems and the final system for testing. These activities are equally applicable to object-oriented systems. However, there are important differences between object-oriented systems and systems developed using a functional model:

1. Objects as individual components are often larger than single functions.
2. Objects that are integrated into sub-systems are usually loosely coupled and there is no obvious 'top' to the system.
3. If objects are reused, the testers may have no access to the source code of the component for analysis.

These differences mean that white-box testing approaches based on code analysis have to be extended to cover larger-grain objects and that alternative approaches to integration testing may have to be adopted. However, once a system has been integrated, the fact that it has been developed as an object-oriented system should not be apparent to system users.

In an object-oriented system, four levels of testing can be identified:

1. *Testing the individual operations associated with objects*   These are functions or procedures and the black-box and white-box approaches discussed above may be used.

2. *Testing individual object classes*   The principle of black-box testing is unchanged but the notion of an equivalence class must be extended to cover related operation sequences. Similarly, structural testing requires a different type of analysis. This is discussed in section 20.3.1.

3. *Testing clusters of objects*   Strict top-down or bottom-up integration is inappropriate to create groups of related objects. Other approaches such as scenario-based testing should be used. These are discussed in section 20.3.2.

4. *Testing the object-oriented system*   Verification and validation against the system requirements specification is carried out in exactly the same way as for any other type of system.

Testing techniques for object-oriented systems have matured rapidly and there is now a good deal of information available on object-oriented testing techniques (Binder, 1999). The following sections give an overview of a basic approach to object-oriented system testing.

20.3.1   Object class testing

The approach to test coverage discussed in section 20.1.3 was concerned with ensuring that all statements in a program were executed at least once and that all paths through the program were executed. When testing objects, complete test coverage should include:

1. the testing in isolation of all operations associated with the object;
2. the setting and interrogation of all attributes associated with the object;
3. the exercise of the object in all possible states. This means that all events that cause a state change in the object should be simulated.

Consider, for example, the weather station from Chapter 12 whose interface is shown in Figure 20.16. It has only a single attribute, which is its identifier. This is a constant that is set when the weather station is installed. You therefore only need a test that checks if it has been set up. You need to define test cases for reportWeather, calibrate, test, startup and shutdown. Ideally, you should test methods in isolation but, in some cases, some test sequences are necessary. For example, to test shutdown you need to have executed the startup method.

To test the states of the weather station, you use a state model as shown in Figure 12.14. Using this model, you can identify sequences of state transitions that have to be tested and define event sequences to force these transitions. In principle,

Figure 20.16
The weather station
object interface

WeatherStation
identifier
reportWeather () calibrate (instruments) test () startup (instruments) shutdown (instruments)

you should test every possible state transition sequence although in practice this may be too expensive. Examples of state sequences that should be tested in the weather station include:

Shutdown → Waiting → Shutdown

Waiting → Calibrating → Testing → Transmitting → Waiting

Waiting → Collecting → Waiting → Summarising → Transmitting → Waiting

If inheritance is used, this makes it more difficult to design object class tests. Where a superclass provides operations that are inherited by a number of subclasses, all of these subclasses should be tested with all inherited operations. The reason for this is that the inherited operation may make assumptions about other operations and attributes and these may have been changed when inherited. Equally, when a superclass operation is overridden, the overwriting operation must be tested.

The notion of equivalence classes may also be applied to object classes. Tests that fall into the same equivalence class might be those that use the same attributes of the objects. Therefore, equivalence classes should be identified which initialise, access and update all object class attributes.

20.3.2 Object integration

When object-oriented systems are developed, the levels of integration are less distinct. Clearly, operations and data are integrated to form objects and object classes. Testing these object classes corresponds to unit testing. There is no direct equivalent to module testing in object-oriented systems. However, Murphy *et al.* (1994) suggest that groups of classes which act in combination to provide a set of services should be tested together. They call this *cluster testing*.

Neither top-down nor bottom-up integration is really appropriate for object-oriented systems. In these systems, there is no obvious 'top' that provides a goal for the integration nor is there a clear hierarchy of objects that can be created. Clusters therefore have to be created using knowledge of their operation and the features of the system that are implemented by these clusters. There are three possible approaches to integration testing that may be used:

1. *Use-case or scenario-based testing*   Use-cases or scenarios (see Chapter 6) describe one mode of use of the system. Testing can be based on these scenario descriptions and object clusters created to support the use-cases that relate to that mode of use.

2. *Thread testing*   Thread testing is based on testing the system's response to a particular input or set of input events. Object-oriented systems are often event-driven so this is a particularly appropriate form of testing to use. To use this approach, you have to identify how the processing of events threads its way through the system.

3. *Object interaction testing*   A related approach to testing groups of interacting objects is proposed by Jorgensen and Erickson (1994). They suggest that an intermediate level of integration testing can be based on identifying 'method-message' paths. These are traces through a sequence of object interactions which stop when an object operation does not call on the services of any other object. They also identify a related construct which they call an 'Atomic System Function' (ASF). An ASF consists of some input event followed by a sequence of MM-paths which is terminated by an output event. This is similar to the notion of a thread in a real-time system.

Scenario-based testing is often the most effective of these approaches as it can be organised so that the most likely scenarios are tested first with unusual or exceptional scenarios considered later in the testing process. This satisfies a fundamental principle of testing that most testing effort should be devoted to those parts of the system that receive the most use.

To illustrate scenario-based testing, I again use an example from the weather station system. Scenarios can be identified from the use-cases that you may have developed but these may not include enough information for testing purposes. To supplement these use-cases when planning testing, you can use interaction diagrams that show in more detail how a scenario is implemented by the objects in a system.

Consider Figure 20.17 (taken from Chapter 12) which shows the sequence of operations in the weather station when it responds to a request to collect data for the mapping system. You can use this diagram to identify operations that will be tested and to help design the test cases to execute the tests.

Therefore, you can see that issuing a request for a report will result in the following thread of methods to be executed:

CommsController:request → WeatherStation:report → WeatherData:summarise

When choosing scenarios to devise system tests, it is important to ensure that you execute each method in each class at least once. Therefore, you should create a checklist of object classes and methods and, when a scenario is chosen, you should then tick the methods that have been executed. Of course, it isn't possible to execute all combinations of methods but this at least ensures that all individual methods have been tested as part of a sequence.

Figure 20.17
Collect weather
data sequence chart

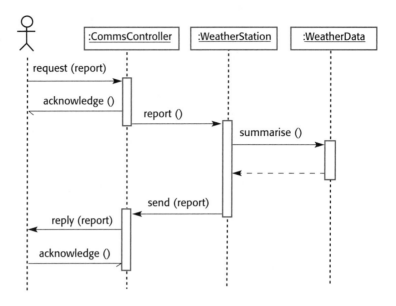

The sequence diagram can also be used to identify inputs and outputs that have to be created for the test:

1. An input of a request for a report should have an associated acknowledgement and a report should ultimately be returned from the request. During the testing, you should create summarised data that can be used to check that the report is correctly organised.

2. An input request for a report to **WeatherStation** results in a summarised report being generated. You can test this in isolation by creating raw data corresponding to the summary that you have prepared for the test of **CommsController** and checking that the **WeatherStation** object correctly produces this summary.

3. This raw data is also used to test the **WeatherData** object.

Of course, I have simplified the sequence chart in Figure 20.17 so that it does not show exceptions. A complete scenario test must also take these into account and ensure that these are correctly handled by the objects.

20.4 Testing workbenches

Testing is an expensive and laborious phase of the software process. As a result, testing tools were among the first software tools to be developed. These tools now

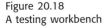

Figure 20.18
A testing workbench

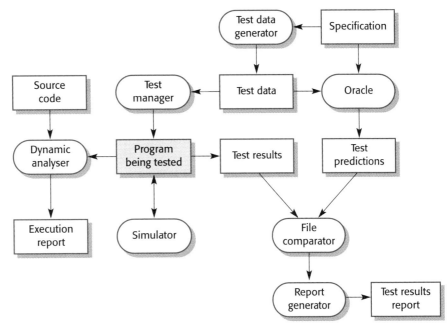

offer a range of facilities and their use significantly reduces the cost of the testing process. Different testing tools may be integrated into testing workbenches.

Figure 20.18 shows some tools which may be included in a testing workbench and the interactions between these tools. Tools included are:

1. *Test manager*   Manages the running of program tests. The test manager keeps track of test data, expected results and program facilities tested.

2. *Test data generator*   Generates test data for the program to be tested. This may be accomplished by selecting data from a database or by using patterns to generate random data of the correct form.

3. *Oracle*   Generates predictions of expected test results. Oracles may be either previous program versions or prototype systems. Back-to-back testing involves running the oracle and the program to be tested in parallel. Differences in their outputs are highlighted.

4. *File comparator*   Compares the results of program tests with previous test results and reports differences between them. Comparators are essential in regression testing where the results of executing old and new versions are compared. Differences in these results indicate potential problems with the new version of the system.

5. *Report generator*   Provides report definition and generation facilities for test results.

6. *Dynamic analyser*   Adds code to a program to count the number of times each statement has been executed. After the tests have been run, an execution profile is generated showing how often each program statement has been executed.

7. *Simulator*   Different kinds of simulator may be provided. Target simulators simulate the machine on which the program is to execute. User interface simulators are script-driven programs which simulate multiple simultaneous user interactions. Using simulators for I/O means that the timing of transaction sequences is repeatable.

The testing requirements for large systems depend on the application which is being developed. Consequently, testing workbenches invariably have to be adapted to suit the test plan of each system. Examples of adaptations are:

1. New tools may have to be added to test specific application characteristics. Some existing testing tools may not be required.
2. Scripts may have to be written for user interface simulators and patterns defined for test data generators. Report formats may also have to be defined.
3. Sets of expected test results may have to be prepared manually if no previous program versions are available to serve as an oracle.
4. Special-purpose file comparators may have to be written which include knowledge of the structure of the test results on file.

A significant amount of effort and time is usually needed to create a comprehensive testing workbench. Complete test workbenches as shown in Figure 20.18 are therefore only used when large systems are being developed. For these systems, the overall testing costs may be up to 50 per cent of the total development costs so it is cost-effective to invest in high-quality CASE tool support for testing.

KEY POINTS

▶ It is more important to test the parts of the system which are commonly used rather than parts which are only rarely exercised.

▶ Equivalence partitioning is a way of deriving test cases. It depends on finding partitions in the input and output data sets and exercising the program with values from these partitions. Often, the value which is most likely to lead to a successful test is a value at the boundary of a partition.

▶ Black-box testing does not need access to source code. Test cases are derived from the program specification.

▶ Structural testing relies on analysing a program to determine paths through it and using this analysis to assist with the selection of test cases.

▶ Integration testing should focus on testing the interactions between the components in a system and component interfaces.

▶ Interface defects may arise because of errors made in reading the specification, specification misunderstandings or errors or invalid timing assumptions. Interface testing is intended to discover defects in the interfaces of objects or modules.

▶ When testing object classes, you should design tests that exercise all of the operations associated with a class, assign and evaluate all object attributes and test the object in all possible states.

▶ Object-oriented systems should be integrated around natural clusters of objects such as those associated with a particular use-case or set of use-cases or with object threads.

FURTHER READING

Testing Object-oriented Systems: Models, Patterns and Tools. This is an immense book (1000+ pages) that provides very complete coverage of object-oriented testing. Its completeness means that it shouldn't be the first thing that you read on object-oriented testing (most books on object-oriented development have a testing chapter) but it is the object-oriented equivalent of Beizer's book. (R. V. Binder, 1999, Addison Wesley Longman.)

'How to design practical test cases'. A how-to article on test case design by an author from a Japanese company that has a very good reputation for delivering software with very few faults. (T. Yamaura, *IEEE Software*, 15(6), November 1998.)

'Regression testing in an industrial environment'. This paper discusses the importance of regression testing and gives practical advice on the process. (A. K. Onoma, W-T Tsai, M. Poonawala and H. Suganuma, *Comm ACM*, 41(5), May 1998.)

Software Testing Techniques. This is the definitive book on defect testing for programs which are developed using a function-oriented approach. It is incredibly detailed and thorough. Beizer's approach is practical rather than theoretical and he gives detailed advice for system testers. (B. Beizer, 1990, Van Nostrand Rheinhold.)

EXERCISES

20.1 Discuss the differences between black-box and structural testing and suggest how they can be used together in the defect testing process.

20.2 What testing problems might arise in numerical routines designed to handle very large and very small numbers?

20.3 Derive a set of test cases for the following components:

- A sort routine which sorts arrays of integers.
- A routine which takes a line of text as input and counts the number of non-blank characters in that line.
- A routine which examines a line of text and replaces sequences of blank characters with a single blank character.
- An object that implements variable length character strings. Operations should include concatenation, length (to give the length of a string) and substring selection.
- An object representing a keyed table where entries are made and retrieved using some alphabetic key.

20.4 Program the first three of these routines using a language of your choice and, for each routine, derive its cyclomatic complexity.

20.5 Show, using a small example, why it is practically impossible to exhaustively test a program.

20.6 By examining the code of the routines which you have written, derive further test cases in addition to those you have already considered. Has the code analysis revealed omissions in your initial set of test cases?

20.7 Implement (using Java or C++) an object class called SYMBOL_TABLE which could be used as part of a compilation system. You should include operations to add a name and associated type information to the table, to delete a name, to modify the information associated with a name and to search the table. You should maintain information about where the object is declared. Organise a program inspection of this object (see Chapter 19) and keep a careful account of the errors discovered. Test the object using a black-box approach and compare errors which are revealed by testing with those discovered by inspection.

20.8 Explain why interface testing is necessary given that individual units have been extensively validated through unit testing and program inspections.

20.9 Find out about top-down and bottom-up testing strategies. Discuss why these may be inappropriate for object-oriented systems.

20.10 Derive test cases to test the states of the microwave oven whose state model is defined in Figure 7.5.

21 Critical systems validation

Objectives

The objective of this chapter is to discuss verification and validation techniques that are used in the development of critical systems. When you have read this chapter, you will:

❏ be aware of the arguments for and against the use of formal methods in critical systems verification;

❏ understand how the reliability of a software system can be measured and how reliability growth models are used to predict reliability;

❏ understand how safety assurance is reliant on both system validation and process assurance;

❏ understand the idea of safety proofs and how these may be used to demonstrate that hazards cannot arise in a system.

Contents

21.1 Formal methods and critical systems
21.2 Reliability validation
21.3 Safety assurance
21.4 Security assessment

The verification and validation of a critical system has obviously much in common with the validation of any other system. The V & V processes should demonstrate that the system meets its specification and that the system services and behaviour support the customer's requirements. However, the nature of critical systems is such that it is usually necessary to augment normal analysis and testing with additional processes that are designed to produce evidence that the system is trustworthy. There are two reasons why this is necessary:

1. *Costs of failure* The costs and consequences of critical systems failure are potentially much greater than for non-critical systems. Consequently, it is cost-effective to spend more on verification and validation so that faults may be detected and removed before the system is delivered.

2. *Validation of dependability attributes* Customers for critical systems must be convinced that the specified dependability attributes (availability, reliability, safety and security) have been met by the system. Assessing these attributes requires specific verification and validation activities that I discuss later in this chapter.

For these reasons, the costs of V & V for critical systems is usually much higher than for other classes of system. It is not uncommon for verification and validation to take up more than 50 per cent of the total development costs for critical software systems. This cost is, of course, justified, if an expensive system failure is avoided. For example, in 1996 a mission-critical software system on the Ariane 5 rocket failed and several satellites were destroyed. The consequential loss was hundreds of millions of dollars.

Although the critical systems validation process should mostly focus on validating the system, there should be related activities that verify that defined system development processes have been used. As I discuss in Chapters 18 and 24, system quality is affected by the quality of processes used to develop the system. In short, good processes lead to good systems. Therefore, to produce systems that have high dependability requirements, you need to be confident that a sound development process has been followed.

This process assurance is an inherent part of the ISO 9000 standards for quality management that I discuss briefly in Chapter 24. These standards require the documentation of processes that are used and associated activities that ensure that these processes have been followed. This normally requires the generation of tangible evidence such as signed forms that certify the completion of process activities and product quality checks. ISO 9000 standards specify what tangible process outputs should be produced and who is responsible for producing and checking these forms. In section 21.3.3, I illustrate this using a standard form that records the hazard analysis process.

21.1 Formal methods and critical systems

There is a continuing debate in the critical systems community about the role of formal methods in the safety-critical and security-critical software development process. The use of formal mathematical specification and associated verification is mandated in UK defence standards for safety-critical software (MOD, 1995). However, many critical systems developers are not convinced that formal methods are cost-effective and argue that they may even reduce rather than increase system dependability.

Formal methods may be used at two levels in the development of critical systems:

1.   A formal specification of the system may be developed and mathematically analysed for inconsistency. This technique is effective in discovering specification errors and omissions, as I discussed in Chapter 9. In that chapter, I illustrate the use of a formal technique to specify part of the insulin pump software that I described in Chapter 16.

2.   A formal verification that the code of a software system is consistent with the specification may be developed. This requires a formal specification and is effective in discovering programming and some design errors. A transformational development process (Chapter 3) or a Cleanroom process (Chapter 19) may be used to support the formal verification process.

The argument for the use of formal specification and associated program verification is that formal specification forces a detailed analysis of the specification. It may reveal potential inconsistencies or omissions which might not otherwise be discovered until the system is operational. Formal verification demonstrates that the developed program meets its specification so that implementation errors do not compromise dependability.

The argument against the use of formal specification is that it requires specialised notations. These can only be used by specially trained staff and cannot be understood by domain experts. Hence, problems with the system requirements can be concealed by formality. Software engineers cannot recognise potential difficulties with the requirements because they don't understand the domain; domain experts cannot find these problems because they don't understand the specification. Although the specification may be mathematically consistent it may not specify the system properties that are really required.

Verifying a non-trivial software system takes a great deal of time and requires specialised tools such as theorem provers and mathematical expertise. It is therefore an extremely expensive process and the costs are non-linear. As the system size increases, the costs of formal verification increase disproportionately. Many people therefore think that formal verification is not cost-effective. The same level of safety or security can be achieved at lower cost by using other validation techniques such as inspections and system testing. It is currently impossible either to confirm or refute this assertion as so few systems have been developed using formal methods.

It is sometimes claimed that the use of formal methods for system development leads to more reliable and safer systems. There is no doubt that a formal system specification is less likely to contain anomalies that must be resolved by the system designer. However, formal specification and proof do not guarantee that the software will be reliable in practical use. The reasons for this are:

1. *The specification may not reflect the real requirements of system users* Lutz (1993) discovered that many failures experienced by users were a consequence of specification errors and omissions which could not be detected by formal system specification. Furthermore, users rarely understand formal notations, so cannot read the formal specification directly to find errors and omissions.

2. *The proof may contain errors* Program proofs are large and complex so, like large and complex programs, they usually contain errors.

3. *The proof may assume a usage pattern which is incorrect* If the system is not used as anticipated, the proof may be invalid.

In spite of their disadvantages, my view is that formal methods have an important role to play in the development of safety-related and security-related software. Formal specifications are very effective in discovering specification problems which are the most common causes of system failure. Formal verification increases confidence in the most critical components of these systems. The use of formal approaches is increasing as procurers demand it and as more and more engineers become familiar with these techniques. However, it will be many years before their use is universal for critical systems development.

21.2 Reliability validation

As I explained in Chapter 17, a number of different metrics have been developed that may be used to specify a system's reliability requirements. To validate if the system meets these requirements, you have to measure the reliability of the system as perceived by a typical system user.

The process of measuring the reliability of a system is illustrated in Figure 21.1. This process involves four stages:

1. Existing systems of the same type are studied to establish an operational profile. An operational profile identifies different classes of system inputs and

Figure 21.1
The reliability
measurement
process

the probability of these inputs in normal use. I discuss this in the following section.

2. A set of test data is constructed (sometimes with the help of test data generators) that reflect the operational profile.

3. The system is tested with these data and the number of failures is observed. The times of these failures are also logged. As discussed in Chapter 17, the time units chosen should be appropriate for the reliability metric used.

4. After a statistically significant number of failures have been observed, the software reliability can then be computed. You can then work out the appropriate reliability metric value.

This approach is sometimes called statistical testing. The aim of statistical testing is to assess system reliability. This contrasts with defect testing whose aim is to discover system faults. Prowell *et al.* (1999) discuss statistical testing in their book on Cleanroom software engineering.

This conceptually attractive approach to reliability measurement is not easy to apply in practice. The principal difficulties which arise are due to:

1. *Operational profile uncertainty*   The operational profiles may not be an accurate reflection of the real use of the system.

2. *High costs of test data generation*   Defining a large amount of test data takes a long time if it is not possible to generate this data automatically.

3. *Statistical uncertainty when high reliability is specified*   It is important to generate a statistically significant number of failures to allow accurate reliability measurements.

Developing an accurate operational profile is certainly possible for some types of system that have a standardised pattern of use. For other systems, however, there are many different users who each have their own ways of using the system. As I discussed in Chapter 16, different users can get quite different impressions of reliability because they use different system services and facilities.

By far the best way to generate the large data set that is required for reliability measurement is to use some form of test data generator that can be set up to automatically generate inputs matching the operational profile. However, it is not usually possible to automate the production of all test data for interactive systems. Data sets for these systems have to be generated manually with correspondingly higher costs.

Statistical uncertainty is a general problem when trying to measure the reliability of a system. To make an accurate prediction of reliability, you need to do more than simply cause a single system failure. You have to generate a reasonably large number of failures to be confident that your measurement is accurate. The problem then is the better you get at minimising the number of faults in a system, the harder it becomes to measure the effectiveness of fault minimisation techniques. If very high levels of reliability are specified, it is often impractical to generate enough system failures to check these specifications.

21.2.1   Operational profiles

The operational profile of the software reflects how it will be used in practice. It consists of a specification of classes of input and the probability of their occurrence. When a new software system replaces an existing manual or automated system, it is reasonably easy to assess the probable pattern of usage of the new software. It should roughly correspond to the existing usage with some allowance made for the new functionality which is (presumably) included in the new software. For example, an operational profile can be specified for telecommunication switching systems because telecommunication companies know the call patterns which these systems have to handle.

Typically, the operational profile is such that the inputs which have the highest probability of being generated fall into a small number of classes as shown on the left of Figure 21.2. There is an extremely large number of classes where inputs are highly improbable but not impossible. These are shown on the right of Figure 21.2. The ellipsis (. . .) means that there are many more of these unusual inputs which are not shown.

Musa (1993, 1998) suggests guidelines for the development of operational profiles. In the application domain in which he worked (telecommunication systems), there is a long history of collecting usage data, so the process of operational profile development is relatively straightforward. For a system taking about 15 person-years

Figure 21.2
An operational
profile

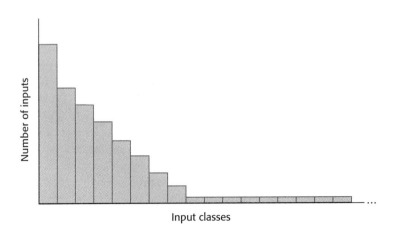

Input classes

of development, an operational profile was developed in about 1 person-month. In other cases, operational profile generation took longer (2–3 person-years) but the cost, of course, is written off over a number of system releases. Musa reckons that his company (a telecommunications company) had at least a 10-fold return on the investment required to develop an operational profile.

However, when a software system is new and innovative it is more difficult to anticipate how it will be used. Systems are used by a range of users with different expectations, backgrounds and experience. There is no historical usage database. Computer users often make use of systems in ways which are not anticipated by their developers. The problem is further compounded by the fact that the operational profile may change as the system is used. When the abilities and confidence of users change as they gain experience with the system, they may use it in more sophisticated ways. Because of these difficulties, Hamlet (1992) suggests that it is often impossible to develop a trustworthy operational profile. It is therefore difficult to estimate the degree of uncertainty in the reliability measurements.

21.2.2 Reliability prediction

During software validation, managers have to assign effort to system testing. As testing is very expensive, it is important to stop testing as soon as possible and not to 'over-test' the system. Testing can stop when the required level of system reliability has been achieved. Sometimes, of course, reliability predictions may reveal that the required level of reliability will never be achieved. In this case, the manager must make difficult decisions about rewriting parts of the software or renegotiating the system contract.

A reliability growth model is a model of how the system reliability changes over time during the testing process. As system failures are discovered, the underlying faults causing these failures are repaired so that the reliability of the system should improve during system testing and debugging. To predict reliability, the conceptual reliability growth model must then be translated into a mathematical model. I do not go into this level of detail here but simply discuss the conceptual notion of reliability growth.

There are various models which have been derived from reliability experiments in a number of different application domains. The simplest reliability growth model is a step function model (Jelinski and Moranda, 1972) where the reliability increases by a constant increment each time a fault is discovered and repaired (Figure 21.3). This model assumes that software repairs are always correctly implemented so that the number of software faults and associated failures decreases with time. As repairs are made, the rate of occurrence of software failures (ROCOF) should therefore decrease as shown in Figure 21.3. Note that the time periods on the horizontal axis reflect the time between releases of the system for testing so they are normally of unequal length.

In practice, however, debugging sometimes fails to fix software faults and the code change may introduce new faults into the system. The probability of occurrence of

Figure 21.3
Equal-step function
model of reliability
growth

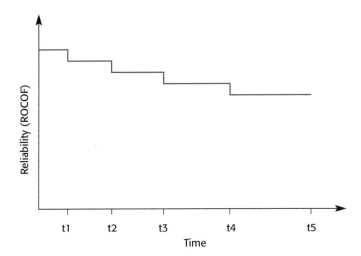

these faults may be higher than the occurrence probability of the fault which has been repaired. Therefore, the system reliability may worsen rather than improve.

The simple equal-step reliability growth model also assumes that all faults contribute equally to reliability and that each fault repair contributes the same amount of reliability growth. However, not all faults are equally probable. Repairing the most common faults contributes more to reliability growth than repairing faults which only occur occasionally. Therefore, the growth of reliability is not constant in each time increment.

Later models, such as that suggested by Littlewood and Verrall (1973), take these problems into account by introducing a random element into the reliability growth improvement effected by a software repair. Thus, each repair does not result in an equal amount of reliability improvement but varies depending on the random perturbation (Figure 21.4).

Figure 21.4
Random-step
function model of
reliability growth

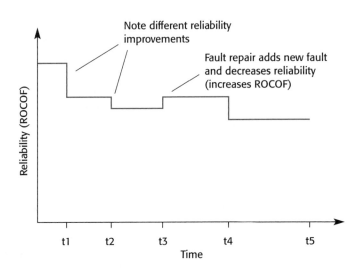

Figure 21.5
Reliability prediction

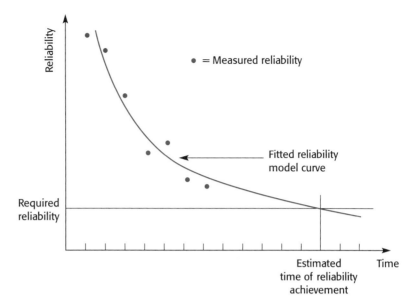

Littlewood and Verrall's model allows for negative reliability growth when a software repair introduces further errors. It also models the fact that as faults are repaired, the average improvement in reliability per repair decreases. The reason for this is that the most probable faults are likely to be discovered early in the testing process. Repairing these contributes most to reliability growth.

The above models are discrete models that reflect incremental reliability growth. When a new version of the software with repaired faults is delivered for testing it should have a lower ROCOF than the previous version. However, to predict the reliability that will be achieved after a given amount of testing, continuous mathematical models are needed. Many different models, derived from different application domains, have been proposed and compared (Musa *et al.*, 1987; Abdel-Ghaly *et al.*, 1986).

Simplistically, reliability can be predicted by matching the measured reliability data to a known reliability model. This model is then extrapolated to the required level of reliability. The time that this will be achieved can then be read off the graph (Figure 21.5). Therefore, testing and debugging must continue until that time.

Predicting system reliability from a reliability model has two principal benefits:

1. *Planning of testing*   Given the current testing schedule, the time when testing will be completed can be predicted. If this is after the planned delivery schedule for the system then additional testing resources may have to be deployed to accelerate the rate of reliability growth.

2. *Customer negotiations*   Sometimes the reliability model shows that the growth of reliability is very slow and that a disproportionate amount of testing effort is required for relatively little benefit. It may be worth renegotiating the

reliability requirements with the customer. Alternatively, it may be that the model predicts that the required reliability is unlikely ever to be reached. In this case, requirements renegotiation is essential.

Readers who are interested in more detail about reliability growth and reliability growth models should refer to Musa's book and the articles by Littlewood referenced here. Various authors have described their practical experience of the use of reliability growth models (Schneidewind and Keller, 1992; Sheldon *et al.*, 1992; Ehrlich *et al.*, 1993).

21.3 Safety assurance

Safety assurance and reliability validation are quite different processes. It is possible to specify reliability quantitatively using some metric and then to measure the reliability of the completed system. Safety cannot be meaningfully specified in a quantitative way and so it cannot therefore be measured when a system is tested.

Safety validation is therefore concerned with establishing a confidence level in the system which might vary from 'very low' through to 'very high'. This is a matter for professional judgement. In many cases, this confidence is partly based on the experience of the organisation developing the system. If a company has previously developed a number of control systems that have operated safely then it is reasonable to assume that they will continue to develop safe systems of this type. However, such an assessment must be backed up by tangible evidence from the system design, the results of system verification and validation and the system development processes that have been used.

21.3.1 Verification and validation

The verification and validation of safety-critical systems has much in common with the testing of any other systems with high reliability requirements. There must be extensive testing to discover as many defects as possible and statistical testing should be used to assess the system reliability. However, because of the ultra-low failure rates required in many safety-critical systems, statistical testing cannot always provide a quantitative estimate of the system reliability because of the unrealistically large number of tests required. The tests simply give evidence that is used with other evidence such as the results of reviews and static checking (see Chapter 19) to judge the system safety.

Extensive reviews are essential during a safety-oriented development process. Parnas *et al.* (1990) suggest five types of review that should be mandatory for safety-critical systems:

1. review for correct intended function;
2. review for maintainable, understandable structure;
3. review to verify that the algorithm and data structure design are consistent with the specified behaviour;
4. review the consistency of the code and the algorithm and data structure design;
5. review the adequacy of the system test cases.

An assumption that underlies work in system safety is that the number of system faults which can lead to hazards is significantly less than the total number of faults which may exist in the system. Safety assurance can concentrate on these faults with hazard potential. If it can be demonstrated that these faults cannot occur or, if they occur, the associated hazard will not result in an accident, then the system is safe. This is the basis of safety arguments which I discuss in the next section.

21.3.2   Safety arguments

Proofs of program correctness have been proposed as a software verification technique for over 25 years. However, these have been little used except in research laboratories. The practical problems of constructing a correctness proof are so great that few organisations have considered them to be cost-effective in normal system development. However, as I discussed earlier in this chapter, for some critical applications, it may be economic to develop correctness proofs to increase confidence that the system meets its safety or security requirements.

Although it may not be cost-effective to develop correctness proofs for most systems, it is sometimes possible to develop a safety argument that demonstrates that the program meets its safety obligations. It is not necessary to prove that the program meets its specification. It is only necessary to demonstrate that program execution cannot result in an unsafe state.

The most effective technique for demonstrating the safety of a system is proof by contradiction. This means assuming that the unsafe state (identified by the hazard analysis) can be reached by executing the program. You then systematically analyse the code and show that the pre-conditions for this hazardous state are contradicted by the post-conditions of all program paths leading to that state. If this is the case, the initial assumption of an unsafe state is incorrect. If this is repeated for all identified hazards then the software is safe.

As an example, consider the code in Figure 21.6 which might be part of the implementation of the insulin delivery system. Some comments have been added to this code to relate it to the fault tree shown in Figure 17.6.

Developing a safety argument for this code involves demonstrating that the dose of insulin administered is never greater than some maximum level which is established for each individual diabetic. Therefore, it is not necessary to prove that the system delivers the 'correct' dose, merely that it never delivers an overdose to the patient.

To construct the safety argument, you identify the pre-condition for the unsafe state which, in this case, is that currentDose > maxDose. You then demonstrate that

Figure 21.6 Insulin
delivery code

```
-- The insulin dose to be delivered is a function of
-- blood sugar level, the previous dose delivered and
-- the time of delivery of the previous dose

    currentDose = computeInsulin () ;

    // Safety check - adjust currentDose if necessary

    // if statement 1

    if (previousDose == 0)
    {
        if (currentDose > 16)
            currentDose = 16 ;
    }
    else
        if (currentDose > (previousDose * 2) )
            currentDose = previousDose * 2 ;

    // if statement 2

    if ( currentDose < minimumDose )
            currentDose = 0 ;
    else if ( currentDose > maxDose )
            currentDose = maxDose ;
    administerInsulin (currentDose) ;
```

all program paths lead to a contradiction of this unsafe assertion. If this is the case, the unsafe condition cannot be true. Therefore, the system is safe.

Safety arguments, such as that shown in Figure 21.7, are much shorter than formal system verifications. You first identify all possible paths that lead to the potentially unsafe state. You work backwards from this unsafe state and consider the last assignment to all state variables on each path leading to it. Previous computations (such as if-statement 1 in Figure 21.7) do not have to be considered in the safety argument. In this example, all you need be concerned with are the set of possible values of currentDose immediately before the administerInsulin method is executed.

In the safety argument shown in Figure 21.7, there are three possible program paths which lead to the call to the administerInsulin method:

1. Neither branch of if-statement 2 is executed. This can only happen if currentDose is either greater than or equal to minimumDose and less than or equal to maxDose.

2. The then branch of if-statement 2 is executed. In this case, the assignment setting currentDose to zero is executed. Therefore, its post-condition is currentDose = 0.

3. The else if-branch of if-statement 2 is executed. In this case, the assignment setting currentDose to maxDose is executed. Therefore, its post-condition is currentDose = maxDose.

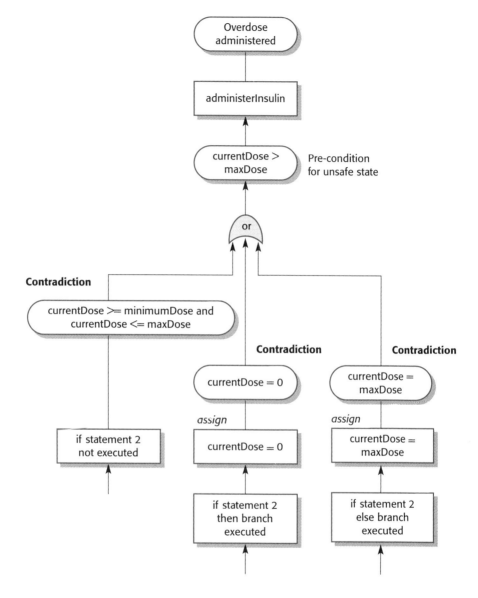

Figure 21.7
Informal safety
argument based
on demonstrating
contradictions

In all three cases, the post-conditions contradict the unsafe pre-condition, so the system is safe.

21.3.3 Process assurance

I have already discussed the importance of assuring the quality of the system development process in the introduction to this chapter. This is important for all critical systems but it is particularly important for safety-critical systems. There are two reasons for this:

1. Accidents are rare events in critical systems and it may be practically imposs-
    ible to simulate them during the testing of a system.

2. Safety requirements, as I discussed in Chapter 16, are sometimes 'shall not'
    requirements that exclude unsafe system behaviour. It is impossible to demon-
    strate conclusively through testing and other validation activities that these require-
    ments have been met.

The life-cycle model for safety-critical systems development makes clear that
explicit attention should be paid to safety during all stages of the software process.
This means that specific safety assurance activities must be included in the process.
These include:

1. The creation of a hazard logging and monitoring system that traces hazards from
    preliminary hazard analysis through to testing and system validation.

2. The appointment of project safety engineers who have explicit responsibility
    for the safety aspects of the system.

3. The extensive use of safety reviews throughout the development process.

4. The creation of a safety certification system whereby safety-critical components
    are formally certified for their assessed safety.

5. The use of a very detailed configuration management system (see Chapter 29)
    which is used to track all safety-related documentation and keep it in step with
    the associated technical documentation. There is little point in having stringent
    validation procedures if a failure of configuration management means that the
    wrong system is delivered to the customer.

To illustrate what is involved in process validation, I use the hazard analysis process which is an essential part of safety-critical systems development. Recall from
Chapter 17 that hazard analysis is concerned with the identification and analysis of
hazards. The process is a continuing one throughout the system development. It is
important to be able to demonstrate that hazards have been properly considered at
all stages in the process.

If the development process includes clear traceability from hazard identification
through to the system itself then an argument can be made why these hazards will
not result in accidents. This may be supplemented by safety arguments as discussed
in section 21.3.2. Where external certification is required before a system is used
(e.g. in an aircraft), it is usually a condition of certification that this traceability can
be demonstrated.

The central safety document is the hazard log where hazards identified during
the specification process are documented and traced. This hazard log is then used
at each stage of the software development process to assess how that development

Figure 21.8
A simplified hazard
log page

Hazard Log.   **Page 4: Printed 20.02.99**
System: Insulin Pump System | *File: InsulinPump/Safety/HazardLog*
Safety Engineer: James Brown | *Log version: 1/3*
Identified Hazard | Insulin overdose delivered to patient
Identified by | Jane Williams
Criticality class | 1
Identified risk | High
Fault tree identified | YES *Date* 24.01.99 *Location* Hazard Log, Page 5
Fault tree creators | Jane Williams and Bill Smith
Fault tree checked | YES *Date* 28.01.99 *Checker* James Brown

System safety design requirements

1. The system shall include self-testing software that will test the sensor system, the clock and the insulin delivery system.

2. The self-checking software shall be executed once per minute.

3. In the event of the self-checking software discovering a fault in any of the system components, an audible warning shall be issued and the pump display should indicate the name of the component where the fault has been discovered. The delivery of insulin should be suspended.

4. The system shall incorporate an override system that allows the system user to modify the computed dose of insulin that is to be delivered by the system.

5. The amount of override should be limited to be no greater than a pre-set value that is set when the system is configured by medical staff.

stage has taken the hazards into account. A simplified example of a hazard log entry for the insulin delivery system is shown in Figure 21.8. This documents the process of hazard analysis and shows design requirements that have been generated during this process.

As shown in Figure 21.8, individuals who have some safety responsibilities should be explicitly identified. It is important to appoint a project safety engineer who should not be involved in the system development. The responsibility of this engineer is to ensure that appropriate safety checks have been made and documented. The system procurer may also require an independent safety assessor to be appointed from an outside organisation who reports directly to the client on safety matters.

In many types of application, system engineers who have safety responsibilities must be certified engineers. In the UK, this means that they have to have been accepted as a member of one of the engineering institutes (civil, electrical, mechanical, etc.) and have to be chartered engineers. Inexperienced, poorly qualified engineers may not take responsibility for safety. This does not currently apply to software engineers. However, future process standards for safety-critical software development may require that project safety engineers should be formally certified engineers with a defined minimum level of training.

Run-time safety checking

The notion of defensive programming was introduced in Chapter 18 where redundant statements were added to programs to check for possible system faults. A similar technique can be used in safety-critical systems. Checking code can be added that checks a safety constraint and that throws an exception if that constraint is violated. The safety constraints that should always hold at particular points in a program may be expressed as assertions. Assertions are predicates that describe conditions which must hold before the following statement can be executed. In safety-critical systems, the assertions should be generated from the safety specification. They are intended to assure safe behaviour rather than behaviour which conforms to the specification.

Assertions can be particularly valuable to assure the safety of communications between components of the system. For example, in the insulin delivery system, the dose of insulin administered involves generating signals to the insulin pump to deliver a specified number of insulin increments (Figure 21.9). The number of insulin increments associated with the allowed maximum insulin dose can be pre-computed and included as an assertion in the system.

Therefore, if there has been an error in the computation of currentDose, the state variable that holds the amount of insulin to be delivered, or if this value has been corrupted in some way then this will be trapped at this stage. An excessive dose of insulin will not be delivered as the check in the method ensures that the pump will not deliver more than maxDose.

From the safety assertions that are included as program comments, code to check these assertions can be generated as illustrated in Figure 21.9. In principle, much of this code generation could be automated using an assertion preprocessor. However, these are rarely available and assertion code is normally generated by hand.

Figure 21.9 Insulin administration

```
static void administerInsulin ( ) throws SafetyException {

    int maxIncrements = InsulinPump.maxDose / 8 ;
    int increments = InsulinPump.currentDose / 8 ;

    // assert currentDose <= InsulinPump.maxDose

    if (InsulinPump.currentDose > InsulinPump.maxDose)
        throw new SafetyException (Pump.doseHigh) ;
    else
        for (int i = 1 ; i <= increments; i++)
        {
            generateSignal () ;
            if (i > maxIncrements)
                throw new SafetyException ( Pump.incorrectIncrements) ;
        } // for loop

} //administerInsulin
```

21.4 Security assessment

The assessment of system security is becoming increasingly important as more and more systems are connected to the Internet. As I discussed in Chapter 16, security requirements are similar to safety requirements in some respects in that they are often 'shall not' requirements. That is, they specify system behaviour that is disallowed rather than behaviour that is expected of the system. However, it is not usually possible to define this behaviour as simple constraints that may be checked by the system.

A fundamental difference between safety and security is that safety problems are usually accidental whereas attacks on a system are malicious. Even in systems that have been in use for many years, an ingenious attacker can discover a new form of attack and can penetrate what was thought to be a secure system. For example, the RSA algorithm for data encryption that was thought to be secure was cracked in 1999.

There are four complementary approaches to security checking:

1. *Experience-based validation*   In this case, the system is analysed against types of attack that are known to the validation team. This type of validation is usually carried out in conjunction with tool-based validation.

2. *Tool-based validation*   In this case, various security tools such as password-checkers are used to analyse the system. This is really an extension of experience-based validation where the experience is embodied in the tools used.

3. *Tiger teams*   In this case, a team is set up and given the objective of breaching the system security. They simulate attacks on the system and use their ingenuity to discover new ways to compromise the system security.

4. *Formal verification*   A system can be verified against a formal security specification. However, as in other areas, formal verification for security is not widely used.

It is very difficult for end-users of a system to verify its security. Consequently, as discussed by Gollmann (1999), bodies in North America and in Europe have established sets of security evaluation criteria that can be checked by specialised evaluators. Software product suppliers can submit their products for evaluation and certification against these criteria.

Therefore, if you have a requirement for a particular level of security, you can choose a product that has been validated to that level. However, many products are not security-certified and the certification applies to individual products. When the certified system is used in conjunction with other uncertified systems, such as locally developed software, then the security level of the overall system cannot be assessed.

KEY POINTS

▶ Because of the high costs of failure of critical systems, verification and validation techniques such as formal specification and proof that are normally too expensive may be cost-effective for critical systems.

▶ Statistical testing is used to estimate software reliability. It relies on testing the system with a test data set which reflects the operational profile of the software. Test data may be generated automatically.

▶ Reliability growth models model the change in reliability as faults are removed from software during the testing process. Reliability models can be used to predict when the required reliability will be achieved.

▶ Safety proofs are an effective product safety assurance technique. They show that an identified hazardous condition can never occur. They are usually simpler than proving that a program meets its specification.

▶ It is important to have a well-defined, certified process for safety-critical systems development. The process must include the identification and monitoring of potential hazards.

▶ Security validation may be carried out using experience-based analysis, tool-based analysis or by using 'tiger teams' to simulate attacks on the system.

FURTHER READING

Software Reliability Engineering: More Reliable Software, Faster Development and Testing. This is probably the definitive book on the use of operational profiles and reliability models for reliability assessment. It includes details of experiences with statistical testing. (J. D. Musa, 1998, McGraw-Hill.)

Safety-critical Computer Systems. This excellent textbook includes a particularly good chapter on the place of formal methods in the development of safety-critical systems. (N. Storey, 1996, Addison-Wesley.)

Safeware: System Safety and Computers. Includes a good chapter on the validation of safety-critical systems with more detail than I have given here on the use of safety arguments based around fault trees. (N. Leveson, 1995, Addison-Wesley.)

EXERCISES

21.1 Describe how you would go about validating the reliability specification for a supermarket system that you specified in Exercise 17.3. Your answer should include a description of any validation tools which might be used.

21.2 Explain why it is practically impossible to validate reliability specifications when these are expressed in terms of a very small number of failures over the total lifetime of a system.

21.3 Using the literature as background information, write a report for management (who have no previous experience in this area) on the use of reliability growth models.

21.4 Is it ethical for an engineer to agree to deliver a software system with known faults to a customer? Does it make any difference if the customer is told of the existence of these faults in advance? Would it be reasonable to make claims about the reliability of the software in such circumstances?

21.5 Explain why ensuring system reliability is not a guarantee of system safety.

21.6 The door lock control mechanism in a nuclear waste storage facility is designed for safe operation. It ensures that entry to the storeroom is only permitted when radiation shields are in place or when the radiation level in the room falls below some given value (dangerLevel). That is,

(i)   If remotely controlled radiation shields are in place within a room, the door may be opened by an authorised operator.
(ii) If the radiation level in a room is below a specified value, the door may be opened by an authorised operator.
(iii) An authorised operator is identified by the input of an authorised door entry code.

The Java code shown in Figure 21.10 is used to control the door locking mechanism. Note that the safe state is that entry should not be permitted.

Develop a safety argument that shows that this code is potentially unsafe. Modify the code to make it safe.

21.7 Using the specification for the dosage computation given in Chapter 9 (Figure 9.11), write the Java method computeInsulin as used in Figure 21.6. Construct an informal safety argument that this code is safe.

21.8 Suggest how you would go about validating a password protection system for an application that you have developed. Explain the function of any tools that you think may be useful.

21.9 Assume you were part of a team which developed software for a chemical plant which went wrong and caused a serious pollution incident. Your boss is interviewed on television and states that the validation process is comprehensive and that there are no faults in the software. She asserts that the problems must be due to poor operational procedures. The system operators reject this and propose to go on strike. Discuss how you might handle this situation.

Figure 21.10 Door
lock controller

```
1    entryCode = lock.getEntryCode () ;
2    if (entryCode == lock.authorisedCode)
3    {
4        shieldStatus = Shield.getStatus () ;
5        radiationLevel = RadSensor.get () ;
6        if (radiationLevel < dangerLevel)
7            state = safe ;
8        else
9            state = unsafe ;
10       if (shieldStatus == Shield.inPlace() )
11           state = safe ;
12       if (state == safe)
13           {
14               Door.locked = false ;
15               Door.unlock () ;
16           }
17       else
18       {
19           Door.lock () ;
20           Door.locked := true ;
21       }
22   }
```

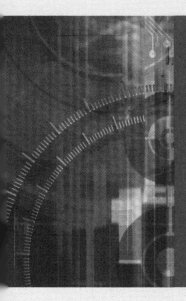

PART SIX

Management

22 Managing people

Objectives

The objective of this chapter is to discuss the importance of people in the software engineering process. When you have read the chapter, you will:

❑ understand simple models of human memory, problem solving and motivation and some implications of this for software managers;

❑ understand the key issues of team working, namely team composition, team cohesiveness, team communications and team organisation;

❑ understand some of the issues involved in selecting and retaining staff in a software development organisation;

❑ have been introduced to the P-CMM – a model that is a framework for enhancing the capabilities of software developers in an organisation.

Contents

22.1   Limits to thinking
22.2   Group working
22.3   Choosing and keeping people
22.4   The People Capability Maturity Model

The people working in a software organisation are its greatest assets. They represent intellectual capital and it is up to software managers to ensure that the organisation gets the best possible return on its investment in people. In successful companies and economies, this is achieved when people are respected by the organisation. They should have a level of responsibility and reward that is commensurate with their skills.

Effective management is therefore about managing the people in an organisation. Project managers have to solve technical and non-technical problems by using the people in their team in the most effective way possible. They have to motivate people, plan and organise their work and ensure that the work is being done properly. Poor management of people is one of the most significant contributors to project failure.

I base my discussion of management on cognitive and social factors rather than any, currently fashionable, management theory. Software engineering is a cognitive and social activity, so these factors are important in developing an understanding of how people write software. If managers have some understanding of these fundamentals, they can do a better job of getting the best from the people who work for them.

22.1 Limits to thinking

There is great diversity in individual abilities reflecting differences in intelligence, education and experience but most of us seem to be subject to some basic constraints on our thinking. These are a consequence of the way in which information is stored and modelled in our brains. You don't need to understand cognitive information processing in detail. However, I think that an awareness of the limits to the way we think is important. It helps explain why some software engineering techniques are effective and gives you insights into interactions between people in a software development team.

22.1.1   Memory organisation

Software systems are abstract entities and engineers have to remember their characteristics during the development process. For example, programmers must understand and remember the relationship between a source code listing and the dynamic behaviour of the program. They apply this stored knowledge in further program development.

The organisation of human memory seems to be hierarchical with three distinct, connected areas (Figure 22.1):

Figure 22.1
Human memory
organisation

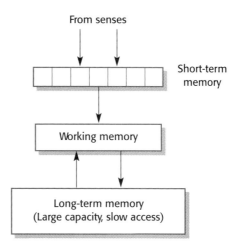

1. *A limited capacity, fast-access, short-term memory*   Input from the senses is received here for initial processing. This memory is comparable with registers in a computer; it is used for information processing and not information storage.

2. *A larger capacity, working memory area*   This memory area has a longer access time than short-term memory. It is used for information processing but can retain information for longer periods than short-term memory. It is not used for long-term information retention. By analogy with a computer, this is like RAM where information is maintained for the duration of a computation.

3. *Long-term memory*   This has a large capacity, relatively slow access time and unreliable retrieval mechanisms (we forget things). Long-term memory is used for the 'permanent' storage of information. To continue the analogy, long-term memory is like disk memory on a computer.

Problem information is input to the short-term memory from reading documents and talking to people. This is integrated with other relevant information from long-term memory in the working memory. The result of this integration forms the basis for problem solutions. These are stored in long-term memory for future use. Of course, the solution may be incorrect. As more information becomes available, long-term memory must be modified. However, incorrect information is not completely discarded but is retained in some form. We know this because we learn from our mistakes.

The limited size of short-term memory constrains our cognitive processes. In a classic experiment, Miller (1957) found that the short-term memory can store about seven quanta of information. A quantum of information is not a fixed size but is rather a coherent information entity. It may be a telephone number, the purpose of an object or a street name. Miller also describes the process of 'chunking' where information quanta are collected together into chunks.

If a problem involves the input of more information than the short-term memory can handle, there has to be information processing and transfer during the input

Figure 22.2
Cognitive 'chunks'
in a sort program

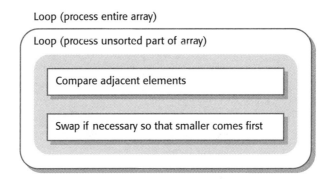

process. This can result in information being lost. Errors arise because this information processing cannot keep up with the memory input.

Shneiderman (1980) suggests that an information chunking process is used in understanding programs. Program readers abstract the information in the program into chunks which are built into an internal semantic structure. Programs are not understood on a statement-by-statement basis unless a statement represents a logical chunk. Figure 22.2 shows how a simple sorting program might be 'chunked' by someone trying to understand it.

Once the internal semantic structure representing the program has been established, this knowledge is transferred to long-term memory. If it is regularly used, it is not usually forgotten. It can be reproduced in different notations without much difficulty. Therefore, we seem to learn in terms of high-level abstractions and not in terms of low-level details.

The knowledge acquired during software development and stored in long-term memory falls into two classes:

1. *Semantic knowledge*   This is the knowledge of concepts such as the operation of an assignment statement, the notion of an object class, how a hash search technique operates and how organisations are structured. This knowledge is acquired through experience and learning and is retained in a representation-independent fashion.

2. *Syntactic knowledge*   This is detailed representation knowledge such as how to write an object description in the UML, what standard functions are available in a programming language, whether an assignment is written using an '=' or a ':=' sign, etc. This knowledge seems to be retained in an unprocessed form.

This knowledge organisation is illustrated in Figure 22.3, adapted from Shneiderman's (1992) book on user interface design. This diagram suggests that semantic and task knowledge is organised and structured. Relationships between different knowledge fragments have been constructed. By contrast, syntactic knowledge is arbitrary and disorganised. It is therefore easier to forget and to make mistakes using this type of knowledge.

Semantic knowledge is acquired by experience and through active learning. New information is consciously integrated with existing semantic structures. Syntactic

Figure 22.3 Syntactic
and semantic
knowledge

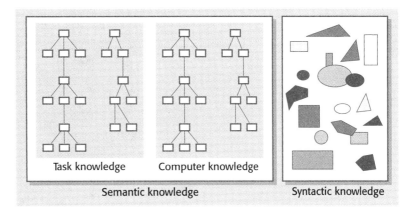

knowledge, however, seems to be acquired by memorisation. New syntactic knowledge is not immediately integrated with existing knowledge but may interfere with
it. It is more easily forgotten than deeper semantic knowledge.

The different acquisition modes for syntactic and semantic knowledge help
explain how experienced programmers learn a new programming language. They
have no difficulty understanding language concepts such as assignments, loops, conditional statements, etc. The language syntax, however, tends to get mixed up with
the syntax of familiar languages. Therefore, an Ada programmer learning Java might
write the assignment operator as ':=' rather than '='.

As an understanding of a concept develops, it is stored in memory as semantic
knowledge. Semantic knowledge appears to be stored in an abstract conceptual form.
The concept details can be regenerated in a number of different concrete representations (Soloway *et al.*, 1982; Card *et al.*, 1983).

For example, consider the binary search algorithm where an ordered collection is
searched for a particular item. This involves examining the mid-point of the collection and using knowledge of the ordering relationship to check if the key item is in
the upper or the lower part of the collection. A programmer who understands this
algorithm can easily produce a version in Java, Ada or other programming language.

This model explains why, for many people, learning to program is a skill that
seems to arrive all at once, after a period of difficulties. Programming skills require
an understanding of the semantic concepts and a separation of semantic and syntactic concepts. Instructors sometimes have difficulties understanding student problems.
They have successfully understood and processed the semantic information, so only
have to consider syntactic information. They may therefore find it hard to explain
the semantic concepts in ways that novice programmers can understand.

22.1.2   Problem solving

Devising and writing a program is a problem solving process. To develop a software system, you must understand the problem, work out a solution strategy then

Figure 22.4
Problem solving

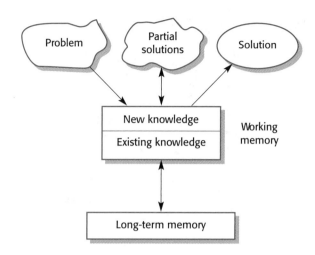

translate it into a program. The first stage involves the problem statement entering working memory from short-term memory. It is integrated with existing knowledge from long-term memory and analysed to work out an overall solution. Finally, the general solution is refined into an executable program (Figure 22.4).

Problem solving generally requires task and computer concepts to be integrated. Organisational factors such as the need to complete a solution within budget are important. Thus, a user may be expert in the task concepts, a software designer an expert in the computer concepts and a manager an expert in the organisation factors. During the software engineering process, all of this expertise may have to be used and integrated.

The development of the solution (the program) involves building an internal semantic model of the problem and a corresponding model of the solution. When this model has been built, it may be represented in any appropriate syntactic notation. The process of program design is therefore an iterative process involving several steps:

1. Integrate existing computer and task knowledge to create new knowledge and hence understand the problem. Curtis (Curtis *et al.*, 1988) suggests that application experience is particularly important at this stage.

2. Construct a semantic model of the solution. Test this against the problem and refine it until it is satisfactory.

3. Represent the model in some programming language or design notation.

When managers have to make decisions on who should be involved in a long-term project, they should consider overall problem solving ability and domain experience rather than specific programming language skills. Once a problem has been understood, experienced programmers will have roughly the same degree of difficulty in writing a program, irrespective of the programming language used. Language skills are necessary and take time to develop (particularly for complex languages like C++) but in my experience it is much easier to learn a specific programming language than it is to develop problem solving skills.

The translation from semantic model to program is more likely to be error-free if the programming language includes constructs that match the lowest-level semantic structures that the programmer understands. These vary from individual to individual but probably correspond with concepts such as assignments, loops, conditional statements, information hiding, objects, inheritance, etc. The closer the fit between the programming language and these concepts, the easier it is to write the program.

Programs written in high-level languages like Java should therefore contain fewer errors than those written in assembly code because low-level semantic concepts can be encoded directly as language statements. However, problems may arise if functional and object-oriented concepts are mixed up. These can be a problem if a company has standardised on one type of method for analysis (e.g. SADT) but uses an object-oriented design and programming process.

The model also explains why structured programming (see Chapter 18) is the best strategy for organising program control. It is based on semantic concepts such as loops and conditional statements. The programmer's short-term memory is not overloaded and so he or she is less likely to make mistakes. Structured programs are easier to understand because you can read them from top to bottom. The abstractions involved in forming chunks can be made sequentially without looking at other parts of the program. Short-term memory can be devoted to a single section of code. Information from working memory about other parts of the program which interfere with that section does not have to be retrieved.

22.1.3   Motivation

One of the roles of project managers is to motivate the people who work for them. Maslow (1954) suggested that people are motivated by satisfying their needs and that needs were arranged in a series of levels as shown in Figure 22.5. The lower levels of this hierarchy represent fundamental needs for food, sleep, etc. and the need to feel secure in an environment. Social needs are concerned with the need to feel part of a social grouping. Esteem needs are the need to feel respected by others and self-realisation needs are concerned with personal development. Human priorities are to satisfy lower-level needs like hunger before the more abstract, higher-level needs.

People working in software development organisations are not usually hungry or thirsty and generally do not feel physically threatened by their environment. Therefore, ensuring the satisfaction of social, esteem and self-realisation needs is most significant from a management point of view:

1. Satisfying social needs means allowing people time to meet their co-workers and providing places for them to meet. Informal, easy-to-use communication channels such as electronic mail are very important.

Figure 22.5 Human
needs hierarchy

2. To satisfy esteem needs you need to show people that they are valued by the organisation. Public recognition of achievements is a simple yet effective way of doing this. Obviously, people must also feel that they are paid at a level that reflects their skills and experience.

3. Finally, to satisfy self-realisation needs you need to give people responsibility for their own work, assign them demanding (but not impossible) tasks and provide a training programme where people can develop their skills.

In a psychological study into motivation, Bass and Dunteman (1963) classified professionals into three types:

1. *Task-oriented* who are motivated by the work they do. In software engineering, they are technicians who are motivated by the intellectual challenge of software development.

2. *Self-oriented* who are principally motivated by personal success and recognition. They are interested in software development as a means of achieving their own goals.

3. *Interaction-oriented* who are motivated by the presence and actions of co-workers. As software development becomes more user-centred, interaction-oriented individuals are becoming more and more involved in software engineering.

Interaction-oriented personalities usually like to work as part of a group whereas task-oriented and self-oriented people often prefer to work alone. Women are more likely to be interaction-oriented than men. They are often more effective communicators.

Each individual's motivation is made up of elements of each class but one type of motivation is usually dominant at any one time. However, personalities are not static and individuals can change. For example, technical people who feel they are not being properly rewarded can become self-oriented and put personal interests before technical concerns.

The problem with Maslow's model of motivation is that it takes an exclusively personal viewpoint on motivation. It does not take adequate account of the fact that people feel themselves to be part of an organisation, a professional group and, usually, some culture. People are not just motivated by personal needs but are also motivated by the goals of these broader groups. Being a member of a cohesive group is highly motivating to most people. People with fulfilling jobs often like to go to work because they are motivated by the people they work with and by the work that they do.

22.2 Group working

Most professional software is developed by project teams ranging in size from two to several hundred people. However, as it is clearly impossible for everyone in a large team to work together effectively on a single problem, these large teams are usually split into a number of groups. Each group is responsible for a sub-project that is developing some sub-system. As a general rule, software engineering project groups should normally have no more than eight members. When small groups are used, communication problems are reduced. The whole group can get round a table for a meeting and can meet in each other's offices. Complex communication structures are not required.

Putting together a group which works effectively is therefore a critical management task. It is obviously important that the group should have the right balance of technical skills and experience and personalities. However, successful groups are more than simply a collection of individuals with the right balance of skills. A good group has a team spirit so that the people involved are motivated by the success of the group as well as their own personal goals. Therefore, managers should promote explicit 'team building' activities to help establish this essential feeling of group loyalty.

There are a number of factors that influence group working:

1. *Group composition* Is there the right balance of skills, experience and personalities in the team?
2. *Group cohesiveness* Does the group think of itself as a team rather than as a collection of individuals who are working together?
3. *Group communications* Do the members of the group communicate effectively with each other?
4. *Group organisation* Is the team organised in such a way that everyone feels valued and is satisfied with their role in the group?

22.2.1 Group composition

Many software engineers are motivated primarily by their work. Software development groups, therefore, are often composed of people who have their own idea on how technical problems should be solved. This is borne out by regularly reported problems of interface standards being ignored, systems being redesigned as they are coded, unnecessary system embellishments, etc. Selecting the right members for a project group is essential if these kinds of problem are to be avoided.

A group which has complementary personalities may work better than a group which has been selected solely on technical ability. People who are motivated by the work are likely to be the strongest technically. People who are self-oriented will probably be best at pushing the work forward to finish the job. People who are interaction-oriented help with communications within the group. I think that it is particularly important to have interaction-oriented people in a group. They like to talk to people and can detect tensions and disagreements at an early stage. They can help resolve personality problems and differences before they have a serious impact on the group.

It is sometimes impossible to choose a group with complementary personalities. In this case, the project manager has to control the group so that group members do not let their individual goals transcend organisational and group objectives. This control is easier to achieve if all group members participate in each stage of the project. Individual initiative is most likely when group members are given instructions without being aware of the part that their task plays in the overall project.

For example, say an engineer is given a program design for coding and notices possible design improvements. If these improvements are implemented without understanding the rationale for the original design, they might have adverse implications on other parts of the system. If the whole group are involved in the design from the start, they will understand why design decisions have been made. They may identify with these decisions rather than oppose them.

Within a group, the group leader has an important role. He or she may be responsible for providing technical direction and project administration. Group leaders must keep track of the day-to-day work of their group, ensure that people are working effectively and work closely with project managers on project planning.

Leaders are normally appointed and report to the overall project manager. However, the appointed leader may not be the real leader of the group as far as technical matters are concerned. The group members may look to another group member for leadership. He or she may be the most technically competent engineer or may be a better motivator than the appointed group leader.

Sometimes, it is effective to separate technical leadership and project administration. People who are technically competent are not always the best administrators. When they are given an administrative role, this reduces their overall value to the group. It is best to support them with an administrator who relieves them of day-to-day administrative tasks.

If an unwanted leader is imposed on a group, this is likely to introduce tensions. The members will not respect the leader and may reject group loyalty in favour of individual goals. This is a particular problem in a fast-changing field such as software engineering where new members may be more up to date and better educated than experienced group leaders. Some people with experience may resent the imposition of a young leader with new ideas.

22.2.2   Group cohesiveness

In a cohesive group, members think of the group as more important than the individuals in it. Members of a well-led, cohesive group are loyal to the group. They identify with group goals and with other group members. They attempt to protect the group, as an entity, from outside interference. This makes the group robust and able to cope with problems and unexpected situations. The group can cope with change by providing mutual support and help.

The advantages of a cohesive group are:

1. *A group quality standard can be developed*   Because this standard is established by consensus, it is more likely to be observed than external standards imposed on the group.

2. *Group members work closely together*   People in the group learn from each other. Inhibitions caused by ignorance are minimised as mutual learning is encouraged.

3. *Group members can get to know each other's work*   Continuity can be maintained should a group member leave.

4. *Egoless programming can be practised*   Programs are regarded as group property rather than personal property.

Egoless programming (Weinberg, 1971) is a style of group working where designs, programs and other documents are considered to be the common property of the group rather than the individual who developed them. If engineers think of their work in this way, they are more likely to offer it for inspection by other group members, to accept criticism, and to work with the group to improve the program. Group cohesiveness is improved because all members feel that they have a shared responsibility for the software.

As well as improving the quality of designs, programs and documents, egoless programming also improves communications within the group. It encourages uninhibited discussion without regard to status, experience or gender. Individual members actively cooperate with other group members throughout the course of the project. This all serves to draw the members of the group together and makes them feel part of a group.

Group cohesiveness depends on many factors, including the organisational culture and the personalities in the group. Managers can encourage cohesiveness in a number of ways. They may organise social events for group members and their families. They may try to establish a sense of group identity by naming the group and establishing a group identity and territory. They may get involved in explicit group building activities such as sports and games.

However, in my experience, one of the most effective ways of promoting cohesion is to ensure that group members are treated as responsible and trustworthy and given access to information. Often, managers feel that they cannot reveal certain information to all of the group. This invariably creates a climate of mistrust. Simple information exchange is a cheap and efficient way of making people feel that they are part of a group.

Strong, cohesive groups, however, can sometimes suffer from two problems:

1. *Irrational resistance to a leadership change*   If the leader of a cohesive group has to be replaced by someone outside of the group, the group members may band together against the new leader. Group members may spend time resisting changes proposed by the new group leader with a consequent loss of productivity. Whenever possible, new leaders are therefore best appointed from within groups.

2. *Groupthink*   Groupthink (Janis, 1972) is the name given to a situation where the critical abilities of group members are eroded by group loyalties. Consideration of alternatives is replaced by loyalty to group norms and decisions. Any proposal favoured by the majority of the group may be adopted without proper consideration of alternatives.

To avoid groupthink, formal sessions may be organised where group members are encouraged to criticise decisions. Outside experts may be introduced to review the group's decisions. People who are naturally argumentative, questioning, and disrespectful of the *status quo* may be appointed as group members. They act as a devil's advocate, constantly questioning group decisions, thus forcing other group members to think about and evaluate their activities.

22.2.3   Group communications

It is essential that there should be good communications between members of a software development group. The group members must exchange information on the status of their work, the design decisions that have been made and changes to previous decisions that are necessary. Good communications also strengthens group cohesiveness as group members come to understand the motivations, strengths and weaknesses of other people in the group.

Some key factors which influence the effectiveness of communications are:

1. *Group size*   As a group increases in size, it becomes more difficult to ensure that all members communicate effectively with each other. The number of one-way communication links is $n * (n - 1)$ where n is the group size, so you can see that, with a group of seven or eight members, it is quite possible that some people will rarely communicate. Status differences between group members mean that communications are often one-way communications. Higher-status members tend to dominate communications with lower-status members who are often reluctant to start a conversation or to make critical remarks.

2. *Group structure*   People in informally structured groups communicate more effectively than in groups with a formal, hierarchical structure. In hierarchical groups, communications tend to flow up and down the hierarchy. People at the same level may not talk to each other. This is a particular problem in a large

project with several development groups. If people working on different sub-systems only communicate through their managers, this often leads to delays and misunderstandings.

3. *Group composition*   If there are too many people in the group who have the same personality types, these may clash and communications may be inhibited. Communication is usually better in mixed-sex groups (Marshall and Heslin, 1975) than in single-sex groups. Women tend to be more interaction-oriented than men and female group members may act as interaction controllers and facilitators for the group.

4. *The physical work environment of the group*   The organisation of the work-place is a major factor in facilitating or inhibiting communications. I discuss this in section 22.3.1.

22.2.4   Group organisation

Small programming groups are usually organised in a fairly informal way. The group leader gets involved in the software development with the other group members. A technical leader may emerge who effectively controls software production. In an informal group, the work to be carried out is discussed by the group as a whole and tasks allocated according to ability and experience. High-level system design is car-ried out by senior group members but low-level design is the responsibility of the member who is allocated to a particular task.

Informal groups can be very successful particularly where the majority of group members are experienced and competent. The group functions as a democratic unit, making decisions by consensus. Psychologically, this improves group spirit with a resultant increase in cohesiveness and performance. If a group is composed mostly of inexperienced or incompetent members, informality can be a hindrance. No definite authority exists to direct the work, causing a lack of coordination between group members and, possibly, eventual project failure.

An interesting organisational variant of democratic group organisation is described by Beck in his book on 'extreme programming' (Beck, 2000). In this approach, many decisions that are usually seen as management decisions such as decisions on schedule are devolved to group members. Programmers work together in pairs to develop code and take a collective responsibility for the programs that are developed. This approach has reportedly worked successfully but, like Clean-room development discussed in Chapter 19, I suspect it requires highly qualified and motivated staff for it to be successful.

As I discuss in Chapter 23, individual ability has the most significant influence on programmer productivity. To make the most effective use of highly skilled pro-grammers, Baker (1972) and others (Aron, 1974; Brooks, 1975) suggested that teams should be built around an individual, highly skilled chief programmer. The under-lying principle of the chief programmer team was that skilled and experienced staff should be responsible for all software development. They should not be concerned

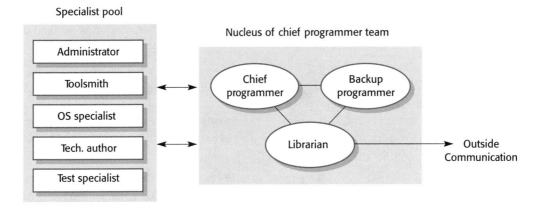

Specialist pool

Nucleus of chief programmer team

Administrator

Toolsmith

OS specialist

Tech. author

Test specialist

Chief programmer

Backup programmer

Librarian

Outside Communication

Figure 22.6 A chief programmer team

with routine matters and should have good technical and administrative support for their work. Their communications with people outside the group should be limited (Figure 22.6).

The key members of a chief programmer team are:

1. a chief programmer who takes full responsibility for the design, programming, testing and installation of the system;
2. an experienced backup programmer whose job is to support the chief programmer and take responsibility for software validation;
3. a librarian whose role is to assume all the clerical functions associated with a project such as configuration management, finalising documentation, etc.

Depending on the size and type of the application, other experts might be drawn from a specialist pool to work temporarily or permanently with a team. These might be administrators, operating system or language specialists, test engineers, etc.

The rationale for this approach comes from the fact that there are immense differences in programming ability amongst software engineers. The best programmers may be up to 25 times as productive as the worst programmers. It therefore makes sense to use the best people in the most effective way and to provide them with as much support as possible. Therefore, although the proposals for a chief programmer team are more than 25 years old, it is still an effective way to organise a small development group.

If the right people are available, using this very structured group organisation can be very effective. However, it suffers from a number of problems:

1. Talented designers and programmers are uncommon. The approach relies on an excellent chief programmer and deputy chief programmer. If they make mistakes, there is no one to question their decisions. In a democratic group, anyone can question decisions and hence may discover problems with them.
2. The chief programmer takes all the responsibility and can claim all the credit for success. However, group members may be resentful if their role in the

project is not recognised. Their need for esteem may not be satisfied if all the credit for success is given to the chief programmer.

3. Projects may be threatened if both the chief programmer and his or her deputy are ill or leave the organisation. Managers may not wish to accept this risk.

4. Organisational structures may not be able to accommodate the introduction of this type of group. Large companies may have a well-developed grading structure. Appointing chief programmers outside this structure may be very difficult. In small companies, it may simply be impossible for one of them to be completely devoted to one task.

Chief programmer teams may therefore be a risky strategy for organisations to adopt. However, we can learn from the experiences of this type of group. It makes sense to support technically talented people with project librarians, administrators, etc. Their abilities can therefore be used in the best way. Making specialists available for short times can be more productive than using programmers with general experience for a longer period.

22.3 Choosing and keeping people

One of the roles of a project manager is to choose staff to work on the project. In exceptional cases, project managers can appoint the people who are best suited to the job irrespective of their other responsibilities or budget considerations. More normally, however, project managers do not have a free choice of staff. They may have to use whoever is available in an organisation, they may have to find people very quickly and they may have a limited budget. This limited budget may constrain the number of (expensive) experienced engineers who may work on the project.

If a manager has some choice of staff who can work on the project, the factors which may influence his or her decision are shown in Figure 22.7. There is no way of rating these factors in terms of importance as this varies depending on the application domain, the type of project and the skills of other members of the project team.

The decision on who to appoint to a project is usually made using three types of information:

1. information provided by candidates about their background and experience (their resumé or CV);
2. information gained by interviewing candidates;
3. recommendations from other people who have worked with the candidates.

Some companies make use of various types of test to assess candidates. These include programming aptitude tests and psychometric tests. Psychometric tests are

Figure 22.7 Factors
governing staff
selection

Factor	Explanation
Application domain experience	For a project to develop a successful system, the developers must understand the application domain.
Platform experience	This may be significant if low-level programming is involved. Otherwise, not usually a critical attribute.
Programming language experience	This is normally only significant for short duration projects where there is insufficient time to learn a new language.
Educational background	This may provide an indicator of the basic fundamentals which the candidate should know and of their ability to learn. This factor becomes increasingly irrelevant as engineers gain experience across a range of projects.
Communication ability	This is important because of the need for project staff to communicate orally and in writing with other engineers, managers and customers.
Adaptability	Adaptability may be judged by looking at the different types of experience which candidates have had. This is an important attribute as it indicates an ability to learn.
Attitude	Project staff should have a positive attitude to their work and should be willing to learn new skills. This is an important attribute but often very difficult to assess.
Personality	This is an important attribute but difficult to assess. Candidates must be reasonably compatible with other team members. No particular type of personality is more or less suited to software engineering.

intended to produce a psychological profile of the candidate indicating attitude and suitability for certain types of task. Some managers consider these tests to be useless; others think they provide useful information for staff selection. As discussed above, problem solving ability seems to be related to the building of semantic models which is a long-term process. Aptitude and psychometric tests usually rely on the rapid completion of questions. It has not been convincingly demonstrated that there is a link between problem solving ability and aptitude tests.

Project managers are sometimes faced with difficulties in finding people with appropriate skills and experience. Teams have to be built using relatively inexperienced engineers. This may lead to problems because of a lack of understanding of the application domain or the technology used in the project.

One reason for this is that, in some organisations, technically skilled staff quickly reach a career plateau. To progress further, they must take on managerial responsibilities. Promotion of these people to managerial status means that useful technical skills are lost. To avoid this loss of technical skills, some companies have developed parallel technical and managerial career structures of equal worth.

Experienced technical people are rewarded at the same level as managers. As an engineer's career develops, they may specialise in either technical or managerial activities and move between them without loss of status or salary.

22.3.1   Working environments

The workplace has important effects on people's performance and their job satisfaction. Psychological experiments have shown that behaviour is affected by room size, furniture, equipment, temperature, humidity, brightness and quality of light, noise and the degree of privacy available. Group behaviour is affected by architectural organisation and telecommunication facilities. Communications within a group are affected by the building architecture and the organisation of the workspace.

There is a real and significant cost in failing to provide good working conditions. When people are unhappy about their working conditions, staff turnover increases. More costs must therefore be expended on recruitment and training. Software projects may be delayed because of lack of qualified staff (DeMarco and Lister, 1999).

Software development staff often work in large open-plan office areas, sometimes with cubicles, and only senior management have individual offices. McCue (1978) carried out a study that showed that the open-plan architecture favoured by many organisations was neither popular nor productive. The most important environmental factors identified in that design study were:

1. *Privacy*   Programmers require an area where they can concentrate and work without interruption.

2. *Outside awareness*   People prefer to work in natural light and with a view of the outside environment.

3. *Personalisation*   Individuals adopt different working practices and have different opinions on decor. The ability to rearrange the workplace to suit working practices and to personalise that environment is important.

In short, people like individual offices that they can organise as they like. There is less disruption and fewer interruptions than in open-plan workspaces. In open-plan offices, people are denied privacy and a quiet working environment. They are limited in the ways that they can personalise their own workspace. Concentration can be difficult and performance is degraded.

Providing individual offices for software engineering staff can make a significant difference to productivity. DeMarco and Lister (1985) compared the productivity of programmers in different types of workplace. They found that factors such as a private workspace and the ability to cut off interruptions had a significant effect. Programmers who had good working conditions were more than twice as productive than equally skilled programmers who had to work in poorer conditions.

Development groups need areas where all members of the group can get together as a group and discuss their project, both formally and informally. Meeting

Figure 22.8 Office
and meeting room
grouping

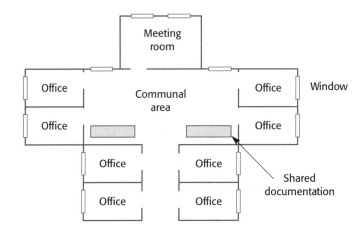

rooms must be able to accommodate the whole group in privacy. Individual privacy
requirements and group communication requirements seem to be exclusive objectives. McCue suggested that these conflicting needs could be accommodated by grouping individual offices round larger group meeting rooms (Figure 22.8).

A similar model is suggested by Beck (2000) in his description of an environment for 'extreme programming'. However, he suggests retaining an open-plan area
with all programming activities taking place in the communal area and individual
cubicles for the group members when they wish to work alone. Clearly, the key
requirement is to provide both individual and group space so that people can work
alone or as a group when necessary.

This type of communication helps people solve their problems and exchange information in an informal but effective way. Weinberg (1971) cites an anecdotal example
of how an organisation wanted to stop programmers 'wasting time' talking to each
other around a coffee machine. They removed the machine, then immediately
had a dramatic increase in requests for formal programming assistance. As well
as gossiping around the machine, people were solving each other's problems. This
illustrates that companies need informal meeting places as well as formal conference rooms.

22.4 The People Capability Maturity Model

The Software Engineering Institute (SEI) in the USA is engaged on a long-term programme of software process improvement. Part of this programme is the Capability
Maturity Model (CMM) for software processes which I discuss in Chapter 25.
This is concerned with best practice in software engineering. To support this
model, they have also proposed a People Capability Maturity Model (P-CMM)

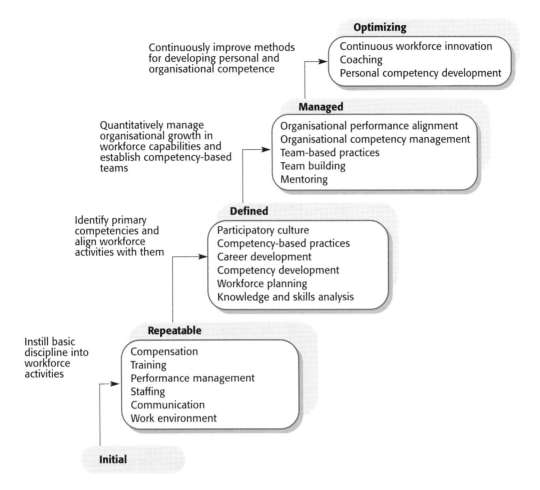

Optimizing
- Continuous workforce innovation
- Coaching
- Personal competency development

Continuously improve methods for developing personal and organisational competence

Managed
- Organisational performance alignment
- Organisational competency management
- Team-based practices
- Team building
- Mentoring

Quantitatively manage organisational growth in workforce capabilities and establish competency-based teams

Defined
- Participatory culture
- Competency-based practices
- Career development
- Competency development
- Workforce planning
- Knowledge and skills analysis

Identify primary competencies and align workforce activities with them

Repeatable
- Compensation
- Training
- Performance management
- Staffing
- Communication
- Work environment

Instill basic discipline into workforce activities

Initial

Figure 22.9 The people capability maturity model

(Curtis *et al.*, 1995). This can be used as a framework for improving the way in which an organisation manages its human assets.

Like the CMM, the P-CMM is a five-level model as shown in Figure 22.9. The five levels are:

1. *Initial*   Ad hoc, informal people management practices used.
2. *Repeatable*   Establishment of policies for developing the capability of the staff.
3. *Defined*   Standardisation of best people management practice across the organisation.
4. *Managed*   Quantitative goals for people management established and introduced.
5. *Optimising*   Continuous focus on improving individual competence and work-force motivation.

Curtis *et al.* (1995) state that the strategic objectives of the P-CMM are:

1. to improve the capability of software organisations by increasing the capability of their workforce;

2. to ensure that software development capability is an attribute of the organisation rather than a few individuals;
3. to align the motivation of individuals with that of the organisation;
4. to retain human assets (i.e. people with critical knowledge and skills) within the organisation.

The P-CMM is a practical tool for improving the management of people in an organisation because it provides a framework for motivating, recognising, standardising and improving good practice. It reinforces the need to recognise the importance of people as individuals and to develop their capabilities. Of course, the complete application of this model is very expensive and probably unnecessary for most organisations. However, I believe that the model is a helpful guide that can lead to significant improvements in the capability of organisations to produce high-quality software.

KEY POINTS

▸ Software management is principally concerned with managing people. Managers should therefore have some understanding of human factors so that they do not make unrealistic demands on themselves or their staff.

▸ Humans have a fast, short-term memory, a working memory and a long-term memory. Knowledge may be arbitrary syntactic knowledge and deeper semantic knowledge. Problem solving involves integrating semantic information from the long-term memory with new information in the short-term memory.

▸ Factors which might be used to select staff include application domain experience, adaptability and personality.

▸ Software development groups should be small and cohesive. Group leaders should be technically competent and should have administrative and technical support.

▸ Communications within a group are influenced by factors such as the status of group members, the size of the group, the sexual composition of the group, personalities and available communication channels.

▸ Providing a private working environment with appropriate computing and communication facilities can improve the productivity and satisfaction of programmers.

▸ The People-Capability Maturity Model provides a framework and associated advice for improving the capabilities of people in an organisation and improving the organisation's capability to gain benefits from its human assets.

FURTHER READING

Peopleware: Productive Projects and Teams, 2nd edition. This is a new edition of the classic book on the importance of treating people properly when managing software projects. It's easy to read and one of the few books that recognises the importance of the place where people work. Strongly recommended. (T. DeMarco and T. Lister, 1999, Dorset House.)

Overview of the People Capability Maturity Model. A summary of the SEI's model that can be downloaded from their web site which is accessible from this book's web pages. (B. Curtis, W. E. Hefley, S. Miller, Software Engineering Institute, report CMU/SEI-95-MM-01.)

Software Management, 4th edition. This is an IEEE tutorial text which has several articles about managing and motivating people. (D. J. Reifer, 1993, IEEE Press.)

Working with Computers: Theory versus Outcome. This book is a collection of papers on human factors. They are mostly written by cognitive scientists with an interest in software development. (G. van der Veer, T. R. Green, J.-M. Hoc and D. M. Murray (eds), 1988, Academic Press.)

EXERCISES

22.1 Briefly describe the human memory hierarchy and explain why the organisation of this hierarchy suggests that object-oriented systems are easier to understand than systems based on functional decomposition.

22.2 What is the difference between syntactic and semantic knowledge? From your own experience, suggest a number of instances of each of these types of knowledge.

22.3 As a training manager, you are responsible for the initial programming language training of a new graduate intake to your company whose business is the development of defence aerospace systems. The principal programming language used is Ada, which was designed for defence systems programming. The trainees may be computer science graduates, engineers or physical scientists. Some but not all of the trainees have previous programming experience; none have previous experience in Ada. Explain how you would structure the programming training for this group of graduates.

22.4 What factors should be taken into account when selecting staff to work on a software development project?

22.5 Explain why keeping all members of a group informed about progress and technical decisions in a project can improve group cohesiveness.

22.6 Explain what you understand by 'groupthink'. Describe the dangers of this phenomenon and explain how it might be avoided.

22.7 You are a programming manager who has been given the task of rescuing a project that is critical to the success of the company. Senior management have given you an open-ended budget and you may choose a project team of up to five people from any other projects going on in the company. However, a rival company, working in the same area, is actively recruiting staff and several staff working for your company have left to join them.

Describe two models of programming team organisation that might be used in this situation and make a choice of one of these models. Give reasons for your choice and explain why you have rejected the alternative model.

22.8 Why are open-plan and communal offices sometimes less suitable for software development than individual offices? Under what circumstances do you think that open-plan environments might be better?

22.9 Why is the P-CMM an effective framework for improving the management of people in an organisation? Suggest how it may have to be modified if it is to be used in small companies.

22.10 Should managers become friendly and mix socially with more junior members of their group?

22.11 Is it ethical to provide the answers which you think the tester wants rather than saying what you really feel when taking psychological tests?

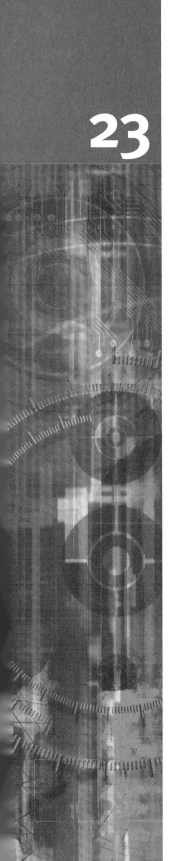

23 Software cost estimation

Objectives

The objective of this chapter is to introduce techniques for estimating the cost and effort required for software production. When you have read this chapter, you will:

❏ understand the fundamentals of software costing and pricing and the complex relationship between them;

❏ have been introduced to three metrics that are used for software productivity assessment;

❏ appreciate that a range of different techniques should be used when estimating software costs and schedule;

❏ understand the principles of the COCOMO 2 model for algorithmic cost estimation.

Contents

23.1 Productivity
23.2 Estimation techniques
23.3 Algorithmic cost modelling
23.4 Project duration and staffing

In Chapter 4, I introduced the project planning process. During that process, a project is split into a number of activities which are enacted in parallel or in sequence. The earlier discussion of project planning concentrated on ways to represent these activities, their dependencies and the allocation of people to carry out these tasks.

In this chapter, I turn to the problem of associating estimates of effort and time with the identified project activities. Project managers must estimate the answers to the following questions:

1. How much effort is required to complete an activity?
2. How much calendar time is needed to complete an activity?
3. What is the total cost of an activity?

Project estimation and project scheduling are carried out together. However, some cost estimation may be required at an early stage of the project before detailed schedules are drawn up. These estimates may be needed to establish a budget for the project or to set a price for the software for a customer.

Once a project is under way, estimates should be updated regularly. This assists with the planning process and allows the effective use of resources. If actual expenditure is significantly greater than the estimates then the project manager must take some action. This may involve applying for additional resources for the project or modifying the work to be done.

There are three parameters involved in computing the total cost of a software development project:

• hardware and software costs, including maintenance;
• travel and training costs;
• effort costs (the costs of paying software engineers).

For most projects, the dominant cost is the effort cost. Computers that are powerful enough for software development are relatively cheap. Although travel costs can be significant where a project is developed at different sites, they are relatively low for most projects. Furthermore, the use of electronic mail, fax and teleconferencing can reduce the travel required.

Effort costs are not simply the costs of the salaries of the software engineers involved in the project. Organisations compute effort costs in terms of overhead costs where they take the total cost of running the organisation and divide this by the number of productive staff. Therefore, the following costs are all part of the total effort cost:

1. costs of providing, heating and lighting office space;
2. costs of support staff such as accountants, secretaries, cleaners and technicians;
3. costs of networking and communications;
4. costs of central facilities such as a library, recreational facilities, etc.;
5. costs of social security and employee benefits such as pensions and health insurance.

Figure 23.1 Factors
affecting software
pricing

Factor	Description
Market opportunity	A development organisation may quote a low price because it wishes to move into a new segment of the software market. Accepting a low profit on one project may give the opportunity of more profit later. The experience gained may allow new products to be developed.
Cost estimate uncertainty	If an organisation is unsure of its cost estimate, it may increase its price by some contingency over and above its normal profit.
Contractual terms	A customer may be willing to allow the developer to retain ownership of the source code and reuse it in other projects. The price charged may then be less than if the software source code is handed over to the customer.
Requirements volatility	If the requirements are likely to change, an organisation may lower its price to win a contract. After the contract is awarded, high prices may be charged for changes to the requirements.
Financial health	Developers in financial difficulty may lower their price to gain a contract. It is better to make a smaller than normal profit or break even than to go out of business.

Typically, this overhead factor is somewhere around twice the software engineer's salary depending on the size of the organisation and its associated overheads. Therefore, if a software engineer is paid $90,000 per year, the total cost to the organisation is $180,000 per year or $15,000 per month.

Software costing should be carried out objectively with the aim of accurately predicting the cost to the contractor of developing the software. If the project cost has been computed as part of a project bid to a customer, a decision then has to be made about the price quoted to the customer. Classically, price is simply cost plus profit. However, the relationship between the project cost and the price to the customer is not usually so simple.

Software pricing must take into account broader organisational, economic, political and business considerations. Factors which may be taken into account are shown in Figure 23.1. Therefore, there may not be a simple relationship between the price to the customer for the software and the development costs. Because of the organisational considerations involved, project pricing usually involves senior management in the organisation as well as software project managers.

23.1 Productivity

Productivity in a manufacturing system can be measured by counting the number of units which are produced and dividing this by the number of person-hours required to produce them. However, for any software problem, there are many different solutions which have different attributes. One solution may execute more efficiently while another may be more readable and easier to maintain. When solutions with different attributes are produced, comparing their production rates is not really meaningful.

Nevertheless, the productivity of engineers in the software development process may have to be estimated by managers. These estimates may be needed for project estimation and to assess whether process or technology improvements are effective. These productivity estimates are usually based on measuring some attributes of the software and dividing this by the total effort required for development. There are two types of measure which have been used:

1. *Size-related measures*   These are related to the size of some output from an activity. The most common size-related measure is lines of delivered source code. Other measures which may be used are the number of delivered object code instructions or the number of pages of system documentation.

2. *Function-related measures*   These are related to the overall functionality of the delivered software. Productivity is expressed in terms of the amount of useful functionality produced in some given time. Function points and object points are the best known measures of this type.

Lines of source code per programmer-month is a widely-used metric in productivity measurement. This is computed by counting the total number of lines of source code which are delivered. The count is divided by the total time in programmer-months required to complete the project. This time therefore includes the time required for analysis and design, coding, testing and documentation.

This approach was first developed when most programming was in FORTRAN, assembly language or COBOL. Then, programs were typed on cards, with one statement on each card. The number of lines of code was easy to compute. It corresponded to the number of cards in the program deck. However, programs in languages like Java or C++ consist of declarations, executable statements, and commentary. They may include macro instructions that expand to several lines of code. There may be more than one statement per line. There is not, therefore, a simple relationship between program statements and lines on a listing.

Some line counting techniques consider executable statements only; others count executable statements and data declarations; some count each non-blank line in the program, irrespective of what is on that line. Standards for line counting in different languages have been proposed (Park, 1992) but these are not widely known. Productivity comparisons across organisations are impossible unless each organisation uses the same method for counting lines of code.

Comparing productivity across different programming languages can also give misleading impressions of programmer productivity. The more expressive the programming language, the lower the apparent productivity. This anomaly arises because all software development activities are considered together when computing productivity but the metric used only applies to the programming process.

Figure 23.2 System
development times

	Analysis	Design	Coding	Testing	Documentation
Assembly code	3 weeks	5 weeks	8 weeks	10 weeks	2 weeks
High-level language	3 weeks	5 weeks	8 weeks	6 weeks	2 weeks

	Size	Effort	Productivity
Assembly code	5000 lines	28 weeks	714 lines/month
High-level language	1500 lines	20 weeks	300 lines/month

For example, consider a system which might be coded in 5000 lines of assembly code or 1500 lines of high-level language code. The development time for the various phases is shown in Figure 23.2. The assembler programmer has a productivity of 714 lines/month and the high-level language programmer less than half of this, 300 lines/month. Yet the development costs for the high-level language system are lower and it is produced in less time.

An alternative to using code size as the estimated product attribute is to use some measure of the functionality of the code. This avoids the above anomaly as functionality is independent of implementation language. MacDonell (1994) briefly describes and compares several different function-based measures.

The best-known of these measures is the function-point count. This was proposed by Albrecht (1979) and refined by Albrecht and Gaffney (1983). Function points are language-independent so productivity in different programming languages can be compared. Productivity is expressed as function points produced per person-month. Function points are biased towards data-processing systems which are dominated by input and output operations. A function point is not a single characteristic but is a combination of program characteristics. The total number of function points in a program is computed by measuring or estimating the following program features:

• external inputs and outputs
• user interactions
• external interfaces
• files used by the system.

Each of these is individually assessed for complexity and given a weighting value that varies from 3 (for simple external inputs) to 15 for complex internal files. Either the weighting values proposed by Albrecht may be used or values based on local experience.

The unadjusted function-point count (UFC) is computed by multiplying each raw count by the estimated weight and summing all values.

UFC = $\sum$(number of elements of given type) $\times$ (weight)

This initial function-point count is then further modified by factors whose value is based on the overall complexity of the project. This takes into account the degree of distributed processing, the amount of reuse, the performance, etc. The unadjusted function-point count is multiplied by the project complexity factors to produce a final function-point count.

Symons (1988) notes that the subjective nature of complexity estimates means that the function-point count in a program depends on the estimator. Different people have different notions of complexity. There are wide variations in function-point count depending on the estimator's judgement. For this reason, there are differing views about the value of function points (Furey and Kitchenham, 1997). However, users argue that, in spite of their flaws, they are effective in practical situations (Kemerer, 1993).

Object points (Banker *et al.*, 1992) are an alternative to function points when 4GLs or comparable languages are used for software development. Object points are used in the COCOMO 2 estimation model discussed later in this chapter. Object points are not object classes that may be produced when an object-oriented approach is taken to software development. Rather, the number of object points in a program is a weighted estimate of:

1. The number of separate screens that are displayed. Simple screens count as 1 object point, moderately complex screens count as 2 and very complex screens count as 3 object points.

2. The number of reports that are produced. For simple reports, count 2 object points, for moderately complex reports, count 5 and for reports which are likely to be difficult to produce, count 8 object points.

3. The number of 3GL modules that must be developed to supplement the 4GL code. Each 3GL module counts as 10 object points.

The advantage of using object points rather than function points is that they are easier to estimate from a high-level software specification. Object points are only concerned with screens, reports and 3GL modules.

If function points or object points are used they can be estimated at an early stage in the development process. Estimates of these parameters can be made as soon as the external interactions of the system have been designed. At this stage, it is very difficult to produce an accurate estimate of the size of a program in lines of source code. Indeed, the programming language which is to be used may not even have been decided. Early estimates are essential when using the algorithmic cost estimation models that are discussed later in this chapter.

Function-point counts can be used in conjunction with lines of code estimation techniques. The number of function points is used to estimate the final code size. Using historical data analysis, the average number of lines of code, AVC, in a particular language required to implement a function point can be estimated. The estimated code size for a new application is computed as follows:

Code size = AVC × Number of function points

Figure 23.3 Factors
affecting software
engineering
productivity

Factor	Description
Application domain experience	Knowledge of the application domain is essential for effective software development. Engineers who already understand a domain are likely to be the most productive.
Process quality	The development process used can have a significant effect on productivity. This is covered in Chapter 25.
Project size	The larger a project, the more time required for team communications. Less time is available for development so individual productivity is reduced.
Technology support	Good support technology such as CASE tools, supportive configuration management systems, etc. can improve productivity.
Working environment	As discussed in Chapter 22, a quiet working environment with private work areas contributes to improved productivity.

Values of AVC vary from 200–300 LOC/FP in assembly language to 2–40 LOC/FP for a fourth-generation language.

The productivity of individual engineers working in an organisation is affected by a number of factors. Some of the most important of these are summarised in Figure 23.3. However, individual differences in ability are more significant than any of these factors. In an early assessment of productivity, Sackman *et al.* (1968) found that some programmers were more than 10 times more productive than others. My experience is that this is still true. Large teams are likely to have a mix of abilities so will have 'average' productivity. In small teams, however, overall productivity is mostly dependent on individual aptitudes and abilities.

There is no such thing as an 'average' value for productivity that applies across application domains and organisations. For large, complex embedded systems, productivity may be as low as 30 lines/programmer-month. For straightforward, well-understood application systems it may be as high as 900 lines/month. When measured in terms of object points, Boehm *et al.* (1995) suggest that productivity varies from four object points per month to 50 object points/month depending on tool support and developer capability.

The problem with measures expressed as volume/time is that they take no account of non-functional software characteristics such as reliability, maintainability, etc. They imply that more always means better. Beck (2000) makes the excellent point that if you have an approach that is based around continuous code simplification and improvement then counting lines of code doesn't mean much.

These measures also do not take into account the possibility of reusing the software produced. What we really want to estimate is the cost of deriving a particular system with given functionality, quality, performance, maintainability, etc. This is only indirectly related to tangible measures such as the system size.

This becomes a particular problem if managers use productivity measurements to judge the abilities of staff. In such situations, engineers may compromise on quality in order to become more 'productive'. It may be the case that the 'less productive' programmer produces more reliable code which is easier to understand and cheaper to maintain. Productivity measures must therefore be used only as a guide. They should not be used without careful analysis.

23.2 Estimation techniques

There is no simple way to make an accurate estimate of the effort required to develop a software system. Initial estimates may have to be made on the basis of a high-level user requirements definition. The software may have to run on unfamiliar computers or use new development technology. The people involved in the project and their skills will probably not be known. All of these factors mean that it is difficult to produce an accurate estimate of system development costs at an early stage in the project.

Furthermore, there is a fundamental difficulty in assessing the accuracy of different approaches to cost estimation techniques. Project cost estimates are often self-fulfilling. The estimate is used to define the project budget and the product is adjusted so that the budget figure is realised. I do not know of reports of controlled experiments with project costing where the estimated costs were not used to bias the experiment. A controlled experiment would not reveal the cost estimate to the project manager. The actual costs would then be compared with the estimated project costs.

Nevertheless, organisations need to make software effort and cost estimates. To do so, one or more of the techniques described in Figure 23.4 may be used (Boehm, 1981).

Hihn and Habib-agahi (1991) describe an experiment where they asked managers to estimate the size of a software system to be developed and the effort required. The managers used expert judgement and estimation by analogy. It was found that they were reasonably accurate in estimating required effort but their estimates of code size were much less accurate. This means that cost estimates based on a code size estimate were also inaccurate.

These approaches to cost estimation can be tackled using either a top-down or a bottom-up approach. A top-down approach starts at the system level. The estimator starts by examining the overall functionality of the product and how that functionality is provided by interacting sub-functions. The costs of system-level activities such as integration, configuration management and documentation are taken into account.

The bottom-up approach, by contrast, starts at the component level. The system is decomposed into components and the effort required to develop each of these

Figure 23.4 Cost estimation techniques

Technique	Description
Algorithmic cost modelling	A model is developed using historical cost information that relates some software metric (usually its size) to the project cost. An estimate is made of that metric and the model predicts the effort required.
Expert judgement	Several experts on the proposed software development techniques and the application domain are consulted. They each estimate the project cost. These estimates are compared and discussed. The estimation process iterates until an agreed estimate is reached.
Estimation by analogy	This technique is applicable when other projects in the same application domain have been completed. The cost of a new project is estimated by analogy with these completed projects. Myers (1989) gives a very clear description of this approach.
Parkinson's Law	Parkinson's Law states that work expands to fill the time available. The cost is determined by available resources rather than by objective assessment. If the software has to be delivered in 12 months and five people are available, the effort required is estimated to be 60 person-months.
Pricing to win	The software cost is estimated to be whatever the customer has available to spend on the project. The estimated effort depends on the customer's budget and not on the software functionality.

is computed. These costs are then added to give the effort required for the whole system development.

The disadvantages of the top-down approach are the advantages of the bottom-up approach and vice versa. Top-down estimation can underestimate the costs of solving difficult technical problems associated with specific components such as interfaces to non-standard hardware. There is no detailed justification of the estimate that is produced. By contrast, bottom-up estimation produces such a justification and considers each component. However, this approach is more likely to underestimate the costs of system activities such as integration. Bottom-up estimation is also more expensive. There must be an initial system design to identify the components to be costed.

Each estimation technique has its own strengths and weaknesses. For large projects, you should use several cost estimation techniques and compare their results. If these predict radically different costs, this suggests that you do not have enough costing information. You should look for more information and repeat the costing process until the estimates converge.

These estimation techniques are applicable where a requirements document for the system has been produced. This should define all users and system requirements. You can therefore make a reasonable estimate of the extent of the system functionality which is to be developed. In general, large systems engineering projects will normally have such a requirements document.

However, in many cases, the costs of many projects must be estimated using only an outline of the user requirements for the system. This means that the estimators have very little information to work with. Requirements analysis and specification is expensive and the managers in a company may need an initial cost estimate for the system before they can have a budget approved for this process.

Under these circumstances, 'pricing to win' is a commonly used strategy. The notion of 'pricing to win' may seem unethical and unbusinesslike. However, it does have some advantages. A project cost is agreed on the basis of an outline proposal. Negotiations then take place between client and customer to establish the detailed project specification. This specification is constrained by the agreed cost. The buyer and seller must agree on what is acceptable system functionality. The fixed factor in many projects is not the project requirements but the cost. The requirements may be changed so that the cost is not exceeded.

When estimating software costs, managers must take into account that there may be important differences between past projects and future projects. A range of new development methods and techniques have been introduced in the last 10 years. Many managers have little experience of these techniques or knowledge of how they affect project costs. Some examples of the changes which may affect estimates based on experience include:

- object-oriented development rather than function-oriented development;
- client–server systems rather than mainframe-based systems;
- use of off-the-shelf software components rather than component development;
- development for and with reuse rather than new development of all parts of a system;
- the use of CASE tools and program generators rather than unsupported software development.

All of these factors make it more difficult for managers to produce accurate estimates of the costs of software production. Their previous experience may not be relevant in helping them estimate software project costs.

23.3 Algorithmic cost modelling

The most systematic, although not necessarily the most accurate, approach to software estimation is algorithmic cost estimation. An algorithmic cost model can be built by analysing the costs and attributes of completed projects. A mathematical formula is used to predict costs based on estimates of project size, number of programmers and other process and product factors. Kitchenham (1990) describes 13 algorithmic cost models that have been developed from empirical observations.

Most algorithmic estimation models have an exponential component. This reflects the fact that costs do not normally increase linearly with project size. As the size of the software increases, extra costs are incurred because of the communication overhead of larger teams, more complex configuration management, more difficult system integration, etc. They may also include multipliers reflecting the attributes of the product being developed, the development platform, the process and the software developers.

In its most general form, an algorithmic cost estimate for software cost can be expressed as:

$$\text{Effort} = A \times \text{Size}^B \times M$$

A is a constant factor which depends on local organisational practices and the type of software that is developed. Size may be either an assessment of the code size of the software or a functionality estimate expressed in function or object points. The value of exponent B usually lies between 1 and 1.5. It reflects the disproportionate effort required for large projects. M is a multiplier made up by combining different process, product and development attributes.

All algorithmic models suffer from the same basic difficulties:

1. It is often difficult to estimate Size at an early stage in a project where only a specification is available. Function point and object point estimates are easier to produce than estimates of code size but may still be inaccurate.

2. The estimates of the factors contributing to B and M are subjective. Estimates vary from one person to another depending on their background and experience.

The number of lines of source code in the finished system is the basic metric used in most algorithmic cost models. Size estimation may involve estimation by analogy with other projects, estimation by converting function points to code size, estimation by ranking the sizes of system components and using a known reference component to estimate the component size or may simply be a question of engineering judgement.

Design decisions, which may not be known when the initial estimates are made, influence the size of the final system. For example, an application which requires complex data management may either use a commercial database or implement its own data manager. If a commercial database is used, the code size will be smaller. The programming language used is also significant. A language like Java might mean that more lines of code are necessary than if C (say) were used. However, this extra code allows more compile-time checking so validation costs are likely to be reduced. How should this be taken into account? Furthermore, the extent of reuse in the software development process must also be estimated and the size estimate adjusted to take this into account.

If algorithmic models are used for project costing, they should be calibrated using data for the type of project being estimated and their outputs must be carefully

Figure 23.5 Estimate
uncertainty

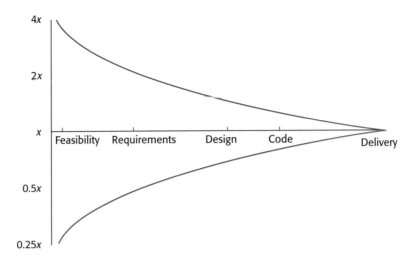

intepreted. The estimator should develop a range of estimates (worst, expected and best) rather than a single estimate. The costing formula should be applied to all of these. Errors in initial estimates are likely to be significant. Estimates are most likely to be accurate when the product is well understood, the model has been calibrated for the organisation using it, and language and hardware choices are predefined.

The accuracy of the estimates produced by an algorithmic model depends on the system information that is available. As the software process proceeds, more information becomes available so estimates become more and more accurate. If the initial estimate of effort required is x months of effort, this range may be from $0.25x$ to $4x$ when the system is first proposed. This narrows during the development process as shown in Figure 23.5. This figure, adapted from Boehm's paper (Boehm *et al.*, 1995), reflects experience of a large number of software development projects.

23.3.1 • The COCOMO model

There are a number of algorithmic models that have been proposed as a basis for estimating the effort, schedule and costs of a software project. These are conceptually similar but use different parameter values. The specific model which I discuss here is the COCOMO model. The COCOMO model is an empirical model. It was derived by collecting data from a large number of software projects, then analysing that data to discover formulae that were the best-fit to the observations. I have chosen COCOMO for the following reasons:

1. It is well documented, in the public domain and is supported by public domain and commercial tools.

2. It has been widely used and evaluated.

Project complexity	Formula	Description
Simple	PM = 2.4 (KDSI)$^{1.05}$ × M	Well-understood applications developed by small teams.
Moderate	PM = 3.0 (KDSI)$^{1.12}$ × M	More complex projects where team members may have limited experience of related systems.
Embedded	PM = 3.6 (KDSI)$^{1.20}$ × M	Complex projects where the software is part of a strongly coupled complex of hardware, software, regulations and operational procedures.

Figure 23.6
The basic COCOMO
81 model

3. It has a long pedigree from its first instantiation in 1981 (Boehm, 1981), through a refinement tailored to Ada software development (Boehm and Royce, 1989) to its most recent version, published in 1995 (Boehm *et al.*, 1995).

The first version of the COCOMO model (now known as COCOMO 81) was a three-level model where the levels reflected the detail of the analysis of the cost estimate. The first level (basic) provided an initial, rough estimate, the second level modified this using a number of project and process multipliers and the most detailed level produced estimates for different phases of the project. Figure 23.6 shows the basic COCOMO formula for different types of project. The multiplier M is similar to that discussed below for COCOMO 2.

COCOMO 81 assumed that the software would be developed according to a water-fall process and that the vast majority of the software would be developed from scratch. However, there have been radical changes to software development since this initial version was proposed. Software may be created by assembling reusable components and linking them via some scripting language. Prototyping and incremental development are commonly used process models. In many cases, off-the-shelf sub-systems are used. Existing software is re-engineered to create new software. CASE tool support for most software process activities is now available.

To take these changes into account, the COCOMO 2 model recognises different approaches to software development such as prototyping, development by component composition, use of 4GLs, etc. The model levels do not simply reflect increasingly complex and detailed estimates. Levels are associated with activities in the software process so that initial estimates may be made early in the process with more detailed estimating carried out after the system architecture has been defined. The levels identified in COCOMO 2 are:

1. *The early prototyping level*   Size estimates are based on object points and a simple size/productivity formula is used to estimate the effort required.

2. *The early design level*   This level corresponds to the completion of the system requirements with (perhaps) some initial design. Estimates are based on function points which are then converted to number of lines of source code. The formula follows the standard form discussed above with a simple set of multipliers associated with it.

Figure 23.7 Object
point productivity

Developer's experience and capability	Very low	Low	Nominal	High	Very high
ICASE maturity and capability	Very low	Low	Nominal	High	Very high
PROD (NOP/month)	4	7	13	25	50

3. *The post-architecture level* Once the system architecture has been designed a reasonably accurate estimate of the software size can be made. The estimate at this level uses a more extensive set of multipliers reflecting personnel capability, product and project characteristics.

The early prototyping level

The early prototyping level was introduced into COCOMO to support the estimation of effort required for prototyping projects and for projects where the software was developed by composing existing components. It is based on an estimate of weighted object points (discussed in section 23.1) that is divided by a standard figure for estimated productivity. Programmer productivity depends on the developer's experience and capability and the capabilities of the CASE tools used to support development. Figure 23.7 shows the different levels of productivity suggested by the developers of the model (Boehm *et al.*, 1995).

At this level, reuse is common so the number of object points used in the schedule estimate is adjusted to take into account the percentage of reuse (%reuse) that is expected. Therefore, the final formula for schedule computation is:

$$PM = (NOP \times (1 - \%reuse/100))/PROD$$

PM is the effort in person-months, NOP is the number of object points and PROD is the productivity as shown in Figure 23.7.

The early design level

The estimates produced at this stage are based on the standard formula for algorithmic models, namely

$$Effort = A \times Size^B \times M$$

Based on his own large data-set, Boehm proposes that the coefficient A should be 2.5 for estimates made at this level. The size of the system is expressed in KSLOC, namely the number of thousands of lines of source code. This is computed by estimating the number of function points in the software and converting this to KSLOC using standard tables which relate software size to function points for different programming languages. This size estimate refers to the code that is implemented manually rather than generated or reused.

The exponent B reflects the increased effort required as the size of the project increases. This is not fixed as in the first version of COCOMO but can vary from 1.1 to 1.24 depending on the novelty of the project, the development flexibility, the risk resolution processes used, the cohesion of the development team and the process maturity level (see Chapter 25) of the organisation. The way in which this exponent is computed is discussed in the following section.

The multiplier M is based on a simplified set of seven project and process drivers which include product reliability and complexity (RCPX), reuse required (RUSE), platform difficulty (PDIF), personnel capability (PERS), personnel experience (PREX), schedule (SCED) and support facilities (FCIL). These can be estimated directly on a six-point scale where 1 corresponds to very low values for these multipliers and 6 corresponds to very high values. Alternatively, they can be computed by combining values of the more detailed multipliers used in the post-architecture level.

This results in an effort computation as follows:

$$PM = A \times Size^B \times M + PM_m \text{ where}$$

$$M = PERS \times RCPX \times RUSE \times PDIF \times PREX \times FCIL \times SCED$$

The last term in the formula (PM_m) is a factor that is used when a significant percentage of the code is generated automatically. Some manual input is usually needed to tailor this code but the productivity level is much higher than for manually created code. Therefore, the effort required (PM_m) is computed separately using the following formula and then added to the effort computed for manually developed code.

$$PM_m = (ASLOC \times (AT/100))/ATPROD$$

ASLOC is the number of automatically generated lines of source code and ATPROD is the productivity level for this type of code production. However, some effort is required to interface generated code with the remainder of the system. This depends on the percentage of the total system code which is automatically generated (AT). The actual productivity therefore depends on the number of modules which are generated. The smaller the amount of generated code, the greater the overhead involved in integrating this with other code in the system.

The post-architecture level

The estimates produced at the post-architecture level are based on the same basic formula that is used in the early design estimates. However, the size estimate for the software should be more accurate by this stage in the estimation process and 17 rather than seven attributes are used to refine the initial effort computation.

The estimate of the total number of lines of source code is adjusted to take two important project factors into account:

- *The requirements volatility*   An estimate is made of the rework which may be required to accommodate changes to the system requirements. This estimate is expressed as the number of lines of source code which must be modified and this number is added to the initial size estimate.

- *The extent of possible reuse*   Extensive reuse means that the number of lines of source code which will actually be developed must be amended. However, Selby (1988) discovered that reuse costs are non-linear because of the initial effort required to discover and select components and because of the effort required to understand reusable components and their interfaces if they need to be modified.

The effects of reuse are taken into account in COCOMO 2 by adjusting the size effort according to the following formula:

$$\text{ESLOC} = \text{ASLOC} \times (\text{AA} + \text{SU} + 0.4\text{DM} + 0.3\text{CM} + 0.3\text{IM})/100$$

where ESLOC is equivalent number of lines of new code, ASLOC is the number of lines of reusable code which must be modified, DM is the percentage of design modified, CM is the percentage of the code that is modified and IM is the percentage of the original integration effort required for integrating the reused software. SU is a factor based on the cost of software understanding which ranges from 50 for complex unstructured code to 10 for well-written, object-oriented code. AA is a factor which reflects the initial assessment costs of deciding if software may be reused. It depends on the amount of testing and evaluation that is required. Its value varies from 0 to 8.

The exponent term in the effort computation formula had three possible values in COCOMO 1. These were related to different levels of project complexity. As projects become more complex, the effects of increasing system size become more significant. However, organisational practices and procedures can control this 'diseconomy of scale' and this is recognised in COCOMO 2. The exponent is estimated by considering five scale factors as shown in Figure 23.8. These factors are rated on a six-point scale from Very low to Extra high (5 to 0). The resulting ratings are added, divided by 100 and the result is added to 1.01 to give the exponent term.

To illustrate this, imagine that an organisation is taking on a project in a domain where it has little previous experience. The project client has not defined the process to be used and has not allowed time in the project schedule for significant risk analysis. A new development team must be put together to implement this system. The organisation has recently put a process improvement programme in place and has been rated as a Level 2 organisation according to the CMM model (see Chapter 25). Possible values for the ratings used in exponent calculation are:

1. *Precedentedness*   This is a new project for the organisation – rated Low (4)
2. *Development flexibility*   No client involvement – rated Very high (1)
3. *Architecture/risk resolution*   No risk analysis carried out – rated Very low (5)

Figure 23.8 Scale
factors used in the
COCOMO 2
exponent
computation

Scale factor	Explanation
Precedentedness	Reflects the previous experience of the organisation with this type of project. Very low means no previous experience; Extra high means that the organisation is completely familiar with this application domain.
Development flexibility	Reflects the degree of flexibility in the development process. Very low means a prescribed process is used; Extra high means that the client sets only general goals.
Architecture/risk resolution	Reflects the extent of risk analysis carried out. Very low means little analysis; Extra high means a complete and thorough risk analysis.
Team cohesion	Reflects how well the development team know each other and work together. Very low means very difficult interactions; Extra high means an integrated and effective team with no communication problems.
Process maturity	Reflects the process maturity of the organisation. The computation of this value depends on the CMM Maturity Questionnaire but an estimate can be achieved by subtracting the CMM process maturity level from 5.

4. *Team cohesion*   New team so no information – rated Nominal (3)
5. *Process maturity*   Some process control in place – rated Nominal (3)

The sum of these values is 16 so the resulting exponent is 1.17.

The attributes (Figure 23.9) that are used to adjust the initial estimates in the post-architecture model fall into four classes:

1. Product attributes are concerned with required characteristics of the software product being developed.
2. Computer attributes are constraints imposed on the software by the hardware platform.
3. Personnel attributes are multipliers that take the experience and capabilities of the people working on the project into account.
4. Project attributes are concerned with the particular characteristics of the software development project.

Figure 23.10 shows an example of how these cost drivers influence effort estimates. I have taken a value for the exponent of 1.17 as discussed in the above example and I assume that RELY, CPLX, STOR, TOOL and SCED are the key cost drivers in the project. All of the other cost drivers have a nominal value of 1 so do not affect the computation of the effort.

Figure 23.9 Project
cost drivers

Product attributes

RELY	Required system reliability	DATA	Size of database used
CPLX	Complexity of system modules	RUSE	Required percentage of
DOCU	Extent of documentation required		reusable components

Computer attributes

| TIME | Execution time constraints | STOR | Memory constraints |
| PVOL | Volatility of development platform | | |

Personnel attributes

ACAP	Capability of project analysts	PCAP	Programmer capability
PCON	Personnel continuity	AEXP	Analyst experience in project domain
PEXP	Programmer experience in project domain	LTEX	Language and tool experience

Project attributes

| TOOL | Use of software tools | SITE | Extent of multi-site working and |
| SCED | Development schedule compression | | quality of site communications |

Figure 23.10 The
effect of cost drivers
on effort estimates

Exponent value	1.17
System size (including factors for reuse and requirements volatility)	128,000 DSI
Initial COCOMO estimate without cost drivers	**730 person-months**

Reliability	Very high, multiplier = 1.39
Complexity	Very high, multiplier = 1.3
Memory constraint	High, multiplier = 1.21
Tool use	Low, multiplier = 1.12
Schedule	Accelerated, multiplier = 1.29
Adjusted COCOMO estimate	**2306 person-months**

Reliability	Very low, multiplier = 0.75
Complexity	Very low, multiplier = 0.75
Memory constraint	None, multiplier = 1
Tool use	Very high, multiplier = 0.72
Schedule	Normal, multiplier = 1
Adjusted COCOMO estimate	**295 person-months**

In the example, I have assigned maximum and minimum values to the key cost drivers to show how they influence the effort estimate. The values taken are those from the COCOMO 2 reference manual (Boehm, 1997). You can see that high values for the cost drivers lead to an effort estimate that is more than three times the initial estimate whereas low values reduce the estimate to about 1/3 of the original.

This highlights the vast differences between different types of project and the difficulties of transferring experience from one application domain to another.

This formula proposed by the developers of the COCOMO 2 model reflects their experience and data but, in my view, it seems too complex for practical use. There are too many attributes and too much scope for uncertainty in estimating their values. In principle, each user of the model should calibrate the model and the attribute values according to its own historical project data as this will reflect local circumstances which affect the model. In practice, however, few organisations have collected enough data from past projects in a form that supports model calibration. Practical use of COCOMO 2 would normally start with the published values for the model parameters.

23.3.2 Algorithmic cost models in project planning

Project managers can use an algorithmic cost model to compare different ways of investing money to reduce project costs. This is particularly important where there must be hardware/software cost trade-offs and where there may be a need to recruit new staff with specific project skills.

Consider an embedded system to control an experiment that is to be launched into space. Spaceborne experiments have to be very reliable and are subject to stringent weight limits. The number of chips on a circuit board may have to be minimised. In terms of the COCOMO model, the multipliers based on computer constraints and reliability are greater than 1.

There are three components to be taken into account in costing this project:

1. The cost of the target hardware to execute the system.
2. The cost of the platform (computer plus software) to develop the system.
3. The cost of the effort required to develop the software.

Figure 23.11 shows some possible options that may be considered. These include spending more on target hardware to reduce software costs or investing in better development tools.

Additional hardware costs may be acceptable in this case because the system is a specialised system that does not have to be mass-produced. If hardware is embedded in consumer products, however, investing in target hardware to reduce software costs is rarely acceptable because it increases the unit cost of the product.

Figure 23.12 shows the hardware, software and total costs for the options A–F shown in Figure 23.11. Applying the COCOMO 2 model without cost drivers predicts an effort of 45 p.m. to develop an embedded software system for this application. The average cost for one person-month of effort is $15,000.

The relevant multipliers are based on storage and execution time constraints (TIME and STOR), the availability of tool support (cross-compilers, etc.) for the development system (TOOL) and development team's experience platform experience

Figure 23.11
Management options

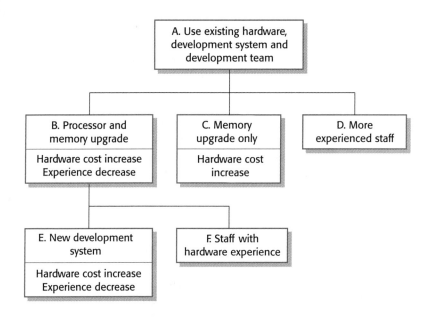

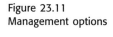

Option	RELY	STOR	TIME	TOOLS	LTEX	Total effort	Software cost	Hardware cost	Total cost
A	1.39	1.06	1.11	0.86	1	63	949,393	100,000	1,049,393
B	1.39	1	1	1.12	1.22	88	1,313,550	120,000	1,402,025
C	1.39	1	1.11	0.86	1	60	895,653	105,000	1,000,653
D	1.39	1.06	1.11	0.86	0.84	51	769,008	100,000	897,490
E	1.39	1	1	0.72	1.22	56	844,425	220,000	1,044,159
F	1.39	1	1	1.12	0.84	57	851,180	120,000	1,002,706

Figure 23.12 Costs of management options

(LTEX). In all options, the reliability multiplier (RELY) is 1.39, indicating that significant extra effort is needed to develop a reliable system.

The software cost (SC) is computed as follows:

$$SC = \text{Effort estimate} \times RELY \times TIME \times STOR \times TOOL \times EXP \times \$15,000$$

Option A represents the cost of building the system with existing support and staff. It represents a baseline for comparison. All other options involve either more hardware expenditure or the recruitment (with associated costs and risks) of new staff. Option B shows that upgrading hardware does not necessarily reduce costs because the experience multiplier is more significant. It is actually more cost-effective to upgrade memory rather than the whole computer configuration.

Option D appears to offer the lowest costs for all basic estimates. No additional hardware expenditure is involved but new staff must be recruited onto the project. If these are already available in the company, this is probably the best option to choose. If not, they must be recruited externally and this involves significant costs and risks. These may mean that the cost advantages of this option are much less significant than suggested by Figure 23.12. Option C offers a saving of almost $50,000 with virtually no associated risk. Conservative project managers would probably select this option rather than the riskier Option D.

The comparisons show the importance of staff experience as a multiplier. If good quality people with the right experience are recruited, this can significantly reduce project costs. This is consistent with the discussion of productivity factors in section 23.1. It also reveals that investment in new hardware and tools may not be cost-effective. Such strategies are often promoted by developers who like to work with new systems. However, the loss of experience is a more significant effect on the system cost than the savings which come from the new hardware system.

23.4 Project duration and staffing

As well as estimating the effort required to develop a software system and the overall cost of that effort, project managers must also estimate how long the software will take to develop and when staff will be needed to work on the project. The development time for the project is called the project schedule. Increasingly, organisations are demanding shorter development schedules so that their products can be brought to market before their competitor's.

The relationship between the number of staff working on a project, the total effort required and the development time is not linear. As the number of staff increases, more effort may be needed. People must spend more time communicating. More time is required to define interfaces between the parts of the system. Doubling the number of staff (for example) does not mean that the duration of the project will be halved.

The COCOMO model includes a formula to estimate the calendar time (TDEV) required to complete a project. The time computation formula is the same for all COCOMO levels:

$$TDEV = 3 \times (PM)^{(0.33+0.2*(B-1.01))}$$

PM is the effort computation and B is the exponent computed as discussed above (B is 1 for the early prototyping model). This computation predicts the nominal schedule for the project.

However, the predicted project schedule and the schedule which is required by the project plan are not necessarily the same thing. The planned schedule may be shorter or longer than the nominal predicted schedule. However, there is obviously a limit to the extent of schedule changes and this is predicted by the COCOMO 2 model:

$$\text{TDEV} = 3 \times (\text{PM})^{(0.33+0.2*(\text{B}-1.01))} \times \text{SCEDPercentage}/100$$

SCEDPercentage is the percentage increase or decrease in the nominal schedule. If the predicted figure then differs significantly from the planned schedule, it suggests that there is a high risk that there will be problems delivering the software as planned.

To illustrate the COCOMO development schedule computation, assume that a software project has been estimated to require 60 months of development effort (Option C in Figure 23.12). Assume that the value of exponent B is 1.17.

From the schedule equation, the time required to complete the project is:

$$\text{TDEV} = 3(60)^{0.36} = 13 \text{ months}$$

In this case, there is no schedule compression or expansion so the last term in the formula has no effect on the computation.

An interesting implication of the COCOMO model is that the time required to complete the project is a function of the total effort required for the project. It does not depend on the number of software engineers working on the project. This confirms the notion that adding more people to a project that is behind schedule is unlikely to help that schedule to be regained. Myers (1989) discusses the problems of schedule acceleration. He suggests that projects are likely to run into significant problems if they try to develop software without allowing sufficient calendar time.

Dividing the effort required on a project by the development schedule does not give a useful indication of the number of people required for the project team. Generally, the number of people employed on a software project builds up from a relatively small number to a peak and then declines.

Only a small number of people are needed at the beginning of a project to carry out planning and specification. As the project progresses and more detailed work is required, the number of staff builds up to a peak. After implementation and unit testing is complete, the number of staff required starts to fall until it reaches one or two when the product is delivered. A very rapid build-up of project staff often correlates with project schedule slippage. Project managers should therefore avoid adding too many staff to a project early in its lifetime.

The effort build-up can be modelled by what is called a Rayleigh curve (Londeix, 1987) and Putnam's estimation model (Putnam, 1978) incorporates a model of project staffing based around these curves. Putnam's model also includes development time as a key factor. As development time is reduced, the effort required to develop the system grows exponentially.

KEY POINTS

▶ Factors that affect productivity include individual aptitude (the dominant factor), domain experience, the development process, the size of the project, tool support and the working environment.

▶ There are various techniques of software cost estimation. In preparing an estimate, several of these should be used. If the estimates diverge widely, this means that inadequate estimating information is available.

▶ Software is often priced to gain a contract and the functionality of the system is then adjusted to meet the estimated price.

▶ Algorithmic cost modelling suffers from the fundamental difficulty that it relies on attributes of the finished product to make the cost estimate. At early stages of the project, these attributes are impossible to estimate accurately.

▶ The COCOMO costing model is a well-developed model that takes project, product, hardware and personnel attributes into account when formulating a cost estimate. It also includes a means of estimating development schedules.

▶ Algorithmic cost models are valuable to management as they support quantitative option analysis. They allow the cost of various options to be computed and, even with errors, the options can be compared on an objective basis.

▶ The time required to complete a project is not simply proportional to the number of people working on the project. Adding more people to a late project can make it later.

FURTHER READING

Software Project Management: Readings and Cases. A selection of papers and case studies on software project management that is particularly strong in its coverage of algorithmic cost modelling. (C. F. Kemerer (ed.), 1997, Irwin.)

'Cost models for future software life cycle processes: COCOMO 2'. A comprehensive introduction to the COCOMO 2 cost estimation model which includes the rationale for the formulae used. (B. Boehm *et al.*, *Annals of Software Engineering*, 1, Balzer Science Publishers, 1995.)

'Nine management guidelines for better cost estimating'. Sound practical advice on cost estimation. (A. Lederer and J. Pasad, *Comm. ACM*, 35(2), February 1992.)

EXERCISES

23.1   Describe two metrics that have been used to measure programmer productivity. Comment briefly on the advantages and disadvantages of these metrics.

23.2   In the development of large, embedded real-time systems, suggest five factors which are likely to have a significant effect on the productivity of the software development team.

23.3   Cost estimates are inherently risky irrespective of the estimation technique used. Suggest four ways in which the risk in a cost estimate can be reduced.

23.4   A software manager is in charge of the development of a safety-critical software system which is designed to control a radiotherapy machine to treat patients suffering from cancer. This system is embedded in the machine and must run on a special-purpose processor with a fixed amount of memory (8 Mbytes). The machine communicates with a patient database system to obtain the details of the patient and, after treatment, automatically records the radiation dose delivered and other treatment details in the database.

The COCOMO method is used to estimate the effort required to develop this system and an estimate of 26 person-months is computed. All cost driver multipliers were set to 1 when making this estimate.

Explain why this estimate should be adjusted to take project, personnel, product and organisational factors into account. Suggest four factors that might have significant effects on the initial COCOMO estimate and propose possible values for these factors. Justify why you have included each factor.

23.5   Give three reasons why algorithmic cost estimates prepared in different organisations are not directly comparable.

23.6   Explain how the algorithmic approach to cost estimation may be used by project managers for option analysis. Suggest a situation where managers may choose an approach that is not based on the lowest project cost.

23.7   Implement the COCOMO model using a spreadsheet such as Microsoft Excel. Details of the model can be downloaded from the COCOMO 2 web site. I have included a link to this site in the book's web pages.

23.8   Some very large software projects involve the writing of millions of lines of code. Suggest how useful the cost estimation models are likely to be for such systems. Why might the assumptions on which they are based be invalid for very large software systems?

23.9   Is it ethical for a company to quote a low price for a software contract knowing that the requirements are ambiguous and that they can charge a high price for subsequent changes requested by the customer?

23.10 Should measured productivity be used by managers during the staff appraisal process? What safeguards are necessary to ensure that quality is not affected by this?

24 Quality management

Objectives

The objectives of this chapter are to introduce software quality management and to describe specific quality management activities. When you have read this chapter, you will:

❑ understand the quality management process and the key process activities of quality assurance, quality planning and quality control;

❑ understand the importance of standards in the quality management process;

❑ understand the notion of a software metric and the differences between predictor metrics and control metrics;

❑ understand how measurement may be helpful in assessing some quality attributes and the current limitations of software measurement.

Contents

24.1 Quality assurance and standards
24.2 Quality planning
24.3 Quality control
24.4 Software measurement and metrics

Achieving a high level of product or service quality is the objective of most organisations. It is no longer acceptable to deliver poor quality products and then repair problems and deficiencies after they have been delivered to the customer. In this respect, software is the same as any other manufactured product such as cars, televisions or computers.

However, software quality is a complex concept that cannot be defined in a simple way. Classically, the notion of quality has been that the developed product should meet its specification (Crosby, 1979). In an ideal world, this definition should apply to all products but, for software systems, there are problems:

1.   The specification should be oriented towards the characteristics of the product that the customer wants. However, the development organisation may also have requirements (such as maintainability requirements) which are not included in the specification.

2.   We do not know how to specify certain quality characteristics (e.g. maintainability) in an unambiguous way.

3.   As I discussed in Part 1, which covered requirements engineering, it is very difficult to write complete software specifications. Therefore, although a software product may conform to its specification, users may not consider it to be a high-quality product.

Obviously, efforts should be made to improve specifications but currently we have to accept that these will be imperfect. We should recognise the problems with existing specifications and put procedures in place to improve quality within the constraints imposed by an imperfect specification. In particular, software attributes such as maintainability, portability or efficiency may be critical quality attributes that are not specified explicitly but which affect the perceived quality of the system. I discuss these quality attributes in section 24.2 which covers quality planning.

The responsibility of quality managers in an organisation is to ensure that the required level of product quality is achieved. In principle, quality management simply involves defining procedures and standards which should be used during software development and checking that these are followed by all engineers. In practice, however, there is more to quality management than this.

Good quality managers aim to develop a 'quality culture' where everyone responsible for product development is committed to achieving a high level of product quality. They encourage teams to take responsibility for the quality of their work and to develop new approaches to quality improvement. While standards and procedures are the basis of quality management, experienced quality managers recognise that there are intangible aspects to software quality (elegance, readability, etc.) which cannot be embodied in standards. They support people who are interested in these intangible aspects of quality and encourage professional behaviour in all team members.

Software quality management can be structured into three principal activities:

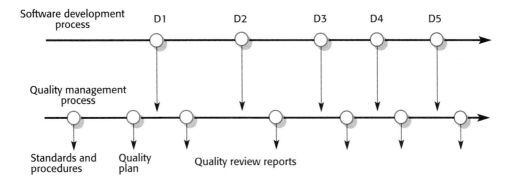

Software development process   D1   D2   D3   D4   D5

Quality management process

Standards and procedures   Quality plan   Quality review reports

Figure 24.1 Quality management and software development

1. *Quality assurance*   The establishment of a framework of organisational proced-ures and standards which lead to high-quality software.

2. *Quality planning*   The selection of appropriate procedures and standards from this framework and the adaptation of these for a specific software project.

3. *Quality control*   The definition and enactment of processes which ensure that the project quality procedures and standards are followed by the software devel-opment team.

Quality management provides an independent check on the software develop-ment process. The deliverables from the software process are input to the quality management process and are checked to ensure that they are consistent with organ-isational standards and goals (Figure 24.1). As the quality assurance and control team should be independent, they can take an objective view of the process and can report problems and difficulties to senior management in the organisation.

Quality management should be separated from project management so that quality is not compromised by management responsibilities for project budget and schedule. An independent team should be responsible for quality management and should report to management above the project manager level. The quality man-agement team should not be associated with any particular development group but should take organisation-wide responsibility for quality management.

An international standard that can be used in the development of a quality man-agement system in all industries is called ISO 9000. ISO 9000 is a set of standards that can be applied to a range of organisations from manufacturing through to ser-vice industries. ISO 9001 is the most general of these standards and applies to organ-isations concerned with the quality process in organisations which design, develop and maintain products. A supporting document (ISO 9000-3) interprets ISO 9000 for software development. Several books describing the ISO 9000 standard are avail-able (Johnson, 1993; Oskarsson and Glass, 1995; Peach, 1996).

ISO 9001 is a generic model of a quality process. It describes various aspects of that process and defines which standards and procedures should exist within an organisation. As it is not industry-specific, these are not defined in detail. Within any specific organisation, a set of appropriate quality processes should be defined and documented in an organisational quality manual.

Figure 24.2 Areas
covered by ISO 9001
model for quality
assurance

Management responsibility	Quality system
Control of non-conforming products	Design control
Handling, storage, packaging and delivery	Purchasing
Purchaser-supplied products	Product identification and traceability
Process control	Inspection and testing
Inspection and test equipment	Inspection and test status
Contract review	Corrective action
Document control	Quality records
Internal quality audits	Training
Servicing	Statistical techniques

Figure 24.2 shows the areas which are covered in ISO 9001. I do not have space here to discuss this standard in any depth. Ince (1994) and Oskarrson and Glass (1995) give a more detailed account of how the standard can be used to develop software quality management processes.

The quality assurance procedures in an organisation are documented in a quality manual which defines the quality process. In some countries, bodies exist which will certify that the quality process as expressed in the quality manual conforms to ISO 9001. Increasingly, customers look for ISO 9000 certification in a supplier as an indicator of how seriously that supplier takes quality.

Figure 24.3 ISO
9000 and quality
management

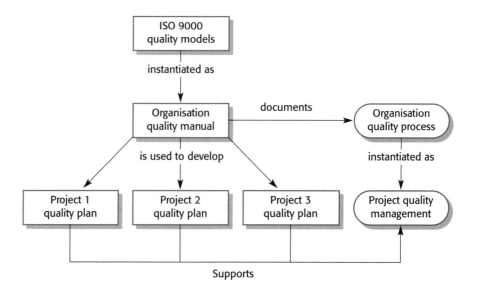

The relationship between ISO 9000, the quality manual and individual project quality plans is shown in Figure 24.3. This is derived from a model given in Ince's book (1994).

24.1 Quality assurance and standards

Quality assurance (QA) activities define a framework for achieving software quality. The QA process involves defining or selecting standards that should be applied to the software development process or software product. These standards may be embedded in procedures or processes which are applied during development. Processes may be supported by tools that embed knowledge of the quality standards.

There are two types of standard that may be established as part of the quality assurance process:

1. *Product standards* These are standards that apply to the software product being developed. They include document standards such as the structure of the requirements document which should be produced, documentation standards such as a standard comment header for an object class definition and coding standards which define how a programming language should be used.

2. *Process standards* These are standards that define the processes which should be followed during software development. They may include definitions of specification, design and validation processes and a description of the documents which must be generated in the course of these processes.

There is a very close relationship between product and process standards. The product standards apply to the outputs of the software process and, in many cases, the process standards include specific process activities that ensure that product standards are followed. I discuss the important relationship between process and product quality in section 24.1.2.

There are a number of reasons why software standards are important:

1. They provide an encapsulation of best, or at least most appropriate, practice. This knowledge is often only acquired after a great deal of trial and error. Building it into a standard avoids the repetition of past mistakes. Standards capture wisdom that is of value to the organisation.

2. They provide a framework around which the quality assurance process may be implemented. Given that standards encapsulate best practice, quality control simply involves ensuring that standards have been properly followed.

Figure 24.4 Product and process standards

Product standards	Process standards
Design review form	Design review conduct
Requirements document structure	Submission of documents to CM
Procedure header format	Version release process
Java programming style	Project plan approval process
Project plan format	Change control process
Change request form	Test recording process

3. They assist in continuity where work carried out by one person is taken up and continued by another. Standards ensure that all engineers within an organisation adopt the same practices. Consequently, learning effort when starting new work is reduced.

The development of software engineering project standards is a difficult and time-consuming process. National and international bodies such as the US DoD, ANSI, BSI, NATO and the IEEE have been active in the production of standards. These are general standards that can be applied across a range of projects. Bodies such as NATO and other defence organisations may require that their own standards are followed in software contracts.

National and international standards have been developed covering software engineering terminology, programming languages such as Ada and C++, notations such as charting symbols, procedures for deriving and writing software requirements, quality assurance procedures and software verification and validation processes (IEEE, 1994).

Quality assurance teams who are developing standards should normally base organisational standards on national and international standards. Using these standards as a starting point, the quality assurance team should draw up a standards 'handbook'. This should define the standards that are appropriate for their organisation. Examples of standards that might be included in such a handbook are shown in Figure 24.4.

Software engineers sometimes consider standards to be bureaucratic and irrelevant to the technical activity of software development. This is particularly likely when the standards require tedious form-filling and work recording. Although they usually agree about the general need for standards, engineers often find good reasons why standards are not necessarily appropriate to their particular project.

To avoid these problems, quality managers who set the standards need to be adequately resourced and should take the following steps:

1. Involve software engineers in the development of product standards. They should understand the motivation behind the development of the standard and be

committed to these standards. The standards document should not simply state a standard to be followed but should include a rationale of why particular standardisation decisions have been made.

2. Review and modify standards regularly to reflect changing technologies. Once standards are developed they tend to be enshrined in a company standards handbook and there is often a reluctance to change them. A standards handbook is essential but it should evolve with changing circumstances and technology.

3. Provide software tools to support standards wherever possible. Clerical standards are the cause of many complaints because of the tedious work involved in implementing them. If tool support is available, there is not a great deal of additional effort involved in development to the standards.

Process standards may cause difficulties if an impractical process is imposed on the development team. Such standards are often simply guidelines which must be sympathetically interpreted by individual project managers. There is no point in prescribing a particular way of working if it is inappropriate for a project or project team. Each project manager should therefore have the authority to modify process standards according to individual circumstances. However, standards that relate to product quality and the post-delivery process should only be changed after careful consideration.

The project manager and the quality manager can avoid the problems of inappropriate standards by careful quality planning. They should decide which of the standards in the handbook should be used without change, which should be modified and which should be ignored. New standards may have to be created in response to a particular project requirement. For example, standards for formal specifications may be required if these have not been used in previous projects. These new standards must be allowed to evolve during the project.

24.1.1   Documentation standards

Documentation standards in a software project are particularly important as documents are the only tangible way of representing the software and the software process. Standardised documents have a consistent appearance, structure and quality and should therefore be easier to read and understand.

There are three types of documentation standards:

1. *Documentation process standards*   These standards define the process which should be followed for document production.
2. *Document standards*   These are standards that govern the structure and presentation of documents.
3. *Document interchange standards*   These are standards that ensure that all electronic copies of documents are compatible.

Figure 24.5
A document
production process
including quality
checks

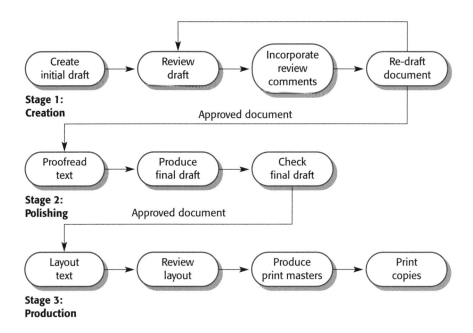

Process standards define the process used to produce documents. This means defining the procedures involved in document development and the software tools used for document production. Checking and refinement procedures which ensure that high-quality documents are produced should also be defined.

Document process quality standards must be flexible and must be able to cope with all types of document. For working papers or memos, there is no need for explicit quality checking. However, where documents are formal documents used for further development or are released to customers, a formal quality process should be adopted. Figure 24.5 is a model of one possible process.

Drafting, checking, revising and redrafting is an iterative process. It should continue until a document of acceptable quality is produced. The acceptable quality level depends on the document type and the potential readers of the document.

Document standards should apply to all documents produced in the course of the software development. Documents should have a consistent style and appearance and documents of the same type should have a consistent structure. Although document standards should be adapted to the needs of a specific project, it is good practice for the same 'house style' to be used in all of the documents produced by an organisation.

Examples of document standards which may be developed are:

1. *Document identification standards* As large systems projects may produce thousands of documents, each document must be uniquely identified. For formal documents, this identifier may be the formal identifier defined by the configuration manager. For informal documents, the style of the document identifier should be defined by the project manager.

2. *Document structure standards*   Each class of document produced during a software project should follow some standard structure. Structure standards should define the sections to be included and should specify the conventions used for page numbering, page header and footer information, and section and subsection numbering.

3. *Document presentation standards*   Document presentation standards define a 'house style' for documents and they contribute significantly to document consistency. They include the definition of fonts and styles used in the document, the use of logos and company names, the use of colour to highlight document structure, etc.

4. *Document update standards*   As a document evolves to reflect changes in the system, a consistent way of indicating document changes should be used. You can use different colours of cover to indicate a new document version and change bars in the margin to indicate modified or added paragraphs.

Document interchange standards are important as electronic copies of documents are interchanged. The use of interchange standards allows documents to be transferred electronically and re-created in their original form.

Assuming that the use of standard tools is mandated in the process standards, interchange standards define the conventions for using these tools. Examples of interchange standards include the use of an agreed standard macro set if a text formatting system is used for document production or the use of a standard style sheet if a word processor is used. Interchange standards may also limit the fonts and text styles used because of differing printer and display capabilities.

24.1.2   Process and product quality

An underlying assumption of quality management is that the quality of the development process directly affects the quality of delivered products. This assumption is derived from manufacturing systems where product quality is intimately related to the production process. Indeed, in automated mass production systems, once an acceptable level of process quality has been attained, product quality naturally follows. Figure 24.6 illustrates this approach to quality assurance.

Figure 24.6
Process-based
quality

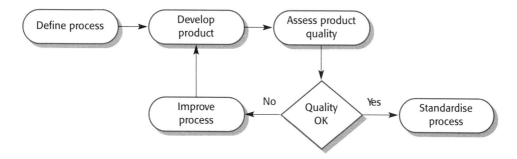

Process quality is particularly important in software development. The reason for this is that it is difficult to measure software attributes, such as maintainability, without using the software for a long period. Quality improvement focuses on identifying good quality products, examining the processes used to develop these products, then generalising these processes so that they may be applied across a range of projects. However, the relationship between software process and software product quality is complex. Changing the process does not always lead to improved product quality.

There is a clear link between process and product quality in manufacturing because the process is relatively easy to standardise and monitor. Once manufacturing systems are calibrated, they can be run again and again to output high-quality products. Software is not manufactured but is designed. As software development is a creative rather than a mechanical process, the influence of individual skills and experience is significant. External factors, such as the novelty of an application or commercial pressure for an early product release, also affect product quality irrespective of the process used.

Nevertheless, process quality has a significant influence on the quality of the software. Process quality management involves:

1. Defining process standards such as how reviews should be conducted, when reviews should be held, etc.
2. Monitoring the development process to ensure that the standards are being followed.
3. Reporting the software process to project management and to the buyer of the software.

A danger of process-based quality assurance is that the prescribed process may be inappropriate for the type of software which is being developed. For example, process quality standards may specify that a specification must be complete and approved before implementation can begin. However, some systems may require prototyping which involves program implementation. The quality team may suggest that this prototyping should not be carried out because its quality cannot be monitored. In such situations, senior management must intervene to ensure that the quality process supports rather than hinders product development.

I return to the relationships between process and product quality in the next chapter which is concerned with process improvement.

24.2 Quality planning

Quality planning should begin at an early stage in the software process. A quality plan should set out the desired product qualities. It should define how these are

Figure 24.7 Software
quality attributes

Safety	Understandability	Portability
Security	Testability	Usability
Reliability	Adaptability	Reusability
Resilience	Modularity	Efficiency
Robustness	Complexity	Learnability

to be assessed. It therefore defines what 'high quality' software actually means. Without such a definition, different engineers may work in an opposing way so that different product attributes are optimised. The result of the quality planning process is a project quality plan.

The quality plan should select those organisational standards that are appropriate to a particular product and development process. New standards may have to be defined if the project uses new methods and tools. Humphrey (1989), in his classic book on software management, suggests an outline structure for a quality plan. This includes:

1. *Product introduction* A description of the product, its intended market and the quality expectations for the product.
2. *Product plans* The critical release dates and responsibilities for the product along with plans for distribution and product servicing.
3. *Process descriptions* The development and service processes which should be used for product development and management.
4. *Quality goals* The quality goals and plans for the product, including an identification and justification of critical product quality attributes.
5. *Risks and risk management* The key risks which might affect product quality and the actions to address these risks.

When writing quality plans, you should try to keep them as short as possible. If the document is too long, engineers will not read it and this will defeat the purpose of producing a quality plan.

There is a wide range of potential software quality attributes (Figure 24.7) that should be considered during the quality planning process. In general, it is not possible for any system to be optimised for all of these attributes so a critical part of quality planning is selecting critical quality attributes and planning how these can be achieved.

The quality plan should define the most significant quality attributes for the product being developed. It may be that efficiency is paramount and other factors have to be sacrificed to achieve this. If this is set out in the plan, the engineers working on the development can cooperate to achieve this. The plan should also define the quality assessment process. This should be a standard way of assessing whether some quality, such as maintainability, is present in the product.

24.3 Quality control

Quality control involves overseeing the software development process to ensure that quality assurance procedures and standards are being followed. As discussed earlier in the chapter (see Figure 24.1), the deliverables from the software process are checked against the defined project standards in the quality control process.

The quality control process has its own set of procedures and reports that must be used during software development. These procedures should be straightforward and easily understood by the engineers developing the software.

There are two complementary approaches to quality control:

1. Quality reviews where the software, its documentation and the processes used to produce that software are reviewed by a group of people. They are responsible for checking that the project standards have been followed and that software and documents conform to these standards. Deviations from the standards are noted and brought to the attention of project management.

2. Automated software assessment where the software and the documents which are produced are processed by some program and compared to the standards which apply to that particular development project. This automated assessment may involve a quantitative measurement of some software attributes. I discuss software measurement and metrics in section 24.4.

24.3.1 Quality reviews

Reviews are the most widely used method of validating the quality of a process or product. They involve a group of people examining part or all of a software process, system or its associated documentation to discover potential problems. The conclusions of the review are formally recorded and passed to the author or whoever is responsible for correcting the discovered problems.

Figure 24.8 briefly describes several different types of review. Program inspections have already been covered in Chapter 19. Progress reviews are part of the management process as discussed in Chapter 4. In this chapter, I concentrate on reviews as part of the quality management process. The different review processes have much in common and I have already described the process of setting up a review in Chapter 19.

The remit of the review team is to detect errors and inconsistencies and point them out to the designer or document author. Reviews are document-based but are not limited to specifications, designs or code. Documents such as process models, test plans, configuration management procedures, process standards and user manuals may all be reviewed.

The review team should include those project members who can make an effective contribution. For example, if a sub-system design is being reviewed, designers of related sub-systems should be included in the review team. They may bring important

Figure 24.8 Types
of review

Review type	Principal purpose
Design or program inspections	To detect detailed errors in the requirements, design or code. The review should be driven by a checklist of possible errors.
Progress reviews	To provide information for management about the overall progress of the project. This is both a process and a product review and is concerned with costs, plans and schedules.
Quality reviews	To carry out a technical analysis of product components or documentation to find mismatches between the specification and the component design, code or documentation and to ensure that defined quality standards have been followed.

insights into sub-system interfaces which could be missed if the sub-system is considered in isolation.

The review team should have a core of 3–4 people who are selected as principal reviewers. One member should be a senior designer who can take the responsibility for making significant technical decisions. The principal reviewers may invite other project members to contribute to the review. They may not be involved in reviewing the whole document. Rather, they concentrate on those parts which affect their work. Alternatively, the review team may circulate the document being reviewed and ask for written comments from other project members.

Documents to be reviewed must be distributed well in advance of the review to allow reviewers time to read and understand them. Although this delay can disrupt the development process, reviewing is ineffective if the review team have not properly understood the documents before the review takes place.

The review itself should be relatively short (two hours at most). The author of the document being reviewed should 'walk through' the document with the review team. One team member should chair the review and another should formally record all review decisions. During the review, the chair is responsible for ensuring that all written comments are considered. On completion of the review, the actions are noted and forms recording the comments and actions are signed by the designer and the review chair. These are then filed as part of the formal project documentation. If only minor problems are discovered, a further review may be unnecessary. The chairman is responsible for ensuring that the required changes are made. If major changes are necessary, a follow-on review may be arranged.

24.4 Software measurement and metrics

Software measurement is concerned with deriving a numeric value for some attribute of a software product or a software process. By comparing these values to each other and to standards which apply across an organisation, it is possible to draw conclusions about the quality of software or software processes. For example, say an organisation plans to introduce a new software testing tool. Before introducing the tool, the number of software defects discovered in a given time may be recorded; after introducing the tool, this process is repeated. If more defects are discovered in the same amount of time after introducing the tool then it would appear that it provides useful support for the software validation process.

A number of large companies such as Hewlett-Packard (Grady, 1993) and AT&T (Barnard and Price, 1994) have introduced metrics programmes and are using collected metrics in their quality management processes. Most of the focus has been on collecting metrics on program defects and the verification and validation processes. Offen and Jeffrey (1997) and Hall and Fenton (1997) discuss the introduction of such programmes in industry. The ami handbook (Pulford et al., 1996) gives detailed advice on measurement and using measurement for process improvement.

However, the use of systematic software measurement and metrics is still relatively uncommon. There is a reluctance to introduce measurement because the benefits are unclear. One reason for this is that, in many companies, the software processes used are still poorly organised and are not sufficiently mature to make use of measurements. Another reason is that there are no standards for metrics and hence limited support for data collection and analysis. Most companies will not be prepared to introduce measurement until such standards and tools are available.

A software metric is any type of measurement which relates to a software system, process or related documentation. Examples are measures of the size of a product in lines of code, the Fog index (Gunning, 1962) which is a measure of the readability of a passage of written text, the number of reported faults in a delivered software product and the number of person-days required to develop a system component.

Metrics may be either control metrics or predictor metrics. Control metrics are usually associated with software processes; predictor metrics are associated with software products. Examples of control or process metrics are the average effort and time required to repair reported defects. Examples of predictor metrics are the cyclomatic complexity of a module, the average length of identifiers in a program and the number of attributes and operations associated with objects in a design. Both control and predictor metrics may influence management decision making as shown in Figure 24.9. I cover process metrics and their role in process improvement in Chapter 25. The focus here is on measurement to predict software product quality.

It is often impossible to measure software quality attributes directly. Attributes such as maintainability, complexity and understandability are affected by many different factors and there are no straightforward metrics for them. Rather, we have to measure some internal attribute of the software (such as its size) and assume that a relationship exists between what we can measure and what we want to know. Ideally, there should be a clear and validated relationship between the internal and the external software attributes.

Figure 24.10 shows some external quality attributes which might be of interest and internal attributes which can be measured and which might be related to the

Figure 24.9 Predictor and control metrics

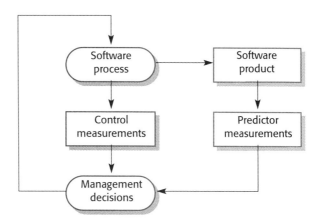

Figure 24.10 Relationships between internal and external software attributes

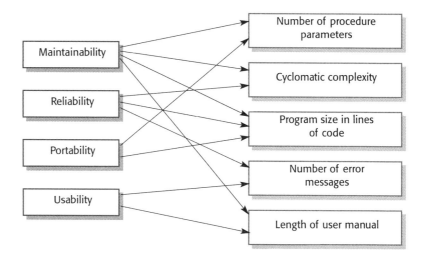

external attribute. The diagram suggests that there may be a relationship between external and internal attributes but it does not say what that relationship is. If the measure of the internal attribute is to be a useful predictor of the external software characteristic, three conditions must hold (Kitchenham, 1990):

1. The internal attribute must be measured accurately.
2. A relationship must exist between what we can measure and the external behavioural attribute.
3. This relationship is understood, has been validated and can be expressed in terms of a formula or model.

Model formulation involves identifying the functional form of the model (linear, exponential, etc.) by analysis of collected data, identifying the parameters which are to be included in the model and calibrating these using existing data. Such model development, if it is to be trusted, requires significant experience in statistical techniques. A professional statistician should be involved in the process.

24.4.1 The measurement process

A software measurement process that may be part of a quality control process is shown in Figure 24.11. Each of the components of the system is analysed separately and the different values of the metric compared both with each other and, perhaps, with historical measurement data collected on previous projects. Anomalous measurements should be used to focus the quality assurance effort on components that may have quality problems.

The key stages in this process are:

1. *Choose measurements to be made* The questions that the measurement is intended to answer should be formulated and the measurements required to answer these questions defined. Measurements which are not directly relevant to these questions need not be collected. Basili's GQM (Goal-Question-Metric) paradigm (Basili and Rombach, 1988), discussed in the following chapter, is a good approach to use when deciding what data is to be collected.

2. *Select components to be assessed* It may not be necessary or desirable to assess metric values for all of the components in a software system. In some cases, a representative selection of components may be chosen for measurement. In others, components which are particularly critical such as core components that are in almost constant use may be assessed.

3. *Measure component characteristics* The selected components are measured and metric values are computed. This normally involves processing the component representation (design, code, etc.) using an automated data collection tool. This may be specially written or may already be incorporated in CASE tools that are used in an organisation.

Figure 24.11 The process of product measurement

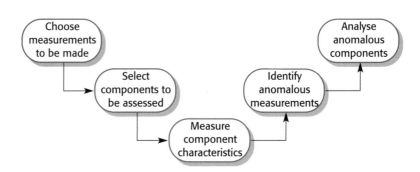

4. *Identify anomalous measurements*   Once the component measurements have been made, these should then be compared to each other and to previous measurements which have been recorded in a measurement database. You should look for unusually high or low values for each metric as these suggest that there could be problems with the component exhibiting these values.

5. *Analyse anomalous components*   Once components which have anomalous values for particular metrics have been identified, you should examine these components to decide whether or not the anomalous metric values mean that the quality of the component is compromised. An anomalous metric value for complexity (say) does not necessarily mean a poor quality component. There may be some other reason for the high value and it may not mean that there are component quality problems.

Collected data should be maintained as an organisational resource and historical records of all projects should be maintained even when data has not been used during a particular project. Once a sufficiently large measurement database has been established, comparisons across projects may then be made and specific metrics can be refined according to organisational needs.

24.4.2   Product metrics

Product metrics are concerned with characteristics of the software itself. Unfortunately, software characteristics that can be easily measured such as size and cyclomatic complexity do not have a clear and universal relationship with quality attributes such as understandability and maintainability. The relationships vary depending on the development processes and technology and the type of system that is being developed. Organisations interested in measurement have to construct a historical database. This can then be used to discover how the software product attributes are related to the qualities of interest to the organisation.

Product metrics fall into two classes:

1. Dynamic metrics which are collected by measurements made of a program in execution.
2. Static metrics which are collected by measurements made of the system representations such as the design, program or documentation.

These different types of metric are related to different quality attributes. Dynamic metrics help to assess the efficiency and the reliability of a program whereas static metrics help to assess the complexity, understandability and maintainability of a software system.

Dynamic metrics are usually fairly closely related to software quality attributes. It is relatively easy to measure the execution time required for particular functions and to assess the time required to start up a system. These relate directly to the

Figure 24.12
Software product
metrics

Software metric	Description
Fan-in/Fan-out	Fan-in is a measure of the number of functions that call some other function (say X). Fan-out is the number of functions which are called by function X. A high value for fan-in means that X is tightly coupled to the rest of the design and changes to X will have extensive knock-on effects. A high value for fan-out suggests that the overall complexity of X may be high because of the complexity of the control logic needed to coordinate the called components.
Length of code	This is a measure of the size of a program. Generally, the larger the size of the code of a program component, the more complex and error-prone that component is likely to be.
Cyclomatic complexity	This is a measure of the control complexity of a program. This control complexity may be related to program understandability. The computation of cyclomatic complexity is covered in Chapter 20.
Length of identifiers	This is a measure of the average length of distinct identifiers in a program. The longer the identifiers, the more likely they are to be meaningful and hence the more understandable the program.
Depth of conditional nesting	This is a measure of the depth of nesting of if-statements in a program. Deeply nested if-statements are hard to understand and are potentially error-prone.
Fog index	This is a measure of the average length of words and sentences in documents. The higher the value for the Fog index, the more difficult the document may be to understand.

system's efficiency. Similarly, the number of system failures and the type of failure can be logged and related directly to the reliability of the software as discussed in Chapter 16.

Static metrics, on the other hand, have an indirect relationship with quality attributes. A large number of these metrics have been proposed and experiments carried out to try to derive and validate the relationships between these metrics and system complexity, understandability and maintainability. Figure 24.12 describes several static metrics which have been used for assessing quality attributes. Of these, program or component length and control complexity seem to be the most reliable predictors of understandability, system complexity and maintainability.

Since the early 1990s, there have been a number of studies of object-oriented metrics. Some of these have been derived from the older metrics shown in Figure 24.12 but others are unique to object-oriented systems. A number of object-oriented metrics are explained in Figure 24.13. These metrics are less mature than the metrics in Figure 24.12 which are intended for function-oriented designs so their usefulness as predictor metrics is still being established.

Figure 24.13
Object-oriented
metrics

Object-oriented metric	Description
Depth of inheritance tree	This represents the number of discrete levels in the inheritance tree where subclasses inherit attributes and operations (methods) from superclasses. The deeper the inheritance tree, the more complex the design as, potentially, many different object classes have to be understood to understand the object classes at the leaves of the tree.
Method fan-in/fan-out	This is directly related to fan-in and fan-out as described above and means essentially the same thing. However, it may be appropriate to make a distinction between calls from other methods within the object and calls from external methods.
Weighted methods per class	This is the number of methods included in a class weighted by the complexity of each method. Therefore, a simple method may have a complexity of 1 and a large and complex method a much higher value. The larger the value for this metric, the more complex the object class. Complex objects are more likely to be more difficult to understand. They may not be logically cohesive so cannot be reused effectively as superclasses in an inheritance tree.
Number of overriding operations	These are the number of operations in a superclass which are overridden in a subclass. A high value for this metric indicates that the superclass used may not be an appropriate parent for the subclass.

The specific metrics that are relevant depend on the project, the goals of the quality management team and the type of software that is being developed. All of the metrics shown in Figures 24.12 and 24.13 may be useful in some situations. Equally, however, there will be other situations where they are inappropriate. When introducing software measurement as part of the quality management process, organisations should experiment to discover the most appropriate metrics for their needs.

24.4.3 Analysis of measurements

One of the problems with collecting quantitative data about software and software projects is understanding what that data really means. It is easy to misinterpret data and to make inferences that are incorrect. Measurements must be carefully analysed to understand what they really mean.

To illustrate how collected data can be interpreted in different ways consider the following scenario:

A manager decides to monitor the number of change requests submitted by customers based on an assumption that there is a relationship between these change requests and product usability and suitability. The higher the number of change requests, the less the software meets the needs of the customer.

Processing change requests and changing the software is expensive. The organisation therefore decides to modify its process to increase customer satisfaction and, at the same time, reduce the costs of change. It is intended that the process changes will result in better products and fewer change requests.

Process changes are initiated which involve more customer involvement in the software design process. Beta-testing of all products is introduced and customer-requested modifications are incorporated in the delivered product. New versions of products, developed with this modified process, are delivered. In some cases, the number of change requests is reduced; in others, it is increased. The manager is baffled and cannot assess the effects of the process changes on the product quality.

To understand why this kind of thing can happen, you have to understand why change requests are made. One reason is that the delivered software does not do what customers want it to do. Another possibility is that the software is very good and is widely and heavily used, sometimes for purposes for which it was not originally designed. Because there are so many people using it, it is natural that more change requests are generated.

A third possibility is that the company producing the software is responsive to customers' change requests. Customers are therefore satisfied with the service they receive. They generate a lot of change requests because they know that these requests will be taken seriously. Their suggestions will probably be incorporated in later versions of the software.

The number of change requests might decrease because the process changes have been effective and have made the software more usable and suitable. Alternatively, the number might have decreased because the product has lost market share to a rival product. There are consequently fewer product users. The number of change requests might increase because there are more users, because the beta-testing process has convinced users that the company is willing to make changes or because the beta-test sites were not typical of most usage of the program.

To analyse the change request data, we do not simply need to know the number of change requests. We need to know who made the request, how they use the software and why the request was made. We need to know if there are external factors such as modifications to the change request procedure or market changes which might have an effect. With this information, it is then possible to find out if the process changes have been effective in increasing product quality.

This illustrates that interpreting quantitative data about a product or a process is an uncertain process. Processes and products that are being measured are not insulated from their environment and changes to that environment may make comparisons of data invalid. Quantitative data about human activities cannot always be taken at face value. Underlying reasons that might account for the measured value should be investigated.

KEY POINTS

▶ Software quality management is concerned with ensuring that software has a low number of defects and that it reaches the required standards of maintainability, reliability, portability, etc. Quality management activities include quality assurance that sets the standards for software development, quality planning and quality control that checks the software against the defined standards.

▶ An organisational quality manual should document a set of quality assurance procedures. This may be based on the generic model suggested in the ISO 9000 standards.

▶ Software standards are important to quality assurance as they represent an identification of 'best practice'. The quality control process is concerned with checking that the software process and the software being developed conform to these standards.

▶ Reviews of the software process deliverables are the most widely used technique for assessing quality.

▶ Software measurement can be used to gather quantitative data about software and the software process. The values of the software metrics which are collected may be used to make inferences about product and process quality.

▶ Product quality metrics are particularly valuable for highlighting anomalous components which may have quality problems. These components should then be analysed in more detail.

▶ There are no standardised and universally applicable software metrics. Organisations must select metrics and analyse measurements based on local knowledge and circumstances.

FURTHER READING

'Making sense of measurement for small organisations'. This is an interesting article about the practical application of metrics. It makes the point that all uses of metrics have to take their context into account. (K. Kautz, *IEEE Software,* March/April 1999.)

ISO 9000 and Software Quality Assurance. This is a readable introduction to ISO 9000 and its relevance to software quality assurance. Its structure is based on the quality standard with a chapter on each topic. (D. Ince, 1994, McGraw-Hill.)

IEEE Software, March 1997. This is a special issue on software measurement which has particularly useful articles on introducing a measurement programme.

A quantitative approach to software management: The ami handbook. This is an excellent 'how-to' guide which discusses how to introduce a measurement programme and use the results for process improvement. (K. Pulford, A. Kuntzmann-Combelles and S. Shirlaw, 1996, Addison-Wesley.)

EXERCISES

24.1   Explain why a high-quality software process should lead to high-quality software products. Discuss possible problems with this system of quality management.

24.2   What are the stages involved in the review of a software design?

24.3   Discuss the assessment of software quality according to the quality attributes shown in Figure 24.7. You should consider each attribute in turn and explain how it might be assessed.

24.4   Design an electronic form that may be used to record review comments and which could be used to mail comments electronically to reviewers.

24.5   Briefly describe possible standards which might be used for:

- the use of control constructs in C, C++ or Java;
- reports which might be submitted for a term project in a university;
- the process of making and approving changes to a program (see Chapter 29);
- the process of purchasing and installing a new computer.

24.6   Assume you work for an organisation that develops database products for microcomputer systems. This organisation is interested in quantifying its software development. Write a report suggesting appropriate metrics and suggest how these can be collected.

24.7   Explain why design metrics are, by themselves, an inadequate method of predicting design quality.

24.8   Consult the literature and find other design quality metrics that have been suggested apart from those discussed here. Consider these metrics in detail and assess whether they are likely to be of real value.

24.9   Do software standards stifle technological innovation?

24.10   A colleague who is a very good programmer produces software with a low number of defects but consistently ignores organisational quality standards. How should the managers in the organisation react to this behaviour?

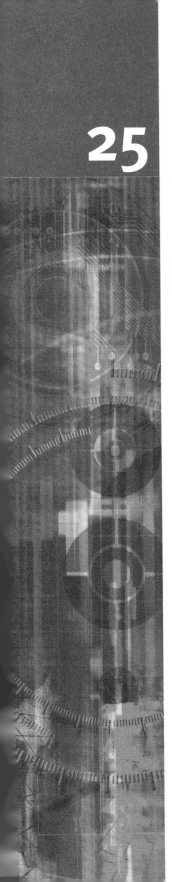

25 Process improvement

Objectives

The objective of this chapter is to explain how software processes can be improved to produce better software. When you have read this chapter, you will:

- ❑ understand the principles of software process improvement and why process improvement is worthwhile;

- ❑ understand how software process factors influence software quality and the productivity of software developers;

- ❑ understand the SEI's Process Capability Maturity Model (CMM) which may be used to assess the quality of the software process in large organisations;

- ❑ understand why CMM-based improvement is not applicable to all types of software process.

Contents

25.1 Process and product quality
25.2 Process analysis and modelling
25.3 Process measurement
25.4 The SEI Process Capability Maturity Model
25.5 Process classification

Over the past few years, there has been a great deal of interest in the software engineering community in process improvement. Process improvement means understanding existing processes and changing these processes to improve product quality and/or reduce costs and development time. Most of the literature on process improvement has focused on improving processes to improve product quality and, in particular, to reduce the number of defects in delivered software. Once this has been achieved cost or schedule reduction might become the principal improvement goals.

As discussed in Chapter 24, there is a strong relationship between the quality of the developed software product and the quality of the software process used to create that product. By improving the software process, it is hoped that the related product quality is correspondingly enhanced. Software processes are inherently complex and involve a very large number of activities. Like products, processes also have attributes or characteristics as shown in Figure 25.1.

It is not possible to make process improvements that optimise all process attributes simultaneously. For example, if a rapid development process is required then it may be necessary to reduce the process visibility. Making a process visible means producing documents at regular intervals. This will slow down the process.

Process improvement does not simply mean adopting particular methods or tools or using some model of a process that has been used elsewhere. Although organisations which develop the same type of software clearly have much in common, there are always local organisational factors, procedures and standards which influence the process. The simple introduction of published process improvements is

Figure 25.1 Process characteristics

Process characteristic	Description
Understandability	To what extent is the process explicitly defined and how easy is it to understand the process definition?
Visibility	Do the process activities culminate in clear results so that the progress of the process is externally visible?
Supportability	To what extent can the process activities be supported by CASE tools?
Acceptability	Is the defined process acceptable to and usable by the engineers responsible for producing the software product?
Reliability	Is the process designed in such a way that process errors are avoided or trapped before they result in product errors?
Robustness	Can the process continue in spite of unexpected problems?
Maintainability	Can the process evolve to reflect changing organisational requirements or identified process improvements?
Rapidity	How fast can the process of delivering a system from a given specification be completed?

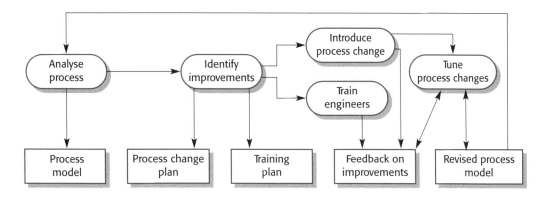

Figure 25.2
The process
improvement
process

unlikely to be successful. Process improvement should always be seen as an activity that is specific to an organisation or a part of a larger organisation.

A generic model of the process improvement process is illustrated in Figure 25.2. Process improvement is a long-term, iterative process. Each of the activities shown in Figure 25.2 might last several months. Successful process improvement requires organisational commitment and resources. It must be sanctioned by senior management and must have an associated budget to support improvements.

There are a number of key stages in the process improvement process:

1. *Process analysis*   Process analysis involves examining existing processes and producing a process model to document and understand the process. In some cases, it may be possible to analyse the process quantitatively Measurements made during the analysis add extra information to the process model. Quantitative analysis before and after changes have been introduced allows an objective assessment of the benefits (or the problems) of the process change.

2. *Improvement identification*   This stage is concerned with using the results of the process analysis to identify quality, schedule or cost bottlenecks where process factors might adversely influence the product quality. Process improvement should focus on loosening these bottlenecks by proposing new procedures, methods and tools to address the problems.

3. *Process change introduction*   Process change introduction means putting new procedures, methods and tools into place and integrating them with other process activities. It is important to allow enough time to introduce changes and to ensure that these changes are compatible with other process activities and with organisational procedures and standards.

4. *Process change training*   Without training, it is not possible to gain the full benefits from process changes. They may be rejected by the managers and engineers responsible for development projects. All too commonly, process changes have been imposed without adequate training and the effects of these changes have been to degrade rather than improve product quality.

5. *Change tuning* Proposed process changes will never be completely effective as soon as they are introduced. There needs to be a tuning phase where minor problems are discovered, modifications to the process are proposed and are introduced. This tuning phase should last for several months until the development engineers are happy with the new process.

Once a change has been introduced, the improvement process can iterate with further analysis used to identify process problems, propose improvements, etc. It is impractical to introduce too many changes at the same time. Apart from the problems of training that this causes, introducing too many changes makes it impossible to assess the effect of each change on the process.

25.1 Process and product quality

As discussed in Chapter 24, process improvement is based on the assumption that the critical factor that influences product quality is the quality of the product development process. These ideas of process improvement stemmed from the work of an American engineer called W. E. Deming who worked with Japanese industry after World War 2 to improve quality. Japanese industry has been committed to a process of continuous process improvement (the Japanese word for this is *kaizen*) for many years. This has largely contributed to the generally high quality of Japanese manufactured goods.

Deming (and others) introduced the idea of statistical quality control. This is based on measuring the number of product defects and relating these defects to the process. The process is improved with the aim of reducing the number of product defects. The process is improved until it is repeatable. That is, the results of the process are predictable and the number of defects reduced. It is then standardised and a further improvement cycle begins.

Where manufacturing is involved, the process/product relationship is very obvious. Improving a process so that defects are avoided will lead to better products. This link is less obvious when the product is intangible and dependent, to some extent, on intellectual processes which cannot be automated. Software quality is not dependent on a manufacturing process but on a design process where individual human considerations are significant. In some classes of product, the process used is the most significant determinant of product quality. However, for innovative applications in particular, the people involved in the process may be more important than the process used.

For software products (or any other intellectual products such as books, films, etc. where quality principally depends on the design), there are four factors that can affect product quality. These are shown in Figure 25.3.

Figure 25.3 Principal
software product
quality factors

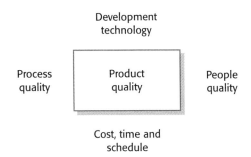

Development
technology

Process
quality

Product
quality

People
quality

Cost, time and
schedule

The influence of each of these factors depends on the size and type of the project. For very large systems that are composed of separate sub-systems, developed by different teams, the principal determinant of product quality is the software process. The major problems with large projects are integration, project management and communications. There is usually a mix of abilities and experience in the team members and, as the development process usually takes place over a number of years, the development team is volatile. It may change completely over the lifetime of the project. Therefore, particularly skilled or talented individuals don't usually have a dominant effect over the lifetime of the project.

For small projects, however, where there are only a few team members, the quality of the development team is more important than the development process used. If the team has a high level of ability and experience, the quality of the product is likely to be high. If the team is inexperienced and unskilled, a good process may limit the damage but will not, in itself, lead to high-quality software.

Where teams are small, good development technology is particularly important. The team cannot devote a lot of time to tedious administrative procedures. Engineers spend much of their time designing and programming the system, so good tools can significantly affect their productivity. For large projects, a basic level of development technology is essential for information management. Paradoxically, however, sophisticated tools are less important. Team members spend a relatively smaller proportion of their time in development activities and more time communicating and understanding other parts of the system. This is the dominant factor affecting their productivity. Development tools make no difference to this.

The base of the rectangle in Figure 25.3 is absolutely critical. If a project, irrespective of size, is under-budgeted or planned with an unrealistic delivery schedule, the product quality will be affected. A good process requires resources for its effective implementation. If these resources are insufficient, the process cannot work effectively. If resources are inadequate, only excellent people can save a project. Even then, if the deficit is too great, the product quality will be degraded.

All too often, the real cause of software quality problems is not poor management, inadequate processes or poor quality training. Rather, it is the fact that organisations must compete to survive. Many software projects are deliberately under-budgeted in order to win a development contract. Pricing to win (see Chapter 23) is an inevitable consequence of a competitive system. It is not surprising that product quality under such a system is difficult to control.

25.2 Process analysis and modelling

Process analysis and modelling involve studying existing processes and developing an abstract model of these processes that captures their key characteristics. Several generic process models were introduced in Chapter 1. Throughout the book, I have used process model fragments to discuss specific activities such as requirements engineering, software design, etc. Huff (1996) gives a good overview of the general topic of software process modelling.

Process analysis is concerned with studying existing processes to understand the relationships between different parts of the process. The initial stages of process analysis are inevitably qualitative where the analyst is simply trying to discover the key features of the model. Later stages may be more quantitative. The process is analysed in more detail using various metrics that are automatically or manually collected. After analysis, the process may be described using a process model.

The starting point for process analysis should be whatever 'formal' process model is used. Many organisations have such a formal model which may be imposed on them by the software customer. This standard defines the critical activities and life-cycle deliverables which must be produced.

Formal models can serve as a useful starting point for process analysis. However, they rarely include enough detail or reflect the real activities of software development. Formal process models are fairly abstract and only define the principal process activities and deliverables. It is usually necessary to 'look inside' the model to find the real process that is being enacted. Furthermore, the actual process which is followed often differs significantly from the formal model, although the specified deliverables will usually be produced.

Techniques of process analysis include:

1. *Questionnaires and interviews* The engineers working on a project are questioned about what actually goes on. The answers to a formal questionnaire are refined during personal interviews with those involved in the process.

2. *Ethnographic studies* As discussed in Chapter 6, ethnographic studies may be used to understand the nature of software development as a human activity. Such analysis reveals subtleties and complexities which may not be discovered using other techniques.

Each of these approaches has advantages and disadvantages. Questionnaire-based analysis can be carried out fairly quickly once the right questions have been discovered. However, if the questions are badly worded or inappropriate, you will end up with an incomplete or inaccurate model of the process. Furthermore, questionnaire-based analysis appears like a form of assessment. The engineers being questioned may give the answers which they think the questioner wants to hear rather than the truth about the process used.

Ethnographic analysis is more likely to discover the true process used. However, is a prolonged and expensive activity which can last for several months. It relies on external observation of the process. A complete analysis must continue from the initial stages of a project through to product delivery and maintenance. This will probably be impractical, when projects last several years. Ethnographic analysis, therefore, is most useful when an in-depth understanding of process fragments is required.

The output of process analysis is a process model that may be expressed at a greater or lesser level of detail. The process models used in this book are abstract, simplified models which present a generic view of the processes concerned. At this abstract level, these processes are the same in many different organisations. However, these generic models have different instantiations depending on the type of software being developed and the organisational environment. Detailed process models are not usually transferable from one organisation to another.

Generic process models are a useful basis for discussing processes. However, they do not include enough information for process analysis and improvement. Process improvement needs information about activities, deliverables, people, communications, schedules and other organisational processes that affect the software development process. Figure 25.4 explains what might be included in a detailed process model.

The timing of and the dependencies between activities, deliverables and communications must also be recorded in a process model. Sometimes activities can be carried out in parallel and sometimes in sequence. They may be interleaved so that the same engineer is involved in several activities. Deliverables may be dependent on other deliverables or on some communications between engineers working on the process.

In the examples of process models in this book, I show the approximate sequence of activities from left to right. Activities that may be carried out in parallel are, as far as possible, aligned vertically.

Detailed process models are extremely complex. It is very difficult to construct a single model that incorporates all of the above elements. To illustrate the complexity of a model, consider the process fragments below. These describe the process of testing a single module in a large system which uses a strictly controlled configuration management process (see Chapter 29). The software being tested and the test data are under configuration control. Figure 25.5 shows the role responsible for the testing process, process inputs and outputs and pre- and post-conditions.

Figure 25.6 decomposes the process 'Test module' into a number of separate activities. This fragment shows only the activities in the relatively simple activity of module testing. There are four streams of activities concerned with preparing test data, writing a test harness for the module, running the tests and reporting on the tests. The activities in the preparation streams would normally be interleaved. Obviously, the preparation activities precede the execution and reporting activities.

I have left out information on process pre- and post-conditions and process inputs and outputs in this diagram. This information would make the model complex and difficult to understand. Rather than trying to get all information into a single model,

Process model element	Description
Activity (represented by a round-edged rectangle with no drop shadow)	An activity has a clearly defined objective, entry and exit conditions. Examples of activities are preparing a set of test data to test a module, coding a function or a module, proofreading a document, etc. Generally, an activity is atomic, i.e. it is the responsibility of one person or group. It is not decomposed into sub-activities.
Process (represented by a round-edged rectangle with drop shadow)	A process is a set of activities which have some coherence and whose objective is generally agreed within an organisation. Examples of processes are requirements analysis, architectural design, test planning, etc.
Deliverable (represented by a rectangle with drop shadow)	A deliverable is a tangible output of an activity which is predicted in a project plan.
Condition (represented by a parallelogram)	A condition is either a pre-condition which must hold before a process or activity can start or a post-condition which holds after a process or activity has finished.
Role (represented by a circle with drop shadow)	A role is a bounded area of responsibility. Examples of roles might be configuration manager, test engineer, software designer, etc. One person may have several different roles and a single role may be associated with several different people.
Exception (not shown in examples here but may be represented as a double-edged box)	An exception is a description of how to modify the process if some anticipated or unanticipated event occurs. Exceptions are often undefined and it is left to the ingenuity of the project managers and engineers to handle the exception.
Communication (represented by an arrow)	An interchange of information between people or between people and supporting computer systems. Communications may be informal or formal. Formal communications might be the approval of a deliverable by a project manager; informal communications might be the interchange of electronic mail to resolve ambiguities in a document.

Figure 25.4 Elements of a process model

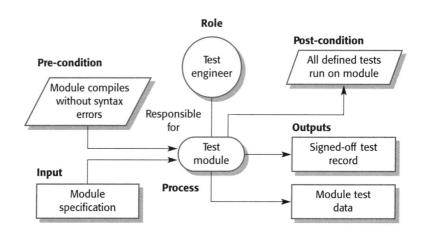

Figure 25.5 The module testing process

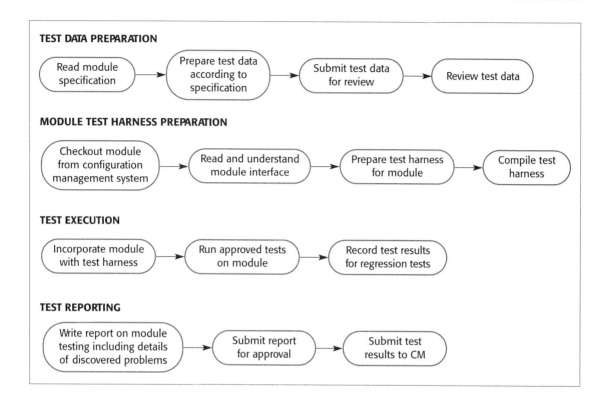

TEST DATA PREPARATION

Read module specification → Prepare test data according to specification → Submit test data for review → Review test data

MODULE TEST HARNESS PREPARATION

Checkout module from configuration management system → Read and understand module interface → Prepare test harness for module → Compile test harness

TEST EXECUTION

Incorporate module with test harness → Run approved tests on module → Record test results for regression tests

TEST REPORTING

Write report on module testing including details of discovered problems → Submit report for approval → Submit test results to CM

Figure 25.6 The activities involved in module testing

you may need to make several different models at different levels of abstraction. These should be related using common elements such as activities or deliverables. Some models should be primarily concerned with process activities, others with control information that drives the process execution.

25.2.1 Process exceptions

Software processes are very complex entities. While there may be a defined process model in an organisation, this can only ever represent the ideal situation where the development team is not faced with any unanticipated problems. In reality, unanticipated problems are a fact of everyday life for project managers. The 'ideal' process model must be modified dynamically as solutions to these problems are found. Examples of the kinds of exception that a project manager must deal with include:

1. several key people becoming ill at the same time just before a critical project review;
2. a communications processor failure which means that electronic mail is out of action for several days;

3. an organisational reorganisation which means that managers have to spend much of their time working on organisational matters rather than on project management;

4. an unanticipated request for new project proposals being made. Effort must be transferred from the project to work on a proposal.

In general, the effect of an exception is that, somehow, the resources, budgets or schedules of a project are changed. It is difficult to predict all exceptions in advance and to incorporate them into a formal process model. Many exceptions are therefore handled by managers dynamically changing the 'standard' process to cope with these unexpected circumstances.

25.3 Process measurement

Process measurements are quantitative data about the software process. Humphrey (1989), in his book on process improvement, argues that the collection of process metrics is essential for process improvement. Humphrey also suggests that measurement has an important role to play in small-scale, personal process improvement (Humphrey, 1995). Process metrics, in their own right, can be used to assess whether or not the efficiency of a process has been improved. For example, the effort and time devoted to testing can be monitored. Effective improvements to the testing process should reduce the effort, testing time or both. However, process measurements on their own cannot be used to determine if product quality has improved. Product metrics (see Chapter 24) must also be collected and related to the process activities.

Three classes of process metric can be collected:

1. *The time taken for a particular process to be completed*   This can be the total time devoted to the process, calendar time, the time spent on the process by particular engineers, etc.

2. *The resources required for a particular process*   The resources might be total effort in person-days, travel costs, computer resources, etc.

3. *The number of occurrences of a particular event*   Examples of events that might be monitored include the number of defects discovered during code inspection, the number of requirements changes requested, the average number of lines of code modified in response to a requirements change, etc.

The first two types of measurement can be used to help discover if process changes have improved the efficiency of a process. Say there are fixed points in a software development process such as the acceptance of requirements, the completion of architectural design, the completion of test data generation, etc. It may be possible to measure the time and effort required to move from one of these fixed points to another. The measured values may be used to suggest areas where the process might be improved. After changes have been introduced, measurements of system attributes can show if the process changes have actually been beneficial.

Measurements of the number of events which occur can have a more direct bearing on software quality. For example, increasing the number of defects discovered by changing the program inspection process will probably be reflected in improved product quality. However, this has to be confirmed by subsequent product measurements.

The fundamental difficulty in process measurement is knowing what to measure. Basili and Rombach (1988) have proposed what they call the GQM (Goal–Question–Metric) paradigm. This is used to help decide what measurements should be taken and how they should be used. This approach relies on the identification of:

1. *Goals*   What the organisation is trying to achieve. Examples of goals might be improved programmer productivity, shorter product development time, increased product reliability, etc.

2. *Questions*   These are refinements of goals where specific areas of uncertainty related to the goals are identified. Normally, a goal will have a number of associated questions which need to be answered. Examples of questions related to the above goals are:

   • how can the number of debugged lines of code be increased?
   • how can the time required to finalise product requirements be reduced?
   • how can more effective reliability assessments be made?

3. *Metrics*   These are the measurements that need to be collected to help answer the questions and to confirm whether or not process improvements have achieved the desired goal. In the above examples, measurements which might be made include the productivity of individual programmers in lines of code and their level of experience, the number of formal communications between client and contractor for each requirements change and the number of tests required to cause product failure.

The advantage of this approach applied to process improvement is that it separates organisational concerns (the goals) from specific process concerns (the questions). It focuses data collection and suggests that collected data should be analysed in different ways depending on the question it is intended to answer. Basili and Green (1993) describe how this approach has been used in a long-term, measurement-based process improvement programme.

The GQM approach has been developed and combined with the SEI's capability maturity model (discussed below) in the ami method (Pulford *et al.*, 1996) of software process improvement. The developers of the ami method propose a staged approach to process improvement where measurement is introduced when an organisation has introduced some discipline into its processes. It provides guidelines and practical advice on implementing measurement-based process improvement.

25.4 The SEI Process Capability Maturity Model

The Software Engineering Institute (SEI) at Carnegie-Mellon University is a DoD-funded institute whose mission is software technology transfer. It was established to improve the capabilities of the US software industry and, specifically, the capabilities of those organisations who receive DoD funding for large defence projects. In the mid-1980s, the SEI initiated a study of ways of assessing the capabilities of contractors. They were particularly interested in contractors who were bidding for software projects funded by the US Department of Defense.

The outcome of this capability assessment work was the SEI Software Capability Maturity Model. This has been tremendously influential in convincing the software engineering community, in general, to take process improvement seriously. The SEI model classifies software processes into five different levels as shown in Figure 25.7.

These five levels are defined as follows:

1. *Initial level* At this level, an organisation does not have effective management procedures or project plans. If formal procedures for project control exist, there are no organisational mechanisms to ensure that they are used consistently. The organisation may successfully develop software but the characteristics of the software (quality, etc.) and the software process (budget, schedule, etc.) will be unpredictable.

2. *Repeatable level* At this level, an organisation has formal management, quality assurance and configuration control procedures in place. It is called the repeatable level because the organisation can successfully repeat projects of the same

Figure 25.7 The SEI capability maturity model

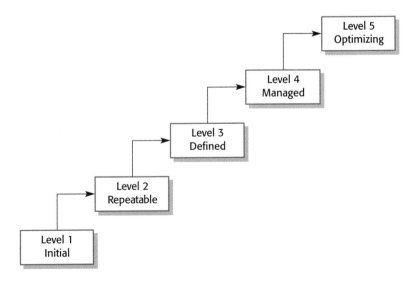

type. However, there is a lack of a formal process model. Project success is dependent on individual managers motivating a team and on organisational folk-lore acting as an intuitive process description.

3. *Defined level* At this level, an organisation has defined its process and thus has a basis for qualitative process improvement. Formal procedures are in place to ensure that the defined process is followed in all software projects.

4. *Managed level* A Level 4 organisation has a defined process and a formal programme of quantitative data collection. Process and product metrics are collected and fed into the process improvement activity.

5. *Optimising level* At this level, an organisation is committed to continuous process improvement. Process improvement is budgeted and planned and is an integral part of the organisation's process.

The maturity levels in the initial version of the model were criticised as being too imprecise. After experience with using the model for capability evaluation as discussed in the following section, a revised version was adopted (Paulk *et al.*, 1993). The five levels were retained but were defined more specifically in terms of key process areas (Figure 25.8). Process improvement should be concerned with establishing these key processes and not with simply reaching some arbitrary level in the model. A similar approach, based on key practices, has been used to derive a requirements engineering process maturity model (Sommerville and Sawyer, 1997).

The SEI work on this model has been influenced by methods of statistical quality control in manufacturing. Humphrey (1988), in the first widely published description of the model states:

W. E. Deming, in his work with the Japanese industry after World War II, applied the concepts of statistical process control to industry. While there are important differences, these concepts are just as applicable to software as they are to automobiles, cameras, wristwatches and steel.

While there are certainly some similarities, I do not think that results from manu-facturing engineering can be transferred directly to software engineering. As I have already discussed in section 25.1, factors such as the skill and experience of the development engineers affect product quality. These are often as important as process factors.

The SEI maturity model is an important contribution but it should not be taken as a definitive capability model for all software processes. The model was devel-oped to assess the capabilities of companies developing defence software. These are large, long-lifetime software systems which have complex interfaces with hard-ware and other software systems. They are developed by large teams of engineers and must follow the development standards and procedures laid down by the US Department of Defense.

Figure 25.8 Key
Process Areas
(©1993 IEEE)

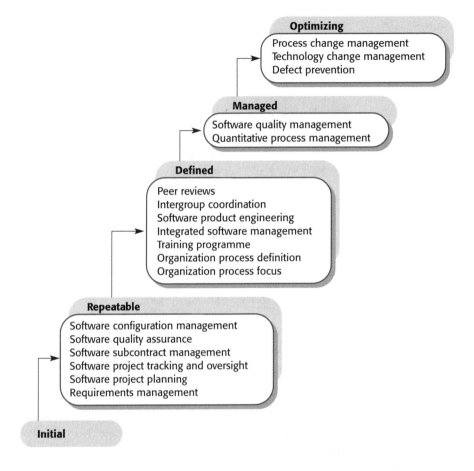

The first three levels of the SEI model are relatively simple to understand. The key process areas include practices which are currently used in industry. Some organisations have reached the higher levels of the model (Diaz and Sligo, 1997) but the standards and practices that are applicable at that level are not widely understood. In some cases, the best practice might diverge from the SEI model because of local organisational circumstances.

Problems at the higher levels do not negate the usefulness of the SEI model. Most organisations are at lower levels of process maturity. There are, however, three more serious problems with the SEI model. These may mean that it is not a good predictor of an organisation's capability to produce high-quality software.

The major problems with the capability maturity model are:

1. The model focuses exclusively on project management rather than product development. It does not take into account an organisation's use of technologies such as prototyping, formal or structured methods, tools for static analysis, etc.

2. It excludes risk analysis and resolution as a key process technology (Bollinger and McGowan, 1991). We have discussed the importance of risk assessment

in Chapter 1. Its advantage is that it discovers problems before they seriously affect the development process.

3.   The domain of applicability of the model is not defined. The authors of the model clearly recognise that the model is not appropriate for all organisations. However, they do not describe the type of organisations where they think the model should and should not be used. The consequence of this is that the model has been oversold as a way to tackle software process problems. For smaller organisations, in particular, the model is too bureaucratic. Humphrey has recognised this and has now developed smaller-scale process improvement strategies (Humphrey, 1995).

The authors of the SEI model admitted (Humphrey and Curtis, 1991) that technology assessment was excluded because they could not find any standard way of assessing technology usage. Furthermore, they suggest that the management processes that are defined in the model are essential before technology can be effectively used. Therefore, at the lower levels of the model, the use of particular technologies is not significant as far as product quality is concerned.

This is, again, an over-simplification. The effective use of technologies such as prototyping and static analysis of programs can have a significant effect on product quality. This does not depend on how these are incorporated into the software process. The routine use of tools and methods by an organisation can clearly separate it from other organisations at the same level. It may mean that its product quality is superior to those products developed by organisations at a higher maturity level.

There are significant differences between commercial and defence software development. The problems of developing very large software systems are not necessarily shared by all organisations involved in software development. In particular, commercial software development can respond more quickly to technological change. This is evident in the way it has moved towards Internet-based systems and the use of distributed architectures. Defence software, on the other hand, has a long procurement process, a long lifetime and, for good reasons, tends to be more conservative in adopting new techniques. Some of the ideas underlying the SEI model are generally relevant but the model is not completely applicable outside the domain for which it was designed.

Paulk has compared the Capability Maturity Model with the ISO 9000 standard for quality management as discussed in Chapter 24 (Paulk, 1995). He looked at the key process areas at each level of the CMM and compared these to the ISO 9000 requirements for the quality management processes which should defined (see Figure 24.2). For the vast majority of areas, there is a clear correlation between the key processes and the ISO 9000 standard. The CMM is more detailed and prescriptive and includes a framework for process improvement. This is not covered in ISO 9000. In general, organisations whose process maturity is rated at Level 2 or 3 are likely to be ISO 9000 compliant. However, because of the abstract definition of ISO 9000, some Level 1 organisations can also satisfy the ISO 9000 standard.

Based on their experience with software process maturity, the SEI have now developed a number of other capability maturity models. A systems engineering capability maturity model assesses systems engineering processes as discussed in Chapter 2; the systems acquisition capability maturity model focuses on company's acquisition processes for software and hardware; the people capability maturity model (see Chapter 22) is concerned with organisational processes for improving the capabilities and competencies of its staff. Details of all of these are available from the SEI web site which is linked from this book's web pages.

25.4.1 Capability assessment

In discussions of process maturity and the SEI model, it is sometimes forgotten that the intention of the model was to allow the US Department of Defense to assess the capabilities of software contractors. At the time of writing, there is no published requirement for contractors to have reached a given level of maturity. However, there is an assumption in the community that organisations at the higher maturity level do have an advantage in bidding for contracts. In future, organisations will probably be expected to have reached a certain level of maturity (probably Level 3) before they can bid for DoD software contracts.

The model is intended to represent the capabilities of organisations rather than the maturity of particular projects. This makes sense from a contractual point of view but because an organisation is rated at Level 1 (say), this does not mean that all of its projects are at that level. Within the organisation, there may be particular projects or groups working at a much higher maturity level.

Capability assessment is based on a standard questionnaire that is designed to identify the key processes in the organisation. This is applied during an evaluation visit where project managers from a number of different projects are interviewed. After discussion of their responses to the questionnaire and refinement of these responses, an evaluation score is reached. A model of this assessment process is shown in Figure 25.9.

I think that the main problem with the current model is its stratification into levels and the judgemental association of numbers with these levels. The assessment guidelines require an organisation to have all the practices at a particular level in place before it can be accredited at that level. Thus, an organisation which has 80 per cent of Level 2 practices in place (say) and 70 per cent of Level 3 practices would receive a Level 1 rating. A better approach would be a finer-grain capability classification where the specific practices which are standard in an organisation are identified.

The SPICE approach to capability assessment and process improvement (Paulk and Konrad, 1994; El Amam et al., 1997) is more flexible than the SEI model. SPICE has been proposed as an ISO standard process improvement framework. It includes maturity levels comparable with the SEI levels but also identifies key processes areas such as customer–supplier processes that cut across these levels. As the level of maturity increases, the performance of these key processes must improve.

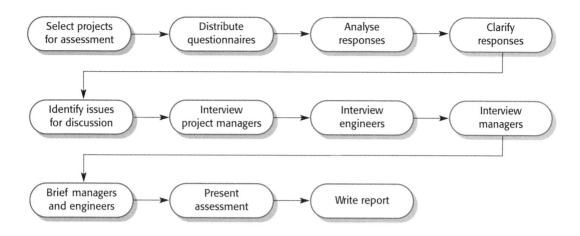

Figure 25.9
The capability
assessment process

The Bootstrap project had the goal of extending and adapting the SEI maturity model to make it applicable across a wider range of companies. The Bootstrap model (Haase *et al.*, 1994; Kuvaja *et al.*, 1994) uses the SEI's maturity levels but also proposes:

* guidelines for a company-wide quality system to support process improvement,
* an important distinction between organisation, methodology and technology,
* a base process model (based on the model used in the European Space Agency) which may be adopted.

The evolution of the SEI's Capability Maturity Model is taking these alternative approaches into account. During the lifetime of this book, I anticipate that a new version of the CMM will be available which incorporates the best features of other approaches. This will become the world-wide standard for software process assessment and improvement.

25.5 Process classification

The process maturity classification proposed in the SEI model is appropriate for large, long-lifetime software projects undertaken by large organisations. There are many other types of software project and organisation where this view of process maturity should not be applied directly.

Rather than attempt to classify processes into levels, with fairly arbitrary boundaries drawn between these levels, I believe a more general approach to process classification can be applied across a broader spectrum of organisations and projects. Different types of process can be identified:

1. *Informal processes* These are processes where there is not a strictly defined process model. The process used is chosen by the development team. Informal processes may use formal procedures such as configuration management but the procedures to be used and the relationships between procedures are not predefined.

2. *Managed processes* These are processes where there is a defined process model in place. This is used to drive the development process. The process model defines the procedures used, their scheduling and the relationships between the procedures.

3. *Methodical processes* These are processes where some defined development method or methods (such as systematic methods for object-oriented design) are used. These processes benefit from CASE tool support for design and analysis processes.

4. *Improving processes* These are processes which have inherent improvement objectives. There is a specific budget for process improvements and procedures in place for introducing such improvements. As part of these improvements, quantitative process measurement may be introduced.

These classifications obviously overlap and a process may fall into several classes. For example, the process may be informal in that it is chosen by the development team. The team may choose to use a particular design method. They may also have a process-improvement capability. In this case, the process would be classified as *informal, methodical* and *improving*.

These classifications are useful because they serve as a basis for multi-dimensional process improvement. They help organisations choose an appropriate process for different types of product development. Figure 25.10 shows different types of product and the type of process that might be used for their development.

Figure 25.10 Process applicability

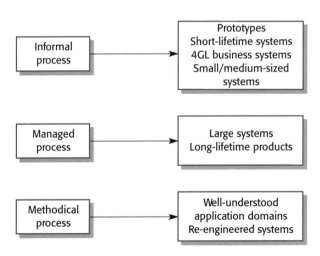

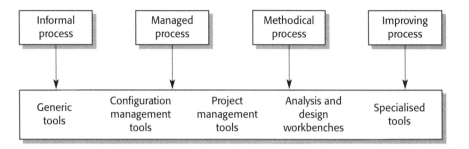

Figure 25.11 Process tool support

The classes of system shown in Figure 25.10 may overlap. Therefore, small systems which are re-engineered can be developed using a methodical process. Large systems always need a managed process. However, if the domain is not well understood, it may be difficult to choose an appropriate design method. Large systems may therefore be developed using a managed process that is not based on any particular design method.

Process classification provides a basis for choosing the right process to be used when a particular type of product is to be developed. For example, say a program is needed to support a transition from one type of computer system to another. This has a relatively short lifetime. Its development does not require the standards and management procedures which are appropriate for software which will be used for many years.

Process classification recognises that the process affects product quality. It does not assume, however, that the process is always the dominant factor. It provides a basis for improving different types of process. Different types of process improvement may be applied to the different types of process. For example, the improvements to methodical processes might be based on better method training, better integration of requirements and design, improved CASE tools, etc.

Most software processes now have some CASE tool support so they are *supported processes*. Methodical processes are now usually supported by analysis and design workbenches. However, processes may have other kinds of tool support (for example, prototyping tools, testing tools) irrespective of whether or not a structured design method is used.

The tool support that can be effective in supporting processes depends on the process classification. For example, informal processes can use generic tools such as prototyping languages, compilers, debuggers, word processors, etc. They will rarely use more specialised tools in a consistent way. Figure 25.11 shows that a spectrum of different tools can be used in software development. The effectiveness of particular tools depends on the type of process that is used.

Analysis and design workbenches are only likely to be cost-effective where a methodical process is being followed. Specialised tools are developed as part of the process improvement activity to provide specific support for improving certain process activities.

KEY POINTS

▶ Process improvement involves process analysis, standardisation, measurement and change. Training is essential if process improvement is to be effective.

▶ Process models include descriptions of activities, sub-processes, roles, exceptions, communications, deliverables and other processes.

▶ Measurement should be used to answer specific questions about the software process used. These questions should be based on organisational improvement goals.

▶ Three types of process metrics are time metrics, resource utilisation metrics and event metrics.

▶ The SEI process maturity model classifies software processes as initial, repeatable, defined, managed and optimising. It identifies key processes that should be used at each of these levels.

▶ The SEI model is appropriate for large systems developed by large teams of engineers. It should not be applied without adaptation to local circumstances.

▶ Processes can be classified as informal, managed, methodical and improving. This classification can be used to identify process tool support.

FURTHER READING

Trends in Software: Software Process Modelling and Technology. This book includes a good selection of overview papers which cover different aspects of software processes, including process modelling, process support and the use of the CMM. (A. Fuggetta and A. Wolf (eds.), 1996, John Wiley and Sons.)

The Capability Maturity Model for Software. This is a comprehensive description of the SEI's process assessment and improvement framework. It includes descriptions of all of the key processes and rationale for their inclusion. (M. Paulk, C, V, Weber and B. Curtis, 1995, Addison-Wesley.)

IEEE Software, **10**(4), July 1993. This is a special issue of the journal devoted to articles on process maturity. It includes a description of version 1.1 of the capability maturity model as well as articles discussing process improvement and process modelling.

EXERCISES

25.1   Suggest process models for the following processes:

- Lighting a wood fire
- Cooking a three-course meal (you choose the menu)
- Writing a small (50 line) program

25.2   Under what circumstances is product quality likely to be determined by the quality of the development team? Give examples of the types of software product that are particularly dependent on individual talent and ability.

25.3   Assume that the goal of process improvement in an organisation is to increase the number of reusable components which are produced during development. Suggest three questions in the GQM paradigm to which this might lead.

25.4   Describe three types of software process metric that may be collected as part of a process improvement process. Give one example of each type of metric.

25.5   Give two advantages and two disadvantages of the approach to process assessment and improvement which is embodied in the SEI process maturity model.

25.6   Suggest two application domains where the SEI capability model is unlikely to be appropriate. Give reasons why this is the case.

25.7   Consider the type of software process used in your organisation. How many of the key process areas identified in the SEI model are used? How would this model classify your level of process maturity?

25.8   Suggest three specialised software tools which might be developed to support a process improvement programme in an organisation.

25.9   Explain why a methodical process is not necessarily a managed process as defined in section 25.5.

25.10   Are process improvement programmes which involve measuring the work of people in the process and changing the process inherently dehumanising? What resistance to a process improvement programme might arise?

PART SEVEN

Evolution

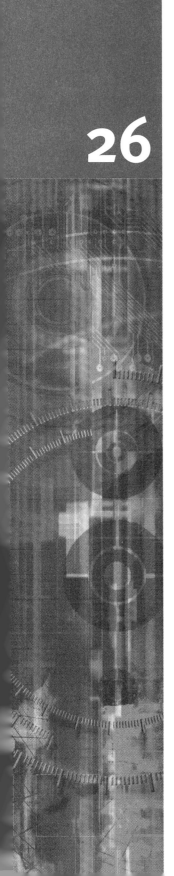

26 Legacy systems

The objectives of this chapter are to introduce legacy systems and to describe how many of these systems have been designed. When you have read this chapter, you will:

❏ understand what is meant by a 'legacy system', and know why these systems are critical to the operation of many businesses;

❏ have been introduced to common legacy system structures;

❏ understand the principles of function-oriented design – the most commonly used design strategy for current legacy systems;

❏ understand how legacy systems can be assessed to decide if they should be scrapped, maintained, re-engineered or replaced.

Contents

26.1 Legacy system structures
26.2 Legacy system design
26.3 Legacy system assessment

Companies spend a lot of money on software systems and, to get a return on that investment, the software must be usable for a number of years. The lifetime of software systems is very variable but many large systems remain in use for more than 10 years. Some organisations still rely on software systems that are more than 20 years old. Many of these old systems are still business-critical. That is, the business relies on the services provided by the software and any failure of these services would have a serious effect on the day-to-day running of the business. These old systems have been given the name *legacy systems*.

These legacy systems are not, of course, the systems that were originally delivered. External and internal factors, such as the state of the national and international economies, changing markets, changing laws, management changes and structural reorganisation, mean that businesses undergo continual change. These changes generate new or modified software requirements, so all useful software systems inevitably change as the business changes. Therefore, legacy systems incorporate a large number of changes which have been made over many years. Many different people have been involved in making these changes and it is unusual for any one person to have a complete understanding of the system.

Businesses regularly replace their equipment and machinery with modern systems. However, scrapping legacy systems and replacing them with more modern software involves significant business risk. As I discussed in Chapter 4, most managers try to minimise risks and therefore do not want to face the uncertainties of new software systems. Replacing a legacy system is a risky business strategy for a number of reasons:

1. There is rarely a complete specification of the legacy system. The original specification may have been lost. If a specification exists, it is unlikely that it incorporates details of all of the system changes that have been made. Therefore, there is no straightforward way of specifying a new system which is functionally identical to the system that is in use.

2. Business processes and the ways in which legacy systems operate are often inextricably intertwined. These processes have been designed to take advantage of the software services and to avoid its weaknesses. If the system is replaced, these processes will also have to change, with potentially unpredictable costs and consequences.

3. Important business rules may be embedded in the software and may not be documented elsewhere. A business rule is a constraint which applies to some business function and breaking that constraint can have unpredictable consequences for the business. For example, an insurance company may have embedded its rules for assessing the risk of a policy application in its software. If these rules are not maintained, the company may accept high-risk policies which will result in expensive future claims.

4. New software development is itself risky so that there may be unexpected problems with a new system. It may not be delivered on time and for the price expected.

Keeping legacy systems in use avoids the risks of replacement but making changes to existing software usually becomes more expensive as systems get older. Legacy software systems which are more than a few years old are particularly expensive to change for several reasons:

1. Different parts of the system have been implemented by different teams. There is, therefore, no consistent programming style across the whole system.

2. Part or all of the system may be implemented using an obsolete programming language. It may be difficult to find staff who have knowledge of these languages and expensive outsourcing of system maintenance may be required.

3. System documentation is often inadequate and out of date. In some cases, the only documentation is the system source code. Sometimes the source code has been lost and only the executable version of the system is available.

4. Many years of maintenance have usually corrupted the system structure, making it increasingly difficult to understand. New programs may have been added and interfaced with other parts of the system in an *ad hoc* way.

5. The system may have been optimised for space utilisation or execution speed rather than written for understandability. This causes particular difficulties for programmers who have learned modern software engineering techniques and who have not been exposed to the programming tricks that have been used.

6. The data processed by the system may be maintained in different files which have incompatible structures. There may be data duplication and the data itself may be out of date, inaccurate and incomplete.

Businesses which have a large number of legacy systems are therefore faced with a fundamental dilemma. If they continue using the legacy systems and making changes as required, their costs will inevitably increase. If they decide to replace their legacy systems with new systems, this will be costly and the new systems may not provide as effective business support as the legacy systems. Consequently, many businesses are looking at software engineering techniques which extend the lifetime of legacy systems and which reduce the costs of keeping these systems in use. I discuss some of these techniques in Chapter 27, which covers software evolution in general and in Chapter 28, which covers software re-engineering.

26.1 Legacy system structures

Legacy systems are not simply old software systems although the software components of these systems are the main focus of this chapter. Legacy systems are socio-technical computer-based systems (discussed in Chapter 2) so they include

Figure 26.1 Legacy
system components

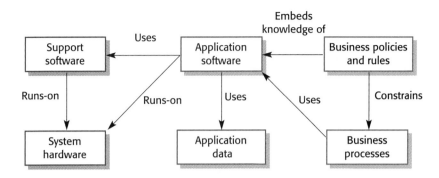

software, hardware, data and business processes. Changes to one part of the system inevitably involve further changes to other components. Decisions about these systems are not always governed by objective engineering criteria but are affected by broader organisational strategies and politics.

Figure 26.1 illustrates the different logical parts of a legacy system and their relationships:

1. *System hardware*   In many cases, legacy systems have been written for mainframe hardware which is no longer available, which is expensive to maintain and which may not be compatible with current organisational IT purchasing policies.

2. *Support software*   The legacy system may rely on a range of different support software from the operating system and utilities provided by the hardware manufacturer through to the compilers used for system development. Again, these may be obsolete and no longer supported by their original providers.

3. *Application software*   As I discuss later, the application system which provides the business services is usually composed of a number of separate programs which have been developed at different times. Sometime the term *legacy system* means this application software system rather than the entire system.

4. *Application data*   These are the data which are processed by the application system. In many legacy systems, an immense volume of data has accumulated over the lifetime of the system. This data may be inconsistent and may be duplicated in different files.

5. *Business processes*   These are processes which are used in the business to achieve some business objective. An example of a business process in an insurance company would be issuing an insurance policy; in a manufacturing company, a business process would be accepting an order for products and setting up the associated manufacturing process.

6. *Business policies and rules*   These are definitions of how the business should be carried out and constraints on the business. Use of the legacy application system may be embedded in these policies and rules.

Figure 26.2
Layered model of
a legacy system

Socio-technical system

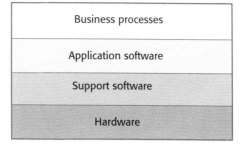

An alternative way of looking at these different components of a legacy system is as a series of layers as shown in Figure 26.2. Each layer depends on the layer immediately below it and interfaces with that layer. If interfaces are maintained, then it should be possible to make changes within a layer without affecting either of the adjacent layers.

In practice, however, this simple encapsulation rarely works and changes to one layer of the system may require consequent changes to layers that are both above and below the changed level. The reasons for this are:

1. Changing one layer in the system may introduce new facilities and higher layers in the system may then be changed to take advantage of these facilities. For example, a new database introduced at the support software layer may include facilities to access the data through a web browser and business processes may be modified to take advantage of this facility.

2. Changing the software in the system may slow it down so that new hardware is needed to improve the system performance. The increase in performance from the new hardware may then mean that further software changes which were previously impractical become possible.

3. It is often impossible to maintain hardware interfaces, especially if a radical change to a new type of hardware is proposed. For example, if a company moves from mainframe hardware to client–server systems (discussed in Chapter 11) these usually have different operating systems. Major changes to the application software may therefore be required.

The application software in a legacy system is not a single application program but usually includes a number of different programs. The system may have started as a single program processing one or two data files but, over time, changes may have been implemented by adding new programs which share the data and which communicate with other programs in the system. Similarly, the initial system data files are added to as new information is required. This is illustrated in Figure 26.3. Different programs share data files so that changes to one program that affect data inevitably result in changes to other programs.

Figure 26.3 Legacy
application systems

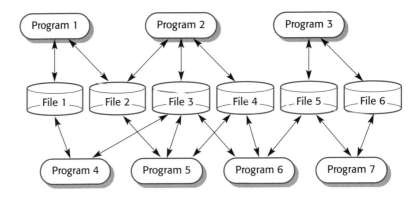

Figure 26.4
Database-centred
systems

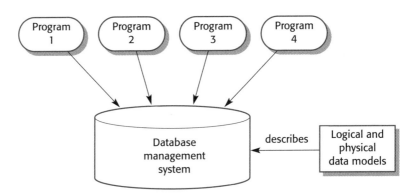

The different programs in the legacy application system have usually been written by different people and are often written in different programming languages or in different versions of a programming language. For example, the original software may have been developed in COBOL-72 but later programs implemented in a new version of the language, COBOL-80. Compilers and support software for all of these languages may have to be maintained. This all adds to the complexity of the system and increases the costs of making changes to it.

While there are still legacy systems that use separate files to maintain their data, a large number of business systems have centralised their data management around a database system (Figure 26.4). The advantage of adopting this structure is that the data in the system is described using logical and physical data models. Redundancy and data duplication are less likely and it is easier to assess the impact of system changes which affect the system data. Databases also provide transaction processing capabilities where changes to the data can be made in a recoverable way. This allows interactive updates of the data to be made.

The requests for interactive updates of the data come from different terminals and different times. For example, a banking system may have hundreds of terminals used by counter staff in branches and by the public as ATMs. These individual transactions are all made against the central accounts database and they must be collected and organised in such a way that they do not interfere with each other.

Figure 26.5
Transaction
processing using
a TP monitor

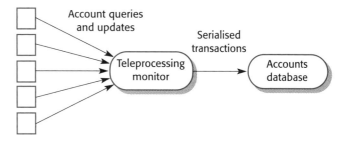

A teleprocessing monitor, such as IBM's CICS system, is a software system which can handle and buffer inputs from many different sources. In banking systems, a TP monitor accepts transactions from branch terminals and ATMs and may carry out some local processing. It then buffers these transactions and presents them as a serialised list to the account database which updates the customer's account and confirms that the transaction has been processed. This is illustrated in Figure 26.5.

There are two major legacy issues in database-centred systems:

1.   The database management system which is used may be obsolete and incompatible with other DBMSs used by a business. Relational database management systems are now the most effective database management systems for business applications. However, many legacy systems rely on older database systems that are based on hierarchical and network models. These systems were designed to allow the performance of the system to be optimised rather than for simple data management. Modern hardware may make this performance optimisation unnecessary but the costs of changing to a relational data model are very high.

2.   The teleprocessing monitor which is used may have been designed for use with a particular database system and for mainframe hardware. Therefore, it may not be possible to use the same TP monitor with a new database. This part of the system may also have to be replaced and this increases the costs and risks of system change.

26.2 Legacy system design

Virtually all of today's legacy systems were designed before object-oriented development was widely used in industry. Rather than being organised as a set of interacting objects, the programs in these systems are usually structured as a collection of subroutines or functions. Each subroutine provides part of the functionality of the system and is called, as required, by other subroutines. In some languages,

Figure 26.6
A function-oriented
view of design

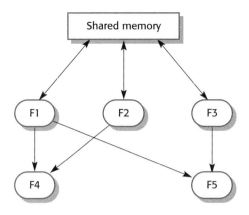

subroutines have their own private data but also access shared data areas. In other languages, such as older versions of COBOL, data is shared and accessible by all subroutines.

A function-oriented design strategy relies on decomposing a program into a set of interacting functions or subroutines with a centralised system state shared by these functions (Figure 26.6). The local state information in functions is only maintained while they are in execution. This design strategy is embedded as 'top-down design' or 'structured design' in a number of structured methods which were invented in the 1970s and early 1980s (Myers, 1975; Wirth, 1976; Constantine and Yourdon, 1979). Hundreds of thousands of application programs have been developed using these methods and associated CASE tools.

Function-oriented design conceals the details of an algorithm in a function but system state information is not hidden. This can cause problems because a function can change the state in a way that other functions do not expect. Changes to a function and its use of the system state may cause unanticipated changes in the behaviour of other functions. This is a particular problem with legacy systems as the programs have usually been changed by many different people. It is unusual for one person to completely understand how the different parts of a program interact.

A functional approach to design is most effective when the amount of system state information is minimised and information sharing is explicit. Systems whose responses depend on a single stimulus or input and which are not affected by input histories are naturally functionally oriented. Many business data-processing systems are concerned with processing discrete records. The processing of one record is not dependent on the results of processing the previous record. It is therefore quite natural to use a function-oriented approach when designing these systems.

Business data processing systems are the largest class of legacy systems. There are two main types of business system:

1. *Batch processing systems*   Data is input and output in batches from a file rather than input and output to a user terminal. Examples of batch processing systems are payroll systems, billing systems, etc.

Figure 26.7
An input–process–
output model

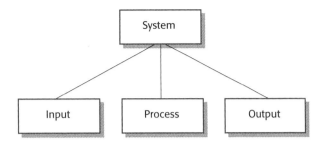

2. *Transaction processing systems*   Data is input and output as a series of trans-
    actions against a database with the transaction generated from a user terminal.

Of course, these different types of system may share data. Therefore a bank uses
a transaction processing system to manage account transactions but generates bank
statements for customers using a batch processing system.

Both batch processing and transaction processing systems generally follow an
input–process–output model as illustrated in Figure 26.7. These systems collect inputs
from one or more sources, carry out some processing on these inputs and then generate outputs that are related, in some way, to the inputs. For example, a telephone
billing system takes inputs which are customer records and telephone meter readings from an exchange switch, computes the costs for each customer and then generates printed bills as output.

The input, processing and output components may themselves be further decomposed into an input–process–output structure. For example:

1. An input component may read some data (input) from a user terminal, check
    the validity of that data and correct some errors (process), then queue the valid
    data for processing (output).

2. A processing component may take a transaction from a queue (input), perform
    some computations on the data and create a new data record recording the results
    of the computation (process), then queue this new record for printing (output).

3. An output component may read records from a queue (input), format these accord-
    ing to the output form (process) and then send them to a printer (output).

The design of function-oriented systems is often modelled using data-flow diagrams. I introduced data-flow diagrams in Chapter 7. Data-flow diagrams are a functional representation where each round-edged rectangle in the data flow represents
a function which implements some data transformation and each arrow represents
a data item which is processed by the function. Files or data stores are represented
as rectangles in the data-flow notation which I use for data-flow diagrams. Data-
flow diagrams show end-to-end processing, i.e. all of the functions which act on
data as it moves through the different stages of the system.

To illustrate how the data-flow diagram can describe a function-oriented design,
consider Figure 26.8 which shows the design of a salary payment system. This would

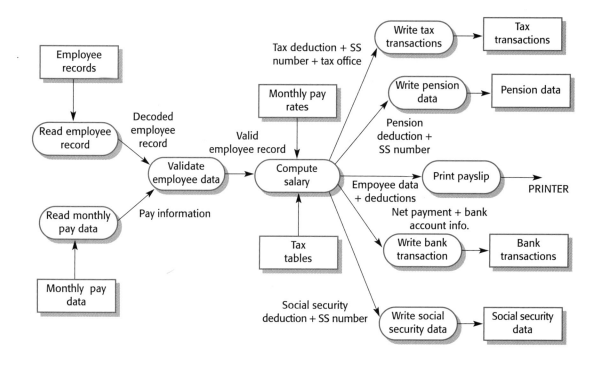

Figure 26.8
Data-flow diagram
of a payroll system

normally be implemented as a batch processing system. In this system, information about employees in the organisation is read into the system, monthly salary and deductions are computed and payments are made. You can see how this system follows the basic input–process–output structure which I discussed above:

1. The functions on the left of the diagram, 'Read employee record', 'Read monthly pay data' and 'Validate employee data', input the data for each employee and check that data.

2. The 'Compute salary' function works out the total gross salary for each employee and the various deductions which are made from that salary. The net monthly salary is then computed.

3. The output functions on the right of the diagram write a series of files which hold details of the deductions made and the salary to be paid. These files are processed by other programs once details for all employees have been computed. A payslip for the employee recording the net pay and the deductions made is printed by the system.

An example of a transaction processing system is the software which controls automatic bank teller machines (ATMs). The service provided to a user is independent of previous services provided so can be thought of as a single transaction. Figure 26.9 illustrates a simplified functional design of such a system. I have used a function-oriented design description language rather than Java. Java is an object-

Figure 26.9
Design description
of an ATM

```
INPUT

loop
    repeat
        Print_input_message (" Welcome - Please enter your card") ;
    until Card_input ;

    Account_number := Read_card ;
    Get_account_details (PIN, Account_balance, Cash_available) ;
```

```
PROCESS

    if Invalid_card (PIN) then
        Retain_card ;
        Print ("Card retained - please contact your bank") ;
    else
    repeat
        Print_operation_select_message ;
        Button := Get_button ;
        case Get_button is
            when Cash_only =>
                Dispense_cash (Cash_available, Amount_dispensed) ;
            when Print_balance =>
                Print_customer_balance (Account_balance) ;
            when Statement =>
                Order_statement (Account_number) ;
            when Check_book =>
                Order_checkbook (Account_number) ;
        end case ;
        Print ("Press CONTINUE for more services or STOP to finish") ;
        Button := Get_button ;
    until Button = STOP ;
```

```
OUTPUT

    Eject_card ;
    Print ("Please take your card ) ;
    Update_account_information (Account_number,  Amount_dispensed) ;

end loop ;
```

oriented language and I don't think it is natural to use it to describe function-oriented designs.

In this design, the system is implemented as a continuous loop and actions are triggered when a card is input. Functions such as Dispense_cash, Get_account_number, Order_statement, Order_checkbook, etc. can be identified which implement system actions. The system state maintained by the program is minimal. The user services operate independently and do not interact with each other.

Each ATM in the bank's network is generating a transaction, so the banking system must have some way of managing potentially simultaneous transactions and updating its database in a controlled way. This is usually achieved using a tele-processing monitor as shown in Figure 26.5.

Keeping legacy systems in operation is one good reason why function-oriented design will continue to be used for many years. However, the use of this approach is not confined to legacy systems. It may be appropriate to use this technique for new systems development:

1. Where data processing systems are to be implemented which rely on processing transactions and updating a database. The program processing the transactions does not need to maintain information about previous transactions, so objects maintaining private data are unnecessary. These follow the input–process–output model that I have discussed.

2. Where a company has invested heavily in structured methods, associated CASE tools and staff training. The risks and costs of changing to an object-oriented approach to program design may be not justified.

Although many software developers consider function-oriented design to be an outdated approach, object-oriented development may not offer significant advantages in these situations. An interesting challenge that we face is to ensure that function-oriented and object-oriented systems can work together.

26.3 Legacy system assessment

Organisations which depend on many legacy systems and which have a limited budget for maintaining and upgrading these systems have to decide how to get the best return on their investment. This means that they should make a realistic assessment of their legacy systems and then decide on what is the most appropriate strategy for evolving these systems. There are four strategic options:

1. *Scrap the system completely*   This option should be chosen when the system is not making an effective contribution to business processes. This occurs when business processes have changed since the system was installed and they are no longer completely dependent on the system. This situation is most common when mainframe terminals have been replaced by PCs and off-the-shelf software on these machines has been adapted to provide the computer support that the business process needs.

2. *Continue maintaining the system*   This option should be chosen when the system is still required but where it is fairly stable and users do not request a large number of system changes.

3. *Transform the system in some way to improve its maintainability*   This option should be chosen when the system quality has been degraded by regular change and where regular change to the system is still required. This is covered in Chapter 28 which discusses techniques of system re-engineering.

4. *Replace the system with a new system*   This option should be chosen when other factors such as new hardware mean that the old system cannot continue in operation or where off-the-shelf systems are available which allow the new system to be developed at a reasonable cost.

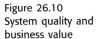
Figure 26.10
System quality and
business value

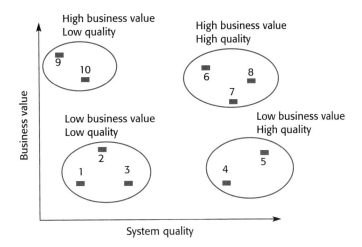

Naturally, these options are not exclusive, so where a system is composed of several different programs, different options may be applied to different parts of that system.

When you are assessing a legacy system, you have to look at it from two different perspectives (Warren, 1998). From a business perspective, you have to make an assessment of the value of that system to the business. From a system perspective, you have to make an assessment of the quality of the application software and the system's support software and hardware. The combination of the business value and the system quality is then used to help inform the decision on what to do with the legacy system.

To illustrate this assessment, let's assume that an organisation has 10 legacy systems. The quality and the business value of each of these systems is assessed and compared with others by plotting it on a chart showing relative business value and system quality. This is illustrated in Figure 26.10.

From Figure 26.10, you can see that there are four clusters of systems:

1. *Low quality, low business value*   Keeping these systems in operation will be expensive and the rate of the return to the business will be fairly small. These are candidates for scrapping.

2. *Low quality, high business value*   These systems are making an important business contribution so cannot be scrapped. However, their low quality means that operational costs are high so these are candidates for system transformation or replacement if a suitable system is available.

3. *High quality, low business value*   These are systems which don't contribute much to the business but which may not be very expensive to maintain. It is not worth the risk of replacing these systems, so normal system maintenance may be continued or they may be scrapped.

4. *High quality, high business value*   These must be kept in operation but their high quality means that it is not necessary to invest in transformation or system replacement. Normal system maintenance should be continued.

Ideally, objective assessment should be used to inform decisions about what to do with a legacy system. However, in many cases, these decisions are not really objective but are based on organisational or political considerations. For example, if two businesses merge, the systems used by the most politically powerful partner will usually be used by the merged business and other systems may be scrapped. If senior management in an organisation make a decision to move to a new hardware platform, then this may require applications to be replaced. If there is no budget available for system transformation in a particular year, then system maintenance may be continued even although this will result in higher long-term costs.

26.3.1   Business value assessment

The assessment of the business value of a system is a subjective judgement and there is no reliable objective method that can be used. As with all subjective processes, if you simply rely on one opinion then you are likely to get a very skewed value. Therefore, I recommend that you adopt a viewpoint-oriented approach (see Chapter 6) where you identify a number of business viewpoints and make a value assessment from each of these viewpoints. Viewpoints which should be considered and possible questions are:

1. *End-users of the system*   How effective do they find the system in supporting their business processes? How much of the system functionality is used?

2. *Customers*   Is the use of the system transparent to customers or are their interactions constrained by the system? Are they kept waiting because of the system? Do system errors have a direct impact on customers?

3. *Line managers*   Do managers think that the system is effective in contributing to the success of their unit? Are the costs of keeping the system in use justified? Is the data managed by the system critical for the functioning of the manager's unit?

4. *IT managers*   Are there difficulties in finding people to work on the system? Does the system consume resources which could be deployed more effectively on other systems?

5. *Senior managers*   Does the system and associated business process make an effective contribution to the business goals?

Once viewpoints have been identified, people from each of these viewpoints should be interviewed and their answers collated. This will give you an overall picture of the value of the system to the business and you can then make an informed assessment of its business value.

26.3.2 System quality assessment

We have seen in Figure 26.2 that a legacy system is not just an application software system but also includes business processes and the hardware and support software environment of the system. In order to assess the quality of the system, you have to look at all of the levels in the system. Once you have collected information about all aspects of the system, you are then in a position to make a judgement about the system quality and where it should be positioned in Figure 26.10. However, there is no systematic method of making this judgement. It depends on the individual systems and the businesses which use these systems.

Business process assessment

Assessing the quality of a business process is closely related to assessing the business value of the system. During the business value assessment, you will have to ask questions about the business process and this will give you some understanding of the effectiveness of that process in supporting business goals.

However, as the process is part of the legacy system, you may wish to discover more detailed information about the process to help you make a judgement whether or not the process is of high quality. This is important because poor quality processes require improvement and this leads to associated changes to the system software.

To assess the process, I recommend a comparable viewpoint-oriented approach to that used for business value assessment. Examples of questions which you might ask are:

1. Is there a defined model of the process and are there procedures in place to check that the model is followed?

2. Do different parts of the organisation have the same processes for the same functions?

3. How have the people involved in the process adapted it to make it more suited to their work?

4. Are there relationships with other business processes necessary? If so, are they clear to the people involved in the process?

5. Is the process effectively supported by the legacy application software? Does it provide the information required? Does the process require the same data to be entered several times in different places?

You should not be surprised if the answers that you get to these questions from different people are totally different. Management in an organisation may think that they have high-quality processes but the actual processes used may be totally different from that assumed by managers. When making process assessments, you should always focus on the actual process which is used and you should not rely only on process documentation to make judgements of the process quality.

Environment assessment

From Figure 26.2, we can see that the environment of an application software system includes the support software (operating systems, compilers, utilities, etc.) used by the system and the hardware platform on which the application system executes. You need to assess this environment as environmental factors are often the drivers of changes to the application software.

Assessing the system's environment is again a judgemental process that is informed by measurements of the system and its maintenance processes. Examples of data which may be useful include the costs of maintaining the system hardware and support software, the number of hardware faults which occur over some time period and the frequency of patches and fixes applied to the system support software.

Factors that you should consider during the environment assessment are shown in Figure 26.11. Notice that these are not all technical characteristics of the environment. You also have to consider the reliability of the suppliers of the hardware and support software. If these suppliers are no longer in business, this means that there may not be maintenance support for their systems.

Figure 26.11 Factors used in environment assessment

Factor	Questions
Supplier stability	Is the supplier is still in existence? Is the supplier financially stable and likely to continue in existence? If the supplier is no longer in business, are the systems maintained by someone else?
Failure rate	Does the hardware have a high rate of reported failures? Does the support software crash and force system restarts?
Age	How old is the hardware and software? The older the hardware and support software, the more obsolete it will be. It may still function correctly but there could be significant economic and business benefits to moving to more modern systems.
Performance	Is the performance of the system adequate? Do performance problems have a significant effect on system users?
Support requirements	What local support is required by the hardware and software? If there are high costs associated with this support, it may be worth considering system replacement.
Maintenance costs	What are the costs of hardware maintenance and support software licences? Older hardware may have higher maintenance costs than modern systems. Support software may have high annual licensing costs.
Interoperability	Are there problems interfacing the system to other systems? Can compilers etc. be used with current versions of the operating system? Is hardware emulation required?

Figure 26.12 Factors
used in application
assessment

Factor	Questions
Understandability	How difficult is it to understand the source code of the current system? How complex are the control structures which are used? Do variables have meaningful names that reflect their function?
Documentation	What system documentation is available? Is the documentation complete, consistent and up to date?
Data	Is there an explicit data model for the system? To what extent is data duplicated in different files? Is the data used by the system up to date and consistent?
Performance	Is the performance of the application adequate? Do performance problems have a significant effect on system users?
Programming language	Are modern compilers available for the programming language used to develop the system? Is the programming language still used for new system development?
Configuration management	Are all versions of all parts of the system managed by a configuration management system? Is there an explicit description of the versions of components that are used in the current system?
Test data	Does test data for the system exist? Is there a record of regression tests carried out when new features have been added to the system?
Personnel skills	Are there people available who have the skills to maintain the application? Are there only a limited number of people who understand the system?

Application software assessment

Assessing the quality of existing application software is different from the quality assurance activities that take place during software development (see Chapter 24). The legacy system may have been developed using techniques and standards that are no longer in use, the system structure will inevitably have been corrupted through change and the documentation of the system may be out of date.

Some of the factors which you might use to make a judgement of the quality of the application software are shown in Figure 26.12. Finding the answers to the questions associated with these factors helps you assess the system quality. You may also collect quantitative system data that will give you more information on which to base your judgement.

Examples of quantitative data which might be collected are:

1. *The number of system change requests* System changes tend to corrupt the system structure and make further changes more difficult. The higher this value, the lower the quality of the system.

2. *The number of different user interfaces used by the system*   This is an important factor in forms-based systems where each form can be considered as a separate user interface. The more different interfaces, the more likely that there will be inconsistencies and redundancies in these interfaces.

3. *The volume of data used by the system*   The higher the volume of data (number of files, size of database, etc.), the more complex the system.

Although this data is often useful, it can be very expensive to collect. This may mean that it is impractical to collect it for the assessment of the system. Furthermore, there are no absolute values that may be used. The age and size of the system have to be taken into account when making quality judgements based on measurements.

KEY POINTS

▶ A legacy system is an old system that still provides essential business services.

▶ Legacy systems are not just application software systems. They are socio-technical, computer-based systems, so include business processes, application software, support software and system hardware.

▶ Most legacy systems include a number of different programs and shared data associated with these programs. This data may be held in files or in an obsolete database management system.

▶ Most legacy systems have been designed from a functional perspective and are composed of sets of interacting functions which communicate through parameters and global shared data areas.

▶ In the business systems domain, most legacy systems are either batch processing systems or transaction processing systems. In both cases, their general organisation can be represented using an input–process–output model.

▶ The business value of a legacy system and the quality of the application software and its environment should be assessed to help decide whether to replace, transform or maintain the system.

▶ The business value of a system is an assessment of the effectiveness of the system in supporting business goals.

▶ The quality of the system depends on the quality of the business processes, the quality of the application software itself and the quality of the hardware and software which is used to support the system.

FURTHER READING

'Legacy information systems: Issues and directions'. An overview of the problems of legacy systems with a particular focus on the problems of legacy data. (J. Bisbal, D. Lawless, B. Wu and J. Grimson, *IEEE Software*, September/October 1999.)

The Renaissance of Legacy Systems. This book is mostly concerned with a method for the evolution of legacy systems. However, it includes a good general discussion of these systems, case studies which illustrate legacy system structures and a chapter on system assessment. (I. Warren, 1998, Springer.)

'Cash cow in the tar pit: Reengineering a legacy system'. A readable description of practical experiences of a legacy system evolution project. (W. S. Adolph, *IEEE Software*, May 1996.)

EXERCISES

26.1   Explain why legacy systems may be critical to the operation of a business.

26.2   Suggest three reasons why software systems become more difficult to understand when different people are involved in changing these systems.

26.3   What difficulties are likely to arise when different components of a legacy system are implemented in different programming languages?

26.4   Why is it necessary to use a teleprocessing monitor when requests to update data in a system come from a number of different terminals? How do modern client–server systems reduce the load on the teleprocessing monitor?

26.5   Most legacy systems use a function-oriented approach to design. Explain why this approach to design may be more appropriate for these systems than an object-oriented design strategy.

26.6   Expand the 'Compute salary' function in Figure 26.8 and draw a data-flow diagram which shows the computations carried out in that function. You need the following information to do this:

*   The employee record identifies the grade of an employee which can be used to look up the table of pay rates.

*   Employees below a particular grade may be paid overtime pay at the same rate as their normal hourly pay rate. The extra hours for which they are to be paid are indicated in their employee record.

*   The tax deducted depends on the employee's tax code (indicated in the record) and his or her annual salary. Monthly deductions for each code and a standard

salary are indicated in the tax tables. These are scaled up or down depending on the relationship between the actual salary and the standard salary used.

26.7 Under what circumstances might an organisation decide to scrap a system when the system assessment suggests that it is of high quality and high business value?

26.8 Suggest 10 questions that might be put to end-users of a system when carrying out a business process assessment.

26.9 Explain why problems with support software might mean that an organisation has to replace its legacy systems.

26.10 The management of an organisation has asked you to carry out a system assessment and has suggested to you that they would like the results of that assessment to show that the system is obsolete and that it should be replaced by a new system. This will mean that a number of system maintainers are made redundant. Your assessment actually shows that the system is well maintained and is of high quality and high business value. How would you report these results to the management of the organisation?

27 Software change

Objectives

The objectives of this chapter are to introduce software change and to describe a number of ways of modifying software. When you have read this chapter, you will:

❑ understand three different strategies for changing software systems, namely software maintenance, architectural evolution and software re-engineering;

❑ understand the principles of software maintenance and why software is so expensive to maintain;

❑ understand how legacy systems may be transformed to distributed client–server systems to extend their life and to make effective use of modern hardware.

Contents

27.1 Program evolution dynamics
27.2 Software maintenance
27.3 Architectural evolution

It is impossible to produce systems of any size which do not need to be changed. Once software is put into use, new requirements emerge and existing requirements change as the business running that software changes. Parts of the software may have to be modified to correct errors that are found in operation, improve its performance or other non-functional characteristics. All of this means that, after delivery, software systems always evolve in response to demands for change.

Software change is very important because organisations are now completely dependent on their software systems and have invested millions of dollars in these systems. Their systems are critical business assets and they must invest in system change to maintain the value of these assets. As I suggested in Chapter 1, a key problem for organisations is implementing and managing change to their legacy systems so that they continue to support their business operations.

There are a number of different strategies for software change (Warren, 1998):

1. *Software maintenance*   Changes to the software are made in response to changed requirements but the fundamental structure of the software remains stable. This is the most common approach used to system change. I discuss maintenance later in this chapter in section 27.2.

2. *Architectural transformation*   This is a more radical approach to software change then maintenance as it involves making significant changes to the architecture of the software system. Most commonly, systems evolve from a centralised, data-centric architecture to a client–server architecture. I discuss architectural evolution in section 27.3.

3. *Software re-engineering*   This is different from other strategies in that no new functionality is added to the system. Rather, the system is modified to make it easier to understand and change. System re-engineering may involve some structural modifications but does not usually involve major architectural change. I cover software re-engineering in Chapter 28.

The above strategies are not mutually exclusive. Re-engineering may be necessary to make the software easier to understand before its architecture is changed or components are reused. Some parts of a system may be replaced by off-the-shelf components while other, stable, parts are maintained. As I discussed in Chapter 26, the choice of the most appropriate strategy depends on both the technical quality of the system and its business value.

Equally, different strategies may be applied to different parts of a system or to different programs that make up a legacy information system. A program which is well structured and which does not need frequent maintenance may be maintained; another program which is used by many different people in different locations may have its architecture modified so that its user interface runs on a client computer, and a third program in the same system may be replaced by an off-the-shelf alternative. However, if the system data is re-engineered this will normally require changes to all of the programs in the system.

For some systems, none of these change strategies is appropriate and you have to replace the system. As I discussed in Chapter 26, it may be possible to replace part or all of the system with an off-the-shelf (COTS) system. However, there may be no suitable COTS alternative and you therefore have to develop a new customised system. In such a situation, it may be possible to reuse major parts of the original system in the development of the replacement.

Software change inevitably generates many different versions of a software systems and its components. It is critically important to keep track of these different versions and to ensure that the appropriate versions of components are used in each system version. The management of changing software products is called configuration management. I discuss this in Chapter 29.

27.1 Program evolution dynamics

Program evolution dynamics is the study of system change. The majority of work in this area has been carried out by Lehman and Belady (1985). From these studies, they proposed a set of 'laws' (Lehman's Laws) concerning system change. They claim these 'laws' are invariant and widely applicable. Lehman and Belady examined the growth and evolution of a number of large software systems. The proposed laws were derived from these measurements. The laws (hypotheses, really) are shown in Figure 27.1.

Figure 27.1
Lehman's Laws

Law	Description
Continuing change	A program that is used in a real-world environment necessarily must change or become progressively less useful in that environment.
Increasing complexity	As an evolving program changes, its structure tends to become more complex. Extra resources must be devoted to preserving and simplifying the structure.
Large program evolution	Program evolution is a self-regulating process. System attributes such as size, time between releases and the number of reported errors are approximately invariant for each system release.
Organisational stability	Over a program's lifetime, its rate of development is approximately constant and independent of the resources devoted to system development.
Conservation of familiarity	Over the lifetime of a system, the incremental change in each release is approximately constant.

The first law states that system maintenance is an inevitable process. As the system's environment changes, new requirements emerge and the system must be modified. When the modified system is reintroduced into the environment, this promotes more environmental changes so the evolution process recycles.

The second law states that, as a system is changed, its structure is degraded. This is commonly observed in legacy systems as I discussed in Chapter 26. The only way to avoid this happening is to invest in preventative maintenance where you spend time improving the software structure without adding to its functionality. Obviously, this means additional costs, over and above those of implementing required system changes.

The third law is, perhaps, the most interesting and the most contentious of Lehman's laws. It suggests that large systems have a dynamic of their own that is established at an early stage in the development process. This determines the gross trends of the system maintenance process and limits the number of possible system changes. Lehman and Belady suggest that this law is a result of fundamental structural and organisational factors.

Once a system exceeds some minimal size it acts in the same way as an inertial mass. Its size inhibits major change because changes introduce new faults that degrade the functionality of the system. If a large change increment is proposed, this will introduce many new faults that will limit the useful change delivered in the new version of the system.

Large systems are usually produced by large organisations. These have their own internal bureaucracies that set the change budget for each system and control the decision-making process. Major system changes require organisational decision making and changes to the project budget. Such decisions take time to make. During that time, other, higher-priority system changes may be proposed. It may be necessary to shelve the original changes to a later date. The rate of change of the system is therefore governed by the organisation's decision-making processes.

Lehman's fourth law suggests that most large programming projects work in what he terms a 'saturated' state. That is, a change to resources or staffing has imperceptible effects on the long-term evolution of the system. Of course, this is also suggested by the third law which suggests that program evolution is largely independent of management decisions. This law confirms that large software development teams are unproductive as the communication overheads dominate the work of the team.

Lehman's fifth law is concerned with the change increments in each system release. Adding new functionality to a system inevitably introduces new system faults. The more functionality added in each release, the more faults there will be. Therefore, a large increment in functionality in one system release means that this will have to be followed by a further release where the new system faults are repaired. Relatively little new functionality will be included in this release. The law suggests that you should not budget for large functionality increments in each release without taking into account the need for fault repair.

Lehman's observations seem generally sensible. They should be taken into account when planning the maintenance process. It may be that business considerations require them to be ignored at any one time. For example, for marketing reasons, it may necessary to make several major system changes in a single release. The likely consequences of this are that one or more releases devoted to error repair are likely to be required.

It may appear that the radical differences which are obvious between releases of program products violate Lehman's Laws. For example, Microsoft Word has been transformed from a simple word processor which operated in 256K of memory to a gigantic, feature-laden system. It now needs many megabytes of memory and a fast processor to operate. Its evolution seems to contradict the fourth and fifth of Lehman's laws. However, I suspect that this program is not really a sequence of revisions. Rather, the same name has been retained for marketing reasons but the program itself has been largely rewritten between releases.

27.2 Software maintenance

Software maintenance is the general process of changing a system after it has been delivered. The changes may be simple changes to correct coding errors, more extensive changes to correct design errors or significant enhancements to correct specification errors or accommodate new requirements. As I said in the introduction, software maintenance does not normally involve major architectural changes to the system. Changes are implemented by modifying existing system components and, where necessary, by adding new components to the system.

There are three different types of software maintenance:

1. *Maintenance to repair software faults*   Coding errors are usually relatively cheap to correct; design errors are more expensive as they may involve the rewriting of several program components. Requirements errors are the most expensive to repair because of the extensive system redesign which may be necessary.

2. *Maintenance to adapt the software to a different operating environment*   This type of maintenance is required when some aspect of the system's environment such as the hardware, the platform operating system or other support software changes. The application system must be modified to adapt it to cope with these environmental changes.

3. *Maintenance to add to or modify the system's functionality*   This type of maintenance is necessary when the system requirements change in response to organisational or business change. The scale of the changes required to the software is often much greater than for the other types of maintenance.

In practice, there isn't a clear-cut distinction between these different types of maintenance. Software faults may be revealed because a system has been used

Figure 27.2
Maintenance effort
distribution

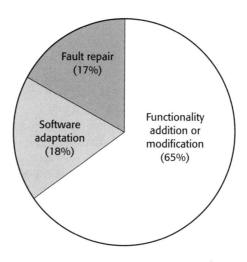

in an unanticipated way and the best way to repair these faults may be to add new functionality to help users with the system. When adapting the software to a new environment, functionality may be added to take advantage of new facilities supported by the environment. Adding new functionality to a system may be necessary because faults have changed the usage patterns of the system and a side-effect of the new functionality is to remove the faults from the software.

While these different types of maintenance are generally recognised, different people sometimes give them different names. Corrective maintenance is universally used to refer to maintenance for fault repair. However, adaptive maintenance sometimes means adapting to a new environment and sometimes means adapting the software to new requirements. Perfective maintenance sometimes means perfecting the software by implementing new requirements and, in other cases, maintaining the functionality of the system but improving its structure and its performance. Because of this naming uncertainty, I have avoided the use of all of these terms in this chapter.

It is difficult to find up-to-date figures for the relative effort devoted to the different types of maintenance. A rather old survey by Lientz and Swanson (1980) discovered that about 65 per cent of maintenance was concerned with implementing new requirements, 18 per cent with changing the system to adapt it to a new operating environment and 17 per cent to correct system faults (Figure 27.2). Similar figures were reported by Nosek and Palvia (1990) 10 years later. For custom systems, I guess that this distribution of costs is still roughly correct.

From these figures we can see that repairing system faults is not the most expensive maintenance activity. Rather, evolving the system to cope with new environments and new or changed requirements consumes most maintenance effort. Maintenance is therefore a natural continuation of the system development process with associated specification, design, implementation and testing activities. A spiral model, such as that shown in Figure 27.3, is therefore a better representation of the

Figure 27.3
Spiral model of
development

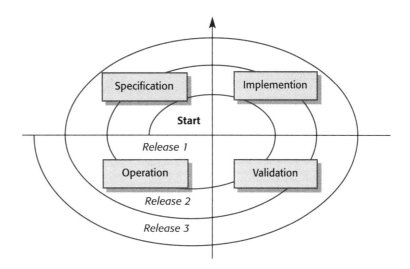

software process than representations such as the waterfall model (see Figure 3.1) where maintenance is represented as a separate process activity.

The costs of system maintenance represent a large proportion of the budget of most organisations that use software systems. In the 1980s, Lientz and Swanson found that large organisations devoted at least 50 per cent of their total programming effort to evolving existing systems. McKee (1984) found a similar distribution of maintenance effort across the different types of maintenance but suggests that the amount of effort spent on maintenance is between 65 and 75 per cent of total available effort. As organisations have replaced old systems with off-the-shelf systems, such as enterprise resource planning systems, this figure may not have come down. Although the details may be uncertain, we do know that software change remains a major cost for all organisations.

Maintenance costs as a proportion of development costs vary from one application domain to another. For business application systems, a study by Guimaraes (1983) showed that maintenance costs were broadly comparable with system development costs. For embedded real-time systems, maintenance costs may be up to four times higher than development costs. The high reliability and performance requirements of these systems may require modules to be tightly linked and hence difficult to change.

It is usually cost-effective to invest effort when designing and implementing a system to reduce maintenance costs. It is more expensive to add functionality after delivery because of the need to understand the existing system and analyse the impact of system changes. Therefore, any work done during development to reduce the cost of this analysis is likely to reduce maintenance costs. Good software engineering techniques such as precise specification, the use of object-oriented development and configuration management all contribute to maintenance cost reduction.

Figure 27.4 shows how overall lifetime costs may decrease as more effort is expended during system development to produce a maintainable system. Because

Figure 27.4
Development and
maintenance costs

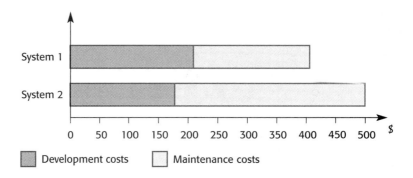

of the potential reduction in costs of understanding, analysis and testing, there is a significant multiplier effect when the system is developed for maintainability. For System 1, extra development costs of $25,000 are invested in making the system more maintainable. This results in a saving of $100,000 in maintenance costs over the lifetime of the system. This assumes that a percentage increase in development costs results in a comparable percentage decrease in overall system costs.

One important reason why maintenance costs are high is that it is more expensive to add functionality after a system is in operation than it is to implement the same functionality during development. The key factors that distinguish development and maintenance and which lead to higher maintenance costs are:

1. *Team stability*   After a system has been delivered, it is normal for the development team to be broken up and people work on new projects. The new team or the individuals responsible for system maintenance do not understand the system or the background to system design decisions. A lot of the effort during the maintenance process is taken up with understanding the existing system before implementing changes to it.

2. *Contractual responsibility*   The contract to maintain a system is usually separate from the system development contract. The maintenance contract may be given to a different company rather than the original system developer. This factor, along with the lack of team stability, means that there is no incentive for a development team to write the software so that it is easy to change. If a development team can cut corners to save effort during development it is worthwhile for them to do so even if it means increasing maintenance costs.

3. *Staff skills*   Maintenance staff are often relatively inexperienced and unfamiliar with the application domain. Maintenance has a poor image among software engineers. It is seen as a less skilled process than system development and is often allocated to the most junior staff. Furthermore, old systems may be written in obsolete programming languages. The maintenance staff may not have much experience of development in these languages and must learn these languages to maintain the system.

4. *Program age and structure*   As programs age, their structure tends to be degraded by change and so they become harder to understand and change. Furthermore, many legacy systems have been developed without modern software engineering techniques. They were never well structured and they were often optimised for efficiency rather than understandability. The documentation for old systems may be lost or inconsistent. Old systems may not have been subject to configuration management, so time is often wasted finding the right versions of system components to change.

The first three of these problems stem from the fact that many organisations still make a distinction between system development and maintenance. Maintenance is seen as a second-class activity and there is no incentive to spend money during development to reduce the costs of system change. The only long-term solution to this problem is to accept that systems rarely have a defined lifetime but continue in use, in some form, for an indefinite period.

Rather than develop systems, maintain them until further maintenance is impossible and then replace them, we have to adopt the notion of evolutionary systems. Evolutionary systems are systems that are designed to evolve and change in response to new demands. They can be created from existing legacy systems by improving their structure through re-engineering (see Chapter 28) and by evolving the architecture of these systems as discussed in section 27.3.

The last issue in the list above, namely the problem of degraded system structure is, in some ways, the easiest problem to address. Re-engineering techniques may be applied to improve the system structure and understandability. If appropriate, architectural transformation (discussed later in this chapter) can adapt the system to new hardware. Preventative maintenance work (essentially incremental re-engineering) can be supported to improve the system and make it easier to change.

27.2.1 The maintenance process

Maintenance processes vary considerably depending on the type of software being maintained, the development processes used in an organisation and the people involved in the process. In some organisations, maintenance may be an informal process. Most maintenance requests come from conversations between the system users and developers. In other companies, it is a formalised process with structured documentation produced at each stage in the process. However, at an abstract level, all maintenance processes have the same fundamental activities of change analysis, release planning, system implementation and releasing a system to customers.

The maintenance process is triggered by a set of change requests from system users, management or customers. The cost and impact of these changes are assessed to see how much of the system is affected by the change and how much it might cost to implement the change. If the proposed changes are accepted, a new release of the system is planned. During release planning, all proposed changes (fault repair, adaptation and new functionality) are considered. A decision is then made on which

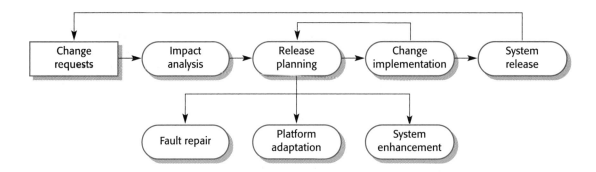

Figure 27.5
An overview of the
maintenance process

changes to implement in the next version of the system. The changes are implemented and validated and a new version of the system is released. The process then iterates with a new set of changes proposed for the new release. Figure 27.5, adapted from Arthur (1988), shows an overview of this process.

Ideally, the change implementation stage of this process should modify the system specification, design and implementation to reflect the changes to the system (Figure 27.6). New requirements that reflect the system changes are proposed, analysed and validated. System components are redesigned and implemented and the system is re-tested. If appropriate, prototyping of the proposed changes may be carried out as part of the change analysis process.

During this process, the requirements are analysed in detail and, frequently, implications of the changes emerge that were not apparent in the earlier change analysis process. This means that the proposed changes may be modified and further customer discussions may be required before they are implemented.

Change requests sometimes relate to system problems which must be tackled very urgently. These urgent changes can arise for three reasons:

1. the emergence of a system fault which must be repaired to allow normal operation to continue;
2. environmental changes which have unexpected effects on the system;
3. unanticipated business changes which might be due to the emergence of new competitors or new legislation.

In these cases, it is usually more important to make the change quickly than to ensure that the formal change process is followed. Rather than modify the requirements

Figure 27.6 Change
implementation

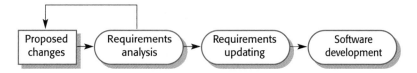

Figure 27.7
The emergency
repair process

and design, an emergency fix is made to the code of the system to implement the change (Figure 27.7). However, the danger of this approach is that the requirements, the software design and the code gradually become inconsistent. It is difficult to avoid this happening because it may be difficult to implement the change quickly. Maintenance engineers may be told to deal with new emergency fixes to the software and the proper repair is delayed. If the engineer who made a code change then leaves a team before the design is updated, it is difficult for his or her replacement to retrofit the changes to the requirements and the design.

A further problem with emergency system repairs is that they have to be completed as quickly as possible. A workable solution rather than the best solution as far as system structure is concerned may be chosen. This accelerates the process of software ageing so that future changes become progressively more difficult and maintenance costs are increased.

Ideally, when emergency code repairs are made the change request should remain outstanding after the code faults have been fixed. It can then be reimplemented more carefully after further analysis. Of course, the code of the repair may be reused. An alternative, better solution to the problem may be discovered when more time is available for analysis. In practice, however, it is almost inevitable that these changes will have a low priority and, after further system changes are made, it is unrealistic to redo the emergency repairs.

27.2.2 Maintenance prediction

Managers hate surprises, especially if these result in unexpectedly high costs. It therefore makes sense for them to try to predict what system changes are likely to be requested, what parts of the system are likely to cause the most difficulties for maintenance staff and the overall maintenance costs for a system in a given time period. Figure 27.8 illustrates these different predictions and associated questions.

These different predictions are obviously closely related:

1. Whether or not a system change should be accepted depends, to some extent, on the maintainability of the system components affected by that change.
2. Implementing system changes tends to degrade the system structure and hence reduce its maintainability.
3. Maintenance costs depend on the number of changes and the costs of change implementation depend on the maintainability of system components.

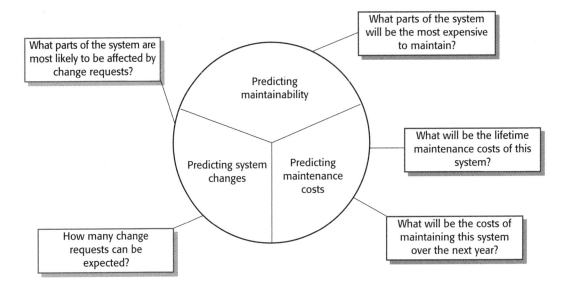

Figure 27.8
Maintenance
prediction

Predicting the number of change requests for a system requires an understanding of the relationship between the system and its external environment. Some systems have a very complex relationship with their external environment and changes to that environment inevitably result in changes to the system. To make a judgement of the relationships between a system and its environment, you should assess:

1. *The number and complexity of system interfaces*   The larger the number of interfaces and the more complex these interfaces, the more likely it is that demands for change will be made.

2. *The number of inherently volatile system requirements*   As I discussed in Chapter 6, requirements which reflect organisational policies and procedures are likely to be more volatile than requirements which are based on stable domain characteristics.

3. *The business processes in which the system is used*   As business processes evolve, they generate system change requests. The more business processes that use a system, the more the demands for system change.

To predict system maintainability you need to understand the number and the types of relationship between the different components of the system and the inherent complexity of these components. There have been various studies of the different types of complexity in a system (McCabe, 1976; Halstead, 1977) and of the relationships between complexity and maintainability (Kafura and Reddy, 1987; Banker et al., 1993). It is not surprising that these studies have found that the more complex a system or component, the more expensive it is to maintain.

Banker *et al.* (1993) carried out a study using a number of commercial programs written in COBOL. They assessed these using various complexity metrics, including procedure size, module size and density of branching which is a measure of control complexity. By comparing the complexity of different parts of the program with the records of actual program maintenance they found that using good programming practice to reduce system complexity paid off in reduced maintenance costs.

Complexity measurements have been found to be particularly useful in identifying individual program components that are likely to be particularly expensive to maintain. In Kafura and Reddy's study (1987) they examined a number of system components and found that maintenance effort tended to be focused on a small number of complex components. The implications of this are that it may be cost-effective to replace particularly complex system components with simpler alternatives.

After a system has been put into service you may be able to use process data to help predict maintainability. Examples of process metrics which may be useful for assessing maintainability are:

1. *Number of requests for corrective maintenance*   If the number of failure reports is increasing, this may indicate that more errors are being introduced into the program than are being repaired during the maintenance process. This may indicate a decline in maintainability.

2. *Average time required for impact analysis*   This reflects the number of program components that are affected by the change request. If this time increases, it implies that more and more components are affected and that maintainability is decreasing.

3. *Average time taken to implement a change request*   This is not the same as the time for impact analysis although it may correlate with it. The activities involved are making changes to the system and its documentation rather than simply assessing what components are affected. This change time depends on the difficulty of programming so that non-functional requirements such as performance are met. If the time to implement a change increases, this may indicate a decline in maintainability.

4. *Number of outstanding change requests*   If this number increases with time, it may imply a decline in maintainability.

You use predicted information about change requests and predictions about system maintainability to make predictions of maintenance costs. Most managers combine this information with intuition and experience to make an estimate of costs. The COCOMO 2 model of cost estimation (Boehm *et al.*, 1995) suggests that an estimate for software maintenance effort can be based on the effort to understand existing code and the effort to develop the new code. Readers should look at Boehm's paper for details of this estimation technique.

27.3 Architectural evolution

During system maintenance most individual changes which are made are localised and do not affect the architecture of the system. However, since the 1980s, the economics of computer-based systems have changed radically, so that distributed rather than centralised systems are often the most cost-effective solution to business problems. Therefore, many companies are faced with the need to evolve their centralised mainframe systems to distributed client–server systems as discussed in Chapter 11.

There are a number of different drivers that contribute to this change:

1. *Hardware costs*   The costs of buying and maintaining a distributed client–server system are usually much less than the costs of buying a mainframe computer of equivalent power.

2. *User interface expectations*   Many legacy mainframe systems provide form-based, character interfaces. However, most users now expect graphical user interfaces and easier interaction with the system. These interfaces require much more local computation and can only be provided effectively in a client–server system.

3. *Distributed access to systems*   Companies are, increasingly, physically distributing their organisation rather than maintaining all facilities on a single site. Their computer systems may have to be accessed from different locations and from different types of equipment. Customers and staff may access systems from their homes and this has to be supported.

By migrating to a distributed architecture, organisations can dramatically reduce hardware costs, can develop a system which has a more effective interface and a more modern 'look and feel' and can support distributed working. In the process of migration, there will inevitably be some conversion of the system to an object-oriented model and this is likely to reduce the costs of future system maintenance.

However, modifying the architecture of a legacy system is a major challenge and a very expensive process. Key factors which influence this decision are shown in Figure 27.9. Before embarking on architectural migration, organisations should make a careful assessment of their legacy systems to ensure that they will gain real business value from the architectural transformation.

A fundamental difficulty in migrating many centralised legacy systems to a distributed architecture is that the systems are not structured in such a way that the basic architectural components can be identified and separated from other components. Ideally, we would like legacy systems to have a structure as shown in the diagram on the left of Figure 27.10. In this case, the user interface, the services provided by the system and the database are clearly separated. Individual services are well defined. Within the service layer, it is possible to distinguish between the

Figure 27.9 Factors influencing system distribution decisions

Factor	Description
Business importance	Returns on the investment of distributing a legacy system depend on its importance to the business and how long it will remain important. If distribution provides more efficient support for stable business processes then it is more likely to be a cost-effective evolution strategy.
System age	The older the system, the more difficult it will be to modify its architecture because previous changes will have degraded the structure of the system.
System structure	The more modular the system, the easier it will be to change the architecture. If the application logic, the data management and the user interface of the system are closely intertwined, it will be difficult to separate functions for migration.
Hardware procurement policies	Application distribution may be necessary if there is a company policy to replace expensive mainframe computers with cheaper servers.

Figure 27.10 Ideal and realistic legacy system structures

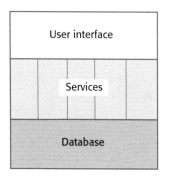
Ideal model for distribution

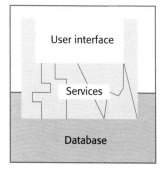
Real legacy systems

different services. With this type of structure, the distributable elements can be identified in the system and can be rewritten to run on client computers.

In practice, most legacy systems are more like the right side of Figure 27.10 where user interface facilities, services and data access are intermingled. Services may overlap. Different parts of the service are implemented in different system components. User interface and service code are integrated in the same components and there may not be a clear distinction between the system services and the system database. In these cases, it may not be possible to identify the parts of the system which can be distributed.

In situations where it is impractical to separate the legacy system into distributable components and implement these components on a distributed system an

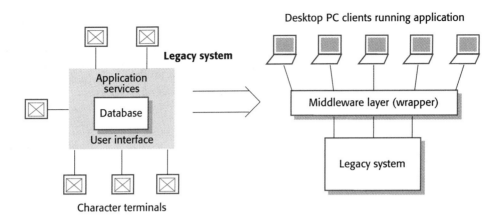

Desktop PC clients running application

Legacy system

Application services

Database

User interface

Character terminals

Middleware layer (wrapper)

Legacy system

Figure 27.11 Legacy system distribution

alternative approach can be used. The legacy system may be frozen and the complete system packaged (wrapped) as a server. The user interface is reimplemented on the client and special-purpose middleware translates requests from the client into interactions with the unchanged legacy system. This situation is illustrated in Figure 27.11.

Although the user interface and services provided by a legacy system are usually integrated, when planning a distribution strategy it may be helpful to consider them as being organised into a number of logical layers (Figure 27.12). The layers in this diagram represent potential candidates for distribution.

1. The presentation layer is concerned with the display and organisation of the screens presented to end-users of the system.
2. The data validation layer is concerned with checking the data input by and output to the end-user.
3. The interaction control layer is concerned with managing the sequence of end-user operations and the sequence of screens presented to the user.
4. The application services layer is concerned with providing the basic computations provided by the application.
5. The database layer provides application data storage and management.

Figure 27.12 Layered distribution model

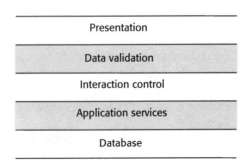

Presentation

Data validation

Interaction control

Application services

Database

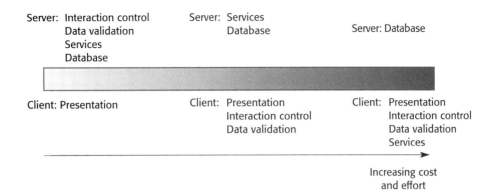

Server: Interaction control Data validation Services Database	Server: Services Database	Server: Database

Client: Presentation

	Client: Presentation Interaction control Data validation	Client: Presentation Interaction control Data validation Services

Increasing cost
and effort

Figure 27.13
Spectrum of
distribution options

It is impractical to distribute the database for most legacy systems but there is a spectrum of alternative distribution options as shown in Figure 27.13. In the simplest option, the client computer is concerned only with the presentation of the user interface and all other functions are retained on the server. In the most radical distribution option, the server only manages the system data and all other functionality is distributed to the client. Of course, these are not exclusive options. You may decide to start with presentation distribution and distribute other logical layers when time and resources are available. Furthermore, as I discuss in Chapter 11, other distribution options involving multi-tier servers are also possible.

When a legacy system is wrapped and accessed through a middleware layer as in Figure 27.11, it is possible to implement a distribution strategy which starts on the left of Figure 27.13 and, over time, moves further and further to the right. As new services are implemented, these take over the legacy system functions in the server, thus transferring more and more processing to the client. Eventually, this gradual distribution of functionality may mean that most of the initial legacy system is unused and it acts only as a database server for the distributed system.

Once this stage has been reached, you must then decide if it is worth retaining the legacy system or if you should replace it with a database management system. Factors that you should consider include the system hardware, the available expertise, whether or not a DBMS is already in use, whether it can cope with the amount of data to be managed and costs of data re-engineering.

27.3.1   User interface distribution

Many legacy systems were designed before graphical user interfaces were available. They use forms-based interfaces which run on specialised terminals that can only display characters. These terminals have limited processing power and display characteristics, so all display and associated computation functions are handled by a central mainframe system. Even when these terminals have been replaced by PCs, the character-based interface may still be maintained through a terminal emulation program running on the PC.

Figure 27.14 User
interface distribution

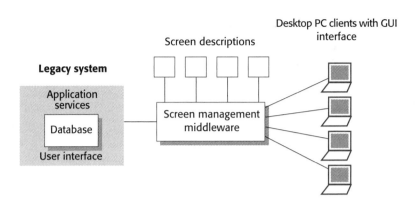

User interface distribution takes advantage of the local processing power available on desktop PCs to provide a more responsive graphical interface to system users. User interface services (presentation, interaction control and validation) are moved to the desktop machine and the character-based forms interface is replaced by a GUI interface where the user can point at menus, fields, etc. The data being processed and most or all of the application services remain on the server system.

If the legacy system is structured so that the user interface services are clearly identifiable then the legacy system can be modified to implement user interface distribution. To distribute the user interface, those parts of the system which deal with user interaction are reimplemented on the client computer and communicate with the application through the same interface as the character-based UI.

In many cases, however, user interface code and the application logic are tightly integrated and it is very difficult to separate the user interface code from other code in the legacy system. In this case, the distributed user interface can be implemented as illustrated in Figure 27.14.

The screen management middleware in Figure 27.14 communicates with the application and behaves in exactly the same way as a user terminal. The screen management system uses a description of each screen to interpret the data on the display. It then sends this to the client where the user interface software presents this within a graphical interface. This can now often be implemented fairly easily using XML (St Laurent and Cerami, 1999) to describe the interface structure. There is therefore no need to change the legacy system itself. All that is required is to write the screen management middleware and the user interface software for the client computer.

There are two implementation strategies for user interface distribution:

1. Implement the interface using the window management system which is native to the client PC and implement communications with the server.
2. Implement the user interface using a WWW browser.

Figure 27.15
Advantages and
disadvantages of UI
migration strategies

Strategy	Advantages	Disadvantages
Implementation using the window management system	Access to all UI functions so no real restrictions on UI design Better UI performance	Platform dependent May be more difficult to achieve interface consistency
Implementation using a web browser	Platform independent Lower training costs owing to user familiarity with the WWW Easier to achieve interface consistency	Potentially poorer UI performance Interface design is constrained by the facilities provided by web browsers

In the first case, the user interface is programmed in a conventional programming language such as Java or in a scripting language such as Visual Basic. Calls are made to functions in the client operating system to implement the user interface. In the second case, implementation involves using the facilities in HTML and in web browsers to construct a user interface based on WWW pages. Computations which are required may be implemented on the client using Java or on the web server using a CGI interface or servlets. Each of these approaches has different advantages and disadvantages as described in Figure 27.15.

Converting interfaces to web-based interfaces is attractive because of the platform independence and widespread availability of web browsers. Java applets can be used to provide local client-side computation, so these interfaces can be comparable to interfaces developed using the window management system. However, some users may still use versions of browsers which are either incapable of running Java or the latest versions of HTML or which are not properly configured. Interface designers often have to design to these lower-capability systems and this restricts the functionality of web-based interfaces.

A basic difficulty which arises in converting forms-based interfaces into graphical user interfaces comes from the different approaches which each of these take to interaction control and validation. In a forms-based system, the computer system controls the interaction and applies data validation rules as soon as the data is entered. Most applications require form fields to be completed in a particular sequence and display forms only when other forms have been completely and correctly filled in.

In a GUI, the user is in control and uses a model of interaction where he or she points and clicks to select the fields. It is unnatural for the order of this to be controlled by the machine. If control is implemented, this can result in additional network traffic between the client and the server. Data validation may only be possible after a form has been completely filled in or the system may be slowed down by frequent communications between the client and the server.

KEY POINTS

▶ Software change strategies include software maintenance, architectural evolution and software re-engineering.

▶ There appear to be a number of invariant relationships (Lehman's Laws) which affect the evolution of a software system. These have been derived from empirical observations and show that maintenance costs are inevitable. They provide guidelines on how to manage the maintenance process.

▶ There are three principal types of software maintenance. These are maintenance to repair defects in the software, maintenance to adapt the software to a different operating environment and maintenance to add to or modify the functionality of the system.

▶ The cost of software change usually exceeds the cost of software development. As companies manage an increasing number of legacy systems, more of their software budget is taken up in legacy system maintenance.

▶ High maintenance costs are due to lack of staff stability, development contracts that don't encourage the production of maintainable code, shortages of the skills required to maintain a system and system structures that have degraded owing to age and regular system change.

▶ Architectural evolution involves modifying the architecture of a system from a centralised, data-centric architecture to a distributed architecture. Both the user interface and system functionality may be distributed.

▶ A common architectural evolution strategy for legacy systems is to encapsulate the legacy system as a server and to implement a distributed user interface which accesses the system functionality through special-purpose middleware.

FURTHER READING

The Renaissance of Legacy Systems. This book includes a chapter which discusses various strategies for migrating centralised systems to client–server systems. (I. Warren, 1998, Springer.)

Software Evolution and Reuse. Discusses a number of industrial case studies where research techniques have been applied. (S. Hallsteinsen and M. Paci, 1997, Springer.)

EXERCISES

27.1 Explain why a software system that is deployed in a changing organisation is always subject to requests for change. Why do these changes become increasingly expensive?

27.2 Explain the rationale underlying Lehman's Laws. Under what circumstances might the laws break down?

27.3 Explain the difficulties of measuring program maintainability. Suggest why you should use several different complexity metrics when trying to assess the maintainability of a program.

27.4 As a software project manager in a company that specialises in the development of software for the offshore oil industry, you have been given the task of discovering those factors which affect the maintainability of the particular systems which are developed by your company. Suggest how you might set up a programme to analyse the maintenance process to discover appropriate maintainability metrics for your company.

27.5 Explain why encapsulating a mainframe legacy system and using it as a server should only be considered as a short-term solution to the problems of architectural evolution.

27.6 Discuss the advantages and disadvantages of distributing each of the layers in Figure 27.12.

27.7 Two major international banks with different customer information databases merge and decide that they need to provide access to all customer information from all bank branches. Giving reasons for your answer, suggest the most appropriate strategy for providing access to these systems and briefly discuss how the solution might be implemented.

27.8 Do software engineers have a professional responsibility to produce maintainable code even if this is not explicitly requested by their employer?

28 Software re-engineering

Objectives

The objective of this chapter is to explain the process of software re-engineering to improve the maintainability of a software system. When you have read this chapter, you will:

❑ understand why re-engineering is sometimes a cost-effective option for software system evolution;

❑ understand the activities such as reverse engineering and program restructuring which may be involved in the software re-engineering process;

❑ understand the differences between software and data re-engineering and understand why data re-engineering is an expensive and time-consuming process.

Contents

28.1 Source code translation
28.2 Reverse engineering
28.3 Program structure improvement
28.4 Program modularisation
28.5 Data re-engineering

In Chapters 26 and 27, I introduced legacy systems and different strategies for software evolution. Legacy systems are old software systems which are essential for business process support. Companies rely on these systems so they must keep them in operation. Software evolution strategies include maintenance, replacement, architectural evolution and, the topic of this chapter, software re-engineering.

Software re-engineering is concerned with reimplementing legacy systems to make them more maintainable. Re-engineering may involve redocumenting the system, organising and restructuring the system, translating the system to a more modern programming language and modifying and updating the structure and values of the system's data. The functionality of the software is not changed and, normally, the system architecture also remains the same.

From a technical perspective, software re-engineering may appear to be a second-class solution to the problems of system evolution. The software architecture is not updated so distributing centralised systems is difficult. It is not usually possible to radically change the system programming language, so old systems cannot be converted to object-oriented programming languages such as Java or C++. Inherent limitations in the system are maintained because the software functionality is unchanged.

However, from a business point of view, software re-engineering may be the only viable way to ensure that legacy systems can continue in service. It may be too expensive and too risky to adopt any other approach to system evolution. To understand the reasons for this, we must make a rough assessment of the legacy system problem.

The amount of code in legacy systems is immense. In 1990, it was estimated (Ulrich, 1990) that there were 120 *billion* lines of source code in existence. The majority of these systems have been written in COBOL, a programming language best suited to business data processing, or FORTRAN. FORTRAN is a language for scientific or mathematical programming. These languages have limited program structuring facilities and, in the case of FORTRAN, very limited support for data structuring.

Although many of these programs have now been replaced, most of them are probably still in service. Meanwhile, since 1990, there has been a huge increase in computer use for business process support. Therefore, I guess that there must now be roughly 250 billion lines of source code in existence which must be maintained. Most of this is not written in object-oriented languages and much of it still runs on mainframe computers.

There are so many systems in existence that complete replacement or radical restructuring is financially unthinkable for most organisations. Maintenance of old systems is increasingly expensive so re-engineering these systems extends their useful lifetime. As discussed in Chapter 26, re-engineering a system is cost-effective when it has a high business value but is expensive to maintain. Re-engineering improves the system structure, creates new system documentation and makes it easier to understand.

Re-engineering a software system has two key advantages over more radical approaches to system evolution:

Figure 28.1
Forward engineering
and re-engineering

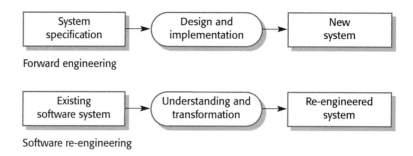

1. *Reduced risk*   There is a high risk in redeveloping software that is essential for an organisation. Errors may be made in the system specification, there may be development problems, etc.

2. *Reduced cost*   The cost of re-engineering is significantly less than the costs of developing new software. Ulrich (1990) quotes an example of a commercial system where the reimplementation costs were estimated at $50 million. The system was successfully re-engineered for $12 million. If these figures are typical, it is about four times cheaper to re-engineer than to rewrite.

The term re-engineering is also associated with business process re-engineering (Hammer, 1990). Business process re-engineering is concerned with redesigning business processes to reduce the number of redundant activities and improve process efficiency. It is usually reliant on the introduction or the enhancement of computer-based support for the process. Process re-engineering is often a driver for software evolution as legacy systems may incorporate implicit dependencies on the existing processes. These have to be discovered and removed before process re-engineering is possible. Therefore, the need for software re-engineering may emerge in a company when it becomes clear that the scale of the changes required by the business process re-engineering cannot be accommodated through normal program maintenance.

The critical distinction between re-engineering and new software development is the starting point for the development. Rather than start with a written specification, the old system acts as a specification for the new system. Chikofsky and Cross (1990) call conventional development *forward engineering* to distinguish it from software re-engineering. This distinction is illustrated in Figure 28.1. Forward engineering starts with a system specification and involves the design and implementation of a new system. Re-engineering starts with an existing system and the development process for the replacement is based on understanding and transformation of the original system.

Figure 28.2 illustrates a possible re-engineering process. The input to the process is a legacy program and the output is a structured, modularised version of the same program. At the same time as program re-engineering, the data for the system may also be re-engineered. The activities in this re-engineering process are:

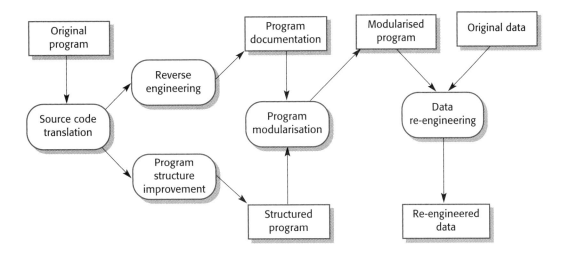

Figure 28.2
The re-engineering
process

1. *Source code translation*   The program is converted from an old programming language to a more modern version of the same language or to a different language.

2. *Reverse engineering*   The program is analysed and information extracted from it which helps to document its organisation and functionality.

3. *Program structure improvement*   The control structure of the program is analysed and modified to make it easier to read and understand.

4. *Program modularisation*   Related parts of the program are grouped together and, where appropriate, redundancy is removed. In some cases, this stage may involve architectural transformation as discussed in Chapter 27.

5. *Data re-engineering*   The data processed by the program is changed to reflect program changes.

Program re-engineering may not necessarily require all of the steps in Figure 28.2. Source code translation may not be needed if the programming language used to develop the system is still supported by the compiler supplier. If the re-engineering relies completely on automated tools then recovering documentation through reverse engineering may be unnecessary. Data re-engineering is only required if the data structures in the program change during system re-engineering. However, software re-engineering always involves some program restructuring.

The costs of re-engineering obviously depend on the extent of the work that is carried out. There is a spectrum of possible approaches to re-engineering as shown in Figure 28.3. Costs increase from left to right so that source code translation is the cheapest option and re-engineering as part of architectural migration is the most expensive.

Figure 28.3
Re-engineering
approaches

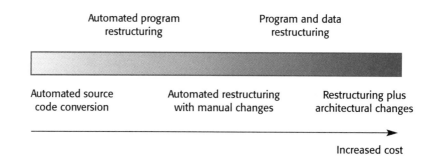

Apart from the extent of the re-engineering, the principal factors that affect re-engineering costs are:

1. *The quality of the software to be re-engineered* The lower the quality of the software and its associated documentation (if any), the higher the re-engineering costs.

2. *The tool support available for re-engineering* It is not normally cost-effective to re-engineer a software system unless you can use CASE tools to automate most of the program changes.

3. *The extent of data conversion required* If re-engineering requires large volumes of data to be converted, this significantly increases the process cost.

4. *The availability of expert staff* If the staff responsible for maintaining the system cannot be involved in the re-engineering process, this will increase the costs. System re-engineers will have to spend a great deal of time understanding the system.

The main disadvantage of software re-engineering is that there are practical limits to the extent that a system can be improved by re-engineering. It isn't possible, for example, to convert a system written using a functional approach to an object-oriented system. Major architectural changes or radical reorganising of the system data management cannot be carried out automatically, so involve high additional costs. Although re-engineering can improve maintainability, the re-engineered system will probably not be as maintainable as a new system developed using modern software engineering methods.

28.1 Source code translation

The simplest form of software re-engineering is program translation where source code in one programming language is automatically translated to source code in

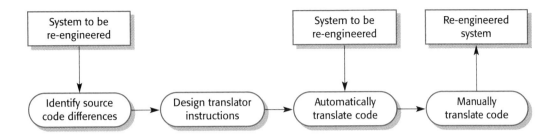

Figure 28.4
The program
translation process

some other language. The structure and organisation of the program itself are unchanged. The target language may be an updated version of the original language (e.g. COBOL-74 to COBOL-85) or may be a translation to a completely different language (e.g. FORTRAN to C).

Source-level translation may be necessary for the following reasons:

1. *Hardware platform update*   The organisation may wish to change its standard hardware platform. Compilers for the original language may not be available on the new hardware.

2. *Staff skill shortages*   There may be a lack of trained maintenance staff for the original language. This is a particular problem where programs were written in a non-standard language that has now gone out of general use.

3. *Organisational policy changes*   An organisation may decide to standardise on a particular language to minimise its support software costs. Maintaining many versions of old compilers can be very expensive.

4. *Lack of software support*   The suppliers of the language compiler may have gone out of business or may discontinue support for their product.

Figure 28.4 illustrates the process of source code translation. There may be no need to understand the operation of the software in detail or to modify the system architecture. The analysis involved can focus on programming language considerations such as the equivalence of program control constructs.

Source code translation is only economically realistic if an automated translator is available to do the bulk of the translation. This may be a specially written program, a bought-in tool to convert from one language to another or a pattern matching system. In the latter case, a set of instructions how to make the translation from one representation to another has to be written. Parameterised patterns in the source language are defined and associated with equivalent patterns in the target language.

In many cases, completely automatic translation is impossible. Constructs in the source language may have no direct equivalent in the target language. There may be embedded conditional compilation instructions in the source code which are not supported in the target language. In these circumstances, you need to make changes manually to tune and improve the generated system.

28.2 Reverse engineering

Reverse engineering is the process of analysing software with the objective of recovering its design and specification. The program itself is unchanged by the reverse engineering process. The software source code is usually available as the input to the reverse engineering process. Sometimes, however, even this has been lost and the reverse engineering must start with the executable code.

Reverse engineering is not the same thing as re-engineering. The objective of reverse engineering is to derive the design or specification of a system from its source code. The objective of re-engineering is to produce a new, more maintainable system. Of course, as we can see from Figure 28.2, reverse engineering to develop a better understanding of a system is often part of the re-engineering process.

Reverse engineering is used during the software re-engineering process to recover the program design which engineers use to help them understand a program before reorganising its structure. However, reverse engineering need not always be followed by re-engineering:

1. The design and specification of an existing system may be reverse engineered so that they can serve as an input to the requirements specification for that program's replacement.

2. Alternatively, the design and specification may be reverse engineered so that they are available to help program maintenance. With this additional information, it may not be necessary to re-engineer the system source code.

The reverse engineering process is illustrated in Figure 28.5. The process starts with an analysis phase. During this phase, the system is analysed using automated tools to discover its structure. In itself, this is not enough to re-create the system design. Engineers then work with the system source code and its structural model. They add information to this which they have collected by understanding the system. This information is maintained as a directed graph that is linked to the program source code.

Figure 28.5
The reverse
engineering process

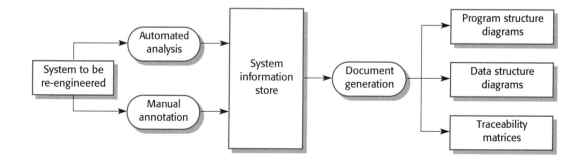

Information store browsers are used to compare the graph structure and the code and to annotate the graph with extra information. Documents of various types such as program and data structure diagrams and traceability matrices can be generated from the directed graph. Traceability matrices show where entities in the system are defined and referenced. The process of document generation is an iterative one as the design information is used to further refine the information held in the system repository.

Tools for program understanding may be used to support the reverse engineering process. These usually present different system views and allow easy navigation through the source code. For example, they allow users to select a data definition, then move through the code to where that data item is used. Examples of such program browsers are discussed by Cleveland (1989), Oman and Cook (1990) and Ning *et al.* (1994).

After the system design documentation has been generated, further information may be added to the information store to help re-create the system specification. This usually involves further manual annotation of the system structure. The specification cannot be deduced automatically from the system model.

28.3 Program structure improvement

The need to optimise memory use and the lack of understanding of software engineering by many programmers have meant that many legacy systems are not well structured. Their control structure is tangled with many unconditional branches and unintuitive control logic. This structure may also have been degraded by regular maintenance. Changes to the program may have made some code unreachable but this can only be discovered after extensive analysis. Maintenance programmers often dare not remove code in case it may be accessed indirectly.

Figure 28.6 illustrates how complex control logic can make a relatively simple program difficult to understand. The program is written in a notation similar to FORTRAN which was often used to write this type of program. However, I have not made the program even more difficult to understand by using cryptic variable names. The example in Figure 28.6 is a controller for a heating system. A panel switch may be set to On, Off or Controlled. If the system is controlled, then it is switched on and off depending on a timer setting and a thermostat. If the heating is on, Switch-heating turns it off and vice versa.

Typically, programs develop this complex logic structure as they are modified during maintenance. New conditions and associated actions are added without changing the existing control structure. In the short term, this is a quicker and less risky solution as it reduces the chances of introducing faults in the system. In the long term, however, it leads to incomprehensible code. Complex code structures can also arise when programmers tried to avoid duplicating code. This was sometimes necessary when programs were constrained by limited memory.

Figure 28.6 A control
program with
spaghetti logic

```
Start:   Get (Time-on, Time-off, Time, Setting, Temp, Switch)
         if Switch = off goto off
         if Switch = on goto on
         goto Cntrld
off:     if Heating-status = on goto Sw-off
         goto loop
on:      if Heating-status = off goto Sw-on
         goto loop
Cntrld:  if Time = Time-on goto on
         if Time = Time-off goto off
         if Time < Time-on goto Start
         if Time > Time-off goto Start
         if Temp > Setting then goto off
         if Temp < Setting then goto on
Sw-off:  Heating-status := off
         goto Switch
Sw-on:   Heating-status := on
Switch:  Switch-heating
loop:    goto Start
```

Figure 28.7
A structured control
program

```
loop
    -- The Get statement finds values for the given variables from the system's
    -- environment.
    Get (Time-on, Time-off, Time, Setting, Temp, Switch) ;
    case Switch of
        when On => if Heating-status = off then
                        Switch-heating ; Heating-status := on ;
                    end if ;
        when Off => if Heating-status = on then
                        Switch-heating ; Heating-status := off ;
                    end if ;
        when Controlled =>
            if Time >= Time-on and Time < = Time-off then
                if Temp > Setting and Heating-status = on then
                    Switch-heating; Heating-status = off ;
                elsif Temp < Setting and Heating-status = off then
                    Switch-heating; Heating-status := on ;
                end if ;
            end if ;
    end case ;
end loop ;
```

Figure 28.7 shows the same control system which I have rewritten using structured
control statements. The program may be read sequentially from top to bottom so it
is much easier to understand. The three switch positions, on, off and controlled, are
clearly identified and linked to their associated code. I have not used Java here as
the original program is not object-oriented.

Figure 28.8
Condition
simplification

```
-- Complex condition
if not (A > B and (C < D or not ( E > F) ) )...

-- Simplified condition
if A <= B and (C>= D or E > F)...
```

Figure 28.9
Automated program
restructuring

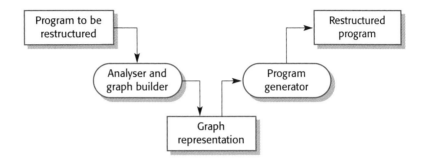

As well as unstructured control, complex conditions can also be simplified as part of the program restructuring process. Figure 28.8 shows how a conditional statement including 'not' logic may be made more understandable.

Bohm and Jacopini (1966) proved that any program may be rewritten in terms of simple if-then-else conditionals and while-loops and that unconditional goto statements were not required. This theorem is the basis for automatic program restructuring. Figure 28.9 shows the stages in the automatic restructuring of a program. It is first converted to a directed graph, then a structured equivalent program, without goto statements, is generated.

The directed graph that is generated is a program flow graph which shows how control moves through the program. Simplification and transformation techniques can be applied to this graph without changing its semantics. These detect and remove unreachable parts of the code. Once simplification has been completed, a new program is generated. While-loops and simple conditional statements are substituted for goto-based control. This program may be in the original language or in a different language (e.g. FORTRAN may be converted to C).

Problems with automatic program restructuring include:

1. *Loss of comments*   If the program has in-line comments, these are invariably lost as part of the restructuring process.

2. *Loss of documentation*   Similarly, the correspondence between external program documentation and the program is also lost. In many cases, however, both the comments and the documentation of a program are out of date, so this is not an important factor.

3. *Heavy computational demands*   The algorithms embedded in restructuring tools are complex. Even with fast, modern hardware it can take a long time to complete the restructuring process for large programs.

If the program is data-driven with components tightly coupled through shared data structures, restructuring the code may not lead to a significant improvement in understandability. Program modularisation, as discussed in the following section, may also be necessary. If the program is written in a non-standard language dialect, standard restructuring tools may not work properly and significant manual intervention may be required.

In some cases, it may not be cost-effective to restructure all of the programs in a system. Some may be of better quality than others and some may not be subject to frequent change. Arthur (1988) suggests that data should be collected to help identify those programs which could benefit most from restructuring. For example, the following metrics may be used to identify the candidates for restructuring:

• failure rate;
• percentage of source code changed per year;
• component complexity.

Other factors such as the degree to which programs or components meet current standards might also be taken into account in making restructuring decisions.

28.4 Program modularisation

Program modularisation is the process of reorganising a program so that related program parts are collected together and considered as a single module. Once this has been done, it becomes easier to remove redundancies in these related components, to optimise their interactions and to simplify their interface with the rest of the program. For example, in a program that processes seismographic data, all operations associated with graphical presentation of the data may be collected together into a single module. If the system is to be distributed, the modules created can be encapsulated as objects and accessed through a common interface.

Several different types of module may be created during the program modularisation process. These include:

1. *Data abstractions*   These are abstract data types that are created by associating data with processing components. I discuss this in section 28.4.1.

2. *Hardware modules*   These are closely related to data abstractions and collect together all of the functions which are used to control a particular hardware device.

3. *Functional modules*   These are modules which collect together functions that carry out similar or closely related tasks. For example, all of the functions concerned with input and input validation may be incorporated in a single module. This type of modularisation should be considered where it is impractical to recover program data abstractions.

4. *Process support modules*   These are modules where all of the functions and the specific data items required to support a particular business process are grouped. For example, in a library system, a process support module may include all of the functionality required to support the issue and return of books.

Program modularisation is usually carried out manually by inspecting and editing the code. To modularise a program, you have to identify relationships between components and work out what these components do. Browsing and visualisation tools help but it is impossible to automate this process completely.

28.4.1 Recovering data abstractions

To save memory space, many legacy systems rely on the use of shared tables and common data areas. The information in these areas is globally accessible and may be used by different parts of the system in different ways. Making changes to these global data areas is expensive because of the costs of analysing change impacts across all uses of the data.

To reduce the costs of change to these shared data areas, the program modularisation process may focus on the identification of data abstractions. Data abstractions or abstract data types collect together data and associated processing and are resilient to change. Data abstractions hide the data representation and provide constructor and access functions to modify and inspect the data. So long as the interface is maintained, changes in the data type should not affect other parts of the program.

The steps involved in converting shared global data areas to objects or abstract data types are:

1. Analyse common data areas to identify logical data abstractions. It will often be the case that several abstractions are combined in a single shared data area. These should be identified and logically restructured.

2. Create an abstract data type or object for each of these abstractions. If the programming language does not have data hiding facilities, simulate an abstract data type by providing functions to update and access all fields of the data.

3. Use a program browsing system or cross-reference generator to find all references to the data. Replace these with calls to the appropriate functions.

This process seems to be time-consuming but relatively straightforward. In practice, however, it can be very difficult because of the ways in which shared data areas are used. In older versions of languages like FORTRAN which have limited data structuring facilities, programmers may have designed complex data management strategies which they have implemented using shared arrays. The array therefore may actually be used as a different kind of data structure. Further problems are caused by indirect addressing of shared structures and addressing by offsets from some other structure.

If the target machine for the original program had a limited memory, this causes other problems. The programmers may have used knowledge about data lifetimes and embedded this in the program. To avoid allocating extra space, they use the same data area to store different abstractions at different points in the program. These can only be discovered after a detailed static and dynamic analysis of the program.

28.5 Data re-engineering

So far, most of the discussion of software evolution has focused on the problems of changing programs and software systems. However, in many cases, there are associated problems of data evolution. The storage, organisation and format of the data processed by legacy programs may have to evolve to reflect changes to the software. The process of analysing and reorganising the data structures and, sometimes, the data values in a system to make it more understandable is called *data re-engineering*.

In principle, data re-engineering should not be necessary if the functionality of a system is unchanged. In practice, however, there are a number of reasons why you may have to modify the data as well as the programs in a legacy system:

1. *Data degradation*   Over time, the quality of data tends to decline. Changes to the data introduce errors, duplicate values may have been created and changes to the external environment may not be reflected in the data. This is inevitable because data lifetimes are often very long. For example, personal banking data comes into existence when an account is opened and may have to persist for at least the lifetime of the customer. As the customer's circumstances change, these changes may not be properly included in the bank's data. Program re-engineering can bring data quality problems to light and thus highlight the need for associated data re-engineering.

2. *Inherent limits that are built into the program*   When originally designed, developers of many programs included built-in constraints on the amount of data which could be processed. However, programs are now often required to process much more data than was originally envisaged by their developers. Data re-engineering may be required to remove the limitations. For example, Rochester and Douglass (1993) describe a funds management system that was originally designed to handle up to 99 funds. The company running the system was managing more than 2000 funds and had to run 23 separate copies of the system. They therefore decided to re-engineer the system and its associated data.

3. *Architectural evolution*   If a centralised system is migrated to a distributed architecture it is essential that the core of that architecture should be a data management system that can be accessed from remote clients. This may require a large data re-engineering effort to move data from separate files into the server

database management system. The move to a distributed program architecture may be initiated when an organisation decides to move from file-based data management to a database management system.

As with program re-engineering, there are a spectrum of approaches to data re-engineering which reflect the reasons why data re-engineering may be required. These are shown in Figure 28.10.

Rickets *et al.* (1993) describe some of the problems with data which can arise in legacy systems made up of several cooperating programs:

1. *Data naming problems*   Names may be cryptic and difficult to understand. Different names (synonyms) may be given to the same logical entity in different programs in the system. The same name may be used in different programs to mean different things.

2. *Field length problems*   This is a problem when field lengths in records are explicitly assigned in the program. The same item may be assigned different lengths in different programs or the field length may be too short to represent current data. To solve this problem, other fields may be reused in some cases so that usage of a named data field across the programs in a system is inconsistent.

3. *Record organisation problems*   Records representing the same entity may be organised differently in different programs. This is a problem in languages like COBOL where the physical organisation of records is set by the programmer and reflected in files. It is not a problem in languages like C++ or Java where the physical organisation of a record is the compiler's responsibility.

4. *Hard-coded literals*   Literal (absolute) values, such as tax rates, are included directly in the program rather than referenced using some symbolic name.

5. *No data dictionary*   There may be no data dictionary defining the names used, their representation and their use.

Figure 28.10
Approaches to data
re-engineering

Approach	Description
Data cleanup	The data records and values are analysed to improve their quality. Duplicates are removed, redundant information is deleted and a consistent format applied to all records. This should not normally require any associated program changes.
Data extension	In this case, the data and associated programs are re-engineered to remove limits on the data processing. This may require changes to programs to increase field lengths, modify upper limits on the tables, etc. The data itself may then have to be rewritten and cleaned up to reflect the program changes.
Data migration	In this case, data is moved into the control of a modern database management system. The data may be stored in separate files or may be managed by an older type of DBMS. This situation is illustrated in Figure 28.11.

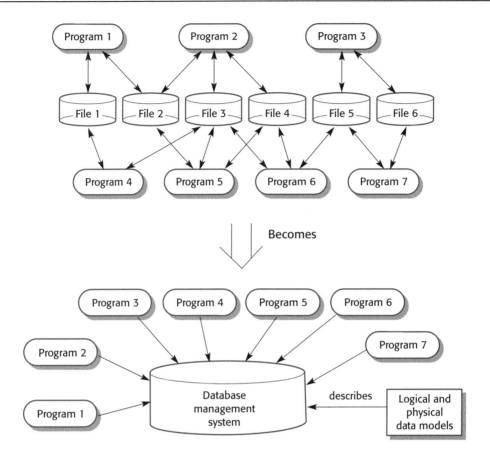

Figure 28.11
Data migration

As well as inconsistent data definitions, data values may also be stored in an inconsistent way. After the data definitions have been re-engineered, the data values must also be converted to conform to the new structure. Rickets *et al.* also describe some possible data value inconsistencies. These are shown in Figure 28.12.

Detailed analysis of the programs that use the data is essential before data re-engineering. This analysis should be aimed at discovering the function of identifiers in the program, finding the literal values which should be replaced with named constants, discovering embedded data validation rules and data representation conversions. Tools such as cross-reference analysers and pattern matchers may be used to help with this analysis. A set of tables should be created which show where data items are referenced and the changes to be made to each of these references.

Figure 28.13 illustrates the process of data re-engineering, assuming that data definitions are modified, literal values named, data formats reorganised and the data values converted. The change summary tables hold details of all the changes to be made. They are therefore used at all stages of the data re-engineering process.

Figure 28.12 Data
value inconsistencies

Data inconsistency	Description
Inconsistent default values	Different programs assign different default values to the same logical data items. This causes problems for programs other than those that created the data. The problem is compounded when missing values are assigned a default value that is valid. The missing data cannot then be discovered.
Inconsistent units	The same information is represented in different units in different programs. For example, in the US or the UK, weight data may be represented in pounds in older programs but in kilograms in more recent systems. A major problem of this type has arisen in Europe with the introduction of a single European currency. Legacy systems have been written to deal with national currency units and data has to be converted to euros.
Inconsistent validation rules	Different programs apply different data validation rules. Data written by one program may be rejected by another. This is a particular problem for archival data which may not have been updated in line with changes to data validation rules.
Inconsistent representation semantics	Programs assume some meaning in the way items are represented. For example, some programs may assume that upper-case text means an address. Programs may use different conventions and may therefore reject data which is semantically valid.
Inconsistent handling of negative values	Some programs reject negative values for entities which must always be positive. Others, however, may accept these as negative values or fail to recognise them as negative and convert them to a positive value.

Figure 28.13 The
data re-engineering
process

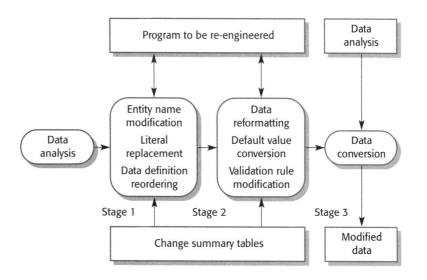

In Stage 1 of this process, the data definitions in the program are modified to improve understandability. The data itself is not affected by these modifications. It is possible to automate this process to some extent using pattern matching systems such as awk (Aho *et al.*, 1988) to find and replace definitions or to develop XML descriptions of the data (St Laurent and Cerami, 1999) and use these to drive data conversion tools. However, some manual work is almost always necessary to complete the process. The data re-engineering process may stop at this stage if the goal is simply to improve the understandability of the data structure definitions in a program. If, however, there are data value problems as discussed above, Stage 2 of the process may then be entered.

If an organisation decides to continue to Stage 2 of the process, it is then committed to Stage 3, data conversion. This is usually a very expensive process. Programs have to be written which embed knowledge of the old and the new organisation. These process the old data and output the converted information. Again, pattern matching systems may be used to implement this conversion.

KEY POINTS

▸ The objective of system re-engineering is to improve the system structure and make it easier to understand. The cost of future system maintenance should therefore be reduced.

▸ The re-engineering process includes source code translation, reverse engineering, program structure improvement, program modularisation and data re-engineering.

▸ Source code translation is the automatic conversion of a program written in one programming language to another language. It may be necessary when the original programming language is obsolete.

▸ Reverse engineering is the process of deriving a systems design and specification from its source code. Tools such as program browsers may be used to assist this process.

▸ Program structure improvement involves replacing unstructured control constructs such as gotos with while-loops and conditional statements. This can be automated.

▸ Program modularisation involves reorganising the source code of a program to group related items together. This makes them easier to understand and change.

▸ Data re-engineering may be necessary because of inconsistent data management by the programs in a legacy system. The objective of data re-engineering may be to re-engineer all programs to use a common database.

▸ The costs of data re-engineering are significantly increased if existing data has to be converted to some new format.

FURTHER READING

'Examining data quality'. This special section includes a number of papers which discuss data quality issues and the impact of poor data quality. (G. K. Tayi and D. P. Ballou, *Comm. ACM*, 41(2), Feb. 1998.)

Software Re-engineering. This is an IEEE tutorial that includes most of the important papers on re-engineering which were published before 1992. Many of the papers referenced in this chapter are reprinted in it. (R. S. Arnold, 1994, IEEE Press.)

'DoD legacy systems: Reverse engineering data requirements'. This is a good description of the practical problems which arise with legacy systems. The paper focuses on data re-engineering where systems managing similar but incompatible data were combined. Other papers in this special issue on reverse engineering are also relevant. (P. Aiken, A. Muntz, R. Richards, *Comm. ACM*, 37(5), May 1994.)

EXERCISES

28.1 Under what circumstances do you think that software should be scrapped and rewritten rather than re-engineered?

28.2 Compare the control constructs (loops and conditionals) in any two programming languages which you know. Write a short description of how to translate the control constructs in one language to the equivalent constructs in the other.

28.3 Translate the unstructured routine shown in Figure 28.14 into its structured equivalent and work out what it is supposed to do.

28.4 Write a set of guidelines that may be used to help find modules in an unstructured program.

28.5 Suggest meaningful names for the variables used in the program shown in Figure 28.14 and construct data dictionary entries for these names.

28.6 What problems might arise when converting data from one type of database management system to another (e.g. hierarchical to relational or relational to object-oriented)?

28.7 Explain why it is impossible to recover a system specification by automatically analysing system source code.

28.8 Using examples, describe the problems with data degradation which may have to be tackled during the process of data cleanup.

28.9 The Year 2000 problem where dates were represented as two digits posed a major program maintenance problem for many organisations. What were the implications of this problem for data re-engineering?

Figure 28.14
An unstructured
program

```
routine BS (K, T, S, L)
B:= 1
NXT:  if S >= B goto CON
L = -1
goto STP
CON:  L := INTEGER (B / S)
L := INTEGER ((B+S) / 2)
if T (L) = K then return
if T(L) > K then goto GRT
B := L+1
goto NXT
GRT:  S := L-1
goto NXT
STP: end
```

28.10 A company routinely places contractual conditions on freelance programmers working on re-engineering their applications which prevents them from taking on contracts with similar companies. The reason for this is that re-engineering inevitably reveals business information. Is this a reasonable position for a company to take given that they have no obligations to contractors after their contract has finished?

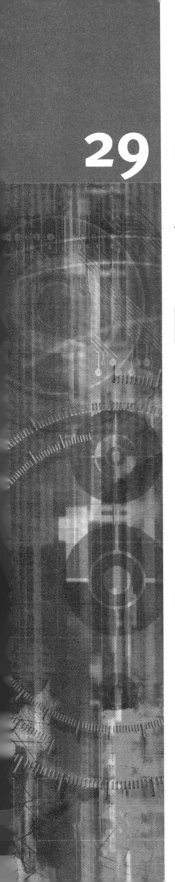

29 Configuration management

Objectives

The objective of this chapter is to introduce the process of managing the code and documentation of an evolving software system. When you have read this chapter, you will:

❑ understand why software configuration management is important;

❑ have been introduced to four principal configuration management activities – configuration management planning, change management, version and release management and system building;

❑ understand how CASE tools for configuration management may be used to support configuration management processes.

Contents

29.1 Configuration management planning
29.2 Change management
29.3 Version and release management
29.4 System building
29.5 CASE tools for configuration management

Configuration management (CM) is the development and application of standards and procedures for managing an evolving system product. You need to manage evolving systems because, as they evolve, many different versions of the software are created. These versions incorporate proposals for change, corrections of faults and adaptations for different hardware and operating systems. There may be several versions under development and in use at the same time. You need to keep track of the changes that have been implemented and how these changes have been included in the software.

Configuration management procedures define how to record and process proposed system changes, how to relate these to system components and the methods used to identify different versions of the system. Configuration management tools are used to store versions of system components, build systems from these components and track the releases of system versions to customers.

Configuration management is sometimes seen as part of a more general software quality management process as discussed in Chapter 24. The same manager may share quality management and configuration management responsibilities. Software is released by the developers to a quality assurance team who are responsible for checking that the system is of acceptable quality. It is then passed to the configuration management team who become responsible for controlling changes to the software. Controlled systems are sometimes called *baselines* as they are a starting point for controlled evolution.

There are many reasons why systems exist in different configurations. Configurations may be produced for different computers, for different operating systems, incorporating client-specific functions and so on (Figure 29.1). Configuration managers are responsible for keeping track of the differences between software versions, for ensuring that new versions are derived in a controlled way and for releasing new versions to the right customers at the right time.

The configuration management process and associated documentation should be based on standards. An example of such a standard is IEEE 828-1983, which defines a standard for configuration management plans. Within an organisation, these standards should be published in a configuration management handbook or as part of a quality handbook. External standards may be used as a basis for more detailed organisational standards that are tailored to a specific environment. It doesn't really

Figure 29.1
System families

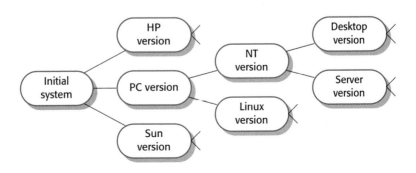

matter which standard is taken as a starting point as all of them include comparable processes. In both the ISO 9000 quality standards (Ince, 1994) and the SEI's Capability Maturity Model (Paulk *et al.*, 1993), organisations must define and follow formal CM standards for quality certification.

In a traditional software development process based on the 'waterfall' model (see Chapter 3), software is delivered to the configuration management team after development is complete and the individual software components have been tested. This team then takes over the responsibility for building the complete system and for managing system testing. Faults which are discovered during system testing are passed back to the development team for repair. They then fix the fault and deliver a new version of the repaired component to the CM team.

This approach has influenced the development of configuration management standards and these standards have an embedded assumption that a waterfall model of the software process will be used for system development (Bersoff and Davis, 1991). This means that they cannot be readily applied to alternative approaches to software development such as evolutionary prototyping or incremental development. To cater for this style of development, some organisations have developed a modified approach to configuration management which supports concurrent development and system testing. This approach relies on a very regular (often daily) build of the whole system from its components:

1. The development organisation sets a delivery time (say 2 p.m.) for system components. If developers have new versions of the components that they are writing they must deliver them by that time. Components may be incomplete but should provide some basic functionality which can be tested.

2. A new version of the system is built from these components by compiling and linking them to form a complete system.

3. This system is then delivered to the testing team who carry out a set of predefined system tests. At the same time, the developers are still working on their components, adding to the functionality and repairing faults discovered in previous tests.

4. Faults that are discovered during system testing are documented and returned to the system developers. They repair these faults in a subsequent version of the component.

The main advantages of using daily builds of software is that the chances of finding problems that stem from component interactions early in the process are increased. Furthermore, daily building encourages thorough unit testing of components. Psychologically, developers are put under pressure not to 'break the build', i.e. deliver versions of components which cause the whole system to fail. They are therefore reluctant to deliver new component versions which have not been properly tested. Less system testing time is spent discovering and coping with software faults that should have been found during unit testing.

The successful use of daily builds requires a very stringent change management process to keep track of the problems that have been discovered and repaired. It also leads to a very large number of system and component versions that must be managed. Good configuration management is therefore essential for this approach to be successful.

29.1 Configuration management planning

A configuration management plan describes the standards and procedures which should be used for configuration management. The starting point for developing the plan should be a set of general, company-wide configuration management standards and these should be adapted as necessary for each specific project. The CM plan should be organised into a number of chapters and should include:

1. the definition of what entities are to be managed and a formal scheme for identifying these entities;

2. a statement of who takes responsibility for the configuration management procedures and for submitting controlled entities to the configuration management team;

3. the configuration management policies that are used for change control and version management;

4. a description of the records of the configuration management process which should be maintained;

5. a description of the tools to be used for configuration management and the process to be applied when using these tools;

6. a definition of the configuration database which will be used to record configuration information.

Other information such as the management of software from external suppliers and the auditing procedures for the CM process may also be included in the CM plan.

An important part of the CM plan is the definition of responsibilities. It should define who is responsible for the delivery of each document or software component to quality assurance and configuration management. It may also define the reviewers of each document. The person responsible for document delivery need not be the same as the person responsible for producing the document. To simplify interfaces, it is often convenient to make project managers or team leaders responsible for all of the documents produced by their team.

29.1.1 Configuration item identification

In the course of developing a large software system, thousands of documents are produced. Many of these are technical working documents which present a snapshot of ideas for further development. These documents are subject to frequent and regular change. Others are inter-office memos, minutes of group meetings, outline plans and proposals, etc. These documents may be of interest to a project historian. However, they are not needed for future maintenance of the system.

During the configuration management planning process, you decide exactly which items (or classes of item) are to be controlled. Documents or groups of related documents under configuration control are formal documents or *configuration items*. Project plans, specifications, designs, programs and test data suites are normally maintained as configuration items. However, all documents which may be necessary for future system maintenance should be controlled.

The document naming scheme must assign a unique name to all documents under configuration control. There are always relationships between these documents. For example, design documents will be associated with programs. These relationships can be recorded implicitly by organising the naming scheme so that related documents have a common root to their name. This leads to a hierarchical naming scheme where examples of names might be:

PCL-TOOLS/EDIT/FORMS/DISPLAY/AST-INTERFACE/CODE
PCL-TOOLS/EDIT/HELP/QUERY/HELPFRAMES/FR-1

The initial part of the name is the project name, PCL-TOOLS. In this project, there are four separate tools. The tool name is used as the next part of the name. Each tool is made up of different named modules. This decomposition process continues until the base-level formal documents are referenced (Figure 29.2). The leaves

Figure 29.2
Configuration
hierarchy

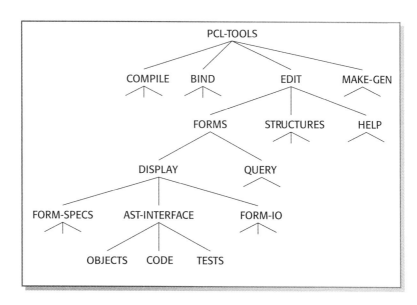

of the documentation hierarchy are the formal project documents. Figure 29.2 shows that three formal documents are required for each managed entity. These are an object description (OBJECTS), the code of the component (CODE) and a set of tests for that code (TESTS).

The problem with naming schemes of this sort is that they are project based. Identifiers associate components with a particular project. This may reduce the opportunities for reuse. Copies of reusable components should normally be taken out of such a scheme and renamed according to their application domain. Other problems may arise if the document naming scheme is used as a direct basis for designing a storage structure for storing the managed components. Users of the documents then have to know their name to find them and all documents of the same type (e.g. design documents) are not held together in one place. There may also be problems in relating the naming scheme to the identification scheme used by a version management system.

29.1.2 The configuration database

The configuration database is used to record all relevant information relating to configurations. Its principal functions are to assist with assessing the impact of system changes and to provide management information about the CM process. As well as defining the configuration database schema, procedures for recording and retrieving project information must also be defined as part of the CM planning process.

A configuration data base must be able to provide answers to a variety of queries about system configurations. Typical queries might be:

1. Which customers have taken delivery of a particular version of the system?
2. What hardware and operating system configuration is required to run a given system version?
3. How many versions of a system have been created and what were their creation dates?
4. What versions of a system might be affected if a particular component is changed?
5. How many change requests are outstanding on a particular version?
6. How many reported faults exist in a particular version?

Ideally, the configuration database should be integrated with the version management system that is used to store and manage the formal project documents. This approach, supported by some integrated CASE tools, makes it possible to link changes directly with the documents and components affected by the change. Links between documents, such as design documents, and program code may be maintained so that it is relatively easy to find everything which must be modified when a change is proposed.

However, many companies do not use integrated CASE tools for configuration management but maintain their configuration database as a separate system. The configuration items may be stored in files or in a version management system such as RCS (Tichy, 1985), a well-known version management system for Unix. This configuration database stores information about the configuration items and references their file names in the version management system. While this is a relatively cheap and flexible approach, its disadvantage is that configuration items may be changed without going through the configuration database. Therefore, you can't be sure that the configuration database is an up-to-date description of the state of the system.

29.2 Change management

Change is a fact of life for large software systems. As discussed in earlier chapters, organisational needs and requirements change during the lifetime of a system. This requires corresponding changes to be made to the software. A defined change management process and associated CASE tools ensure that these changes are recorded and applied to the system in a cost-effective way.

The change management process (Figure 29.3) should come into effect when the software or associated documentation is put under the control of the configuration management team. It may be initiated during system testing or after the software has been delivered to customers. Change management procedures should be designed to ensure that the costs and benefits of change are properly analysed and that changes to a system are made in a controlled way.

The first stage in the change management process is to complete a change request form (CRF) where the requester sets out the change required to the system. As well

Figure 29.3 The change management process

```
Request change by completing a change request form
Analyse change request
if change is valid then
    Assess how change might be implemented
    Assess change cost
    Record change request in database
    Submit request to change control board
    if change is accepted then
        repeat
            make changes to software
            record changes and link to associated change request
            submit changed software for quality approval
        until software quality is adequate
        create new system version
    else
        reject change request
else
    reject change request
```

Figure 29.4
A partially completed
change request form

Change Request Form

Project: Proteus/PCL-Tools   **Number:** 23/94
Change requester: I. Sommerville   **Date:** 1/12/98
Requested change: When a component is selected from the structure, display the
name of the file where it is stored.

Change analyser: G. Dean   **Analysis date:** 10/12/98
Components affected: Display-Icon.Select, Display-Icon.Display

Associated components: FileTable

Change assessment: Relatively simple to implement as a file name table is
available. Requires the design and implementation of a display field. No changes to
associated components are required.

Change priority: Low
Change implementation:
Estimated effort: 0.5 days
Date to CCB: 15/12/98   **CCB decision date:** 1/2/99
CCB decision: Accept change. Change to be implemented in Release 2.1.
Change implementor: **Date of change:**
Date submitted to QA: **QA decision:**
Date submitted to CM:
Comments

as recording the change required, the CRF records the recommendations regarding the change, the estimated costs of the change and the dates when the change was requested, approved, implemented and validated. It may also include a section where the maintenance engineer outlines how the change is to be implemented. Change requests should be registered in the configuration database. The CM team can therefore track the status of change requests and the change requests which are associated with specific software components.

An example of a change request form, which has been partially completed, is shown in Figure 29.4. The change request form is usually defined during the CM planning process. For some contracts, however, particularly government contracts, the change request form must conform to a specified client standard.

Once a change request form has been submitted, it is analysed to check that the change is valid. Some change requests may be due to misunderstandings rather than system faults; others may refer to already known faults. If the analysis discovers that a change request is invalid, duplicated or has already been considered, the change should be rejected. The reason for the rejection should be returned to the person who submitted the change request.

For valid changes, the next stage of the process is change assessment and costing. The impact of the change on the rest of the system must be checked. A technical analysis must be made of how to implement the change. The cost of making the change and possibly changing other system components to accommodate the change is then estimated. This should be recorded on the change request form. This assessment process may use the configuration database where component interrelationships are recorded. The impact of the change on other components may then be considered.

Unless the change simply involves correcting minor errors on screen displays or in documents, it should be submitted to a change control board (CCB) who decide whether or not it should be accepted. The change control board considers the impact of the change from a strategic and organisational rather than a technical point of view. It decides if the change is economically justified and if there are good organisational reasons to accept the change.

The term 'change control board' sounds very formal. It implies a rather grand group which makes change decisions. Formally structured change control boards which include senior client and contractor staff are a requirement of military projects. For small or medium-sized projects, however, the change control board may simply consist of a project manager plus one or two engineers who are not directly involved in the software development. In some cases, there may be only a single change reviewer who gives advice on whether or not changes are justifiable.

When a set of changes has been approved, the software is handed over to the development or maintenance team for implementation. Once these have been completed, the revised software must be revalidated to check that these changes have been correctly implemented. The CM team, rather than the system developers, then builds a new version or release of the software.

When new versions of the system are created though daily system builds, a simpler change management process is used. Problems and changes must still be recorded but changes that only affect individual components and modules need not be independently assessed. They are passed directly to the system developer. They either accept them or make a case why they are not required. Changes which affect system modules produced by different development teams should be still be assessed by some kind of change control authority who decides if they should be implemented.

As software components are changed, a record of the changes made to each component should be maintained. This is sometimes called the derivation history of a component. The best way to maintain such a record is in a standardised comment prologue kept at the beginning of the component (see Figure 29.5). This should

Figure 29.5 Component header information

```
// PROTEUS project (ESPRIT 6087)
//
// PCL-TOOLS/EDIT/FORMS/DISPLAY/AST-INTERFACE
//
// Object: PCL-Tool-Desc
// Author: G. Dean
// Creation date: 10th November 1998
//
// © Lancaster University 1998
//
// Modification history
// Version    Modifier    Date         Change       Reason
// 1.0        J. Jones    1/12/1998    Add header   Submitted to CM
// 1.1        G. Dean     9/4/1999     New field    Change req. R07/99
```

reference the change request associated with the software change. Specialised tools may be used to process the derivation histories and produce reports about component changes.

29.3 Version and release management

Version and release management are the processes of identifying and keeping track of different versions and releases of a system. Version managers devise procedures to ensure that different versions of a system may be retrieved when required and are not accidentally changed. They may also work with customer liaison staff to plan when new releases of a system should be distributed. New system versions should always be created by the CM team rather than the system developers, even when they are not intended for external release. This makes it easier to maintain consistency in the configuration database as only the CM team can change version information.

A system *version* is an instance of a system that differs, in some way, from other instances. New versions of the system may have different functionality, performance or may repair system faults. Some versions may be functionally equivalent but designed for different hardware or software configurations. If there are only small differences between versions, one of these is sometimes called a *variant* of the other.

A system *release* is a version that is distributed to customers. Each system release should either include new functionality or be intended for a different hardware platform. There are always many more versions of a system than releases as versions are created within an organisation for internal development or testing that are never released to customers.

Version management is now always supported by CASE tools as discussed in section 29.5. These tools manage the storage of each system version and control access to system components. They must be checked out from the system for editing. When re-entered in the system, a new version is created and named by the version management system.

29.3.1 Version identification

Within a large software system, there are hundreds of software components each of which may exist in many different versions. Procedures for version management should define an unambiguous way of identifying each component version. Specific versions of components may then be recovered as required for further change.

There are three basic techniques which may be used for component identification:

1. *Version numbering* The component is given an explicit and unique version number. This is the most commonly used identification scheme.

2. *Attribute-based identification* Each component has a name (which is not unique across versions) and an associated set of attributes which differs for each version of the component (Estublier and Casallas, 1994). Components are therefore identified by the combination of name and attribute set.

3. *Change-oriented identification* Each system is named as in attribute-based identification but is also associated with one or more change requests (Munch *et al.*, 1993). The system version is identified by associating the name with the changes implemented in the component.

Version numbering

In a simple version numbering scheme, the component or system name is augmented by a version number. Therefore, we can talk about Solaris 2.6 (version 2.6 of the Solaris system) and version 1.4 of component getToken. The first version may be called 1.0, subsequent versions are 1.1, 1.2 and so on. At some stage, a new release is created (release 2.0) and the process starts again at version 2.1, 2.2, etc. The scheme is a linear one based on the assumption that system versions are created in sequence. Many version management tools (see section 29.5) such as RCS support this approach to version identification.

This approach and the derivation of a number of different system versions from previous versions of the system is illustrated in Figure 29.6. The arrows in this diagram point from the source version to a new system version that is created from the source. Notice that the derivation of versions is not necessarily linear and versions with consecutive version numbers may be produced from different baselines. This is shown in Figure 29.6 where version 2.2 is created from version 1.2 rather than version 2.1. In principle, any existing version may be used as the starting point for a new version of the system.

This scheme is simple but requires a good deal of associated information management to keep track of the differences between versions and the relationships between system change proposals and versions. It may therefore be difficult to find

Figure 29.6 Version derivation structure

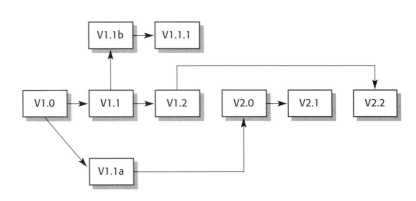

specific system or component versions when they are required, especially if there is no integrated link between the configuration database and the stored versions of the system.

Attribute-based identification

A fundamental problem with explicit version naming schemes is that they do not reflect the many different attributes which may be used to identify versions. Examples of these identifying attributes are:

- Customer
- Development language
- Development status
- Hardware platform
- Creation date

If each version is identified by a unique set of attributes, it is easy to add new versions that are derived from any of the existing versions. These are identified using a unique set of attribute values. They share most of these values with their parent version so relationships between versions are maintained. Versions can be retrieved by specifying the attribute values required. Functions on attributes support queries such as 'the most recently created version', 'the version created between given dates', etc. For example, the version of the software system AC3D developed in Java for Windows NT in January 1999 would be identified

AC3D (language = Java, platform = NT4, date = Jan1999)

Attribute-based identification may be implemented directly by the version management system. More commonly, however, it is implemented on top of a hidden version naming scheme and the configuration database maintains the links between identifying attributes and underlying system and component versions.

Change-oriented identification

Attribute-based identification of system versions removes some of the problems of version retrieval which are found with simple numbering schemes. However, to retrieve a version, you still have to know its associated attributes. Furthermore, you still need to use a separate change management system to discover the relationships between versions and changes.

Change-oriented identification is used for systems rather than components so that versions of individual components are hidden from users of the CM system. Each proposed system change has an associated *change set* that describes the changes made to the different system components to implement that change. Change sets may be applied in sequence so that, in principle at least, a version of the system which incorporates any arbitrary set of changes may be created. Therefore, no explicit version identification is required. The CM team interacts with the version management system indirectly through the change management system.

In practice, of course, it isn't possible to apply arbitrary sets of changes to a system. Different change sets may be incompatible so that applying change set A followed by change set D may create an invalid system. Furthermore, change sets may conflict in that different changes affect the same code of the system. To address these difficulties, version management tools which support change-oriented identification allow system consistency rules to be specified which limit the ways in which change sets may be combined.

29.3.2   Release management

A system release is a version of the system that is distributed to customers. System release managers are responsible for deciding when the system can be released to customers, managing the process of creating the release and the distribution media and documenting the release to ensure that it may be re-created exactly as distributed if this is necessary.

A system release is not just the executable code of the system. The release may also include:

1. *configuration files* defining how the release should be configured for particular installations;
2. *data files* which are needed for successful system operation;
3. *an installation program* that is used to help install the system on target hardware;
4. *electronic and paper documentation* describing the system;
5. *packaging and associated publicity* which have been designed for that release.

Release managers cannot assume that customers will always install new system releases. Some system users may be happy with an existing system version. They may consider that it is not worth the cost of changing to a new release. New releases of the system cannot, therefore, depend on the existence of previous releases. Consider the following scenario:

1. Release 1 of a system is distributed and put into use.
2. Release 2 follows which requires the installation of new data files but some customers do not need the facilities of release 2 so remain with release 1.
3. Release 3 requires the data files installed in release 2 and has no new data files of its own.

The software distributor cannot assume that the files required for Release 3 have already been installed in all sites. Some sites may go directly from Release 1 to Release 3, skipping Release 2. Some sites may have modified the data files associated with Release 2 to reflect local circumstances. Therefore, the data files must be distributed and installed with Release 3 of the system.

Figure 29.7 Factors
influencing system
release strategy

Factor	Description
Technical quality of the system	If serious system faults are reported which affect the way in which many customers use the system, it may be necessary to issue a fault repair release. However, minor system faults may be repaired by issuing patches (often distributed over the Internet) that can be applied to the current release of the system.
Lehman's fifth law (see Chapter 27)	This suggests that the increment of functionality which is included in each release is approximately constant. Therefore, if there has been a system release with significant new functionality, it may have to be followed by a repair release.
Competition	A new system release may be necessary because a competing product is available.
Marketing requirements	The marketing department of an organisation may have made a commitment for releases to be available at a particular date.
Customer change proposals	For customised systems, customers may have made and paid for a specific set of system change proposals and they expect a system release as soon as these have been implemented.

Release decision-making

Preparing and distributing a system release is an expensive process, particularly for mass market software products. If releases are too frequent, customers may not upgrade to the new release; if they are infrequent, market share may be lost as customers move to alternative systems. This, of course, does not apply to customised software developed specially for an organisation. However, for this type of software, infrequent releases may mean increasing divergence between the software and the business processes that it is designed to support.

Decisions on when to release a new version of the system should be governed by technical and organisational considerations, as shown in Figure 29.7.

Release creation

Release creation is the process of creating a collection of files and documentation which include all of the components of the system release. The executable code of the programs and all associated data files must be collected and identified. Configuration descriptions may have to be written for different hardware and operating systems and instructions prepared for customers who need to configure their own systems. If machine-readable manuals are distributed, electronic copies must be stored with the software. Scripts for the installation program may have to be written. Finally, when all information is available a master release disk is prepared and handed over for distribution.

The normal distribution medium for system releases is now CD-ROM disks which can store up to 600 Mbytes of data. In addition, many software products are also released by making them available on the Internet and allowing customers to download them. However, many people find the time taken to download large files is too long and prefer CD-ROM distribution.

Release documentation

When a system release is produced, it must be documented to ensure that it can be re-created exactly in future. This is particularly important for customised, long-lifetime embedded systems. Customers may use a single release of these systems for many years and may require specific changes to a particular software release long after its original release date.

To document a release, you have to record the specific versions of the source code components which were used to create the executable code. You must also keep copies of the source and executable code and all data and configuration files. You should also record the versions of the operating system, libraries, compilers and other tools used to build the software. These may be required to build exactly the same system at some later date. In these cases, copies of the platform software and tools may also be stored in the version management system.

29.4 System building

System building is the process of compiling and linking software components into a program which executes on a particular target configuration. When you are building a system from its components, you have to think about the following questions:

1. Have all the components which make up a system been included in the build instructions?

2. Has the appropriate version of each required component been included in the build instructions?

3. Are all required data files available?

4. If data files are referenced within a component, is the name used the same as the name of the data file on the target machine?

5. Is the appropriate version of the compiler and other required tools available? Current versions of software tools may be incompatible with the older versions used to develop the system.

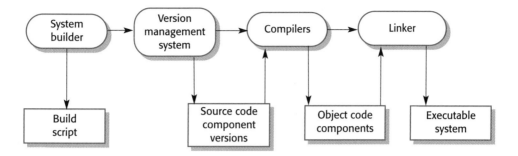

Figure 29.8
System building

Nowadays, CM tools are used to automate the system building process. The CM team writes a build script that defines the dependencies between the different components of the system. It also specifies the tools used to compile and link the system components. The system building tool interprets the build script and calls other programs as required to build the executable system. This is illustrated in Figure 29.8.

Dependencies between components are specified in the build script so that the system building system can decide when components must be recompiled and when existing object code can be reused. Build script dependencies are most commonly specified as dependencies between the files in which the source code components are stored. However, when there are multiple source code files representing different versions of components, it is sometimes unclear which source files were used to derive object-code components. This confusion is particularly likely when the correspondence between source and object code files relies on them having the same name but a different suffix (e.g. .c and .o).

To avoid some of the difficulties of physical file dependencies, some experimental systems, based on module description languages, have been produced (Sommerville and Dean, 1996). These use a description of the logical software structure and a mapping to a storage structure to infer the dependencies between files containing source code components. This approach reduces the scope for error and leads to more understandable descriptions of the system building process.

29.5 CASE tools for configuration management

Configuration management processes are usually standardised and involve the application of predefined procedures. They require careful management of very large amounts of data and attention to detail is essential. When building a system from component versions, a single configuration management mistake can mean that the software will not work properly. Consequently, CASE tool support is essential for configuration management and, since the 1970s, a large number of different tools which address different areas of configuration management have been produced.

Examples of first-generation CM tools include SCCS (Rochkind, 1975) and RCS (Tichy, 1985) for revision control and make (Feldman, 1979) for system building. These are stand-alone tools that address specific activities in the configuration management process. Second-generation tools such as Lifespan (Whitgift, 1991) and DSEE (Leblang and Chase, 1987) provided some integrated CM process support but did not support all CM activities. At the time of writing, integrated CASE toolsets are available (Leblang, 1994) which support configuration planning, change management, version management and system building. However, these integrated CM toolsets are complex and expensive and many organisations still use first- and second-generation CM tool support.

29.5.1 Support for change management

Each person involved in the change management process is responsible for some activity. They complete this activity, then pass on the forms and associated configuration items to someone else. The procedural nature of this process means that a change process model can be designed and integrated with a version management system. This model may then be interpreted so that the right documents are passed to the right people at the right time.

Change management tools may therefore provide the following facilities to support the process:

1. *A form editor* that allows change proposal forms to be created and filled in.

2. *A workflow system* that allows the CM team to specify the different people who must process the change request form and the order of processing. This system will also automatically pass forms to the right people at the right time and inform the relevant team members of the progress of the change. Electronic mail is used to provide progress updates for those involved in the process.

3. *A change database* that is used to manage all change proposals and which may be linked to a version management system. Query facilities which allow the CM team to find specific change proposals are usually provided.

29.5.2 Support for version management

Version management involves managing large amounts of information and ensuring that system changes are recorded and controlled. Version management tools control a repository of configuration items where the contents of that repository are immutable (i.e. cannot be changed). To work on a configuration item, it must be checked-out of the repository into some working directory. After the work is complete, it is then re-entered in the repository and a new version is automatically created.

Figure 29.9 Delta-based versioning

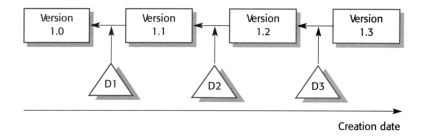

Creation date

All version management systems provide a comparable basic set of capabilities although some have more sophisticated facilities than others. Examples of these capabilities are:

1. *Version and release identification*   Managed versions are assigned identifiers when they are submitted to the system. Different systems support the different types of version identification discussed in section 29.3.1.

2. *Storage management*   To reduce the storage space required by different versions which are largely the same, version management systems provide storage management facilities so that versions are described by their differences from some master version. Differences between versions are represented as a *delta* which encapsulates the instructions required to re-create the associated system version. This is illustrated in Figure 29.9 which shows how backward deltas may be applied to the latest version of a system to re-create earlier system versions.

3. *Change history recording*   All of the changes made to the code of a system or component are recorded and listed. In some systems, these changes may be used to select a particular system version.

4. *Independent development*   Different versions of a system can be developed in parallel and each version may be changed independently. For example, release 1 can be modified after development of release 2 is in progress by adding new level-1 deltas. The version management system keeps track of components which have been checked out for editing and ensures that changes made to the same component by different developers do not interfere. Some systems only allow one instance of a component to be checked out for editing; others resolve potential clashes when the edited components are checked back into the system.

29.5.3   Support for system building

System building is a computationally intensive process. If all of the components of a large system have to be compiled and linked, this can take several hours. There may be hundreds of files involved with the consequent possibility of human error if these are compiled and linked manually. System building tools automate the build process to reduce the potential for human error and, where possible, minimise the time required for system building.

System building tools may be stand-alone tools such as derivatives of the Unix make utility (Feldman, 1979) or may be integrated with version management tools. Facilities provided by system building CASE tools may include:

1. *A dependency specification language and associated interpreter*   Component dependencies may be described and recompilation minimised. I explain this in more detail later in this section.

2. *Tool selection and instantiation support*   The compilers and other processing tools which are used to process the source code files may be specified and instantiated as required.

3. *Distributed compilation*   Some system builders, especially those which are part of integrated CM systems, support distributed, network compilation. Rather than all compilations being carried out on a single machine, the system builder looks for idle processors on the network and sets off a number of parallel compilations. This dramatically reduces the time required to build a system.

4. *Derived object management*   Derived objects are objects which are created from other source objects. Derived object management links the source code and the derived objects and only re-derives an object when this is required by source code changes.

Managing derived objects and minimising recompilation is best explained using a simple example. Consider a situation where a program called comp is created out of object modules scan.o, syn.o, sem.o and cgen.o. For each object module, there exists a source code module called scan.c, syn.c, sem.c and cgen.c. A file of declarations called defs.h is shared by scan.c, syn.c and sem.c (Figure 29.10). In Figure 29.10 arrows mean 'depends-on'. Therefore, comp depends on scan.o, syn.o, sem.o and cgen.o, scan.o depends on scan.c, etc.

Figure 29.10
Component
dependencies

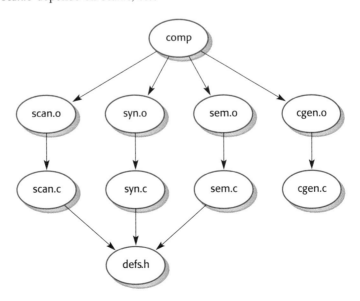

If scan.c is changed, the system building tool can detect that the derived object scan.o must be re-created and calls the appropriate compiler to compile scan.c to create a new derived object, scan.o. It then uses the dependency link between comp and scan.o to detect that comp must be re-created by linking scan.o, syn.o, sem.o and cgen.o. The system can detect that the other object code components are unchanged so recompilation of the associated source code is unnecessary.

Some system builders use the file modification date as the key attribute in deciding whether or not recompilation is required. If a source code file is modified after its corresponding object code file then the object code file is re-created. However, this normally means that there is a derived object only for the most recent source code version. If an earlier version of the source code must be recompiled, then its modification date has to be set artificially to force the system builder to recognise the need for recompilation. Other systems use a more sophisticated approach to derived object management. They tag derived objects with the version identifier of the source code and, within the limits of the storage capacity, they maintain all derived objects. Therefore, it is usually possible to recover the object code of all versions of source code components without recompilation.

KEY POINTS

▶ Configuration management is the management of system change. When a system is maintained, the role of the CM team is to ensure that changes are incorporated in a controlled way.

▶ In a large project, a formal document naming scheme should be established and used as a basis for keeping track of the different versions of all project documents.

▶ The CM team should be supported by a configuration database that records information about system changes and change requests that are outstanding. Projects should have some formal means of requesting system changes.

▶ When setting up a configuration management scheme, a consistent scheme of version identification should be established. Versions may be identified by version number, by an associated set of attributes or by the proposed system changes which they implement.

▶ System releases include executable code, data files, configuration files and documentation. Release management involves making decisions on when to release a system, preparing all information for distribution and documenting each system release.

▶ System building is the process of assembling system components into an executable program to run on some target computer system.

▶ CASE tools are available to support all configuration management activities. These include tools such as RCS to manage system versions, tools to support change management and system building tools.

▶ CASE tools for CM may be stand-alone tools supporting change management, version management and system building or may be integrated systems which provide a single interface to all CM support.

FURTHER READING

System Configuration Management. This is the latest proceedings of a series of workshops on software configuration management. It summarises the latest research and industrial practice in this area. (J. Estublier, 1999, Springer.)

Trends in Software: Configuration Management. This is a collection of papers on different aspects of configuration management by authors who are active researchers and practitioners in this field. It's a good introduction for students and practitioners who are interested in reading on advanced CM topics. (W. Tichy (ed.), 1995, John Wiley and Sons.)

Implementing Configuration Management. This book is written from the perspective of a large system supplier. It discusses the problems of system configuration management where hardware, software and embedded firmware must all be controlled. (F. J. Buckley, 1993, IEEE Press.)

EXERCISES

29.1 Explain why you should not use the title of a document to identify the document in a configuration management system. Suggest a standard for a document identification scheme that may be used for all projects in an organisation.

29.2 Using the entity-relational or object-oriented approach (see Chapter 7), design a model of a configuration database which records information about system components, versions, releases and changes. Some requirements for the data model are as follows:

• It should be possible to retrieve all versions or a single identified version of a component.
• It should be possible to retrieve the 'latest' version of a component.
• It should be possible to find out which change requests have been implemented by a particular version of a system.

- It should be possible to discover which versions of components are included in a specified version of a system.
- It should be possible to retrieve a particular release of a system according to either the release date or the customers to whom the release was delivered.

29.3 Using a data-flow diagram, describe a change management procedure which might be used in a large organisation concerned with developing software for external clients. Changes may be suggested from either external or internal sources.

29.4 Describe the difficulties which can be encountered in system building. Suggest particular problems that might arise when a system is built on a host computer for some target machine.

29.5 With reference to system building, explain why it may sometimes be necessary to maintain obsolete computers on which large software systems were developed.

29.6 A common problem with system building occurs when physical file names are incorporated in system code and the file structure implied in these names differs from that of the target machine. Write a set of programmer's guidelines which help avoid this and other system building problems which you can think of.

29.7 Describe five factors which must be taken into account by engineers during the process of building a release of a large software system.

29.8 Describe two ways in which system building tools can optimise the process of building a version of a system from its components.

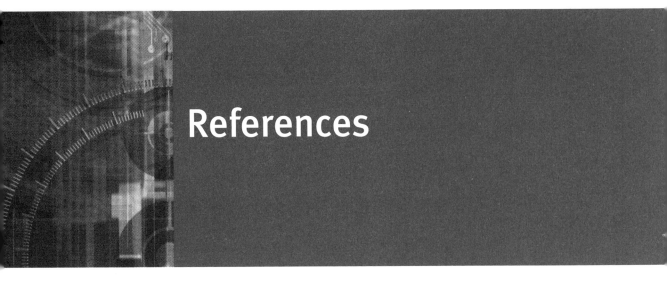

References

Abbott, R. (1983). Program design by informal English descriptions. *Comm. ACM*, **26**(11), 882–94. (Ch. 12)

Abdel-Ghaly, A. A., Chan, P. Y. *et al.* (1986). Evaluation of competing software reliability predictions. *IEEE Trans. on Software Engineering*, **SE-12**(9), 950–67. (Ch. 21)

Ackroyd, S., Harper, R. *et al.* (1992). *Information Technology and Practical Police Work*. Milton Keynes: Open University Press. (Ch. 2)

Adams, E. N. (1984). Optimizing preventative service of software products. *IBM J. Res & Dev.*, **28**(1), 2–14. (Ch. 16)

Aho, A. V., Kernighan, B. W. *et al.* (1988). *The Awk Programming Language*. Englewood Cliffs, NJ: Prentice-Hall. (Chs 8, 28)

Albrecht, A. J. (1979). Measuring application development productivity. *SHARE/GUIDE IBM Application Development Symposium*. (Ch. 23)

Albrecht, A. J. and Gaffney, J. E. (1983). Software function, lines of code and development effort prediction: a software science validation. *IEEE Trans. on Software Engineering*, **SE-9**(6), 639–47. (Ch. 23)

Alexander, C., Ishikawa, S. *et al.* (1977). *A Pattern Language*. Oxford: Oxford University Press. (Ch. 14)

Alford, M. W. (1977). A requirements engineering methodology for real time processing requirements. *IEEE Trans. on Software Engineering*, **SE-3**(1), 60–9. (Ch. 5)

Alford, M. W. (1985). SREM at the age of eight: the distributed computing design system. *IEEE Computer*, **18**(4), 36–46. (Ch. 5)

Aron, J. D. (1974). *The Program Development Process*. Reading, MA: Addison-Wesley. (Ch. 22)

Aron, J. D. (1983). *The Program Development Process: Part 2 – The Programming Team*. Reading, MA: Addison-Wesley. (Ch. 4)

Arthur, L. J. (1988). *Software Evolution*. New York: John Wiley and Sons. (Chs 27, 28)

Avizienis, A. (1985). The N-Version Approach to Fault-Tolerant Software. *IEEE Trans. on Software Engineering*, **SE-11**(12), 1491–501. (Ch. 18)

Avizienis, A. A. (1995). A methodology of N-version programming. In *Software Fault Tolerance* (M. R. Lyu, ed.). Chichester: John Wiley and Sons, 23–46. (Ch. 18)

Baker, F. T. (1972). Chief programmer team management of production programming. *IBM Systems J.*, **11**(1), 56–73. (Ch. 22)

Baker, T. P. and Scallon, G. M. (1986). An architecture for real-time software systems. *IEEE Software*, **3**(3), 50–8. (Ch. 13)

Banker, R. D., Datar, S. M. *et al.* (1993). Software complexity and maintenance costs. *Comm. ACM*, **36**(11), 81–94. (Ch. 27)

Banker, R., Kauffman, R. *et al.* (1992). An empirical test of object-based output measurement metrics in a computer-aided software engineering (CASE) environment. *J. of Management Info. Sys.*, **8**(3), 127–50. (Ch. 23)

Bansler, J. P. and Bødker, K. (1993). A reappraisal of structured analysis: design in an organizational context. *ACM Trans. on Information Systems*, **11**(2), 165–93. (Ch. 3)

Barker, R. (1989). *CASE* Method: Entity Relationship Modelling*. Wokingham: Addison-Wesley. (Ch. 7)

Barnard, J. and Price, A. (1994). Managing code inspection information. *IEEE Software*, **11**(2), 59–69. (Chs 19, 24)

Barnes, J. (1998). *Programming in Ada 95*. Harlow, Essex: Addison-Wesley. (Ch. 13)

Barnes, J. G. P. (1994). *Programming in Ada, 4th edn*. Wokingham: Addison-Wesley. (Ch. 13)

Basili, V. and Green, S. (1993). Software process improvement at the SEL. *IEEE Software*, **11**(4), 58–66. (Ch. 25)

Basili, V. R. and Rombach, H. D. (1988). The TAME project: towards improvement-oriented software environments. *IEEE Trans. on Software Engineering*, **14**(6), 758–773. (Chs 24, 25)

Basili, V. R. and Selby, R. W. (1987). Comparing the effectiveness of software testing strategies. *IEEE Trans. on Software Engineering*, **SE-13**(12), 1278–96. (Ch. 19)

Bass, B. M. and Dunteman, G. (1963). Behaviour in groups as a function of self, interaction and task orientation. *J. abnorm. soc. psychology*, **66**(4), 19–28. (Ch. 22)

Bass, L., Clements, P., *et al.* (1998). *Software Architecture in Practice*. Reading, MA: Addison-Wesley. (Ch. 10)

Baumer, D., Gryczan, G. *et al.* (1997). Framework development for large systems. *Comm. ACM*, **40**(10), 52–9. (Ch. 14)

Beck, K. (1999). Embracing change with extreme programming. *IEEE Computer*, **32**(10), 70–8. (Ch. 3)

Beck, K. (2000). *Extreme Programming Explained*. Reading, MA: Addison-Wesley Longman. (Chs 22, 23)

Beck, K. and Cunningham, W. (1989). A laboratory for teaching object-oriented thinking. *SIGPLAN Notices*, **24**(10). (Ch. 12)

Beizer, B. (1990). *Software Testing Techniques, 2nd edn*. New York: Van Nostrand Rheinhold. (Ch. 20)

Bell, T. E., Bixler, D. C. *et al.* (1977). An extendable approach to computer aided software requirements engineering. *IEEE Trans. on Software Engineering*, **SE-3**(1), 49–60. (Ch. 5)

Bentley, R., Rodden, T. *et al.* (1992). Ethnographically-informed systems design for air traffic control. *Proc. CSCW '92*, Toronto, Canada. (Ch. 6)

Bernstein, P. A. (1996). Middleware: a model for distributed system services. *Comm. ACM*, **39**(2), 86–97. (Ch. 11)

Bersoff, E. H. and Davis, A. M. (1991). Impact of life cycle models on software configuration management. *Comm. ACM*, **34**(8), 104–18. (Ch. 29)

Binder, R. V. (1999). *Testing Object-Oriented Systems: Models, Patterns and Tools*. Reading, MA: Addison-Wesley Longman. (Ch. 20)

Bishop, P., Esp, D. *et al.* (1986). PODS – a project on diverse software. *IEEE Trans. on Software Engineering*, **SE-12**(9), 929–40. (Ch. 18)

Boehm, B. (1997). *COCOMO II Model Definition Manual*. Computer Science Dept., University of Southern California. (Ch. 23)

Boehm, B. (1999). COTS integration: plug and pray? *IEEE Computer*, **32**(1), 135–38. (Ch. 14)

Boehm, B. and Royce, W. (1989). Ada COCOMO and the Ada Process Model. *Proc. 5th COCOMO Users' Group Meeting*, Pittsburgh, Software Engineering Institute. (Ch. 23)

Boehm, B., Clark, B. *et al.* (1995). Cost models for future life cycle processes: COCOMO 2. *Annals of Software Engineering*, **1**, 57–94. (Chs 23, 27)

Boehm, B. W. (1979). Software engineering; R & D trends and defense needs. In *Research. Directions in Software Technology* (P. Wegner, ed.). Cambridge, MA: MIT Press. (Ch. 19)

Boehm, B. W. (1981). *Software Engineering Economics*. Englewood Cliffs, NJ: Prentice-Hall. (Ch. 23)

Boehm, B. W. (1988). A spiral model of software development and enhancement. *IEEE Computer*, **21**(5), 61–72. (Chs 3, 4)

Boehm, B. W., Gray, T. E. *et al.* (1984). Prototyping versus specifying: A multi-project experiment. *IEEE Transactions on Software Engineering*, **SE-10**(3), 290–303. (Ch. 8)

Boehm, B. W., McClean, R. L. *et al.* (1975). Some experience with automated aids to the design of large-scale reliable software. *IEEE Trans. on Software Engineering*, **SE-1**(1), 125–33. (Ch. 16)

Bohm, C. and Jacopini, G. (1966). Flow diagrams, Turing machines and languages with only two formation rules. *Comm. ACM*, **9**(5), 366–71. (Ch. 28)

Bollinger, T. and McGowan, C. (1991). A critical look at software capability evaluations. *IEEE Software*, **8**(4), 25–41. (Ch. 25)

Bolognesi, T. and Brinksma, E. (1987). Introduction to the ISO specification language LOTOS. *Computer Networks*, **14**(1), 25–59. (Ch. 9)

Booch, G. (1987). *Software Components with Ada: Structures Tools and Subsystems*. Menlo Park, CA: Benjamin Cummings. (Ch. 14)

Booch, G. (1994). *Object-oriented Analysis and Design with Applications*. Redwood City, CA: Benjamin Cummings. (Chs 1, 3, 6, 7, 12)

Booch, G., Rumbaugh, J. *et al.* (1999). *The Unified Modeling Language User Guide*. Reading, MA: Addison-Wesley Longman. (Chs 1, 3, 7, 12)

Bourne, S. R. (1978). The Unix Shell. *Bell Sys. Tech. J.*, **57**(6), 1971–90. (Chs 8, 14)

Brazendale, J. and Bell, R. (1994). Safety-related control and protection systems: standards update. *IEE Computing and Control Engineering J.*, **5**(1), 6–12. (Ch. 17)

Brilliant, S. S., Knight, J. C. *et al.* (1990). Analysis of faults in an N-version software experiment. *IEEE Trans. on Software Engineering*, **16**(2), 238–47. (Ch. 18)

Brinch-Hansen, P. (1973). *Operating System Principles*. Englewood Cliffs, NJ: Prentice-Hall. (Ch. 13)

Brooks, F. P. (1975). *The Mythical Man Month*. Reading, MA: Addison-Wesley. (Chs 4, 22)

Brown, A. W., Earl, A. N. *et al.* (1992). *Software Engineering Environments*. London: McGraw-Hill. (Ch. 10)

Burns, A. (1991). Scheduling hard real-time systems: a review. *BCS/IEE Software Engineering J.*, **6**(3), 116–128. (Ch. 13)

Burns, A. and Wellings, A. (1990). *Real-time Systems and their Programming Languages*. Wokingham: Addison-Wesley. (Ch. 13)

Burns, A. and Wellings, A. (1997). *Real-time Systems and Programming Languages, 2nd edn*. Harlow, UK: Addison-Wesley. (Ch. 13)

Button, G. and Sharrock, W. (1997). The production of order and the order of production. *Proc. ECSCW'97*, Lancaster, UK, Kluwer. (Ch. 6)

Buxton, J. (1980). *Requirements for Ada Programming Support Environments: Stoneman*. Washington D.C: US Department of Defense. (Ch. 10)

Card, S., Moran, T. P. *et al.* (1983). *The Psychology of Human–Computer Interaction*. Hillsdale, NJ: Lawrence Erlbaum Associates. (Ch. 22)

Carroll, J. M. (1992). *The Nurnberg Funnel: Designing Minimalist Instruction for Practical Computer Skill*. Boston MA: MIT Press. (Ch. 15)

Checkland, P. (1981). *Systems Thinking, Systems Practice*. Chichester: John Wiley and Sons. (Ch. 2)

Checkland, P. and Scholes, J. (1990). *Soft Systems Methodology in Action*. Chichester: John Wiley and Sons. (Ch. 2)

Chen, P. (1976). The entity relationship model – Towards a unified view of data. *ACM Trans. on Database Systems*, **1**(1), 9–36. (Ch. 7)

Chikofsky, E. J. and Cross, J. H. (1990). Reverse engineering and design recovery: a taxonomy. *IEEE Software*, **7**(1), 13–17. (Ch. 28)

Cleveland, L. (1989). A program understanding support environment. *IBM Sys. J.*, **28**(2), 324–44. (Ch. 28)

Coad, P. and Yourdon, E. (1990). *Object-oriented Analysis*. Englewood Cliffs, NJ: Prentice-Hall. (Chs 7, 12)

Cobb, R. H. and Mills, H. D. (1990). Engineering software under statistical quality control. *IEEE Software*, **7**(6), 44–54. (Ch. 19)

Codd, E. F. (1979). Extending the database relational model to capture more meaning. *ACM Trans. on Database Systems*, **4**(4), 397–434. (Ch. 7)

Codenie, W., De Hondt, K. *et al.* (1997). From custom applications to domain-specific frameworks. *Comm. ACM*, **40**(10), 70–7. (Ch. 14)

Cohen, B., Harwood, W. T. *et al.* (1986). *The Specification of Complex Systems*. Wokingham: Addison-Wesley. (Ch. 9)

Constantine, L. L. and Yourdon, E. (1979). *Structured Design*. Englewood Cliffs, NJ: Prentice-Hall. (Chs 3, 26)

Cooling, J. E. (1991). *Software Design for Real-time Systems*. London: Chapman and Hall. (Ch. 13)

Coulouris, G., Dollimore, J. *et al.* (1994). *Distributed Systems: Concepts and Design*. Wokingham: Addison-Wesley. (Ch. 11)

Crosby, P. (1979). *Quality is Free*. New York: McGraw-Hill. (Ch. 24)

Curtis, B., Hefley, W. E. *et al.* (1995). *Overview of the People Capability Maturity Model*, Software Engineering Institute. (Ch. 22)

Curtis, B., Krasner, H. *et al.* (1988). A field study of the software design process for large systems. *Comm. ACM*, **31**(11), 1268–87. (Ch. 22)

Cusamano, M. (1989). The software factory: a historical interpretation. *IEEE Software*, **6**(2), 23–30. (Ch. 14)

Dasarthy, B. (1985). Timing constraints for real-time systems: constructs for expressing them, methods of validating them. *IEEE Trans. on Software Engineering*, **SE-11**(1), 80–6. (Ch. 13)

Date, C. J. and Darwen, H. (1997). *A Guide to the SQL Standard, 4th ed*. Reading, MA: Addison-Wesley. (Ch. 8)

Davis, A. M. (1990). *Software Requirements: Analysis and Specification*. Englewood Cliffs, NJ: Prentice-Hall. (Ch. 5)

Davis, A. M. (1993). *Software Requirements: Objects, Functions and States*. Englewood Cliffs, NJ: Prentice-Hall. (Ch. 5)

Dehbonei, B. and Mejia, F. (1995). Formal development of safety-critical software systems in railway signalling. *Applications of Formal Methods* (M. Hinchey and J. P. Bowen, eds). London, Prentice-Hall, 227–52. (Ch. 9)

DeMarco, T. (1978). *Structured Analysis and System Specification*. New York: Yourdon Press. (Chs 1, 7)

DeMarco, T. and Lister, T. (1985). Programmer performance and the effects of the workplace. *Proc. 8th Int. Conf. on Software Engineering*, London, IEEE Press. (Ch. 22)

DeMarco, T. and Lister, T. (1999). *Peopleware: Productive Projects and Teams*. New York: Dorset House. (Ch. 22)

Diaper, D. (1989). *Task Analysis for Human–Computer Interaction*. Chichester: Ellis Horwood. (Ch. 15)

Diaz, M. and Sligo, J. (1997). How software process improvement helped Motorola. *IEEE Software*, **14**(5), 75–82. (Ch. 25)

Dijkstra, E. W. (1968a). Goto statement considered harmful. *Comm. ACM*, **11**(3), 147–8. (Ch. 18)

Dijkstra, E. W. (1968b). Cooperating sequential processes. In *Programming Languages* (F. Genuys, ed.). London: Academic Press, 43–112. (Ch. 13)

Diller, A. (1994). *Z: An Introduction to Formal Methods, 2nd edn*. New York: John Wiley and Sons. (Ch. 9)

Dix, A., Finlay, J. *et al.* (1998). *Human–Computer Interaction, 2nd edn*. London: Prentice-Hall. (Ch. 15)

Easterbrook, S. (1993). Domain modelling with hierarchies of alternative viewpoints. *Proc. RE'93*, San Diego, USA. (Ch. 6)

Easterbrook, S. and Nuseibeh, B. (1996). Using viewpoints for inconsistency management. *BCS/IEE Software Engineering J.*, **11**(1), 31–43. (Ch. 6)

Easterbrook, S., Lutz, R. *et al.* (1998). Experiences using lightweight formal methods for requirements modeling. *IEEE Trans. on Software Engineering*, **24**(1), 4–14. (Ch. 9)

Eckstein, R., Loy, M. *et al.* (1998). *Java Swing*. Sebastopol, CA: O'Reilly and Associates Inc. (Ch. 15)

ECMA (1991). *A Reference Model for Frameworks of Computer-Assisted Software Engineering Environments*. Tech. Rept. European Computer Manufacturers Association. (Ch. 10)

Ehrlich, W., Prasanna, B. *et al.* (1993). Determining the cost of a stop-test decision. *IEEE Software*, **9**(4), 33–42. (Ch. 21)

El Amam, K., Drouin, J. *et al.* (1997). *SPICE: The Theory and Practice of Software Process Improvement and Capability Determination*. Los Alamitos, CA: IEEE Computer Society Press. (Ch. 25)

Ellison, R. J., Fisher, D. A. *et al.* (1999a). Survivability: protecting your critical systems. *IEEE Internet Computing* **3**(6), 55–63. (Ch. 16)

Ellison, R. J., Linger, R. C. *et al.* (1999b). Survivable network system analysis: a case study. *IEEE Software*, **16**(4), 70–7. (Ch. 16)

Endres, A. (1975). An analysis of errors and their causes in system programs. *IEEE Trans. on Software Engineering*, **SE-1**(2), 140–9. (Ch. 16)

Estublier, J. and Casallas, R. (1994). The Adele Configuration Manager. In *Configuration Management* (W. Tichy, ed.). Chichester: John Wiley and Sons, 99–134. (Ch. 29)

Fagan, M. E. (1976). Design and code inspections to reduce errors in program development. *IBM Systems J.*, **15**(3), 182–211. (Ch. 19)

Fagan, M. E. (1986). Advances in software inspections. *IEEE Trans. on Software Engineering*, **SE-12**(7), 744–51. (Ch. 19)

Fayad, M. E. and Schmidt, D. C. (1997). Object-oriented application frameworks. *Comm. ACM*, **40**(10), 32–38. (Ch. 14)

Feldman, S. I. (1979). MAKE – a program for maintaining computer programs. *Software-Practice and Experience*, **9**(4), 255–65. (Ch. 29)

Finkelstein, A., Kramer, J. *et al.* (1990). Viewpoint oriented software development. *Proc. 3rd Int. Workshop on Software Engineering and its Applications*, Toulouse, France. (Ch. 6)

Forte, G. (1992). Tools fair: out of the lab, onto the shelf. *IEEE Software*, **9**(3), 70–9. (Ch. 8)

Fowler, M. and Scott, K. (1997). *UML Distilled: Applying the Standard Object Modelling Language*. Reading, MA: Addison-Wesley. (Chs 1, 6)

Frewin, G. D. and Hatton, B. J. (1986). Quality management – procedures and practises. *IEE/BCS Software Engineering J.*, **1**(1), 29–38. (Ch. 19)

Fromme, B. and Walker, J. (1993). An open architecture for tool and process integration. *Proc. 6th Conf. on Software Engineering Environments*, Reading, UK, IEEE Press. (Ch. 10)

Fuggetta, A. (1993). A classification of CASE technology. *IEEE Computer*, **26**(12), 25–38. (Ch. 3)

Fujiwara, E. and Pradhan, D. K. (1990). Error-control coding in computers. *IEEE Computer*, **23**(7), 63–72. (Ch. 18)

Furey, S. and Kitchenham, B. (1997). Point/Counterpoint: function points. *IEEE Software*, **14**(2), 28–31. (Ch. 23)

Futatsugi, K., Goguen, J. A. *et al.* (1985). Principles of OBJ2. *12th ACM Symp. on Principles of Programming Languages*, New Orleans. (Ch. 9)

Gamma, E., Helm, R. *et al.* (1995). *Design Patterns: Elements of Reusable Object-Oriented Software*. Reading, MA: Addison-Wesley. (Chs 10, 14)

Gane, C. and Sarson, T. (1979). *Structured Systems Analysis*. Englewood Cliffs, NJ: Prentice-Hall. (Ch. 3)

Garlan, D. and Shaw, M. (1993). An introduction to software architecture. *Advances in Software Engineering and Knowledge Engineering*, **1**, 1–26. (Ch. 10)

Garlan, D., Allen, R. *et al.* (1995). Architectural mismatch: why reuse is so hard. *IEEE Software*, **12**(6), 17–26. (Ch. 14)

Garlan, D., Kaiser, G. E. *et al.* (1992). Using tool abstraction to compose systems. *IEEE Computer*, **25**(6), 30–8. (Ch. 10)

Gilb, T. and Graham, D. (1993). *Software Inspection*. Wokingham: Addison-Wesley. (Ch. 19)

Goldberg, A. and Robson, D. (1983). *Smalltalk-80. The Language and its Implementation*. Reading, MA: Addison-Wesley. (Ch. 15)

Gollmann, D. (1999). *Computer Security*. Chichester: John Wiley and Sons. (Ch. 21)

Gomaa, H. (1993). *Software Design Methods for Concurrent and Real-time Systems*. Reading, MA: Addison-Wesley. (Ch. 13)

Gordon, V. S. and Bieman, J. M. (1995). Rapid prototyping: lessons learned. *IEEE Software*, **12**(1), 85–95. (Ch. 8)

Gotterbarn, D., Miller, K. *et al.* (1999). Software engineering code of ethics is approved. *Comm. ACM*, **42**(10), 102–7. (Ch. 1)

Grady, R. B. (1993). Practical results from measuring software quality. *Comm. ACM*, **36**(11), 62–8. (Ch. 24)

Grady, R. B. and Van Slack, T. (1994). Key lessons in achieving widespread inspection use. *IEEE Software*, **11**(4), 46–57. (Ch. 19)

Graham, I. (1994). *Object-Oriented Methods, 2nd edn.* Wokingham: Addison-Wesley. (Ch. 12)

Greenbaum, J. and Kyng, M. (1991). *Design at Work: Cooperative Design of Computer Systems.* Hillsdale, NJ: Lawrence Erlbaum Associates. (Ch. 15)

Griss, M. L. and Wosser, M. (1995). Making reuse work at Hewlett-Packard. *IEEE Software*, **12**(1), 105–7. (Ch. 14)

Grudin, J. (1989). The case against user interface consistency. *Comm. ACM*, **32**(10), 1164–73. (Ch. 15)

Guimaraes, T. (1983). Managing application program maintenance expenditures. *Comm. ACM*, **26**(10), 739–46. (Ch. 27)

Gunning, R. (1962). *Techniques of Clear Writing.* New York: McGraw-Hill. (Ch. 24)

Guttag, J. (1977). Abstract data types and the development of data structures. *Comm. ACM*, **20**(6), 396–405. (Ch. 9)

Guttag, J. V., Horning, J. J. *et al.* (1985). The Larch family of specification languages. *IEEE Software*, **2**(5), 24–36. (Ch. 9)

Guttag, J., Horning, J. *et al.* (1993). *Larch: Languages and Tools for Formal Specification.* Heidelberg: Springer-Verlag. (Ch. 9)

Haase, V., Messnarz, R. *et al.* (1994). Bootstrap: fine tuning process assessment. *IEEE Software*, **11**(4), 25–35. (Ch. 25)

Hall, A. (1990). Seven myths of formal methods. *IEEE Software*, **7** (5), 11–20. (Ch. 9)

Hall, A. (1996). Using formal methods to develop an ATC information system. *IEEE Software*, **13**(2), 66–76. (Chs 9, 17)

Hall, E. (1998). *Managing Risk: Methods for Software Systems Development.* Reading, MA: Addison-Wesley Longman. (Ch. 4)

Hall, T. and Fenton, N. (1997). Implementing effective software metrics programs. *IEEE Software*, **14**(2), 55–64. (Ch. 24)

Halstead, M. H. (1977). *Elements of Software Science.* Amsterdam: North-Holland. (Ch. 27)

Hamlet, D. (1992). Are we testing for true reliability? *IEEE Software*, **9**(4), 21–27. (Ch. 21)

Hammer, M. (1990). Reengineering work: don't automate, obliterate. *Harvard Business Review*, July–August 1990, 104–112. (Ch. 28)

Hammer, M. and McLeod, D. (1981). Database descriptions with SDM: a semantic database model. *ACM Trans. on Database Systems*, **6**(3), 351–86. (Ch. 7)

Harel, D. (1987). Statecharts: a visual formalism for complex systems. *Sci. Comput. Programming*, **8**(3), 231–74. (Chs 7, 12, 13)

Harel, D. (1988). On visual formalisms. *Comm. ACM*, **31**(5), 514–30. (Chs 7, 13)

Harker, S. D. P., Easton, K. D. *et al.* (1993). The change and evolution of requirements as a challenge to the practice of software engineering. *Proc. RE'93*, San Diego, USA. (Ch. 6)

Hayes, I. (ed.). (1987). *Specification Case Studies.* London: Prentice-Hall. (Ch. 9)

Heath, C. and Luff, P. (1991). Collaborative activity and technological design: task coordination in the London Underground control room. *Proc. ECSCW'91*, Amsterdam, Kluwer. (Ch. 6)

Heninger, K. L. (1980). Specifying software requirements for complex systems. New techniques and their applications. *IEEE Trans. on Software Engineering*, **SE-6**(1), 2–13. (Ch. 5)

Hihn, J. and Habib-agahi, H. (1991). Cost estimation of software intensive projects: a survey of current practices. *Proc. 13th Int. Conf. on Software Engineering*, Austin TX, ACM Press. (Ch. 23)

Hoare, C. A. R. (1974). Monitors: an operating system structuring concept. *Comm. ACM*, **21**(8), 666–77. (Ch. 13)

Hoare, C. A. R. (1985). *Communicating Sequential Processes*. London: Prentice-Hall. (Chs 8, 9)

Huff, C. and Martin, C. D. (1995). Computing consequences: a framework for teaching ethical computing. *Comm. ACM*, **38**(12), 75–84. (Ch. 1)

Huff, C. C. (1992). Elements of a realistic CASE tool adoption budget. *Comm. ACM* **35**(4), 45–54. (Ch. 3)

Huff, K. E. (1996). Software process modeling. In *Trends in Software: Software Process* (A. Fuggetta and A. Wolf, eds). New York: John Wiley and Sons. (Ch. 25)

Hughes, J. A., O'Brien, J. *et al.* (1997). Designing with ethnography: a presentation framework for design. *Proc. DIS'97*, Amsterdam, ACM Press. (Ch. 15)

Hughes, J. A., Randall, D. *et al.* (1992). Faltering from ethnography to design. *Proc. CSCW'92*, Toronto, Canada. (Ch. 6)

Hughes, J., Rodden, T. *et al.* (1994). Moving out from the control room: ethnography in system design. *Proc. CSCW'94*, Greensborough, North Carolina. (Ch. 6)

Hull, R. and King, R. (1987). Semantic database modeling: survey, applications and research issues. *ACM Computing Surveys*, **19**(3), 201–60. (Ch. 7)

Humphrey, W. (1989). *Managing the Software Process*. Reading, MA: Addison-Wesley. (Chs 24, 25)

Humphrey, W. and Curtis, B. (1991). Comment on 'A Critical Look'. *IEEE Software*, **8**(4), 42–47. (Ch. 25)

Humphrey, W. S. (1988). Characterizing the software process. *IEEE Software*, **5**(2), 73–79. (Ch. 25)

Humphrey, W. S. (1995). *A Discipline for Software Engineering*. Reading, MA: Addison-Wesley. (Ch. 25)

IEC (1998). *Draft Standard IEC 6150: Functional safety of electrical/electronic/programmable electronic safety-related systems*. International Electrotechnical Commission, Geneva. (Ch. 17)

IEEE (1993). IEEE recommended practice for software requirements specifications. In *Software Requirements Engineering* (R. H. Thayer and M. Dorfman, eds). Los Alamitos, CA: IEEE Computer Society Press. (Ch. 5)

IEEE (1994). *Software Engineering Standards Collection*. Los Alamitos CA: IEEE Press. (Ch. 24)

Ince, D. (1994). *ISO 9001 and Software Quality Assurance*. London: McGraw-Hill. (Chs 24, 29)

Ince, D. C. and Hekmatpour, S. (1987). Software prototyping – progress and prospects. *Information and Software Technology*, **29**(1), 8–14. (Ch. 8)

ISO/IEC (1998). *Information technology – Guidelines for the management of IT Security*, ISO/IEC. (Ch. 17)

Jackson, M. A. (1983). *System Development*. London: Prentice-Hall. (Chs 1, 3)

Jackson, M. A. (1995). *Requirements and Specifications*. Wokingham: Addison-Wesley. (Ch. 5)

Jacky, J. (1995). Specifying a safety-critical control system. *IEEE Trans. on Software Engineering*, **21**(2), 99–106. (Ch. 9)

Jacky, J. (1997). *The Way of Z: Practical Programming with Formal Methods*. Cambridge: Cambridge University Press. (Ch. 9)

Jacky, J., Unger, J. *et al.* (1997). Experience with Z: developing a control program for a radiation therapy machine. *Proc. ZUM'97*, Reading, Springer. (Ch. 9)

Jacobson, I., Christerson, M. *et al.* (1993). *Object-Oriented Software Engineering*. Wokingham: Addison-Wesley. (Chs 5, 6, 12)

Jacobson, I., Griss, M. *et al.* (1997). *Software Reuse*. Reading, MA: Addison-Wesley. (Ch. 14)

Jahanian, F. and Mok, A. K. (1986). Safety analysis of timing properties in real-time systems. *IEEE Trans.on Software Engineering*, **SE-12**(9), 890–904. (Ch. 17)

Janis, I. L. (1972). *Victims of Groupthink. A Psychological Study of Foreign Policy Decisions and Fiascos*. Boston: Houghton Mifflin. (Ch. 22)

Jelinski, Z. and Moranda, P. B. (1972). Software reliability research. In *Statistical Computer Performance Evaluation* (W. Frieberger, ed.). New York, Academic Press, 465–84. (Ch. 21)

Johnson, P. L. (1993). *ISO 9000: Meeting the New International Standards*. New York: McGraw-Hill. (Ch. 24)

Jones, C. B. (1980). *Software Development – A Rigorous Approach*. London: Prentice-Hall. (Ch. 9)

Jones, C. B. (1986). *Systematic Software Development Using VDM*. London: Prentice-Hall. (Ch. 9)

Jorgensen, P. C. and Erickson, C. (1994). Object-oriented integration testing. *Comm. ACM*, **37**(9), 30–8. (Ch. 20)

Kafura, D. and Reddy, G. R. (1987). The use of software complexity metrics in software maintenance. *IEEE Trans. on Software Engineering*, **SE-13**(3), 335–43. (Ch. 27)

Kemerer, C. F. (1993). Reliability of function points measurement: a field experiment. *Comm. ACM*, **36**(2), 85–97. (Ch. 23)

Kit, E. (1995). *Software Testing in the Real World: Improving the Process*. Reading, MA: Addison-Wesley. (Ch. 20)

Kitchenham, B. (1990). Measuring software development. In *Software Reliability Handbook* (P. Rook, ed.). Amsterdam: Elsevier, 303–31. (Ch. 24)

Kitchenham, B. (1990). Software development cost models. In *Software Reliability Handbook* (P. Rook, ed.). Amsterdam: Elsevier, 487–517. (Ch. 23)

Knight, J. C. and Leveson, N. G. (1986). An experimental evaluation of the assumption of independence in multi-version programming. *IEEE Trans. on Software Engineering*, **SE-12**(1), 96–109. (Ch. 18)

Knuth, D. E. (1971). *The Art of Computer Programming: Fundamental Algorithms*. Reading, MA: Addison-Wesley. (Ch. 14)

Kotonya, G. and Sommerville, I. (1992). Viewpoints for requirements definition. *BCS/IEE Software Engineering J.*, **7**(6), 375–87. (Ch. 6)

Kotonya, G. and Sommerville, I. (1996). Requirements engineering with viewpoints. *BCS/IEE Software Engineering J.*, **11**(1), 5–18. (Ch. 6)

Kotonya, G. and Sommerville, I. (1998). *Requirements Engineering: Processes and Techniques*. Chichester, UK: John Wiley and Sons. (Chs 5, 6)

Kramer, J. and Magee, J. (1985). Dynamic configuration for distributed systems. *IEEE Trans. on Software Engineering*, **SE-11**(4), 424–35. (Ch. 13)

Kuvaja, P., Similä, J. *et al.* (1994). *Software Process Assessment and Improvement: The BOOTSTRAP Approach*. Oxford: Blackwell Publishers. (Ch. 25)

Kyng, M. (1988). Designing for a dollar a day. *Proc. CSCW'88*, Portland OR, ACM Press. (Ch. 15)

Lamping, J., Rao, R. *et al.* (1995). A focus + context technique based on hyperbolic geometry for visualising large hierarchies. *Proc. CHI'95*, ACM Press. (Ch. 15)

Laprie, J.-C., Arlat, J. *et al.* (1995). Architectural issues in software fault tolerance. In *Software Fault Tolerance* (M. R. Lyu, ed.). Chichester: John Wiley and Sons, 47–80. (Ch. 18)

Laudon, K. (1995). Ethical concepts and information technology. *Comm. ACM*, **38**(12), 33–9. (Ch. 1)

Leblang, D. (1994). The CM challenge: configuration management that works. In *Configuration Management* (W. Tichy, ed.). Chichester: John Wiley and Sons, 1–38. (Ch. 29)

Leblang, D. B. and Chase, R. P. (1987). Parallel software configuration management in a network environment. *IEEE Software*, **4**(6), 28–35. (Ch. 29)

Lehman, M. M. and Belady, L. (1985). *Program Evolution: Processes of Software Change*. London: Academic Press. (Ch. 27)

Leveson, N. G. (1985). Software safety. In *Resilient Computing Systems* (T. Anderson, ed.). London: Collins, 123–43. (Chs 16, 17)

Leveson, N. G. (1986). Software safety: why, what and how. *ACM Computing Surveys*, **18**(2), 125–63. (Ch. 17)

Leveson, N. G. (1995). *Safeware: System Safety and Computers*. Reading, MA: Addison-Wesley. (Ch. 18)

Leveson, N. G. and Harvey, P. R. (1983). Analysing software safety. *IEEE Trans. on Software Engineering*, **SE-9**(5), 569–79. (Ch. 17)

Lientz, B. P. and Swanson, E. B. (1980). *Software Maintenance Management*. Reading, MA: Addison-Wesley. (Ch. 27)

Linger, R. C. (1994). Cleanroom process model. *IEEE Software*, **11**(2), 50–8. (Chs 3, 9, 19)

Liskov, B. and Guttag, J. (1986). *Abstraction and Specification in Program Development*. Cambridge, MA: MIT Press. (Ch. 9)

Littlewood, B. (1990). Software reliability growth models. In *Software Reliability Handbook* (P. Rook, ed.). Amsterdam: Elsevier, 401–412. (Ch. 16)

Littlewood, B. and Verrall, J. L. (1973). A Bayesian reliability growth model for computer software. *Applied Statistics*, **22**, 332–46. (Ch. 21)

Londeix, B. (1987). *Cost Estimation for Software Development*. Wokingham: Addison-Wesley. (Ch. 23)

Luqi (1992). Computer-aided prototyping for a command and control system using CAPS. *IEEE Software*, **9**(1), 56–67. (Ch. 8)

Lutz, M. (1996). *Programming Python*. Sebastopol, CA: O'Reilly and Associates. (Ch. 8)

Lutz, R. R. (1993). Analysing software requirements errors in safety-critical embedded systems. *Proc. RE'93*, San Diego, CA, IEEE. (Chs 16, 20, 21)

Lyu, M. (ed.) (1996). *Software Reliability Engineering*. New York: McGraw-Hill. (Ch. 17)

MacDonell, S. G. (1994). Comparative review of functional complexity assessment methods for effort estimation. *BCS/IEE Software Engineering J.*, **9**(3), 107–17. (Ch. 23)

Marshall, J. E. and Heslin, R. (1975). Boys and girls together: sexual composition and the effect of density on group size and cohesiveness. *J. of Personality and Social Psychology*, **35**(5), 952–61. (Ch. 22)

Maslow, A. A. (1954). *Motivation and Personality*. New York: Harper and Row. (Ch. 22)

Matsumoto, Y. (1984). Some experience in promoting reusable software: presentation in higher abstract levels. *IEEE. Trans. on Software Engineering*, **SE-10**(5), 502–12. (Ch. 14)

McCabe, T. J. (1976). A complexity measure. *IEEE Trans. on Software Engineering*, **SE-2**(4), 308–20. (Chs 20, 27)

McCue, G. M. (1978). IBM's Santa Teresa Laboratory: architectural design for program development. *IBM Systems J.*, **17**(1), 4–25. (Ch. 22)

McGuffin, R. W., Elliston, A. E. *et al.* (1979). CADES – Software engineering in practice. *Proc. 4th Int. Conf. on Software Engineering*, Munich, Germany. (Ch. 10)

McKee, J. R. (1984). Maintenance as a function of design. *AFIPS National Computer Conf.*, Las Vegas. (Ch. 27)

Meyer, B. (1999). On to components. *IEEE Computer*, **32**(1), 139–40. (Ch. 14)

Miller, G. A. (1957). The magical number 7 plus or minus two: some limits on our capacity for processing information. *Psychological Review*, **63**, 81–97. (Ch. 22)

Millington, D. and Stapleton, J. (1995). Special report: developing a RAD Standard. *IEEE Software*, **12**(5), 54–6. (Ch. 8)

Mills, H. D., Dyer, M. *et al.* (1987). Cleanroom software engineering. *IEEE Software* **4**(5), 19–25. (Chs 3, 9, 16, 19)

Mills, H. D., O'Neill, D. *et al.* (1980). The management of software engineering. *IBM Sys. J.*, **24**(2), 414–77. (Ch. 3)

MOD (1995). *The Procurement of Safety Critical Software (Revised ed.)*. UK Ministry of Defence, Procurement Executive. (Chs 9, 21)

Mullery, G. (1979). CORE – a method for controlled requirements specification. *Proc. 4th Int. Conf. on Software Engineering*, Munich, IEEE Press. (Ch. 6)

Mumford, E. (1989). User participation in a changing environment – why we need it. In *Participation in Systems Development* (K. Knight, ed.). London: Kogan Page. (Ch. 2)

Munch, B. P., Larsen, J.-L. *et al.* (1993). Uniform versioning: the change-oriented model. *Proc. 4th Workshop on Software Configuration Management*, Baltimore, MD. (Ch. 29)

Murphy, G. C., Townsend, P. *et al.* (1994). Experiences with cluster and class testing. *Comm. ACM*, **37**(9), 39–47. (Ch. 20)

Musa, J. D. (1993). Operational profiles in software reliability engineering. *IEEE Software*, **10**(2), 14–32. (Ch. 21)

Musa, J. D. (1998). *Software Reliability Engineering: More Reliable Software, Faster Development and Testing*. New York: McGraw-Hill. (Ch. 21)

Musa, J. D., Iannino, A. *et al.* (1987). *Software Reliability: Measurement, Prediction, Application*. New York: McGraw-Hill. (Ch. 21)

Musciano, C. and Kennedy, B. (1998). *HTML The Definitive Guide*. Sebastopol, CA: O'Reilly and Associates Inc. (Ch. 15)

Myers, G. J. (1975). *Reliable Software through Composite Design*. New York: Petrocelli/Charter. (Ch. 26)

Myers, W. (1989). Allow plenty of time for large-scale software. *IEEE Software*, **6**(4), 92–9. (Ch. 23)

Nakajo, T. and Kume, H. (1991). A case history analysis of software error–cause relationships. *IEEE Trans. on Software Engineering*, **18**(8), 830–8. (Ch. 16)

Neil, M., Ostrolenk, G. *et al.* (1998). Lessons from using Z to specify a software tool. *IEEE Trans. on Software Engineering*, **24**(1), 15–23. (Ch. 9)

Neilsen, J. (1993). *Usability Engineering*. New York: Academic Press. (Ch. 15)

Nii, H. P. (1986). Blackboard systems, Parts 1 and 2. *AI Magazine*, **7**(3 and 4), 38–53 and 62–9. (Ch. 10)

Nilsen, K. (1998). Adding real-time capabilities to Java. *Comm. ACM*, **41**(6), 49–56. (Ch. 13)

Ning, J. Q., Engberts, A. *et al.* (1994). Automated support for legacy code understanding. *IEEE Software*, **37**(5), 50–7. (Ch. 28)

Norman, D. A. and Draper, S. W. (1986). *User-centered System Design*. Hillsdale, NJ: Lawrence Erlbaum. (Chs 8, 15)

Nosek, J. T. and Palvia, P. (1990). Software maintenance management: changes in the last decade. *Software Maintenance: Research. and Practice*, **2**(3), 157–74. (Ch. 27)

Nuseibeh, B., Kramer, J. *et al.* (1994). A framework for expressing the relationships between multiple views in requirements specifications. *IEEE Trans. on Software Engineering*, **20**(10), 760–73. (Ch. 6)

O'Connor, J., Mansour, C. *et al.* (1994). Reuse in command and control systems. *IEEE Software*, **11**(4), 70–9. (Ch. 14)

Offen, R. J. and Jeffrey, R. (1997). Establishing software measurement programs. *IEEE Software*, **14**(2), 45–54. (Ch. 24)

Oman, P. W. and Cook, C. R. (1990). The book paradigm for improved maintenance. *IEEE Software*, **7**(1), 39–45. (Ch. 28)

Orfali, R. and Harkey, D. (1998). *Client/server Programming with Java and CORBA*. New York: John Wiley and Sons. (Chs 8, 11, 14)

Oskarsson, O. and Glass, R. L. (1995). *An ISO 9000 Approach to Building Quality Software*. Englewood Cliffs, NJ: Prentice-Hall. (Ch. 24)

Ould, M. (1999). *Managing Software Quality and Business Risk*. Chichester: John Wiley and Sons. (Ch. 4)

Ousterhout, J. (1994). *Tcl and the Tk toolkit*. Reading, MA: Addison-Wesley. (Ch. 8)

Ousterhout, J. (1998). Scripting: higher-level programming for the 21st century. *IEEE Computer*, **31**(3), 23–30. (Chs 8, 14)

Park, R. (1992). *Software Size Measurement: A Framework for Counting Source Statements*, Software Engineering Institute. (Ch. 23)

Parnas, D. L., van Schouwen, J. *et al.* (1990). Evaluation of safety-critical software. *Comm. ACM*, **33**(6), 636–51. (Chs 18, 21)

Paulk, M. (1995). How ISO 9000 compares with the CMM. *IEEE Software*, **12**(1), 74–84. (Ch. 25)

Paulk, M. C. and Konrad, M. (1994). An overview of ISO's SPICE Project. *IEEE Computer*, **27**(4), 68–70. (Ch. 25)

Paulk, M. C., Curtis, B. *et al.* (1993). Capability Maturity Model, Version 1.1. *IEEE Software*, **10**(4), 18–27. (Chs 25, 29)

Peach, R. W. (1996). *The ISO 9000 Handbook (3rd edn)*. New York: Irwin Professional Publishers. (Ch. 24)

Perrow, C. (1984). *Normal Accidents: Living with High-Risk Technology*. New York: Basic Books. (Ch. 16)

Perry, W. (1995). *Effective Methods for Software Testing*. New York: John Wiley and Sons. (Ch. 20)

Peterson, J. L. (1981). *Petri Net Theory and the Modeling of Systems*. New York: McGraw-Hill. (Chs 9, 17)

Pfaff, G. and ten Hagen, P. J. W. (1985). *Seeheim Workshop on User Interface Management Systems*. Heidelberg: Springer-Verlag. (Ch. 15)

Pfleeger, C. P. (1997). *Security in Computing, 2nd edn*. Englewood Cliffs: Prentice-Hall. (Ch. 16)

Pope, A. (1998). *CORBA*. Harlow, UK: Addison-Wesley Longman. (Ch. 8)

Preece, J., Rogers, Y. *et al.* (1994). *Human–Computer Interaction*. Wokingham: Addison-Wesley. (Ch. 15)

Pressman, R. S. (1997). *Software Engineering: A Practitioner's Approach*. New York: McGraw Hill. (Ch. 1)

Prieto-Díaz, R. and Arango, G. (1991). *Domain Analysis and Software System Modeling*. Los Alamitos CA: IEEE Press. (Ch. 6)

Prowell, S. J., Trammell, C. J. *et al.* (1999). *Cleanroom Software Engineering: Technology and Process*. Reading, MA: Addison-Wesley Longman. (Chs 3, 9, 19, 21)

Pulford, K., Kuntzmann-Combelles, A. *et al.* (1996). *A Quantitative Approach to Software Management*. Wokingham: Addison-Wesley. (Chs 24, 25)

Putnam, L. H. (1978). A general empirical solution to the macro software sizing and estimating problem. *IEEE Trans. on Software Engineering*, **SE-4**(3), 345–61. (Ch. 23)

Pycock, J. and Bowers, J. (1996). Getting others to get it right: an ethnography of design work in the fashion industry. *Proc. CSCW'96*, Boston, ACM Press. (Ch. 6)

Randell, B. (1975). System structure for software fault tolerance. *IEEE Trans. on Software Engineering*, **SE-1**(2), 220–32. (Ch. 18)

Randell, B. and Xu, J. (1995). The evolution of the recovery block concept. In *Software Fault Tolerance* (M. R. Lyu, ed.). Chichester: John Wiley and Sons: 1–22. (Ch. 18)

Redmill, F. (1998). IEC 61508: Principles and use in the management of safety. *IEE Computing and Control Engineering J.*, **9**(10), 205–13. (Ch. 17)

Reiss, S., P. (1990). Connecting tools using message passing in the field environment. *IEEE Software*, **7**(4), 57–66. (Ch. 10)

Rettig, M. (1994). Practical programmer: prototyping for tiny fingers. *Comm. ACM*, **37**(4), 21–7. (Ch. 8)

Rickets, J. A., DelMonaco, J. C. *et al.* (1993). Data reengineering for application systems. In *Software Reengineering* (R. S. Arnold, ed.). Los Alamitos CA: IEEE Press, 288–93. (Ch. 28)

Rittel, H. and Webber, M. (1973). Dilemmas in a general theory of planning. *Policy Sciences*, **4**, 155–69. (Ch. 2)

Robinson, P. J. (1992). *Hierarchical Object-Oriented Design*. Englewood Cliffs, NJ: Prentice-Hall. (Chs 3, 12)

Rochester, J. B. and Douglass, D. P. (1993). Re-engineering existing systems. In *Software Reengineering* (R. S. Arnold, ed.). Los Alamitos, CA: IEEE Press, 41–51. (Ch. 28)

Rochkind, M. J. (1975). The Source Code Control System. *IEEE Trans. on Software Engineering*, **SE-1**(4), 255–65. (Ch. 29)

Rockwell, R. and Gera, M. H. (1993). The Eureka Software Factory CoRe: a conceptual reference model for software factories. *Proc. 6th Conf. on Software Engineering Environments*, Reading, UK, IEEE Press. (Ch. 10)

Ross, D. T. (1977). Structured analysis (SA). A language for communicating ideas. *IEEE Trans. on Software Engineering*, **SE-3**(1), 16–34. (Chs 5, 6)

Royce, W. W. (1970). Managing the development of large software systems: concepts and techniques. *Proc. IEEE WESTCON*, Los Angeles, CA. (Ch. 3)

Rubin, K. and Goldberg, A. (1992). Object behaviour analysis. *Comm. ACM*, **35**(9), 48–62. (Ch. 12)

Rumbaugh, J., Blaha, M. *et al.* (1991). *Object-oriented Modeling and Design*. Englewood Cliffs, NJ: Prentice-Hall. (Chs 1, 3, 6, 7)

Rumbaugh, J., Jacobson, I. *et al.* (1999a). *The Unified Modeling Language Reference Manual*. Reading, MA: Addison-Wesley. (Chs 1, 3, 7, 11, 13)

Rumbaugh, J., Jacobson, I. *et al.* (1999b). *The Unified Software Development Process*. Reading, MA: Addison-Wesley. (Chs 1, 3, 7, 12)

Sackman, H., Erikson, W. J. *et al.* (1968). Exploratory experimentation studies comparing on-line and off line programming performance. *Comm. ACM*, **11**(1), 3–11. (Ch. 23)

Schmidt, D. C. (1997). Applying design patterns and frameworks to develop object-oriented communications software. In *Handbook of Programming Languages, Vol. 1* (P. Salus, ed.). New York: Macmillan Computer Publishing. (Ch. 14)

Schneidewind, N. F. and Keller, T. W. (1992). Applying reliability models to the space shuttle. *IEEE Software*, **9**(4), 28–33. (Ch. 21)

Schoman, K. and Ross D. T. (1977). Structured analysis for requirements definition. *IEEE Trans. on Software Engineering*, **SE-3**(1), 6–15. (Chs 5, 6)

Selby, R. (1988). Empirically analyzing software reuse in a production environment. In *Software Reuse: Emerging Technology* (W. Tracz, ed.). Los Alamitos, CA: IEEE Computer Society Press. (Ch. 23)

Selby, R. W., Basili, V. R. *et al.* (1987). Cleanroom software development: an empirical evaluation. *IEEE Trans. on Software Engineering*, **SE-13**(9), 1027–37. (Chs 3, 19)

Sessions, R. (1997). *COM and DCOM: Microsoft's Vision for Distributed Objects*. New York: John Wiley and Sons. (Ch. 8)

Sheldon, F. T., Kavi, K. M. *et al.* (1992). Reliability measurement: from theory to practice. *IEEE Software*, **9**(4), 13–20. (Ch. 21)

Shlaer, S. and Mellor, S. (1988). *Object-Oriented Systems Analysis: Modeling the World in Data*. Englewood Cliffs, NJ: Yourdon Press. (Ch. 12)

Shneiderman, B. (1980). *Software Psychology*. Cambridge, MA: Winthrop Publishers Inc. (Ch. 22)

Shneiderman, B. (1992). *Designing the User Interface, 1st edn*. Reading, MA: Addison-Wesley. (Ch. 22)

Shneiderman, B. (1998). *Designing the User Interface, 3rd edn*. Reading, MA: Addison-Wesley. (Chs 8, 15)

Siegel, J. (1998). OMG overview: CORBA and the OMA in enterprise computing. *Comm. ACM*, **41**(10), 37–43. (Ch. 11)

Silberschaltz, A. and Galvin, P. (1998). *Operating System Concepts, 5th edn*. Reading, MA: Addison-Wesley. (Ch. 13)

Soloway, E., Ehrlich, K. *et al.* (1982). What do novices know about programming? In *Directions in Human-Computer Interaction* (A. Badre and B. Shneiderman, eds). Norwood, NJ: Ablex Publishing Co. (Ch. 22)

Sommerville, I. and Dean, G. (1996). PCL: a language for modelling evolving system architectures. *BCS/IEE Software Engineering J.*, **11**(2), 111–21. (Ch. 29)

Sommerville, I. and Sawyer, P. (1997). *Requirements Engineering: A Good Practice Guide*. Chichester: John Wiley and Sons. (Ch. 8)

Sommerville, I., Rodden, T. *et al.* (1993). Integrating ethnography into the requirements engineering process. *Proc. RE'93*, San Diego, CA, IEEE Computer Society Press. (Ch. 6)

Spafford, E. (1989). The Internet worm: crisis and aftermath. *Comm ACM* **32**(6), 678–87. (Ch. 16)

Spivey, J. M. (1990). Specifying a real-time kernel. *IEEE Software*, **7**(5), 21–8. (Ch. 9)

Spivey, J. M. (1992). *The Z Notation: A Reference Manual, 2nd edn*. London: Prentice-Hall. (Ch. 9)

St Laurent, S. and Cerami, E. (1999). *Building XML Applications*. New York: McGraw-Hill. (Chs 27, 28)

Stapleton, J. (1997). *DSDM Dynamic Systems Development Method*. Harlow, UK: Addison-Wesley Longman. (Ch. 8)

Suchman, L. (1983). Office procedures as practical action. *ACM Trans. on Office Information Systems*, **1**(3), 320–28. (Chs 6, 15)

Swartz, A. J. (1996). Airport 95: automated baggage system? *ACM Software Engineering Notes*, **21**(2), 79–83. (Ch. 2)

Symons, C. R. (1988). Function-point analysis: difficulties and improvements. *IEEE Trans. on Software Engineering*, **14**(1), 2–11. (Ch. 23)

Szyperski, C. (1998). *Component Software: Beyond Object-oriented Programming*. Reading, MA: Addison-Wesley. (Ch. 14)

Tanenbaum, A. S. and Woodhull, A. S. (1997). *Operating Systems: Design and Implementation, 2nd edn*. Englewood Cliffs, NJ: Prentice-Hall. (Ch. 13)

Teichrow, D. and Hershey, E. A. (1977). PSL/PSA: a computer aided technique for structured documentation and analysis of information processing systems. *IEEE Trans. on Software Engineering*, **SE-3**(1), 41–8. (Ch. 5)

Thayer, R. H. and Dorfman, M. (1997). *Software Requirements Engineering, 2nd edn*. Los Alamitos, CA: IEEE Computer Society Press. (Ch. 5)

Tichy, W. (1985). RCS – a system for version control. *Software Practice and Experience*, **15**(7), 637–54. (Ch. 29)

Ulrich, W. M. (1990). The evolutionary growth of software reengineering and the decade ahead. *American Programmer*, **3**(10), 14–20. (Ch. 28)

Wall, L., Christiansen, T. *et al.* (1996). *Programming Perl*. Sebastopol, CA: O'Reilly and Associates. (Ch. 8)

Ward, P. and Mellor, S. (1985). *Structured Development for Real-time Systems*. Englewood Cliffs, NJ: Prentice Hall. (Ch. 7, 13)

Warren, I. (ed.) (1998). *The Renaissance of Legacy Systems*. London: Springer. (Chs 26, 27)

Weinberg, G. (1971). *The Psychology of Computer Programming*. New York: Van Nostrand. (Ch. 22)

White, S., Alford, M. *et al.* (1993). Systems engineering of computer-based systems. *IEEE Computer*, **26**(11), 54–65. (Ch. 2)

Whitgift, D. (1991). *Software Configuration Management: Methods and Tools*. Chichester: John Wiley and Sons. (Ch. 29)

Wirfs-Brock, R. J. and Johnson, R. E. (1990). Surveying current research in object-oriented design. *Comm. ACM*, **33**(9), 104–24. (Ch. 14)

Wirfs-Brock, R., Wilkerson, B. *et al.* (1990). *Designing Object-Oriented Software*. Englewood Cliffs, NJ: Prentice-Hall. (Ch. 12)

Wirth, N. (1976). *Systematic Programming: An Introduction*. Englewood Cliffs, NJ: Prentice-Hall. (Ch. 26)

Wood, J. and Silver, D. (1995). *Joint Application Development (2nd edn)*. New York: John Wiley and Sons. (Ch. 8)

Woodcock, J. C. P. and Davies, J. (1996). *Using Z: Specification, Proof, Refinement*. London: Prentice-Hall. (Ch. 9)

Wordsworth, J. (1996). *Software Engineering with B*. Wokingham: Addison-Wesley. (Chs 3, 9, 17)

Wordsworth, J. B. (1991). The CICS application programming interface definition. *Proc. Z User Workshop*, Oxford, Berlin: Springer. (Ch. 9)

Zave, P. (1989). A compositional approach to multiparadigm programming. *IEEE Software*, **6**(5), 15–27. (Ch. 8)

Zave, P. and Schell, W. (1986). Salient features of an executable specification language and its environment. *IEEE Trans. on Software Engineering*, **SE-12**(2), 312–25. (Ch. 8)

Zimmermann, H. (1980). OSI Reference Model – the ISO model of architecture for open systems interconnection. *IEEE Transactions on Communications*, **COM-28**(4), 425–32. (Ch. 10)

Index

4GL 168, 176, 183, 309, 523

A

abstract data type 198, 200
  machine model 223–4
activity networks 79–84
actuator 286
aggregation relationship 265, 276
air traffic control system 21, 30
  architecture 27, 28, 216
  procurement 38
  requirements 32, 136
  specification 194, 201–3
air traffic controller 330
airline reservation system 367, 376
alarm system 26–7, 29, 155, 295–9, 376
  architecture 297
  Java code 298
algebraic specification 196, 198
algorithmic cost estimate 521
  modelling 520–32
ami method 567
analogue displays 336
application assessment 597
  domain 141, 317, 469
    abstraction 317
    requirement 100, 105–6
  family 307, 318–22

APSE 103, 223
aptitude test 503, 504
architectural design 37, 57, 216
  migration 614, 634
  model 151, 217, 218, 224–9
  organisation (building) 505
  transformation 602, 609, 625
architecture description language 217
Ariane 5 468
association relationship 265
ATM 151, 586
  client-server 247
  design description 591
  PDL description 113
  reliability 377–8
  requirements 128
  viewpoints 130, 131
  attack (security) 367, 368
availability 218, 354, 358, 360, 375, 468
awk 638

B

B 197, 204
bar charts 79–84
baseline 642
batch processing 588
behavioural model 153–7
blackboard model 221

Bootstrap 573
brainstorming 129
building monitoring system 226
business-critical system 582
business process re-engineering 624

C

capability assessment 572–3
  maturity model (CMM) 506, 526, 568–73, 643
    key process areas 570
    people 506–8, 572
    system engineering 572
CASE 12, 43, 58, 59, 63, 64, 155, 158
  classification 65–7
  environments 66, 67, 236
  tool 66, 523, 550, 558, 592
    change management 647, 657
    debugging 423
    program understanding 629
    rapid system development 176, 184
    re-engineering 626
    requirements 131, 138, 142, 143
    system building 658–60
    testing 463
    version management 646, 650, 657–8
  toolset 102, 151, 220
    configuration management 642, 656–60
    integrated 221
  workbenches 66, 149, 166–8, 462–4, 575, 592
change control 58
  board 649
  management 142, 143, 144–5, 647–50
    process 647
  request 553, 554, 610, 612
    form 648
chief programmer team 502–3
CICS 194, 587
circular buffer 301–2
Cleanroom 426, 429, 434–7, 471, 501
  process 49, 194, 434, 436, 469
  team 436
client server system 222–3, 240, 242, 244–9, 251,
    585, 614
  2-tier 246, 249
  3-tier 247–9
  design 245
cluster testing 460

COCOMO 522–9, 532, 613
  drivers 525, 528
  levels 523–5
  scale factors 527
code generator 310
code of ethics 15
command and control system 295
command language 333
compiler architecture 233–4
component 262, 311
  abstractions 312
  design 58
  identification 650
  interfaces 311–12
  reuse 307
  testing 441, 458
component-based software engineering 49, 185–8,
    308, 310
computer concepts 494
computer science 7
computer-based system 21, 583
  system engineering 22
concurrent processes 287
configuration control 107
  database 656
  hierarchy 645
  item 645
  management 223, 399, 480, 563, 607
    planning 644–6
    process 642
  manager, non-stop system 293
consistency 331
context models 150–3
contractors and sub-contractors 39
contractual model 177
control, centralised 225–7
  event-based 225
cooperation and awareness 136
CORBA 185, 252–7
  services 256–7
CORE 126
COTS 27, 33, 34, 37, 50, 307, 312, 603
  reuse 315–17
    problems 316
critical path 81, 82
  region 289
  system 194, 201, 356–7, 393
    specification 372
    validation 468
CSP 197
cyclomatic complexity 451

D

damage 367
  assessment 400, 406–8
  limitation 365, 386
data abstraction 632, 633–4
  acquisition system 294, 295, 300–3
    architecture 301
  degradation 634
  dictionary 159–60
  evolution 634
  migration 636
  mining system 251–2
  re-engineering 37, 602, 625, 634–8
    approaches 635
    process 637
  value inconsistencies 636–7
  visualisation 338
data-flow model 58, 109, 150, 152, 153, 218, 231–2,
    589, 590
database programming 183–4
  query language 183
database-centred system 586
DCOM 185, 253
debugging 60
  process 422
defect detection 427
defensive programming 400
deliverable 77
delta 658
denial of service 367
dependability, costs 355
  definition 354
derivation history 649
design editing system 107, 108, 111, 112, 159
  evolution 280–1
  function-oriented 357, 587–92
  patterns 236, 315, 322–4
    elements 323
  process model 57
  top-down 588
development for reuse 317–18
direct manipulation 332, 334
disclosure of confidential information 367
discrete mathematics 193
distributed object architectures 242, 249–52
  advantages 250
distributed system 614
  characteristics 240–1

developers 257
  testing 458
distribution model 616
  options 616
document standards 542
  compound 186
documentation 5, 344–5, 541–3, 583, 655
domain-specific architectures 233–6, 318
DSEE 657

E

e-commerce 7, 11
effort build-up 532
egoless programming 499
embedded system 286
emergent property 21, 22–4, 31, 61, 194, 241, 457
entity-relation model 59, 158
equivalence partitions 444–7, 449
error avoidance 395–7, 434
  checklist 429, 430
  detection 195, 434
  messages 340–1
  recovery 331
error-prone constructs 396
estimation techniques 518–20
  bottom-up 518
  top-down 518
ethical dilemmas 16
ethnography 125, 135–6, 330, 562, 563
evolution costs 11
evolutionary development 9, 44, 46–8
  for prototyping 174, 175–8
  for user interfaces 329
  in Java 182
  problems 177
  requirements 117
exception 226, 401
  handling 401–3
exposure limitation 368
extreme programming 53, 501, 506

F

failure 376
  classification 377

costs 357, 468
severity 360
fault avoidance 362, 393
density 395
detection 362, 393, 400, 403–6
methods 407
preventative 404
retrospective 405
manager 293
minimisation 393–9
recovery 400, 408–9
removal costs 395
repair 400
tolerance 241, 362, 364, 393, 400–9, 411, 412, 413
fault-free software 393–4
fault-tolerant system 362, 400
architecture 401, 410–13
fault-tree analysis 382–4, 386
feasibility study 56, 122, 123
film and picture library system 222
flow graph, program 450–1
Fog index 548
form fill-in 333
formal methods 470
and critical systems 469–70
risks 194
specification 57, 193, 357, 372, 435, 469, 541
air traffic control system 201–3
in the software process 195
process 199
systems development 44, 48–9
transformations 9, 55
verification 483
forms-based interface 617
forward engineering 624
framework (reuse) 262, 314–15
freezer controller 404
function points 514, 515–17, 521
functional system components 27–9

G

generalisation relationship 163
GQM (Goal-Question-Metric) 550, 567
graphical presentation 336
user interface 328
group cohesiveness 499–500
communications 500–1
composition 497–8, 501

leadership 498
organisation 501–3
size 497, 500
working 497–503

H

hazard 379
analysis 480
and risk analysis 381–2
avoidance 365, 386
classes 382
detection and removal 365, 386
log 480–1
probability 385
severity 385
heating system 25, 299–300
help system 341, 342–3
HOOD 272
human and organisational factors 25, 328
human needs hierarchy 496
hypertext 222, 343

I

IEC 61508, safety management 379
implementation and unit testing 45
incremental development 51–3, 172, 178, 313, 435
individual ability 501, 517
information chunking 492
hiding 397–9
presentation 334–9
inheritance 396, 460, 399, 424, 425–31
model 59, 130, 162–4, 264, 276
inspection 60, 420, 546, 567
process, roles 428–9
insulin delivery system 205, 357–9, 463
exceptions 402–3
fault tree 383
reliability 378–9
risk analysis 385
safety argument 477–9
safety checking 482
safety requirements 387
Z schema 206, 208

integration, system 441, 452–8
  bottom-up 454
  incremental 452
  top-down 453
intellectual property 14
interactive system 127
interface definition language (IDL) 254
  design 57
  errors 456
  specification 114–15, 197–204
  types of 455–6
Internet banking system 248
  worm 367
interrupt-driven control 227, 228
inventory management 320
invoice processing system 232
ISO 9000 468, 537, 571, 643
  and quality management 538
  areas covered 538

J

Jackson System Development 58
JavaBeans 185
Joint Application Development 176

K

kaizen 560

L

Larch 197, 198
legacy system 36, 582, 591, 623
  application system 586
  architecture 614
  assessment 592–8
  change management 602
  components 584
  design 587–92
  model 585
  structures 615
library system 165, 320
Lifespan 657

lines of code 514
LINT 433
list specification 199
Lotos 197
Lotus Notes 181

M

maintainability 218, 262, 517
maintenance 583, 602, 605–13, 614
  adaptive 606
  corrective 606
  costs 607, 608, 611
  cost factors 608–9
  effort distribution 605
  perfective 606
  prediction 611–13
  preventative 604
  process 604, 609–11
make 657, 659
management activities 73
  option costs 530
mean-time-to-failure 374, 375
measurement process 550
memory organisation 490–3
  long-term 491, 494
  short-term 330, 491, 494, 495
  working 491, 494
menu selection 332
metrics 103, 104, 567
  control 548, 549
  dynamic 551
  object-oriented 552–3
  predictor 548, 549
  process 566, 613
  product 551–3
  reliability 104
  static 551, 552
microwave oven 155–7, 289
middleware 243, 247, 250, 252, 314, 616, 617, 618
milestone 77, 78
model-based specification 196
model-view-controller 314–15, 324, 334, 335
modular decomposition 229–32
module 217
  description language 656
  functional 632
  hardware 632
  program support 633

monitoring systems 295–300
motivation 495–7
multiprocessor system 243
mutual exclusion 289

N

N–version programming 110, 410, 411, 413
natural language 106, 110, 114, 333
non-functional requirement 100, 101–5, 218, 372, 374

O

OBJ 197
object
    active 266
    aggregation 164–5
    behaviour model 165–6
    class 161, 162, 198
        definition 262
        hierarchy 264
        testing 459–60
    concurrent 265–7
    identification 272
    integration 460–2
    interface specification 279–80
    model 109, 230–1, 274–9, 614
    points 516, 521
    request broker 250, 254–5
    server 26
object-oriented design 58, 261, 267–80, 495
    development 261, 455, 592, 607
    methods 59, 122, 149, 262
    modelling 150, 160–6
    systems 441
    techniques 357
    testing 442, 458–62
Objectory 133
Observer pattern 323–4, 335
OLE 186
operation and maintenance 45, 46
operational profile 471, 472–3
operator error 373
organisational requirement 102
OSI reference model 235–6

P

packing robot system 219
parallelism 396
participatory design 329
PDL 112–14, 115, 132
people management 490
    selection 503–6
performance 218, 224, 355
Petri nets 197, 382
pollution monitoring system 281
pricing to win 519, 520, 561
probability of failure on demand 375
problem solving 493–5
process analysis 562
    applicability 574
    assurance 479–81
    characteristics 558
    classification 573–5
    exceptions 565–6
    improvement 43, 558, 569, 571
        process 559
    iteration 51–5
    management 293–5
    measurement 566–7
    model 8–9, 44, 152, 563
        elements 564
        spiral 53–5, 606–7
    modelling 562–6
    reliability 398–9
    requirement 102
    tool support 575
product line architecture 216, 235, 318–22
    requirement 102
productivity 513–18
    factors affecting 517
    measures 514
professional responsibility 14–17
program analyser, dynamic 451
program and data corruption 367
    browsing 633
    evolution dynamics 603–5
    inspections 138, 427–31
    modularisation 632–4
    proofs 49, 193
    refinement 48
    restructuring 631
    structure improvement 629–32
    translation 627

programmer productivity 514
project duration and staffing 531
  cost estimation 73, 512
    algorithmic 520–31
    techniques 518–20
    uncertainty 522
  management 54, 72, 73, 431, 537, 540
  monitoring 74
  plan 75, 76–7
  planning 73, 75–8, 512
    process 75, 76
    using cost models 529–31
  schedule 76, 77, 531
  scheduling 78–84, 512
    process 79
  team 74, 497
proposal writing 73
prototyping 55, 136, 138
  dynamic high-level languages 181–3
  evaluation 174
  process 173–4, 179, 313
  techniques 180–8
  throw-away 46, 175, 178–80
psychometric test 503, 504

Q

quality assessment 595–8
  assurance 537, 539–44
  attributes 536, 545, 548
  control 537, 546–7
    statistical 560
  factors affecting 561
  management 536, 537, 544, 553, 642
  manual 537
  planning 536, 537, 544–5
  process and product 543–4
  standard 102, 499
questionnaires 346, 562
queue 456

R

railway signalling system 194, 398
rapid application development 176

rate of failure occurrence 375
RCS 647, 651, 657
real-time system 153, 194, 228, 235, 244
  definition 286
  executive 288, 291–5
    components 292
  model 287, 289–90
  programming 290–1
  with Java 291
recovery blocks 411, 412
re-engineering 592, 602, 609, 623
  approaches 626
  process 625
  with 4GL 184
release 650
  management 653–5
  strategy 654
reliability 23, 101, 102, 308, 354, 359, 360, 373, 468, 517
  and safety 364
  engineering 373
  estimation 421
  growth model 436, 473–6
  hardware 373
  measurement 471
  metrics 374–6
  operator 373
  prediction 473–6
  requirements 374, 378, 470
  terminology 361
  validation 470–6
reporting (management) 74
repository model 218, 220–1, 223, 234
requirement 98, 100, 101–5, 106, 379, 480
  examples 99, 100, 103, 104, 106, 107, 108
requirements
  analysis and definition 45, 53, 56, 122
  document 98, 105, 115–18
    standards 116–17
    structure 118
    users 116
  elicitation and analysis 124–37, 172
  emergent 602
  enduring 140
  engineering 98
    process 56, 98, 122
    process maturity 569
  errors 605
  external 103
  functional 100–1, 372
  identification of 142

management 122, 139–45, 186, 399
    planning 142–4
problems 195
reviews 137, 138–9, 399
specification 56, 122
usability 102
validation 56, 137–9, 172
volatility 141, 526, 582
writing 109, 111
resource management system 319
reusable component 185, 186
reuse 44, 50, 65, 216, 307
    benefits 308
    generator based 309–10
    process 312–13
reverse engineering 628
    process 628
reviews 60, 420, 476–7, 546
    types 547
rework 30, 46, 51, 137, 173, 196
ring buffer 301–2
risk 54
    analysis and assessment 53, 77, 86–7, 88, 172, 384
    categories 84
    factors 90
    identification 86
    levels 384
    management 84–90
        process 85
        strategies 89
    monitoring 90
    planning 89–90
    reduction 308
    resolution 525
    types 86, 87
    business 582

S

SADT 126, 495
safety 23, 218, 354, 359, 364, 468
    argument 477–9
    assurance 476–82
    checking, run-time 482
    engineer 481
    management 380
    requirement 379, 480

review 480
specification 379–87
terminology 365–6
validation 380
safety-critical life cycle 379, 380, 480
    system 16, 194, 356, 364, 378, 397, 413, 476
SCCS 657
scenario 125, 132–5, 273
schedule 561
scheduling 288, 294–5
scripting languages 187
search routine 445, 446, 447
    binary search 448, 449
security 23, 218, 354, 367, 468
    assessment 483
    checking 483
    life-cycle 387
    requirements 483
    specification 387–8
    techniques and technologies 387
    terminology 368
Seeheim model 334
semantic knowledge 492, 493
semaphore 289
sensors 286
sequence diagram 134–5, 165–6, 275, 277, 462
size estimation 521
Smalltalk 181, 335
social and organisation requirements 135
Socio-technics 25
Soft Systems Methodology 25
Softbench 228
software architecture 216, 623
    attributes of good software 12–13
    change 602
    costs 512
    crisis 4
    design and implementation 43
    design specification 98
    development 8
    engineering 4, 6–7
        challenges 13
        costs 9–11
        ethics 14–17
        FAQs 6
        method 11, 12
    evolution 8, 43, 63
    factory 309
    life cycle 45
    maintenance 46, 63, 129
    management 545

measurement 547–54
pricing 513
process 8, 43
product 5, 10
quality 536
specification 8, 43, 195
system 5
validation 8, 43, 60
SPICE 572
SQL 248
staff selection 504
stakeholder 124, 126, 216, 321
standards 43, 116–17, 308, 388, 536, 537, 539, 546
    configuration management 642
    documentation 541, 542
    IEEE 540
    metrics 548
    process 539, 540, 541, 542
    product 539, 540
state machine model 153, 154–7, 275, 278–9, 436
    microwave oven 290
Statecharts 155, 278, 279, 289
static analysis 374, 399, 421, 431–4
stimulus/response system 286, 288, 296
Stoneman 220
structural model 59
structural testing 459
Structured Design 58, 588
structured methods 58, 122, 149, 153, 592
structured programming 395, 435
sub-system 21, 217
    development 34
    models 275
survivability 368
syntactic knowledge 492, 493
system 21
    and software design 45
    architecture 288, 297, 524, 614
    boundary 151, 153
    building 452, 643, 655–6
    decommissioning 36
    design 32–3, 287, 288
    engineering 7–8, 21, 117
        disciplines 31
        process 29–31
    environment 24–6
        assessment 596
    evolution 36
system families 642
    faults 361
    installation 35

integration 34–5, 50
model 149, 150
operation 35–6
procurement process 38
reliability 22–3
requirements 56
    definition 31–2, 98, 99, 109–15
specification 37, 55
testing 53, 173

T

task analysis 330
    concepts 494
TCL/TK 185, 313
telecommunication system 182, 472, 359, 376
teleprocessing monitor 247, 316, 587
test case 444, 451
    planning 399, 424, 425, 475
testing 420
    alpha 62
    beta 62
    black-box 443–4, 459
    defect 421, 442–52
    functional 443
    guidelines 446, 457
    integration 452–8
    interface 455–7
    module 450
    path 450–2
    phases 62, 441
    principle 461
    process 60–1, 441, 442–3
        module 564, 565
    regression 423
    scenario-based 461
    statistical 421, 435, 471
    stress 457–8
    structural 447–9
    unit 450
    validation 442
    white-box 448, 458
    workbenches 462–4
top-down development 395
traceability 142
traffic control system 243–4
train control system 374
    protection system 106

transaction 409
   processing 457, 586, 589
transformational development 469
transponder 267
triple modular redundancy 410
type system 403

U

UML 150, 157, 161, 262, 289
   process 167
university library system 100
Unix shell 187, 313
usability attributes 345
   specification 345
use-case 134, 136
   model 270–1, 276
   testing 461
user assistance 332
   interaction 332–4
      styles 332
   interface 36, 328
      design 492
         principles 330
         process 329
      distribution 618
      evaluation 345–7
      migration strategies 619
      prototyping 188–9
      use of colour 338–9
   manual 343
   requirements 56, 98, 99, 106, 149, 176, 518, 529
   support 340–5
   training 173
user-centred design 188, 329

V

V-spec 412
variant 650
VDM 197, 204
verification and validation 60, 177, 420

version 642, 650
   and release management 650–5
   derivation 651
   identification, attributes 652–3
   numbering 651
viewpoint 101, 126, 129
viewpoint-oriented approach 594, 595
   elicitation 125
Visual Basic 187, 188, 313
VORD 128
vulnerability avoidance 368

W

waterfall model 9, 44, 45–6, 47, 48, 51, 53,
      643
weather mapping system 268, 276
   architecture 268
   subsystems 269
weather station system 461
   architecture 272
   interface 280
   objects 273, 442
   testing 459–60
web-based interface 189
web-based system 7, 11
wicked problem 32, 139
working environment 501, 505–6
WWW browser 188

X

XML 618, 638

Z

Z 197, 204
   schemas 204–5
      invariants 207

Author Index

A

Abbott 272
Abdel-Ghaly 475
Ackroyd 25
Adams 363
Aho 182, 638
Albrecht 515
Alexander 322
Alford 110
Arango 141
Aron 501
Arthur 610, 632
Avizienis 412

B

Baker 292, 501
Banker 516, 612, 613
Bansler 59
Barker 158
Barnard 430, 548
Barnes 291

Basili 426, 550, 567
Bass 216, 217, 220, 496
Baumer 314
Beck 53, 273, 501, 506, 517
Beizer 441, 444
Belady 603
Bell 110, 384
Bentley 136
Bernstein 243
Bersoff 643
Bieman 173
Binder 459
Bishop 413
Bodker 59
Boehm 88, 172, 317, 365, 517, 518, 522,
    523, 524, 528, 613
Bohm 631
Bollinger 570
Bolognesi 197
Booch 11, 58, 122, 149, 150, 161, 262,
    322
Bourne 187
Bowers 136
Brazendale 384
Brilliant 412
Brinch-Hansen 289
Brinksma 197
Brooks 72, 501
Burns 288, 291, 295

Button 136
Buxton 220, 223

C

Card 493
Carroll 344
Cerami 618, 638
Checkland 25
Chen 158
Chikofsky 624
Cleveland 629
Coad 161, 262, 273
Cobb 434, 437
Codd 158
Codenie 314
Cohen 198
Colouris 240, 241
Constantine 58, 588
Cook 629
Crosby 536
Cross 624
Cunningham 273
Curtis 494, 507, 571
Cusamano 309

D

Darwen 183
Dasarthy 288
Date 183
Davis 98, 110, 116, 643
Dean 656
Dehbonei 194
DeMarco 11, 149, 153, 154, 505
Diaper 330
Diaz 570
Dijkstra 289
Diller 204
Dix 329
Dorfman 116
Douglass 634
Draper 188, 329
Dunteman 496

E

Eckstein 329
Endres 365
Ellison 368
Erickson 461
Ehrlich 476
Easterbrook 127, 141, 194
El Amam 572

F

Fagan 427
Fayad 314
Feldman 657, 659
Fenton 548
Finkelstein 127
Forte 184
Fowler 11, 134
Frewin 424
Fromme 228
Fugetta 66
Fujiwara 408
Furey 516
Futatsugi 197

G

Gaffney 515
Galvin 289
Gamma 236, 322
Gane 58
Garlan 218, 227
Gera 233, 236
Gilb 426, 428, 429
Glass 537, 538
Goldberg 273, 335
Gollmann 483
Gomaa 289
Gordon 173
Gotterbarn 14
Grady 427, 548
Graham (1994) 262
Graham (1993) 426, 428, 429

Green 567
Greenbaum 329
Grudin 331
Guimares 607
Guttag 197, 198

H

Haase 573
Habib-agahi 518
Hall 84, 194, 195, 372, 548
Halstead 612
Hamlet 473
Hammer 158, 624
Harel 155, 278, 289
Harkey 185, 245, 314
Harvey 382, 384
Hatton 424
Hayes 204
Heath 136
Hekmatpour 173, 174
Heninger 111, 116
Hershey 110
Hihn 518
Hoare 182, 197, 289
Huff 17, 64
Hughes 136, 330
Hull 158
Humphrey 545, 566, 569, 571

I

Ince 173, 174, 538

J

Jackson 11, 58
Jacky 194, 204
Jacobson 133, 161, 262, 309
Jacopini 631
Jahanian 382
Jeffrey 548
Jelinski 473

Johnson 314, 537
Jones 197, 204
Jorgensen 461

K

Kafura 612, 613
Keller 476
Kennedy 329
King 158
Kit 441
Kitchenham 516, 520, 549
Knight 412
Knuth 322
Konrad 572
Kotonya 100, 115, 127
Kume 365
Kuvaja 573
Kyng 329

L

Lamping 338
Laprie 413
Lauson 17
Leblang 657
Lehman 603
Leveson 381, 382, 384, 412
Lientz 606, 607
Linger 44, 49, 194, 434, 437
Liskov 198
Lister 505
Littlewood 362, 474
Londeix 532
Luff 136
Luqi 181
Lutz 185, 187, 365, 470
Lyu 373

M

MacDonnell 515
Martin 17

Maslow 495
Matsumoto 309
McCabe 451, 612
McCue 505
McGowan 570
McGuffin 220
McKee 607
McLeod 158
Mejia 194
Mellor 155, 273, 289
Meyer 311
Miller 491
Millington 176
Mills 44, 49, 51, 194, 363, 426, 434, 437
MOD 469
Mok 382
Moranda 473
Mullery 126
Mumford 25
Murphy 460
Musa 472, 473, 475
Musciano 329
Myers 532, 588

N

Nakajo 365
Neil 194
Neilsen 345
Nii 221
Nilsen 291
Ning 629
Norman 188, 329
Nosek 606
Nuseibeh 127

O

O'Connor 310
Offen 548
Oman 629
Orfali 185, 244, 314
Oskarsson 537, 538
Ould 84
Ousterhout 185, 187, 188, 313

P

Palvia 606
Park 514
Parnas 414, 476
Paulk 569, 571, 572, 643
Peach 537
Perrow 366
Perry 441
Peterson 197, 382
Pfaff 334
Pope 185
Pradham 408
Preece 329
Pressman 4
Price 430, 548
Prieto-Diaz 141
Prowell 49, 194, 434, 471
Pulford 567
Putnam 532
Pycock 136

R

Randell 412
Reddy 612, 613
Redmill 379
Reiss 228
Rettig 180
Rickets 635
Rittel 32
Robinson 58, 262, 272
Robson 335
Rochester 634
Rochkind 657
Rockwell 233, 236
Rombach 550, 567
Ross 126
Royce 45, 523
Rubin 273
Rumbaugh 11, 58, 122, 149, 161, 253, 267, 289

S

Sackman 517
Sarson 58

Sawyer 180, 569
Scallon 292
Schell 182
Schmidt 314
Schneidewind 476
Scholes 25
Schoman 126
Scott 11, 134
Seeheim 334
Selby 25, 49, 426, 437, 526
Sessions 185, 186
Sharrock 136
Shaw 218
Sheldon 476
Shneiderman 188, 329, 330, 332, 333, 338,
      492
Siegal 253
Silberschaltz 289
Silver 176
Sligo 570
Soloway 493
Sommerville 100, 115, 127, 136, 180, 569, 656
Spafford 367
Spivey 194, 197, 204
St Laurent 618, 638
Stapleton 176
Suchman 135, 330
Swanson 606, 607
Swartz 31
Symons 516
Szyperski 309

T

Tanenbaum 289
Teichrow 110
ten Hagen 334
Thayer 116
Tichy 647, 657

U

Ulrich 623, 624

V

Van Slack 427
Verral 474

W

Walker 228
Wall 185, 187
Ward 155, 289
Warren 593, 602
Weber 32
Weinberg 499, 506
Wellings 291, 295
Whitgift 657
Wirfs-Brock 273, 314
Wirth 588
Wood 176
Woodcock 204
Woodhull 289
Wordsworth 194, 197, 204, 372
Wosser 309

X

Xu 412

Y

Yourdon 58, 161, 262, 273, 588

Z

Zave 182
Zimmermann 223, 235